TORIES
THE END OF AN ERROR

Also by Russell Jones

The Decade in Tory
Four Chancellors and a Funeral

TORIES
THE END OF AN ERROR

RUSSELL JONES

London, United KIngdom

Byline Books
London, United Kingdom

First published in 2025
All rights reserved
© Russell Jones, 2025

The right of Russell Jones to be identified as the author of this work has been asserted in accordance with Section 77 of the Copyright, Designs and Patents Act, 1988. No part of this publication may be copied, reproduced, stored in a retrieval system, or transmitted, in any form or by any means without the prior permission of the publisher, nor be otherwise circulated in any form of binding or cover other than that in which it is published and without a similar condition being imposed on the subsequent purchaser.

Byline does not have any control over, or responsibility for, any third-party websites referred to in this book. All internet addresses given in this book were correct at the time of going to press. The author and publisher regret any inconvenience caused if addresses have changed or sites have ceased to exist, but can accept no responsibility for any such changes.

A CIP record for this book is available from the British Library

Cover design by Mecob Designs

Text design by Prepare to Publish

Printed in Great Britain by Clays Ltd

ISBN 978-1-916754-17-1

There are times, perhaps once every thirty years, when there is a sea-change in politics. It then does not matter what you say or what you do. There is a shift in what the public wants and what it approves of.
 – Jim Callaghan, 1979

Contents

Part 1: 'Privileged, sneering elites who take the rest of us for fools'
    January to June 2023   3
    July to December 2023   84

Part 2: 'Can we, for more than five minutes, dispense with the civil war?'
    January to May 2024   135

Part 3: 'Basically Bonkers'
    The General Election of 2024   205
    Repeating the Error   238

Endnotes   249
Supporters   317

Part 1
'Privileged, sneering elites who take the rest of us for fools'

Part I

January to June 2023

The Keynes Mutiny

By the turn of the century, Lehman Brothers had been ticking along nicely for over 150 years. The company had moved on from its modest beginnings, and via a series of well-planned investments, smart acquisitions and wise appointments, it had grown into the fourth-largest investment bank in the USA, employing more than 26,000 people and operating on four continents. Everything was looking rosy, and the board of directors probably didn't think anything could go wrong until, in 2006, they decided to offer a job to Steve Baker.

Within two years of his appointment as Chief Architect of Global Financing and Asset Service Platforms, the architecture of their global financing service platform fell over so spectacularly that it almost took the entire global banking system down with it.

So Baker decided to apply his unique talents to politics and become a Tory MP.[1]

Lehman's downfall had been precipitated by overexposure to Collateralised Debt Obligations,[2] a group of complex and wildly hazardous financial instruments that had been enthusiastically marketed to institutions across the world by Deutsche Bank. The responsibility for the structuring and sale of CDOs fell to their Head of Global Trading (Asia), Sajid Javid.[3] A US Senate investigation later concluded Deutsche Bank's promotion of CDOs had caused 'material damage to ordinary people and the wider global economy'.[4]

But for a much smaller part of the economy, the resulting worldwide financial crisis presented a glorious opportunity. Rishi Sunak spent his 2008 as a partner in a hedge fund which placed bets that British banks would collapse, while at the same time aggressively pushing the Royal Bank of Scotland to accept 'an extremely risky deal' that made any such collapse more likely.[5] When the inevitable happened, the cost to taxpayers of rescuing RBS was £45 billion. However, we should focus on the positives: the bet that it would happen by the company of which Sunak was a partner earned him about five million quid.[6]

Bailing out the banks doubled our national debt overnight. But every crisis is an opportunity, and this was no exception. Despite three of their most senior future figures being integral to the chaos, the Tories saw in this disaster a chance to implement their most cherished ideological fantasy. They would tell everybody Gordon Brown had crashed the banks, sweep to electoral victory in 2010, and then slash the state to the bone and blame all the subsequent pain on Labour. All they needed was a tame media (which wasn't hard to come by), and some intellectual ballast to lend weight to their austerity plan (which was).

Luckily, just as David Cameron was making his final push to become prime minister, two Harvard professors presented a new paper to the annual meeting of the American Economic Association. *Growth in a Time of Debt*, by Carmen Reinhart and Ken Rogoff, built on years of data to conclusively prove that when a country's public borrowing increases, its overall economy suffers.[7]

This was a shocking bit of news for the economic establishment.

It turned on its head the orthodoxy that had held since 1933, when the great economist John Maynard Keynes had argued that in times of recession, a state should spend like crazy.

Keynes's theory sounds counterintuitive, but the logic goes like this: a nation in recession should borrow money, increase its debt, and pump the cash into the economy. This would stimulate growth, and the resulting economic activity would generate lots of tax revenue. The state's debt would then be repaid, and equilibrium would return. You can think of it as a seesaw: when private sector spending is down, state spending should be up. When the economy is on the rise, government spending could go down again.

Keynesian economics proved itself a huge success. It dragged us out of the Great Depression that followed the Wall Street Crash in 1929, and appeared to have worked pretty much every time it had been applied since then.

Yet the core finding of *Growth in a Time of Debt* was the opposite. The new paper seemed to show higher state debt was a drag on economic growth, and therefore the correct response to a recession was not government stimulus, but austerity. The seesaw should be down on both sides at the same time.

For David Cameron and his closest political adherents, these findings were manna from heaven. His economic mastermind George Osborne lauded the paper is if it were a holy writ. 'As Rogoff and Reinhart demonstrate convincingly, all financial crises ultimately have their origins in one thing', he said, and that thing was high state debt.[8] Underpinned by the new research, austerity became the theme of the 2010 election. Cameron slid into Downing Street, tens of billions of pounds were slashed from practically every sector of the UK state, and Gordon Brown shouldered all the blame.

Everything was going according to plan, but for one niggling problem: the economy tanked. *Growth in a Time of Debt* had predicted austerity would supercharge commerce, yet Britain was experiencing the slowest recovery from a recession in – quite literally – recorded history.[9] Despite Cameron and Osborne's repeated assurances that growth was imminent, it never seemed to arrive.

Or at least, it didn't arrive for you and me. For others, it was boom-time. In the dozen years since 2010, the ten wealthiest individuals in Britain saw their fortunes grow from £47 billion to over £182 billion.[10] The gap between the richest 10 per cent of the population and the poorest grew by 50 per cent.[11] When Boris Johnson came to power after a decade of austerity, the richest one per cent of Britons held more wealth than the poorest 70 per cent combined.[12] And money – both for the grotesquely rich and the new armies of struggling poor – had become utterly decoupled from the amount of work or talent that went into creating it. The link between productivity and pay had broken.[13]

As a result, millions no longer saw any value in sweating our lives away, working for a corporate master who would never share the wealth we'd helped to create. So a fifth of British adults simply opted out, and no longer even looked for work.[14] Meanwhile austerity led to plummeting investment, because if a government doesn't have the confidence to finance its country, why should anybody else? By 2022, business investment in the UK was the lowest in the G7 and ranked 28 out of 31 in the Organisation for Economic Co-operation and Development (OECD).[15]

Naturally, with fewer people seeing the value in work, and lower investment, Britain's productivity went off a cliff. After a decade of the Tories, our output was ten per cent lower than the OECD average,[16] and 18 per cent lower than that in the USA,[17] where Obama had responded to the banking crisis with a massive stimulus.

As Britain watched money and opportunity flood to the top, the Conservatives' long-championed individualism transformed into rampant, grasping, profoundly ugly personal greed, with senior figures in pretty much every part of the establishment becoming steeped in scandal. It undermined public trust in all of our great institutions: politics, finance, corporations, royalty, media, the police, the church: they all seemed to grow ever more corrupt and decadent, operating on the basis that it was easier to get rich via greased palms than greased elbows. They were viewed with disgust in towns and cities far away from London; the forgotten places where austerity had inflicted deep wounds, stagnant incomes, unaffordable housing, and increasingly fragile jobs and infrastructure. Out of sight of the comfortable Home Counties and the M4 corridor, huge social pressures grew, which the government and their friends in a cossetted, complicit media largely ignored. The growing anger was ripe for exploitation.

And that's when UKIP emerged from the wreckage of previous right-wing ethno-nationalist experiments, and began accusing foreigners of causing all our problems, as ethno-nationalists always do. They told us some essential Britishness was being lost, and at the risk of agreeing with them, they weren't entirely wrong. But it was being lost to the rich and powerful, not to the poor and ethnic.

Because the link between work and wages wasn't the only thing that had broken. For as long as anybody could remember, social progress had gone hand-in-hand with economic progress. But suddenly those most responsible for our stalling wages decided they could make even money by co-opting progressive views and selling them back to us. They began bombarding us with demands. We didn't have to merely buy Nike trainers that are allegedly produced in sweatshops.[18] We had to adopt the purported Nike philosophy of inclusiveness and kindness, while buying trainers made in sweatshops.

It was a cynical marketing ploy that became known as 'Woke Culture', and the populist right loved it. They'll tell you they hated it, of course, but in truth they were besotted. It allowed populists to weave a narrative that the thing standing between you and a better standard of living was 'Wokeness', rather than the real culprit: precisely the kind of feral capitalism the right advocated. But if you listened to the populists, what was driving your wages down was no longer being able to make racist jokes in the workplace. And kindness wasn't free: it was a luxury opinion that only the metropolitan elite could afford.

Very much to their shame, many Tory MPs were more than happy to nod along with UKIP about both Wokeness and foreigners, delighted that somebody was diverting blame away from the government in Westminster. For years this populist cancer had quietly metastasised, waiting to erupt during the Brexit referendum. And throughout those years, Downing Street had ignored the rising crisis, and confidently waited for growth to miraculously spring from their cutbacks.

But over in the USA something even more implausible was already happening. In 2013 Thomas Herndon, an unsung, 20-something economics student from Massachusetts, was handed a homework assignment. He was tasked with picking a published study and trying to replicate its results, and the one he chose was *Growth in a Time of Debt*.

He immediately ran into problems. No matter what data he shoved into the paper's economic models, he couldn't reproduce its conclusion: that economies performed less well on average when their state debt rose. So he dug deeper into the calculations behind the original paper's results, and what he found astonished him.

As a result of a simple mistake when adding up their spreadsheet data, Rogoff and Reinhart had accidentally left out the growth figures from Austria, Australia, Belgium, Canada and Denmark. With that blunder fixed, the paper's findings were reversed. Its revolutionary, earth-shattering, internationally important economic theory was proved wrong. The paper now agreed with Keynes. State investment boosted growth. Austerity stifled it.

And that's how David Cameron's entire calamitous economic policy – and all of the subsequent damage – was the result of a stupid error in an Excel Spreadsheet.[19]

Austerity, Frigidity, Delinquency, and Insolvency

If you believed the hype, the Conservatives were the natural party of government, delivering rectitude, prosperity and stability for over two centuries. Yet in January of 2023, after a dozen years in charge, the country was dilapidated, divided and diminished, and the Tories had burned their way through five PMs: prime minister David Cameron, prim monster Theresa May, primate minister Boris Johnson, and punctuation mark Liz Truss. Each of them had, in their own special way, made a stupefying mess of the job, taking it in turns to curse us with austerity, frigidity, delinquency, and insolvency. And finally: inadequacy, in the shape of prime miniature Rishi Sunak.

Sunak's premiership hadn't even begun well enough to say it was going from Bad to Worse. The nation would have accepted Bad as a starting point. Bad, we could deal with. But Sunak managed to skip Bad entirely, kicked things off at Worse, and then headed rapidly downhill. At the start of 2023 he'd only been in office for 100 days, yet it already felt like the sun was going down on his career.

Mind you, when you're Rishi Sunak's size, the sun does go down earlier than for the rest of us.

The country he now led was not merely in doo-doo, it was in the deepest and darkest of doo-doo. Britain had suffered well over a decade of volatility, driven by a near-total political failure to even identify – let alone adequately resolve – the fundamental cause of the global financial crisis that began in 2007: the grimly inevitable endgame of the form of capitalism kick-started by Margaret Thatcher, and later warmed over by David Cameron, a lightly glazed polyp who made it halfway to getting elected in 2010.

Cameron had won a mandate for two things: 'Compassionate Conservatism', a pairing of words it's impossible to even think about without deploying air-quotes; and 'Rebalancing the Economy', which he did by making Britain technically richer, but almost everybody who lived in Britain measurably poorer.[20] Nearly all the new money generated by the economic system Cameron espoused headed straight into the tax-averse pockets of the richest one percent, who grabbed 63 per cent of all gains made since 2010.[21]

For the rest of us, that period was primarily notable for two things: everything we valued falling to pieces, and rising anger. An increasingly incensed, fast-growing section of society saw Cameron and his ilk as being in cahoots with the insatiable corporate monsters who had taken all of the cash. For a decade, all the money had flooded away from the centre, and then voters followed. Turbocharged by social media echo-chambers, frighteningly large numbers of us began abandoning established political norms, until even the notion of democracy fell into disrepute, with only 6 per cent of us thinking our views held any sway with the political classes.[22] The same process was being repeated everywhere you looked, as across the western world elections began to swing wildly between a shaky left, hamstrung by fear of radical solutions and cowed by the markets we'd just finished bailing out; and an increasingly scatty far-right, gratuitously apportioning blame for capitalism's failures onto the people most failed by capitalism.

Left, right, lefter, righter, as voters desperately sought a way out of the trap.

Here in Britain, all such volatility was contained within the Conservative Party. Or rather, Parties. There were two of them, you see.

One of the Conservative Parties was a large group of nominally centre-right traditionalists, which would have been vaguely recognisable to Winston Churchill or Harold Macmillan. Despite only one in a hundred of them emerging from a working-class background, they claimed to be an ordinary party for ordinary people, with an ethos based around money, monarchy, orthodoxy, money, faith, the military and money. They did love that money.

The other Conservative Party was a noisy band of feral radicals who seemed unable to decide if they were libertarians or authoritarians, so tried to be both at once, treating their friends with laissez-faire nonchalance, and their critics with dictatorial judgement. They insisted the answer to every problem was 'more of the same', even though every single thing they'd advocated in the six years since they'd taken control of the government had been proven objectively wrong. Unable to cope with this contradiction, they'd given up the hunt for practical solutions, and instead began to claim reality itself was at fault. After a decade of this process, their ethos boiled down to two things: the glorification of a bygone Britain that has never existed; and monotonous nit-picking about a modern Britain that they had largely imagined.

Oh, and they also loved money.

But at least the two sects had finally shaken off their instinct to punch down. They'd taken to punching sideways instead. The two Conservative Parties had been at war for four decades, although you'd hardly know it, because the moderates barely lifted a finger in their own defence. All the sensible ones had wandered off into the wilderness rather than share a room with Boris Johnson, and by 2023 only the dim or spineless remained, frittering away their lives leaking self-defeating quotes to the press while they waited for their own extinction.

As a new PM, it was Rishi Sunak's task to keep both of his parties happy at once, which would have been a tricky enough prospect even for a politician with vision, strength, and skill. Sunak possessed no such attributes. People accused him of plastic managerialism,[23] but I don't think that's fair because he also had a wooden smile for the cameras, a tin ear for politics, clay feet for presentation, a ham fist for strategy, and a brass neck for self-enrichment that set him at odds with the mood of the entire nation. The man had never seen a cock-up he didn't have a head-on collision with, and was so lily-livered you could open a branch of Interflora in his abdomen. I had hoped the format of this book could be a tribute to Rishi Sunak, but I couldn't figure out a way to publish it without a spine.

And he had three strikes against him to begin with.

The first strike: shockingly poor judgement, astonishing the nation with feat after feat of erring-do.

The second: he was so weak you could apply him as a homeopathic remedy.

The third: he was haunted by the ghosts of his immediate predecessors, a bullshitting sex yeti, and a gawping, delusional nothingness who managed to be outmanoeuvred by a lettuce. Both Johnson and Truss were frivolous, shallow, and utterly unsuited to office, yet driven there by (in the first case) charisma, ambition and hogwash; and (in the second) by a power vacuum, nobody sane wanting the job, and a sense of a party shrugging 'what the hell, why not?'.

Yet despite their trifling, superficial natures, they each had an immense effect on the country. And that's the paradox at the heart of Johnson and Truss: they were each trivial, yet each momentous.

Within Sunak, however, there was no such paradox. He rose without consequence.

*

He'd begun his Westminster career in 2015, when he was parachuted into one of the safest Conservative seats in the country. Four years later, he'd become Chancellor of the Exchequer without having demonstrated the slightest political skill. From there, after a brief pause while Liz Truss did her drive-by attack on the British economy, he stepped unopposed into Downing Street without anybody consulting voters, or even Conservative members. The party had chosen a man who had faced no noteworthy electoral test. He hadn't distinguished himself in any significant way. He had no hinterland, experience, or political talent.

They had only themselves to blame for what came next.

It was immediately clear that Sunak lacked any sense of the world around him, or of the winds of change blowing across the country.

Society no longer recognised the established socioeconomic divisions between a working-class left and a middle-class right. Cameron's economically careless Tories had fumblingly dropped the UK in 2010, and then Johnson's self-serving vandalism had stamped all over the wreckage in 2016, splintering it yet further. As a result, new dividing lines appeared everywhere, and Sunak contrived to be on the wrong side of all of them. His party advocated reduced spending in a dilapidated nation yearning for massive investment. They opposed improvements to workers' rights, despite those rights being backed by a majority of voters from every party.[24] They championed a cramped, petty traditionalism in a Britain that was more socially liberal than it had ever been.[25] And they were peevishly nationalistic in a multicultural land of international traders and travellers, where a third more voters saw themselves as 'global citizens' than did not.[26]

The effects of this growing disconnect had been temporarily disguised by Boris Johnson's 2019 victory over Jeremy Corbyn, a man who really had his finger on the pulse of the people, provided those people hadn't had a pulse for 140 years and were called Karl Marx. It didn't matter that Corbyn was a well-liked local MP: he was the least popular opposition leader for almost half a century,[27] and Johnson presumed Labour's massive defeat represented bone-deep approval for the Tories, for Brexit, but most especially for himself.

And to that I say: chinny reckon. In a two-horse Grand National against Corbyn, the Conservatives could have secured a handsome victory on a three-legged donkey.

Still, credit where it's due: Johnson was a master at appealing to people who loathed almost any other Tory, which he did using two simple tricks: perpetual, omnidirectional bullshit; and pretending he was barely a Tory at all. Maybe a bit Tory around the edges, but he wasn't *one of them*: the stereotypically spoiled, vindictive and small-minded chancers who were clumsily bleeding the nation dry, when they weren't flogging it off to their mates. Those people were traditional Tories. He was something else. Something new. Something fun.

But the moment he was in power, he was revealed to be not only a textbook example of *one of them*, but something far worse as well. What started as giddy novelty act quickly descended into a set of behaviours that sickened the public, infected the whole party, and reminded us that, as one of Johnson's own frontbenchers admitted, 'when you peek behind the curtain, Tories are privileged, sneering elites who take the rest of us for fools'.[28]

Yet Johnson had achieved one success: for a short while, he gave the impression that he had resolved the tensions that led to all that infighting. He hadn't. He was simply a phony; a lusty, wild-eyed buffoon, hell-bent on distracting his detractors with belly-slapping gesticulations while he pulled the wool over their credulous eyes. He fibbed to the public. He hoodwinked the press. He bullshat the Queen.[29] And he lied to every Tory cabal that came through his door, reassuring them that they alone had the ear of the leader. Yet no sooner had they left his office, with a victorious grin pasted across their faces, than Johnson was spinning a different yarn to the next faction in the queue.

This strategy had kept things inside the party relatively calm, right until the moment it didn't: the truth turned up on Boris Johnson's doorstep, holding a fistful of receipts. As his lies came undone, every betrayed Tory faction went berserk at once, and then so did the electorate. The sky darkened with the wings of chickens coming home to roost, and Johnson, that object lesson in grandiose, hubristic obscenity, was hurled from office in disgrace.

And then the battle for control of the Tory party started again in earnest. It was like that bit in *Game of Thrones* when King Full Monty died, the fragile peace was over, and suddenly every entitled psychopath in the kingdom decided to fight it out for a go on the Iron Throne. Except in this case the King wasn't dead at all: he was a White Walker, still clattering about the place, destroying all he touched and endangering the whole shebang.

Meanwhile, in the capital the band struck up Benny Hill music, and in rushed Liz Truss with a plan to reinvigorate Britain's economy that she thought was foolproof. But nothing is foolproof to a truly masterful fool, as Truss proved in just 49 days of hectic disorder. And then she too was gone, and we ended up with Rishi Sunak, a small man who seemed smaller the longer you looked at him, had absolutely zero democratic mandate for his job, and wanted us to believe he could govern 67 million angry citizens across four nations, when it was abundantly clear he couldn't govern a slack handful of cabinet colleagues inside a single room.

He entered Downing Street as the Government reeled from the Truss disaster and had a brief window of opportunity to stamp his mark on the party. A key strategic decision needed to be made, and fast: which of his two parties would he back?

Would he stand up to the Tufton Street fanatics, and tell them in no uncertain terms the very evident truth: that the three pillars which had held up the Tory party for 40 years were all rotten? Thatcherism had run out of other people's money. The lysergic promise of Brexit had turned into a very bad trip indeed. And libertarian Trussonomics had been a frenzied calamity. If Sunak rejected those false gods and embraced realities, he would have had a chance to introduce a new Conservatism ... which was really just the old Conservatism again: pragmatism, solidity, a little bit of modest cruelty to keep the *Daily Mail* happy, and a few tentative steps towards the political centre, from where all elections are won.

Or would he embrace populism, reward his batshit fabulists with cabinet posts, and lead the party further down the narrow, nationalistic path towards annihilation? This choice meant Tories would continue to shovel money into the deep pockets of the very rich, while the fabric of the state disintegrated, and voters seethed. Instead of unity, the Conservatives would seek division. Instead of solutions, they'd seek diversions. And instead of traditional conservatism, they'd compete with Nigel Farage's latest rebrand, Reform UK, a jingoistic bar-room fantasia that hoped you'd forget its previous incarnation had led to Brexit, a national embarrassment so bad that nobody – not even Farage – wanted to talk about it anymore.[30]

Sunak made his bold decision. He would be a centrist on Tuesdays, Thursdays and Saturdays. On Mondays, Wednesdays and Fridays he would try to outflank Farage on the right.

Sundays were anybody's guess.

This shilly-shallying made the prime minister appear weak to right-wing voters who valued simplistic authoritarianism. And it made the party look like delusional extremists in the eyes of wavering centre-right voters who detested nativism. He should have been isolating Reform and painting them as deranged zealots, but instead he spent 18 months laying out a landing strip for Nigel Farage's return, while ceding a vast space in the political centre ground to Keir Starmer's dishwater impersonation of Labour.

Days into his premiership, Sunak had already doomed the Conservatives from both left and right.

In his defence, it was hard to imagine any of his Tory contemporaries being better at the job. Or for that matter, being worse. Nobody with much talent or integrity had wanted to join the Conservative Party for years. There were barely any capable Tory MPs left, and the few that had stuck it out now swam in a fetid, degenerate soup of endless disappointment, livened up by spicy chunks of blatant sleaze. Sunak was leader of a Government that only eight per cent of us thought trustworthy, and only twelve per cent thought were competent.[31] Two-thirds of voters believed the Tories were 'institutionally corrupt',[32] and in the eyes of 7 out of every 10 of us, Brexit, the party's defining policy, had ended up a disaster that left the country significantly poorer.[33]

*

Straight away, the new PM seemed acutely gauche. When he waved at the public, it looked like he was testing a faulty motion-sensor. Interacting with a card machine rendered him a flapping, disorderly mess. He allowed himself to be filmed using a hammer the wrong way round.[34] Every public appearance seemed worse than the last. Every week seemed to be the worst one yet. You could never get over the impression that he wasn't an entirely completed project, more of a prime minister concept that you'd scribble onto a pub napkin.

His innate clodhoppery was clear from the off, when he stood on the steps of Downing Street and informed a sniggering Britain that he was about to conjure 'integrity, professionalism and accountability' from the cast of self-serving masturbators, crooks, xenophobes and charlatans that formed the parliamentary Conservative Party.[35] It was a magnificently stupid promise to make. The notion of moral hygiene from this lot was laughable. There were dead rats floating in the Thames that had picked up the rumours swirling around many of Sunak's ministerial appointees, yet despite the near certainty that scandal would quickly overwhelm his cabinet and render his integrity promise ludicrous, he went right ahead and appointed every single ticking timebomb.

To absolutely nobody's surprise, morbidly doltish horse-faced abomination Gavin Williamson had to be sacked barely a fortnight into his tenure at the Ministry of Defence, after he began deploying the novel military tactic of ordering his own side to 'slit their throats'.[36] And then there was another Sunak appointment, Nadhim Zahawi, a child's drawing of perfect greed superimposed onto a competitively evil gonad, who managed to limp on a for a couple of months before years of duplicity about his tax affairs caught up with him, along with a million pound fine from HMRC.[37]

Next up: Dominic Raab, Sunak's deputy and the inspiration for the phrase 'you couldn't be more wrong', who became embroiled in a long-brewing story about his intimidation and mistreatment of practically everybody who came into contact with him, and many others who simply wandered within tomato-hurling distance.[38] In the end, after much effort, Raab achieved his first recorded triumph when he managed to successfully fall on his own sword. It was a bloody and satisfying end to his years-long, widely-reported and officially-documented history of problematic behaviour, which somehow only became apparent to his party's leader half a decade after the rest of Westminster noticed.[39]

All of this happened in the first hundred days of Sunak's gap-year in Number 10, culminating in a week that saw two auspicious memorials: the 50th anniversary of Britain's accession to the EEC,[40] and the second anniversary of the final implementation of Brexit. This was the Tory party's crowning achievement, even though two-thirds of Britons supported holding a referendum to undo the whole thing.[41] The process of leaving the EU had barely begun, and had already led to a 330,000 reduction in the UK labour force.[42] Brexit had cost the treasury £40 billion in lost revenue during the year preceding Sunak's premiership, which is enough to form a stack of £10 notes 250 miles tall.[43] And for all the government's boasts of economic competence, this keynote policy would leave us a further £311 billion worse off within a decade.[44]

His hundredth day in office should have been a moment for celebration. In fact, it was Rishi Sunak's worst week to date, and as we tumbled dejectedly into February 2023, things were about to get a whole lot worse for the prime minister and his mouth-breathing MPs.

Seventy Per Cent Fiction

Nadine Dorries is a woman whose entire life seems to be conducted 'after lunch'.

Since becoming a cabinet minister, she had spent her days strutting around in deluded pride with head held high: a simple enough task, since her head was clearly unburdened by contents. And predictably her ascendency to high office had been driven entirely by ego, it's just that it wasn't *her* ego: it was Boris Johnson's, who seemingly promoted her for gazing lushly at him during PMQs, her eyes illuminated from within by the dancing light of an idiot's lantern.

Her first brush with politics set the tone for everything that had happened since: the Hazel Grove constituency had been a top target seat for the Conservatives in 2001, but then Nadine rocked up. The decision to select her as candidate split the local party between those who thought she was a complete moron, and those who knew it for sure.

Within days of being selected she was deselected again, not least because – and it's hard to believe this, but it's what reports say – she hadn't even been able to get the year of her birth right on her application to stand.[45] Yet no sooner had she been deselected than she was reselected again, due to Conservative Central Office applying pressure on the local party. Headquarters felt selecting more female candidates would burnish the party's reputation, and seemed rather less concerned that one of those candidates being Nadine Dorries would instantly sully it again. By the time her good works were done, the Conservatives had admitted to 'privately writing off' their chances of winning Hazel Grove.[46] Dorries had converted an almost-certain electoral victory into a loss by over 9,000 votes.[47]

She stood again in Mid Bedfordshire, a seat which had become vacant because the previous Conservative MP, Jonathan Sayeed, had the whip removed when it was discovered he'd been running a dodgy sideline showing wealthy people around parliament in return for money.[48] Dorries was clearly eager to correct her predecessors' reputation for putting personal enrichment ahead of public responsibility, which is why she attended only two per cent of meetings of the parliamentary committee she was appointed to, while simultaneously attaining a top-ten placement on the list of MPs giving highly-paid jobs to their own family members.[49] Her daughter managed to get a £45,000 job as her office manager, even though she lived 96 miles away from the office she was supposedly managing.[50]

When a journalist enquired into this odd state of affairs, Dorries informed him of her plans to 'nail your balls to the floor using your own front teeth'.⁵¹ Yet despite her sterling efforts to charm the news media, journalists continued querying Nadine's finances, and she told the BBC she was the victim of a witch-hunt.⁵²

But here's the thing with witch-hunts. Sometimes they catch a witch.

Dorries – who once said, 'I never do anything I know to be wrong and I have common sense by the bucketful'⁵³ – then abandoned being an MP for a month so she could whizz off to Australia for an appearance on *I'm A Celebrity*, which she justified by saying it gave her a platform to promote her pro-life views. It also gave her a platform for collecting £82,000 in appearance fees, and I think we can mark it down as one of her greatest successes, since she was voted off the show in the blink of an eye, failed to mention abortion, and tried to persuade the parliamentary standards committee that she didn't declare her appearance fee because she'd signed a confidentiality agreement with ITV. When this ploy didn't work, she threatened to litigate against the commissioner for standards, using the bold legal argument that she didn't like those standards, and would like to operate under different ones.⁵⁴ Much like her career, her threat of litigation passed without notice, and Dorries was suspended from the parliamentary Conservative party.

'I have not had the whip withdrawn', she said, upon being informed that she had had the whip withdrawn. 'The whip has temporarily been suspended while I was abroad. And I hope that it will be fully reinstated tomorrow'.⁵⁵ It was not reinstated tomorrow, and she had to make a public apology to parliament for the entire farcical episode.

Yet by 2021 Dorries was the toast of the Tory right, by which I mean she was thick, jammy, and often found face down on the kitchen floor. The jammyness was most apparent in her appointment as culture secretary, an event that cannot be explained away without the use of the word 'spoof'. Her first act as minister was to push for the privatisation of Channel 4, because she said it was getting public money. And reality's first act was to wearily sigh, and explain that that's not how Channel 4 is funded, something Nadine was forced to discover in real time during a select committee meeting that redefined the boundaries of cringeworthiness. Fortunately she was able to escape from any embarrassment with a turn of phrase that is almost Churchillian in its poise, dignity and eloquence.

'And so… though it's… yeah… and that'.[56]

Beautiful. We should put that on our money.

To conclude: public service comes in many forms, and the form chosen by Nadine was to add to the gaiety of the nation, while simultaneously diminishing its dignity. So it brought a tear to many an eye when in February 2023 she announced she was standing down due to what she had the temerity to describe as the Conservative Party's 'sheer stupidity'.[57]

Dorries' beef with the party arose from her *Folie à Une* over Boris Johnson, who had told her, 'Nads, stay', something she was kind enough to report to a nation that seemed to be running out of things to laugh about.[58] So she sat nicely, wagging and panting, while he promised he'd reward her with a nice juicy peerage. What Johnson had failed to inform her was that the House of Lords Appointments Commission had already rejected her as a peer, and he already knew as much.[59]

Dorries was livid, and because every single thought that enters her mind must instantly be shared with the world, like a panda showing off its rare baby, she took to every medium available to fulminate noisily about the unfairness of it all. She claimed that 'posh boy' Rishi Sunak had blocked her peerage, and that he was 'not telling the truth', unlike her famously honest, non-posh old Etonian hero, Boris Johnson.[60]

Three months after she said she'd resign with immediate effect, she still hadn't got around to it, and had transformed once again into a gigantic political embarrassment. She hadn't spoken in parliament for over a year, although you couldn't shut her up in other locations.[61] Her local council urged her to quit in a strongly worded letter.[62] Her parliamentary colleagues couldn't decide whether to embrace her, reject her, or drop her off at a no-kill animal shelter. Even Rishi Sunak said she wasn't doing an MP's job properly, and Tory backbenchers had begun moves to force her from her seat if she didn't turn up.[63] They'd just give her another six months and then, ooh, just you watch.[64]

There are as many reasons for Nadine Dorries to be denied a lifetime of unelected political power as there are stars in the sky, not least that she'd just spent years standing in noisy and mildly befuddled opposition to unelected political power. 'I for one will be lobbying for a bill to massively reduce the Lords in size', she tweeted in 2018, arguing for 'positions to be elected'.[65] But the official reason given for denying her a peerage was that she hadn't agreed to stop being an MP within the requisite six-month timeframe. When this was eventually, and presumably very slowly, explained to Dorries, she threw a record-breaking conniption fit and finally, only 81 days after she'd promised to resign with immediate effect, she stood down as an MP in August.[66]

A Wish Called Rwanda

I had imagined lots of ways in which Boris Johnson's political career might end. Shanked in Pentonville. Beaten to death in his Y-fronts after being discovered hiding in somebody's wife's closet. Unnecessarily obvious guest on *Would I Lie To You?* But I hadn't foreseen a third of his party jettisoning him in disgust. For a man obsessed with being world-beating, imagine Johnson's pride when 62 ministers and trade envoys quit to force him from office, more than quintupling the previous mass-resignation record of 11.[67]

Worzel Damage had been brought low by his mishandling of a long series of scandals, by his inability to perform an even longer list of basic functions, and most of all by his own profound failures as a human being. But the defining event in his downfall was Partygate. On 13 April 2022 he was handed a fine for breaching the very rules he'd set,[68] so it suddenly became urgent to draw focus away from those damaging headlines with some big, chewy, Conservative-sounding red meat. And that's why, on the morning after receiving his Partygate fine, Boris Johnson suddenly announced what became *the* running story of the next two years: his Rwanda scheme.[69]

Well, I say 'scheme'. You could barely even call it a pipedream.

At launch it was assigned no budget, no team to implement it, no timeline, and it had no mandate. It was clearly a breach of both domestic and international law, and it hadn't even been signed up to by Rwanda when he dead-catted it into the public consciousness. It also directly contradicted Boris Johnson's 2019 manifesto, which had promised, 'We will continue to grant asylum and support to refugees fleeing persecution, with the ultimate aim of helping them to return home if it is safe to do so'.[70] Rwanda was a piece of desperate posturing that was never meant to actually *happen*, and it would deliver its supposed benefits of cutting migration not long after the opening ceremony of the Winter Olympics in Hell.

Yet it provided a reason for the Tories to exist for the next two years, despite being a MacGuffin so stupid it would be rejected from a Michael Bay movie. And that was good enough for them.

'The deal we have done is uncapped', said Johnson when announcing the policy, 'and Rwanda will have the capacity to resettle tens of thousands of people in the years ahead'. This was necessary, he argued, because Britain, the fifth-richest country that has ever existed, couldn't afford a 'blank cheque to cover the costs' of immigration, but for some reason Rwanda, over a hundred places behind us on the rich-list, would find it simple. Johnson went on to explain that 'Rwanda is one of the safest countries in the world', and that he was confident the plan was 'fully compliant with our international legal obligations'.[71]

None of those claims was true.

Those 'uncapped' tens of thousands turned out to be just 300 individuals, and by 2023 the cost of sending them to Rwanda had risen to £1.8 million per asylum seeker.[72] That's more than three times the amount an average Briton will earn in a lifetime.[73]

As for Rwanda being one of the safest countries: it's run by former guerilla leader Paul Kagame, who insists his country is a democracy. If it is, it's a pretty strange one. Across the whole of Rwanda's constituencies, only a single opposition candidate was allowed to stand against the governing party in the 2017 elections, and in that year's presidential election Paul Kagame managed to secure a frankly astonishing 98 per cent of the vote, making him even more popular than the famously democratic Vladimir Putin, who barely scraped by with 87 per cent.[74]

The US non-profit organisation Freedom House awarded Rwanda a score of only 20 per cent for political rights and for civil liberties. Year after year the nation is classified as 'Not free',[75] possibly because Paul Kagame overturned his constitution's election laws, allowing him to remain president practically indefinitely.[76] Whether or not this is lawful is irrelevant because, as Suella Braverman noted in a report she wrote before she was an MP, Rwanda didn't even have a properly functioning legal system.[77]

The Rwandan government also has a policy of trying to 'silence critics and dissidents living overseas through extrajudicial killings, kidnappings and intimidation'.[78] The nation's braver newspapers speak of 'alarm on police brutality, cold blood killings' across the country,[79] and it was barely 4 years since a dozen refugees in Rwanda complained that reductions in their food rations left had them at risk of starvation, so the local police helped the process along by shooting them all dead.[80]

Despite all this, Johnson promised Britain that his flight of fancy would reduce immigration, which had risen by 350 per cent since he had promised his previous flight of fancy, Brexit, would also reduce immigration.[81]

Logically, every single thing about the Rwanda plan was nonsense. Factually too. And legally. And ethically. And financially. And practically. It was clear to anybody with half a brain that that it would never work, but the Conservative party still contained plenty of people who didn't have half a brain, and within days Rwanda was adopted as an article of faith by the right. They may have overthrown Johnson, ousted Truss, and groused endlessly about Sunak, but they were loyal beyond comprehension to the idea of spending enough money to form a stack of £10 notes 11 miles high so they could send a statistically insignificant number of people to a country they couldn't find on a map. And as the collapsing, disreputable Conservative government ran out of ideas, energy, competence, hope – even of spare leaders – this barbaric, batshit plan became pretty much the only policy left on the table.

The Nuttiest Margins

In February, only one week after Lee Anderson had described his own government as being like 'the band on the Titanic', Rishi Sunak appointed him as deputy chairman, on purpose.

Under a leader with any sense, Anderson would have remained on the backbenches, unacknowledged and unloved, mooing his way through PMQs until it was time for him to be taken away in a van. His unexpected promotion was unrelated to his abilities, because he didn't have any abilities. He was simply intended as a pacifier to the angry right. But here's the thing about the angry right: they don't like being pacified, they like being angry. If you found a solution to one of their myriad petty, calcified resentments, they'd just hunt around for another one and ratchet up the fury yet further.

According to insiders, Lee Anderthal's appointment was based on his popularity with the public.[82] Yet at the time, YouGov recorded him being utterly unknown to 72 per cent of us, and only popular with 5 per cent.[83] Yet still Sunak decided to thrust the gibbering ape into the limelight.

Against pretty stiff competition, it turned out to be one of Sunak's worst decisions. Only 48 hours after appointing him, the PM had to publicly rebuke his new deputy chairman for expressing the exact rationale of Judge Death, advocating the return of capital punishment on the grounds that 'nobody has ever committed a crime after being executed'.[84]

Like every political movement, the Tories had to accommodate a wide range of views, although I doubt any previous party has had to find room for somebody with such an extreme direction of travel as Anderson. He'd begun as not just a Labour supporter, but as a member of Arthur Scargill's militant union, and an active campaigner for Michael Foot to become prime minister. He cited Scargill, along with socialist firebrands Tony Benn and Dennis Skinner, as the greatest influences on his political growth.[85] But something dark lurked within Anderson's mind, and as we've since discovered, he wasn't all that keen on anything dark, which might be why his mind said, 'there goes the neighbourhood', and moved out of the area. His opinions about minorities made Labour uncomfortable, and they suspended him after his Palaeolithic attitudes to the Traveller community led to a community protection warning.

So as an arch political opportunist, Anderson accused Labour of being taken over by the 'hard left' of which he'd been a lifelong member. He joined the Conservatives, and within four years was stalking the Badlands of the party's nuttiest margins.[86]

The strategy of the new populist right was brutally simple and effective. If the left ignored their noisy, offensive bile, the right won, for the simple reason that nobody was opposing them. If the left responded with facts, the right would accuse them of being elitist snobs. And if the left responded with derision, the right would still win: they'd simply turn to voters and whisper, 'See how they mock Lee Anderson. See the contempt they have for him. See their smart-arsery and smug superiority. Well, that's probably how they think of you, too'. And in doing so, populists would turn a certain, susceptible kind of voter against reason, expertise, electoral self-interest, and even demonstrable reality.

But it didn't help to understand the strategy, because the simple act of explaining it to the principal victims of populism – which studies have proven to be less educated people who fall for the trick – only helps to entrench the view that the left are a bunch of condescending know-alls.[87]

There is, of course, a solution to all of this: give poorer people better lives. People listen to populists when their lives are hard, insecure, and shorn of promise. The likes of Donald Trump, Marine Le Pen and Nigel Farage exploit these real problems by blaming it all on foreigners. But it isn't caused by foreigners, it's caused by the kinds of financial inequality produced by late-stage capitalism. The solution is not a more extreme version of capitalism. Nor is it communism. The solution is to materially improve people's lives.

But this cannot be done by merely increasing GDP, despite what politicians of every stripe insist. The richest fifth of Britons sit on 63 per cent of existing wealth, but also take home 36 per cent of new income. The poorest fifth receive only half of a per cent.[88] So any GDP growth within the existing economic order will only increase inequality and create a ready market for the empty bromides of the far-right. Redistribution is the solution, since it robs the populists of an angry, disillusioned constituency who feel left behind by modernity, impoverished by late-stage capitalism, and ignored by conventional politics.

As Good as It Gets

Anderson was bad enough, but Sunak hadn't finished with his hiring spree. He invited Suella Braverman to be his home secretary a mere six days after Liz Truss had sacked her from the same job because of a mindboggling series of security breaches.[89] Nobody trusted Braverman, which was hardly surprising. She wasn't just gaslighting the public, she was doing it to the Cabinet too. On at least six occasions Downing Street had to ask Home Office civil servants to fact-check things Braverman had said in cabinet meetings, because she made 'basic errors' and 'keeps getting facts wrong'.[90]

Braverman's return seems to have made her assume she was unsackable, no matter how blatantly she manoeuvred to replace the PM. So she waited and plotted, with an important part of that plot being guiding the Rwanda bill through parliament. But even the Conservative Party still contained a few MPs who suspected it might be a bad look for a permanent member of the UN Security Council to deliberately break international law, and they pushed back hard against the Rwanda plan. They were led by Theresa May, a tottering, stridulous seabird who lurched to her feet behind Braverman, and openly attacked the government's signature asylum policy.

'The UK has always welcomed those who are fleeing persecution, regardless of whether they come from a safe and legal route', said May, and concluded that passing this bill would 'harm the reputation of the UK on the world stage'.[91]

She was followed by Caroline Nokes, the former immigration minister, who declared her 'absolute horror' of the Rwanda legislation. Chris Skidmore swore he would never support it. Simon Hoare condemned it. Robert Buckland. David Simmonds. Stephen Hammond. One by one, senior Tory backbenchers took to their feet to pull their own government's policy into small, wet pieces, and hurl it back into Braverman's face.[92]

Yet in the end, not a single Tory voted against the bill. Many abstained, but once again the supposedly calming presence of One Nation Conservatives had no effect whatsoever on the shrill, nativist aggression of the rest of the party. Their moderating influence influenced nothing. The maniacs powered the Tories ever further to the right, and the meek cowardice of technically sane Conservative

MPs delivered nothing more than a small, very much temporary victory over morality, practicality, affordability, and legality.

It was as good as things were ever going to get for Suella Braverman.

To celebrate, she headed off to Rwanda to reassure everybody that it wasn't a dangerous autocratic dictatorship, and that she herself wasn't a heartless, cackling sociopath. As a top-ranking general in the battle to defend free speech, she only invited right-wing media to accompany her on the plane to Kigali. She found places for GB News and the *Daily Mail*, which is banned as a source by Wikipedia because of 'poor fact checking, sensationalism and flat-out fabrication'.[93] But the BBC, *Guardian*, and *Independent* – which, despite what you might think, remain some of the most accurate, reliable and trusted news sources on the planet[94] – were barred from Braverman's flight.[95] So there was nobody to question the government's latest series of claims: that all loopholes for asylum seekers had now been closed; that small boats would stop arriving any moment now; and that the Rwanda scheme was so very, very legal that there was no doubt it would be 'authoritatively upheld by the High Court'.

Most importantly: that deportations to Rwanda would start in the summer of 2023.[96]

Yet despite the millions spent, by this point the only people we'd managed to send to Rwanda were our home secretary and a bunch of nodding dogs pretending to be journalists. They followed Braverman to a Rwandan housing development supposedly intended for Britain's asylum seekers, where she was photographed in a widely-shared image: standing with her head thrown back, teeth exposed, howling in some sort of paroxysm.[97] It was hard to know whether she was performing a maniacal laugh, or simply emitting the high, keening sound her species uses to attract a mate. But whichever it was, she broke off momentarily to tell friendly journalists that the flats were 'really beautiful', and that she wanted to hire their interior designer to work on her own home, or hive, or vespiary or whatever.

But you'll note I said *supposedly* intended for asylum seekers. It may shock you to learn that not everything the government told you was strictly accurate. By January 2024 – at which point we still hadn't sent a single asylum seeker overseas – the flats had all been sold off because, in the words of the property developers' sales team, 'The houses are for Rwandans. If you say it's for refugees, I don't think so'.[98]

*

And still Braverman pressed on, determined to persuade the public that Rishi Sunak was 'getting a grip' on the situation. He was quick to agree. 'Make no mistake', he said, clearly hoping to monopolise the making of mistakes, 'if you come here illegally, you will not be able to stay'.[99]

But there's no such thing as coming here illegally, because seeking asylum was something anybody could do, regardless of how they arrived in a country, where they came from, or how many safe countries they'd visited in the interim.[100] It says as much in the 1951 Refugee Convention, of which Britain was not merely a signatory, but one of the key authors.[101] It was drawn up in response to the refugee crisis of World War II, but Braverman now argued the Convention was not 'fit for our modern age', and that we 'live in a completely different time'.

I'll give her that. That much was true. World War II was a gigantic crisis, creating 60 million refugees. But in 2023 the world wasn't experiencing a single, massive conflict: it was experiencing 65 of them at once, springing up on almost every continent.[102] Instead of 60 million forcibly displaced civilians, the UNHCR listed 122.6 million of them.[103]

So if the Refugee Convention was no longer fit for the times, it was because it no longer went far enough.

I Know Thee Not, Old Man

'Hubris', wrote P.J. O'Rourke, 'is one of the great renewable resources', a theory that was about to be put to the test by Boris Johnson, who in March 2023 endured a spectacularly vanity-destroying week in politics.

It began with his appearance before a House of Commons committee, which gathered to pass judgement on whether Johnson had lied to parliament during Partygate, in an exciting sequel to the working group that converged in the woods to debate ursine defecation habits.

This was the event that would determine Johnson's future in politics. A moment for the history books. One that demanded the utmost seriousness. So he rocked up with the bedraggled mien of somebody who had recently eaten quite a lot of tablets, then spent the subsequent days investigating the bins during a heavy finale at Creamfields. He'd been plodged into his suit as though somebody had blindly poured a vat of blancmange into a wardrobe. His blond mop seemed to have been brushed with a toffee apple, and he faced his enemies not so much like a caged beast as a cowed trifle.

The braggadocio was still there though, the bluster, the rampant jumbles of pleonastic gobbledegook. But it now seemed desperate. Once he had been his party's Falstaff, a spittle-flecked raspberry in the face of decency, a lazy, lardy manufacturer of lies and larceny, ready to stick a knife into anybody, then drop his pants and wink at the audience for laughs. But those days were gone. As the committee closed in, he just seemed lost, desperate, and angry.

He might have expected some support from the Tory MPs who formed the majority of those there to judge him. But the ruling fell during one of those transient moments where his party viewed him as an embarrassment again, and barely one of them could make eye contact with him as he placed his hand on the Bible, swore to be truthful, and immediately perjured himself.

'Hand on heart', he said, 'I did not lie to the House'.[104]

This would have been a great defence if, two days earlier, he hadn't published a 52-page document in which he admitted misleading Parliament.[105] That's what you get for £265,000 of the best legal defence money can buy. Not Johnson's money, by the way: yours.[106] The National Audit Office later heavily criticised the Government for such epic waste.[107]

Proceedings were paused so the defendant could go and vote against Sunak's Windsor Framework, which Johnson opposed on the grounds that it would help to Get Brexit Done. You can't claim credit for Brexit if somebody else is doing it better, so he rallied his troops and charged pell-mell into the breach. Only 22 Tory MPs followed him, and his pathetic rebellion failed.[108]

The morning's humiliation behind him, Fat Malfoy traipsed back to the committee chamber, wearing the forlorn look of a man who has just turned the lights on and realised two important things: that this isn't the bathroom at all; and that he should have pulled his trousers down before he began the procedure. Any power he retained existed only in his mind, and even that drained visibly away as he faced the final verdict.

To summarise: *absurdly* guilty, your honour.

Johnson and his acolytes responded with concocted assertions the committee was a kangaroo court, and that the entire thing was either punishment for eating a cake that didn't exist, or an attempt to reverse the Brexit that Johnson had just spent his morning voting against. Yet a majority of those who sat on the committee – a fixed part of the parliamentary system for over thirty years – were not naysaying Remoaners, but Brexiteer Tories.[109] The committee chair had been selected in a free vote by every member of parliament, something the Conservatives had demanded and got.[110] And Johnson's party still held a 70-plus majority in the house, easily enough to overturn any committee findings.

'He just isn't used to being rejected', said one former Johnson staffer as mitigation. 'There's a kind of madness in it, like he's in denial. But then it's hard to overstate how many extraordinary things have happened to him in the past few years. His mother died, he nearly died, his children started hating him'.[111] It was if they'd somehow forgotten that he'd overseen the deaths of 200,000 other people, all of whom had mothers. Or that 50,000 of them had already died by the time Johnson volunteered to be injected with Covid on live TV to prove it was nothing to worry about.[112] And his kids hating him would be poignant if it wasn't, by this stage, the most plausible thing about the man.

And then, just at the moment we were supposed to feel the most sorry for him, Johnson unleashed the moral pugnacity that made him our generation's Sir Plankton Churchill, and started making not-so-subtle threats to the MPs who had pointed out his failings.[113] 'I think that people will judge for themselves, on the basis of the evidence that you've produced, on the fairness of this committee', said Johnson. So that evening on BBC *Question Time*, Fiona Bruce asked the audience to judge for themselves, on the basis of the evidence.

Not one person believed Boris Johnson.[114]

Putting On His Frightening Pants

Boris Johnson's unique combination of bombast, debauchery, incompetence and brute ambition had now ended the careers of three prime ministers, including that of Boris Johnson, which turned out to be the only genuinely funny thing he ever achieved. But with the Partygate fallout, a line had been drawn, and you'd have forgiven Sunak for thinking all of his Christmases had come at once.

Sadly, he'd reckoned without Matt Hancock.

The former health secretary is what happens when you type 'cringe' into ChatGPT; a dauntingly inept, walking, talking advert for Fathers4Justice, who had led us backwards through the pandemic despite Downing Street's most senior advisor repeatedly warning Johnson, 'if we don't sack Matt Hancock, we are going to kill people'.[115]

The fact that they went right ahead and *did* kill people was a rare example of Hancock not disappointing, and many held him personally responsible for snuffing their nana with his signature policy of waiting until hospitals were awash with the Covid virus, then rounding up all the elderly patients he could find and shoving them into care homes without giving them a test first.

At least 20,000 people died as a result.[116]

But who cares about all that! We had more important things to focus on, not least Hancock's detailed plan for rehabilitation. It took the form of him pretending he wasn't on the public payroll for a few weeks, so he could head off to the sun for a lucrative stint on *I'm A Celebrity*, where for £320,000 he agreed to be looked at quite harshly by somebody off *Hollyoaks*, and thus justice was done.[117]

I can't put my finger on why, but the public remained cross with Hancock, and he still had a divorce to fund. So in an increasingly desperate attempt to make a killing out of all that killing, he decided he would publish a gripping, tell-all memoir that nobody would give rubbery tartan shit about.

Perhaps fearing he might lack the skills to say things in his own words, he decided to say them in somebody else's words instead, and asked for the help of *The Telegraph*'s chief Isabel Oakeshott correspondent, Isabel Oakeshott. She had form. She'd co-authored the book detailing the astonishing claim that David Cameron had stuck his tallywacker into a dead pig, and the not-one-bit-astonishing claim that he held regular cocaine-fuelled dinner parties, which for some reason got rather less press attention.[118] It's almost certain that the pig story was entirely invented,[119] which made Oakeshott the ideal person to produce a hagiography of Hancock, and paint him not as a malignant little turd of a man who looked like Peewee Herman reflected in the back of a spoon, but as a misunderstood hero who made all the right calls.

But *just in case* appointing Oakeshott wasn't the right call, Hancock got her to sign a Non-Disclosure Agreement before he shared 100,000 of his most humiliating WhatsApp messages with her. She diligently wrote the book, dutifully cashed the cheque, and then predictably reneged on the NDA, spilling the lot to *The Telegraph*. She said what she's done was in 'the national interest', although was unable to deny *The Telegraph* had paid her a shitload of money to hand over the messages.[120]

It would have been a PR nightmare for anybody but Hancock, whose reputation was by now so low that graphene would bang its head on it. His messages showed a man who had spent his lockdowns mocking those trapped in the quarantine he'd designed, criticising Sunak's infamous Eat Out To Help Out scheme, and threatening to 'frighten the pants off everyone' during the pandemic, thankfully using a different pants-removal strategy than the one he'd deployed on Gina Coladangelo.[121]

But more importantly, the messages showed he'd been given medical and scientific advice telling him not to send untested patients into care homes, but he had ignored it.

When he saw the leaked texts, he claimed they'd been 'doctored', leaving the nation split between those who were aghast at the implication that somebody as ethical as Isabel Oakeshott would dream of doing such a thing, and those who were merely shocked that Matt Hancock knew what 'doctor' meant.[122]

An April Shower of Shit (Part 1)

The human sense of scale isn't designed to comprehend the magnitude of the universe. We evolved to understand distances and sizes that were useful to a Neolithic hunter: down to a grain of sand and up to the horizon. Anything on a larger or smaller scale – which accounts for almost everything in existence – is beyond the scope of our imagination.

So your mind might just about be able to deal with the fact that Matt Hancock was so bad at his job that he'd managed to be sacked by Boris Johnson, but you'll need smelling salts and a long lie down when you learn Kwasi Kwarteng was a man so bad at his job that he managed to be sacked by Liz Truss.

Liz Truss! I don't know if that's rock bottom, but creeping Jesus, I hope we never find out.

So imagine my delight when at the end of March, Hancock and Kwarteng teamed up, for one of those moments when you're so full of shit one arsehole isn't enough. The campaigning group Led By Donkeys set up a fake company supposedly based in South Korea, and easily duped Hancock and Kwarteng into offering their services for cash. Hancock explained that he didn't expect a 'king's ransom', just a modest £10,000 per day, and then Kwarteng said he wanted the same. It's clearly not his strong suit, so I'll step in here to help Kwasi with the maths: the man who destroyed the nation's economy in just 38 days as Chancellor reckoned his market value was more than £3 million a year.[123]

Not for nothing did the Labour MP Chris Bryant describe this as 'the worst parliament in our history'.[124] Statistically speaking, he was right: a record 23 MPs had resigned or been suspended since the last time the country had a say in who led them, and now this. Kwancock – yep, they deserve a portmanteau – were by my estimation about the thousandth leading Tories to have been caught on camera offering to sell their democratic obligations to some shady gobshites for a thick handful of banknotes. And now it was time for Kwarteng's successor to present his latest wild stab at economic competence.

The Chancellor, Jeremy Hunt, assured us he had conjured up a 'budget for growth' that would avoid recession in 2023 and would, at long last, 'prove the doubters wrong'[125]. The doubters could relax: the UK went into recession in October, and it's not hard to understand why.[126] Back in 2010, Labour minister Liam Byrne had famously left a jokey private note reading, 'there's no money left'. This was part of a custom of addressing self-deprecating messages to your successor, going back to (at least) Tory Chancellor Reginald Maudling, who had written a message for his Labour replacement reading, 'Good luck, old cock, sorry to leave it in such a mess'. But the Tories exploited a traditional in-joke for all the electoral value they could get, then used it as cover for their lifelong dream – a chance to cut the state to the bone while blaming the resulting pain and chaos on Labour.

Liam Byrne joked there was no money left. Cameron and Osborne's austerity scratched that same message bone deep into the fabric of our country and kept on cutting. For 13 years they'd relentlessly starved the UK of investment and attention, driven by an ideological preoccupation with small-statism, rather than evidence or judgement. They'd skim-read the *CliffsNotes* about arch neoliberal Friedrich Hayek, Thatcher's favourite economist, and then the more ambitious of them had shouted the general principles at Lee Anderson through the bars of his pen. And that was that. Stop reading: you've already got all the economic wisdom worth having. Hayek's 1943 theories would definitely still apply in the complicated, interconnected, digitally transformed real world of 2023; and if they didn't, well, the real world would just have to change. We must have no state investment, no valuable shared assets, and above all no regulations, so the invisible hand of the market could more efficiently punch Britain in the face.

But the dream of a non-existent state had turned into a nightmare. After a dozen years, nobody was buying the pathetic story that Labour was to blame. And if a government spends all its days denying responsibility for anything, they shouldn't be surprised when their MPs start acting irresponsibly. There was a near constant eruption of scandal, and by April the smarter Tories began to suspect they'd need to find a new career soon. Despite Labour's Keir Starmer projecting all the charisma of John Major depicted as an Easter Island statue, his party still held a consistent 20-point lead in the polls, suggesting more than half of Conservative seats would be lost at a general election.[127]

Consequently, more than half of Conservative underpants were suddenly very full indeed.[128]

In despair, many simply gave up. Every week seemed to bring more news that some Tory MP or other had chosen not to stand for re-election. The resignations were the constant drip, drip, drip in the background of Sunak's ministry, a signifier of a decaying old boiler about to bring the roof down. With over a year to go until the election, a sixth of the party had already decided to call it quits, and more than a few others had had that decision made for them.[129]

Which brings me to Scott Benton, who had the whip withdrawn after committing the basic schoolboy error of undertaking his corruption in front of witnesses.

With minimal prompting from a *Times* journalist posing as a rep from a fake gambling company, Benton had offered to leak confidential government documents and ask parliamentary questions in return for £4,000 a month. In case this wasn't incriminating enough, Benton accidentally told *The Times* this wasn't the first time he'd offered paid services in this way.[130]

A parliamentary inquiry found Benton had given the implicit message that 'he was corrupt and "for sale", and that so were many other Members of the House', which wasn't something the public was supposed be aware of, despite the recent sting operation on Kwarteng and Hancock. Benton, who emits the energy of an estate agent who became an MP after he took a wrong turn on his way to audition for *The Book of Mormon*, was found to have shown all the hallmarks of committing a 'repeat offence'. He was handed a 35-day suspension from parliament, which was almost certain to lead to a by-election that he had a snowball in Hell's chance of winning.[131]

So rather than accept the inevitable and trudge down to the job centre, Benton burst without warning into an exuberant spasm of auto-parodic genius. He claimed the fact that he'd offered to leak reports should be overlooked, because the report into his leaking had been leaked.[132]

It's the satirists I feel sorry for.

His appeal failed, and a committee of MPs upheld the 35-day suspension. Benson stood down, leading to the 13th by-election Rishi Sunak had faced in barely a year.

It was Sunak's worst week to date.

*

It was also a pretty bad week to be on the Committee on Parliamentary Standards, which faced a hectic schedule. April brought so many scandals that they averaged one every three days, which was pretty much the rate Boris Johnson had maintained right up until the explosive sprint finish that ended his run in Downing Street. Johnson may have been 200 gallons of undiluted, voluptuary gibberish formed into the rudimentary shape of a baboon, but man alive, he could get a lick on when came to ludicrous disgrace, and few of us expected ethical superbot Rishi Sunak – with his somewhat limited stride length – to keep up the pace. How wrong we were.

As Scott Benton swept out of the revolving door at the back of the Standards Chamber, Sunak swept in, facing an investigation into his failure to declare an interest over his wife's shares in a childcare firm that had benefitted from policies just announced by his own government.[133]

To help the public retain confidence in the transparency and integrity of his high office, Downing Street flatly refused to publish details of the PM's finances. Under questioning, Sunak said, 'All of my disclosures are declared in the normal way'. But the committee responsible for overseeing the Register of Members' Interests pointed out that the record, which is supposed to be published every six months, 'hasn't seen the light of day since last May'. That was a year earlier.[134]

Sunak had promised 'integrity, professionalism and accountability at every level', but at every level his party seemed determined to stymie him.[135]

A fresh shambles had arisen around Mark Spencer, who in his former role as chief whip was supposed to stop his fellow idiots from blabbing in public about their various prejudices and ineptitudes. Despite this, when Nus Ghani had claimed in 2022 that she lost her ministerial post after being told by a colleague that her 'Muslim woman minister status was making colleagues feel uncomfortable', Spencer rushed onto Twitter to deny he'd ever said those words.[136]

Nobody had claimed he said those words.

They did now, obviously.

After just enough time had passed for Spencer to work out that exposing the party to ridicule was the complete opposite of what his job required – an insight that took him eight long, pained minutes – he deleted the tweets.[137] And then he almost immediately tweeted basically the same message again, 'cos sure, why not?[138]

After an investigation that took almost a year, the government's ethics advisor reached a conclusion: it was inconclusive. No further action would be taken against Spencer, due to the he-said, she-said nature of the accusation, but it didn't sound like Nus Ghani was entirely pleased with this outcome. She observed that the inquiry had established 'no criticism or doubt expressed regarding my version of events', but it had slated the 'omissions', 'shortcomings' and 'inaccurate briefings' in Spencer's side of the story. I'd be interested to discover whether she and Mark Spencer still exchange birthday cards.

*

And still the April shower of shit continued, as news arrived from Wales of an audio recording in which a local councillor had said, 'I think all white men should have a Black man as a slave or Black woman as a slave'. He went on to reassure listeners that this wasn't about skin colour – phew! – but rather about social status, because 'they're lower class than us white people'.

Officials working alongside Conservative councillor Andrew

Edwards identified it as his voice on the recording, and he referred himself to an Ombudsman to evaluate whether he was horrifyingly racist, disgustingly classist, or unsurprisingly both. Who knows, he may even be innocent, although the Tories immediately suspended him, which doesn't suggest the party had much faith in such an outcome. Edwards said it would be unfair for him to comment until the investigation was complete, which, at the time of writing, it isn't. So, dear reader, conclude nothing about this massive racist until we hear the results.[139]

And on to the next bit of embarrassment. In the four months since the leader of the Tory group on Plumsted council had tweeted that it was 'likely' that a rape victim in his own ward was a prostitute whose 'punter didn't pay', the Tory party hadn't got around to sacking him. In April, a space in the scandal diary finally cleared, and he was expelled. Shaun Slator said he was 'disappointed' to be very slowly shuffled out of his career because, in his words, 'I'm not promoting rape, am I?'[140]

No Shaun, you aren't. Well done for that small accomplishment.

Slator said he would be appealing. Not to me, he isn't.[141]

*

Also in April – Jesus, Mary and Joseph and the wee donkey, this is all in the same month! – also in April, Andrew Bridgen, the Norse god of doing the wrong thing, was finally expelled from the Tory Party over his contention that vaccinating people during a global pandemic qualified as 'the biggest crime against humanity since the Holocaust'.[142] He'd lost the parliamentary whip for this at the start of the year, but now he lost his party membership too, along with control over his few remaining marbles.[143]

He announced his intention to stand again at the next election, determined to represent his constituents through thick and thin. He'd provide the thick, and the thin came in the form of leading failed actor and failing lead singer Laurence Fox, who posed happily alongside Bridgen as he transformed into the Reclaim Party's first and last MP.[144]

I don't know what first attracted Bridgen to a party that had recently reached the dizzy heights of 2 per cent in the polls.[145] I will merely observe that Reclaim had Jeremy Hosking, and Jeremy Hosking had deep pockets: he was the party's main financier, and had previously given money to the Tories when Boris Johnson had promised Net Zero, and then to one of Nigel Farage's lucrative political vehicles because it promised to oppose Net Zero.[146] This infallible knack for political coherence and sound character judgement came in handy for Andrew Bridgen when Hosking later parted with a £4.7 million loan to help Bridgen get over his profound failure to win a court case about some potatoes.[147]

Spud-u-Hate had been blessed with a unique gift for being the stupidest person in every gathering he was part of, which may be why he resigned from Reclaim only seven months later, perhaps concerned that Laurence Fox was about to oust him as the party's top embarrassment.[148]

However, the defection of Andrew Bridgen left a space in the Tory ranks for Most Tragicomic Travesty, an accolade almost the entire party fought over with unseemly relish. The crown temporarily landed on the cuboid head of Dominic Raab, a semi-professional Jason Statham lookalike from the cheapest agency in Buckinghamshire.

His haircuts cost £8, which is £2 a side.

Raab resigned from the cabinet in April after a report found his eight denials over eight separate accusations of bullying weren't an accurate reflection of reality.[149] In the land where Raab's mind wanders, he had 'acted with professionalism and integrity', and merely required high standards from his underlings. In the land where the rest of us live, he was a howling, fruit-hurling tyrant who presided over a 'culture of fear', refused to listen to advice, and tended to end his meetings 'literally shaking with rage'.[150] The report said he was 'unreasonably and persistently aggressive [and] difficult to deal with', and concluded that he was an intimidating man.

Not intellectually. But in other ways.

Take to the Un-Lifeboats!

It was Rishi Sunak's worst week to date.

It was also curtains-up time at Suella Braverman's theatre of the absurd. The home secretary existed in a fog of contradiction, at once enraptured by the opportunities for sadism her role presented, and obsessed with escaping that role so she could replace Sunak as the next calamitous, short-term leader of the Conservative Party. You could never be sure whether she *personally* despised foreigners, or if she just reckoned Tory members did, and, as part of her machinations to become party leader, had merely deployed the cynical tactic of pandering to their every worst instinct. You can draw your own conclusions, which is exactly what Conservative peer Sayeeda Warsi did.

'Whether [Braverman's] consistent use of racist rhetoric is strategy or incompetence doesn't matter,' said Warsi. 'Both show she is not fit to hold high office'.[151]

Braverman's latest stunt was equal parts eye-catching and mind-numbing. In April, she announced her plan to house asylum seekers in a theatrically horrible prison barge, the Bibby Stockholm, which had just been purchased from a Dutch government that had been shamed into selling it after the vessel was criticised for being an 'oppressive environment'.[152]

'That sounds like my kinda party,' said Braverman, flipped opened the Home Office chequebook, and parted with £22 million of your pounds.[153]

The head of the Home Affairs Committee said she was 'just flabbergasted that a value-for-money assessment was not carried out' when the contract was signed; but for Joseph Gerbils and her endlessly hungry ambition, fiscal prudence and humane effectiveness came second to gaining positive headlines from *The Telegraph*. That a formerly-great publication now served a readership in constant conflict with the troubling details of reality; but if she was ever going to be party leader, this was the cohort Braverman needed to win over, and fast. So in the rush to sign a contract, the home secretary didn't spend a lot of time contemplating all the things that could go wrong.

And boy oh boy, did they go wrong.

It quickly emerged that the Bibby Stockholm didn't come with lifejackets.[154] Not that you'd need any: you couldn't reach the water anyway, since it also didn't have any emergency exits, and firemen had to point out that it would prove borderline impossible to tackle a blaze on board,[155] because the corridors had been narrowed so we could cram in more human cattle.[156] The boat was designed to accommodate 222 people. Our Government planned to store over 500.[157]

The manufacturer's website describes a vessel with 'natural ventilation'.[158] But after it had been adapted to hold more than double the safe number of migrants, the head of the UK's Health Security Agency told us to relax: inmates burning alive or drowning wouldn't be much of a problem anyway, since the vessel now had such poor air-flow that there was a high risk of death from respiratory infections before a single blazing human body had a chance to hit the water.

Whatever the opposite of a lifeboat is, this was it; but the government simply shrugged, and went ahead with its mad plans anyway.[159]

Or at least, tried to. Unfortunately, they immediately fell over their own feet, because by this point even the promise of indeterminate incarceration in a suffocating aquatic firetrap wasn't nasty enough to please the Tory right.

The Braverman-supporting local MP for the proposed site of the Bibby Stockholm, the lavishly named Richard Grosvenor

Plunkett-Ernle-Erle-Drax, suddenly discovered he didn't support Braverman at all.[160] Drax said he'd launch a legal action to prevent the asylum seekers that he wanted to be treated cruelly from being treated cruelly anywhere near him, thank you very much.[161] It was an act of extreme Nimbyism from a man whose back yard is an inherited, 28 square-kilometre country estate.[162] The family money – irony of ironies – came from his ancestors going to somebody else's country and stealing people's jobs. Or to be more accurate, stealing people, and forcing them to do jobs, since the Drax family had been some of our very best slavers.[163]

The current Drax said the pivotal role his ancestors played in the Caribbean slave trade was deeply regrettable, but 'no one can be held responsible today for what happened many hundreds of years ago'. His steadfast rejection of responsibility for the past didn't stretch to rejecting the money accruing from it: Barbadian politicians demanded reparations from Drax, but instead he agreed to flog the former slave plantations for £3 million.[164]

Back here at home, he insisted our country was too full to accommodate migrants.[165] And from his point of view, mathematics suggests he's right: if everybody in Britain had a home the size of his, the UK could contain only 8700 people. Contrast his humble abode with the life of asylum seekers on the Bibby Stockholm, who, a parliamentary inquiry later found, were being crammed six-to-a-room in a cabin designed for one.[166]

By the time Braverman had overcome Drax's attempt to put a legal block on the exact thing he wanted to happen, it was August, and 35 asylum-seekers were forlornly led up the gangplank towards their floating prison. Only 15 of them made it. The rest refused to go inside,[167] and who can blame them, because within minutes of their arrival Legionnaires' disease was found on the vessel, and it was abandon-ship again.[168] Not immediately though: the Home Office knowingly left them on board with the deadly pathogen for four days.[169]

The part that it was okay to say out loud was the claim that the barge would save the taxpayer millions that were currently being spent keeping asylum seekers in hotels. Subtextually, it was all part of the ongoing pageant of cruelty that had turned into a competitive sport for the Conservative front bench. What it cost, what it achieved – those things were largely irrelevant. So was accuracy. Immigration delivery minister Tom Pursglove had said the price of this fiasco was 'undoubtedly' cheaper than housing asylum seekers in hotels, but I'd advise you to invest heavily in doubts, because Pursglove was spectacularly wrong.[170] By November 2023, the asylum accommodation ship was 530 per cent more expensive per-person than the hotel-based system it replaced.

Senior Conservatives were infuriated, not merely by the sheer incompetence, but by the nativism, the cruelty, the resentment of it all. Multiple MPs, peers and senior activists turned on Braverman in the press, describing her as a 'real racist bigot', while another despaired at the damage she was doing to the party's good name, which presumably they still thought it had.[171] 'The country is not as grotesque as she makes it out to be', they said, warning that the 'Conservative reputation on discrimination has dropped to a new low'.

Part of this was due to Braverman's increasingly noisy attempts to gain the attention of the party faithful's xenophobe contingent, desperate for their votes when Sunak inevitably fell from power. In the previous months she'd said small boat arrivals amounted to an 'invasion', and then appeared to accuse British men of Pakistani origins of holding 'cultural attitudes completely incompatible with British values'.[172]

'Suella's comments pander to the unpleasant base instinct of a small section of the British population', said a Conservative former minister, 'She's not stupid, she believes she has a licence to say these things because she's not white. But all her language does is exacerbate hatred'.

Another senior Tory said, 'The politics of this leadership plan stink', and there were more than a few placing the blame at the feet of Rishi Sunak, insisting he should, 'stop the culture wars and create change. But his inaction shows how insecure he is in his own ability'.[173]

Meanwhile Braverman's supposedly cheap contract for barges and hotels had by now spiralled to £1.6 billion, enough to form a pile of £10 notes towering almost 10 miles into the sky. Yet after nearly a year of loading the Bibby Stockholm with desperate migrants, it held just 70 people. Tragically, this number quickly fell to 69 following the death by suicide of 27-year-old Leonard Farruku,[174] who we should remember was a real human being with hopes and fears, and a mum and dad. It's easy to reduce arguments about asylum-seekers to a debate about impersonal statistics, but every refugee is an actual person, and you should stop thinking of yourself as somebody with ethics if you can't come to terms with that.

Sadly, Leonard Farruku found it impossible to come to terms with what you or I would describe as an overcrowded, infectious, floating death-trap for incarcerating people who had broken no laws, but which the Bibby website still describes as 'luxury living' designed to keep people 'happy and comfortable during their stay'.[175]

The Latest Brexit Betrayal

The relentless and official dehumanisation of immigrants had been a central feature of Brexit, a policy that in April, almost seven years after it had begun, once again found itself in a need of saving.

This was hardly a new experience. Nigel Farage had been Brexit's first saviour, saving it tirelessly for 23 years, day in, day out, with an upright zeal that lasted right up to the instant – which was approximately one twinkling second after the referendum closed – that his campaign required somebody to take responsibility for what came next, at which point he sodded off. You probably don't even remember the man, because in July of 2016 he had stepped away from the public gaze forever, telling the throng of journalists invited along to witness his monastic withdrawal into humble obscurity, 'I want my life back [and] I won't be changing my mind again, I can promise you'.[176]

You've never said a truer word, Nigel.

No really, I've checked. All your other words were even less true.

Brexit's next scheduled saviour was supposed to be Boris Johnson, but his enthronement was abruptly cancelled when his own running-mate, Michael Gove, revealed to the world's press the shock news that Johnson was a shambolic, deceitful absurdity who wasn't remotely capable of the job.[177] Instead Gove, a man with a face only a motherfucker could love, decided that he himself would take on the mantle, overruling the objections of – let me check my notes – Michael Gove, who had said in 2012, 'I'm not equipped to be prime minister'.

And then, 'I'm constitutionally incapable of it'.

And then, 'I don't have it in me. I don't have what it takes'.

And then, 'I don't want to do it and there are people who are far better equipped than me to do it'.

And then, 'If anyone wants me to sign a piece of parchment in my own blood saying I don't want to be prime minister, then I'm perfectly happy to do that'.[178]

Sadly there was a change of plan. All of Michael Gove's blood remained in his body, so in June of 2016 he decided he did want to be prime minister after all. On the face of it, the joint-leader of the Leave campaign[179] should have been a shoo-in to lead a party committed to saving Brexit, but in fact the job went to somebody who opposed the very idea of quitting the EU. Gove himself came a distant third.[180]

But our laughter was short-lived, because now Brexit had to be saved by Theresa May, a clattering, haunted Anglepoise lamp who seemed to have learned her political dictum from the Dulux colour chart. As we know, the European Union lives in a blizzard of treaties and memoranda, which May hoped would be overthrown by her detailed characterisation of Brexit as being 'red, white and blue'.[181] Unfortunately the EU wanted the Brexit agreement to contain a bit more detail than: what are the colours in your national flag?

So in a fluster, she made the foolish mistake of attempting to properly define Brexit, rather than merely save it. This went down badly with the 17 million people who each had their own vague idea of what it is they may or may not have voted for in 2016.

'What do we want?', went their battle-cry.

'Not this!'

'When do we want it?;

'Ummmm...'

Exhausted by the process, May took inspiration from the stage at her party conference, and collapsed under the weight of her own ridiculousness, leaving Boris Johnson to return for a second attempt at saving Brexit.

It didn't come a moment too soon for Johnson, who was having to scrape by on the quarter of a million quid *The Telegraph* handed over in exchange for 800 words of bullshit every Sunday.[182] But he majestically sacrificed all that to save Brexit again. Saving Brexit was a vital element in Johnson's lifelong plan to persuade us he could be court-jester and king at the same time. It's called multitasking, and despite claims that men can't multitask, Johnson managed to be a scrounger, moocher, freeloader, schnorrer and junketeer, all at the same time.

He was also a Brexiteer whenever it provided an immediate advantage to himself, and as such he promised that if we made him prime minister, he would Get Brexit Done. In fact, he so enjoyed Getting Brexit Done that he had to Do It Again on a practically weekly basis. His oven-ready deal skipped the middleman and went straight into the toilet, so Johnson reverted to type, and delivered an endlessly refreshed diet of moonshine and procrastination.

But there was a problem: the moment he'd signed his triumphant Brexit agreement, all that hazy hogwash was suddenly replaced by a legally binding framework. And even worse, by a strict schedule. The vast pile of Brexit cans that he'd kicked down the road now began to bang into an immovable deadline. It was like that scene in *World War Z* where the zombies pile up against the Jerusalem wall. And in 2021, they spilled over into chaos.

'Don't give up on Brexit,' bellowed Johnson, safe inside his moated Tudor mansion. 'These are just teething troubles,' he hollered as the zombies bit into your neck. Inevitably, he was hurled from office in a cloud of inarticulate, unprincipled twaddle, and Brexit needed a new saviour.

In swept Liz Truss.

And then out swept Liz Truss, leaving Brexit in trouble again.

By 2023, perhaps only Lois Lane had been saved as many times as Brexit; and just like her, Brexit seemed to immediately get itself into a rare old pickle again, just in time for the next cartoonish episode.

It was now Rishi Sunak's turn to save Brexit, and it wasn't going well. Despite the Windsor Framework, our decision to leave the EU had never been less popular, and by the end of the year only one person in ten felt better off as a result of the referendum decision.[183] Even so, the main presumptive candidates to replace Sunak – bookies' favourite Kemi Badenoch, sea dog's favourite Penny Mordaunt, and nobody's favourite Suella Braverman – still jostled to prove their Brexit-saving credentials.

Sunak had campaigned for the leadership on a promise of a 'red tape bonfire' that would 'unleash the full potential of Britain post-Brexit',[184] and at the start of the year had backed a plan to instantly scrap 4,000 laws in an orgy of political recklessness and document shredding not witnessed since Partygate.[185] Badenoch was put in charge of delivery. Now was her chance to surge ahead of her rivals.

In pursuit of Purity of Brexit Essence, the Tories had made a big song-and-dance about igniting a bonfire of those 4,000 laws, and to hell with the consequences. Sadly, the consequences didn't care, and after four months of reading the small print Kemi Badenoch had to admit that only one fifth of those 4,000 laws could actually be removed. And even then, it would have to be done very slowly and carefully.

Brexiteers responded with the nuance and moderation you would expect.

'Latest Brexit betrayal', shouted *The Telegraph*.[186]

'Brexit is being surrendered', droned posturing Regency undertaker Jacob Rees-Mogg.[187]

'You need a tough minister, but she is a lame minister,' said an MP from the European Research Group, 'Kemi is proving to be a huge disappointment.'

'This blows her leadership chances,' said another. 'She will lose a third of the party'.

Losing a third of Tories sounded like great news to most voters, but it was bad news for Semi GoodEnough's career hopes, until it became clear the cause of this entire mess – gird your loins for a shock – was the ERG's very own Jacob Rees-Mogg, Badenoch's ministerial predecessor, who had overseen the drafting of the legislation. And guess what? 'Kemi inherited a mess', said a Government insider, 'but now she's got a grip of the process'.[188]

However, her supposed grip was entirely dependent on her not fully understanding what that process was. Legal experts described Badenoch's amended bill to scrap the laws as 'unprecedented', 'undemocratic' and an 'invitation to litigation', not least because it bypassed scrutiny from MPs. And our laws being scrutinised by MPs is the entire point of our system of legislative democracy.[189]

The bonfire of EU laws had accidentally set fire to parliamentary sovereignty, and the whole idea was quietly scrapped.[190]

Driving Miss Crazy

In the eyes of the Tory right – the group most likely to decide Sunak's successor – the gloss had come off Badenoch, so the new favourite was Suella Braverman again. She wasn't going to let the opportunity pass, and spent her days attention-seeking, self-promoting, and making attempts to lodge herself in the public imagination that fell only one step short of following you home and screaming her name through your letterbox.

But in May it emerged she had a shy trait too: she'd been caught speeding and was given the option to accept a fine and points on her license, or alternatively to attend a speed awareness course.[191]

Minor stuff, but Braverman, something of a human hand-grenade, managed to blow it up into an almighty row. She had been loath to accept points on her licence, fearing it could affect her insurance premiums; but she'd been even more reluctant to be known as the hard-line, take-no-prisoners home secretary who got laughed at by other attendees at a remedial course for people who had broken the law. So she asked civil servants to arrange a private, one-to-one course. And as every minister knows, because every minister signs up to the ministerial code, that's not the job of civil servants, and ministers aren't allowed to ask them such things.

Thus we entered yet another week of dithering, as Westminster worked itself into a hot pink lather (again) over whether Braverman would have to resign (again) for breaking the ministerial code (again). Sunak raced tepid-foot to the rescue, revealing the mastery of detail and ethical fortitude he had promised us. 'I don't know the full details of what has happened,' he said, 'nor have I spoken to the home secretary.'[192]

Stirring stuff.

There were several ways to explain away the PM's lack of response. Maybe Inaction Man had concluded it was just a storm in a teacup. Perhaps he was too weak to take on a right-wing darling. Or perhaps he was aware that any measures he took would create a ripple of crises across his party, because it was soon revealed three other Tory MPs had also claimed driving fines on expenses: energy minister Amanda Solloway, Simon Hoare and Bim Afolami. Hundreds of pounds were swiftly repaid.[193]

As for Braverman, she showed a surprising amount of morality on the subject.

'Pretending we haven't made mistakes, carrying on as if everyone can't see that we have made them, and hoping that things will magically come right is not serious politics. I have made a mistake; I accept responsibility; I resign.'[194]

No, sorry, hold on: that's what she said the *previous* time she resigned for breaking the ministerial code. This time, she decided the code no longer mattered, and stayed in her job.

Destined for Oblivion

The mood in Government was terrible, with Tory MPs batting their resentments back and forth like gobshite tennis. Boris Johnson was 'like a bad smell that does not seem to go away'. It was 'blindingly obvious' that Suella Braverman was 'not up to the job and her attitude, tone and lack of administrative ability are detrimental to the Government'.[195] She was 'peddling inflated rhetoric and giving speeches that trash the Conservative brand'.[196]

She wasn't alone in the trashcan. April had been bad enough, but as we entered May, Marcus Fysh was facing investigations into discrepancies in his statements of income and expenditure, which would eventually lead to him being ordered to apologise for yet another breach of the MPs' code of conduct.[197] While this investigation was beginning, another was ending, with former health minister Steve Brine being found guilty of failing to declare he was being paid by a health recruitment firm when he'd lobbied the Government during the pandemic.[198]

But spare a thought for heartbreakingly banal backbench room-meat Henry Smith, who had to repay £1,763 of expenses over his misuse of parliamentary stationery. After 13 years in Westminster, the fact that a quibble over photocopier supplies qualifies as his biggest impact on the national stage is unbelievably poignant.[199]

It was against this background that the Tories faced May's local elections. The omens were not good. After a dozen years in power there were no more excuses that could be made, although that didn't stop the Conservatives from trying. They performed their usual routine in the run-up to polling day – stabbing wildly at traditional panic buttons of migration, Europe, and the existential horror of poor, benighted billionaires having to pay equitable tax – without realising the electorate had long since disconnected the wiring from those buttons. The orders to panic were no longer getting through. Sunak made bold announcements, and voters just merely shrugged. It was a terminal sign.

What's more, the PM couldn't escape the long shadow of Boris Johnson, or the significantly shorter one of Liz Truss. And however much he wanted to, his own team wouldn't let him. Conservative Chairman Greg Hands insisted Boris Johnson was a 'campaigning asset',[200] which is why the Porno Honey Monster was let out in public once more, and immediately broke the law.[201] He filmed a piece to camera inside a moving car while not wearing a seatbelt, so Greg Hands had to spend five excruciating minutes on live TV, studiously avoiding the question of how somebody could simultaneously be a brilliant campaigning asset, the subject of a yet another embarrassing police inquiry, and a man of integrity.[202]

Mind you – and it's damning him with the faintest of praise – by comparison with a good many Tory candidates, Johnson looked like a positive saint. In Bracknell, they fielded a nominee who was the former deputy leader of the fascist organisation Britain First. In Bolton, the Conservative candidate had floated the idea on Facebook that we 'shoot the Pakis on the spot', whereas in Lincolnshire they had to make do with a contender who got suspended for sharing racist and homophobic content. Over in Devon, the nominee had to step aside when he suggested that the Holocaust wouldn't have happened if 'more Jews had guns'.[203]

In Lee Anderson's seat of Ashfield, there must be something in the water, because the Conservatives had to suspend a local council candidate when it was revealed he favoured 'stoning' migrants.[204] Also dropped: the Conservative's Blackpool councillor Carl Mather, whose superpower was to see paedophiles everywhere, like the star of a movie called *The Sick Sense*. He claimed the civil service was merely a 'paedo club', insisted that the entire Labour party 'likes to abuse children', and alleged Joe Biden was basically interchangeable with Jimmy Savile.[205]

It was clear people were not likely to vote for candidates like this, so the Tories decided the solution was the make it difficult for people to vote at all. May's local elections were the first since the government had introduced the requirement to produce photo ID when voting, and here are four facts to give this a bit of context.

1. Britain recorded fewer than one voter fraud conviction every two years.[206]
2. Since 2018, more Tory MPs had been arrested for sexual offences than the total number of voter fraud convictions.[207]
3. Voter ID legislation disproportionately excludes ethnic minorities from voting, because they are significantly less likely to possess the required ID.[208]
4. Ethnic minorities are half as likely to vote Conservative than white Britons.[209]

At the May 2023 local elections, over 26,000 voters were turned away at polling stations. They didn't possess any of the acceptable ID. A year later, at the General Election of 2024, research suggests 850,000 legitimate voters were turned away from polling stations, with people of colour being three times more likely to be refused a vote than white people.[210]

Long-standing accusations that the voter ID legislation had been a deliberate attempt to suppress the anti-Tory vote would have been hard to prove, were it not for steampunk C3PO Jacob Rees-Mogg. He popped up at a conference of National Conservatism, looking like a Babadook attempting to pass unnoticed in a knitting circle, and told the collected media that voter ID was merely a 'clever scheme' designed to 'gerrymander' votes.[211]

File under: *saying the quiet part out loud*.

Across town, Conservative peer Peter Cruddas went even further. He gave a speech to yet another batty little Tory faction – the Conservative Democratic Organisation, which it turns out was neither recognisably Conservative, particularly democratic, or especially well organised. Cruddas deplored the prospect of a Starmer victory, fearful that Labour would, 'abolish voter ID, making it impossible for the Conservative party to win an outright majority in the future'.[212]

You have to feel sorry for the Tories. They'd presented the country with a wretched pageant of racist, fascist, paranoid candidates, offered the electorate nothing but galumphing carelessness and a post-vindaloo-level shower of shit, and then made a blatant effort to corrupt democracy: and *still* voters turned against them. The local elections turned out to be yet another catastrophe for Sunak. His professed worst-case scenario had been losing 1000 councillors. In the event, he managed to find an even-worse-case scenario: he lost 1063, an outcome that seemed to catapult Greg Hands into a different universe, from where he beamed his response. 'What I'm hearing on the doorstep is that people are giving Rishi Sunak a chance'.[213] A chance to fuck off, maybe, but that's all.

The response from the PM's cheerleaders was lift music to his ears. *The Telegraph* said the party was 'destined for oblivion'.[214] A source within Government said, 'We almost feel like the next election is out of our hands now'. For Tory MPs of the saner variety, the results were inevitable given the cost-of-living crisis, the outrage about sewage in our waterways, the by-now unavoidable consequences of austerity, and the pandemonium of the previous two years. But for those paddling in the shallow end of the gene pool, it came down to one thing: Rishi Sunak had been horrid to Boris Johnson.

To be honest, I've always felt that was a bit of a stretch. The Johnson loyalists seem to have forgotten that the first minister to quit the cabinet on that fateful day – the blank little pebble that precipitated the landslide of resignations – was Sajid Javid. Sunak, our new, principled prime minister, had only resigned when it was clear that somebody else's principles might get all the limelight. And then 60 others had followed, many of them longstanding Johnson loyalists. But for the libertarian right, Boris had not repeatedly lied to parliament, Liz had not crashed the economy, and if the Government had a fault – which was doubtful – that fault should be laid at the tiny feet of Rishi Sunak. Around two dozen of the most Brexity Tories marched into the office of the chief whip to speak what we must still refer to as their minds.

'What was so astonishing was the level of hostility towards the Government,' said one attendee.[215] Another, a senior backbencher, said, 'The disillusion with the Government is palpable,' and MPs seemed to be lining up to put the boot in.

'A storm is brewing'.

'The membership are angry'.

'The party are giving up on Rishi,' said a moderate former minister, convinced that the Tories were, once again, contemplating ousting a leader. God knows who would want the job next, but many on the right agitated for the return of Boris the Menace, so he could kick-start another year-long gobshite jamboree.

This sense was reenforced at the conference of the Conservative Democratic Organisation, which one minister had described as a 'budget front organisation for Bring Back Boris', and another boiled down to the rather more pithy, 'insane'.[216] The group was a hermetically sealed drunk-tank for those who had overdone the culture war Kool-Aid, and was to be attended former ministers Jacob Rees-Mogg and Nadine Dorries, the Mick Fleetwood and Samantha Fox of the Tory right.

The CDO were in direct competition – not with Labour, but with another contingent of mad populists, who called themselves National Conservatives. Back in 2020 Daniel Kawczynski, a prattling tower of ceaseless backbench inadequacy, had been reprimanded by his party for attending a conference of National Conservatives, because Tory officials described as the movement as 'far-right'. Kawczynski was, the Conservatives said, 'formally warned that his attendance at this event was not acceptable'. The party 'utterly condemn[ed]' National Conservatism, and Kawczynski was made to give a formal apology.[217]

Three years later, in 2023, half the Conservative party attended.

The get-together saw appearances by Suella Braverman and Michael Gove, alongside right-wing commentator Douglas Murray, who had once written that 'conditions for Muslims in Europe must be made harder across the board', and David Starkey, who was sacked from his university post after arguing that even though 15 per cent of African slaves had died during transportation, it still didn't qualify as genocide, because in his words, 'so many damned blacks' had survived.[218]

Another attendee was Danny Kruger, the Tory backbencher who, after 13 years of Conservative government, claimed our nation's troubles were a result of 'Marxism, narcissism and paganism', and placed the blame for Britain's woes on John Lennon, who at this point had been dead for more than four decades.[219]

Britain's population faced a desperate housing crisis, terrifying job insecurity, institutional and national decline, calamitous trade, disintegrating infrastructure, a pensions time-bomb, harrowing poverty, vast queues for healthcare, an existential climate disaster, and world-leading inequality. The solution, argued Kruger, was the return of 'the normative family - held together by marriage, by mother and father sticking together for the sake of the children',[220] which is a bit rich coming from a guy who wouldn't even have been born were it not for his father divorcing his first wife.[221]

It was even more of a strain to hear this from Kruger, who had worked as political secretary to Boris Johnson, the twice-divorced father of a rumoured 12 children, half of them illegitimate,[222] who had left one of his wives at home to battle cancer so he could play a few rounds of Mixed Press-Ups with a pole-dancing bikini model to whom he'd handed £126,000 of public money.[223]

Such lavish and unbridled fuckery leads me inevitably to Miriam Cates, an evangelical Christian who brought her Shag For Britain campaign to the conference.[224] The political cause she ardently believes in – individualism – had 'completely failed to deliver babies', she told attendees, so we should all remember that 'children are not an economic burden'.[225] It's a persuasive argument, only slightly undermined by the fact she's a member of a Government that *literally* passed a law to define children as an economic burden, when for fiscal reasons it placed a two-child cap on benefits.[226]

And it represented yet another bold interpretation of scripture from the Conservative Christians, a self-selecting groupoid dementedly focused on half a dozen passages from the Bible relating to human sexuality, which they insisted were literal divine commandments, while they dismissed as 'personal choice' the thousands of verses urging care for migrants, the poor and the marginalised. God probably didn't mean all that stuff. Who knows? He's ineffable.

The National Conservatives had officially abbreviated to themselves to NatCons, but Twitter had unofficially abbreviated them to the rather more phonetically embarrassing NatCs. To help secure that monicker, Miriam Cates claimed that 'Cultural Marxism' was 'destroying our children's souls',[227] which brought a genuinely shocked response from the Government's own antisemitism tsar,

John Mann, who said the term Cultural Marxism was a 'conspiracy theory with anti-Semitism at its core'.[228] But this barely put a dent in NatC orator Douglas Murray, who said there was nothing wrong with 'with nationalism in a British context', and we shouldn't rule it out just because Germany had 'mucked up twice'.[229]

Ah yes, the great mucking up at Auschwitz-Birkenau.

Michael Gove celebrated the NatC's success, claiming it was 'evidence of the intellectual energy we have in the centre-right at the moment'.[230] None of them had yet realised their populism wasn't remotely popular. Every lurch to the right alienated yet more voters.

In a panic, Sunak farted out a fresh miasma of policy guesswork: it was time to get back in touch with the mood of the country! So after a report from the globally respected health thinktank the Nuffield Trust found the rolling catastrophe in social care 'represents the consequences of letting one of our most important public services languish in constant crisis for years',[231] the Tories announced cuts of a further £250 million from social care funding.[232] And then they told a nation of animal lovers that they were cancelling the ban on animal testing for cosmetics, which led to over 80 major beauty brands expressing dismay at the move.[233]

It was Rishi Sunak's worst week to date.

*

His struggles to distract from the local election drubbing had been farcical. His party was so divided that even the tiny, crackpot far-right groups had subdivided into factionalism and schisms. His pledge to reduce interest rates had turned into interest rates rising for the twelfth consecutive time.[234] His Brexit policy was wildly unpopular, his small boats strategy was failing, and both of them were contributing to the very inflation he was failing to control: a former Bank of England economist said the UK's fiscal problems were worse than elsewhere in the world due to 'the effects of Brexit and limiting immigration'.[235]

But at least he had a better election than UKIP, which saw its district and county councillors reduced from very nearly 500 to very exactly zero. 'It certainly wasn't a disaster', said the party's chairman, Ben Walker, and I eagerly await his ruling on what *does* qualify as a disaster.[236] Brexit, perhaps.

What's that old phrase? *You can fool all of the people some of the time, and some of the people all of the time.* Well, UKIP had done its job, and for a brief period had fooled enough of us to agree to holing our own futures below the waterline. In the resulting mayhem, Nigel Farage's old party was also utterly sunk.

But luckily for Nigel a lifeboat had turned up in 2019, in the form of near-identical xenophobia vehicle The Brexit Party. Farage leaped aboard, and then, as Brexit became wildly and predictably unpopular, its loudest advocates disowned the word, rebranded themselves as Reform UK, and set about collecting votes from people who thought Priti Patel was a bit of a wet liberal.

Reform UK was founded on unusual principles, meaning none. Rather than being a political party like Labour or the Conservatives, in which members have voting powers over policy and personnel, Reform UK was founded as a private company. It didn't have answerable politicians, it had three shareholders, the largest being Nigel Farage, the richest being Richard Tice, and the spare being the former chairman of UKIP, Paul Oakden, a man who was so useless that he had even managed to be sacked for incompetence by Andrew Bridgen. Can you imagine?

Bridgen claimed Oakden had spent the entirety of the eight weeks he spent in his employment frittering away his time on dating websites rather than working, and said Oakden 'shouldn't be in politics' because he was a 'political suicide bomber'. Little of this seemed to bother Farage or Tice, and Oakden was now part-owner of a bombastic, parochial protest movement with ambitions to run a country.

I repeat: *You can fool some of the people all of the time.*

The Ascent of Mordaunt

We had reached April, and Adam Afriyie, who had repeatedly stood in the House of Commons to promote vaping, kickstarted yet another Tory lobbying scandal after it was reported that he'd neglected to mention his family stood to profit from being the third-largest shareholders in a major vaping company.[237]

And while the country was still furious about the endless stream of untreated excrement being poured into our rivers, streams and coastlines, Damian Green did a one-man performance of the Four Yorkshiremen sketch, describing a blissful childhood spent bathing in torrents of fresh turds. He now answers to the name Damian Brown and took to the airways with a heartwarming nostalgia-fest, chuckling over the good old days when doing lengths through human excrement 'was regarded as acceptable'.[238] It didn't wash, although I hope to God *he* has.

*

The few remaining grown-ups had bigger issues on their minds. As May began, the Conservative chair of the Intelligence and Security committee, Julian Lewis, backed an amendment that would close loopholes allowing foreign political donations. He was concerned that British parties – not least his own – had 'clearly welcomed Russian money', most of it via a type of private organisation called an Unincorporated Association. There were hundreds of such groups, many of them entirely benign, but others almost entirely opaque, channelling hundreds of thousands of pounds towards MPs, mainly those from the right of the Conservative party.[239]

It was a legal loophole allowing dark money to be channelled directly into the heart of our government, and it might be hard to conclusively prove it in court, but you'd have to be deranged to conclude such money wasn't capable of undermining democracy.

Lewis contended that such donations could and should be considered a malign influence: in effect, a hostile act. And therefore, 'the amendment is eminently reasonable, it shouldn't be controversial for political parties to want to ensure the transparency of their foreign political donations'.[240]

Tom Tugendhat, the security minister, took a different view. 'The law already makes robust provision', he said, so new legislation was unnecessary because 'foreign donations are banned'.[241] I don't know what his definition of 'banned' is, but since Boris Johnson had become prime minister, the Conservative Party had accepted £2.6 million in such 'shadowy' donations.[242] At least £243,000 of Tory donations were directly traceable to individuals and businesses linked to Putin's Russia.[243]

So imagine my shock when Tory MPs were whipped to overturn Julian Lewis's proposal to tighten the law. Dark money donations via Unincorporated Associations remained legal.[244]

Tugendhat's next duty was to set the tone for the Coronation of our new, yet also rather old, King. It was, said Tugendhat, swelling with patriotic pride, 'a chance for the United Kingdom to showcase our liberty and democracy', whereupon Suella Braverman banned peaceful protest.

Almost immediately the Home Office sent 'intimidatory' letters to members of the anti-monarchy campaign group Republic, threatening them with a year in prison.[245] At this point the group had gone no further than discussing the possibility of a legal, peaceful protest with senior police officers, who said they would be 'happy for [Republic] to proceed'. But it seems even *thinking* about doing a protest was enough to trigger Braverman.[246]

Lee Anderson, meanwhile, tweeted that anybody who didn't support the monarchy should 'emigrate'.[247] Somebody very patient should be tasked with sitting Anderson down, and explaining to him what 'ending freedom of movement' means. A forlorn hope. One week after telling people not to have opinions, Anderson was the guest speaker at a Young Conservative event promoting free speech and opposing cancel culture.[248]

*

Every living former prime minister arrived for the Coronation: John Major, Tony Blair, Gordon Brown, David Cameron, Theresa May and Boris Johnson lined up; the evolutionary depiction of *The Ascent of Man* shown in reverse order. Liz Truss was there too, like somebody who had made a single-episode cameo on *Star Trek*, and then eked it out into a lifetime of ComicCon appearances.

But the main attraction was, of course, Penny Mordaunt, who had taken it upon herself to perform the vital task of pointlessly holding a sword upright for fucking hours. It was enough to instantly make her the Conservative Party's Next Big Hope. It didn't seem to matter that her record of, y'know, *doing politics* wasn't great. Her expertise in homeopathy – a form of advanced poppycock for people who think cups of water can remember things – hadn't helped her to succeed during her previous big TV moment, a spectacular bellyflop that saw her ousted from much-forgotten TV diving show *Splash!* And only 27 of her colleagues had bothered to support her when she stood to replace Liz Truss, mainly because she'd been bounced around eight ministerial jobs in as many years, which doesn't immediately suggest she'd excelled at any of them.

Mordaunt was basically a placeholder for scoundrels, constantly being shuffled around to fill a hole left by the most recent minister to be sacked for ineptitude or depravity. She'd succeeded Priti Patel (booted for holding unauthorised secret meetings with Israeli forces);[249] Amber Rudd (booted for misleading parliament during the Windrush scandal);[250] and then Gavin Williamson (booted for leaking information from a top-level meeting of the National Security Council).[251] And each time, Mordaunt had been transferred out of the role again the moment an opportunity arose, parked until the call came for her to temporarily replace the next embarrassment booted from office.

In fact, until that palaver with the sword, Mordaunt's main

claim to fame was *Not Being In The Royal Navy*, and I don't wish to boast, but that applies to me too. And probably to you, and your mum, and cat, and most of your furniture. But it all changed for Penny on Coronation Day, when she won the hearts and minds of a party that I'd always assumed lacked both. A star was born, as she radiated a dignified composure notably absent from other senior Conservatives. She wasn't caught shagging somebody behind a pew or pilfering from the collection plate. She didn't fall over or shit herself in public. And she managed to pull off a look that perfectly combined the Poundland logo with an extra from *Buck Rogers in the 25th Century*.

The threat such unexpected statesmanship presented to the prime minister – an unflattering comparison with his own performance, which seemed based on Buck Rogers' diminutive robot sidekick, Twiki – was enough to send convulsions through the parliamentary party, and suddenly Suella Braverman and Kemi Badenoch realised they had to up their game, lower their standards, or – as we shall inevitably discover – both.

Russian Roulette

Labour remained miles ahead in polls; the government was beset by inertia, ineptitude and scandal; the public mood was shading from contempt to indignation and back again; and voters longed for a general election.

It was beginning to look like many of Sunak's backbenchers did too.[252] Even the MPs who hadn't already announced they were quitting were practically lining up to embrace the sweet release of electoral oblivion. But many seemed to have no idea what was coming. More than half of 2023's Tory intake had never experienced being in opposition. They acted as though Conservative rule was the natural order of things, so discipline in the year before an election was an optional extra. Delerium erupted on all sides. The party's various batshit contingencies indulged in increasingly absurd experiments with public messaging. As May rolled into June, Jacob Rees-Mogg, the haunting offspring of a Cyberman and a cursed dildo, was wheeled out on Sky News to assert that Britain leaving the EU had made it impossible for Russia to successfully invade Ukraine.[253]

I've thoroughly fact-checked this, and can confirm that Ukraine had, in fact, been invaded. It had happened 383 days earlier, and it made quite a few headlines. But maybe JRM had been too busy presenting GB News to keep up with ... the news.

The Conservative grip on reality weakened, but the one on Brexit was tightened to the point of strangulation, even though the main promise of leaving the EU – a reduction in immigration – had failed utterly. Fortunately a new false idol had appeared in the shape of the Rwanda plan, which was attracting all kinds of weird acolytes. Even David Cameron, the comparatively moderate former PM who had charmed us all with his polished manners, lacquered hair and varnished face, popped up uninvited to scold us all. He insisted we should not criticise the government for spending money we didn't have on an illegal plan to send an insignificant number of Albanians to a quasi-dictatorship in central Africa: not unless we had a better idea.[254]

But millions of us had a *much* better idea – stop doing it – it's just that the Government wasn't listening. Rwanda was advertised as a cheap and effective disincentive to immigration, yet in the year since the deterrent had been announced illegal immigration had risen by 26 per cent.[255] Meanwhile the cost of sending just 7 asylum seekers to Rwanda in June was the same as paying their asylum allowances for 235 years – at least it would have been if any of them had actually made it to Rwanda.[256] The flight was ruled unlawful and never left the ground. It was yet another disaster for Sunak, who the previous November had promised to bring immigration down to the levels last seen in 2019, around 200,000 people.[257] By May he'd quietly dropped that promise and started boasting about his new limit of 500,000 migrants.[258] Finally he could relax. There was no way he could more than double his original stupid, arbitrary migration target and *still* fail.

He still failed. Migration exceeded 600,000.[259]

*

In a way, this was a rare stroke of luck for Sunak. The right-wing media's relentless, one-sided obsession with reducing immigration meant his latest noisy failure left little room for headlines about his other blunders. Which is a shame, because they were legion.

Back in January, in the shadow of the inevitable fallout from his appointments of Dominic Raab, Gavin Williamson and Nadhim Zahawi, Sunak had performed the first of many resets. Gone were professionalism, accountability and … whatever the third one was. It doesn't matter, forget about it, because now we had a brand-new set of promises that nobody had voted for, but which we were asked to clutch to our chests and then, like the PM himself, quietly drop again as soon as it was convenient.

Rather than a programme of government, Sunak was engaged in a flailing ballet of opportunistic gimmicks, each one born of paranoia and desperation, and each one granted the lifespan of a mayfly. This time, it was five pledges: make sure the national debt was falling; get the economy growing; halve inflation to 5.4 per cent so we could get interest rates under control; cut NHS waiting lists; and stop the small boats.

These were, he informed us, the 'people's priorities', although he refused utterly to let the people have an election to confirm that we wanted him to deliver any of them. Instead he confidently assured us they'd all happen by end of the year, no ifs, no buts. 'I ask you to judge us on the effort we put in and the results we achieve', he said, his dead eyes barely breaking contact with the endless vista of misery he presided over, as he calmly loaded a revolver and prepared to play Russian Roulette with his own premiership.[260]

The pledges had been made in January. Now it was June, halfway through the year, and time for a review. Sunak pointed the gun to his head, took a deep breath, and began to methodically pull the trigger.

Click. Inflation wasn't down: it had climbed to highest level for three decades.[261]

Click. The economy shrank in March,[262] slid into recession again in the final quarter of the year[263] and people were suffering the worst decline in living standards of any advanced economy.[264]

Click. Government debt soared past 100 per cent of GDP for the first time in 62 years.[265]

Click. Interest rates rose for the twelfth successive month.[266]

Click. NHS waiting lists in England rose to a record 7.4 million people,[267] over 13 per cent of the country's entire population in a queue for treatment.[268]

And then the final, unavoidable, inevitable pull of the trigger. The deterrent effect of the Rwanda policy resulted in a 22 per cent increase in small boat arrivals,[269] just as the High Court ruled that removing asylum seekers to Rwanda was unlawful.[270]

Boom!

It was Rishi Sunak's worst week to date.

Not The Best Idea In The World

Threats emerged of yet another confidence vote to remove yet another unelected prime minister, and he only survived because his party was 100 per cent malevolent, but only 9 per cent competent. Plots hatched, and there was an endless stream of skulduggery from skulls few would care to dig into – Boris Johnson's continuity delusion squad, a motley crew of shrill ideologues whose response to every electoral setback was another step to the right. They openly fantasised about Johnson's return to power, sure that bringing back a disgraced and laughable figure of contempt would win over an electorate that mostly hated him. His acolytes spent their days calculating the threshold necessary for the no-confidence letters that would oust Sunak.

'54 letters [are] not hard between now and November,' boasted one former minister.

'FFS: who on earth is spouting this bonkersness?' asked a colleague in a Tory WhatsApp group, 'Are you determined to turn our party into a skip fire?'

Apparently, they were. Even some of Johnson's most trenchant backers rebelled against the notion of his return, and despaired to the press. 'A lot of us reluctantly decided he had to go [in 2022] so the story would stop', said one. 'He's gone, but it's still going'.[271]

When, days later, the privileges committee investigating Boris Johnson's extensive and perfectly obvious lies to parliament finally produced its report, it was curtains for Johnson. And – entirely on-brand for a guy addicted to £840-per-roll gold wallpaper – they were pretty expensive curtains too.[272] Under the Tories, ordinary citizens are ineligible for civil legal aid unless they have an income below £31,884.[273] Boris Johnson had found time to earn more than £5 million in just the previous six months, yet got his entire legal bill paid for by taxpayers. It came to £265,000, a sum it would take an average Briton half a lifetime to earn.[274]

It didn't help him much, not least because while his lawyers were preparing their case they had stumbled upon Johnson's social diary, in which he had listed all the times he'd invited friends to Chequers during the socially-distanced months of the pandemic. His legal team had an official duty to share the diary with the Cabinet Office, and the Cabinet Office had a legal obligation to share it with the police.

It was at this point that a light switched on in the flyblown netherscape between Johnson's ears, and it dawned on him that it might not have been the best idea in the world to keep detailed written records of all the times he'd done something illegal. And then along came his sister to reveal she too had broken pandemic restrictions, so she could go to her second home and play tennis.[275] When Boris stood accused of throwing yet more parties at the stately home we had loaned him, Rachel Johnson decided to further polish the clan's public standing by proudly informing listeners to her radio show that she had also visited Chequers during the lockdown months.[276]

'The whole family have a massive sense of entitlement,' said a Johnson-era minister. 'It's part of the grandeur that he thinks is his due.'[277]

By this point you'd be forgiven for assuming Boris Johnson was working for the prosecution, a conclusion amply supported by his next move: he fired his own defence team for the heinous sin of adhering to the law.[278] And then, at the very moment he most needed allies inside Westminster, he threatened to sue the Cabinet Office for doing its legal duty. The main reason his threat didn't come to fruition was that he'd just sacked his lawyers.[279]

It's hard to believe Boris Johnson hadn't managed to make a success of Brexit.

*

All of this upset Jacob Rees-Mogg, a clinically evil owl that had been imprisoned inside a pencil. He argued that holding Johnson to the standards we expect from MPs would make MPs 'look foolish',[280] and that Parliament should not be allowed to act as though it was … what's the word? … sovereign. It was quite a turn-around for a man who had stood in Parliament a year earlier to say: 'Now that we have left the European Union the sovereignty of Parliament has been restored',[281] and had written in *The Spectator*, 'From sovereignty flows accountability. It will be Parliament, rather than the Council of Europe, which will give its voice.'[282]

So now sovereign Parliament gave its voice. Accountability flowed. Boris Johnson became the first prime minister in history to be found to have deliberately misled the House of Commons. He had also deliberately misled the privileges committee, perjuring himself with the same old lies under oath. And then to make matters worse, he leaked the report before it was officially published, which MPs later ruled was an attempt to 'impugn parliamentary process' while he orchestrated a 'campaign of abuse and attempted intimidation of the committee'.[283]

Yet for all the strength of their findings, the standards committee had no power to impose a punishment. All it could do was make a recommendation to MPs, who would then vote on whether to implement the recommendation. A near-record 90-day suspension was proposed, enough to force a by-election in Johnson's Uxbridge constituency. But the cowardly lion had no intention of hanging around for voters to pass judgement on him. He didn't even wait around for the parliamentary vote, and quit with immediate effect, while publicly insisting, 'I take my responsibilities seriously'.[284]

He had missed 187 Commons votes since he had stepped down as prime minister, and in Parliament he had mentioned his constituency of Uxbridge only four times in the seven years he'd been its MP, two of them on a single day in 2015.[285] Yet Johnson asserted his resignation wasn't yet another example of him running away from responsibility.[286] No: he was quitting because there was a 'witch-hunt under way'.[287]

But here's the thing with witch-hunts: sometimes they catch a witch, and this one had easily found a fat, blond, shambolic one, who was wielding his famous Inexhaustible Bullshit Spell. The suspension recommendation was endorsed by a huge margin of 354 votes to 7 – although that apogee of moral certitude Rishi Sunak made sure he missed the vote[288] – and Johnson's parliamentary security pass was revoked.[289]

But at least nobody could now say Boris Johnson was a politician without convictions.

*

Three days later, he started his new job writing for the *Daily Mail*.[290]

The parliamentary appointments body, which must approve any jobs taken by former ministers, said Johnson had committed a 'clear breach' of the rules in taking the role. The *Mail* didn't care: they'd mercilessly demand the rigorous application of justice for anybody they disagreed with, but had never seemed especially bothered about rules governing Their Sort Of People. Johnson breaking yet another set of regulations didn't matter, and they seemed convinced that the £1 million per year they were paying their 'erudite new columnist' would be worth every penny.[291]

To drum up business, Johnson had done a promo piece to camera, warning that he would fill the *Daily Mail* with 'completely unexpurgated stuff', and Westminster trembled at the very thought of what was in the works.[292] Across SW1, breath was bated and hooks were tentered, as politicos turned to his first column, only to discover it tackled the weighty issues of Johnson's cheddar habit, his utter lack of willpower, and the sad news that he'd had to give up injecting fat-reducing fluids directly into his stomach 'because they were making me feel ill'.[293] Personally I was amazed he needed to take weight-loss drugs at all, what with all the running he did.

Nobody could have been overwhelmed by the quality of his column, but perhaps his least whelmed readers were Johnson's former colleagues.[294]

'His actions are akin to mutiny.'

'My hopes for the future of Boris Johnson is that he will shut up and go away.'

'This is the grand finale of the Boris madness. Good riddance.'[295]

But the Boris madness was infectious. In his wake, somebody called Nigel Adams – no, me neither – also quit as an MP in protest at the attack on Johnson's honour, which is a bit like falling on your sword for the glory of Brigadoon.[296]

Meanwhile Johnson's second-biggest fan – after himself – was still powering through a 24-hour dunce-a-thon which had been so successful that she'd left it running for over a decade. It often felt like the only reason Nadine Dorries was wandering around in public was that wokery meant it was no longer acceptable to place the village idiot in the stocks.

If you had to guess, I doubt many of us would think she had been *elected* to Parliament. We might assume she'd visited Westminster on a hen-do, only to be abandoned there by friends who thought she'd gone a bit too far. Or we might speculate that she'd been part of a reality TV experiment, in which somebody was made an MP having been plucked at random from the crowd at a meat raffle. Perhaps she'd wandered unbidden into Parliament, having become disoriented following a fight outside a flat roofed pub, and nobody had the nerve to show her the way out.

But elected? It just didn't compute.

On the morning of 9 June, just as Johnson was resigning in a colossal huff, she appeared on short-lived right-wing victimisation engine Talk TV, where she reassured viewers that she was going nowhere. 'The last thing I would want to do', she said, 'would be to cause a by-election in my constituency'.[297]

Four hours later she announced she would resign with immediate effect, causing a by-election in her constituency.[298]

It was a huge loss to satirists, for whom her presence in public life was like being the landlord of a pub next door to Oliver Reed's house. It was a huge loss to newsprint, because she's already announced her resignation in February, and now the papers had to print it all over again.[299] And it was a huge loss to Parliament, where she had not spoken since July of 2022.[300] Perhaps she'd been saving herself up for a lifetime in the House of Lords, which is what she claimed Boris Johnson had promised her, even though he'd known for months that any such move had been firmly rejected by the upper house's appointments committee.[301]

We expected little from Dorries, and she delivered in spades. Having resigned with immediate effect, she then stayed on as an MP for months, steadfastly not attending Parliament but steadfastly pocketing the wages, thanks very much. When she wasn't whining about the unfairness of it all on her own highly-paid TV show, she was cropping up on shows hosted by other Tory MPs, getting entangled in rampant brambles of incoherent waffle as she tried to describe the 'sinister forces' set against her.[302] And every time she appeared there was an immediate sense that somewhere on Merseyside, a wedding was missing a pissed auntie.

The Lyin' King

The words 'Boris Johnson's resignation honours' suggest he had voluntarily resigned and had some honour, but we know neither of those things are true. Despite his utter public disgrace, he still found room for some private disgrace, and as he lumbered away from parliament, he delivered one final fart in the face of decency. He lavished gongs upon all and sundry, the latter being 29-year-old Charlotte Owen, who became our youngest ever life peer.

Johnson had awarded her for her work as a 'Former Special Adviser to the former prime minister'.[303] Yet her name did not appear in the official government directory of special advisers, and Downing Street insiders described her as 'more like an executive assistant' who had only been employed to provide maternity cover.[304] Her listing on the House of Lords website didn't help much: under 'Experience' it said, 'There is no experience information to show'.[305]

So perhaps the life peerage was due to her experience before entering top-level politics and/or answering the phone? She claimed to have briefly been an intern at the constituency office of top economic sadist George Osborne. Unfortunately, none the people who had actually worked in that constituency office backed up her claims.[306]

There was wild speculation about Owen's bizarre, unjustified peerage: that it had been given because she held kompromat on Johnson, or she was his lover, or maybe yet another of his illegitimate children (she does bear a passing resemblance). The point of repeating these evidence-free rumours is not to lend them credence, because they almost certainly deserve none. The point is that nothing about any of them seemed implausible. That's the kind of man he was.

And this was clearly illustrated by the other gongs he handed out. A parliamentary report identified 10 Tories who had waged a coordinated campaign to interfere with the Commons investigation into Johnson's lies.[307] And The Lyin' King had just honoured practically all of them.

Let's start with Jacob Rees-Mogg, an aristocratic goth supervillain who had dressed up as a harrowing antique dildo for Halloween, and then the wind changed direction, and he got stuck. Knighthood.

Michael Fabricant, the larval form of David Dickinson, a deranged, reality-repelling ukulele enthusiast and internationally recognised mockery magnet. Knighthood.

Simon Clarke, a mouse-fart made flesh who formed part of the core team that destroyed the economy under Liz Truss. Knighthood.

Andrea Jenkyns, famous for dressing as an irradiated lemon to remorselessly stalk the streets, locked and loaded with a lethal dose of stupidity, giving the middle finger to the public.[308] Damehood.

Priti Patel, the Shetland Pony of the Apocalypse, a proven bully,[309] sacked because she lied multiple times about holding illicit meetings with a foreign power,[310] and described as 'completely potty' by the Royal Navy.[311] Damehood.

Ross Kempsell, who heroically managed not to laugh out loud while Johnson claimed his favourite pastime was making buses out of wine boxes, rather than admitting his real hobby: money, getting squiffy, and shagging. Kempsell was also Boris Johnson's tennis partner, so, aged just 32: life peerage.[312]

Kulveer Singh Ranger, a very much on-brand Johnson advisor who didn't even make it through a year in the House of Lords before he was facing suspension from House of Lords bars after getting hammered and harassing people on the Westminster estate.[313] Life peerage.

Will Lewis, a leading member of the – and this is honestly how it's described – 'brains trust' tasked with saving Boris Johnson after Partygate, who was accused by three officials of advising Johnson and Downing Street staff to 'clean up' their phones, destroying evidence before any inquiry began. He denied the allegations and got a knighthood.[314]

The only significant Johnson groupie to miss out on a gong was Brendan Clark-Smith, an untrammelled collection of clattering idiocy with the resting expression a somebody battling their way through a difficult beer-shit. He missed out on being knighted, possibly because when he had the chance to vote to save the Eton Mess, he opted to spend the day at the cricket instead. 'I fully intended to vote against [suspending Johnson]', he tweeted; but sadly, more pressing matters had dragged him away from his £86,584 role as an MP, and he photographed himself abandoning parliament so he could visit the Oval to support England while wearing a tie covered in kangaroos.[315]

Partygate was fully rewarded. A peerage for Shaun Bailey, the Conservative mayoral candidate who was amongst the first to resign in disgrace. An OBE for Ben Mallett, who had been pictured alongside Bailey in lockdown-breaching party mode. A knighthood for Martin 'Party Marty' Reynolds, the Downing Street aide who had invited more than 100 people to 'bring your own booze'.[316] A Damehood was handed to Shelley Williams-Walker, who had the nickname 'DJ SWW' because she'd been in charge of the playlist at the illegal Downing St party on the eve of Prince Philip's spartan, socially distanced funeral.[317]

And another knighthood was handed to Guto Harri, the comms director brought in to save Johnson's skin, which he emphatically didn't. The project probably wasn't helped by Guto Harri's record of describing Johnson as a 'sexually incontinent [and] divisive' figure who was 'digging his own political grave' and 'dragging the country down' with him.[318]

While you're still being baffled by the list, allow me to make things even more incomprehensible. An OBE to Kelly Jo Dodge, Boris Johnson's hairdresser, which is a bit like awarding a gold star to Shane MacGowan's dental hygienist.

And finally, there was a life peerage for Ben Houchen, the Tory mayor of Tees Valley, who was surrounded by scandal, battling constant allegations of corruption after he apparently sold 110 acres of public land – which was valued at £13.2 million[319] – to two of his friends for £1 per acre.[320] A review later found no evidence of corruption, but found the project was criticised for its excessive secrecy and 'poor value for money for the local taxpayer'[321]

Great value for money for Houchen's friends and their families though, who now pootle around Teesside in £300,000 Rolls Royces.[322] Wages in Tees Valley are 15 per cent below the national average.[323]

This was held as proof that Levelling Up was working, part of Rishi Sunak's grand strategy for regional regeneration, which largely involved selling off those regions for peanuts. They would become 'Freeports', where workers' rights and environmental protections could be reduced, and lower business taxation could be negotiated with their new corporate owners, while workers taxes would remain the same. If you didn't like it, tough: there would be practically no democratic accountability.[324] The goal was, said the Tory manifesto, to 'level-up every part of the country', which they were doing by isolating the weakest parts of the country, and then levelling down their wages, freedoms and rights.

It would be shocking enough, even if it had the desired effect. But it didn't. In 2024, a year after Houchen made it to the Lords and his pals made it to the Rolls Royce dealership, Sunak swore the plan was working, and that his Teesworks project proved the policy was a success. But the previous day, the National Institute of Economic and Social Research had published a report finding 'no evidence of sustained regional regeneration' since the policy had begun five years earlier. In fact, regional inequality had increased.[325]

Covid Inquiry

The Covid Inquiry had been announced in May 2021 by the then prime minister, Darth Bagpuss,[326] and in June 2023 it was time for it to expose what Johnson and his Cabinet had been doing throughout the pandemic.[327] This was not a happy prospect for Rishi Sunak, who had been interning as Chancellor during that period. Severe embarrassment beckoned, which is why the joyless claymation ethics droid decided to sue his own inquiry for having the temerity to ask for the things he'd always promised it could have.[328]

It wasn't a good look for Sunak, a man with a self-proclaimed commitment to transparency. Even Boris Johnson agreed to hand over his WhatsApp messages and notebooks: not because he wanted to, but because it would annoy and humiliate his successor. But Sunak refused, deploying the arrestingly strange argument that the things he or Johnson had done or said during the Britain's biggest crisis since the Second World War could be considered 'unambiguously irrelevant'.[329]

The Inquiry reassured him that they'd only place into evidence things which were relevant, to which Sunak responded that he'd already decided what was relevant, and the Inquiry could trust him, honest guvnor.[330] The chair of the Inquiry was having none of it, and demanded the messages be handed over, to which Downing Street's response can be summarised as: What messages? We deleted them all. Who needs records of what's going on, when we are led by people of integrity like Rishi Sunak or Boris Johnson?

It was a tug of war. Justice pulled. Politics pulled back. Sunak framed this stalemate as constitutional over-reach by unelected judges, which he was heroically fighting in his role as unelected prime minister. It was, he suggested, an unavoidable and entirely coincidental tragedy that this battle would lead to yet more delays, and it wasn't his fault that, to ensure the delays were as lengthy as possible, the Government insisted on a judicial review.[331] This was despite having spent years insisting judicial reviews were a waste of time and should be reformed out of existence.[332]

Eventually the PM's threat to sue his own Inquiry was quietly dropped, but only after he'd wasted £200,000 of taxpayers' money in exchange for the perfectly obvious legal advice that suing the Inquiry was an incredibly stupid idea that was doomed to fail.[333] Yet despite a High Court ruling that the messages must be disclosed, in October Sunak failed to hand them over: he claimed he had changed his phone, and the messages hadn't been backed up.[334] I use WhatsApp. In all likelihood, you do too. So we all know that automatic backups to The Cloud happen constantly. But for some reason Sunak's phone was the exception.

Boris Johnson, a more practiced hand at this kind of thing, handed his phone over with the story that – terrible shame – he'd only gone and forgotten the flipping passcode, like a numpty. Tsk, what were the chances? Not that it mattered, because he'd stopped using the phone in May 2021 after security officials discovered his number had been readily accessible online for the past 15 years, each of which he'd spent being an MP, a member of the Cabinet, or a prime minister.[335] So if the Covid Inquiry wanted to know what he'd done during the pandemic, it would have been quicker to just ask Chinese spies.

Austerity, Illegality, Degeneracy, and Bankruptcy

While Suella Braverman was busy shrieking from the rocks at small boats in the English Channel, on the English Riviera a far uglier crisis was unfolding.

During the previous 18 months, more than 600 unaccompanied asylum-seeking children had passed through hotels in Sussex, provided by the Government as safe, temporary homes until Braverman's department could stop wasting money on Chinook helicopter trips for the Flying Squirrel, and get around to processing some actual immigrants.[336] In a little over a year, at least 136 of those children had gone missing, with a whistle-blower working for a Home Office contractor reporting that kids were, 'literally being picked up from outside the building, disappearing and not being found. They're being taken from the street by traffickers.'[337]

The revelations were new to the public, but the Home Office had known for months. Data from the previous October showed it was even worse than first reported – at least 222 children were missing from Home Office hotels, and the whistle-blower estimated 10 per cent of youngsters disappeared *each week* from one hotel in Hythe. Week after week, kids were reported to have been kidnapped, he claimed, and police warnings had been ignored.[338]

The Government said the local council in Kent had responsibility to deal with this, but even if this were true, they hadn't done so because – like many councils – their finances were unsustainable, and their services were at breaking point. The effects of austerity were making themselves plain. Between 2010 and 2023, the National Audit Office described council spending power as falling by 'something like 50 per cent' in real terms.[339]

As a nation, we are rarely aware of how much local councils do for us. The UK's grotesque over-centralisation of power and media interest makes most people assume there is a similar over-centralisation of responsibility. But that's not the case. Local government delivers huge swathes of our education, social care, environmental regulation and standards, highways and transport, housing, planning, culture and sport: in essence, all the things we interact with on a daily basis. They do so under the regulations defined by Westminster, with funding limits decided by Westminster, and – historically – with significant amounts of income provided by Westminster. But that income had dried up in the baking heat of George Osborne's small-state fixation.

As the social problems caused by austerity grew, the costs for councils of the consequences hit the roof – especially for those who didn't even have a roof. Overall funding might have halved, but the costs of tackling the effects of homelessness more than doubled, which is hardly surprising, since homelessness had increased by 175 per cent under the Tories.[340] Austerity cost us far more than it saved, because it kicked away support structures and paying for the damage became a huge burden. For example, since David Cameron entered Downing Street and began slashing expenditure on youth services, the costs of child social care had increased by 36 per cent. More than 4.3 million of our children lived in poverty, a rise of over a million since austerity was implemented. It amounts to almost 30 per cent of all Britain's kids, and 46 per cent of families with three or more children living at home.[341] And of course, due to the Conservative sell-off of social housing, combined with their lackadaisical approach to building new homes, the number of young adults forced to remain living with their parents has increased to 3.8 million.[342]

Pressure on councils increased at both ends: the social costs of austerity skyrocketed just as overall council funding was slashed. Essential and spiralling spending on care forced the axe to fall even deeper on their other responsibilities. Pest control budgets fell by two-thirds, and street cleaning by a fifth, which just led to yet more problems with environment and disease control, all of which were also the responsibility of your local council.

Spending on culture: down 38 per cent. On highways and local transport: down over 50 per cent on average, but some areas saw an almost total cessation of spending. North Yorkshire, Bath, Somerset and Lambeth saw cuts to expenditure on roads and transport of 96 per cent. Potholes became so prevalent it often felt like you were driving across the lunar surface.

There were deep cuts to housing budgets across 84 per cent of England's council regions, which fell largely on the poor, and explained the rise in so-called Red Wall seats, where lower income voters turned to right-wing populists in the hope of reducing migration. But immigrants weren't taking all the houses: austerity was. Knowsley on Merseyside saw an 84 per cent fall in council housing expenditure. In South Tyneside, it was down a staggering 94 per cent.[343]

Councils trimmed provision to the bone, and then hacked into the bone and kept on cutting in a desperate attempt to make ends meet. It didn't work. Technically, councils cannot go bankrupt, but in effect that's what was happening. In 2023, Nottingham, Woking and Birmingham councils went effectively insolvent for the first time. For Thurrock and Croydon, 2023 was the third time they'd gone bust since David Cameron had cheerfully announced austerity would make us all richer. As Sunak became PM, half of all the councils in the UK warned that without reform – which means more funding – they'd be bankrupt within five years.[344] Remember that as a future Tory opposition blames these problems on Labour.

But in the meantime, Conservatives had identified a new scapegoat: the parents of disabled children. Those selfish pricks kept on insisting their kids were given the Special Educational Needs and Disabilities resources that were their legal right. Under vast financial pressure, councils regularly refused to provide SEND services, but at least 96 per cent of parental appeals against refused funding were eventually upheld, an outcome that appalled Gillian Keegan, our ninth education secretary in 10 years.[345] It was, she said, proof of 'lots of parents taking councils to tribunal to get [their children into] … normally very expensive independent schools'.[346]

Keegan's accusation wasn't supported by the slightest bit of evidence.[347]

Meanwhile Michael Gove, running the Levelling Up programme, deplored all this levelling up, and insisted those 96 per cent of parents of children with special needs must be the elite, wealthy minority who had 'the loudest voices, or the deepest pockets, or the most persistent lawyers'.[348] The failure was not a result of austerity's 50 per cent cut in funding. No, all of this was the result of greedy disabled children and shoddy left-wing councils who hadn't been able to make a go of what the Tories had left them with: a sparse handful of coins, a guilty conscience, and a tattered mop with which to clean up the consequences.

So it's not a surprise those overstretched councils couldn't afford to protect the children being regularly kidnapped from incompetent Home Office hotels, while Braverman was proposing spending £551 million on a 360-degree, all-terrain, panoptic governmental failure to deport 300 people.[349] And it wasn't even legal, as we discovered in news which pushed hundreds of trafficked kids out of the headlines: the Appeal Court ruled it was unlawful for the Government to send asylum seekers to Rwanda. The place simply wasn't safe. A bit like Home Office hotels in Hythe.

'While I respect the court, I fundamentally disagree with their conclusions', said Sunak, and announced that he'd send it to the Supreme Court for a final adjudication.[350]

Definitely final.

Definitely.

July to December 2023

The New Conservatives

The best thing about this Conservative Government was the 40 years of my life before it existed.

Not only had they just failed to prevent hundreds of children from being kidnapped, but as we entered July, they found time to make life even more pointlessly miserable for the ones who had thus far managed to dodge the traffickers. Immigration minister Robert Jenrick ordered Home Office staff to paint over Disney murals at an asylum centre, just in case the place seemed too welcoming for traumatised, parentless children. The workers tasked with implementing this bit of meaningless cruelty said they were 'horrified' by the instructions to whitewash out Mickey Mouse and Winnie the Pooh, and initially refused to do it.[1]

Leaving the murals would have cost nothing. Painting them out was merely another empty gesture from a government committed to leaping theatrically through a seemingly endless series of reductive cruelty hoops, and not even the latest right-wing Tory cabal could bring themselves to defend it: they were too busy publishing their own programme for government, because it transpired that Lee Anderson was having so much fun being deputy chairman of one political party that he'd decided to start a second one.

'The last thing the Conservative Party needed was a new sub-group of fanatics,' said one senior Tory, and yet here we were.[2] Conservatives had essentially turned into a dozen parties masquerading as one, like a stack of children in an adult trench coat, and just about as stable. The latest addition to the pile called themselves The New Conservatives, a bunch of chinless twonks from the lower-second, diligently pulling the wings off things because they hadn't got over mummy abandoning them at the school gate. The New Conservatives became a magnet for the type of Tory MP who – quite literally – believed a woman playing Doctor Who was pushing men into a life of crime, and its members took the opportunity to put their deliriums down in writing and call it a manifesto.[3] It featured two key recommendations.[4]

The first was to reduce by 117,000 the number of visas granted to care workers, which would stop unwanted nurses coming into the country. It didn't matter that the UK had a massive crisis in the care sector, with a record 165,000 unfilled posts, while half a million Britons were on a waiting list for social care.[5] Or that we had an ageing population and a shrinking workforce, which was the major underlying factor behind steadily increasing tax demands. During the previous 40 years, the number of people aged over 65 had increased by 52 per cent. There were more than 10 million retired people, all expecting a pension, many requiring NHS services and long-term care. Meanwhile the UK's birthrate was at a record low, and it wasn't being helped by the increasing inequality and stifled life-chances for the young. Of the British women who decided not to have children, 80 per cent said financial insecurity, low wages and poor housing were the leading factors.[6]

Older voters – from the most financially lucky generation to have ever lived[7] – may have consistently backed parties and policies that promised lower migration,[8] but older voters were the ones who would be most thoroughly fucked if nobody paid the taxes that funded their retirements, or did the care work they would rely on in later life. Without migration, this trend would inevitably drive Britain into either bankruptcy, a *Soylent Green* solution for overpopulated old-folks' homes, or some kind of Gilead-inspired enforced breeding programme.

So it's no great surprise that in 2024 Kemi Badenoch endorsed a 'Breed for Britain' policy.[9]

The second recommendation from the New Conservatives was to demand that anybody planning to move to Britain should already have a skilled job with an income of at least £38,700.[10] That was, they argued, the bare minimum required to afford a life in the UK, even though it meant 70 per cent of British workers would be officially too poor to live here.[11]

The news came as a shock to Johnny Mercer, but I'd hazard a guess that if you're Johnny Mercer, *anything* involving people poorer than yourself involves something of a journey into the unknown. Mercer, a Poundland Richard Hammond who was pretending to be veterans minister, occupied that magical zone where you can be awfully proud of the military, but still shrug them off in a heartbeat when reality becomes politically uncomfortable.

Foodbank use in the UK had grown enormously since David Cameron had been elected, with just one of the myriad providers – the Trussell Trust – reporting the number of people requiring their emergency food parcels had soared from 40,000 per year in 2010 to almost 3 million by 2023.[12] And in the latest embarrassment to the Government and Johnny Mercer, an RAF base had been forced to set up a foodbank on-site, as military personnel were now paid too little to feed themselves.[13] This was, said Mercer, not a profound failure by the Government in which he held a ministerial role, but a 'personal decision' by those military personnel.[14]

It's normal – cruel, often unnecessary, but normal – that those without work should fall on hard times. But relentless cuts to welfare made times harder than any in recent memory for many. Benefits for low-income households were £140 per month below the real cost of food, energy and essential basics, plunging the poorest into debt no matter how much they scrimped and saved.[15] And you no longer needed to be unemployed to suffer: a fifth of people being referred to foodbanks came from working households.[16] Wages had fallen so far behind the cost of living that many of us no longer had to choose between heating and eating. There was no choice. We could do neither.

Half of NHS trusts already provided (or were planning) an on-site foodbank to assist nursing staff who were unable to survive,[17] an atrocity that led Britain's first surviving heart-and-brain donor Simon Clarke to accuse nurses of doing 'something wrong with your budgeting', and urge them to 'to take responsibility in their lives'.[18] Clarke had been part of the Liz Truss Government when her budget left Britain's homeowners £300 billion worse off.[19] He took so much responsibility that he remained an MP, and continued to call for more Trussonomics.

The Same Old Conservatives

After a prolonged and largely fruitless search, in July of 2023, a Brexit Benefit had finally been identified: a new system of safety labels that Britain could implement, now that we were free from the EU. They would allow us to finally take control of the regulation of goods we bought and sold, and to make the most of our freedom to diverge from requirements defined in Brussels.

'We have listened to industry and we are taking action to deliver,' said a delighted business minister Kevin Hollinrake, as he announced they were taking no action whatsoever. The plans to diverge from EU standards were quietly dropped. Brexit Benefits remained at zero.

And the latest in a long line of Vote Leave promises transformed into vapour and drifted away on the winds of fate.[20]

This would probably have been terrible news for the former Minister of Brexit Opportunities, but he suddenly had other problems. Lovecraftian nightmare Jacob Rees-Mogg was one of several MPs suddenly under investigation by Ofcom, a media regulator imbued with all the virility of a wet tissue. There had been claims that Rees-Mogg, Philip Davies and Esther McVey might be evincing some kind of bias when they granted softball interviews to other sitting Tory MPs on their various highly paid GB News shows.[21]

The broadcaster also provided an outlet for Lee Anderson, in much the same way Thames Water provided an outlet for excrement, and the man was back again, celebrating Ben Bradley's decision to stand as the first mayor of the East Midlands.

'Ben is the smartest person in politics I know,' wrote Anderson, who had clearly not yet been introduced to the Downing Street cat.[22] He had, however, managed to get hold of some cat food, which – and I know sometimes this can sound like I'm making things up, but honestly – which he had taken to carrying around in his pocket, so he could produce it on his GB News show, and try to force his guests to eat it.[23]

Rees-Mogg, Davies, McVey, Anderson – each of them was unbelievably terrible in every measurable way, but fortunately Sajid Javid had a solution to Tory ministers being, as he put it, 'not very good at their jobs'. He argued that MP salaries should be doubled on the grounds that you needed to attract rich people like himself to Westminster, because poor people 'did not come with the skills that parliament needs'. And doubling the salaries of people who weren't particularly good at their jobs would, he reasoned, immediately make them good at their jobs.[24]

ULEZ If You Want To

The loss of Boris Johnson, David Warburton and Nigel Adams presented Sunak with three simultaneous by-elections, which he fully expected to lose. Uxbridge and South Ruislip, however, was Johnson's former constituency, and the Tories threw everything they had at it, treating it as a dry run for London mayoral election due in early 2024. They developed a two-pronged strategy.

One: pretend Boris Johnson had never existed.

Two: spread around bullshit as though he'd never left.

Tory election leaflets made no mention of the former PM. They didn't even include Conservative branding.[25] They campaigned as though the Conservatives weren't responsible for anything, which to be honest sounds about right: high-level irresponsibility was by now almost a mantra for government, most especially when it came to climate change. Susan Hall, the Tory candidate for Mayor, tweeted: 'Why do Labour politicians not listen to the public - WE DO NOT WANT ULEZ'.[26]

But seemingly she wasn't keen on listening to Tory politicians either.

'The world's first Ultra Low Emission Zone is an essential measure to help improve air quality in our city', said London Mayor Boris Johnson in his 2015 press release. It would 'protect the health of Londoners and lengthen our lead as the greatest city on earth', he continued, and David Cameron wholeheartedly agreed. 'I welcome this announcement which is a world first and great news for London', Cameron wrote, and even promised his Government was 'backing this initiative with £25 million of support'.[27]

That £25 million – which, in case it's not clear, was *your* £25 million – was now thrown away on the bonfire of culture war Conservative ambition, after which London's Tory councillors wasted a further £1 million on a failed legal challenge to *their own policy*. Their rather threadbare legal argument was that the current Mayor of London, Sadiq Khan, didn't have the legal authority to implement ULEZ, even though that's exactly what the previous mayor, Boris Johnson, had done when he announced it in 2015.[28] Johnson seemed to have forgotten about all that, and in 2023 used his *Daily Mail* column to call the ULEZ scheme that he'd designed a 'bone-headed' idea.[29]

Unsurprisingly, opposition to ultra-low emissions zones became talismanic for the Tories, with campaigns leaping up all over the place to spread the message. Thirty-six Facebook groups suddenly appeared, spreading a combination of misinformation, open racism directed at Sadiq Khan, and posts that it's hard to see as anything short of death threats. Members included an anonymous figure holding a Molotov cocktail, who posted: 'If Khan gets in the PURGE must begin with NO REGRETS'. One racist with a neat line in spoonerisms called Sadiq Khan a 'khaki punt', while others called him a 'terrorist sympathiser' and promoted white supremacism and antisemitic conspiracy theories.

It looked to a casual observer as though opposition to ULEZ was arising spontaneously from a disgruntled electorate, but almost all 36 groups were run by the same handful of people: two Conservative HQ staffers, a Tory mayor, Conservative councillors and party officials. One administrator operated across all 36 groups: Rachel Cromie, a Tory councillor who had worked as the party's digital campaign manager. Before that, she'd been head of a consultancy founded by a former senior employee of Cambridge Analytica, the company behind 87 million Facebook hacks, and commonly alleged to have helped to unethically and possibly unlawfully manipulate public opinion during the Brexit campaign. Seven serving Tory MPs were also members of the groups, including Chris Philp, the policing minister.[30]

Of course, none of the groups' administrators made their false-grassroots status public during the by-election, so the constant fearmongering about the dangers of breathable air helped the Tories, if only a little. As expected, the party lost David Warburton's seat with a massive 29 per cent swing, and Labour overturned Nigel

Adams' majority of 20,000, with the largest swing since 1945.[31] But in Johnson's former seat, the centre of the anti-ULEZ campaign, the Tories just about hung on by a scant 495 votes.[32] For once, it was not Sunak's worst week to date.

But not to worry, because the next one was.

*

In the aftermath of the by-elections, yet more of Sunak's colleagues announced they wouldn't be standing at the General Election. By this point, more than 40 had opted to spend more time with their families, their trust funds, their mistresses or their drug dealers. *Not Being an MP* had turned into a pretty lucrative career choice too: severance pay for those leaving parliament had been doubled to £19,000 just in time for the Liz Truss debacle.[33] Payouts to the MPs she burned through cost the taxpayer £3 million. Truss herself took £18,660 in severance pay.[34]

So not every Conservative was entirely unhappy about what already felt like certain electoral defeat. In preparation, they were either announcing their plans to abandon ship with a fat handful of cash or were manoeuvring to take over from Sunak in 2024.

At this point the leading candidates vying to cram into the tiny, Rishi-shaped hole at the top of the party were Suella Braverman and Kemi Badenoch. But neither of them had had a good month. The House of Lords rejected Braverman's plans to remove the limit on how long she could lock up children without charge, which had been a highlight of her latest histrionic spasm of unpleasantness. She had named it the Illegal Immigration Bill, so peers did exactly what it said on the tin, and ensured it remained illegal.[35]

As Braverman's star fell, Kemi Badenoch grasped the opportunity to boost her chances with a blaze of publicity about her wonderful new trade deal, sweeping onto the airwaves to boast there was 'so much potential' in an agreement which covered an area containing 500 million people.[36] The clear implication was that this would replace the trade with 400 million customers that had been so calamitously damaged by the Brexit she supported. For this to be fantastic news for the country, all that was required was absolutely nobody looking at the small print.

Sadly, somebody did. She'd predicted the new arrangements would add a laughable 0.08 per cent to our GDP, which is one fiftieth of the 4 per cent of GDP Brexit was simultaneously costing us.[37] The benefits were insignificant enough to qualify as a rounding-error, but got worse when the OBR fact-checked her claims, and found her deal would actually add only half of what Kemi NotGoodEnough had boasted: 0.04 per cent. And it would take 15 years for us to see even that measly improvement.[38]

An Embarrassment of (Very, Very) Riches

Let's just admit that Liz Truss was not for everybody. In fact, she was hardly for anybody. Since leaving office she had spent her time wandering around with the soft voice, glazed eyes and vacant smile of that woman that lives on your street and poisons cats. And she just wouldn't go away. Every time you turned on the TV, there she was, like a harbinger of failure. It was barely a month since Boris Johnson had dishonoured the honours system, but now it was August, and time for Truss to have her turn.

She handed out 16 honours, which works out as one for every four days she'd spent in office. If Tony Blair had distributed gongs at the same rate, he'd have granted enough honours to send every man, woman and child in Stamford Bridge to the House of Lords. But Blair gave no resignation honours, and neither did Gordon Brown. They aren't an ancient tradition, despite what Truss apologists claimed, and like foodbanks and corruption, they only became normalised under David Cameron, an overinflated shop dummy wearing a plastic face off the front of a Thomas the Tank

Engine, who did prime minister impressions while waiting for his bank account to fill up.

Still – and I'm grasping at straws here – at least we have finally found one thing at which Liz Truss outdid Gordon Brown: handing out meaningless baubles to lickspittle back-office toadies and constitutional vandals, such as Vote Leave boss and founder of Conservative Friends of Russia, Matthew Elliott.[39] Or to Jon Moynihan, who – when he wasn't being the main fundraiser for the Truss leadership bid – had urged her to ignore the Office for Budgetary Responsibility,[40] a decision which ended up crashing the economy and launching a years-long cost-of-living crisis that pushed at least 300,000 people into poverty, and probably still gives you nightmares.[41]

Truss's honours list could have been even worse, were it not for the fact that two of her appointees were too embarrassed to accept.[42] But embarrassment remained something of a novelty in Tory ranks, as Rishi Sunak was keen to demonstrate as July moved into August.

*

Back in March the Government had given a boost to childminders, offering them financial advantages if they registered through an agency. It was a rare moment when it looked like the Conservatives had delivered something useful, with no ulterior motive, and Sunak celebrated by going to Parliament to state that he had no interest to declare, and would not personally benefit from the decision.

'All my disclosures are declared in the normal way', he said.[43]

We could believe him because of that Integrity, Professionalism, Accountability thing he once said. However, parliamentary inquiries are rather more cynical, and looked into his claims. It was discovered Sunak hadn't correctly declared that his wife had a financial interest in one of the childcare agencies able to directly benefit from the budget.[44] He had also managed to break the MP's code of conduct by disclosing details of the investigation before it was made public.[45]

But whatever the Sunak family was making from childcare was small change compared with what it made from oil. While Sunak was still giving lip service to action on climate change, he broke the record for the most frequent domestic flights taken by any PM in British history. To travel between areas of the country, he'd used a chartered RAF flight or helicopter ride on average once every 8 days. Separately, he'd accepted more than £70,000 worth of private jet and helicopter travel in a year, all of them paid for by Tory donors, so he could travel to Conservative Party events.[46]

His defence was that flights got him to his destination faster, and this meant he could use his time wisely. He then gave a practical demonstration of this wisdom by taking a flight to Aberdeen to announce hundreds of new licenses for oil and gas drilling, which he assured the nation was 'entirely consistent with our plan to get to net zero'.[47]

The future always seems further away than the past. That's why the 2050 deadline of Net Zero cannot possibly be only as far away as the TV launch of *Big Brother*, or the release of Coldplay's first album. But it is. The crisis looms very close indeed, but instead of planning for the future, Sunak was focused on his immediate political survival. He urged us to consider the need to improve energy security, to bring down costs, and, more than anything, to cheer up the right of his party. But those oil and gas licences would neither reduce prices nor improve supply: their output would be sold on global markets, at prices set internationally.[48]

So Sunak's strategy was to undermine his core climate reduction policy by burning more carbon, just so he could deliver impossible savings that would never arrive. He placed all his hope for humanity's future on an imaginary Carbon Capture facility that he wanted to be built in Scotland.[49] It was to be based on the world's only existing large-scale carbon capture plant, the Orca facility in Iceland, which cost £15 million and can extract 4,000 tons of CO_2 per year.[50] The UK emits 96,000 times that much CO_2.[51] There was absolutely no possibility this would be a viable solution. Only stopping burning carbon fuels would work, but Sunak was encouraging more of it.

His decision was the work of a 'dangerous radical' who was pursuing policies of 'moral and economic madness', according to radical enviro-mentalists Just Stop Oil.

No, sorry, not Just Stop Oil – that was actually said by the Secretary General of the United Nations.[52]

Not even his fellow Tory MPs could understand the reasoning: 'This is the wrong decision at precisely the wrong time', said one, accusing Sunak of being on the 'wrong side of history'.[53] Zac Goldsmith agreed: he'd resigned from his role as international environment minister the previous month, and now lashed out, calling Michael Gove a 'monster' for continuing to rubbish green policies. Gove had been instrumental in the scrapping of a multibillion pound deal to help developing nations adapt to climate changes, and now Goldsmith accused Sunak of having 'no authentic interest whatsoever' in environmental issues.[54]

But let me come to Sunak's defence: it's wrong to say he had no interest. He had a £1.5 billion interest, which was the value of the deal the prime minister's family firm had signed with BP just before the new licences were put on sale. The wealth of Sunak and his wife increased by £122 million in the subsequent year, leaving the PM richer than the King.[55]

The deal with BP was the second largest that Infosys, the Indian company owned by Sunak's wife's family, had ever signed. It dwarfed the other £172 million of British public sector contracts Infosys had already been handed. Another major client of Infosys was the oil and gas giant Shell, whose CEO had joined Sunak's new Business Council only two weeks earlier.[56]

Sunak insisted none of this was of 'legitimate public interest', and we can believe him because of that Integrity, Professionalism, Accountability thing he once said. He'd clearly provided an ethical example for his colleagues in the Worst Parliament in History, because hot on his heels came Theresa Villiers, who was discovered to have held £70,000 of undisclosed shares in Shell while she was Conservative environment secretary.[57]

By this point, the Tories could not see a wound without giving in to the urge to rub salt into it. During the pandemic they'd given billions to their mates for PPE we couldn't use, and now, in August, they suddenly decided to hand out another £225 million for a private business to set that PPE on fire.[58] The equipment had been produced in China, had never left China, and now it was being incinerated in China, where it released 6,000 tonnes of CO2. That's the annual output of 3,750 UK households.[59]

Small Boats Week

A combination of Boris Johnson and Liz Truss had fatally weakened the Tory brand. Conservatives might not have loved their soubriquet of The Nasty Party, but at least they were once viewed as sensible, hard-headed pragmatists who would look after your money. If they were occasionally cruel, many voters accepted it as tough love, intended to slap some reality into the British public, and get us to buckle down for the good of the country.

All of that was gone now. Conservatives were no longer hard-headed and sensible; they were a bunch of numbskull fantasists. All that remained was the cruelty, so Suella Braverman decided to lean into that. With this in mind, she launched Small Boats Week, an attempt to transform growing public concern over Channel crossings into *epic* public concern about Channel crossings. She didn't appear to want to fix much, simply inflate an issue around which she could build her leadership ambitions. What she actually delivered was a desperate combination of over-the-top villainy and under-the-bottom competence.

The week began with immigration minister Robert Jenrick claiming the Labour Party was using 'every trick and tactic to delay and prevent us from removing people'. It wasn't true. Any legal delays to deportations were actually caused by our courts slowly groping their way through the rambling and incoherent 281 changes to migration policy introduced by the Tories between 2010 and the end of 2023.[60] It's nearly two changes of procedure per month for over a decade.

Day Two of Small Boats Week saw asylum seekers being marched onto a Slightly Larger Boat, the Bibby Stockholm. More than half didn't make it up the gangplank, objecting to the Legionnaires' disease that awaited them.[61] Lee Anderson said they should, 'fuck off back to France' if they didn't like being held in detention centres full of deadly pathogens, which doesn't immediately suggest he understands the word 'detention'.[62]

In public, Tory MPs were obliged to defend Anderson. In private they were fuming, calling him a 'fascist' who 'does not represent the same party as me'. One former Tory minister said Anderson was 'making the Tories the even nastier party', which may well have been the ultimate goal of the Braverman wing, but only two days into Small Boats Week, Government backbenchers already described the whole thing as 'chaotic and unsophisticated', and nothing more than 'cheap populism'.[63]

Day Three of Small Boats Week began with justice secretary Alex Chalk declaring that the Government telling people to 'Fuck off back to France' was merely 'a reflection of a tolerant nation',[64] and gave a live demo of this tolerance by suggesting life imprisonment for lawyers who defended asylum seekers.[65] Conservative HQ then initiated what the Bar Council described as a 'targeted campaign' against one asylum lawyer,[66] who immediately began receiving death threats.[67]

While the Home Office was keeping itself entertained with this little jape, on Day Four of Small Boats Week an organised crime gang broke into a border facility and stole a hard drive full of evidence, preventing planned legal action against a group of people smugglers. And then it was revealed a £400,000 drone used to track gangs had crashed into the sea.[68]

And then six migrants drowned.[69]

We had been reassured that all of this frenetic action would deliver the advertised impact on migration. So to wrap up Small Boats Week, 756 migrants arrived in small boats, which was the highest daily total for the year so far.[70]

The conclusion Sunak's Conservatives drew from this public debacle wasn't that their obsessions had driven them beyond the realms of the possible: it was that they hadn't gone far enough. So their next demand was that we should leave the European Court of Human Rights, something that would be 'a completely foolish idea and absolutely wrong', according to Bob Neill, the Tory chair of the Commons Justice Committee.[71] He went on: 'If Conservatives don't believe in the rule of law, what do we believe in? Are we going to put ourselves in the same company as Russia and Belarus?'[72]

To conclude: Braverman's attempt to turn immigration into a 'wedge issue' had definitely raised its importance in the public mind. But it had no effect whatsoever on migrant numbers. It strengthened Labour's lead on immigration,[73] and brought to public attention the fact that it would take until 2036 to clear the asylum backlog created by the Conservatives.[74] As Small Boats Week drew to a close, David Davis observed: 'The primary thing that's been revealed has been the startling incompetence' of Braverman,[75] and even Priti Patel, the larval form of Maleficent, called the Government's asylum policies 'alarming and staggering'.[76]

And I don't want to alarm you further, but Sunak followed this up with NHS Week.

A Fucking Good Job

Let's leave the shitstorm of 2023 politics for a moment and rewind a few decades, to a time when to save a few quid, thousands of Britain's public buildings had been constructed with a material that could easily be mistaken for shaving foam. Fortunately, it turned out that Reinforced Autoclaved Aerated Concrete would only become prone to collapse if cuts to the maintenance of public buildings forced RAAC to exceed its lifespan, and then it became wet, which of course never happens in the rainiest country in Europe.

The Conservative Government had known about the pending crisis for years, but for once they had not sat on their arses and done nothing. They'd got off their arses and done *less than* nothing, which is where Michael Gove enters the story.

The Blair/Brown Government had instigated a nationwide school building and repairs programme, which identified the looming issue with RAAC and put in place a plan to fix it, with an allocated budget and a timeframe. Michael Gove abandoned the whole lot as part of his first £7 billion of cuts to education.[77] To kickstart this process, Gove had cancelled more than 700 school repair projects. Over 88 per cent of secondary schools had seen their budgets slashed.[78] Real-terms funding per pupil had been frozen for 14 years, by the end of which investment in school buildings and materials was 25 per cent lower than it had been when the Tories came to power.

And for each of those 14 drizzly years, RAAC concrete became more and more wet and crumbly until finally, in 2018, the roof of a primary school collapsed, and the situation demanded immediate action. So the Tories immediately ordered a lengthy investigation and kept their fingers crossed that any expenditure could wait until Labour were in office again.

When the investigation into RAAC reported in 2023, Chancellor Jeremy Hunt said he'd spend 'what it takes' to repair the schools, which is exactly what the Tories had criticised Gordon Brown for doing when Labour had allocated funds two wasted decades earlier.[79] Since then the problem had grown, and the costs had risen. By now over a third of school buildings were past their safe estimated lifespan.[80] The Conservatives' obsession with political gamesmanship and short-term savings had, once again, left a legacy of huge expense.

Yet for all Hunt's promises of spending whatever it takes, the Government allocated 40 per cent less than their own official RAAC assessment recommended as the bare minimum required just to maintain safe buildings.[81]

But RAAC wasn't the only problem. Record numbers of schools had been denied funding for other repairs, with maintenance down over 60 per cent on the previous year. Government building contractors reported 'many hundreds of schools that are unsafe, cold and damp'.[82] A national survey of teachers found 68 per cent of them worked in buildings that leaked, almost half had mould in classrooms, and one fifth reported the problem was 'severe'. There were reports – and not isolated reports either – of fungus growing on carpets, asbestos hanging from the ceilings, and concrete falling into classrooms. Almost two-thirds of all Britain's teachers reported that the physical condition of their schools was negatively affecting learning.[83]

While overseeing this mess, Rishi Sunak helped to fund a £40 million swimming pool at his alma mater Winchester College, one of the most privileged and expensive private schools in the world.[84] And then he led the battle to oppose Winchester from having to pay VAT. He refused to discuss his family's healthcare arrangements, because they were private. Also, because they were private. He claimed that whether or not he used a private GP was 'not really relevant', but it absolutely was.[85] How can he – how can anybody – be trusted to make just and equitable decisions about something that will never affect them?

For the rest of us, inaccessible healthcare and unsafe schools remained something we'd just have to deal with. The wealth of

Britain's billionaires might have increased 1000 per cent in the last couple of decades,[86] but our income had stalled, pushing over 900,000 children into poverty.[87] And as a result, despite enduring almost one-and-a-half decades of pay freezes, and despite working in a building held up by froth, 80 per cent of primary teachers were now spending their own money to provide destitute children with food and adequate clothing.[88]

Number 10 was eager to keep their political embarrassments down to one or two per day, so refused to reveal exactly how huge was the price of fixing the RAAC crisis made worse by their vast, sprawling carelessness. Labour tried to force the release of documents relating to expenditure on school repairs, but the Tories whipped their MPs to block the motion.[89] At the time of writing, nobody knows how much this mess will cost, but an independent study by structural engineers estimated an average of at least £5 million per building.[90] And there are at least 234 schools,[91] 14 hospitals[92] and 5 prisons, plus countless other courts, offices, colleges, health centres and other public buildings where RAAC is still being discovered.[93] It's likely to exceed £1.5 billion, which is one 0.15 per cent of the total wealth of the UK's billionaires.[94]

I, for one, am stumped about how we will ever find the money to fix it.

*

With all of this in mind, imagine the balls on Gillian Keegan, the education minister responsible for resolving the RAAC problem, who was caught on camera lamenting the fact that nobody had thanked her for doing a 'fucking good job'.[95]

Later the same day, renowned bully Gavin Williamson was ordered to apologise for doing a fucking bad job.[96]

And then Chris Pincher resigned his seat after doing a bad job of fucking.

First, the case of Gavin Williamson, whose enforced apology

related to his proven habit of bullying civil servants to the point where he turned into a vibrating rage monster. In Pincher's case, his latest return to the headlines was the epilogue to his more famed 2022 scandal, in which he'd spent £1,700 per year to join an exclusive club for Conservatives, where he could become repeatedly disguised in drink and grope a series of unsuspecting men in – quite genuinely – a place called Cads' Corner.[97]

Although Pincher had already announced plans to stand down at the General Election, he had appealed against his temporary suspension from Parliament. When he lost the appeal he hurled his toys from the pram and stood down immediately.[98] And then, just as the Government was coming to terms with having to face yet another by-election because of yet another outrage, the seemingly endless conveyor belt of scandals turned over one more time, bringing with it Marcus Fysh, who, after the conclusion of investigations begun in May by the Parliamentary Commissioner for Standards, was forced to mouth an obligatory apology for breaching the MPs' code of conduct.[99] Tobias Ellwood had to resign from the Commons defence committee after appearing to compliment the Taliban on their managerial competence,[100] and the following day, another months-long investigation by the parliamentary standards authority found Sunak had indeed broken the MPs' code of conduct by not declaring his wife's interests in a childminding company that could benefit from his Government's policies.[101]

It was Rishi Sunak's worst week to date.

Mrs Braverman Goes To Washington

Our home secretary hadn't managed to fly anybody to Rwanda yet, but she had managed to board a plane to the USA, to splashily demand that the United Nations rewrite its definition of 'refugee'. This was part of her vision of a world where being gay and persecuted would not be grounds for asylum.[102] It didn't seem to matter that a quarter of all nations criminalised homosexuality, or that it was punishable by death in a dozen countries.[103]

People on this side of the Atlantic were shocked by Braverman's ghastly posturing, but few were in Washington; partly because it was all of a piece with the derangements of Trumpism, but mainly because she ended up giving her speech in a tiny room, which still somehow managed to be three-quarters empty. Only nine people attended.[104] It was almost as though nobody knew who she was, why she was there, or why they should care. Still, she got what she wanted: back in London her speech made waves, like a turd dropping into a toilet.

'It's a tone deaf cynically manufactured piece of nonsense,' said a senior Tory MP. 'Rather than seeking scapegoats left, right and centre, she should get on with her job. Unfortunately, it seems she isn't up to it.'[105] What that MP hadn't realised was that for Braverman, effective governance came secondary to winning over the Tory membership via blatant acts of self-promotion. Multiple Conservative backbenchers made official internal complaints about her 'poisonous' speech. They noted that it had been signed off by operatives inside Number 10, leading her colleagues to question the 'instincts of some of the people at the top of the party'.[106]

So the next day, the home secretary brushed off angry accusations of homophobia, and told journalists who were following her one-woman tour of Washington's broom cupboards that migration was out of control because: 'we do see many instances where people purport to be gay when they're not actually gay'.

The Home Office admitted there was absolutely no evidence to support this claim.[107] It was entirely made up. They also confirmed that only 1.5 per cent of asylum seekers even referenced their sexuality, gay, straight or otherwise.[108] Even if every single one of them claimed to be gay (and they didn't), and even if every single one was also lying (and they weren't), it still wouldn't explain the

98.5 per cent of asylum seekers that Braverman had failed to process.

Poor Suella. She'd tried everything – breaking laws, shaming her party, exposing immigrants to deadly pathogens, shrugging off homophobia, and spouting easily-disprovable statistical bullshit – and still nobody took her seriously. If this was a leadership bid – and it absolutely was – it was either going extremely badly, or exceptionally well, if only by comparison with her previous bid, when she'd managed to come sixth in a competition that was won by Liz Truss.[109]

Braverman's manoeuvres had contributed to Rishi Sunak's worst week to date. So to cheer himself up as we entered October, he popped off to the Conservative Party Conference, a pan-directional dingbat fiesta for people awaiting extinction, held in a hermetically sealed, turd-bestrewn playpen that for some reason they'd set up in Manchester, one of the top five most left-wing places in the UK.[110]

They'd invited along Frank Luntz, a plain-speaking Republican pollster who slowly and clearly explained to them that everything they were doing was fucking up the country and dooming their party to almost total annihilation. Only one in ten voters under 50 backed the Tories, and for people under 24 it was down to one in a hundred. The party's elderly base, upon which electoral survival depended, was now dying off at such a rate, explained Luntz, that the average age of a Tory voter was 'Deceased.'[111]

To warm up the audience before the prime minister's address, Suella Braverman ratcheted up the rhetoric to a point where it became so offensive that the Chair of the London Assembly accused her of 'basically vilifying gay people and trans people' in a 'homophobic rant'.[112] Andrew Boff, who had been a Conservative member for over 50 years, was thrown out of the hall for protesting that the home secretary was sending 'a signal to people who don't like people who are LGBT+'.[113]

And then – and I'm aware it sounds like I'm making this up – Braverman stamped on a guide dog.[114]

And she hadn't even got to the worst part yet, as she started Doctor Strangeing whole new realities into existence with her claims that a 'hurricane' of immigrants was just around the corner. It was the long-awaited follow-up to her March warning that 100 million migrants were on the loose and, 'Let us be clear – they are coming here'.[115]

Spoiler: 100 million migrants did not come here.

You'd think this kind of thing would appeal to Nigel Farage, who had attended the conference in his role as the totemic figurehead of their main right-wing rival, leading to rumours he was about to quit Reform and join the Conservatives. 'I think Nigel is broadly a Tory and always has been', opined Jacob Rees-Mogg, but later that day Farage said he'd taken one look at this torrent of awfulness, and asked himself, 'Would I want to join…? No, no and no'.[116]

The news that there was at least one person in the country who didn't want to replace him cheered Sunak up no end, and he grinningly took to the stage for his keynote speech. It looked like he'd been tutored in how to smile in a way that would allow him to blend in with the humans, but it made little difference. He almost vanished on a giant stage bestrewn with the phrase 'Long-term decisions', which even in-house Tory fanfiction *The Spectator* described as the worst slogan ever.[117]

Undeterred, the PM announced his first long-term decision: abandoning a long-term project out of short-term expediency. After months of dithering, Sunak had rushed from Euston to Manchester to announce that the fast train from Euston to Manchester would no longer be going as far as Manchester. Or to Euston, for that matter: to save money it would stop 5 miles north of its London terminal.[118]

So the £65 billion Tories had spent on HS2 would still be transformational, just not in the right way.[119] The National Audit Office confirmed that without its final stage, services north of Birmingham would end up with even less passenger spaces than they had before the entire project was begun, and therefore – mind-blowingly – the

Conservatives' multibillion-pound project to boost rail travel would result in the Government having to actively discourage people from using trains.[120]

But Thunderbird 0.5 now assured us his stunted, perfunctory HS0.5 still qualified as a money-saving masterplan. That narrative lasted quite a long time, by recent standards: it was a month before it was revealed that since the cancellation, the Tories had wasted a further £1.4 million on compulsory purchases to clear the path for a stretch of the project that wasn't even happening.[121] And the entire venture had been mishandled so catastrophically that the price of the HS2 station conveniently placed just outside London had risen to £4.8 billion.[122] The cost of that single station would be higher than the total cost of Spain's entire 437km high-speed rail line from Madrid to Extremadura.[123]

Along the way, we'd blown more than £280 million on private consultants, despite the Government promising to limit their use.[124] Somehow all those consultants had failed to notice that the purchase of rolling stock hadn't been included in the original HS2 estimates back in 2015, which might explain why the budget for the project seemed to have spiralled so much, but didn't explain why we'd spaffed a couple of hundred million on a bunch of freelancers lacking the wit to realise a train service might require some trains.[125] And when they did realise, they ordered trains with the doors in the wrong position, costing a further £200 million to make them compatible with existing platforms.[126]

Any savings made by the cancellation of the last leg of HS2 were immediately wiped out by the reduced income expected from a now hopelessly impaired train line. Combined with the useless freelancers and the incorrect rolling stock, and the whopping £652,000 paid to HS2's chief executive – which included a £34,000 bonus, for the love of God – the total cost of the decision to downgrade the line came to £2 billion, which I think we can agree is quite a lot of money to spend on not going to Manchester.[127]

The good news was that HS2 track was still going to Birmingham, which you'd imagine would cheer up West Midlands mayor Andy Street, the most powerful Conservative outside of Westminster. Think again: Street called the cancellation 'an incredible political gaffe' which would 'shaft the north'.[128]

Perhaps by way of an apology, the Tories had gifted his city an epic architectural folly in the form of a purpose-built £460 million HS2 station, which Downing Street ordered to be completed to full specification even though the project was cancelled. It would remain almost entirely unused.[129]

You won't be shocked to learn that the Institute for Government described the handling of HS2 – planning, execution and cancellation – as a fiasco.[130]

Embarrassed, Sunak went on to suggest the cancellation was necessary, because it would allow him to focus on reducing tax, but a furious Boris Johnson argued – correctly, for once – that it would 'make no difference' to tax.[131] I doubt BoJo was over the moon about Great British Railways either. The state-owned body he'd announced in 2021 was intended to oversee the rail network. Two years later, it still hadn't been officially launched, yet it employed more than 200 private consultants on full pay, who said they spent their days 'twiddling their thumbs', while the timetable for giving them anything – literally anything – to do was pushed back to 2026.[132]

Sunak did, however, provide 'absolute commitments' to invest in local transport using the money he'd saved by turning HS2 into a multibillion pound white elephant. His long-term commitments lasted approximately two weeks, before they were quietly deleted from the Government website, and transport minister Mark Harper admitted they had not been commitments at all, but merely 'examples of the sorts of things money could be spent on'.[133]

Relentless Shouting, Screaming and Hitting

As conference delegates headed back to their constituencies to prepare for obliteration, a poll presented the electorate's views of the Conservatives in a word cloud. The top three words were Useless, Rubbish, and Incompetent.[134] At a more granular level, the top three words beginning with C were Corrupt, Crap and Confused, although I can think of a rather saltier one that I'd like to add to the list, which brings me to Peter Bone.

After entering Parliament in 2005, Bone had risen through the ranks to become exactly what he was when he started: a loudmouth backbencher of no particular merit. He featured prominently on a list of MPs who 'boosted their ratings on the internet by saying very little, very often'.[135]

The man looks like he drank out of the wrong chalice in an Indiana Jones movie, and all that's left is a grisly combination of hollow-cheeked cynicism, physical decrepitude and eye-popping depravity, like the painting Keith Richards keeps in his attic. And not much about his behaviour was designed to make you warm to him. In the wake of the 2009 expenses scandal, the Tory party had consulted public relations experts to guide them through the fundamentals of how human beings might be expected to behave, and the main recommendation was to dial-down the grasping self-interest for a while. Bone had ignored that advice, and nepotistically continued to employ his then-wife, paying her a salary 'in the 'top bracket' of what was permissible.[136] Yet he'd earned the title of 'Britain's meanest boss' when he bragged that he was paying an employee who *wasn't* related to him just 87 pence per hour.[137]

And then, just in case your blood pressure was falling dangerously low, he supported the filibustering of Parliament to deliberately prevent the passing of a bill to block 'up-skirting', which brings us to October 2023, when his primordial beliefs about mistreatment of underlings and his idiosyncratic views on the displaying of genitalia combined to make headlines again.[138]

Bone's parliamentary assistant characterised working for the MP as 'a siege mentality in terms of the relentless shouting, the screaming, the hitting'.[139] It had been building for more than four years, until things came to a head during a work trip. Bone had 'verbally belittled, ridiculed, abused and humiliated' his assistant during the overnight stay, and 'repeatedly physically struck and threw things' at him. That evening, somehow confusing his parliamentary aide with a free on-call plumbing service, Bone instructed him come to his hotel room to 'fix the shower', waited until his victim was kneeling in the cubicle, then dropped his towel and waved his genitals in the poor man's face.[140]

The party suspended Bone pending an investigation by the Parliamentary Commissioner for Standards, which found against him on the grounds that, as a result of all this bloody wokery, pelting members of your team with various objects, punching them, and then flopping out your ancient tallywacker was likely to be frowned upon.[141]

A recall petition in Bone's Wellingborough constituency demanded a by-election, which led him to complain that it 'seems bizarre' that he'd have to be judged by voters in this way. After all, the offences had 'occurred more than 10 years ago'.[142]

Peter Bone had dedicated those years to a heroic battle against undeserving people being given public money. Yet when the Conservatives gave Bone a severance package of over £5,500 to which he was not legally entitled, he happily took it.[143] The payout formed part of the nearly £1 million given to sacked ministers and disgraced Tory MPs during a single year.[144]

He wasn't legally entitled to stand as a candidate again either, so in an act of contempt for his voters that was bewildering to the point of psychosis, it was decided his girlfriend should stand instead. Perhaps the two of them considered this a clever strategy. As it turned out, that was a faulty premise. The result was a disaster for the Conservatives, with Labour overturning Bone's majority of 18,000 when the election fell in February of 2024.[145]

But we're getting ahead of ourselves, because it was still only October 2023, and the Tories still had a few constituencies to lose before Bone got his turn. As part of his campaign to retain the seat formerly held by Chris Pincher, the new candidate Andrew Cooper had taken it upon himself to tell people who couldn't afford to feed their children to 'fuck off'. You have to salute him for deploying such a bold tactic, but – and nobody could have predicted this – it was ultimately unappealing to voters.[146] Labour toppled a 19,000 Tory majority.

And Nadine Dorries' former seat of Mid Bedfordshire fell to Labour that same day. In its entire existence the constituency had never elected a Labour MP, and Dorries had won by over 24,000 votes in 2019. Her loss represented largest overturned majority in the post-war era.[147]

Mad and Dangerous

On 25 October Sunak completed his first and last full year in office, and reviews poured in from his delighted party.

'He's increasingly weak'.[148]

'He exists in torpor'.

'Clearly Rishi Sunak isn't working as leader of our party'.[149]

He wasn't being helped by the constant reminders of his predecessors. A further 24 fixed penalty notices were issued for Partygate, hitting headlines right in the middle of the public inquiry into the Government's handling of Covid, in which Sunak, as the then-Chancellor, had played a major role.[150] Much of this is covered elsewhere,[151] and little new information emerged, but what did was dynamite.

In the depths of the pandemic the UK's most senior civil servant, Simon Case, had written to colleagues saying, 'He [Boris Johnson] cannot lead and we cannot support him in leading with this approach.

The team captain cannot change the call on the big plays every day'. Case added that the at the heart of Government, the ministers with greatest responsibility – Matt Hancock, Gavin Williamson, Johnson, Gove and Sunak – formed a 'weak team', and that, 'This is in danger of becoming Trump/Bolsonaro level mad and dangerous.'[152]

As for Johnson, he'd already become infamous for insisting we should 'let the bodies pile high', but new quotes made it clear this wasn't some slip of the tongue. He had agreed that, 'Covid is just Nature's way of dealing with old people', and had insisted the real hero of the movie *Jaws* was the mayor who had kept the beaches open and actively encouraged the public to dive in and become fish-food.[153]

Dominic Cummings, a part-time hobo who had perfected the glassy-eyed stare of a school caretaker on the receiving end of a dawn raid by a specialist branch of the Met, had complained to colleagues about having to 'sit here for 2 hours just to stop him saying stupid shit'.

Another leading advisor had described Covid as being 'the wrong crisis for [Boris Johnson's] skillset', which was the skillset of a children's entertainer on administrative leave pending the outcome of a tribunal. Johnson had suggested to the country's two leading medical scientists – who presumably possessed Olympic-standard poker faces – that Covid could be cured by directing a 'special hairdryer' up your nose.

This was, said the scientists, a 'low point', at least until it got even lower: Johnson had become bored by Covid, and demanded Dominic Cummings invent some sort of 'dead cat' story to get it 'off the front pages'.[154]

The chaos inside Number 10 clearly horrified the guy next door at Number 11. Hairdryer cures and negligent genocide were against the ethics Sunak seemed so very proud of, although that doesn't explain why Sunak had also said the Government should 'just let people die'.

'This all feels like a complete lack of leadership', wrote the Government's chief scientific adviser.[155] Perhaps feeling she could fill the vacuum, Johnson's then-girlfriend, current-wife, and future-author of an inevitable tell-all bonkbusting memoir, an unelected 32-year-old Theatre Studies graduate called Carrie Symonds, had taken to sending orders to civil servants via text message, often directly contradicting official policy. Instead of telling his staff to ignore this, Johnson placed the blame on her for his own regular U-turns, which of course only made civil servants think she must have some sort of unacknowledged authority and led to yet more confusion. In the end, after repeated protests from senior officials, Johnson ordered somebody to go and talk to Carrie, and suggest that she 'get a job with the Royal Family', or go on lots of foreign holidays to 'get her out of our hair'.[156]

But she wasn't the only one causing bedlam. Simon Case accused Cummings of presiding over a 'fucking extraordinary' turn of events, characterised by Cummings' habit of 'constantly briefing out his plans and screwing up the rest of us in the process'.[157]

In return, Cummings had complained that Simon Case's Cabinet office was 'terrifyingly shit', and described core Cabinet ministers as 'useless fuckpigs', 'morons' and 'cunts'.[158] When this was put to him at the Inquiry, he responded: 'I think I was reflecting a widespread view among competent people'.[159]

This was – and for once I'm pretty confident about this assertion – Rishi Sunak's worst week to date, not least because just at the moment an appalled public yearned to see justice, chief culprit Boris Johnson announced he was taking a lucrative role on GB News, adding to the £4.8 million he had already earned during the year.[160] And then Bob Stewart was found guilty of a racially aggravated public order offence (although later cleared on appeal).[161] And then Crispin Blunt was arrested on suspicion of rape.[162]

*

While this was going on, Sunak took a break from his gap-year as prime minister and spent the day pretending to be Elon Musk's desktop bobble-head. This followed a startling speech from Sunak, in which he warned that the risk of human extinction from AI was on the same scale as from nuclear war,[163] but after giving it serious consideration, he thought the billionaires charging pell-mell towards the end of the world should definitely be allowed to regulate themselves.[164]

And so it came to pass that one week later he sat cross-legged and laughing as he interviewed Elon Musk on stage, chuckling as Sissy SpaceX – in exciting news for fans of the Terminator franchise – predicted humanoid robots that 'can chase you anywhere',[165] launched an AI programme with a 'rebellious streak', and warned that absolutely everybody's livelihoods were about to vanish, except for his.[166]

Sam Coates, Sky News's political editor, described it as, 'One of the maddest events I've ever covered'.[167] But of course, that was just the mainstream media, and proper conservatives wouldn't respond in such terms. As it turns out, they didn't respond in normal terms at all, because they were too busy howling their despair at the Godless skies.[168]

'I despair at No 10's naivety', said one.

Another: 'It's utterly breathtaking. Unbelievable crassness. Who thought this was a good idea?'

A minister said: 'People are worried about their finances, climate change, pandemics, war in Eastern Europe and the Middle East. And now the PM has provided Elon Musk with an interview platform to say, sometime soon, that they and their children will not have jobs, a life without meaning'.

'It's head in hands. Basically, a Conservative prime minister provided a platform for a conspiracist to say their children's lives were going to be meaningless'.

'For crying out loud, we have a general election inside a year and the PM is offering the electorate dystopia. Thick, thick, thick'.

Narcissistic Crap

November, and we find the former Tory chair, Bim Afolami, facing a parliamentary inquiry after he'd failed to declare £2,000 a month he was being paid by a lobbying firm.[169] Another former Tory chair, Brandon Lewis, accepted a six-figure sum to work for a company owned by two Russians who were under sanctions.[170] And then Jake Berry, yet another former Tory chair, accused the party of a 'cover up' over one of their MPs who he claimed was a serial rapist.[171]

Being Tory chair sounds like a relentless, high-stakes game of jackass whack-a-mole.

No sooner had this left the headlines than Sunak's director of communications resigned, less than a year into the job. She was the fourth person to have quit that operationally vital role in the previous 18 months, indicative of a party in freefall, beset by scandal, and unable to hang on to any talent.[172]

And you could see it everywhere. In the 23 years between Thatcher's election and the Brexit referendum, the average tenure of a Chancellor had been 1726 days. The average since the referendum was 447.[173] Those 23 years had seen six Chancellors of the Exchequer. Since the Brexit referendum we had burned through seven. Seven Health Secretaries too. Nine education ministers, three in a single week. Thirteen housing ministers – six of them just since the previous February. Grant Shapps alone had held five ministerial jobs in less than a year, although naturally he has an advantage, because there were four of him.[174]

And, of course, five prime ministers.[175]

We'd also had eight Home Secretaries, assuming you count Suella Braverman twice. She was a divisive figure: you either loathed her or hated her. After being sacked by Liz Truss, Chinchilla the Hun had spent six harrowing days in the political wilderness before being appointed to the same role again by Rishi Sunak, as part of a deal they had struck: she would deliver the support of the party's right flank, and in return Sunak would be too timid to stop her shooting her big mouth off and turning the entire party into a grotesque Nigel Farage tribute act.[176] Which is precisely what she spent the rest of the year doing, as the party's polling tumbled and tumbled.[177]

She didn't seem to understand that there simply weren't enough far right votes, and she didn't appear to care that her relentless pursuit of those few votes was helping to condemn the Tories to oblivion. She didn't seem to care about anything, really, except for her own insatiable leadership ambitions. She constantly mouthed profoundly horrible and dehumanising rhetoric about immigrants, and it had been going on with increasing frequency for months. Back in April, she'd claimed child exploitation gangs were 'almost all British-Pakistani' and explained to the *Daily Mail* that it was 'not racist to tell the truth'.[178]

Sure, but it's definitely racist to spread dangerous and false slurs about an ethnic minority, and that's exactly what she'd done. Her own Home Office had published research showing members of grooming gangs are predominantly white males under 30, and the Independent Press Standards Organisation made the *Mail* publish a correction.[179]

Only days after a firebomb attack on a refugee centre in Dover – which police said met the threshold of a terrorist incident – she claimed there was an 'invasion on our southern coast', which was enough to make even Robert Jenrick wince.[180] He was a major rival for the affections of the Conservative right, but distanced himself from Braverman's rhetoric. 'We do have to choose our language carefully', he said.[181] By September over a dozen Tory MPs, including ministers who sat in the same cabinet as Braverman, had made formal complaints to the chief whip about her incendiary speeches on immigration.[182]

But whether Braverman's claims were true or not is beside the point. Their real purpose was to efficiently conflate various paranoid right-wing conspiracies about immigrants, and in that respect she delivered. Corrections meant nothing, because by the time they arrived, ugly prejudices had been reinforced by lies emerging directly from the home secretary, and then had been repeated across social media. The damage was done. So Braverman moved on to her next bit of social vandalism, describing rough sleeping as a lifestyle choice.

'The British people are compassionate', she had tweeted, but that compassion was misguided because, she claimed, many of those sleeping on the streets were 'from abroad', and therefore, I presume, didn't count as proper humans, worthy of sympathy.[183] It was bullshit anyway. According to the Office for National Statistics, 81 per cent of rough sleepers were born in the UK. But the home secretary never missed a chance to blow on her dog-whistle.[184]

Every time you thought she couldn't get any lower, knock knock knock, here's Suella, banging on the floorboards.

*

Who did this benefit? Not the Tories. It just megaphoned the rhetoric of the far-right, normalised Nigel Farage, boosted the appeal of the Conservatives' main rivals, and drove voters into the arms of Reform and their even less palatable stable-mates.

If you believe Tommy Robinson, you'd think he was the noble and patriotic co-founder of the English Defence League, on a holy mission to protect our borders from criminals.

If you believed our courts, Tommy Robinson is a lying, self-serving, racist grifter with a lifelong commitment to ugly little crimes.[185] He's been jailed for fraud, jailed for assault, jailed for travelling on a false passport, and jailed for interfering with a trial. He has convictions for drug offences and defamation,[186] he isn't called Tommy Robinson, and he isn't even English – he's an Irish citizen called Stephen Yaxley-Lennon,[187] who later unlawfully crossed our borders to avoid British Justice.[188]

Such minor details don't seem to concern his supporters, who had announced their intention to gather at the Cenotaph to oppose a protest calling for a ceasefire in Gaza. At least 300,000 people were expected to join the peace march, taking a route through London that wouldn't come within one mile of the Cenotaph. But that was another minor detail that didn't concern Tommy Robinson and his thick-necked, brass-knuckled, smooth-brained brethren.

They'd been stoked into fury by Braverman, who deplored calls for a ceasefire on 11 November, because it would ruin the meaning of Armistice Day. She'd spent the previous week luxuriating in the theatricality of rage, writing provocative newspaper articles depicting peace protestors as 'hate marchers'.[189] A senior Tory called her comments, 'wholly offensive and ignorant', and said it was 'clear that the home secretary is only looking after her misguided aspirations for leader'.[190]

Many Tories believed Braverman was determined to get sacked. 'It is as if she wants to be fired so she can get on with a leadership bid', said one former cabinet colleague.[191] She chose to ignore Number 10's orders to tone down her language, and her next article claimed the police had an inherent lefty bias. 'Double standards' meant right-wing protestors faced harsh policing, whereas leftwinger marches were being 'largely ignored'.[192]

If this was true – and it patently wasn't, with left-wing protests resulting in two-and-a-half times as many arrests as right-wing ones[193] – the police would still have been justified at the Cenotaph riots later that week. By the end of Remembrance Day, they'd arrested 92 of Tommy Robinson's right-wing protestors.[194] Enraged by peaceful protest and engorged by Braverman's rhetoric, they had chanted 'you're going home in a fucking ambulance',[195] as they threw missiles and metal fences at the police. They flew Swastikas at the memorial to Britain's war dead.[196] Antisemitic chants were heard in their defence of Israel's fight with Hamas. Nine officers were injured as they arrested almost half of the 200 proto-fascists, who in some cases had shouted Braverman's inflammatory article verbatim,[197] and were found to be carrying knives, knuckle-dusters, batons and class-A drugs.[198] Multiple high-ranking officers from forces across the country said Braverman's claims of police bias had been a factor in the 'unprecedented' attacks on officers from the right wingers.[199]

And the lefty hate-marchers? It turns out they were predominantly families with children, who carried cardboard cutouts of doves, and placards asking for a ceasefire. By the end of Remembrance Sunday not a single arrest had been recorded from the entire 300,000 crowd.[200]

You'd think this was bad news for Suella Braverman, but not a bit of it. Finally, she had conquered being Woke, although in a limited and specific way: she didn't have to wake up early on Tuesday morning, because Sunak sacked her on Monday. It was the second time this had happened to her in barely a year.

As appropriate for a home secretary who behaved like a stroppy toddler, smashing her room up because nobody had paid attention to her for two straight minutes, the parliamentary party went into a conniption fit about the entire thing. Two senior MPs threatened to quit if her sacking went ahead. It went ahead. They didn't quit.[201] Andrea Jenkyns wrote to the backbench 1922 Committee, saying, 'Enough is enough ... It is time for Rishi Sunak to go and replace him with a "real" Conservative party leader'.[202] A dozen right-wing Tories arranged a playdate entitled The New Conservatives, which was attended by supporters of Braverman including Lee Anderson, who said, 'Thank goodness we have a home secretary who refuses to be cancelled', struggling to get his mind around her very public cancellation as home secretary.[203]

Meanwhile a senior MP from the party's centre accused Braverman of 'narcissistic crap [as] she continues to act with total self-indulgence'.[204]

The entire episode was as close to a demonstration of total governmental psychopathy as you'd ever want to witness.

All Change!

Only 40 days had passed since the PM had unveiled his previous relaunch. 'I will tell it as it is,' he had told a sceptical Conservative Party Conference back in October. 'I will lead in a different way, because that is the only way to create the sort of change in our politics and in our country that we all desperately want to see'.[205]

For the last month, Sunak had frantically tried to distance himself from the previous 13 years, the consequences of which were catching up with his Government from every direction at once. A combination of Brexit and austerity had royally screwed the UK, and both policies were now wildly unpopular. So Sunak decided to bring back David Cameron, the guy who had instigated – let me check my notes – oh yes, Brexit and austerity.

Depending which faction you asked, the return of Cameron was either the second coming of Home Counties Jesus, or a dirty protest. But in the interests of balance I should note that, following a recent critical reassessment, Cameron had climbed the charts of *Britain's Best Ever Prime Minister*, and now sat proudly just inside the top million.

To facilitate the reshuffle, Cameron, Igglepiggle made of mechanically reclaimed ham, was given a life peerage and the chance to pretend to be foreign secretary until it was time for the Tories to be voted out of office again.[206] But for now, he was stood tersely in front the cameras again, looking for all the world like cross Lego.

All Change Back Again!

With the reboot of Cameron, it had taken only one month for Sunak to transform from the Change Candidate into the Change Back Again candidate.

The reshuffle set Steve Barclay on his travels again too. I'm aware your face has just gone blank at that name, which is appropriate, because he's so featureless that I wouldn't be shocked to learn he can't recognise himself in a mirror. He's so lacking in personality that he failed his Myers Briggs test. His DNA profile reads '404 error'. His spirit animal is a geography teacher. You could walk straight through him like the Canterville Ghost – in fact he's so unmemorable that even while writing this, I had to go back to the start of the paragraph to remind myself who I'm describing.

So before both of us forget again, here's a quick refresher course.

In 2020 Steve Barclay had been an entirely invisible Chief Secretary to the Treasury, after which he was simultaneously and imperceptibly the Chancellor of the Duchy of Lancaster and Boris Johnson's Chief of Staff. He used his roles to promise a 'smaller state' and got off to a cracking start by shrinking his own duties: he lost both jobs.[207]

After that he was sent off to do absolutely nothing helpful at the NHS. The *Health Service Journal* said of his appointment, 'never has a politician arrived in the post of health secretary trailing a worse reputation among NHS leaders', but thankfully it was a problem with a short shelf life, because Barclay returned to the backbenches after only 63 eventless days.[208]

A month later, Sunak appointed him health secretary for a second time, which might have been deliberate, or might have been incompetence, but is more likely a result of nobody noticing Barclay had done it before. He was effortlessly ineffectual in resolving the waves of industrial action that washed across the entire stressed-out NHS. He opted not to hold talks with striking nurses, and instead held a string of secret meetings with the Ministry of Sound and an upmarket interior design firm called The Bon Collective. His department refused to explain what was going on in the minister's mind, potentially because none of them knew who the minister was.[209] Had he really prioritised frilly cushions and dance music over the backlog for NHS treatment, which had risen from a post-Covid

6.5 million[210] to a post-Barclay 7.8 million?[211] It appeared so.

He'd performed so well as two Heath Secretaries that in November Sunak decided to promote him to none. He was shoved down several steps, becoming environment secretary, even though he was married to an executive at a water company that was under investigation for illegally pumping raw sewage into our rivers.[212]

This was clearly an inspiration for the new minister selected to oversee our nation's health: Victoria Atkins, whose husband was the managing director of British Sugar.[213] Previously she'd been drugs minister while her husband ran Britain's largest cannabis farm.[214]

Clearly Atkins and Barclay were serious contenders for the title of Britain's Top Hypocrite, a major challenge to James Cleverley, who – in a devastating one-two sucker punch from irony – was the MP for Braintree. Fortunately, Cleverley reclaimed the Insincerity Crown when he became home secretary and had to deliver the Rwanda policy despite having ridiculed the Rwanda policy as 'batshit'.[215]

Ignore the Laws

It was Rishi Sunak's worst week to date. Again. Everybody knew things were bad, but you couldn't invent a more graphic demonstration of the state of the Conservative party than the decision of the Young Conservative Network to resign. All of them. The Young Conservatives were officially dissolved.

In their final, parting message, they blamed 'the lack of ambitious proposals on housing, childcare and education ... factionalism [and] an increasing disconnect between members and the party'.[216] They weren't wrong. But they weren't especially right either, because they went on to insist: 'we still believe that Conservative ideals are popular with the younger generation'. But this was nonsense. The age at which voters became more likely to vote Conservative was rising at an alarming rate. At the general election of 2019, the average age at which somebody 'crossed over' and became a Tory voter was 39. By the election of 2024, it had risen to 63.[217]

And it's not surprising. The mood music of Sunak's Government was startlingly youth-repelling, with constant dog-whistled attacks on queer and trans cultures, dehumanisation of minorities, and snide needling about the wasteful avocado consumption of a generation who were overwhelmed by the highest housing costs in the English-speaking world.[218] Yet you could waste months googling Tory speeches for solutions for these issues. The entire parliamentary party was focused on the barely-noticeable needs of their wealthy elderly base, to the cost of pretty much everybody else – including the poorer half of the elderly base. Over one quarter of pensioner households were worth more than £1 million,[219] but for the rest, poverty was already at an all-time high[220] by the time Jeremy Hunt chose to lay out his electoral stall with a £1,800 per year cut in income for another half a million of them.[221]

And nobody could remember voting for any of this. Not that it mattered. By this point the Tories were the ultimate transmutational political movement: their half-forgotten manifesto was a melange of ahistorical guesswork, and their mission for Britain could mean whatever you wanted it to mean. The party – indeed the entire right-wing ecosystem, encompassing newspapers, opinion channels and social media – existed in a state of constant, suffused indignation. There need not even be an object for that indignation: one could always be found by publication deadline. If all else failed, fall back on Meghan Markle, Gary Lineker, or the dress sense of a female Labour frontbencher.

And the Tories seemed to have an ambition to achieve as many public service breakdowns as possible before being ousted at the next election. They gave the impression their policy units were exclusively staffed by absolutist bridge-burners, igniting every path back to sensible governance. Whatever problem arose, ideology had already ruled out the most practical solution.

You can't fix the housing market if your ethos is to not interfere with markets.

You can't tackle a global climate emergency if you're subservient to a wing of the party that thinks climate science is all made up, and which rejects international cooperation in favour of angry ethnic purity.

You can't resolve a public sector employment shortfall or endemic low pay if you've just spent a dozen years pouring out spiteful rhetoric that the nation's woes are all caused by avaricious Slovakian care workers earning £5 an hour.

And that demented focus on immigration was about to face its ultimate test, which, in keeping with the motif of Sunak's administration, it failed comprehensively.

*

On 15 November, Britain's Supreme Court found that the Rwanda asylum scheme was unlawful.[222] The Government promised an illegal immigration policy, and that's exactly what they gave us.

The ruling triggered a full-body, all-encompassing, 360-degree, multi-channel explosion of paranoia from the Braverman wing of the party. They raged that this wasn't what it seemed to be: an appropriate application of the law, handed down by the highest judicial authority in the land: it was a conspiracy by a Remainer 'blob'.[223] Accurate descriptions of the legal ruling were brushed away as a secret left-wing plot. Rare instances of neutral journalistic accuracy were furiously dismissed as slanted, woke nonsense. The right's persecution complex had accelerated to the point where Nadine Dorries claimed Silicon Valley had a 'big dial' that they turned to 'nudge opinion ever leftwards', but that Google executives had hidden it from her when she visited their office.[224]

Meanwhile the Tory deputy chairman, Lee Anderthal, said we should 'ignore the laws', while his colleague Jonathan Gullis went even further: we should take 'direct action', said Primark Hodor. We should push boats back across the English Channel 'regardless of any conflict that may end up with the French', almost salivating in his eagerness to restart the Hundred Years' War.[225]

Sunak – as you would expect from a man who once boasted of being 'obsessed with details',[226] – said he would not 'not allow a foreign court to block these flights'.[227] Britain's Supreme Court was, at the risk of labouring the point, British, which was a detail Sunak had opted not to be obsessed about.

Sunak had never looked weaker, and Braverman was on him like a fucking puma, accusing him of having 'no credible plan B'.[228] To prove her wrong, he announced that the 'rule of law is fundamental to our democracy', so he was going to ignore the law. Instead, he'd pass a bill that rendered Rwanda safe by parliamentary fiat.

Unfortunately nobody explained today's spin on events to James Cleverley, so while the PM was telling everybody that he'd break the law to defend the law, the new home secretary was on TV insisting we didn't need to, because the Rwanda plan was already acting as a deterrent, even though it hadn't been implemented.[229] Which makes you wonder why it was necessary at all, since clearly the Tories could achieve their aims by just making up nonsensical things that they knew would never happen.

I mean, it worked fine for the Brexit campaign.

So – deep breath – in defence of the fundamentals of British sovereignty, law and democracy, a policy forbidden by Britain's Supreme Court was going to be implemented by a PM with absolutely no electoral mandate, even though the plan didn't appear in the Tory manifesto, so nobody could possibly have voted for it.

Based on this evidence, you could understandably conclude that the entire cabinet were idiots, but research suggests their IQ was actually around 160. That is combined, though. When Sunak's allies comforted us that he was the smartest person in the room, it only reminded us that all the rooms he worked in were full of intellectual pygmies. So it's hardly a surprise that somebody decided they needed a Minister for Common Sense. What's slightly more surprising is that they selected Esther McVey.[230]

They'd named her Minister for Common Sense because Minister For Stoking Culture Wars was a bit too on-the-nose, but we could all see what it was about. It was Sunak's latest attempt to placate the Tory right, but it didn't work. Jacob Rees-Mogg said McVey's, 'silly little title [was] not the proper business of government. This is ridiculously tokenistic, won't impress anybody'.[231] Number 10 insisted this was definitely a necessary ministerial role, and she would be undertaking serious responsibilities, but Sunak's spokesman was incapable of describing what those responsibilities would be.[232]

Saving money, perhaps? Although probably only for the McVie family. She'd stood for leadership in 2019, with a flashy campaign video in which she said she wanted to be a public servant.[233] When she came last in the contest, she suddenly decided she didn't want to be a public servant anymore, so she took a second job at a private broadcaster. She became a presenter on GB News for £900 per episode, as did her husband, Tory MP Philip Davies.[234]

McVey had gone on to criticise the Conservatives' 2022 budget as 'a socialist paradise of tax and spend',[235] and now raged in the *Daily Mail* about John Q Taxpayer seeing his 'hard-earned cash [being] wasted on unnecessary public spending'.[236] But she had been quite happy in 2019 to claim almost £9,000 in taxpayers' money for a personal photographer to capture all her epic successes as housing minister [not pictured].[237]

And then McVey claimed a further £39,000 of taxpayer's money to rent a flat in London, even though she and Philip Davies owned a flat 25 minutes' walk away. They declared an annual income of £10,000 from renting that property out.[238]

The public were furious that this ninny was being paid £118,000 to do something relating to Common Sense that nobody could define. No such munificence for the rest of us, as we entered our second year of agonising mortgage stress. Liz Truss's decision to give an unfunded £45 billion tax cut to the richest people in the country had caused a spike in interest rates,[239] and the average cost of mortgage repayments had soared by £7,000 per year.[240]

Amongst those struggling was George Freeman, who resigned from Cabinet in November because the increased cost of owning a home caused by his own party meant, 'I simply couldn't afford to pay [the mortgage] on a ministerial salary'.[241] So his solution was not to downsize, or to do more with less, or even to give up Netflix and stop eating avocados. Such options were reserved entirely for the poor. Instead Freeman – who had been science minister – decided the best way to afford his mortgage was to return to being a lower-paid backbencher, a move which reduced his income by almost £27,000.

Why is He Just So Bad at Politics?

But at least some Tories were above blaming poverty on the poor. They blamed it on geography instead. When he was asked in parliament why over one third of children in the Stockton North constituency were living in poverty, James Cleverley was heard by several witnesses to say, 'because it's a shithole'. He issued a blanket denial, which quickly transformed into a string-vest denial, as audio recordings of him saying it made gaping holes in his defence.[242] Inevitably – depressingly – the argument then moved from the conditions of children living in squalor, to a did/didn't schoolyard squabble about unparliamentary language. He showed no particular interest in fixing child poverty, because he got a much faster endorphin hit from a quick round of rhetorical parlour-games with his Labour opponents. It marked the beginning of a truly terrible month for the new home secretary.

Firstly, he inherited responsibility for the most prolonged cat-death in history: Rwanda. Despite the costs so far having risen to £290 million, the only people we'd managed to send to there were three Home Secretaries, the latest being Jim But Dim.²⁴³ He returned to the UK fully committed to implementing the thing he'd once called 'batshit', and determined to persuade MPs that they could make a place 'safe' by an act of parliament, rather than by observed reality. Pound for pound, this was only slightly more blithering than voting to abolish gravity.

As the debate began, immigration ministerRobert Jenrick resigned, officially in protest at what he thought were the failings of the Rwanda bill, which still didn't allow Britain to ignore international laws.²⁴⁴ This may be because Britain – with notable exceptions – was still on Planet Earth, where international law applies.

But a principled stand against having to obey international law wasn't the real reason for him quitting. That was just an excuse. A close confidant said in reality Jenrick was, 'distancing himself from Rishi, it's as simple as that. He's young and is in this for the long term, and can see which way it's going'.²⁴⁵ It was all part of Robert Jenrick's long term commitment to the future of Robert Jenrick.

He'd once been as square, limp and wet as a used dishcloth. But blandly moderate attitudes wouldn't get him very far in the modern Conservative Party. So he transformed himself into something that was still square, limp and wet, but was now also brutally right-wing. His colleagues once called him Robert Generic, but now Enoch Towel was fully committed to the party's increasingly nutty, narrow, nationalistic wing.²⁴⁶

Politics is a minority interest at the best of times, but it's only when you become a member of a party that the real craziness sets in. Locked away in mouldy scout huts, voluntarily isolated from anybody with normal worldviews, local parties transform into clanging echo chambers, with little to prevent members from sliding into zealotry. That's equally the case for barmy, leftist Militants of the 1980s, as it is for the increasingly ethno-nationalist Tory shed-heads of the 2020s. Logic and evidence no longer play a part as members vie to outdo one another's fanaticism.

The process was exacerbated in the Tory Party because its membership had plummeted from around 3 million to under 172,000,[247] while Conservative think-tank the Bow Group estimated the average age of a Tory member at 72.[248] This was a shrinking, ageing cohort with attitudes that had ossified when Margaret Thatcher was in her prime, often wildly detached from modernity, and trapped in a death cycle of petty grievances about a fast-moving world that had left them behind. Lashing out became the norm. Competitive othering had taken over the party.

But this cohort would pick the next leader. Any ambitious Tory had to shuffle toward Faragism on race and immigration, or they would never get to the top. Hence Jenrick's decision to tack right.

Meanwhile his major competitor, Kemi Badenoch, was following in the footsteps of earlier right-wingers Dominic Raab and Gavin Williamson. It had been a year since a senior Conservative had faced accusations of workplace bullying, but officials working in Badenoch's private office described her as creating an intimidating and toxic atmosphere, which was so bad that three senior figures had felt they had no choice but to leave. They alleged her behaviour was 'traumatising and bullying' in a way that was 'sustained and personal'. She denied all the allegations, claiming she had done no more than 'lose her rag', but her conduct clearly concerned her ministerial colleagues: they'd taken to visiting Badenoch's offices unannounced to 'check in' on the wellbeing of her team, and officials had put in place measures to ensure those being 'targeted' by Badenoch never had to be left alone with her.[249] Badenoch's spokesman said this was a 'completely false and flagrant smear'.

Whether it was or not, she still she remained a favourite to succeed Sunak, which is the first and only time the words *Sunak* and *succeed* have appeared together.

Yet now she had another competitor to best: Jenrick, whose resignation-slash-campaign-launch left James Cleverley at the dispatch box, trying to persuade a mocking House of Commons that his Rwanda policy was workable, even as the minister responsible for implementing that policy was doing a runner. Cleverley was asked how a bill to legally declare a location permanently safe could possibly comply with international law, when on its front page it clearly stated that the home secretary couldn't say it was compatible with international law.[250]

'Both things are true and neither one cancels out the other', he replied.[251]

Despite the efforts of Schrödinger's Twat, it was already clear that no mass deportations to Rwanda would ever happen. Home Office officials tasked with awarding contracts to fly asylum seekers out of the country admitted 'no airlines have signed up'. Every potential carrier refused a contract, fearing the damage to their reputations.[252]

Sunak's Rwanda promises had been battered on all sides – by the Supreme Court, by international law, by airlines, and by Parliament. So the day after Jenrick resigned, the PM called an emergency press conference, which many hoped, with mounting excitement, would be the announcement of a General Election.

No such luck: the briefing was merely Sunak publicly begging his own MPs to support his plan to fix an immigration crisis that their relentless rhetoric and incompetence had caused. He warned that without decisive action the Tories would be locked out of power for a generation.[253]

And then he locked himself out of Downing Street.

Footage showed 5'7" Rishi Sunak next to his 6'4" Dutch counterpart Mark Rutte, and the PM having to bang on the door to be allowed inside.[254]

'Why is he just so bad at politics?' asked one despairing Tory MP.[255]

And yet for once Sunak avoided catastrophe. Dozens of his backbenchers had complained that his abracadabra-Rwanda-is-safe bill was either too weak, too strong, or too spellbindingly batty for words, but in the end more than two-dozen potential dissenters merely abstained. This left Sunak with enough votes to get it over its first hurdle on the long route to becoming official policy, but with warnings ringing in his ears. 'This bill has been allowed to live another day', said one rebel, 'but without amendments it will be killed next month'.[256]

We were heading towards a very Conservative Christmas, where the nativity scene was just an empty shed: no unwed mothers, no refugees, and certainly no wise men. The PM probably hoped that his reprieve over Rwanda, combined with the exit of Suella Braverman and the looming holiday break, would bring to a close the wild internecine drama that defined 2023. Compared to the years of Brexit, Johnson, Covid and Truss, things did seem slightly calmer: not because there had been less chaos, but rather that the personnel involved were less cartoonish. Yet despite Sunak's efforts to suck all the oxygen out of the political atmosphere, it still felt like the Tory party were running an experiment based on the question: 'what if rollercoasters never ended and weren't fun?'

And now, as 2023 drew to a close, the prime minister could finally focus on making the party slightly less catastrophically unelectable as he headed towards his date with the voters. Or so he hoped. Fate, however, had its own plans. In the final week before Christmas, the Home Office proudly announced new measures to crack down on the spiking of drinks, hoping to end the year with story that would generate some exciting headlines.

It went badly right.

Only hours after the spiking crackdown had been launched, the home secretary told guests at a Downing Street reception that he regularly spiked his wife with 'a little bit of Rohypnol in her drink every night' and explained that it was 'not really illegal if it's only a little bit'.[257] It had, of course, only been James Cleverley's inept clench at a joke, but his apologies were almost drowned out by the sound of his colleagues' face-palming themselves into unconsciousness.

This was starting to look like Sunak's worst week to date, but he was nothing if not determined, and he'd be damned if he didn't end the year on a high. So he took a handful of friendly journalists with him on a photo-op at a shelter for the down-and-out, where they watched slack jawed as he asked a man queuing at a soup kitchen, 'Do you work in business?'[258]

'No, I'm homeless. I'm actually a homeless person'.

'Oh', said Sunak, and paused, blinking. 'Do you want some fruit?'

Part 2

'Can we, for more than five minutes, dispense with the civil war?'

January to May 2024

Ms Badenoch vs The Post Office

Everybody knew an election could happen at any moment, and you didn't need to be Mystic Meg to predict the outcome. A Conservative victory was nigh-impossible, partly because the Tories had turned into every shade and shape of awful, like a Satanic Benetton; partly because the product they were selling was a pile of worthless crap; and partly because the salesmen were hopeless. The quality of the cabinet made you wonder if some sort of randomised lottery system was involved, or maybe a work scheme for people with a congenital competence disorder.

But the main reason a change of Government seemed inevitable could be boiled down to two words: Tory voters. By this point they were like those people who allegedly turn up at A&E with a lubricated garden ornament accidentally inserted into their fundament: we've all heard the stories, so they must exist, but nobody has ever met one. And who would own up to it anyway?

The nation was desperate for this to be over, but we were still months from the end. The Conservative party had turned into the Saint Sebastian of British politics: besotted with its own martyrdom, full of pricks, but refusing to die. They clung to power the way a drunkard clings to a lamppost.

And what for? What did they still want to do? Nobody could pinpoint it. Governments are elected to set a direction, to plot a course and steer a nation. But since Thatcherism became their defining creed, the Conservatives had developed an ideological aversion to any involvement in steering the ship of state, believing instead that the best outcome would emerge if we just let the winds of fortune blow us where they may, secure in the knowledge that The Market would never, under any circumstances, hurl us against the rocks like it had done in 1920. And 1929.[1]

And then again in 1956.

Then in 1961.

And in 1973.

And in 1980, and 1992.

And spectacularly in 2008.

Of course, some financial crashes are unavoidable. Events happen. Nobody can blame the emergence of Covid on the Conservatives, just as nobody can – or should – blame the collapse of Lehman Brothers on Labour. Those parties just happened to be in office when the disaster struck. But most of the time, the economic outcomes for a nation are a result of political choice, and the Conservatives had chosen 14 years of ineptitude, inertia and negligence. The nation reeked of decay, but every major party – not least the Conservatives – seemed dead set against the wishes of a population yearning for a government that cared enough to try to fix things.

One of the things that needed fixing was the Post Office. Between 1999 and 2015, over 900 postmasters working behind ordinary counters in towns and villages across the land had been convicted of a range of crimes, including theft, fraud and false accounting. They were all innocent. Their prosecutions were based on data that Post Office senior management, together with its software suppliers Fujitsu, had known to be false the entire time. It became the worst and most widespread miscarriage of justice that the Criminal Cases Review Commission had ever seen.[2] Thousands of innocent people were accused, four killed themselves, 230 went to prison, and countless lives were needlessly ruined.³ The scandal – long denied – had been covered for years by *Private Eye* and other investigative reporters, but only became widely known to the public in the wake of an ITV Drama, *Mr Bates vs The Post Office*.

The general public were outraged. It was clear that immediate action was needed, and that the cost of compensation for all of those damaged lives would stretch into the billions.

Enter human hand-grenade Kemi Badenoch. In her capacity as trade minister, she had ignored warnings from civil servants to keep her distance from Fujitsu. Instead, she asked the company if it fancied being given even more Government contracts.⁴ Of course, this was in those heady days when the only people who knew about the brewing scandal were Fujitsu, the Post Office, the Government, and the readership of *Private Eye*. Everything changed after 13 million people watched *Mr Bates vs The Post Office*.⁵ Badenoch, who was now business secretary, phoned the Post Office's chairman Henry Staunton, who she had never even bothered to meet, and sacked him on the spot.

'Well, someone's got to take the rap for this', she told him. He took the news phlegmatically, but revealed to *The Sunday Times* that a senior civil servant had instructed him to stall compensation payments, so they'd land on the desk of an incoming Labour Government, allowing the Tories to 'limp on to the election'.⁶

Badenoch was furious. She insisted *The Sunday Times* had printed a 'serious misrepresentation' of the facts and had 'chosen to ignore' the Government's version of events. This was false. The article included a lengthy and unedited statement by Badenoch's department, and another from the Post Office.⁷

At the time of writing, investigations are still ongoing, and who knows whether they will find Badenoch and her department ordered delays in compensation so it would become a Labour problem. It seems like a he-said, she-said situation, so to avoid prejudicing the outcome of inquiries, I will restrict myself to making two observations.

One: Tory backbencher Andrew Bridgen was a member of the parliamentary group looking into the scandal. He told Parliament that in 2015, 'the Post Office knew the convictions were unsafe, as did the Government'.[8] That means there were nine years of almost total governmental inaction.

Two: A new compensation scheme was finally announced 25 days after the new Labour Government took office.[9]

Hot Air Miles

2024 was definitely going to be an election year, so it was vital that the Tories present their best face to the public. This didn't seem to have been communicated to their MPs, who delivered a flood of isolated incidents, starting with Rishi Sunak himself. We were only three days into the year when the PM was investigated by the UK statistics watchdog, after he claimed he'd fulfilled his pledge to clear a 'legacy' backlog of 92,000 asylum applications. He hadn't, and the Office for Statistics Regulation found 98,599 backlog cases still awaiting decisions.[10] He was officially rebuked,[11] the second time in 12 months that the statistics regulator had condemned him for twisting asylum figures.[12]

All of this was part of his endless crusade against immigration, which he and his party – indeed the entire media ecosystem – reminded us on a daily basis was 'out of control'. We did, in fact, have control over our borders. We have done since mandatory passports were introduced during World War 1, and all the more so in recent years, as technological advances have improved our monitoring of ports and coastlines. Just try finding a small boat before the advent of radar.

Nobody is denying illegal immigration happens. So does illegal shopping. We call it shoplifting, but we don't attempt to ban Tesco in the hopes of wiping it out. Over 93 per cent of immigration into the UK is legal, and we practically beg people to come here, not least because – as the Office for National Statistics observed – they add £83 billion to the UK economy every year,[13] which is half the value of our entire state pension bill.[14] Migrant numbers have spiked in recent years, but the vast majority of that is due to – and here's a word you rarely find in summaries of Conservative administrations – decency. In response to the wars in Ukraine and Afghanistan and the political situation in Hong Kong, new humanitarian routes were opened, and over 270,000 additional people were invited to move here.[15]

Yet we remained nowhere near being a top destination for asylum seekers. When adjusted for population size, the UK ranked twentieth against EU countries. The costs of our migrant hotels was high, but that was largely because everybody's housing costs had increased as the economy battled to recover from Liz Truss. Payments to each individual asylum seeker had actually fallen by a third in the previous five years.[16] Any pressures on the migrant system were not due to unsupportable numbers, but almost entirely because we buggered up the economy, and were terrible at the admin.

And why were we terrible? Because the number of asylum caseworkers had been slashed by 35 per cent as departing prime minister Cameron gifted us one last round of austerity before he left Downing Street.[17] Under Theresa May and then Boris Johnson, the remaining caseworkers found themselves reallocated away from handling asylum claims so they could help an overwhelmed civil service cope with the vast increase in needless paperwork resulting from Brexit.[18]

These staff shortages inevitably caused a surge in the backlog of unprocessed asylum cases, so in a panic the Tories increased the number of caseworkers again. But the Institute for Government noted that to save money, new employees were given inadequate training. Despite a 60 per cent increase in staffing since the low point of the May/Johnson years, productivity in handling asylum cases fell by 80 per cent.[19]

But boring and knotty administrative cockups are a complicated story to tell, so a simpler one was invented. In this version of events, the problem was entirely caused by the tiny percentage of people who came to Britain in a small boat. And the crisis could be ended if we deported an even tinier percentage of them to a dangerous central African dictatorship. It was an act of fag-packet desperation from a fag-end Government, based on the bonkers notion that MPs could arbitrarily vote for a new reality. If that was how the world worked, why didn't they just vote to make Gaza safe? Or Chernobyl? Or putting your fingers near Jonathan Gullis's mouth?

Supposedly safe Rwanda had created almost one million refugees since it signed the asylum deal with the British government,[20] and the UK had granted asylum to some of them on the basis that they weren't safe in their own country.[21] But Sunak chose to ignore that reality. In fact, he even managed to ignore himself, when it was revealed that he'd privately expressed doubts about the entire scheme when Boris Johnson announced it in a blind panic. What was supposed to be a tower of legislative strength looked about to collapse like Jenga, and then another dull block was knocked from the pile: just as MPs were preparing for the next round of Rwanda debates, a report emerged showing torture was 'rampant' in Rwanda, where authorities habitually turned a blind eye to extrajudicial executions and disappearances.[22]

For the moderates who were determined to stop the Rwanda scheme, this was final proof that the policy was cuckoo. For the right of the party, however, it was proof that we weren't being cuckoo enough. Up popped Mark Francois, pompously declaring himself spokesman for a laundry list of Tory sects, who had temporarily put aside their infinitesimal differences to demand a firmer – and therefore more undeliverable – Rwanda policy. This new coalition of the obstinate consisted of the Blue-Collar Conservatives, the

New Conservatives, the National Conservatives, the Conservative Democratic Organisation, the Conservative Growth Group, the No Turning Back Group, the Northern Research Group, the European Research Group and finally the Common Sense Group. To ensure Sunak knew he was getting an offer he couldn't refuse, they had named their alliance 'The Five Families'.

There were nine of them.[23]

Andrea Jenkyns didn't limit herself to the subtlety of Don Corleone. She openly called for a political hit on Sunak, tweeting that she hoped the growing rebellion over Rwanda would be accompanied with 'vote of no confidence letters to the 1922, so we can get a new and true Conservative leader'.[24]

This was enough to trigger Lee Anderson, although that's not difficult. He lived in a state of permanent revolt, in a holding pattern just one Newcastle Brown away from starting a punch-up at a wedding. Both he and his fellow deputy chairman, Brendan Clark-Smith, announced they were stepping down so they could vote against the bill in an act of heroic insurrection.[25]

When the mutiny eventually happened, it was one for the history books. Remember Robert Jenrick, who had resigned so he could force the Rwanda bill to be more extreme? He abstained. So did Suella Braverman, opting to do bugger-all rather than enact her dream of watching helpless refugees being illegally deported to a torture hotspot. Brendan Clarke-Smith, a man whose forehead suggests a prodigious depth of bone, had given up his job to vote against Rwanda: he abstained. Mark Francois menaced Downing Street with a series of terrifying ultimatums if his motley mobsters didn't get their own way: he didn't vote against it either.

In fact, only 11 Tory MPs voted against the bill.[26] They'd fallen for their own dead cat, and then chose to sit and watch it rot.

And then Lee Anderson asked for his job back.[27]

∗

You'd think this would qualify as a rare, good week for Sunak, but despite celebrating a one-day parliamentary victory over a handful of numpties, it was clear he wasn't changing the public mood. Pollsters said voters saw Sunak as 'limp, spineless, out of touch, full of himself and false', and the sight of him on their televisions made them 'cringe'.[28]

And still Rwanda was illegal. So the next idea was for Britain to leave the European Court of Human Rights, and degrade the civil liberties of 68 million Britons so we could send a hundred Albanians to Rwanda.

Confident this was an eventuality we should definitely prepare for, our Government hired an aircraft hangar normally used for film production and handed it over to Home Office staff so they could engage in their own form of make-believe. One group of them would pretend to be asylum seekers, another group would pretend to be competent, and between them they'd role-play getting deportees onto a dummy plane.[29] A real plane wasn't available, because every single airline had refused to sign a contract for Rwanda flights, despite being offered £78 million.[30] The roleplaying did lead to one important revelation, though: that to get even one struggling person across the make-believe runway onto their fictional aeroplane would require five officers, which pushed costs even higher. The National Audit Office estimated the price of sending a single person to Rwanda was now £182,000.[31]

Wouldn't it be simpler if we just ... lost them in the system? Well, fortunately this idea appears to have occurred to the Tories too, because the day after the Rwanda vote, the Conservative government quietly admitted they'd lost 5,598 asylum seekers in the system.[32]

Couldn't find them.

But never mind that.

Stop the boats.

By the time the incoming Labour government cancelled the Rwanda deportation scheme, it had burned through £700 million, three prime ministers, four immigration ministers,[33] six Home Secretaries,[34] and the entire political energy of Britain's government for two whole years. Over £130 million had been spent on an IT system to handle the deportations, which was never even turned on.[35] After all that effort, only 4 asylum seekers had moved from the UK to Rwanda, and every single one of them had gone voluntarily.[36]

Art Attack!

Every nation was facing immigration challenges, as an eruption of local conflicts created a constant supply of refugees, and ever-increasing global income inequality made it easy for a bunch of irresponsible, billionaire-backed populists to blame the consequences of their limitless greed on poor foreigners[37]. The wars in Ukraine and Gaza received widespread coverage, and occasionally you'd hear about Sudan or Yemen, but 2024 saw over 40 ongoing armed conflicts, many of them killing tens of thousands, yet almost entirely unreported.[38]

Luckily, Britain was safe from conflicts, if not from populists, and we can thank one man for both of those things: Boris Johnson – who was once acclaimed as our 'Worst prime minister ever'[39] – decided to start frightening off invaders by volunteering to fight for his country, or what was left of it after his premiership.

'Yes, Sah! Lance Corporal Johnson reporting for duty, Sah!', he declared in the *Daily Mail* in January, secure in the knowledge he was 25 years too old for military service, and nowhere near funny enough to join Dad's Army.[40] The fearless Churchillian colossus who had once hidden inside a fridge to avoid a tricky question from a breakfast TV presenter had at least downgraded his ambition.[41] Where once he had aspired to be World King,[42] he now reckoned he could make it all the way to the lowest-ranking non-commissioned officer it is possible to be. He was sure the Army would want him, even though, as Jennifer Arcuri can attest, he'd already done his fair share of dishonourable discharges.[43]

Sunak longed for his predecessors to stop turning up and embarrassing him, even more so when Liz Truss – who had also once been acclaimed our 'Worst prime minister ever'[44] – popped back up a couple of days later. The least popular Premier in the history of British polling launched a new faction called Popular Conservatism.[45] It was designed to unite the Tories around her banner, but in a stunning return to form, the group split in two during its actual launch event. Four speakers had been invited, but only one appeared alongside Truss: Jacob Rees-Mogg, popping up like jump scare.[46]

Kwasi Kwarteng had been expected to make a speech, but at the last moment decided it would be more useful if he quit politics entirely. So he did. Ranil Jayawardena didn't turn up either, but if he had it's doubtful anybody would have known who he was. And Truss's close ally, Simon Clarke, a politician of such stature that you could sneak him into Parliament in a matchbox, was forced to pull out of the unifying event because he was busy being bollocked for calling for the PM to be replaced.

Clarke wrote in *The Telegraph* that Sunak had to go because 'he is not listening to what the British people want'.[47] Polling showed three quarters of British people wanted an immediate election, and the Tories out, but that wasn't the reason for Clarke's no-show at the Truss launch.[48] He'd expected to lead a heroic coup. He led a shambolic rout. Even the right turned on him, with Priti Patel accusing Clarke of 'engaging in facile and divisive self-indulgence [that] only serves our opponents'. Tobias Ellwood accused him of 'throwing his teddies in the corner' because Truss was no longer in Number 10. Few Tory MPs disguised their brutal opinions.

'He's a self-indulgent tosser'.[49]

'Can we, for more than five minutes, dispense with the civil war and leadership speculation?'[50]

'Get a fucking grip'.[51]

'Dangerous, reckless, selfish'.[52]

By this point, news reports about the Conservative Party had the feel of a wildlife documentary: the filmmakers were witnessing something dying but were unable to intervene. And the Tories were increasingly touchy about almost any independent coverage they received, preferring the soothing words of Nadine Dorries, who months earlier had been granted an outlet to twitch and drool through her ideological fever-dreams: a Friday night talk show on *Talk TV*. It was a fantastic platform for Dorries to address the nation on subjects she didn't entirely understand, although it would have been difficult for her to do otherwise. To avoid the dangers of her ad-libbing, *Talk TV* provided her with an autocue that she couldn't read,[53] and the entire thing was so half-baked you'd swear she hadn't paid the gas bill.

In January, the show was cancelled after less than a year on the air, although once again the details of her being fired seemed to glance off the impenetrable surface of Nadine's mind. She insisted the show – which had attracted the attention of just 0.004 per cent of the British viewing public – had not been a flop at all,[54] and that she had only stopped appearing on TV because the commute to the studio was too challenging for her.[55]

Her sudden absence created two vacancies – culture secretary, and Westminster Village Idiot – but fortunately Lucy Frazer was able to fill them both. The new minister responsible for the media accused BBC News of lacking in impartiality, asserting that 'on occasions it has been biased'.[56]

When asked for evidence of this on Sky News, she replied, 'the evidence shows there is a perception of bias'.

'But that's perception, that's not evidence', said Kay Burley.

'That is evidence. Impartiality is about evidence of the perception,' Frazer floundered.[57]

Much of the internet focused on the unlikelihood of yet another minister who thought people being mistaken was exactly the same as a verifiable fact, but in truth, nobody could confuse any of this with concerns about impartiality. Frazer's attack on the BBC could be explained by three things: an instinctive, knee-jerk detestation of anything nationalised; puerile culture war posturing; and a desperate desire to save the Conservative Party, if only for posterity.

Swift to Frazer's aid came Huw Merriman, whose name I didn't just invent, with his own claims of BBC bias. He'd listened to the Radio 4 comedy show *The News Quiz*, and discovered they were laughing at the Government, which he thought was 'completely biased'. And this time, he had proof! The corporation had only presented 'one side of the story' in reports by BBC journalist Neil Buchanan, and Merriman demanded more accuracy.

So here is more accuracy. Neil Buchannan is not a BBC political journalist. He was the presenter of children's crafts show *Art Attack* from 1990 until 2007. And it was broadcast on ITV.[58]

You Can Do a Lot in 5,000 Days

On 18 January 2024 we commemorated 5,000 days since David Cameron had led Conservatives to power with a promise to the nation that his cuts would abolish £6 billion of 'wasteful spending', allowing him to wipe out the deficit, reduce the national debt, and save us all a fortune.[59]

That £6 billion of cuts ended up being ninety times larger: half a trillion pounds of lost public spending and investment.[60] The national debt has increased by an average of £380 million every single day, and by the time we commemorated 5,000 days since Cameron's election win, the nation owed £2,670 billion.[61]

I'm well aware that £2,670 billion is an impossible thing to imagine. We all struggle to grasp truly enormous numbers, so to help put this into context, let's begin with something I hope all of us can picture. Imagine 1000 pounds, sitting in front of you, as a pile of pound coins. Now imagine that once every second you shoved one of those coins down a grid. It would take you 16 minutes and 40 seconds to waste a grand.

Getting rid of a million quid would take you 12 days.

Pushing a billion down the grid would take you a rather more substantial 31 years.

But you'd need to set aside 84,000 years to throw away £2,670 billion.

Luckily, we weren't throwing it away. We were saving it, apparently. That's what we were told: the Conservative government would save money. Debt would vanish. Taxes would fall. And the market would rush in with competitive solutions to all of the things the state did badly, such as the NHS, which was the most efficient health service on earth when Cameron took office,[62] and which, after the Tories spent 5,000 days forcibly injecting private companies into the mix, entered 2024 with a waiting list that was more than ten per cent of the entire country's population.[63]

So what I want to know more than anything else is: where's the money?

It's not as though we're paying less tax than we did in the 1980s. As a working-class teenager from East Manchester in that decade I was poor, certainly, but it mattered less because people of my class – in fact people of every class – had access to youth clubs, sports fields, swimming pools, libraries and parks. Our parents suffered chronic unemployment under Thatcher, but they fell onto a comparatively generous safety net. Moneyed or not, we saw NHS dentists. Comfortable or not, GPs made house calls. Impoverished or not, hospitals had capacity. A university education was free. There were apprenticeships aplenty. We travelled on regular, cheap bus services, ate free school dinners, drank free school milk, and withstood free assaults on our scalps from Nitty Nora the Bug Explorer, whether we liked it or not.

Yet that was an era with far, far fewer taxpayers than the UK had in 2024, and most of them – not the richest, certainly, but most of them – were paying far less in tax. 1980s Britain was a nation with a much, much smaller GDP than it had in 2024. By any classification worth a damn, we were a poorer nation when I was growing up, and yet we could afford all of those things.

So I ask again: where did all the money go? The rising tide was supposed to lift all boats. Unfettered capitalism was supposed to enrich us. Mass privatisation was supposed to empower us. The invisible hand of the market was supposed to comfort us. Yet with the exception of a tiny smattering of frankly terrible people at the very top of society, that's not what happened. Simply being alive became more expensive in 2024 than at any time in living memory, and for all the nation's supposed wealth, our existence was colder, narrower, and less hopeful every day.

Voters, lumbered with the consequences of this galumphing carelessness, were deserting the Tories in droves, and the Government desperately needed something dramatic to change its fortunes. Something original. Something transformative. Something uplifting, edifying, inspiring and inspired.

So they pushed Sunak into his toytown captain's uniform and made him parrot a new slogan while the ship sank under him. And not a moment too soon, because if there was one thing Conservative Britain was sorely lacking, it was empty slogans. The new one revolved around the odd notion that Sunak had a plan, and that the plan was working. Just in case this wasn't clear, he repeated variations on 'stick to the plan' 41 times in a 20-minute press conference.[64] You had to concentrate to conclude that he wasn't just a prerecorded message. He warned that if we didn't stick to the plan we'd have to go 'back to square one' with Labour, which sounded fine with the public, because we all remembered being in square one, and things had been noticeably less shit there.

Sunak's new slogan was unveiled at the same time as the Jospeh Rowntree Foundation produced a report on what this plan had achieved. The government since 2010 had left 14 million Britons living in severe poverty, while more than one million people had suffered early deaths as a result of austerity. Not because of a war or even a pandemic – those figures were listed separately. Those one million people died because of an ideological conviction, backed up by a mistake in a spreadsheet.

Sir Michael Marmot, professor of epidemiology and public health at UCL, described the situation as, 'deeply deeply depressing. It's grim in the extreme. Essentially Britain has become a poor country with a few rich people'.[65]

And those rich people are, essentially, where all the money went.

The Gini number is a measurement of distribution of a nation's wealth, property ownership and income, expressed as a single number between 0 and 100. Societies with greater inequality have a higher Gini number. More equal societies have a low number.

Back when the Thatcher revolution began in 1979, the UK's Gini number was 25, which was pretty much normal for an advanced modern economy.[66] By 2019 it had reached 36 and was rising fast. In just ten years since Cameron entered Downing Street, the ten wealthiest Britons saw their combined fortunes grow from £47 billion to over £182 billion, an increase of 281 per cent.[67] Yet during the same period, Britain's low- and middle-income households saw their wealth slump.

And a 44 per cent increase in our Gini number was bad enough if you only measured income, but the Gini number for accumulated wealth – property, land and shares – had grown from an unremarkable 25 to a stratospheric 73.[68] The wealth of the richest 10 per cent of UK households had grown 574 times more than that of the poorest tenth.[69] Britain's poor had lower incomes than the poor did in Slovenia, which was ranked as the 84th largest economy.[70] We were sixth.[71]

Handing so much of our money to the already wealthy presented Britain with yet another problem, beyond the inequality, the 14 million in poverty, and over one million unnecessary deaths. The very rich had become 'too big to fail'. The Institute for Fiscal Studies reported the next UK government – which everybody knew would be Labour – would inherit the worst fiscal situation for 70 years,[72] but they'd also inherit probably the least taxable group of rich people the world had ever known. At the slightest sniff of redistribution, the ultra-rich threatened to leave, taking their money with them. Just a few dozen people relocating to warmer climes could vastly affect our national balance sheet, so we let them get away with murder. Tax evasion was not just rife, it was industrialised, and the landmark legislation the Tories had introduced in 2017 to crack down on it had resulted in not a single company – not one – being charged in the subsequent seven years.[73]

Not much of this was helped by the example being set at the top of politics. At a time when the UK was paying more in tax than at any time on record – with the average Briton losing 35 per cent of their income in tax[74] – Rishi Sunak, a man who was richer than the King, had organised his personal tax affairs so he was paying an effective rate of just 23 per cent.[75]

The plan *was* working. This was the plan.

A Lettuce From America

Sunak had dedicated practically the entire energy of his premiership to Rwanda, and it had failed. In February, he registered his lowest-ever favourability score.[76]

Anybody with the slightest instinct for politics would cut their losses, let the policy quietly die, and encourage voters to think about something else instead. But the Conservatives had become obsessed with Rwanda, and simply would not stop banging on about it. As a result of its constant, noisy presence in the nation's consciousness, Sunak became intimately associated with failure, and voters were constantly reminded of the previous bit of populist claptrap they'd been sold: Brexit, which now only one in five people thought had brought any benefits whatsoever.[77]

Finding a positive story – any positive story – arising out of Britain leaving the EU now became politically essential, which is why Kemi Badenoch charged off to Parliament to deliver an update on the post-Brexit trade negotiations she was holding with Canada. 'This is a good opportunity for me to state explicitly that the talks have not broken down,' she reassured MPs. It would have been a persuasive statement, but for the Canadian High Commissioner to the UK, who wrote to the House of Commons to confirm that the talks hadn't broken down, but only because no talks were taking place at all.[78]

Still, at least our departure from the EU had been a great opportunity to shake loose the shackles of excessive European red tape. But on the very day Canada was undermining Badenoch, news broke that British officials were lobbying the EU to increase the amount of regulation on the financial sector, fearing our shaky economic condition would make us vulnerable to market shocks again.[79]

And why was our economy so shaky? Because Brexit had cost Britain almost £100 billion in exports.[80] Round and round we went, cause leading into effect and back to cause again, spiralling downwards while everybody pretended it wasn't happening.

All of this was too much for senior Treasury minister Laura Trott, who went on Radio 4 to insist that just because the official data showed state debt was rising, that didn't mean state debt was rising. Untethered from reason and battling heroically against the merciless and unpredictable lash of infant-level mathematics, the Chief Secretary to the Treasury dismissed her own department's figures, which showed debt forecast to increase by a further 3 per cent of GDP, and insisted she had 'different figures', which she then utterly failed to produce.[81]

There were only two ways to get off this unmerry-go-round.

Backtrack on Brexit, or boost the most promising parts of Britain's economy: science and innovation. But you can't conjure thousands of scientists from the UK population overnight: they need training at well-funded universities. And the higher education sector was warning of imminent collapse, due to an unprecedented funding crisis.[82] Their incomes had plummeted since Suella Braverman announced new restrictions on overseas students one year earlier, as yet another sop to the anti-immigration right.[83] The fees paid to Britain's universities by overseas students accounted for almost one fifth of their entire income, and now that income had dried up.[84]

So maybe we could just import enough scientists to boost that most valuable sector of our economy? After all, it was a stated goal of the government to allow skilled workers into the country. We didn't want unskilled, only skilled. But the government's obsession with cutting immigration at all costs undermined that plan too. *The Wellcome Trust* pointed out that international scientific talent was declining to move to the UK due to the cost of visas, which we had set not twice, not three times, but a whopping *seventeen times* the international average.[85]

Thankfully, such restrictions didn't apply to Russians. Despite the ongoing sanctions against Putin's regime, in February Sunak relaxed rules banning Russians from attending the Chevening Scholarship, a master's degree programme for 'future leaders', which for some reason was fully funded from Britain's foreign aid budget. I'd imagine you thought foreign aid was helping poor farmers in developing nations. In fact, it was actively funding training for Russian leaders. The US anti-corruption campaigner Bill Browder called the move 'highly inappropriate' because – and it's surprising this needs to be explained, but apparently that's where we were – 'a programme like this should be for citizens of countries that aren't threatening us with nuclear war'.[86]

So in they flew, a journey made easier after the new home secretary, James Cleverley fired the UK's Independent Chief Inspector of Borders and Immigration. David Neal was sacked because he had told the *Times* and *Daily Mail* about the 15 reports he'd sent to the Home Office, highlighting the security dangers of private jets landing in the UK.[87] Thousands of such flights landed every year, but 687 of them had been categorised as 'high risk'. Of those, only 144 had been checked by Border Force, and 543 flights landed with passengers facing no passport inspections whatsoever.[88] The Home Office had sat on David Neal's reports, refusing to publish them.

But by a fortunate coincidence, his sacking meant two additional 'explosive' reports on the crisis in Home Office asylum hotels now couldn't be published – they would have to wait until after the General Election. A former Tory minister accused the Government of 'hiding behind the sofa', and it wasn't the first time.

The post of Independent Anti-Slavery Commissioner had also been left empty for 20 months, meaning there had been no official body able to publicly comment on the dangers faced by people subject to the Rwanda scheme.[89] When the Anti-Slavery post was eventually filled in February, the new appointee – a former Tory special adviser – reported that her budget had been cut by so much that her staff was reduced to just two people.

A staff of two. The UK contained 130,000 people living in modern slavery.[90]

You could attribute all of this to the law of unintended consequences, if only millions of people hadn't warned of the consequences during the referendum campaign. Of course, not every disaster was accurately predicted in 2016 – it's in the nature of chaos that it's hard to predict everything – but a great deal of what came to pass seemed very likely from the start.

Some felt sympathy for Sunak, stuck dealing with the wreckage of Brexit. But the man supported it all the way. So did Boris Johnson, the voluptuary vandal whose duplicity and ineptitude had made a bad Brexit even worse. As for Liz Truss's backing for leaving the EU: in keeping with her personality, she had been all over the place. She had started as a pro-EU LibDem, but by now was so wildly to the denialist right that even Reform thought she'd taken it a bit far. What were her beliefs now: was she leaf or romaine?

In February, she headed off to Washington to appear at the Conservative Political Action Committee alongside Nigel Farage, a frog and lettuce explaining their worldview to a smattering of MAGA obsessives in a wonky ballroom. The theme of the conference was 'Where Globalism Comes To Die'. The phrase was repeated on pillars behind Truss, a remarkable decision that left cameras framing her against the words 'Die, Die'[91] while she explained her belief that lefties were running everything.[92]

'The Deep State sabotaged my efforts in Britain to cut taxes, reduce the size of government and restore democratic accountability,' proclaimed Truss, who wasn't elected by anybody, and now believed that the international currency markets were a bunch of Marxists.[93]

The entire thing could easily have turned into a national embarrassment, if anybody on the other side of the Atlantic had even bothered to turn up and watch her. Thankfully they didn't, but they did turn up to watch Steve Bannon, who sat one foot away from Truss, stared straight into her face, and announced in a loud, booming voice that Tommy Robinson was a hero.

'That's right,' replied Truss, waving around a copy of her book, which she hoped somebody – anybody – would buy. It roared straight into the bestseller chart at number 70, massively outsold by the *Ultimate Air Fryer Cookbook* and *More Confessions of a Forty-something Fuck Up.*[94]

Worshipping Satan

The emergence of GB News, and its short-lived competitor Talk TV, now feels inevitable. As populism took hold and levels of governmental gaslighting escalated, traditional news channels found themselves trapped by impartiality regulations from a bygone age, and cowed by incessant hammering from both the Cabinet and the right-wing press, who had fully embraced Steve Bannon's dictum that political rivals didn't matter: 'The real opposition is the media. And the way to deal with them is to flood the zone with shit'.[95]

The sheer volume of shit flowing from Downing Street overwhelmed traditional media's capacity to sift fact from falsehood, and journalism's reduced budgets, editorial cowardice and – in far too many cases – complicity left them failing to challenge lies or explain reality in anything like real time. As Gary Kasparov had once explained, 'The point of modern propaganda isn't only to misinform or push an agenda. It is to exhaust your critical thinking'.[96]

Job done. As legacy news media gave up explaining the truth, it wasn't long before viewers began to conclude there was no such thing as truth at all. Predictably, somebody rich and right-wing decided to exploit this trend, launching a news channel which made almost no attempt to be honest, candid or unbiased.

There are many troubling things about this phenomenon, not least of which is GB News's major backer, Sir Paul Marshall. He cuts an odd figure: a fiercely religious founder of a hedge fund that got half of its startup-capital from liberal overlord George Soros.[97] Marshall spent years embedded deeply into the Liberal Democrats, first as a research assistant for erstwhile leader Charles Kennedy, and then as a parliamentary candidate. He was an editor of *The Orange Book*, the philosophical guiding-light for many of the LibDems who would go on to join the 2010 coalition government. Chapters were written by future LibDem leaders Nick Clegg, Vince Cable and Ed Davey.

Admittedly, some signs of an ideological drift were already there: *The Orange Book* was described as a 'lurch to the right' on publication, and it certainly explains why Nick Clegg, a cabbage patch doll of Colin Firth that somebody sculpted from memory, got to join the Cameron cabinet.[98]

Marshall, however, took a different path. Having donated

£200,000 and half of his life to the Lib Dems, he now barrelled headlong towards the wilder shores of right-wing politics. He donated £500,000 to the Tories under Boris Johnson, then became a close advisor to Michael Gove, consulting with the Conservative Party's emotional support turbot during his Brexit campaign, and handing £100,000 to Vote Leave.[99] Marshall's decision to fund the lies that led us out of Europe was driven by raw fury that the EU was about to regulate hedge funds, such as his, so they couldn't reprise their role as handmaidens to the 2007 global financial crash.

'It's popular to bash the banks', said Marshall, 'But it's actually more important to fight the European financial legislation'.[100]

Sadly for Paul Marshall, large swathes of Britain's media landscape kept noticing all the harm Brexit was doing. Noticing things is not a Brexity characteristic. Total, pig-headed denialism is more their thing. So rather than stand for election again, where he would have to argue his badly formulated case in the crucible of reasoned and honest debate, this former Lib Dem turned his back on the democratic route to influencing events, cast aside any hint of liberalism, and instead used his vast pile of money to promote a heap of rabid far-right gibberish, utterly divorced from concerns about consequences.[101]

And that's why GB News exists. Britain's contribution to the worldwide right wing media effort to get you addicted to stupid stuff.

For a long time, Marshall had run a personal Twitter account with the username @prcmarshall, which had attracted a small but dedicated following, including several MPs and leading national journalists. But in 2023 he changed his username to @areopagus123, the name derived from *Areopagtica*, a work by John Milton about the importance of open debate.[102] He then locked his account so nobody could debate him.

This was a wise move on the part of Sir Paul, since he probably wouldn't approve of you knowing his account had liked quite a number of deeply troubling comments by other users, including lip-smacking predictions of civil war in Europe caused by 'fake refugee invaders', a demand to 'start mass expulsions immediately', and an apocalyptic warning about 'the four stages of Islamic conquest'. He also reposted a tweet associating homosexuality with 'worshipping Satan [and] corrupting children'.[103]

Jacob Rees-Mogg, Dehenna Davison, Philip Davies, Esther McVie and Lee Anderson weren't put off by this. Each of them took jobs as – and this is honestly how it's described – 'on-air talent' for GB News, while simultaneously taking salaries as Conservative MPs. They were soon joined by Boris Johnson, and his former communications director Guto Harri. Meanwhile irreparably bovine former culture minister Nadine Dorries joined GB News's less successful rival *TalkTV*, along with fellow Tory Nick de Bois.

And then the self-interviewing began, with ministers who had advocated a boycott of *Channel 4 News* regularly submitting themselves to the white-hot anvil of inquisitorial pressure from their best mates on GB News, who unquestioningly agreed with them about absolutely everything.[104]

You'd assume this one-sided, fact-averse incestuous political love-in would raise concerns with the regulator charged with ensuring broadcasters don't mislead the public or indulge in political bias. But you'd assume wrongly. Ofcom ruled that multiple programmes broadcast by GB News – which appears under the News section of your TV's programme guide and had the tagline 'Britain's News Channel' – were not actually news.[105] They were, in fact, classed as 'current affairs',[106] which is a different enough criteria to allow Lee Anderson to subject his ideological bedfellow Suella Braverman to a serious dose of nodding-along, without breaching any impartiality guidelines.[107]

*

Those behind channels like GB News know they won't attract huge viewing figures – they get only a 0.45% share of linear TV – but they also know their clips are shared widely on social media.[108] Their capacity to generate outrage has led to a 431 per cent increase in their digital footprint. The channel experienced losses of £42 million in 2023, which was 40 per cent worse than the previous year, but its ability to direct the national conversation and reshape our values had grown vastly, and that makes the losses worth it to Paul Marshall and his fellow investors.

We are not born with values. Our environment helps to form them; our families, our childhoods, our friends, our living and working spaces, and the cues we pick up from society. And, because this is a modern world, our values are shaped by our exposure to media. Films and advertising, television and – increasingly – social media platforms.

Like almost any human attribute, the values we hold exist on a continuum. It stretches between two major groupings, which psychologists label Intrinsic and Extrinsic.

People who exhibit Intrinsic values will tend to place importance on things that don't depend on the relative status of other people. Rich or poor, powerful or inconsequential, it doesn't matter. Intrinsics care about universal rights, environmental protection, people having dignity and agency, and being treated fairly. The things that matter to them are community, justice and social motivation. Having bought into a set of values that are available to all of us, and don't depend on constant comparison with others, people with Intrinsic values will tend to be broadly more satisfied, calmer, kinder, more empathetic, and happier.

People who exhibit Extrinsic values, however, are drawn to status, power, prestige, fame, image and wealth. Those attributes can't exist without a differential comparison. For you to be rich, everybody else has to be poorer. For you to be famous, everybody else has to be more anonymous. For you to have power, everybody else needs to be comparatively weak.

What's more, in order to achieve any of those goals, it is necessary avoid cooperation and community, and to objectify and exploit those around you. It cannot be any other way. For you to be rich, you must take money from others. For you to be famous, everybody else must be left in relative inconsequence. For you to gain power, you must diminish the authority of everybody else.

Very few people with Extrinsic values ever become the things they value, because to do so requires them to have a one-in-a-million combination of talent, privilege and luck. So, having bought into a set of values that they can never live up to, they are much more susceptible to frustration, anger, anxiety and stress.

But you can't have a political and economic system based around exploitation if voters live in an Intrinsic values system. They will simply refuse to engage in exploitation. They will vote for parties which share resources fairly, rather than those that seek to direct wealth and opportunity towards a tiny number of millionaires and billionaires. So to support such a system, it has become essential to create a media environment that advocates Extrinsic values, dividing the world into the deserving and the undeserving, winners and losers, us and them. And as consumers of this media are persuaded to move further along the Extrinsic spectrum, they become more and more likely to vote for a right-wing party.[109]

But they become no more talented, no more fortunate, no more privileged. Extrinsic people are no closer to gaining the status they value. The only people to benefit from this rightward drift are – *quelle surprise* – the rich and privileged group who set up a media environment to encourage this trend. Those taken in by the noise emerging from GB News would be happier if they allowed themselves to be tempted by Intrinsic values, those horrible lefty ones that they've told to reject for years. But instead, they dig deeper into a value system that will never allow them to fulfil its promise. With each perceived 'failure' their levels of anxiety grow. With each new setback, they will need to find somebody else to blame.

And that person is always from outside the Extrinsic value system: somebody supporting universal rights, decency and dignity for all, environmental protection, and social justice. In other words: the Woke.

But just occasionally, the denizens of GB News take it all too far.

40 Per Cent Islamophobic

Events in Gaza could scarcely have been worse for those on the ground, but they didn't exactly make things better for Jews or Muslims in Britain either. After the unconscionable attack by Hamas on 7 October 2023, and the wildly disproportionate response from Israel, the scale of racist incidents in the UK skyrocketed. Both antisemitism and Islamophobia shot up by 600 per cent.[110]

British racism doesn't solely target those two groups; nor is it driven entirely by Israel and Palestine. The UK's relentless, decade-long background hum of antagonism towards immigrants could not help but embolden bigots, as clearly shown by data. In the years since Cameron took office and the so-called 'hostile environment' was introduced, racist incidents tripled, reaching 109,000 in England and Wales by 2021.[111]

This coincided with a rise in populism, a political creed which juxtaposes the needs of 'ordinary people' – supposedly a morally good force with a unified nationalist ethos – against the actions of 'the elite' – supposedly a corrupt and self-serving force of trans-nationalist snobs. Of course, no such neat divisions exist, but even if they did it wouldn't matter, because populism has no interest in resolving problems: it exists to exploit them. And the Tories – a textbook establishment party – found the anti-establishment blame-game of populism easier than tackling the poverty and inequality that are the root causes of many of our nation's problems.

The Conservatives adopted this approach because they had nothing left to offer the country. Under Sunak, MPs achieved record low working hours, sitting for 126 minutes per day less than they had during the peak legislative period under the previous Labour administration.[112] A Government that was out of ideas had nothing to debate, so why bother attending Parliament?

Obviously, it's not correct to say every Conservative is a populist or a bigot, or that all Brexit supporters are prejudiced. They emphatically are not. But it is also not possible to separate Brexit from racism. There was five-fold increase in race-related hate crimes in the single week after Britain voted to leave the EU.[113] The referendum emboldened prejudices that more responsible leaders than Farage or Johnson had spent decades opposing. It's not insignificant that there were noticeably more racist incidents in areas that voted to leave the EU.[114]

So it should not come as a shock that many of Brexit's noisiest cheerleaders found themselves facing accusations of racism, not least recent Tory deputy chairman and champion edgelord Lee Anderson, who held the coveted role of Witless Carnival Barker for the party's populist wing: a noisy, brassy conduit for the nativism, the cruelty, and the resentment of it all. The man was every worst-instinct in Britain gathered in one place, wrapped in sausage-skin, bundled into a polyester suit, and taught to make noises with its mouth hole. And those sounds were a never-ending, whining appeal to people who have convinced themselves they would have successfully stormed the beaches of Normandy, but are incapable of withstanding the shock of seeing a trans person in a John Lewis commercial.

In his defence, Anderson did at least recognise he was fortunate to have a job at all, contrasting his commitment to his constituents with the trough-snuffling prevalent amongst those accepting second careers on GB News.

'We are paid handsomely for the job we do', said Anderson, 'And if you need an extra £100,000 a year on top then you should really be looking for another job'.[115]

And then he accepted a £100,000 second job hosting a weekly show on GB News. His salary equated to a typical weekly family food shop for single every minute he was on air,[116] but that particular sort of elitism didn't matter because, as Nigel Farage explained, Anderson had 'the common touch'.[117]

I'd certainly agree that Anderson was in some way touched, as he made crystal clear when he popped up on GB News in February 2024 to claim Islamists had 'got control of [Sadiq] Khan, and they've got control of London [and] he's given our capital city away to his mates'.[118]

'Lee Anderson, being Islamophobic?', you may cry, clutching your pearls. 'Perish the thought!'. But you'd be too late, for all thought had long since perished in the bleak and inhospitable wasteland between his ears.

Within an hour he was suspended from the Conservatives. This was a perfect opportunity for Sunak to demonstrate moral leadership, and as per usual it was an opportunity that he extravagantly fluffed, slowly, repeatedly, publicly and painfully. The PM refused to use the word 'Islamophobic' in his condemnation of Anderson. Instead, he explained that what Anderson said was 'wrong', and he made sure people knew it was 'wrong' by saying 'wrong' over and over again, as if it was his new slogan. He wouldn't be drawn on exactly *why* Anderson was wrong. He just was.

Islamophobic? I guess that's just unknowable.

Bigoted? An impenetrable secret.

Racist? What do words even mean, anyway? All we knew was that Lee Anderson was 'wrong', but Sunak didn't know why. It was a mystery lost to the ages.

Meanwhile Anderson began considering his options before deciding which party he wanted to be kicked out of next. The most obvious solution was to defect to Reform: after all, the previous November Anderson had claimed Farage's party had 'offered me a lot of money to join them. I say a lot of money, I mean a lot of money.'[119] He hinted that the offered bribe equalled his £86,000 salary as an MP, which is more than three quarters of what he was being paid to *not* be an MP.

The PM's failure to condemn bigotry meant Anderson's prejudices were widely repeated across media for a week, piling injury upon injury on a Government that was desperate for some positive news. What was rather less well-reported were the words Anderson had said immediately before his luckless stumble into wrongness.

'I heard some of the comments Suella [Braverman] made earlier this week', he had said, 'and I don't actually believe that the Islamists have got control of our country'.[120]

Anderson was, in fact, rejecting as too extreme the writings of Suella Braverman in *The Telegraph* a few days earlier, in which she had claimed: 'Islamists are in charge of Britain now'. She went on to assert Islamists had 'hijacked a by-election', wielded malign 'influence in our judiciary, our legal profession and our universities', and had 'bullied our country into submission'.[121]

You could, at a pinch, write off Anderson's racism as a slip of the tongue from a not famously agile mind. But Braverman's was a planned, intentional opinion piece in a national newspaper, written by a graduate of the Sorbonne who Sunak had appointed as home secretary. And if Sunak had admitted Anderson was Islamophobic, he'd have to admit Braverman was even worse.

So you didn't need to read between too many lines to conclude it wasn't so much what Anderson had said, as how he said it. That given the opportunity many Tories would have loved to express the same idea about Islam; they just didn't like hearing it in a Nottinghamshire accent. They preferred their racism expressed carefully and eloquently in a *Telegraph* column. They'd rather tiptoe around it, as Zac Goldsmith had during his London mayoral bid;[122] or have it boomingly delivered with a sub-Jeremy-Clarkson ironic wink by Boris Johnson.

Sunak utterly denied his party had any problems with 'Islamophobic tendencies', but he should probably have paid a bit more attention.[123] Fortunately I'm here to help, by reminding him that Margaret Thatcher was criticised for Islamophobia as far back as 2001. Michael Gove's 2006 book on extremism was described as 'holding apparent hostile opinions towards Muslims', while Conservative peer Baroness Warsi said the party was, 'poisoned by Islamophobic views at every level', as she recalled David Cameron's 'concerns about some of the extreme views that [Gove] had'.[124]

Lynton Crosby, a long-time Tory strategist, advised Boris Johnson's London mayoral campaign to ignore 'fucking Muslims',[125] while Johnson himself wrote that the Islamic faith had left nations 'literally centuries behind' civilised Britain, momentarily forgetting that more than half of the Muslim people in the world had been oppressed by British Imperial control for most of those centuries.[126] Instead of acknowledging the historical facts of what Britain had done to the Islamic World in the thousand years between the First Crusade and the 1950s, he claimed 'the real problem with the Islamic World is Islam'.[127] And just in case his mindset wasn't already clear enough, he emphasised 'the problem is Islam. Islam is the problem', and therefore he concluded that Islamophobia seemed like a 'natural reaction'.[128]

In 2021, Johnson said he wouldn't continue to use what he described as his own 'offending language' now he was PM, but he didn't apologise for it.[129] Nor did he apologise after his article describing Muslim women as looking like 'bank robbers' caused a 375 per cent spike in Islamophobic attacks.[130]

A 2019 report from the British NGO *Muslim Engagement and Development* identified 40 per cent of Boris Johnson's cabinet as having a history of Islamophobia. In a single year they found 120 racist incidents from Tory MPs and candidates.[131] A fish rots from the head, and here were Conservative MPs, mayors, senior members of the cabinet, leading advisors, deputy chairmen, even prime ministers openly spouting bigotry. So it's hardly surprising that the bigots further down the party's food-chain felt emboldened. Between 2015 and 2020, the Conservative Party's complaints database listed

727 anti-Muslim incidents among the membership. The party's report concluded: 'Judging by the extent of complaints and findings of misconduct by the party itself that relate to anti-Muslim words and conduct, anti-Muslim sentiment remains a problem within the party'.[132]

Yet only a couple of years later, Rishi Sunak had reached the evidence-free conclusion that the party no longer had Islamophobic tendencies. Instead, he told the media that Anderson's comments were 'wrong' and 'wrong', but also 'wrong', an abstract term that placed unconcealed bigotry in the same category as a lapse in mental arithmetic.

After 'wrong' became the excuse du jour, it wasn't so much memorised by the lightweights sent out to defend the party, as practically carved onto the surface of their smooth brains. Illegal immigration minister Michael Tomlinson could have been replaced by a tape-loop during his interview about Anderson on LBC, in which he was asked repeatedly whether Anderson's statement was Islamophobic, and replied, 'It was wrong' nine consecutive times. The interview was suspended by Nick Ferrari for being as inane and pointless as a ringtone from a wrong number.[133]

Yet Tomlinson was just avoiding the same battle that Sunak was dodging, the one about the place of racism in the Conservative party. God knows, no race, faith, community or political party is immune to this tendency, but the Tories had form of the worst kind, dating back to mind-boggling events such as the 1964 Smethwick election, where their candidate's campaign slogan was – with sincere apologies for repeating it – 'If you want a n****r for a neighbour, vote Labour'.

Not for a moment had those sentiments gone away: they'd simply become disguised by more palatable language, or dog-whistled by those who were either racist themselves, or who sought career advantage by pandering to racists. Islamophobia was openly expressed by venal leaders such as Boris Johnson: it had become tacitly accepted by weak leaders like Rishi Sunak, who had appointed

Lee Anderson, and then prioritised his need for votes over the morality of how he got them.

By now, Sunak had reached a record low approval rating among Tory members, even lower than that achieved by Liz Truss.[134] His most popular rival for party leadership could boast the support of only 32 per cent of Tory members.[135] Only 45 per cent of Tory voters backed their most popular policy, Rwanda.[136] Yet research found 58 per cent of Conservative Party members held Islamophobic views.[137] It was not a stretch to claim the Tories' strongest connective tissue was racism.

Did the likes of Braverman and Anderson drag the party further to the right, or did they simply answer the call of their membership? It's hard to be sure, but the margins of acceptable Conservatism now bled into what we would traditionally call the far right. And Sunak's electoral hopes increasingly depended on pandering to opinions decent society finds repellent.

A Work of Fiction

And all of it was ultimately pointless. It was already a baked-in certainty that the Conservatives would badly lose the next election, so there was absolutely nothing to be gained by harming Muslims. And, it turned out, there was absolutely no reason to worry about what happened to the nation's finances either.

Jeremy Hunt had given such threadbare details of his fiscal plans that the Office for Budget Responsibility couldn't produce any predictions worth a damn. The head of the OBR, Richard Hughes, said any official forecasts would inevitably be 'a work of fiction', and then corrected himself, adding, 'That is probably being generous when someone has bothered to write a work of fiction [because] the Government hasn't even bothered to write down what its departmental spending plans are'.[138]

Large expenditure commitments were kicked down a long,

long road, partly in hope that they'd somehow magically vanish, and partly to let Labour handle the mess the Conservatives had made. While the Government loudly promised it would cut migration numbers, Jeremy Hunt froze spending on border controls, making any progress impossible.[139] He sanctioned vastly expensive cuts to national insurance,[140] and funded them by slicing yet more from public investment, opening a gaping £20 billion chasm in the nation's finances, and leaving hospitals, schools, and other vital services unable to fulfil their duties.

Regardless, Hunt had to do a budget, because that's what Chancellors do. And what Conservatives do is offer tax cuts. Various kites were flown, partly to soften up the public ahead of possible pre-election tax cuts, and partly to see whether the public would believe any such cuts were possible. Polling showed that even amongst Tory voters, only one in five backed further tax cuts if it meant reduced government spending.[141] Over two-thirds of voters wanted tax to remain as it was, or even climb higher, in return for better public services. The Joseph Rowntree Foundation warned Hunt that his plans would damage public services so badly, that they would risk a 'second lost decade' of static or falling living standards, and permanent damage to the public realm.[142] The OBR's chief economist said performance during the 12 years of Tory rule had been 'abysmal', and Jeremy Hunt's final budget was so shoddy that the head of the OBR, Richard Hughes, later told a Commons Treasury committee that it may have broken the law. Hunt had neglected to reveal almost £10 billion of unfunded spending, which would have 'materially changed' the watchdog's forecasts.[143]

*

And yet after all the kite-flying over potential tax changes, Hunt decided he wasn't going to go ahead with them after all. He had a better idea. He would simply steal some of Labour's most popular policies, and then deliberately vandalise them.

He decided to remove many of the benefits for people claiming non-domicile status – UK residents who avoid tax because they have a permanent home outside of the UK. Those benefitting from non-dom status are predominantly the very wealthy, such as Rishi Sunak's wife, who was reported to have saved £20 million in UK tax by registering as non-dom while she lived in Kensington, or in Sunak's north Yorkshire constituency.[144] Labour had been planning to scrap non-dom status, and use the resulting tax revenue to fund free breakfast clubs for schoolchildren, hundreds of thousands of additional dental appointments, and tackling NHS waiting lists.

Instead, Hunt decided to scrap non-dom, and use the income to cut national insurance, thus ensuring schools, hospitals and your teeth remained rotten, and pressuring Labour to abandon its plans.[145]

It's a marvellous way to think about public service: knowing a policy would be harmful to the public, and knowing it goes against the wishes of voters, but doing it anyway because it sets a trap for Labour.[146]

In the end, it turned out the only part of the public realm Jeremy Hunt wanted to protect was Jeremy Hunt. Facing a strong chance that he'd lose his once incredibly safe seat in the forthcoming election, the Chancellor donated £100,000 of his own fortune to his local party. Under David Cameron and Theresa May combined, he'd donated just £4,447.[147]

*

The thing is: I've run a company, and I can promise you that for business leaders, tax cuts are nowhere near as important as having a stable economy that allows you to make strategic plans. They are nowhere near as important as having access to a large market, and customers who feel confident to spend. Nowhere near as valuable as a good education system that provides skilled employees. Nowhere near as vital as having a system of trading laws you can predict. Nothing like as important as confidence about the value of our currency in 6 months' time.

Since Cameron became prime minister – and certainly since the 2016 referendum – Britain had thrown away all such plans, all such stability. Instead, the message of Government was that The Market would provide. The Tories ran a 14-year experiment in The Market Providing, which turned into a slow-motion catastrophe, with occasional double-speed disasters thrown in just to keep things exciting.

And it resulted in everything being shit. Britain had shit productivity because we had shit training, and that's because we didn't invest in education.

We had shit manufacturing figures because we had shit infrastructure. We neglected it for over a decade, which meant moving goods around – or even getting a workforce to the factory on time – remained a ludicrously difficult and stressful endeavour.

We had shit efficiency because we didn't seem to give a hairy day-glow fuck about regional inequality, so millions of people – each of them packed with potential – had been abandoned and left to rot in dead-end towns while we shovelled money and tax cuts to the rich.

We had shit international trade because we left the EU, and then we told the world we didn't care about laws. So nobody trusted that today's agreements would still be observed in 3 months' time; and even if they did still trust us, traders knew it would cost a small fortune to import or export anything, and goods would rot in understaffed ferry terminals while pointless post-Brexit red tape was processed.

We had shit investment because the rest of the world had watched all of this happening from behind the sofa, and they'd largely concluded the UK wasn't a smart bet. It was a shit bet, in fact, and getting worse every year. Despite what Sunak said over and over again, there were no viable, believable plans. The Government had abandoned its duty, and by now it only seemed to exist to serve and reflect the prejudices of a tiny, elderly, irrational base, and the few dozen donors who bankrolled the party.

In a normal, advanced economy, all those things – strategy, training, infrastructure, stability, and a plan to make the most of each citizen – should be the primary purpose of the Government. Instead, it was every man for himself, in the demented belief this would make us competitive, rather than chaotic. And those who had sold us this nonsense now insisted – just like old communists – that the problem wasn't the ideology; it was that the ideology hadn't been properly implemented. All we needed to do was the same, but to a greater extreme. Just become even more ideological, and The Promised Land would emerge. Any day now. Just you wait.

The rest of the world had done waiting. The experiment had failed utterly, even by its own shonky definition. The plan – if you could even call it a plan – persuaded nobody. Nobody with any sense could imagine a business anywhere in the world which wouldn't give up a 5 per cent tax on profits in return for a bigger chance of there actually *being* profits.

The only exceptions are companies which cannot reasonably gain any more customers, because there are no more customers to gain: the giant corporations such as Amazon or Google, or Britain's former public services, now transformed into vast monopolies in private hands. Unable to expand further, they have to find a new way to boost the value of their assets. And what's a good way to do that? Donate to a government that churns out money and debt, organising the economy so that property and land prices are endlessly inflated, oblivious to the harm this does to everybody in the country who doesn't hold any of those assets.

The Institute for Fiscal Studies laid out the scale of the failure in a startling assessment of the years since Cameron had entered Number 10.[148] The period was, 'remarkable not only for poor economic performance and the scale of public spending retrenchment, but also for the loosest monetary policy in history,' it said, explaining this monetary looseness had done little but over-inflate asset prices, benefiting only those who already owned land or property. These gains had nothing to do with productivity – they were simply rentier economics, a model in which a so-called 'investor' captures an asset, and then charges others to access it. It may look like the economy is growing, but only because a smaller and smaller group of people are charging a larger and larger fee for an increasingly rare product that people cannot live without.

Meanwhile for the rest of us, the situation was terrible. The cost of housing had gone past laughable, and was now a horror story we saw in the eyes of everybody under 40, but couldn't even begin to explain to people over 70. And as for growth, that meant nothing, because it only enriched those with property. If we had continued the trend left by Labour, GDP per capita would be 35 per cent higher in 2024 than it actually was. This equates to almost £11,000 of lost income per person each year, while average house prices increased by almost £100,000 over the same period.[149] Those hoping to buy a home would need a £20,000 pay increase every single year just to stand still.

But in fact, our growth rates were £4,000 per person lower than those of France, Germany and the USA, each of which had responded to the 2008 financial crisis with stimulus, rather than austerity. Inflation may make it look like your wage packet has grown, but in real terms it has remained static for a record-breaking length of time: there has been no longer period without wage growth since the Napoleonic Wars, more than 200 years ago.

Yet the Conservative Government had pursued only one policy to resolve this crisis with any degree of consistency: constant tax cuts for corporations. And in the end it achieved nothing. As the IFS pointed out, 'uncertainty created around policies intended to encourage businesses to invest in the UK has most likely served only to discourage such investment'.[150]

In short, it didn't matter how low corporation tax was: nobody wanted to invest in chaos. And even if they did, the cost of those tax breaks far exceeded the amount of new investment they generated. The tax relief for corporations rolled out in 2023 cost the British people £30 billion, but it only created £10.5 billion of new investment.[151] In a single year, we'd lost almost £20 billion in entirely pointless welfare for corporations.

An April Shower of Shit (Part 2)

'There cannot be a crisis next week', said Henry Kissinger, 'My schedule is already full'.[152] Rishi Sunak, however, boasted a much more can-do attitude, and an almost infinite calendar of calamity. The previous April had been terrible enough, but this one presented unsuspecting voters with a truly extraordinary extravaganza of auto-parodic fuckups.

First out of the gate, William Wragg, who at the tender age of 36 still managed to be described as a 'senior Tory' and had become vice-chairman of the backbench 1922 Committee. This pre-eminence over the other Tories became obvious in April when Wragg decided he would use the Grindr dating app to share what he euphemistically described as 'compromising things' with some randomer he may or may not have met in a pub. And then – and this is the really clever part – he waited until the perfectly obvious extortion racket tried to extort him, and then opted not to tell the authorities, but rather to do exactly what his blackmailers wanted. Parliamentary security was for lesser beings, although none have yet been found, so Wragg handed over the direct contact details of several of his colleagues, so that they too could become targets for blackmail attempts.[153]

'I've been a bit of a clod', said Wragg in a masterful demonstration of understatement. He should have been prouder: he was punching above his weight in the relentless struggle to be declared Britain's Stupidest MP. And yet somehow, despite being outwitted by his own penis, he still managed to maintain more dignity than invertebrate prime minister Sunak, who didn't remove the whip from Wragg, and instead chose to just sit idly by for a few days while the nation laughed at the entire ludicrous incident.

But you don't get to be a senior Tory by the age of 36 without being proactive, so while he hung around, waiting to be sacked for a farcical security lapse, Wragg kept himself busy by accidentally revealing his Wi-Fi password to readers of *The Observer* after agreeing to pose for photographs.[154] And still no action from Sunak.

Eventually Wragg and his wayward wang got tired of waiting to see if the prime minister would do something prime ministerial. Wragg would have to do the job himself, so he resigned the whip, and announced he'd stand down at the next election, explaining that his 'misspent youth was in politics', but now he wanted to clean up his act by distancing himself from Britain's Government.[155]

It was Rishi Sunak's worst week to date.

And the timing was terrible too. It was a month until this lot had to face the country in local elections, yet barely a day passed without news of some former minister or senior backbencher announcing they were doing a runner, while at the grassroots level volunteers complained of being 'emotionally exhausted' by the constant mayhem. They described the Government they were just about to campaign to re-elect as 'the worst I have ever seen'.[156]

'The party at the moment is not remotely ready to fight an election', said the chair of one local association. 'The number of people helping is minuscule compared with 2017 or 2019. The membership is generally thought to have dropped by about 45 per cent since 2022'.

On the backbenches, the mood seemed if anything even worse, with one withering Tory MP asking, 'How do you go into this campaign saying, "I'm the man for the country", and there's 70 MPs behind you saying, "no fucking way?"'

Governance ground to a halt, but – and it's genuinely astonishing that this wasn't openly discussed at the time – that was hardly a new thing. There hadn't been a properly functioning operation in Number 10 since the referendum had been announced in 2015.

Leadership was non-existent. Downing Street insiders expressed dismay that, with the exception of the National Security Council, it had 'become rare to get called to any meetings at all'. The tradition of regular, almost daily cabinet-level summits to discuss policy had stopped. There hadn't been a meeting for weeks, and insiders said, 'a lot of us feel like we've become zombie government'.[157]

Sunak could have ended the agony by scheduling a General Election for early May, on the day already allocated for the local elections, thus avoiding the further reputational damage the by-election results would inevitably cause. But he fluffed it, because knackered Downing Street staff had already made plans for a General Election in the second half of the year, and he didn't want to disappoint them.

Woman Buys House

The one bright spot on the Tory horizon was the slim possibility that Labour's deputy leader, Angela Rayner, might have made a minor tax error years before she became an MP. Team Tory hoped this insignificant nothing-burger could be converted into a scandal large enough to destroy the opposition.

They'd prayed for a similar outcome during Partygate, when the *Daily Mail* dedicated weeks, nay months of front pages to Labour's Keir Starmer, hoping to turn a photo of him having a beer at a time when the Covid regulations permitted such a thing into a cross between Watergate and the Profumo affair. After the Metropolitan Police cleared Starmer, saying there was 'no case to answer', the Conservatives' Richard Holden had written Durham Police, demanding another investigation.[158] Once again, no case to answer, just a prolonged exercise in political mudslinging and a hell of a lot of wasted police time.

The background to the Angela Rayner case came down to this:

she had followed legal advice during the sale of a home almost a decade earlier, but it seemed possible – unlikely, but possible – that there was a small amount of outstanding tax. This was the cue for open political warfare from every Tory paper, while the entire energy of government went on the attack. But it wasn't a universally popular strategy, and many Tories saw it for what it was: 'One of the most grotesque spectacles of hypocrisy I have ever witnessed', in the words of Conservative former minister Nick Boles. Matthew Parris, the ex-Tory MP and now *Times* columnist, described 'the hounding' of Rayner as, 'outrageous: brutal, snobbish and completely out of proportion to any mistake she may (or may not) have made'.[159]

The leading outrageous brutal snobs were Richard Holden again, now in the role of Tory Party chairman; and James Daly, who was so incensed that he wrote to the police demanding they investigate whatever it was he thought might have happened: the exact details were anybody's guess. *Sky News* asked him four times to describe the allegations he laid at Rayner's feet, and four times he didn't have a clue. The closest he got was, 'I asked the police to investigate certain matters regarding, er, certain things'.[160]

And that's not a lot for an investigation to go on.

In fact it's *nothing* for an investigation to go on.

Regardless, Greater Manchester Police had to try. Clearly under huge political pressure, they opened the case for a second time, allocated at least a dozen officers to it,[161] and came to the same conclusion: no criminal wrongdoing whatsoever.[162] The investigation took a month, during which *The Telegraph* dedicated 28 shrieking headlines to Rayner's alleged malfeasance in a single week, while hiding the scale of it deep, deep in their small print. Shuffled away in the pathless backwoods of the paper there appeared a minor article, in which the *Telegraph* revealed tax experts thought any bills Rayner had left outstanding 'would likely only be about £500'.[163]

Contrast this with the four Tory MPs who had made over £5.4 million in profits from selling taxpayer-funded second homes, and would not say whether they had paid capital gains tax on the profits.[164] Or with one of the Conservative party's largest donors, Lord Bamford, who along with his brother, was under investigation for potential tax liabilities of £500 million.[165] In case Jeremy Hunt is reading this and needs help with the maths, that's one million times more tax liability. Yet I can't find a single article relating to Lord Bamford's tax situation in *The Telegraph*.

Britain's press is notoriously, appallingly biased, but the largest bias is not revealed by what they print: it's revealed by what they decide not to.

It's All Gone Wrong Again

The Tories needed money: £34 million, ideally, which was the legal limit on what they were allowed to raise in the year before an election. They'd stood against the state funding of politics, and were insistent that not a single penny of taxpayers' money should go political parties.[166]

Fortunately, a hero was about to appear: Frank Hester, who had become close to the Conservatives after David Cameron invited him on trade missions to India and China in 2013.[167] By 2023, Hester's firm had received payments totalling £137 million from the Department of Health and Social Care, which had somehow failed to be published in the Government's official procurement website.[168] He was still taking £800,000 every week in public money when suddenly, he decided to become the largest donor the Conservatives have ever had, gifting them £10 million.

Giving an acquaintance of the PM a £137 million public contract and then accepting £10 million of it back in party donations is *not* the same as the state funding of politics. Totally different thing. Let's just be clear about that.

Anyway, it was all going as planned, until March, when it was revealed that Hester had said looking at Diane Abbott makes you 'want to hate all black women', and that she should be shot.[169]

There was outrage. The memory of Lee Anderson's run-in with racism was still fresh and raw, and now here was another Tory figure openly spouting outrageous bigotry, combined once again with fantasies of political violence. Fortunately, the Conservatives had stocked up on the word 'wrong' during the Anderson debacle and were quick to roll it out again.

'I'm uncomfortable talking about this now, because he was clearly wrong', said energy minister Graham Stuart. The headlines remained bad, and it became clear 'wrong' didn't quite cut it, so after a brief intermission the Tories went for 'rude' instead. A Tory spokesman admitted 'Mr Hester has made clear that while he was rude, his criticism had nothing to do with her gender nor the colour of her skin', somehow overlooking that the entire scandal hinged on Hester's views about a woman who is black. Mel Stride also failed to notice the references to race and gender, when he said the remarks were 'inappropriate' but were not 'gender-based or race-based'.[170]

This didn't go down well either, but Downing Street still spent the rest of the day refusing to call their biggest donor a racist: he had merely said something that was 'clearly unacceptable', but which they were prepared to accept in return for a few million quid. But by the evening pressure had become unbearable, and through gritted teeth they released a statement admitting Hester's words were 'racist and wrong'.[171]

We all knew why they didn't want to admit it was racist: there were constant calls for his massive donation to be handed back, even from within the party. Scottish Conservatives boasted that they had never taken money from Hester, and issued a statement saying, 'the UK Conservative party should carefully review the donations it has received from Hester in response to his remarks'.[172]

'Nope, no way, not going to happen', responded a senior Conservative official. 'They'll have spent it, and I don't see where they'd get that amount of money from again'.[173]

Have they tried handing £137 million of taxpayer's money to another friend of David Cameron's, and waiting to see how much of it bounces back?

Three days after the story broke, the Conservatives accepted a further donation of £150,000 from Hester's company. By the time the election was done, he'd donated a total of £15 million.[174]

It Has Been Zero Days Since the Last Embarrassment

Imagine for a moment that you're a 78-year-old former Conservative campaign manager, asleep in your bed at 3 am, when suddenly the phone rings and an urgent voice says, 'I've got in with some bad people and they've got me locked in a flat and they want £5,000 to release me'.

You explain that you don't have £5,000 on you at this very moment, what with you being in your nightie and all, so the voice becomes angrier and demands that you immediately leave your house to source a new figure of £6,500, because that's inflation for you. And then the man on the phone suggests that you take the money from your own life savings, and it'll all be fine, cos he'll just secretly steal money from his own campaign funds to repay you.[175]

And then you realise that the voice belongs to your own MP, Mark Menzies.

It had been a long, fraught road for Menzies and his poor constituents in Fylde. In 2014 he'd had to resign from a Government position when it was reported that he'd hired a teenaged Brazilian male sex worker, then given him a private tour of the Palace of Westminster before asking him to procure a big pile of amphetamines.

'A number of these allegations are not true', Menzies had insisted while sweating wildly and chewing his own teeth to dust, 'and I look forward to setting the record straight in due course'. It's a decade later, and we're still waiting.[176]

Two years after that incident, he was back in the headlines, this time for a heartwarming story involving a dog, which quickly became less heartwarming when it was alleged he'd almost killed the beast by pouring dangerous amounts of booze into it. Fortunately Menzies was able to clarify the situation to police, who had been called by concerned neighbours. He hadn't given alcohol poisoning to a dog, he explained; he had merely stood around taking photos while his friend gave alcohol poisoning to a dog, after which the two men got into a pissed-up brawl that spilled out onto the street. And who can expect more from their MP than that? Menzies wasn't charged, but somebody must have been, because the vet bill for pumping the poor hound's stomach exceeded £500.[177]

Further problems with intoxicants plagued our hero, when in August 2023 he turned up late and stupefyingly drunk at The Last Night of the Proms, and quickly launched into a kicky, pokey tantrum when he discovered he hadn't been allocated VIP seats.[178] He maintained that he'd merely struck somebody inadvertently with a flag during an overenthusiastic bout of musical patriotism. But that kind of behaviour is far from rare at the Proms, and security staff aren't usually called upon to ask you to stop kicking the other patrons' chairs, as had been the case with the honourable member for Fylde.

It's not so much a track record as a skid-mark, so you'd expect the Tories to be ready for action whenever a story emerged about Mark Menzies, but you'd be wrong.

Katie Fieldhouse – the 78-year-old woman Menzies had phoned from captivity, perhaps expecting her to launch a Liam Neeson-style takedown of the criminal gang he'd accidentally joined – had informed the Tories about the incident on 3 January, and then the Tories had opted to sit on it for three and a half months. The Conservative Party's chief of staff had reassured her about Menzies' latest brush with the law, telling her: 'It is fraud, but you are not duty-bound to report it because it's not Conservative Party money'.[179]

Fieldhouse had had enough and went to the papers.[180] She reported that her MP's behaviour wasn't a solitary incident, as though any of us really thought it would be. Menzies, she alleged, had previously used £14,000 of political donations to pay his private medical bills.

'I strongly dispute the allegations put to me', said Menzies, again.

'As there is an investigation ongoing, I will not be commenting further', said Menzies, again.[181]

He resigned the from the party, and he wasn't alone. Small armies of senior advisors were quitting before the inevitable happened, joining a mad rush to the exits, desperate to land their next job in politics before *I Advised The Tories To Cover Up Mark Menzies* was added to their CV. At least a dozen MPs had already set up private consultancy firms, keen to start a profitable new career before years of public misbehaviour killed off their previous calling.[182]

'They are jumping before they are pushed given the terrible outlook for the party', said an insider. 'It's a very sensible thing'.[183]

By this stage 64 Tory MPs had already announced they were standing down. Another 18 former Tory MPs were also sitting as independents, having lost the whip due to some gobsmacking scandal or other.[184] In fact, so many had been forced to resign that by this point Former Tories outnumbered Liberal Democrats in parliament. And it turns out it was lucrative business, to be so absolutely fucking terrible that you managed to get sacked by a party that still found room for Jonathan Gullis. If a suspended MP could hang on until the General Election, they could each pocket an extra £29,000 in redundancy money.[185]

Such entrepreneurial spirit would normally be right in the Conservative wheelhouse, but the actions of Wragg, Bone, Menzies and company hadn't gone down entirely well with their remaining colleagues. A senior cabinet minister described the behaviour of his own party as 'utter madness', and pondered, 'Do we really reflect society as a whole? I hope not for the sake of humanity'.

But many Tory MPs still seemed mystified by the actions of people who had sat next to them on the green benches for over a decade, even when those actions had been widely reported in the press. I guess this is what you get when you only read *The Telegraph*, a publication that was by now entirely dedicated to the shocking news that a woman had legally bought her own house with her own money, which she hadn't even stolen from donations.

'How can somebody possibly get a dog pissed?', asked one Tory backbencher, startled by the novel experience of coming face-to-face with a verifiable fact. Another sagely noted, 'There have been so many other mad things that we'd forgotten that it happened'.[186]

It seemed the only part of the British economy that had become more productive under the Tories was Number 10's crisis management team. As the 'Mark Menzies Kidnapped Himself' story ate up bandwidth in a news cycle that was struggling to cope, a quarter of Grant Shapps turned up on TV to remind us that, 'Just because an accusation is made, or something is written, doesn't mean it is necessarily proven', which must have come as a shock to the swarm of *Telegraph* journalists traducing Angela Rayner.[187]

All of this went down brilliantly with a Conservative Party readying itself for local elections in early May. Some faint hope remained amongst the more dementedly optimistic Tories – not of electoral triumph, obviously, but at least that they might avoid complete disaster. However, as even the most ardent of the party's romantic dreamers pointed out, 'You can't rule out a complete panicked meltdown'.[188]

They had no positive story to present to voters, so had focused entirely on negative attacks on Labour, but it seemed to no avail. A cabinet minister privately remarked: 'The issue we have is that even if we land a hit [on Labour], we get one or two days out of it until it's wiped out by something else. It's like those workplace signs: "0 days since the last crisis".'[189]

It was Rishi Sunak's worst week to date.

*

The prime minister's five pledges were now five curses. He hadn't delivered on four of them, and the fifth, falling inflation, didn't mean lives were improving for ordinary Britons, it just meant they were still getting worse, but at a slightly slower rate. And that was basically what Keir Starmer was offering to the electorate, so didn't help Sunak at all. With a shrug, the PM's handful of promises were quietly shuffled out of the limelight, and a desperate scrabble began for some other offering to the country.

Sunak's minders popped him on a cushion, pointed him towards the camera, and left him to do his show-and-tell about whatever had emerged from that morning's fumble inside the Downing Street Policy Tombola. His latest wheeze was to eliminate wheezing: the legal age for buying cigarettes would be raised every year, ensuring younger people would never be able to access them. A bit like their pensions.

In all fairness, I applaud Sunak for trying to eliminate smoking. It's a genuinely good idea, workable, not inconvenient to existing smokers, and cost free (except to tobacco companies, and who likes them anyway?) Nevertheless, the policy's principal accomplishment was highlighting the prime minister's weakness. He couldn't even get his party to agree that cancer was bad. Sunak wanted to save lives. The intellectual giants on his libertarian right argued that adults should be free to smoke themselves to death if they wanted to, but also argued that those same adults should not, under any circumstances, be free to use voluntary euthanasia. Painful death was the only death they were in favour of.

Opposition to the anti-smoking legislation was led by almost every one of the sociopaths vying to replace Sunak. Suella Braverman, Kemi Badenoch and Robert Jenrick, plus several serving ministers, Julia Lopez, Steve Baker, and of course Liz Truss, keen to make a splash as part of the promotional tour for her hilarious new book about how brilliant she was.[190]

Truss's publishers had paid her an advance of £1,512, which, even if you're foolish enough to try to cobble together a living as a writer, still qualifies as 'hilariously shit'.[191] It's less than half what Andrew Bridgen's brother used to pay him to sit in a darkened room for a single day and think about potatoes, and it may explain why it feels like it takes longer to read *10 Years to Save The West* than it took Truss to write it.[192]

'This book is not a traditional political memoir', writes Truss, and that's very true, because memoirs are usually written by somebody who remembers things that actually happened.[193] No such limitations applied to Truss. The blame for her policies lay with the Bank of England, with the International Monetary Fund, with Joe Biden and with the Conservative Party, which she derided as a nest of socialists. She blamed the OBR, who had written a report warning that her budget would be a disaster, which she refused to publish and may not even have read. She presented this documented failure of prime ministerial duty as evidence that she had done nothing wrong, and that the OBR had caused the disaster. She barely recognised the vast harm caused to Britain's economy by her delusional view of the world, and her utter lack of empathy wasn't helped by her admitted reaction to the death of Elizabeth II.

'Why me, why now?' wailed Truss, shocked to her core by the revelation that frail, 96-year-old women sometimes die.[194]

For a brief moment in the book, Truss conducts a thought experiment, contemplating a future where she hadn't been stymied by the notoriously left-wing radicals of the international banking system. And then, having experimented with thought, she returns to her default pre-thought state, and emphatically insists that every single person on the planet is wrong except for herself.

There is evidence to suggest she is wrong. Merely by publishing her book she managed to break the ministerial code.[195] And it's hard to read her complaints about Britain being undone by 'unelected bureaucrats' without remembering that she was an unelected prime minister.[196] It's tricky to buy into her worldview that she's infallible without remembering the time she reportedly considered paying for tax cuts for millionaires by abolishing cancer treatment on the NHS.[197] Her book is so relentlessly skewwhiff, self-serving and petulant that after finishing it you're left thinking that the only conceivable way she could have made it to the top of the slippery pole was that she was holding it upside down. Which is exactly what she did with her own hardback while launching it on Fox News.

Twice.[198]

But what she'd chosen to print was nothing compared to the delusions of her book tour. She'd popped over to the USA to sit on a stage with a man who described Tommy Robinson as a 'hero'.[199] Robinson has convictions for violence, mortgage fraud, stalking, drug possession, actual bodily harm, the false use of a passport, and contempt of court after he almost caused the trial of a grooming gang to collapse.[200] Having mounted a platform next to a Robinson supporter, Truss then performed a perfectly executed dive into conspiracy theories, telling a frankly mystified *Wall Street Journal* that the 'deep state' was out to get Donald Trump, now that it had finished getting her. Back home in Britain, Truss took time out from her busy schedule of arguing about lettuces on live radio, to deny every single thing we know about her past. A former Lib Dem who campaigned to remain in the EU, she now claimed she had simply been 'too busy' to back Brexit, as though she believes being right takes more time than being wrong.

But now she had plenty of time on her hands, so she comforted us with the news that she wouldn't rule out another go at being PM, which is a bit like me refusing to rule out going on a hot date with Gillian Anderson.[201] And then it was back to the USA, trying to capitalise on a MAGA audience who didn't have a fucking clue who she was, and who now had to experience Truss delivering her unique brand of stilted, batshit stage presence to half-empty halls. 'They've heard it all before', said one commentator, 'and by American authors'.

Try as she might to drum up business, her book secured just 0.29 per cent of the advance offered to Boris Johnson for his own disreputable memoir.[202]

*

Truss's reemergence was a nightmare for Sunak, and he was furious. It was his worst week to date. He made public statements distancing himself from his predecessor, and reminding us that he'd opposed her economic policies, which must be why he'd continued to use the Chancellor she'd appointed, Jeremy Hunt.

Even so, openly criticising Truss was a good move, according to Downing Street sources: 'He's come to the conclusion that he has nothing to lose because he's still 20 points behind in the polls and the party is far from united. The trouble is, of course, it is too late.'[203]

All Sunak wanted to do was make the entire country forget Truss and Johnson had ever existed, and all Truss and Johnson wanted to do was leap in front of every available TV camera and insist things had gone perfectly on their watch. And Albino Baloo was back in the news again: it had, after all, been several hours since his last face-palm inducing headline. Now it was time for Johnson to be dragged in front of the parliamentary committee on business appointments, a toothless watchdog designed to generate mealy-mouthed reassurances that everything wasn't spectacularly corrupt.

Yet even the committee expressed surprise at Johnson's response to its modest scrutiny, calling him 'evasive', and complaining that he had 'avoided answering specific questions' and 'refused to be open' about his relationship with a hedge fund company, immediately before he visited the Venezuelan president on its behalf.

The *Sunday Time*s alleged Johnson had been paid for the trip, which included a private jet on which he was accompanied by the hedge fund's founder.[204] Johnson at first denied it, and then claimed that when he and his financier decided to nip off to South America for a private, off-the-record chat with the Venezuelan leader – who had been handed an 18-year sentence for corruption by a panel of exiled judges – 'no commercial matters were discussed'.[205]

So just popping round for a natter, then? You and your hedge fund, on a private jet?

Sounds entirely plausible.

But cynical old Eric Pickles, the Tory chair of the committee, wasn't buying it. He said the relationship between the former PM, the dodgy dictator of an unbelievably corrupt petro-state, and a bunch of City wide-boys 'remains ambiguous'; and Pickles said that for all Johnson's denials, his responses 'lacked candour', which makes Pickles the final person on the planet to recognise this trait in Boris Johnson.[206]

The key problem was that, as Pickles observed, the entire system was designed around The Theory of Decent Chaps: the curious notion that anybody in government must be a good egg who wouldn't possibly lie, cheat, steal, take back-handers, undermine democracy, bullshit the public, shirk responsibility, or drive a coach-and-horses through the feeble guidelines we'd put in place. But whoever came up with this theory had reckoned without Boris Johnson and his followers. His influence on our politics left the Decent Chaps approach in tatters, and Pickles said the rules 'no longer have relevance in the modern world and are unenforceable'.

Absolutely Mental Health

The party was in a febrile mood. The majority of Tory MPs had no experience of opposition, and acted as though a losing an election was not merely an offence against the natural order of things, but also as if it would have no material effect on their ability to wield power. So there was no need to stop the plotting, to think deeply about policy, or even to listen to voters. Tim Montgomerie, founder of *ConservativeHome*, predicted 'some kind of leadership contest in two weeks' time' because, he said, 'Rishi Sunak can't do politics'.[207]

The PM's decision to appoint Lee Anderson had gone predictably badly, but as the local elections approached, Sunak didn't even have the sense to respond when his remaining MPs started backing another party, which Conservative rules classified as a sackable offence.[208] Nick Fletcher told the media he understood why Anderson buggered off to Reform UK and called him 'Ashfield's greatest champion'. Sunak totally ignored it.[209]

Maybe he was focused on interesting new ways to wriggle out of blame for his party's 14-year-long experiment in healthcare failure, which he'd stupidly promised to turn around in just one year, using zero new money. The Government bashfully admitted waiting lists had reached 7.6 million, which is – and there's no getting around this – over ten per cent of the entire country waiting to see a doctor. It sounds terrible, but then along came the ONS to make it sound worse, because they'd suddenly discovered another 2 million cases. Unsurprisingly the Government was even more bashful about this, and it got practically no press coverage. But the figures in April suggested as many as 10 million Britons were waiting for an NHS appointment or treatment.[210]

Sunak urgently needed a scapegoat, and wouldn't you know it – it turned out to be disabled people again. Lucky old disabled people, with their trouble-free existences, constantly dipping into the public purse for wanton fripperies such as life-saving medications and machines that allowed them to breathe.

And wouldn't you just know it: bloody disabled people had – it transpires – been responsible for a creating a 'sicknote culture', which is definitely a real thing that actually exists.

What happens with a sicknote culture is this: doctors who we pay to determine whether sick people are unable to work had – the conniving bastards – determined that lots of sick people were unable to work. And since raising your hand in parliament was enough to make Rwanda safe, it stands to reason that Tories could also pass a vote to cure anxiety. Naturally, telling severely mentally ill people they were about to be flung into poverty would snap them right out of that depression.

Sunak's medically and economically idiotic plan was just part of a longstanding, decades-long story perpetuated by various right-wing politicians and outlets. The narrative dripped from every *Daily Mail* headline. Somebody somewhere is having things easier than you, and – don't question it – it was almost certainly the poor and disabled. Let's get them!

Benefit fraud does exist, of course, and over the last decade it has cost us around £2.2 billion a year.[211] It sounds a lot – it *is* a lot – but it pales into insignificance compared to the amount lost to tax fraud, which is at least nine times greater.[212] And yet Britons were 23 times more likely to be prosecuted for benefits fraud than for tax fraud.[213] In 2017, the Tories launched landmark new powers to hand down enormous fines to tackle tax avoidance and evasion. In the five years since that legislation was introduced, they had failed to fine a single 'enabler'.[214]

A crackdown on fraud might have been necessary but aiming it at the disabled was a wild misfire.

Red meat to the Tories, though, or so you'd assume. But a quarter of Tory Councillors thought adult social care was already underfunded – because it was, as was most of our benefits system.[215] Sick pay in the UK was amongst the lowest in Europe, just 19 per cent of the average UK salary. In Germany, it is 70 per cent, payable for up to 78 weeks. In Norway, Iceland, Denmark and Luxembourg sickness benefit is 100 per cent of salary.

The Worst Parliament in History

A Parliament has existed in Westminster for over 750 years, and there have been some noticeably awful ones: the Mad Parliament of 1258, the Bad Parliament of 1377, and the Merciless Parliament of 1378. Awful parliaments then took a 640-year break so they could get a really good run-up to this: the Parliament that took the biscuit, and then probably tried to shag the biscuit, or ground it up and snorted it, or just sold it to their mates from the rugger club.

The Telegraph – even *The Telegraph*, by all that's holy – described it as 'the worst Parliament in history', and not without cause.[216] Of the MPs elected in 2019, a record number had been expelled from their parties or been forced to resign on the heels of some scandal or other.

Matt Hancock was kicked out of the cabinet because he couldn't keep his clammy mouth off his colleague during lockdown,[217] and then he was suspended from the Tory party because he couldn't keep his clammy mouth away from a camel's penis on *I'm A Celebrity, Get Me Out of Here*. Owen Paterson was jettisoned because he'd taken £100,000 to lobby Parliament in an 'egregious case of paid advocacy'.[218] Andrew Bridgen, gone for his Holocaust tweets. Rob Roberts, the whip withdrawn because he'd texted his 21-year-old intern who was in an 'awful state' due to a mental health crisis, and suggested having some unconditional sex with him might be the answer.[219]

Maybe this is what inspired David Warburton to hoof 'line after line' of cocaine in a young woman's house, before – despite the young woman's insistence that she didn't want to do anything sexual with him – he allegedly stripped naked, got into her bed and 'ground his body against hers and groped her breasts'.[220]

Who can forget Michelle Mone and her long, ultimately futile battle to avoid admitting involvement in a most-likely unlawful scheme to extract £29 million from a *definitely* unlawful Covid VIP lane?[221] David Cameron, with all the moral depth of a graphene scorpion, hoovering up £3.3 million by lobbying for Greensill Capital in what Parliament called 'a significant lack of judgement' and the rest of us called 'shifty moneygrubbing mendacity'.[222]

Christopher Pincher, suspended after eight allegations of sexual misconduct.[223] Scott Benton: lobbying scandal. Gavin Williamson: bullying. Dominic Raab: tomato-based bullying. Peter Bone. Crispin Blunt. Mark Menzies. William Wragg.

At least some of it was funny: ex-tractor fan Neil Parish had been suspended after – and you can't even say this without it sounding like it's in italics – *accidentally* watching hardcore porn in the chamber of the House of Commons while attempting to look at farm machinery. He defended himself by saying he had been 'very well behaved in Parliament' apart from bashing the bishop to pictures of a combine harvester. Parish protested that other MPs had behaved 'much worse', as then, as if to prove it, Julian Knight was suspended in July while police investigated multiple accusations of sexual assault.[224] Knight denied it all, and charges were later dropped. But how did it get that far? Two senior Tories – one an MP, the other a former advisor – said the Whips Office had been aware of the concerns for five years, but had taken no action until the police and media became aware.[225]

No sooner had this bit of unpleasantness washed across the newspapers than another arrived: the science secretary, Michelle Donelan, had lost a libel case against two academics she had wrongly accused of 'sharing extremist views', and then, having been ordered to pay a £34,000 libel settlement, she secretly paid it with taxpayers' money.[226]

Scandal upon scandal, outrage upon outrage. Any programme for government there might once have been seemed to have entirely evaporated, replaced by a sincere commitment to offend each discrete section of society in turn, with a series of tailor-made Fuck Yous. The mood of the country was a combination of sour exhaustion and bilious rage: we'd have rioted if we weren't so knackered, if we could have afforded the petrol for the Molotov cocktails, and if there was anything left for us to smash up in this dilapidated land. So it's hardly a surprise that even *The Telegraph* concluded: 'Not since the Addled Parliament of 1614 has there been [a Government] with so few positive achievements'.[227]

Witless Dickington

Two febrile years earlier, as it became obvious that Partygate was about to end Boris Johnson's premiership, the Nookie Monster had launched *Operation Save Big Dog*, a hare-brained scheme intended to keep him in power.[228] Considering how well that turned out, you'd assume the Conservatives would have learned a lesson, but no. In April it was time for Operation Save Rishi.[229]

The essence of this plan was to do absolutely nothing for a few days, in the hope that political disasters were like the Tyrannosaurus Rex in *Jurassic Park*: they can't get you if you stand still. And for a brief moment it looked as though it might pay off. By Sunday morning, after a week in which the Government attempted to do absolutely nothing, *Sky News* were moved to call it 'one of the better weeks that [Sunak's] had in his premiership',[230] and then literally one hour later, Dan Poulter, a former Tory health minister, defected to Labour in furious protest at the state the Tories had left the NHS, and the imagined success of Sunak's week reverted to type again.[231]

Against all odds, things took a turn for the even worse the following day, as foreign secretary David Cameron was accused of acting 'like a Kardashian sister' because he'd decided to splash out on 'one of the best luxury private jets money can buy' for a five-day jaunt around central Asia.[232] Did it matter that in the same week, it was reported that the British army couldn't afford enough ammunition to protect the country?[233] Probably. So perhaps there were better uses of taxpayers' money than coughing up a few hundred grand so the Sanguine Penguin can flaunt the dignity of Kim Kardashian in front of those vitally important strategic allies, Tajikistan, Kyrgyzstan,

Uzbekistan, Turkmenistan, Kazakhstan and Mongolia.[234]

But I don't want to spend too much time thinking about the Cameron's grotesque spending habits, because I'm too busy thinking about this: what had happened to the RAF jet given to Boris Johnson when he'd been foreign secretary, on which he'd insisted on spending £900,000 to have a union jack painted upside-down on the side?[235] That had happened only three years previously. Where was it now?

And what happened to the second jet Johnson had insisted upon when he became PM, on which he decided it would be a good idea to spend another £800,000 of taxpayers' money on paint?[236] I might be corrected by top mathematician Laura Trott, but I think I'm right in saying that's two jets available for a foreign secretary to use. So why was it necessary to hire a new plane at all, let alone one of the costliest on the planet?

And why, when Liz Truss was foreign secretary, was it necessary to spend £15,000 on in-flight catering for a single trip? The average in-flight meal costs £7.88 per person.[237] Why did Truss and her officials require £1,400 per person?[238]

The constant stream of nest-feathering calamities had led to a terrible atmosphere in the party. Nobody was doing anything of worth. Half the party was engaged in a relentless series of norm violations, and the other half ran 10 paces behind them with a script full of empty apologies. The entire Government was racing endlessly in circles like an excuse hamster. On the odd occasion they stopped running in circles, it was just because they felt like doing a bit of rancorous argufying while voters looked on agog. Tory MPs behaved as though the business of government was just something to keep them busy until the next leadership campaign. You'd call it 'managed decline' if there was any sense of things being managed. Instead, it was like watching the final series of a once-popular show, where the actors have clocked off, the viewers have tuned out, and the writers are bereft of ideas: at once wildly over-the-top, painfully chaotic, and boring.

Even the rare successes turned out to be failures in disguise. Sunak's much-delayed, ultimately doomed Rwanda plan scraped through Parliament, something Conservative MPs had eagerly anticipated ever since Boris Johnson plucked it out of thin air and convinced them it was a good idea. But just as the bill was passing, Sunak was forced to admit flights wouldn't leave for at least another three months, which meant there would be no good news for xenophobes before what still seemed a probable election date in Autumn.[239]

His colleagues had barely recovered from that disappointment when along came another: the Home Office department responsible for processing deportations to Rwanda, which suddenly needed hundreds more staff to deliver on the Conservatives' key policy, had been ordered to make staff redundant instead.[240] No matter how much you hear Tory MPs insist the party was fully committed to Rwanda, remember that behind the scenes they were dismantling the project before a single flight had taken off.

A Natural Response

Almost a year earlier, in June of 2023, the Government had launched their detailed and unbeatable plan to oust Sadiq Khan. The first step was to find a candidate capable of following in Johnson's footsteps as Witless Dickington, the pussy-bothering Conservative Mayor of London.

Paul Scully, the minister for London, threw his hat into the ring with the boast that he would 'reach out beyond any sense of core vote or tribal lines', and in that respect, he was right: neither tribe wanted him. He failed to make the shortlist to be Tory Mayor of London despite being – and you should read this out loud, cos it's amazing – the only Tory MP put forward.[241]

So instead, the party chose Daniel Korski, a former special

advisor to David Cameron, who at least did better than Paul Scully. Korski managed to remain a candidate for an impressive 16 days before being accused of groping a television producer inside Downing Street a decade earlier.[242] He dropped out of the race, protesting his innocence pending an internal investigation that never happened, not least because Conservative Central Office already knew about the groping accusations. They knew when they selected him as a candidate. They chose him anyway, cos what the hell, why not?[243]

And so the party ended up fielding its third-favourite candidate, and then tried to persuade us all that she should be our first: Susan Hall, the batty neighbour from a seventies sitcom that they can't repeat anymore because attitudes have changed. After a long and messy process, the Conservatives had ended up with a candidate who had liked messages on Twitter endorsing Enoch Powell,[244] joined a Facebook group 'rife with Islamophobia' one day after its racism had been revealed in national newspapers, [245] and then joined another group which discussed ways to murder Sadiq Khan.[246] Upon being selected as the party's candidate, she met with *The Standard* for a celebratory photo-shoot, which was enough to cause the Conservatives to make an official complaint that merely photographing Susan Hall constituted 'clear mockery'.[247]

The Tories treated the London mayoral election as a dry run for the forthcoming General Election, and we can mark that down as a rare success. Hall – the prattle of Britain – was comprehensively trounced by Labour, losing by the largest margin in the mayoralty's history. Her response, beamed live from whatever the fuck planet she was on, was that she was 'proud' to have 'so nearly' defeated Sadiq Khan.[248]

Stay in school, kids.

By the time that little tour de farce was over, it was Friday, and Sunak's day-planner informed him it was time to be a populist again. So in a sterling effort to tittilate the readership of the *Daily Mail*, he proposed changing disability benefits to a voucher system. Yep, the centrepiece of Sunak's grand plan to end what he called the UK's worklessness crisis was vouchers for people who are unable to work. To be fair, worklessness really was a crisis for Britain, with almost 22 per cent of the working-age population being economically inactive.[249]

But a voucher wouldn't make a single disabled person one iota less disabled. It would merely make lives harder for those living with disabilities, create a glorious opportunity for voucher counterfeiting rackets, and add a small fortune in admin costs to the branches of the civil service responsible.[250]

However, if you've spent years telling the electorate a story about a plague of benefits fraud, it's necessary to implement benefits crackdowns, and plenty of them. It didn't matter that the previous – and I've checked the maths here – one gazillion benefits crackdowns had resulted in even more people claiming benefits. Crackdowns were definitely the solution. Forcing people into low-paid, poor-quality jobs that were often wildly inappropriate to their lives and skills was the answer. It definitely wasn't coaching the unemployed and supporting them into more suitable jobs.

Thus, the latest crackdown, this one intended to target what the PM suggested was a plague of fake disabilities, built around 'subjective and unverifiable claims'. Sunak presented no evidence of this. It was just a subjective and unverifiable claim.[251]

The causes of the worklessness crisis were self-evident. It wasn't malingerers, or people looking for the luxury of life on benefits. Britain's unemployment benefits are the worst in Europe, offering just 17 per cent of in-work income.[252] The truth is, years of being beaten with sticks rather than fed carrots have exacerbated any injury, disability or mental health crisis a person is experiencing. If you have a minor back injury and are given time to recover, you are likely to return to work. If benefits sanctions force you to take a warehouse job after 2 weeks, that minor injury is more likely to turn into a chronic, long-term problem. Similarly with depression or anxiety. Except in a tiny minority of cases, sticks don't work.

But the carrot has been allowed to rot. For a decade, those who would normally be able to return to work following a little medical or healthcare treatment have instead been abandoned by a health service starved of resources. Separate reports by Lord Darzi and the Health Foundation laid bare 'the consequences of a decade of underinvestment in the NHS'. Doctors and nurses were found to be working harder than at any time in the service's history, but productivity was falling because staff were 'hamstrung by outdated equipment and crumbling infrastructure'.

That was a political choice.

Had the UK, since 2010, matched the public healthcare spending of the other EU countries, the NHS would have received £33 billion more capital investment. Instead, 'weak investment in wider public services has contributed to the nation's deteriorating health'.[253] And the end result was 10 million people waiting for treatment,[254] half of them for more than four months.[255]

That was a political choice.

So, to a large extent, was the prevalence of Long Covid, which was impacting almost 2 million additional Britons.[256] No Government can be blamed for the pandemic, but one Government can definitely be blamed for its lackadaisical approach to tackling it.[257] Boris Johnson went on TV to explain his policy to the outbreak: 'take it on the chin' and 'allow the disease, as it were, to move through the population'.[258] So it did, and despite our island status providing us with an unassailable natural defence against the incoming pandemic, we ended up with among the worst per capita Covid deaths in Europe.[259]

In fact the Tory response had been so poor that a Harvard professor of epidemiology and infectious disease had responded, 'I could not believe it. My colleagues here in the US assumed that reports of the UK policy were satire'.[260] Not very funny satire though. Matt Hancock unlawfully shoved infected patients into unprotected care homes.[261] Around 45,000 people in those care homes died of Covid.[262] During the same period in South Korea – which pursued policies of early and strict lockdowns, with not a single suitcase full of booze at the centre of government – absolutely no care home residents died of Covid. Not one.[263]

That was also a political choice.

So was Brexit, which has resulted in a collapse in investment. Business investment in the UK had grown steadily since the 2008 global financial crisis, but the trend abruptly stopped at precisely the moment of the 2016 referendum. Across the EU, business investment is 2 per cent higher than it was before Brexit. In Britain, it is 31 per cent lower.[264] But we weren't only being squeezed by lack of investment: inflation was eating into our wealth too. Inflation reduction was one of the key pledges Sunak had made, but he didn't even consider tackling the main cause. Bank of England economist Adam Posen said 80 per cent of UK inflation was explained by Brexit.[265]

That was also a political choice.

Perhaps the most insidious factor in our worklessness is the effect that living under vampire capitalism has on our collective psyches. I'm not claiming all capitalism is bad – of course it isn't. Properly managed, it can be an excellent driver of economic and social change. But for years, dating back to the revolution under Ronald Reagan and Margaret Thatcher, it hasn't been managed, it's been unleashed. And it's raged across societies, dividing and debauching them in the service of a tiny sliver of the population at the very, very top.

Sure the economy might technically be growing – we're always told GDP is up 1 per cent, 2 per cent, 3 per cent. But are you, personally, 2 or 3 per cent richer? Probably not. Average UK workers are £200 a week worse off in 2024 than we were when Lehman Brothers collapsed at the start of this book, while Rishi Sunak made £5 million off the failure of RBS.[266] A growing economy and shrinking wages makes no sense until you realise where all that money is going to. It's worth repeating: of the $42 trillion of new wealth generated worldwide between 2019 and 2021, almost two-thirds went to the richest 1%.[267]

And it's a lesson the rest of us have learned, even if we didn't know the exact figures. The background hum of vast inequality and unfairness informs our attitudes to work. Career ambition once had a purpose. Consecutive governments of both the left and right promised it would lead to higher earnings, more fulfilment, a home, a retirement, and the likelihood of better things for your children. But what happens when it becomes obvious that the promise has been broken? What is the point of all that hard work and sacrifice if all the rewards go to a tiny group who refuse to share?

Combine the Government's attitude to our health, and our attitude to a system that is designed to rip us off, and naturally you're going to end up with a huge portion of the population who simply don't want to play that game anymore.

Sunak called it 'a worklessness crisis'.

I call it a natural response.

Re-Inventing Rishi… Again

The Tories couldn't have looked more nervous if they'd been in the waiting room at a vasectomy clinic; or worse, a tax inspector's office. In fact they were so anxious there was a danger of Rishi Sunak paying them in vouchers. Something needed to change, although they were unanimous in their view that whatever needed to change, it definitely wasn't the Government.

Depending on who you asked, we were still minutes, days, weeks or months away from an election being announced, so there was time for at least another half dozen versions of Rishi Sunak to emerge before polling day.

The Tories could have abandoned their tactic of being funded by embarrassing racists, and instead sold collectable sticker books of all Rishi's rebranding exercises. Remember Dishy Rishy? By May he was more Eunuch Sunak. He'd already been through more relaunches than the Space Shuttle, generating just as much hot air, and culminating in just as many disasters, but now it was time for another. It was time for Sunak to don a muscle suit and pretend to be a strong man. It was like being led by Mr Benn.

'The next few years will be some of the most dangerous [...] our country has ever known', he tersely announced in his best tough-guy voice.[268] He'd obviously decided the best way to appeal to voters was to scare us shitless. I guess making us piss ourselves laughing counts as a near miss.

The reveal party for the bold new Rishi had all the right ingredients. He did that point-with-a-thumb thing that for some reason people think is a key prime ministerial trait. He waved at cameras as though he was trying to get the attention of waitress. He even tried to pretend he cared about our survival in the forthcoming World War Three, by arranging his eyebrows into a sad expression that he'd learned from a dog.

But it was a waste of time, because we were already terrified. Not of Putin and nuclear war, but of more prosaic things that in a functioning country wouldn't keep us awake at night: a gas bill, for example; or fear that in the unlikely event we ever get to see a GP, the health centre would fall in on us because somebody in power decided to construct it out of foam.[269] But Sunak wanted us to forget all of that, and focus on his brand new credentials as a man of action who was tough enough to see off the Red Army, having just successfully seen off Natalie Elphicke.

The MP for Dover had defected to Labour days before, in what I think it's fair to say was a move calculated to unite every party in abject horror. She'd been so far to the right of the Tory party that and even some Conservatives expressed surprise that she hadn't joined the BNP.[270]

Elphicke had succeeded her husband Charlie to become the MP

for Dover. For legal reasons, for a long time I wasn't at liberty to say what I think about Charlie Elphicke, because for legal reasons, for a long time Charlie Elphicke wasn't at liberty. 'I'm a naughty Tory, I'm a naughty Tory', he had sung as he committed one of the sex crimes[271] for which he was convicted.[272]

In recent years, the Disney corporation has taken to producing its movies in a facility called The Volume: a 360° wall of computerised GCI artificiality that renders everything small, meaningless and dull, but allows the cheap production of empty crap for mass consumption. Keir Starmer had taken inspiration from this, and created a form of flat, fake, wraparound politics that allowed room for Elphicke in a party that still contained John McDonnell. It caused a ripple of consternation and worry across the party and the wider left.

It was also a bit too much for Vidal Sassoon's nemesis, Michael Fabricant, who accused Elphicke of wanting to 'drown migrants' and 'start a war with France'. It was, said Fabo, 'utterly amazing that someone with those views is accepted into Labour', yet both he and his entire party assured us they were entirely relaxed that she'd been at home in the Tory party until three days earlier.[273]

Sure they were. You could cut the Tories' relaxation with a knife.

With Elphicke gone, a vacancy had arisen for Sheriff of The Nuttiest Tory Badlands. Esther McVey was quick to the draw, keen to remind the Tory right of her credentials as a tackler of the really big issues, and a stout defender of freedom of expression. So she banned the wearing of rainbow lanyards.[274] And then, inspired by Rishi Sunak's habit of constant dithering, she reversed out of that ban the following day,[275] most of which had been spent stifling giggles while Downing Street explained that McVey's ban on officials wearing rainbow lanyards wouldn't mean she would 'ban officials wearing them'.[276]

She was the minister for common sense, you know?

We know now that a General Election was announced just one week later. But if, at the time, any such plans had been in place, everything else that happened in the run-up makes even less sense. The Conservatives seemed to be actively working for the opposition. Chris Philp, a shaved Afghan hound who had been trained to do impressions of a policing minister, beamingly revealed that prisoners wouldn't, after all, be released 70 days early due to the chronic overcrowding his party has overseen. In fact it would only be 18 days.[277] This was because the party of law and order had closed over 10,000 prison places since 2010, and overcrowding had reached the worst levels in British history. At least 10 of our largest prisons were at over 150 per cent capacity. Durham was at 173 per cent.

And the state of the jails was so bad that in the week Philp was making his announcement, it was revealed a group of prisoners had broken through the walls of their jail, not in a twenty-year, Shawshank-style act of endless patience and contraband pick-axes, but by tunnelling through the decrepit walls in half an hour using plastic cutlery.[278]

Yet while Philp was shuffling convicts out of the back door, Michael Gove was planning to shove thousands more in through the front. The free speech absolutist's latest wheeze: singling out protests he didn't like, and forcing them to pay the police to break up their own marches.[279] In effect, this meant you would still be able to protest against a Government that only cared what rich people said, but only if you were a rich person. For the rest of us, a new world beckoned, in which we must stay at home, a sardonic sign in one hand, and in the other, a self-funded truncheon with which to knock our placard to the ground.

Gove's efforts were wasted, and not just because he was so certain voters would kick him out of office that he had joined the mass exodus of MPs opting to jump before they could be pushed.[280] No, Gove's efforts were wasted because, despite campaign groups warning he was perilously close to introducing a police state, it had become impossible to turn us into a police state given the state of our police.[281] Mass jailings remained theoretical in a land where flat broke constabularies had to give orders to avoid doing anything that might result in mass arrests.[282]

Perhaps these stories, each of which emerged in just three days before the election was called, explain why Sunak decided he could wait no longer. After 14 years of public underinvestment and private wealth-extraction, nothing worked. The public longed for a reckoning. The Tories could only offer a wreckening, and the signs of it were everywhere. Nobody expected this Government to fix the NHS, or improve the economy, or bring the long, meandering snipe-hunt for Brexit benefits to a successful conclusion. But we expected law and order. We even, to some extent, expected adherence to the cult of Rwanda. After all, Sunak had said, 'Enough is enough: No more prevarication; No more delay; No ifs, no buts. These flights are going to Rwanda'. But suddenly the guarantee that the PM would pointlessly spend £200 million to send a handful of Albanians to Kigali before the election was dropped too.[283]

It was almost impossible to imagine a worse set of people to sit on a front bench, until you checked out the backbench alternatives. Few of us shed a tear when Iranian president Ebrahim Raisi, the Butcher of Tehran came to a sticky end in a helicopter crash,[284] but Michael Fabricant didn't even wait for confirmation of his death before tweeting 'We can only hope. (For the worst)'.[285]

Michael Fabricant had three enemies in life: international diplomacy, Toni and Guy.

Part 3
'Basically bonkers'

The General Election of 2024

I'm Just Rish!

The period since 2010 had felt like a long illness. The election of 2024 felt like a grateful death. Britain had endured some notably terrible election campaigns as the Conservatives burned their way through five prime ministers, but 2024 stole the show.

It was worse than 2010, when David Cameron, a thumb with a mouth-slit, sold us on the notion of 'Compassionate Conservatism' (sic), and urged us to 'Vote for change'. It turned out to be small change, because his Government's growth forecasts had to be slashed every single year.[1]

It was worse than 2015, when Cameron managed to win the next election due to the media's constant antisemitic slandering of his Labour opponent,[2] and the promise of a 'Long Term Economic Plan',[3] which he'd based around a maths error.[4] The economy was supposed to grow, but it seemed to have a mind of its own, which is more than you could say for most of his parliamentary colleagues, who voted for a Brexit that explains 80 per cent of UK inflation,[5] and costs us £100 billion a year.[6] The £45bn cost of Labour bailing out RBS is commonly portrayed as a once-in-a-generation economic calamity that the nation barely survived.[7] By 2025, our decision to leave the EU was costing us just as much every five-and-a-half months. And for what? The only Brexit benefit identified by the minister responsible for finding Brexit benefits – Jacob Rees-Mogg – was the opportunity for slightly improved signage inside the Dartford Tunnel.[8]

And the election of 2024 was worse than Theresa May's 2017 campaign, during which she had tottered mechanically from photo-op to photo-op, cawing out 'Strong and stable leadership' with brain-mangling regularity, until you felt you'd been Rick-rolled by an over-anxious Meccano giraffe that had swallowed a kazoo.[9]

It was even worse than Boris Johnson's 2019 election, during which the famously fictive Tory leader stole a journalist's phone,[10] and hid in a fridge,[11] and then the Conservatives changed their social media name to *FactCheckUK* so they could proliferate misinformation.[12] You can't claim we weren't warned. But at least we'd been given the choice whether to be led by that dauntingly inept, scapegrace buffoon. Nobody elected Rishi Sunak, not even his own party members. And faced with the opportunity, Britain simply could not wait to kick him and his entire party right in the ballots.

*

Several years ago I shared a flat with an African pygmy hedgehog named Flora, a pointless pet with a short lifespan, whose defining characteristic was that she'd only evacuate while running on her wheel. Round and round she would go, getting nowhere, knee-deep in her own manure, flinging shit across my home in great stinking arcs every single day, until it was time for her to elaborately and expensively die.

The only difference between Flora and Rishi Sunak's party was that the hedgehog had all her pricks on the outside.

Running in circles had been Rishi Sunak's signature move for over a year. He'd made the same mistake so often that I'm surprised he didn't pick up a repetitive strain injury. No matter when he called a General Election, it would have ended in disaster for Conservatives, but Sunak had wandered obliviously past every single less-calamitous opportunity. Tory campaign strategist Isaac Levido had made it clear to Sunak that going for a summer poll would be the wrong move, but he was ignored.[13]

Of course it was the wrong moment. That much should have been obvious to anybody with an ounce of political instinct. It wouldn't have saved his Government, but Sunak could have endured less damage if he'd gone to the country before the local elections in May. An earlier election would have allowed his party to focus its energies on just one near-fatal kicking from voters, rather than two. It would have saved the Tories from losing 500 councillors upon whom their General Election ground-campaign depended.[14] And none of those foot-soldiers would have just lived through the demoralising effects of Susan Hall.

But no: Sunak ruled out those dates.[15]

The second least-bad moment for an election would have been in the Autumn, before it got too cold for the Conservatives' geriatric volunteers to trudge around their constituencies, being bollocked by voters. September would have meant Nigel Farage, Sunak's major challenger from the right, would be in America, fighting for the re-election of Donald Trump. It would have given Sunak's Government time to get at least one Rwanda flight off the ground, follow it up with a media blitzkrieg, and then rush to a plebiscite quickly, before the general public became aware that the Rwanda plan wasn't stopping small boats.

But no, Sunak ruled that out too. And bizarrely, despite the Conservatives having total control over when to call a General Election, none of them had any clue it was happening. Ministers spent the morning of 22 May boosting public confidence by suggesting society was about to collapse.[16] Britons were admonished to urgently stock up on supplies, using money we didn't have to buy food we couldn't afford, and sewage-filled water we didn't dare drink, which we could keep in a house that hadn't been built, in the spare room the Tories had taxed out of existence,[17] in preparation for whatever disaster they had planned next.

Much to their surprise, the next disaster was exclusive to Tory MPs, because that afternoon Rishi Sunak announced he would face the judgment of the country on 4 July.

As election announcements go, it wasn't half bad. It was three-quarters bad. The guy whose campaign was all about his plan working didn't even have the foresight to take an umbrella with him in a torrential downpour.[18] Instead, Sunak opted to go outside and get cinematically piss wet through as he performed his climactic big number.[19]

'I'm just Rish', he sang, the only Ken in history to be smaller than his own action figurine. Prime ministers aspire to grow into the job. Sunak appeared to have shrunk into his, an effect not helped by the sound of protesters off camera, backing his announcement with a tinny rendition of *Things Can Only Get Better*.[20] It was hard to look at him without thinking about the chef from *Ratatouille* after being abandoned by the rat.

'How fucking incompetent do you have to be to launch a campaign that badly?' asked former Scottish Tory leader Ruth Davidson,[21] while another minister went for the rather more pithy, 'It was shite'.[22]

Parliament would be prorogued the following day, but there was still time for some Conservative MPs to try to squeeze in one more leadership election before they were booted from office, and they began threatening Sunak with letters of no confidence.[23] The mood was terrible. Inside Westminster, gloomy cabinet ministers were seen shoving their ministerial red boxes towards their Labour opposite numbers, saying 'You might as well have this now'.[24]

The election announcement was still echoing along Downing Street, and it had already been written off as a total disaster. Was there a strategy behind any of this? It was hard to know. From the outside it looked like an election as improv: a real-time *Whose Lie Is It Anyway?* in which members of the public called out ideas such as 'fuck off', or 'no, seriously, fuck off', and then the Conservatives did the opposite.

*

Day two of the campaign was, if anything, even worse than the first, with Sunak caught taking questions from – very much in air-quotes – 'ordinary members of the public', who turned out to be Conservative councillors cosplaying as humans. They'd donned the trustworthy reflective tabard of the simple peasant, but, in their hurry to perfect their disguises, they had forgotten to change their faces, and were immediately identified.[25]

From there, Sunak went straight to Wales, a nation which had just failed to qualify for the Euros, where he took it upon himself to ask the locals if they were, 'looking forward to all the football?'. In the three agonising seconds of silence that followed, viewers on a high-definition TV could identify the precise moment when Rishi Sunak's soul left his body.[26]

Dozens more Tories stood down, with many of them having dated their resignation letters a month earlier. The Conservative whips were reported to have begged their MPs to stagger their departures, so it didn't look like the entire Tory movement had quit at once.[27] Any fool looking at this trend would realise the party's big beasts would do anything to avoid being the subject of 2024's Portillo Moment – the humiliated personification of every voter's contempt and anger. Yet their resignations still caught party insiders by surprise. High-spending Tory donors poured £2.5 million into key battleground seats for senior MPs such as Penny Mordaunt and Michael Gove,[28] only for him to step down eleven minutes later.[29]

I'll give the Conservatives this: they have impeccable comic timing.

'Who do you trust?', Sunak had asked when he announced the

snap election, and behind him half his team broke off from phoning their bookie to prompt the answer: not you![30] While Sunak held his first major rally of the campaign, many of his MPs opted instead to go to a bar, get pissed, and complain to salivating journalists.

A recent member of the cabinet called Sunak, 'just a spoiled child. He just hasn't been able to bear the criticism and the backbiting and he has basically said "stuff you all! I'm going to call an election!"'.[31]

'This really is the kamikaze election', said another former minister.

I doubt even people who attended Sunak's rally could tell you what happened. It certainly wasn't about policy, because practically every extant pledge was curtly shelved. The bill to ban no-fault evictions, which Tories had been promising since Theresa May was prime minister in 2019,[32] was unceremoniously dropped.[33] The proposed smoking ban – just about the only good idea Sunak had ever had – was excluded from the parliamentary schedule,[34] which Sunak said made him 'disappointed', as if he'd abandoned his proudest legacy by mistake.[35]

*

The paradox of modern politics is that the skills required to win an election are the opposite of those required to run a government. One is a short sprint of empty promises and oversimplification; the other, an exhausting marathon of full in-trays and fastidious compromises. Therefore logic dictates that anybody who becomes our head of government must be either an administrative genius or an electioneering marvel.

None of this explains Rishi Sunak, though.

The election had been called on a Wednesday. By Friday, the PM's team took the unusual step of abandoning the campaign trail, staying at home, banging their heads against a desk, and doing some groaning. That's not how it was spun, of course: Sunak was merely spending a day at his constituency.

But we all knew the truth. As one campaign insider admitted,

'Prime ministers don't normally spend the first weekend of the campaign at home talking to their advisers'.[36] But the whole re-election operation had got off to a calamitous start, and desperation visibly leaked from Sunak, even while he affected an air of stolid nonchalance. For the benefit for the cameras he'd wave and grin his way up Downing Street, the very acme of insouciant confidence; but you got the distinct sense that the moment the door closed behind him, he'd start sobbing like he was watching *Toy Story 3*. Or more likely, appearing in it.

Of course, it was perfectly possible that Labour's Keir Starmer was equally lousy at electioneering, but nobody ever found out because the Tories were so hilariously bad at, y'know, *doing politics* that Starmer didn't even need to try. Which is fortunate, because Keir Starmer turned out to be as hollow and soulless as the chalk outline around the corpse of socialism. Sunak's new bestie Elon Musk had joyfully predicted millions of jobs were about to be replaced by a partially effective AI bot, but nobody had envisaged the first to go would be Leader of the Labour Party.[37] Starmer espoused his vision for the nation in the tone of a man who hates visions for nations, yet here he was, destined for power: a plywood abomination, making a virtue out of offering absolutely nothing to anybody. The man came across as an auditor of all things. Everything was to be enumerated and balanced in his ledger: hope, enthusiasm, imagination, even his own personality. The sum total of Keir Starmerness available to the public would not exceed the sum of his parts; nor would it fall a microgram short, or your money back.

The fact that – despite all of this being patently obvious to the public – Starmer's party was still 20 points ahead of the Tories tells you all you need to know about how far opinion of the Conservatives had fallen.

Meanwhile the LibDem's had accurately predicted they would be ignored by most media outlets, which had somehow concluded that the party which ended up with 72 MPs was less important than Reform, which ended up with just five. So in an effort to grab headlines, the LibDem leader Sir Ed Davey transformed into a Frank Spencer tribute act. He was filmed deliberately falling off a paddleboard five consecutive times,[38] which you'd imagine would be big news, but it was overshadowed by astonishing discovery that the LibDems had a leader at all. Until that moment, it was generally assumed they just spontaneously erupted, like moss, to fill the tiny gaps between the two main parties.

A Fast Catamaran

Exhaustion was the enemy. Only weeks after a gruelling round of disastrous local election campaigning, the Conservatives' largely elderly volunteers were being asked to do it all again, in the face of certain defeat. Few could be bothered. MPs reported knocking on doors accompanied only by their dogs, because no party members were willing to join in.[39]

And only days into the election campaign, Sunak already seemed to be just going through the motions, by which I mean he was rummaging in shit. I first supposed he'd rolled up his sleeves as a traditional political signal that he was all about getting things done. But it turns out he'd been groping elbow-deep in the Number 10 policy toilet, from which he plucked his latest glistening masterpiece: Sunak would force people to pretend they were soldiers for one day per month,[40] a concept clearly inspired by a Venn diagram combining the fever dreams of Mark Francois with the attendance record of Nadine Dorries.[41]

In Sunak's defence, his Government had brought back slum housing, food shortages, DIY dentistry, acceptable racism, rickets and scurvy,[42] so National Service seemed the logical next step on his path to secure victory in the General Election of 1947. But given that his party's last remaining hope lay in the apathy of younger voters, it was a pretty bold tactic to present 18-year-olds with an urgent reason to race to the polling station.

Unfortunately, Tory policy wonks had been wonkier than usual of late, so Sunak's colleagues had to spend days without slightest idea how National Service might work. Would it be paid? Would it be compulsory? And – with my eternal thanks to *The Telegraph* for asking the most pressing question facing the nation – would 10-year-old Prince George have to do it?[43]

None of the above. It would never happen. The former head of the navy, Admiral Alan West, called the return of National Service 'basically bonkers'. Richard Dannatt, the former chief of general staff, called it 'electoral opportunism. This task cannot just be imposed on the armed forces as an extra thing to do'.[44]

It was then revealed the entire National Service plan had been rejected by one of Sunak's own defence ministers only two days before Sunak announced it.[45] The Conservatives had slashed £10 billion from defence spending, leaving our military without the resources to provide their existing recruits with bullets, so there was no hope of finding any spare cash for this vacuous nonsense.[46]

But suddenly, Sunak had a plan to pay for it all. He would crack down on tax avoidance.[47] It's so obvious now! Cracking down tax avoidance was easy the whole time, and had been easy for the previous 14 years. The Tories just ...

What? Forgot?

They say they're One Nation Conservatives. If so, that nation is The Cayman Islands.

It looked like the policy had been not so much planned and announced, as had its shoelaces tied together before being shoved in a mad tumble onto the steps of Downing Street. After days of being thoroughly banjaxed, Tory MPs began to suggest their own definitions of their brand-new signature policy. Anne-Marie Trevelyan suggested parents would be prosecuted if their adult children didn't join in with the batty thing she'd just dreamed up.[48] *Au contraire*, said James

Cleverly, National Service would be 'mandatory', but there would be 'no criminal sanctions' for anybody who decided not to bother,[49] a move clearly inspired by Nadhim Zahawi's approach to paying tax.[50]

Sunak hoped the National Service wheeze would transform his electoral prospects. It worked: he transformed them from dreadful to terminal. But backing out of the policy would be too politically embarrassing, even for him. His only hope was that something even more calamitous would drive it from the headlines, which was pretty much guaranteed, because he was leader of the Conservative Party. Or what was left of it. Almost one quarter of his MPs were standing down. When Sunak launched his surprise election the Tories lacked 150 candidates. After a week of vigorous campaigning, he had managed to convert that into an even greater shortfall of 191.[51]

Conservative HQ scrabbled desperately to fill the gaps, but new faces turned out to be old faeces, helpings from the smorgasbord of odium and obsolescence that had already contrived to be kicked out of the party. Bob Stewart, suspended for racism but now legally certified as Not At All Racist Actually,[52] was welcomed back,[53] as was Matt Hancock, the dad from a gravy advert, restored to the Tory fold just in time to be publicly humiliated once again.[54]

None of this helped. For every returning disgrace, half a dozen existing Tories stood down, some in with quite lavish displays of contempt. Lucy Allen performed a stunning 5.9 difficulty-level Defection/Suspension combo, after she began campaigning for Reform,[55] which at that stage was something not even Nigel Farage had yet decided to do.[56] For one Conservative, Mark Logan, stepping down wasn't enough: in the middle of the election campaign, he defected to Labour.[57]

But what about Steve Baker, the man who started all of this with his calamitous turn at Lehman Brothers? He hadn't officially announced he was standing down, but he might as well have, since he opted to fly off to Greece rather than battle to lose his seat.[58] When he did return, it was to deliver an interview on the BBC, at the end of which he was asked what he'd do if, as predicted, he lost his job. His extraordinary response was to rap out an Action Man dream he once had after consuming an imperial pound of stilton.

'Skydiving, motorcycling, fast catamaran sailing', he barked at Victoria Derbyshire, in the style of somebody up against the clock on the Generation Game Conveyor Belt round.

'I was talking about work', she replied, 'but that's fine'.[59]

Meanwhile Tory candidate Robert Largan had such confidence in his party that he began producing campaign artwork featuring a bright red background, emblazoned with the words 'Labour for Largan'.[60] He claimed he wasn't attempting to con progressive constituents into accidentally voting for a Conservative, but rather that so many Labour voters had said they were about to back him that he decided to 'form a club' for them. It was soon discovered he'd previously pretended to be a Reform candidate too,[61] and a Green.[62] Derbyshire police weren't happy, and opened yet another incident report about yet another Tory MP.[63]

And then Jacob Rees-Mogg entered the campaign, and my heebies have never been so jeebied. His bid for re-election centred around the most pressing issue facing the nation: the consistency of bananas. The *Daily Mail* granted a blaring headline to the gangly abomination's description of the fruit as 'slimy and unpleasant'.[64]

'You can talk, mate', said a banana. Don't Panic!

Most prime ministers boast of being single minded, but two weeks into the campaign, Rishi Sunak's commitment to efficiency had reduced him to a lot less than that. He decided on a quick exit from a D-Day event in Normandy, managing to compress The Longest Day down to a couple of hours as part of his efforts to streamline everything, including the number of Tory MPs. And I was not alone in doubting his strategy. Penny Mordaunt went so far as to described it as 'wrong', which, as we've already seen, places it in the same category as the type of racist outburst that gets you jettisoned into another party.[65]

The political truism, 'Never apologise, never explain' is often attributed – like most things are – to Churchill, but it was probably coined by an Oxford don named Benjamin Jowett a hundred years earlier. Sunak, being a fine student of political theory, apologised and explained.[66] His excuse was that he had left early because he needed to record an interview with ITN, which wasn't even scheduled to be broadcast until one week later, so it could have been done at any time. To be fair, his apology did seem heartfelt, and it was clear he knew he'd screwed up, largely because his colleagues described his exit from the Normandy beaches as, 'a shitshow, a total disaster'.

However, when selling yourself as a detail-oriented and decisive leader, it's perhaps not ideal that your excuse for beshitting the national bed is that Special Advisors made you do it, but that was the message was from Downing Street: that Sunak was Captain Ill-Mannering being run by Spads Army.[67]

'Stupid boy', said his party.

'Don't panic!', replied Downing Street.

'We're doomed', despaired his MPs.

And so Operation Damage Control leaped once more into action, banged its head on the doorframe, and had to have an immediate lie down. Sunak's media appearances were cancelled, leaving TV news, constrained by election laws that mandate equal airtime for each party, with no alternative but to endlessly repeat promo clips for the ITN interview that had caused the crisis in the first place.[68]

It was Sunak's worst week to date. But then again, can you name a previous week that wasn't? He'd spent his entire premiership wandering listlessly from calamity to catastrophe and back again, like a latter-day Micawber, chanting a mantra that something will turn up. What turned up next was Nigel Farage, with a smile like the brass plate on a coffin lid, reassuring those with the memory of a goldfish that he shared their grievances, having personally caused most of them.

Grievances are Farage's business, and business is good.

Not all the blame can rest on Rishi Sunak, because practically the entire Conservative party had spent the previous ten years acting like a resentment pimp, hustling for discontentment that Nigel Farage could later exploit. Sunak was merely doing what bad leaders do: following the trend. He could – he should – have spent the preceding years denouncing Farage's obsessions, isolating him, and using the alarming data arising from Brexit to demonstrate to the country how harmful a further implementation of Farage's policies would be. Instead, Sunak prioritised his party's right flank over the national good and his own electoral hopes, and spent two years helping to normalise Reform. He had opted run his entire campaign as a Nigel Farage tribute act, so his legs were knocked from under him when – with chilling inevitability – the real thing announced his lucrative comeback World Tour of Clacton.[69]

Farage – a man who would deport his own teeth for not being white enough, and would carve a wind instrument out of his own mother's skull if it provided him with a new way to blow his own trumpet – largely campaigned about immigrants, but a big part of his pitch was the classic move of all populists: that the seat of power is full of elitists; that the government doesn't work for the man on the Clapham Omnibus; and that he alone has the solution.

It's nonsense, of course. He has no solutions. Solutions aren't his thing. What gets his yellow-stained heart going is unrest. It's scheming, plotting, madness and destruction. Not governing. Governing is boring. It requires diligence, compromise and responsibility. It demands a leader to operate within the constraints of realpolitik, and to both predict and accept consequences. And where's the fun in that? The last time Farage had any political responsibility was as a member of the EU Fisheries Commission, when, during three years, he attended only 1 of its 42 meetings.[70] Unsurprisingly, in the three months after winning Clacton, he didn't hold a single constituency surgery, claiming – falsely – that he'd been given official advice not to do so.[71] He did, however, find time to hold down nine simultaneous second jobs,[72] admitting his side-hustles earned him more than £1 million in his first year working as an MP.[73]

It's hard to see how Farage could possibly be prioritising his responsibilities as an MP over the interests of the gold bullion company that paid him twice as much to be their brand ambassador.[74] But then again, responsibility, as a concept, seems to have eluded Nigel Farage entirely. It was much better to lead a merry and interminable dance of people who are unburdened by facts and don't care about consequences. As Hannah Arendt said, 'The ideal subject of totalitarian rule is not the convinced Nazi or the convinced Communist, but people for whom the distinction between fact and fiction (i.e., the reality of experience) and the distinction between true and false (i.e., the standards of thought) no longer exist'. Such people fell for Farage's trick, and it was very lucrative, so there was no reason for him to stop. Just keep the wheel turning. And when it all fails, blame somebody else, do a rebrand, and start again. Rinse and repeat, whitewashing racism into patriotism while the country goes down the plughole. Immigrants came to Britain because they aspired to better themselves. Nigel Farage just wanted to worsen everyone else.

He'd spent months sitting out election fever, but now decided he would go head-to-head with the Conservatives over the trophy for Most Batshit Vision of Britain. In Sunak's topsy-turvy UK, poor people were skint because we'd given them all the money, while those who were drowning in riches remained too poor to pay tax. In Farage's arsy-versy Britain, foreigners had ruined the country so much that everybody wanted to come and live here, and we no longer needed a state: the bulldog spirit would protect us from the tyranny of spivs. The only fly in Nigel's ointment was the sheer number of conspiracy-theorists, wackadoos, and actual living breathing Nazis on his team.

So let's do a quick tour of the beliefs of Reform candidates:[75]

There were members of the British National Party. A candidate with the world's worst grasp of Middle Eastern politics, who claimed Jews were conspiring with 'third-world Muslims', and that the British Government was 'injecting' the country with African men. Reform ran a man who called women the 'sponging gender' and proposed denying them healthcare. One who wished for anybody who disagreed with him on immigration to be 'robbed, beaten or attacked'.[76]

Multiple Hitler fans, of course, such as the one who said it would have been 'far better' for Britain to not oppose the Nazis, and another who called Hitler 'brilliant' at 'inspiring people into action'. Candidates who claimed the 'black people of Britain' were 'savages'. Candidates who used homophobic slurs, and who openly called for the murder of Nicola Sturgeon.

There were candidates who thought canned foods turned people transgender. Candidates who thought the 9/11 was an 'inside job'. Candidates who thought King Charles was under direct control of the World Economic Forum. Candidates who thought the pandemic was the work of the pharmaceutical industry. Candidates who thought – deep breath – that the CIA manufactured special televisions that put people to sleep so they would not become alert to the subjects of other mad conspiracy theories.

Reform had candidates serving sentences for kicking dogs, and if that's not bad enough, candidates – James McMurdock, who actually got elected – who had been jailed for repeatedly kicking his girlfriend.[77] Candidates who performed psychic tarot readings for £200 a go on porn website OnlyFans. Candidates who thought the Royal National Lifeboat Institute was a 'taxi service for illegal immigrants'. And, needless to say, plenty of candidates who thought climate change was a hoax.

Please Sir, I Want Some More TV Channels

Like each of his Conservative predecessors, Sunak had spent almost his entire premiership attempting to harmonise with the mood music sung by Reform. Fortunately, Team Rishi had learned from their predecessors' mistakes, and used that knowledge as a springboard into even more impressive mistakes.

Fresh from the Normandy debacle, Sunak decided to relaunch his election campaign with a whistle-stop tour of Britain, which began with him leading his sinking ship to Belfast's Titanic Quarter,[78] but only after the party had sent journalists to the wrong location.

Twice.[79]

And then straight to the launch of his car crash prospectus at Silverstone, where the wheels *really* came off.[80] In country left so unequal and bereft that one third of British kids were living in poverty,[81] and 2.7 million children couldn't afford food every day,[82] the word 'poverty' only appeared once in the responsible party's new programme for government, and that was in reference to people living in developing nations.[83] Was this a manifesto? It didn't seem like one. It seemed the political equivalent of one of those experimental freak-out albums from 1972, which had been written in less than two hours on a hurdy-gurdy, by somebody who didn't play that particular instrument, and was then performed with grim, militaristic gusto by an amateur school band.

The Institute of Fiscal Studies immediately said Conservative plans were unlikely to work,[84] and confirmed they'd left a £22 billion 'black hole' in the nation's finance that was 'obvious to anyone who dared to look'.[85] It felt like the Tories couldn't deliver their famed oven-ready Brexit deal, because everybody in the kitchen was too busy cooking the books. But the truth will out. Where Sunak had once offered 'long-term decisions for a brighter future',[86] he was now reduced to turning off the bright future for budgetary reasons. The enshittification of Britain had reached the stage where Jeremy Hunt sent a tweet celebrating tap water in Bramley being drinkable.[87]

Tap water. How very decadent.

Tories being Tories, the manifesto did promise £17 billion in tax cuts.[88] But unlike previous elections, this time the promise of tax cuts didn't produce a feelgood factor in voters. We all knew what they meant: more damage to the crumbling services that we relied upon to make our lives bearable. Tax cuts only affect you if you pay tax, but almost one in five British workers don't earn enough to reach the threshold. Those workers are disproportionately likely to rely on the public services affected by cuts, so perfectly naturally, they saw tax cuts as something that helped the rich, at the expense of the poor.[89]

For the rest of us, tax cuts today simply meant twice as much painful austerity tomorrow, and it was increasingly obvious that Tory tax reductions were bribes made with our own money that they'd stolen from the future.

Yet even this madness didn't go far enough for the Braverman clique, who immediately announced they had another manifesto ready to go, designed to borrow the clothes of Nigel Farage once again.[90]

*

Conservative chair Richard Holden was not having a great time of it. Holden – who had the look of a German pen pal who forgot to stop writing – was the MP for North West Durham, a seat that at the election of 2024 was abolished due to boundary changes. Fortunately the neighbouring seat, Bishop Auckland, was about to become available: Dehenna Davison was one of the 75 Conservatives who had opted to stand down.[91]

'I am bloody loyal to the North East', Holden reassured his constituents, and then moved 260 miles away to the significantly safer Conservative stronghold of Basildon and Billericay.[92]

'I'm quite appalled by his scrabbling for a safe seat', responded a Tory cabinet minister, 'he is a man without substance'.

'It is an astonishing lack of political and human judgement', said Holden's predecessor as party chair, and the leader of the Basildon Conservative Group described Holden's relocation as 'morally bankrupt ... epitomising the worst in public office, lacking integrity and honesty'.[93]

Competence too, with Holden seemingly unable to remember the name of the second place he'd been bloody loyal to in a week. His campaign leaflets didn't end up in Basildon and Billericay, but in Rayleigh and Wickford, where they were pointlessly distributed to the wrong voters, making this one of the Conservative's more successful ground campaigns.[94]

For anybody else, this would be the final straw, but Sunak operated in a blizzard of straws, and one more made no difference. The Holden debacle was barely out of the headlines before candidate Adam Gregg had to stand down in a hurry. He was reported to have been running a 'club night' for kids as young as 13, where they wore clothes bearing the words 'horny' and 'bitch'. Gregg, who at this point seemed to be working for the prosecution, had taken photographs of his club nights, and posted them on social media.[95]

I Bet I Can Make Things Worse

Desperate to win back voters attracted to this sort of farce, Sunak announced the roaring return of big beast Boris Johnson, reassuring panicking Conservatives that Shit Aslan would 'make a difference' to their fortunes.[96]

He didn't, because Johnson opted to go holiday instead.[97]

But first, he tweeted a supportive video that appeared to have been filmed inside somebody's bedroom closet, perhaps while avoiding the latest in a long line of angry husbands.[98] Throughout his life in the public eye, Johnson had often seemed sozzled, soused, steamed, stewed, toasted, fried, baked and bombed, but judging from his ruddy appearance, it looked like somebody had finally gone the whole hog, and boiled him.

As the Conservative's star player abandoned the field, former ministers Chris Skidmore[99] and Zak Goldsmith[100] publicly backed Labour, while most of the recent cabinet had seemingly wandered off the campaign trail in a lysergic haze, and the Conservative digital campaign was suspended.[101] It was two weeks until the election, and party already seemed to be getting slowly disassembled. You half expected them to start singing *Daisy, Daisy* at an ever-decreasing speed and pitch.

Even the *Sunday Sport* began calling out Tory lies. When Sir Bill Cash urged voters to 'remember how good they've had it under the Conservatives',[102] the comedy tabloid, which once boasted of finding Hitler living on the moon, decided it couldn't cope with this level of fantasy, and tweeted, 'When you've smashed clean through "gaslighting" and are now balls-deep in "taking the fucking piss".[103]

Things couldn't get any worse for Sunak. And then, suddenly, things did.

During a televised interview back in February, Rishi Sunak had placed a bet that deportation flights to Rwanda would take off before a general election. So now, to add to his troubles, he had to pay £1,000 to Piers Morgan. Fortunately, help was on hand: Sunak's closest aide placed a £100 bet on the date of the election 3 days before it was announced. And whadayaknow, it paid off!

History repeats itself, first as tragedy, and then as comedy, but in this election the Conservatives seemed determined to collapse history into a single tragicomic instant. After 14 years of a Government obsessed with gambling the country's future for personal gain, his aides had managed to pack exactly the same thing into a couple of hours on 22 May.[104] It was the final nail in a coffin that already looked like a vast, rectangular, metal hedgehog.

Sunak admitted to being 'incredibly angry' at the news, and he was right: nothing about his anger seemed credible. He didn't even manage to look mildly peeved. Over the coming days, more and more insiders were found to have placed bets, including the Scottish secretary,[105] who Sunak punished by putting him on a shortlist of those considered for a post-election peerage.[106] Another of those placing bets had admitted doing so two weeks before the news broke, but Sunak had taken no action.[107]

'Vote for me', he seemed to be saying, 'If you want nothing done, I'm the best man for the job'.

The media, scenting blood, began sniffing out the source of the gamblers' insider scoop.[108] Could this be a clue: that everybody close to Rishi Sunak somehow knew exactly what was happening – except for Rishi, of course, who when asked about those gambling wins launched into his best Manuel impression: I know nothing! [109]

That reference is one in the eye for Nigel Farage, who said Sunak didn't understand our culture.[110]

Sunak insisted he'd dearly love to help get to the bottom of today's bewildering and preposterous scandal, but sadly (he claimed) answering any questions whatsoever might prejudice inquiries.[111] The absence of a legal – or even logical – basis for this excuse wasn't important, because Sunak had chosen the hill he wanted to die on, and that hill, it seemed, was William Hill.

Philip Davies, meanwhile, had placed an £8,000 bet that he'd lose his seat. When confronted about this, he increased the chances of a windfall by replying, 'What's it got to do with you whether I did or didn't. It's nobody's business'.[112]

Few could confuse Davies with a man who knows what's going on – after all, this is a Conservative who voted against his own party's policies more than 250 times[113] – but many of those involved in the gambling scandal had very direct access to privileged information. The Conservative Director of Campaigns ended up spending the rest of the election on a 'leave of absence' because his wife – a Tory candidate – stood accused of whatever you call the BetFred equivalent of insider trading.[114]

The nation was merely shocked to discover that this campaign had been directed at all.

It wasn't even being financed any more. The Conservatives had reportedly run out of cash,[115] and presumably run out of racist donors,[116] so they decided to abandon their original plan of shoring up Red Wall seats, and focus instead on the Tory heartlands. It would be wrong to say they've given up fighting for marginal constituencies, it was just that a 20,000 Conservative majority now qualified as marginal.[117]

It was against this background that Sunak submitted himself to a *Question Time Special*, where he bobbed excitedly on the spot while presenting unsuspecting voters with a misery-packed extravaganza. He waved his arms around as though his puppeteer was having an argument in Italian, and grinningly presented to the nation whatever had emerged from that morning's wild stab at the Policy Dartboard.

'We will boost the economy by sacking experienced staff and forcing intransigent and inexperienced kids to do it for free', said Sunak.[118]

'How will that make the economy grow?', asked the audience.

'Buggered if I know', said Sunak.

'Isn't forcing people to work for nothing a bit ... slavey?'

'Doesn't matter', said Sunak, 'We will ignore foreign courts.'

'The European Court of Human Rights isn't a foreign court. Britain helped set it up.'[119]

'That's OK', said Sunak, 'We've ignored British courts too.'[120]

As the credit rolled, members of the audience shouted, 'Shame on you!' and Sunak dashed off to look up that unfamiliar term.[121]

Brightness Is Relative

The Independent Parliamentary Standards Authority sets the rules under which campaign finance operates, one of which is that public funding cannot be used for party political purposes. The print costs of Labour's do-nothing manifesto had to be paid from Labour's own coffers. LibDems had to find their own 'falling off a paddleboard' budget. And Tories couldn't spend taxpayer's money on Conservative Party websites. Them's the rules.

Or so you'd think, but somehow – and here it's hard to avoid deploying the term 'fish gotta swim' – over 120 Conservative MPs had given more than £100,000 of taxpayers' money to the party's in-house design team, Bluetree. Conservative Campaign Headquarters insisted Bluetree was an entirely independent company, but its address is the same as CCHQ, and the company describes itself as the 'Conservative party UK official website platform', which is run 'inside the party'.[122] And – in case that's not enough – the company's name is a literal description of the Conservative Party logo.

Among the senior figures having their personal campaign websites funded by the taxpayer was Jeremy Hunt, a Chancellor who by this point could have been replaced by a photo of a dachshund chewing a pocket calculator. Having coughed up £32,000 of his own money to the campaign to keep him in an incredibly safe seat,[123] he tweeted: 'Marriage safe...got the wife's vote', with a photo showing Mrs Hunt's postal voting slip. Revealing anybody's vote is a criminal offence.[124] Jeremy Hunt was considered one of the bright ones. Mind you, he once forgot his wife's nationality, so 'bright' is a relative term.[125]

But I'm confident he was brighter than health minister Nick Markham, who – 'birds gotta fly' – stood accused of corruption when it was revealed he'd overridden the objections of officials, and appointed one of his friends and associates on a £1,500-per-day contract as an advisor to the project to build 40 new hospitals, which the Conservatives were never going to deliver.[126] Perhaps Markham thought it would be easier to build 40 hospitals with the budget for 6^{127} if he handed £137,000 of that budget to a chartered occupational psychologist, without going through any competitive tendering process.[128]

'If one of my teammates got caught for cheating they'd be dead to me. That abuse of trust is unforgivable', said James Cracknell, the former Olympian who was standing as a Conservative candidate, yet still called the Tory party 'a shower of shit' in a video posted on Facebook.[129]

At least Cracknell was making public statements. Half the cabinet seemed to have simply vanished, with even soaringly bananas in-house Tory glorification pamphlet *The Spectator* bemoaning the fact 'one of the few ministers who have been prepared to go out and about for the Tories during this campaign' was somebody nobody knew existed.[130] In a government that still had 372 MPs, 25 per cent of all Tory TV and radio interviews were undertaken by Mel Stride, a man who's only notable achievement was undertaking 25 per cent of all TV and radio interviews.[131]

Neither Bim Afolami[132] nor Greg Hands[133] made any mention of the Conservatives on their election leaflets, not even in the small print. Laura Trott, the Chief Secretary to the Treasury, had failed to turn up to so many hustings that in the end the organisers replaced her with a toy squirrel.[134] Based on Trott's previous outings, during which she had proven herself incapable of understanding that high numbers are higher than low numbers, it's a safe bet the squirrel performed better.[135]

The Nazis are Coming

We were into the final week, but Sunak still ploughed on, battling manfully to remain upright with a whole rivière of albatrosses around his neck.

For his colleagues, it was time to begin manoeuvres. Websites were registered in the names of future leadership bids by Suella Braverman and Kemi Badenoch, while Steve Baker announced he would stand for leadership in the unlikely event his catamaran plans fell through. Bad news for Priti Patel, though: the former home secretary turned out to be the least popular potential successor in a poll of Tory members, although being involved in activities that are massively unpopular hadn't held her back in the past.[136] But this time the hurdle she had to overcome was one of size: her own. One of her political allies described her 'presence problem' – no, not that her very presence made voters wonder where the other three horsemen of the apocalypse were, but rather that she couldn't speak in public because, 'you can't see her over the crowd'.[137]

Patel, however, insisted 'short politicians make the best leaders', a not-historically supported claim that appears to have triggered a Conservative student association to wait until somebody was filming their black-tie dinner, and then begin singing songs in praise of Adolf Hitler.[138]

It spoke deeply about the Conservative party's direction of travel. They'd spent years rummaging in the Nigel Farage dressing-up box, desperately looking for cheap theatrics that might broaden their appeal, and something akin to Stockholm syndrome had set in. The line between Conservatives and Reform had blurred to nothing, with both parties spinning the concept of returning Britain to some mythical, wonderful past.

Any such concept is inherently sexist and racist. Because at what point in the past was Britain brilliant for women? Was it great for them before the feminist revolution in the 1970s? Or perhaps in the 1990s, when women were paid 30 per cent less than men?[139]

Was Britain brilliant for LGBTQ+ people, when their sexuality was illegal in the 1950s? Or when they died in stigmatised droves, enduring state-sanctioned homophobia during the 1980s?[140]

Was Britain brilliant for minorities when the BNP raged throughout the 1990s? Or during the casual televised hatred of the 1970s, the race riots of 1958, or Cable Street in 1936, or Liverpool in 1919? Or ever, actually?

No, it wasn't. Life for all of those groups is better now than in the past. So behind the vacuous thesis of a nation that was once great, but is no longer, lies the implication that it was great at a time when all the power belonged with straight, white men. And that therefore our problems emerged alongside greater rights and power for anybody else: women, queer people, those with disabilities, and racial minorities. Coincidence becomes causation. So when the likes of Lee Anderson, Nigel Farage, or – in increasing numbers – Conservatives on the Badenoch wing – said 'I want my country back', it implicitly reeked of racism, homophobia and misogyny. They may have denied those labels, but that is the undeniable logic of the words they spoke.

*

On 27 June, with scarcely a week until election day, an entirely predictable disaster struck the Reform party. Channel 4 News had broadcast undercover footage of a canvasser for Nigel Farage's Clacton bid, referring to Sunak as 'that fucking paki'. The language was shocking. The attitudes behind it, worse: George Jones, the Reform activist in question, said Reform would begin by 'fucking kicking all the Muslims out of the mosques and turning them into Wetherspoons', and suggested carrying out 'target practice' on migrants.[141]

Farage said the incident left him 'dismayed', but it didn't take long before another response emerged, one entirely bound in conspiracy theorising and denialist bullshit.[142] Reform Chairman Richard Tice said, 'It is quite clear Channel 4 News has used an actor, who is using his acting voice to lie about something', and called the report, 'potentially the greatest scandal in broadcast journalism'.[143] Farage had recovered from his initial dismay, and joined in: 'I have to tell you, this whole thing is a complete and total setup. Of that I have no doubt whatsoever'.[144]

Sunak was outraged. 'When my two daughters have to see and hear Reform people who campaign for Nigel Farage calling me an effing paki, it hurts and it makes me angry, and I think he has some questions to answer. And I don't repeat those words lightly. I do so deliberately, because this is too important not to call out clearly for what it is.'[145]

It had been quite a climb to that moral high ground. It was 106 days since Rishi Sunak had said the public should accept Frank Hester's apology for his racist remarks about Diane Abbott,[146] and kept the £15 million.[147] And 119 days since Sunak had refused to label Lee Anderson's remarks Islamophobic.[148]

The consequences of the Tory strategy of kowtowing to racism had bitten Sunak on the arse.

Even Reform insiders knew what their party was like. Georgie David, a Reform candidate, defected to the Tories, saying 'the vast majority of [Reform] candidates are indeed racist, misogynistic, and bigoted'.[149]

Nigel Farage was, for once, on the back foot, as the media and public pressed him hard on the attitudes that defined his party. On a *Question Time* election special, he tried to persuade a hostile and disbelieving audience, 'I've done more to drive the far right out of British politics than anybody else alive. I took on the BNP just over a decade ago'.[150]

It reminds me of that time Snickers took on Marathons. The audience laughter prompted Farage to go Full Trump, and he boycotted BBC political programmes pending an apology for 'their dishonest QT audience'.[151] He was still observing the boycott of the BBC that he'd begun during an earlier mardy strop in 2019, so why he was on *Question Time* in the first place is something Nigel will have to take up with himself.[152]

The Conservatives Deserve to Lose Every Seat

When Theresa May's premiership was falling very visibly to pieces during that legendary conference speech, her party said they 'felt sorry for her'.[153] Nobody had the heart to stick the knife in. She was saved on humanitarian grounds.

No such spirit would rescue Sunak. The nation viewed him with weary contempt. So did much of his party, with a senior figure accusing him of presiding over 'the worst campaign of my lifetime'.[154] Rishi Sunak's career was coming to an end, and here I'm using the definition of career that means going downhill fast, and without control.

In desperation – or perhaps concluding he had nothing more to lose – the PM decided to appear on *This Morning*, where he was forced to wait, perched on a small chair in the background, until Cat Deeley had finished interviewing Britain's most tattooed mum.[155] The optics were terrible, and by optics, I mean those small wet things that hang on the back-bar. When the PM finally got to speak, it was excruciating, as he struggled to answer the question, 'what is your favourite meal'?

'I am a big sandwich person', he eventually explained. Perhaps when his successor, Kemi Badenoch, later revealed to the country that she didn't think sandwiches are real, she was just trying to distance herself from Sunak's audacious culinary experimentation.[156]

Nearly half the public – including a quarter of those who voted for them in 2019 – now agreed with the proposition, 'the Conservatives deserve to lose every seat'.[157] Such was the sense of inevitability that Conservative Right, yet another insignificant groupuscule, announced they were already planning a post-election post-mortem: a dangerous proposal, since in their weakened state a post-mortem could kill them.[158]

A far more personal blame-game was underway, led by Nadine Dorries, who was by now wandering around with the confused look you see on the face of a red setter when you pretend to throw a stick for it, but there is no stick. She placed responsibility for – well, literally everything – at feet of Michael Gove on the grounds that he been in the cabinet for longest.[159]

Finally, something on which Nadine and I can agree: the less time Conservatives spend in office, the better.

In Memoriam

Long story short: the Tories were trounced. The Conservatives, who had 372 MPs in 2019, finished the 2024 General Election with only 121. It was the lowest number of Tory MPs in the party's history, and the largest ever drop in MPs between two national elections – at least until the next one.[160] Because, while Labour would form the incoming Government, it had a mandate that was a mile wide and an inch deep. Keir Starmer's 412 MPs disguised the party only increasing its vote share by 2 points.[161]

Over the course of three books,[162] I've tried to quantify and explain the myriad disasters conceived, composed, and conducted by the Conservative Government that began in 2010, but if you want the short version, it's this: they were selfish, cruel and incompetent, they were slaves to narrow ideological obsessions, and they made us all feel poorer.

The politically independent Resolution Foundation – led by former Tory MP David Willetts – reported Britain's per capita economic growth had been just 4.3 per cent during the 14 years of Conservatives tenure, compared to 46 per cent during the preceding 14 years.[163] Any growth the Tories had managed to achieve had been almost entirely driven by the very immigration that they were desperate to end. It had been diabolical, monomaniacal, occasionally homicidal regime that pushed those at top towards fat, coddled luxury, those at the bottom towards a spiral of frozen starvation, and all of us – rich and poor alike – into a seemingly unacknowledged descent towards a global frying pan.

Perhaps it was this that made the election seem such a deflating experience for progressives. Yes, Labour, if in name only, had power for the first time in 14 years, and the LibDems had gained a huge number of seats. But there was no enthusiasm for Starmer, and the entire nation knew Labour faced, as Bloomberg labelled it, 'the worst economic and fiscal inheritance for any government since the war'.[164]

Where Tony Blair had walked from the Palace to Downing Street through cheering crowds, Starmer faced a country filled with tepid caution and distrust: divided, diminished, and disheartened by the task ahead.

Of course, the Tories simply walked away, except for vainglorious wazzock Steve Baker, who took a fast catamaran. Liz Truss became the first former PM to lose their seat since 1935, and true to form, blamed everybody but herself.[165] Her chief enablers both left Parliament: Simon Clarke lost his seat, while Kwasi Kwarteng had decided not to even try to save his.

We had to wave goodbye to so much talent: Jack Brereton, who couldn't spell his own name.[166] Steven Crabb, who had texted a 19-year-old woman he'd just interviewed for a job and told her he wanted to have sex with her.[167] Michelle Donelan, who had held on to the job of education secretary for an impressive 35 hours.[168] Andrea Jenkyns, who gave herself whiplash while sat at a desk.[169] Gavin Williamson, a prattling, lifetime collection of blunders lent physical form and fitted with the teeth of a starved horse. All of them gone.

So was Richard Grosvenor Plunkett-Ernle-Erle-Drax, who would have to continue his fight against poor migrants in between days counting his money in the vast mansion his ancestors paid for via the deaths of 30,000 slaves.[170] The nation would have to stagger on without the company of Nigel Evans, who once voted to cut legal aid, and then said it was 'wrong, completely wrong, to remove people's right to have expert legal representation' when he discovered those cuts meant no legal aid for himself.[171]

We lost Michael Fabricant, famed for his signature look of an Oompa Loompa losing a fight with a kitchen mop. Jonathan Gullis, meanwhile, had always been a divisive figure, not least because he was so heroically stupid it was like he'd been bitten by a radioactive idiot. But now he was set free on the job market, where he remained well into 2025, interspersing his empty days by complaining to the press that nobody would employ him.[172]

We were robbed of the ethics of Daniel Kawczynski, the guy who claimed £22,000 in expenses for learning Polish, which he already spoke because it's his native language,[173] and then admitted urging a young researcher to go on a date with a wealthy businessman 'older than her father', which the woman described as 'sleazy in the extreme'.[174]

Fare thee well Johnny Mercer, the Poundland Richard Hammond who entered the election oozing the confidence of a man who hadn't yet realised nobody likes things that ooze. Damian Green was finally free to spend his days bathing in shit again. We lost Brendan Clark-Smith, the 2019-intake Red Wall Tory who was the first person in his family to go to university, or to have opposable thumbs.[175] John Redwood left Parliament in a hurry, perhaps because the mothership was due to collect him any moment now. They were all ousted by ungrateful voters who failed to recognise their charms.

Suella Braverman managed to hang on to her seat, but quickly gave up any hope of leading the party, or of being much of an MP, instead dedicating her time to hosting her own show on LBC,[176] where, with her legendary passion for rigorous accuracy, she informed listeners that she had personally visited the anti-migrant wall Italy had built along its land border with Turkey.[177] There are three countries and a couple of seas between Italy and Turkey.

But for eerie old Jacob Rees-Mogg, the worst part wasn't losing his seat. It was that by the time the result came in, it was dawn, which meant it wasn't safe for him to leave the count and return to his crypt until the sun went down again.

Choosing A New Leader

Remakes are the curse of our cautious, superficial age. If feels as though everything new is really just a slightly depressing, warmed-over rehash of something old. The big musical news of 2024 was a reboot of Oasis, themselves a Slade tribute act played at 33 rpm, who only stopped making albums when they ran out of Beatles songs to steal.[178] 2024 also saw *The Office* squeezed out into recoiling Australian living rooms in its third shiteration[179]. The biggest blockbuster success was *Gladiator II*, a beat-by-beat remake of an original that was itself little more than a scriptless, zhuzhed-up reworking of *Spartacus* set in a plastic Colosseum.[180]

In fact, 8 of year's 10 highest-grossing films were remakes, reboots or sequels.[181] But you have to admire the balls, if not the wisdom, of anybody brave enough to touch one of Britain's greatest cultural highlights: *Yes Minister*. And yet that's what happened next. The spin on things this time was that it was no longer a studio-set sitcom with a live audience, a witty and wise script, and effortlessly brilliant performers. Instead, the Tories opted to remake it as reality TV, with the plum role of Jim Hacker – an over-promoted, delusional, publicity-seeking bungler at eternal war with the civil service – recast as a woman. Kemi Badenoch exuded bombastic, vaudevillian swagger in the lead role of 'Kem Hacker'.

Actors often imagine an entire backstory for their characters, or learn the necessary skills to fully embody them on stage and screen. Jenna Ortega learned the cello for her remake of an Addams Family character.[182] Jennifer Lawrence learned how to skin a squirrel.[183] For some reason, Kate Winslett learned to hold her breath for seven minutes to appear an entirely CGI movie.[184] But Badenoch went one further. In her quest fully embody Kem Hacker, she decided to commit the actual criminal offence of computer hacking.[185] And, judging entirely from her warm and engaging performance, she seems to have imagined her character's backstory was working as an orthodontist on the Death Star.

So let's recap the story so far.

A long time ago, in whatever-the-fuck galaxy the Conservatives lived in, an Unmagnificent Seven started their journey. Suella Braverman, who had spent three solid years positioning herself for the leadership race, didn't even make it to the start line. In a bold tactical move, she described herself as 'mad, bad and dangerous', and everybody agreed so hard that they bent time itself.[186] All those years spent seeding division and hatred in service of her career, and then Heinrich Hamster decided not to stand.

The first actual candidate to be knocked out of the leadership race was proto-Braverman Priti Patel, who managed to gain the support of only fourteen people on a planet with 8 billion of us.[187]

Then we lost Mel Stride, who you have already forgotten exists, even if you are Mel Stride or one of his immediate relatives. After Stride, we struck up the last post for Tom Tugendhat, the Conservatives' alleged moderating influence, who might as well have been a hologram for all the good he did.

And then there were three: Ozempic root-vegetable Robert Jenrick, Kem Hacker, and James Cleverly.[188]

Cleverly never seemed to be running for the leadership; he seemed to be running a one-man campaign to disprove nominative determinism. It was stunningly successful. For example, when he found himself 18 points ahead of his rivals to succeed Sunak,[189] his supporters decided to lend their votes to the opponent he feared the least, so he could prove his mettle by very slightly defeating his most mediocre adversary.[190] His backers lent their votes so effectively that Badenoch accidentally ended up with more votes than Cleverly. Jim But Dim was out of the race, and the eventual winner only ended up in the final two because so many of her colleagues thought she was terrible.

Fair play, it's a comedy masterpiece.

The final two, Semi GoodEnough and Enoch Towel, faced selection by Tory members, while the remaining rump of recognisably centre-right Conservative MPs – James Cleverly, Jeremy Hunt and former deputy PM Oliver Dowden – utterly refused to serve in a shadow-cabinet led by either of them.[191] Riding the wave from this overwhelming vote of confidence, Kemi Badenoch became leader of the His Majesty's Official Opposition, having secured the backing of

53,806 Conservative Party members,[192] which was less than a third of them.[193]

Her supporters were outnumbered two-to-one by 'I Can't Be Bothered To Vote'. And sticking rigidly to form, the party membership had chosen the candidate who was the least popular with ordinary voters.[194]

Within a year plots had openly broken out to remove her from post.[195] Former Tory ministers who had openly backed Liz Truss and Boris Johnson penned columns despairing that as a result of the personalities and policies they had actively promoted and pursued, the party was now unable to justify its existence, and either 'fighting for its life', or already 'completely dead'.[196] Polling by the BBC found they'd win just 15 per cent of the vote if an election were held in May 2025, pushing them into fourth place behind Labour, Reform and the Liberal Democrats.[197] You could, of course, just check you know the correct way to spell 'schadenfreude' or say *Beware the Badenoch, My Son*. It would be a justifiable response, given that the calamities experienced by the Conservative Party were largely self-inflicted, and either entirely predictable (in the case of their idiotic policies) or beyond the realm of imagination (in the case of their personal behaviour). But any laughter must surely turn to ash on your lips as you contemplated that the main beneficiary of their collapse was even worse: Nigel Farage.

Repeating the Error

In 2011, I lived in a tiny apartment in central Manchester, from where I watched as riots reached the streets of my beloved hometown.[1] There was nothing I could do to stop the destruction, but the following morning I woke early, headed down to Piccadilly Gardens, and joined hundreds of volunteers as we cleaned up the mess.[2] We had to. This was our home. We loved it.

That sense of pride in our communities belongs to neither the left nor the right. It need not be nationalistic or isolationist, it is not defined by class or wealth, and it doesn't reside solely amongst those with an abundance of flags or deep roots in our country's soil. Civic pride helps to explain why the Conservatives lost the election. Yes, there was the economic self-harm, the corruption, the sexual depravity, the drugs, the ineptitude, the colossal self-absorption, hubris, and casual malice. But the key to their loss was that Tories had spent years on the wrong side of the national mood. By 2024, everywhere you looked you could see a shattered population desperate to rebuild. By contrast, all Sunak and his gang of vandals could offer was yet more pastiche Thatcherism, shorn of any intellectual depth, shrieking blame at everybody not in power, and revelling in the fetishised cruelty at the heart of their brand of Conservatism.

You'd think such a vast rejection of this ethos would feel like a moment for joy. Worryingly, it didn't. Keir Starmer's soaringly drab pitch to the country was that things would not get better; they would just get worse at a slightly slower rate. And, although a dreadful economic inheritance explains many of Labour's budgetary decisions, the Starmer project, bereft of imagination, seems committed to round upon round of self-defeating austerity, thus repeating the error.[3] Many clung to the hope that Labour was managing expectations throughout the build-up to the election, planning to wildly exceed them later. I was amongst them. I worry I had been fooling myself.

Because despite Labour's win, the UK still seethed. Living standards collapsed between 2010 and 2021, while the wealth of the richest 1 per cent of Britons – some of the wealthiest people to have ever lived – increased 31 times more than it did for the other 67 million of us.[4] But let's leave aside those poor mites who have to scrape by on only ten, twenty or maybe fifty million quid, and focus on a yet-higher strata of the viscerally greedy: Britain's 177 billionaires. In a just world, billionaires wouldn't exist at all. They don't need to. It is only through a grotesque failure of economics, politics, and monopolies regulations that such a thing as a billionaire has come to pass. It's a complete failure of capitalism that it is now impossible for a genuine alternative to Amazon to appear. No company should be allowed to dominate a market enough to generate that much wealth for its owners. Nobody needs that much money. You couldn't spend it if you tried. The interest on £1 billion would be around £20 million a year.

But billionaires do exist, so we might as well try to find a use for them.

Let's imagine we introduced a wealth tax on one third of their wealth. Why not? They're never going to spend it. And one third of the wealth of Britain's billionaires would be enough to fund the entire cost of building a million new homes, insulating every other home in the country, re-nationalising the entire water industry, repairing 90 per cent of Britain's schools, and completing the repairs backlog of every single NHS building.[5] It sounds expensive, but by the time we'd finished, even the poorest of those poor, over-taxed billionaires would be left scraping by on £666 million.

Yet via donations, lobbying and open manipulation of our information environment, those billionaires endlessly seek more riches for themselves. And the Tories have been happy to oblige. The wealth of Britain's billionaires almost tripled between 2010 and 2022.[6] Over the same period, the number of kids from working households who grow up in poverty increased by 44 per cent.[7]

Poverty in Britain exists not because we don't have enough money to satisfy the needs of the poor, but because we don't have enough money to satisfy the greed of the rich.

And we can feel it, in our bones. Our natural sense of community has been shattered not by immigration, but by inequality, corruption, and austerity draining the life out of vital local services.[8] Anti-migrant sentiment is merely deferred pain from the underlying socioeconomic cancer that has been metastasising since the days of Thatcherism. Our hometowns fell into neglectful ruin without any help from a handful of Sudanese guys working in your local car wash, or indeed from an abandoned generation of youngsters turning to riot. Our former civic pride has become displaced into raging nationalism, as many voters cast their lot with Nigel Farage, a bleached Grinch who somehow attracted their votes despite honking a denunciation of everything his voters wanted back: fairer distribution of the nation's wealth;[9] a truly nationalised NHS;[10] a state that delivers for the people;[11] and greater equality of opportunity.[12]

I can't blame those voters. They've been abandoned by a Conservative party in permanent hock to corporatism, and when they turned to the Labour party, they found it was much the same. The LibDems still carry the reek of the coalition years, which doesn't seem especially attractive if your key requirement from politics is that things must change. And the Green Party may have original ideas, but it hasn't gained the momentum necessary to sweep to power, so the electorate largely feels a vote for the Greens would be wasted.

There is nowhere else to turn, and the glue of party loyalty has been replaced by consumer politics. Voters shop for parties and drop them if they fail to satisfy. The Tories stopped satisfying. Starmer's Labour never even began. So, in desperation – and yes, sometimes with glee, but I sense more often in despair – voters throw their lot in with the irresponsible xenophobia of Reform.

Much of this is to do with a perception that traditional politicians lack authenticity. It was, after all, clear well before the election of 2024 that Keir Starmer believed in almost nothing, and millions only voted for Labour because they seemed the best hope of finally getting rid of the Tories. It wasn't a mandate, it was an exercise in expediency. In doing so, Britan replaced a party with terrible ideas with one led by a man who boasted of having no ideas whatsoever. Keir Starmer promised that he would 'get things done' while openly admitting he didn't even know what those things would be.[13] Let's face it: it's hard to believe in a politician who candidly reveals that he doesn't even believe in himself.

Whereas Nigel Farage – the next liar to persuade a desperate populace that they could trust him – appeared to believe every word that spilled from his mouth. And in modern politics, where vibe matters more than policy, such authenticity is vital. Whatever Farage said, it was clear he meant it. And his adherents would tell you until they were blue in the face that you could believe what he said … unless he was talking about replacing the NHS with a US-style insurance-based system, in which case his adherents would tell you that you *shouldn't* believe what he said.[14] That's authenticity for you in the post-truth world.

The dismantling of truth is a process that is leading voters away from the politics that has dominated Britain for a century. It goes hand-in-hand with the dismantling of a reasonably fair economy. The mainstream parties all aim to increase Britain's GDP, but GDP is a lousy way of measuring prosperity, especially if all the growth is generated through what are euphemistically labelled 'efficiency savings'. Such streamlining may lead to assets rising in value, and technically the country becomes a little bit richer. But if, like millions of us, you have no such assets, an increase in GDP means nothing. Less than nothing, since for you any efficiency savings mean falling wages, weaker social protections, less job security, and a more tenuous existence. And what's the point of backing a progressive party that only makes life better for the gilded few who already have a home, a pension, and a portfolio of shares? This is the implicit message being sent to mainstream politics from all those voters throwing their lot in with Nigel Farage: ignore us, and we will walk away.

I can't claim to speak for Reform voters, but somebody needs to, and it can't be Farage. You could argue that attempting to delegitimise the far-right is anti-democratic, since any attempt to suppress their vote denies a perfectly valid political opinion. But to be part of a democracy, you have to accept electoral results. And as we've seen from Washington's Capitol riots on January 6, 2021, and from every unconstitutional and undemocratic decision Trump has made since returning to the Oval Office, that's simply not the case. Once the far-right is in power, democracy is in danger. The political representation we've spent hundreds of blood-stained years fighting to attain is handed in a heartbeat to corporate powers, and the rights of citizens evaporate. As Benito Mussolini, the founder of Fascism, made plain, 'Fascism should more appropriately be called Corporatism because it is a merger of state and corporate power'.[15]

Around the world this process is underway and accelerating. Few governments have the courage to confront that basic reality, and fewer still have the sense to do something to curtail the epic enrichment of a gilded few before it inevitably gets even worse, as generational wealth accrues, genuine investment in human capital remains terrible, inequality accelerates, and the capture and control of democratic power advances.

A handful of people have become so spectacularly rich that they can buy nations, either literally – and by 2024 Elon Musk was richer than the GDP of 140 countries[16] – or by simply buying their way into the executive. Musk's $277 million investment in the re-election of Donald Trump sounds like a hefty bill to pay, but it's the equivalent of somebody earning the average UK salary donating the cost of five glasses of wine.[17] Musk, Mark Zuckerberg, Jeff Bezos – even the comparatively poor James Dyson with his lowly £23 billion – have become so rich that a donation capable of redirecting the goals of our democracy is small change for them.[18] And that's a fundamental threat to us all.

Both Labour and the rump of the Conservatives must recognise the dangers and act, or it will not merely be their parties that are flattened by the oncoming tide of billionaire-backed populism: the entire status of Britain's democracy will be at peril. The fact that this is a global problem does not absolve the UK's leaders of the responsibility to tackle it. It is an undeniable fact that across the world an increasingly extreme right-wing is on the rise, with all the accompanying risks to rights, freedoms, and justice. It is supercharged by social media, a point of vulnerability exploited by malign powers, both foreign and domestic, national and – increasingly – private.

The jeopardy is real, and it is insufficiently challenged by a cowed or complicit traditional media that focuses far too much on the luxury problems of a privileged class. And Labour spends so much time prevaricating and obfuscating and triangulating, desperate to avoid the dwindling threat of a dwindling print news media, that it hasn't yet awoken to the far more existential danger posed by the tech-bro, macho-energy, disrupt-everything oligarchy. Labour's first months were dominated by news reports over the battle to protect a tax avoidance loophole used by multimillionaire landowners,[19] and a fight to protect private schools from paying VAT. For months, this is what dominated our headlines.

Why?

Well, because despite only 7 per cent of British kids attending a private school, 44 per cent of the country's most influential journalists, editors and broadcasters went to one.[20] They barely give a thought to the problems of the other 93 per cent of us. Yet seven out of every 10 state schools in England had less funding in 2023 than in 2010.[21] Budgets have been slashed so severely that 94 per cent of schoolteachers in the UK are obliged to use their own long-frozen wages to buy essential classroom supplies.[22] Almost one third of teachers regularly buy food for students whose families can't afford to feed them.[23]

Meanwhile the heroic fight to protect an inheritance tax wheeze for the richest 500-per-year of Britain's 209,000 farmers[24] was led by privately-educated man of the people Jeremy Clarkson – net worth £55 million[25] – who had written in his *Times* column that he had only bought land because, 'the Government doesn't get any of my money when I die. And the price of the food that I grow can only go up'.[26]

Why on earth should the public be forced to fund a tax-break for a multimillionaire who is boasting of price-gouging essential foodstuffs? Yet this is what the media cared about, because that's what far too much of our media is: utterly divorced from the realities experienced by huge swathes of their readership, and not really interested enough to find out. Such journalism is what we rely upon to hold governments to account between elections, and they are failing comprehensively. As a result, so are governments. And therefore, voters turn in despair to the empty promises of populists. The failure of far too much of the media to understand – or even care about – things that happen outside the corridors of power leads to the same blindness that left so many US journalists in shock at the 2024 victory of Donald Trump. They had taken their eyes off the way inequality affected the vast majority of their country.

There is no single explanation that can account for the return of Donald Trump, but a major factor must surely have been the parlous state of everybody's wallets. Famously Bill Clinton said, 'It's the economy, stupid'. Except, of course, Bill Clinton didn't say it, his advisor James Carville did.[27] Then, as now, incomplete reporting is dangerous, and it's the people behind the scenes that you really need to watch out for. Yet more than thirty years later, there's still a kernel of truth in Carville's aphorism. Joe Biden might have been able to boast that GDP grew faster under his leadership than under the previous Trump administration, but making the economy 3.5 per cent larger meant absolutely nothing to voters if they personally remained poor.[28] The world's ten wealthiest people – nine of them Americans, and including the big tech leaders who by 2025 had merged with Trump's fascism[29] – became $64 billion richer *in a single day* when Trump won the election.[30] And that figure constituted a substantial increase to America's GDP, despite not making the other 336 million citizens a single cent richer. So what good is GDP?

For decades, allegedly progressive governments around the world have focused so much on increasing GDP that they've completely ignored the distribution of that money. Of the $42 trillion of new wealth generated worldwide between 2019 and 2021, almost two-thirds went to the richest 1%.[31]

The same process was being repeated everywhere you looked. It accounted for the rise of Viktor Orbán, Giorgia Meloni, Marine Le Pen, Narendra Modi, Recep Tayyip Erdoğan, and Nigel Farage, each of them far-right populists, each of them conjuring bigotry out of the hollow promise of some future equality. None of them had answers, because each of them backed the wealthy against the poor who predominantly voted for them. In 2024, having discreetly nodded along with this process for years, the Tories found their place in the order of things thrown into doubt by the billionaire-backed arrival of brazen political bandwagon-leapers who had lost all sense of shame about barking terrible ideas in public.[32] They promised to be 'political disruptors', which just makes me wonder how we ever fell for the idea of disruptors in the first place. The mantra of disruptors is to 'move fast and break things', which sounds cool in a coked-up Shoreditch hipster kind of way, assuming you don't think about it for a moment. As soon as you do, you realise the thing being broken is often a combination of decency and laws. Disruptors habitually strip-mine entire industries, dismantle the standards that make society function, destroy whatever exists, and monopolise its replacement.

Is this supposed to be a good thing? Furthermore, is this what we want from politicians, the very people we elect to protect us from a dictatorship of grifters?

Probably not, but at least Reform had opinions. They were uniformly awful opinions that didn't stand up to a lick of scrutiny, but they existed. What were Labour's opinions? Can anybody tell me? Everything seemed done for expediency, and without skill. Perhaps Keir Starmer believed his huge majority gave him a moral mandate for what he was doing, but he was wrong: those policies, those ethics, those behaviours had been decisively rejected at the general election that handed him power. Regardless, Labour left the billionaires alone and announced deep cuts to welfare,[33] driving the party's natural voters away in their droves. As Labour tumbled, Reform took a lead in the polls, so Starmer made exactly the same mistake the Tories had made, and tried to ape Farage. The PM began launching further attacks on immigrants, adopting the dehumanising language of not only Reform, but of Enoch Powell too.[34] At the same time, dozens of progressive MPs and think-tanks denounced Labour's first budget as 'austerity by another name':[35] a focus on GDP growth that almost entirely benefits people who don't need any help, combined with further harm to those who do. This had been the fundamental mistake of Cameron and Osborne, triggering our national spiral of decline in the first place. And from the get-go it looked like Labour had a full-body commitment to repeating that error.

Progressives around the world – and particularly here in Britain, my home, and the place I love – need to stop pursuing a policy which only results in more power for the billionaire class who have clearly demonstrated they can't be trusted with it, while the other 99 per cent of us feeling like we're living in a never-ending recession. That's what happened in America, and Trump was the result. Here in Britain,

Farage is the threat, and the solutions are painfully obvious: tell the truth, and redistribute wealth. The super-rich who have manipulated truth for their own ends will, of course, fight like hell. But we should not let that deter us, because as Aristotle pointed out two and a half thousand years ago: 'In a democracy the poor will have more power than the rich, because there are more of them'.[36] So Labour (and every other responsible politician) must protect democracy first, by reinvigorating its powers and processes, and by reining-in those determined to usurp it. Once that's done, every other policy decision becomes easier.

Until progressive governments remember that they represent the majority – the Aristotelian poor, who outnumber everybody else – the populist danger will grow. The Thatcherite system, radically imposed upon the world a generation ago, no longer makes sense to the vast majority of us. It has become idiotic. Labour must understand that the world has changed since James Carvell identified the central issue as, 'the economy, stupid'. Three decades later the central issue is: the stupid economy.

Of course, it is far easier to smash things up than to mend them, and at the time it probably feels more enjoyable. Perhaps that's why Boris Johnson and Nigel Farage do it. They seem like fun guys, with their jokes and their pints, and their dynamite under the values and principles of our society. By comparison, doing basic maintenance is *boring*. Building things is dull, backbreaking work that requires doggedness and skill. Explaining complicated global systems to a population trained to expect empty soundbites is a challenge. And making things right again will be grindingly hard work, but not only must it be done, it must *feel like* it's being done.

And this is the essential lesson. Ordinary people – far from Westminster, miles from Oxbridge, centuries from Eton – must see tangible, material changes to our lives, and quickly, before we lose all faith in the mainstream. Voters want to fix the country: they just don't want the country to remain the obvious fix that it has been for far too long.

The people wielding brooms on that post-riot morning in 2011 were a rainbow of humanity, gathered from all around the world in the People's Republic of Manchester to enact the city's famous, perhaps somewhat mythical, but nonetheless fundamental kindness and inclusivity, and united by one motivation: a determination to restore things. The riots were over. The rampage done.

In the end, community won.

Fourteen years later, I spent the night of the 2024 General Election dancing away a wretched era. But I awoke on the morning after, apprehensive, certainly, but with a spark in my heart and a hope that things can be made whole again. I come back to this thought often when I think about the small-minded negligence and vandalism of the Torygeddon years. In the end, it ended. All things do, save this alone: a yearning to renew.

Endnotes

Part 1
January to June 2023
1. 'The Rt Hon Steve Baker', Gov.UK, https://www.gov.uk/government/people/steve-baker
2. John Carney, 'Lehman Brothers Was Dramatically Over Valuing Its CDOs', Business Insider, 17 Mar 2010, https://www.businessinsider.com/lehman-brothers-was-dramatically-over-valuing-its-cdos-2010-3
3. 'Sajid Javid: From risky business to business secretary', Euromoney, 13 May 2015, https://www.euromoney.com/article/b12km259jtpqtd/sajid-javid-from-risky-business-to-business-secretary
4. Richard Partington, 'John McDonnell questions chancellor's suitability for office', The Guardian, 5 Aug 2019, https://www.theguardian.com/politics/2019/aug/05/john-mcdonnell-questions-chancellors-suitability-for-office
5. Jessica Elgot, 'PM must face questions about hedge fund at heart of financial crash, says Labour', The Guardian, 2 Jun 2024, https://www.theguardian.com/politics/article/2024/jun/02/pm-must-face-questions-about-hedge-fund-at-heart-of-financial-crash-says-labour?CMP=Share_iOSApp_Other
6. Jack Peat, 'Sunak in the spotlight amid accusations that he profited from the financial crash', The London Economic, 3 Jun 2024, https://www.thelondoneconomic.com/business-economics/economics/sunak-in-the-spotlight-amid-accusations-that-he-profited-from-the-financial-crash-376058/
7. Ruth Alexander, 'Reinhart, Rogoff... and Herndon: The student who caught out the profs', BBC News, 20 Apr 2013, https://www.bbc.co.uk/news/magazine-22223190
8. James Lyons, 'George Osborne's favourite "godfathers of austerity" economists admit to making error in research', Mirror, 17 Apr 2013, https://www.mirror.co.uk/news/uk-news/george-osbornes-favourite-economists-reinhart-1838219
9. Tejvan Pettinger, 'Economic record of Osborne and Cameron – 2010-2016', Economics Help, 14 Jul 2016, https://www.economicshelp.org/blog/21496/economics/economic-record-of-osborne-and-cameron-2010-2016/
10. Anna Fleck, 'The UK'S Rich Are Getting Richer', Statista, 23 May 2022, https://www.statista.com/chart/27505/uks-richest-are-getting-richer/
11. 'The true cost of austerity and inequality', Oxfam, Sep 2023, https://www-cdn.oxfam.org/s3fs-public/file_attachments/cs-true-cost-austerity-inequality-uk-120913-en_0.pdf
12. 'Richest 1% grab nearly twice as much new wealth as rest of the world put together', Oxfam, 16 Jan 2023, https://www.oxfam.org.uk/media/press-releases/richest-1-grab-

nearly-twice-as-much-new-wealth-as-rest-of-the-world-put-together/
13. 'Wages of typical UK employee have become decoupled from productivity', London School fo Economics, 3 Nov 2021, https://www.lse.ac.uk/News/Latest-news-from-LSE/2021/k-November-21/Wages-of-typical-UK-employee-have-become-decoupled-from-productivity
14. Michael Race, 'More than a fifth of UK adults not looking for work', BBC, 12 Mar 2024, https://www.bbc.co.uk/news/business-68534537
15. 'Revealed: Investment in UK is lowest in G7 for third year in a row, new data shows', IPPR, 18 Jun 2024, https://www.ippr.org/media-office/revealed-investment-in-uk-is-lowest-in-g7-for-third-year-in-a-row-new-data-shows
16. 'International comparisons of UK productivity (ICP), final estimates: 2021', Office for National Statistics, 11 Jan 2023, https://www.ons.gov.uk/economy/economicoutputandproductivity/productivitymeasures/bulletins/internationalcomparisonsofproductivityfinalestimates/2021/pdf
17. 'Productivity: Key Economic Indicators', House of Commons Library, 16 Aug 024, https://commonslibrary.parliament.uk/research-briefings/sn02791/
18. 'China compels Uighurs to work in shoe factory that supplies Nike', The Washington Post, 29 Feb 2020, https://www.washingtonpost.com/world/asia_pacific/china-compels-uighurs-to-work-in-shoe-factory-that-supplies-nike/2020/02/28/ebddf5f4-57b2-11ea-8efd-0f904bdd8057_story.html
19. Professor Hannah Fry [@frysquared], TikTok, https://www.tiktok.com/@fryrsquared/video/7326976812322393377
20. 'Rebalancing the economy: article by David Cameron', David Cameron, GOV.UK, 29 May 2010, https://www.gov.uk/government/news/article-for-the-yorkshire-post
21. 'Richest 1% grab nearly twice as much new wealth as rest of the world put together', Oxfam, 16 Jan 2023, https://www.oxfam.org.uk/media/press-releases/richest-1-grab-nearly-twice-as-much-new-wealth-as-rest-of-the-world-put-together/
22. Toby Helm, 'Young adults have dramatic loss of faith in UK democracy, survey reveals', The Guardian, 10 Apr 2022, https://www.theguardian.com/politics/2022/apr/10/young-adults-loss-of-faith-in-uk-democracy-survey
23. John Oxley, 'Rishi Sunak and the triumph of managerialism', The Spectator, 22 Oct 2022, https://www.spectator.co.uk/article/sunak-and-the-triumph-of-managerialism/
24. Heather Stewart, 'Voters of all parties back Labour's plans to boost workers' rights, poll shows', The Guardian, 15 Jul 2024, https://www.theguardian.com/politics/article/2024/jul/15/voters-of-all-parties-back-labours-plans-to-boost-workers-rights-poll-shows
25. Andy Beckett, 'Britain is the most socially liberal it's ever been. Could somebody let our politicians know?', The Guardian, 21 Apr 2023, https://www.theguardian.com/commentisfree/2023/apr/21/britain-socially-liberal-politicians-conservative-politics
26. Edward Elliot, 'Behind Global Britain: Public Opinion on the UK's Role in the World', Henry Jackson Society, 30 Apr 2019, https://henryjacksonsociety.org/publications/behind-global-britain-public-opinion-on-the-uks-role-in-the-world-2/
27. Alain Tolhurst, 'Jeremy Corbyn 'most unpopular opposition leader of past 45 years', says poll', PoliticsHome, 20 Sep 2019, https://www.politicshome.com/news/article/jeremy-corbyn-most-unpopular-opposition-leader-of-past-45-years-says-poll
28. Jonathan Freedland, 'The Brexit 'n' Boris formula was a winner for the Tories. Now it's falling apart', The Guardian, 17 Dec 2021, https://www.theguardian.com/commentisfree/2021/dec/17/brexit-boris-johnson-tories-voters-lies-trust
29. 'Boris Johnson lied to the Queen – in normal times no Prime Minister would survive this', Scottish Sun, 25 Sep 2019, https://www.thescottishsun.co.uk/news/scottish-news/4760102/boris-lied-to-the-queen/

30 Steve Anglesey, 'Nigel Farage doesn't want to talk about the disaster of Brexit', The New European, 7 Jun 2024, https://www.theneweuropean.co.uk/nigel-farage-doesnt-want-to-talk-about-the-disaster-of-brexit/
31 Peter Kellner, 'Rishi Sunak, our 'nothing' prime minister', The New European, 27 Sep 2023, https://www.theneweuropean.co.uk/rishi-sunak-our-nothing-prime-minister/
32 Adam Bienkov, 'The Conservative Party is 'Institutionally Corrupt' Say Voters', Byline Times, 27 Jan 2023, https://www.bylinesupplement.com/p/the-conservative-party-is-institutionally
33 Adam Bienkov, 'Brexit has Made Britain a More Expensive and Poorer Country, Say Voters', Byline Times, 3 Feb 2023, https://www.bylinesupplement.com/p/brexit-has-made-britain-a-more-expensive
34 Rhys Jones, 'Rishi Sunak mocked for using hammer 'wrong' during live TV report', Independent, 24 Nov 2024, https://www.independent.co.uk/tv/news/rishi-sunak-hammer-live-news-b2453005.html
35 'Rishi Sunak's first speech as Prime Minister: 25 October 2022', Gov.uk, 15 Oct 2022, https://www.gov.uk/government/speeches/prime-minister-rishi-sunaks-statement-25-october-2022
36 Pippa Crerar, 'Senior civil servant claims Gavin Williamson told them to 'slit your throat'', The Guardian, 7 Nov 2022, https://www.theguardian.com/politics/2022/nov/07/senior-civil-servant-claims-gavin-williamson-told-them-slit-your-throat
37 Anna Isaac, 'Nadhim Zahawi 'agreed on penalty' to settle tax bill worth millions', The Guardian, 20 Jan 2023, https://www.theguardian.com/uk-news/2023/jan/20/nadhim-zahawi-agreed-on-penalty-to-settle-tax-bill-worth-millions
38 Jasper King, 'Dominic Raab 'hurled three tomatoes across a room at staff in fit of rage'', Metro, 12 Nov 2022, https://metro.co.uk/2022/11/12/dominic-raab-hurls-three-tomatoes-at-staff-in-fit-of-rage-17746668/
39 Jon Stone and William Mata, 'https://www.independent.co.uk/news/uk/politics/dominic-raab-bullying-investigation-timeline-b2323494.html', Independent, 20 Apr 2023, https://www.independent.co.uk/news/uk/politics/dominic-raab-bullying-investigation-timeline-b2323494.html
40 'Into Europe', UK parliament, https://www.parliament.uk/about/living-heritage/transformingsociety/tradeindustry/importexport/overview/europe/
41 Kate Devlin, 'Brexit poll: Two-thirds of Britons now support future referendum on rejoining the EU', Independent, 1 Jan 2023, https://www.independent.co.uk/news/uk/politics/brexit-poll-referendum-rejoin-eu-b2250813.html
42 Benjamin Fox, 'Brexit cost 330,000 drop in UK labour force, new research finds', Euractiv, 18 Jan 2023, https://www.euractiv.com/section/justice-home-affairs/news/brexit-cost-330000-drop-in-uk-labour-force-new-research-finds/
43 Joel Hills, 'Brexit costs government £40 billion a year in lost tax revenue', ITV News, 20 Dec 2022, https://www.itv.com/news/2022-12-20/brexit-costs-government-40-billion-a-year-in-lost-tax-revenue
44 Tim Baker, 'Brexit: New report suggests UK £311bn worse off by 2035 due to leaving EU', Sky News, 11 Jan 2023, https://news.sky.com/story/brexit-new-report-suggests-uk-311bn-worse-off-by-2035-due-to-leaving-eu-13046256
45 'So how did Nadine Dorries MP get selected?', Liberal Conspiracy, 27 Oct 2009, https://web.archive.org/web/20091028081545/http://liberalconspiracy.org/2009/10/27/no-no-nadine/
46 'Tories in seat fight 'shambles'', Manchester Evening News, 17 Feb 2007, https://www.manchestereveningnews.co.uk/news/greater-manchester-news/tories-in-seat-fight-shambles-1192894

47 Electoral Calculus, 15 Oct 2001, https://www.electoralcalculus.co.uk/electdata_2001ob.txt
48 Matthew Tempest, 'Tours scandal Tory MP Sayeed steps down', BBC News, 14 Mar 2005, https://www.theguardian.com/politics/2005/mar/14/conservatives.uk
49 'Revealed: The MPs who skip select committee', Politics, 8 Apr 2009, https://web.archive.org/web/20100612111306/http://www.politics.co.uk/news/news/legal-and-constitutional/revealed-the-mps-who-skip-select-committee-$1286524.htm
50 Hollywatt, 'MPs' expenses surpass pre-scandal levels as 150 give jobs to family', Telegraph, 12 Sep 2013, https://www.telegraph.co.uk/news/newstopics/mps-expenses/10306675/MPs-expenses-surpass-pre-scandal-levels-as-150-give-jobs-to-family.html
51 Darren Boyle, 'Tory MP tells Sunday Mirror reporter 'I'll nail your balls to the floor' in Twitter rant', Press Gazette, 25 Nov, 2013, https://pressgazette.co.uk/publishers/nationals/tory-mp-tells-sunday-mirror-reporter-ill-nail-your-testicles-floor-twitter-rant-over-doorstep/
52 Hélène Mulholland, 'Cameron rebukes Tory MP over 'McCarthyite witch-hunt' comment', The Guardian, 22 May 2009, https://www.theguardian.com/politics/2009/may/22/mps-expenses-conservatives
53 'MPs' expenses in detail', BBC News, 7 Sep 2009. http://news.bbc.co.uk/1/hi/uk_politics/8104383.stm
54 Rowena Mason, 'Nadine Dorries apologises to MPs over I'm a Celebrity appearance fee', The Guardian, 11 Nov 2013, https://www.theguardian.com/politics/2013/nov/11/nadine-dorries-im-a-celebrity-apology
55 Hélène Mulholland, 'Nadine Dorries kept waiting for Tory whip to be restored', The Guardian, 27 Nov 2012, https://www.theguardian.com/politics/2012/nov/27/nadine-dorries-rebuild-bridges-tory-whip
56 Kate Plummer, 'Awkward moment Nadine Dorries learnt how Channel 4 is funded resurfaces', Indy100, 5 Apr 2022, https://www.indy100.com/politics/nadine-dorries-channel-4-funded
57 Press Association, "I have to remove myself': Nadine Dorries to step down as an MP', The Guardian, 9 Feb 2023, https://www.theguardian.com/politics/2023/feb/09/i-have-to-remove-myself-nadine-dorries-to-step-down-as-an-mp
58 Press Association, "I have to remove myself': Nadine Dorries to step down as an MP', The Guardian, 9 Feb 2023, https://www.theguardian.com/politics/2023/feb/09/i-have-to-remove-myself-nadine-dorries-to-step-down-as-an-mp
59 Kate Devlin, 'Boris Johnson told 'months ago' peerage for Nadine Dorries had been rejected', Independent, 14 June 2023, https://www.independent.co.uk/news/uk/politics/nadine-dorries-peerage-rejected-johnson-b2357191.html
60 Nick Duffy, 'Nadine Dorries rails at 'posh boy' Rishi Sunak and claims she was 'bullied' out of peerage', iNews, 12 June 2023, https://inews.co.uk/news/politics/nadine-dorries-posh-boy-rishi-sunak-bullied-lords-peerage-2407260
61 Josiah Mortimer, 'Anger as Nadine Dorries' Year-Long Silence in Parliament is Deemed 'Within the Rules' By Standards Watchdog', Byline Times, 14 Aug 2023, https://bylinetimes.com/2023/08/14/anger-as-nadine-dorries-year-long-silence-in-parliament-is-deemed-within-the-rules-by-standards-watchdog/
62 Shefford Town Council [@SheffordTC], Twitter, 17 Aug 2022, https://twitter.com/SheffordTC/status/1692234844804088035
63 Chas Geiger, 'Nadine Dorries not doing MP's job properly, says Rishi Sunak', BBC News, 2 Aug 2023, https://www.bbc.co.uk/news/uk-politics-66382232
64 Becky Morton, 'Nadine Dorries faces move to force her out of Parliament', BBC News, 7 Aug 2023, https://www.bbc.co.uk/news/uk-politics-66427982

65 Nadine Dorries [@NadineDorries], 18 Apr 2018, https://twitter.com/NadineDorries/status/986718638718836739

66 Adam Forrest 'Nadine Dorries finally quits seat after 12 weeks', Independent, 30 Aug 2023, https://www.independent.co.uk/news/uk/politics/nadine-dorries-resigns-tories-byelection-b2401059.html

67 Camilla Turner, 'Boris Johnson suffers most ministerial resignations in modern history', Telegraph, 6 Jul 2022, https://www.telegraph.co.uk/politics/2022/07/06/boris-johnson-suffers-ministerial-resignations-24-hours-since/

68 Samuel Osborne, 'Boris Johnson fined: Prime minister apologises after receiving fixed penalty notice for lockdown-breaking party', Sky News, 13 Apr 2022, https://news.sky.com/story/boris-johnson-fined-prime-minister-apologises-after-receiving-fixed-penalty-notice-for-lockdown-breaking-party-12588712

69 Radina Gigova, 'UK announces controversial plan to send asylum-seekers to Rwanda', CNN, 15 Apr 2022, https://edition.cnn.com/2022/04/14/europe/uk-rwanda-migrant-deal-gbr-intl/index.html

70 'Conservative Party Manifesto 2019, Conservatives.com, https://cchq2019.webflow.io/our-plan

71 'PM speech on action to tackle illegal migration: 14 April 2022', Gov.uk, 14 Apr 2022, https://www.gov.uk/government/speeches/pm-speech-on-action-to-tackle-illegal-migration-14-april-2022

72 Rajeev Syal, 'Rwanda plan to cost UK £1.8m for each asylum seeker, figures show', The Guardian, 1 Mar 2024, https://www.theguardian.com/uk-news/2024/mar/01/rwanda-plan-uk-asylum-seeker-cost-figures

73 'Average Lifetime Earnings UK – Who Makes the Most Money?', Quotezone, 12 Jan 2024, https://www.quotezone.co.uk/home-insurance/guides/average-lifetime-arnings-uk

74 Andrew Roth, 'Putin's vote share nears outer limits but still the only way is up', The Guardian, 18 Mar 2024, https://www.theguardian.com/world/2024/mar/18/putin-vote-share-outer-limits-russia-election

75 'Rwanda', Freedom House, 2023, https://freedomhouse.org/country/rwanda/freedom-world/2024

76 Jason Burke, 'Paul Kagame re-elected president with 99% of vote in Rwanda election', The Guardian, 2 Aug 2017, https://www.theguardian.com/world/2017/aug/05/paul-kagame-secures-third-term-in-rwanda-presidential-election

77 Lizzie Dearden, 'Revealed: Suella Braverman's trips to Rwanda to teach government lawyers', Independent, 27 Nov 2022, https://www.independent.co.uk/news/uk/politics/suella-braverman-rwanda-law-migrants-b2233102.html

78 Henry Ridgewell, 'Report: Rwanda Using Violence to Silence Critics Across the Globe', Voice of America, 11 Oct 2023, https://www.voanews.com/a/report-rwanda-using-violence-to-silence-critics-across-the-globe/7306031.html

79 Ange Iliza, 'Activist raises alarm on police brutality, cold blood killings', Rwanda Today, 24 Feb 2023, https://rwandatoday.africa/rwanda/news/activist-raises-alarm-on-police-brutality-cold-blood-killings-4135984

80 Kevin Schofield, 'Suella Braverman Insists Rwanda Is Safe Despite Deaths Of 12 Refugees', HuffPost, 2 Apr 2023, https://www.huffingtonpost.co.uk/entry/suella-braverman-insists-rwanda-is-safe-country-despite-12-protester-deaths_uk_642947dce4b00c95175297f7

81 Hein de Haas, 'No, Brexit didn't help UK 'take back control' – it made immigration rise. Here's how', Big Issue, 4 Dec 2023, https://www.bigissue.com/opinion/brexit-net-migration-rishi-sunak-uk-immigration/

82 James Heale [@JAHeale], Twitter, 7 Feb 2023, https://twitter.com/JAHeale/status/1622963115565481988
83 'Lee Anderson fame & popularity tracker', YouGov, https://yougov.co.uk/topics/politics/trackers/fame-and-popularity-lee-anderson-public-figure
84 Peter Walker, 'Rishi Sunak rebukes Tory vice-chair for backing death penalty', The Guardian, 9 Feb 2023, https://www.theguardian.com/politics/2023/feb/09/lee-anderson-tory-vice-chair-backed-death-penalty-and-naval-standoffin-channel
85 Patrick Maguire, 'Who is Lee Anderson, the pro-death penalty Tory deputy chairman?', The Times, 10 Feb 2023, https://www.thetimes.co.uk/article/who-is-lee-anderson-mp-tory-deputy-chairman-kxhlm9lvb
86 'Nottinghamshire Labour councillors quit to join Tories', BBC News, 20 Mar 2018, https://www.bbc.co.uk/news/uk-england-nottinghamshire-43471848
87 Kumru, T, 'The People Know Best: An Empirical Research On Why Lower Educated People Are More Likely To Vote For Left- And Right-Wing Populist Parties In The Netherlands', University of Twente, 2018, https://essay.utwente.nl/74817/
88 'The Scale of Economic Inequality in the UK', Equality Trust, 2022, https://equalitytrust.org.uk/scale-economic-inequality-uk/
89 Adam Forrest, 'Suella Braverman re-appointed home secretary six days after exit over security breach', Independent, 25 Oct 2022, https://www.independent.co.uk/news/uk/politics/suella-braverman-home-secretary-sunak-b2210304.html
90 Aubrey Allegretti, Rowena Mason and Rajeev Syal, 'Civil servants 'have to fact-check' Suella Braverman's claims to cabinet', The Guardian, 23 May 2023, https://www.theguardian.com/politics/2023/may/23/civil-servants-have-to-fact-check-suella-bravermans-claims-to-cabinet
91 Richard Vaughan, 'Theresa May condemns Rishi Sunak's Channel migrant laws for 'shutting the door' on asylum seekers', iNews, 13 Mar 2023, https://inews.co.uk/news/politics/theresa-may-condemns-rishi-sunak-channel-migrant-laws-shutting-door-asylum-seekers-2206636
92 Eleanor Langford, 'All the Conservative MPs who abstained or spoke out against the Government's Illegal Migration Bill', iNews, 14 Mar 2023, https://inews.co.uk/news/conservative-mps-criticised-government-illegal-migration-bill-2207299
93 Jasper Jackson, 'Wikipedia bans Daily Mail as 'unreliable' source', The Guardian, 8 Feb 2017, https://www.theguardian.com/technology/2017/feb/08/wikipedia-bans-daily-mail-as-unreliable-source-for-website
94 'New data shows Guardian is the top quality and most trusted newspaper in the UK', The Guardian, 17 Jun 2020, https://www.theguardian.com/gnm-press-office/2020/jun/17/new-data-shows-guardian-is-the-top-quality-and-most-trusted-newspaper-in-the-uk
95 'Braverman criticised for shutting out Guardian and BBC from Rwanda trip', The Guardian, 18 Mar 2023, https://www.theguardian.com/politics/2023/mar/18/braverman-criticised-for-shutting-out-guardian-and-bbc-from-rwanda-trip
96 Charles Hymas, 'Migrant flights to Rwanda 'by this summer'', The Telegraph, 18 Mar 2023, https://www.telegraph.co.uk/politics/2023/03/18/migrant-flights-rwanda-summer/
97 Connie Dimsdale, 'Suella Braverman's Rwanda visit under fire after 'gleeful' conduct joking about interior design', Metro, 19 Mar 2023, https://inews.co.uk/news/suella-braverman-rwanda-visit-interior-design-2219390
98 Adam Bychawski, 'Exclusive: Rwandan homes praised by Braverman 'won't go to asylum seekers'', Democracy Now, 24 Jan 2024, https://www.opendemocracy.net/en/rwanda-scheme-asylum-seekers-bwiza-riverside-estate-suella-braverman/

99 Charley Adams & Dominic Casciani & Jacob Evans, 'Plan for lifetime ban for Channel migrants is unworkable, say charities', BBC News, 6 Mar 2023, https://www.bbc.co.uk/news/uk-64848101
100 Refugee Action, 'Want The Real Facts About Refugees?' https://www.refugee-action.org.uk/about/facts-about-refugees/
101 Lara Keay, 'What does the UN 1951 Refugee Convention say – and can you change it? https://news.sky.com/story/what-does-the-un-1951-refugee-convention-say-and-can-you-change-it-12970185 - :~:text=It gives refugees the right,refugees to breach immigration rules".
102 'Conflicts in 2023', Wikipedia, https://en.wikipedia.org/wiki/Category:Conflicts_in_2023
103 'Refugee statistics', UNHCR, https://www.unhcr.org/refugee-statistics/
104 Jill Lawless, 'Under oath, Boris Johnson denies he lied over 'partygate'', Associated Press, 22 Mar 2022, https://apnews.com/article/boris-johnson-partygate-coronavirus-rules-uk-parliament-dec689d91755940254e94c2d23704298
105 'Partygate: I misled MPs but not intentionally, says Boris Johnson', BBC News, 21 Mar 2023, https://www.bbc.co.uk/news/uk-politics-65012965
106 'Boris Johnson's partygate legal fees cost taxpayer £265,000', Sky News, 21 Jul 2023, https://news.sky.com/story/boris-johnsons-partygate-legal-fees-cost-taxpayer-265-000-12924534
107 Joshua Nevett, 'Watchdog criticises decision to pay Johnson's £265,000 Partygate bill', BBC News, 19 Sep 2023, https://www.bbc.co.uk/news/uk-politics-66852723
108 Richard Wheeler, 'Windsor Framework: Full list of the 29 MPs who voted against the implementation of Stormont Brake in today's House of Commons vote', News Letter, 22 Mar 2023, https://www.newsletter.co.uk/news/politics/windsor-framework-full-list-of-the-29-mps-who-voted-against-the-implementation-of-stormont-brake-in-todays-house-of-commons-vote-4075436?r=3700
109 Tamara Kovacevic and Anthony Reuben, 'What is the Privileges Committee and who are its members?', BBC News, 15 Jun 2023, https://www.bbc.co.uk/news/uk-politics-65878925
110 Alice Lilly, 'Privileges Committee investigation into Boris Johnson', Institute for Government, 15 Jun 2023, https://www.instituteforgovernment.org.uk/explainer/privileges-committee-investigation-boris-johnson
111 Gaby Hinsliff, "An opportunist in search of an opportunity': what next for Boris Johnson?', The Observer, 19 Mar 2023, https://www.theguardian.com/politics/2023/mar/19/what-next-for-boris-johnson-partygate-pandemic-return-as-leader
112 Kate Whannel, 'Boris Johnson wanted to be injected with Covid on TV - ex-adviser', BBC News, 7 Nov 2023, https://www.bbc.co.uk/news/uk-politics-67347456
113 Nick Hopkins, 'Boris Johnson: why is he in so much trouble – and can his political career survive?', The Guardian, 24 Mar 2023, https://www.theguardian.com/politics/2023/mar/24/boris-johnson-partygate-brexit-political-career
114 Paul Brand [@PaulBrandITV], Twitter, 23 Mar 2023, https://twitter.com/paulbranditv/status/1639008291748470786
115 Tony Diver, 'Dominic Cummings told PM 'if we don't sack Matt Hancock we are going to kill people'', The Telegraph, 26 May 2021, https://www.telegraph.co.uk/politics/2021/05/26/dominic-cummings-matt-hancock-should-have-sacked-15-20-covid/
116 "Matt Hancock left thousands to die and he deserves corporate manslaughter charges", Mirror, 20 Apr 2022, https://www.mirror.co.uk/news/politics/matt-hancock-left-thousands-die-26841501

117 Tom Ambrose, 'Matt Hancock donates just 3% of I'm a Celebrity fee', The Guardian, 27 Jan 2023, https://www.theguardian.com/politics/2023/jan/27/matt-hancock-donates-three-per-cent-of-im-a-celebrity-fee

118 Ian Johnston, 'https://www.independent.co.uk/news/uk/politics/david-cameron-feud-with-lord-ashcroft-pm-indulged-in-drug-taking-and-debauchery-billionaire-donor-alleges-in-new-book-10510417.html', Independent, 25 Sep 2015, https://www.independent.co.uk/news/uk/politics/david-cameron-feud-with-lord-ashcroft-pm-indulged-in-drug-taking-and-debauchery-billionaire-donor-alleges-in-new-book-10510417.html

119 James Kirkup, 'A pig, some drugs and a disappointed billionaire: the life of David Cameron', The Telegraph, 21 Sep 2015, https://www.telegraph.co.uk/news/politics/david-cameron/11880588/A-pig-some-drugs-and-a-disappointed-billionaire-the-life-of-David-Cameron.html

120 'Isabel Oakeshott reveals why she leaked Matt Hancock's WhatsApp messages', BBC News, 2 Mar 2023, https://www.bbc.co.uk/news/av/uk-64822872

121 Helen Catt, 'Matt Hancock: Leaked messages suggest plan to frighten public', BBC News, 5 Mar 2023, https://www.bbc.co.uk/news/uk-64848106

122 Christy Cooney & Becky Morton, 'Matt Hancock disputes claim he rejected care home Covid advice', BBC News, 1 Mar 2023, https://www.bbc.co.uk/news/uk-politics-64807127

123 Jon Ungoed-Thomas, 'Top Tory MPs ask for £10,000 a day to work for fake Korean company', The Guardian, 25 Mar 2023, https://www.theguardian.com/politics/2023/mar/25/top-tory-mps-ask-for-10000-a-day-to-work-for-fake-korean-company

124 Andrew Adonis, 'Is this the worst parliament in history?', Prospect, 21 Aug 2023, https://www.prospectmagazine.co.uk/politics/62661/parliament-worst-history-government-tories

125 Jennifer Scott, 'Budget 2023: UK economy will avoid recession in 2023 and inflation set to plummet, says chancellor', Sky News, 15 Mar 2023, https://news.sky.com/story/budget-2023-jeremy-hunt-says-economy-will-avoid-recession-in-2023-12834284

126 'Economic update: when will the UK exit recession?', ICAEW, 29 Feb 2024, https://www.icaew.com/insights/viewpoints-on-the-news/2024/feb-2024/economic-update-when-will-the-uk-exit-recession

127 'Voting intentions in a general election in the United Kingdom from July 2017 to January 2024', Statista, https://www.statista.com/statistics/985764/voting-intention-in-the-uk/

128 Tom Head, 'Latest polls show Rees-Mogg on course to LOSE his seat as MP', The London Economic, 9 Apr 2023, https://www.thelondoneconomic.com/news/election-forecast-tories-lose-seats-mps-jacob-rees-mogg-346446/

129 Sarah Priddy, 'MPs standing down from the Commons ahead of the next general election', House of Commons Library, 1 Feb 2024, https://commonslibrary.parliament.uk/research-briefings/cbp-9808/

130 Aubrey Allegretti and Donna Ferguson, 'Tory MP Scott Benton has whip suspended after newspaper sting', The Guardian, 5 Apr 2023, https://www.theguardian.com/politics/2023/apr/05/rishi-sunak-facing-calls-suspend-whip-scott-benton

131 'Scott Benton, Second Report of Session 2023-2024', House of Commons Committee on Standards, 14 Dec 2023, https://committees.parliament.uk/publications/42581/documents/211708/default/

132 Paul Burnell, 'Scott Benton: Lobbying scandal MP loses suspension appeal', BBC News, 21 Feb 2024, https://www.bbc.co.uk/news/uk-england-lancashire-68348594

133 Vicki Young and Joshua Nevitt, 'Rishi Sunak investigated over declaration of interest',

BBC News, 17 Apr 2023, https://www.bbc.co.uk/news/uk-politics-65301099
134. Chris Mason, 'Chris Mason: How big a deal is inquiry into Rishi Sunak's declarations?', BBC News, 17 Apr 2023, https://www.bbc.co.uk/news/uk-politics-65302234
135. 'Rishi Sunak's first speech as Prime Minister: 25 October 2022', Gov.uk, 15 Oct 2022, https://www.gov.uk/government/speeches/prime-minister-rishi-sunaks-statement-25-october-2022
136. Peter Walker, 'What is the Nusrat Ghani v Mark Spencer row about?', The Guardian, 6 Apr 2023, https://www.theguardian.com/politics/2023/apr/06/what-is-the-nusrat-ghani-v-mark-spencer-row-about
137. Gabriel Pogrund [@Gabriel_Pogrund], Twitter, 22 Jan 2022, https://twitter.com/Gabriel_Pogrund/status/1485017363661602821
138. Press Association, 'Chief whip comes forward as person behind 'Muslimness' sacking claim', The Observer, 22 Jan 2022, https://www.theguardian.com/politics/2022/jan/22/tory-mp-says-muslimness-given-as-reason-for-losing-job
139. 'Tories suspend Haverfordwest councillor for alleged slave remark', BBC News, 13 Apr 2023, https://www.bbc.co.uk/news/uk-wales-politics-65266125
140. Ben Glaze, 'Tory councillor under fire for suggesting alleged rape victim 'likely' to be a prostitute', Mirror, 2 Jan 2023, https://www.mirror.co.uk/news/politics/tory-councillor-under-fire-suggesting-28858299
141. Joe Coughlan, 'Rape tweet Conservative Shaun Slator expelled from party', BBC News, 15 Apr 2023, https://www.bbc.co.uk/news/uk-england-london-65285105
142. Peter Walker, 'Tory MP Andrew Bridgen loses whip over 'dangerous' Covid vaccine claims', The Guardian, 11 Jan 2023, https://www.theguardian.com/politics/2023/jan/11/tory-mp-andrew-bridgen-loses-whip-over-covid-vaccine-comments
143. Alex Smith and Press Association, 'Andrew Bridgen: MP expelled by Tories after Covid vaccine comments', BBC News, 26 Apr 2023, https://www.bbc.co.uk/news/uk-england-leicestershire-65402195
144. Kate Whannel, 'Ex-Tory Andrew Bridgen joins Laurence Fox's Reclaim party', BBC News, 10 May 2023, https://www.bbc.co.uk/news/uk-politics-65543018
145. 'Ipsos political monitor tables', Ipsos, March 2023, https://www.ipsos.com/sites/default/files/ct/news/documents/2023-04/ipsos-political-monitor-tables-march-2023.pdf
146. Seth Thévoz, 'Revealed: Brexit donor behind net-zero backlash has $130m in fossil fuels', Open Democracy, 22 Mar 2022, https://www.opendemocracy.net/en/dark-money-investigations/jeremy-hosking-brexit-donor-net-zero-invest-fossil-fuels/
147. Gabriel Pogrund, 'MP Andrew Bridgen ordered to quit home in fight over family potato firm', The Sunday Times, 3 Sept 2022, https://www.thetimes.com/uk/law/article/mp-andrew-bridgen-ordered-to-quit-home-in-fight-over-family-potato-firm-wc30j2j6s
148. 'Andrew Bridgen: Ex-Tory MP quits Reclaim Party after seven months', BBC News, 20 Dec 2023, https://www.bbc.co.uk/news/uk-politics-67770990
149. Detailed in Four Chancellors and a Funeral by Russell Jones, pages 292–6 (Unbound, 2024).
150. 'Dominic Raab Created A "Culture Of Fear" By "Belittling" Civil Servants, Sources Say', PoliticsHome, 15 Nov 2022, https://www.politicshome.com/news/article/dominic-raab-culture-of-fear-belittling-civil-servants-bullying-allegations
151. Sam Francis, 'Suella Braverman rhetoric fuels racism, claims Tory peer', BBC News, 13 Apr 2023, https://www.bbc.co.uk/news/uk-politics-65249872
152. Nick Eardley and Oliver Snow, 'Asylum seeker barge plan could face legal challenge', BBC News, 4 Apr 2023, https://www.bbc.co.uk/news/uk-65172368
153. David Hughes and Dominic McGrath, 'Bibby Stockholm asylum barge costing

taxpayers £22m, says Home Office chief', Irish News, 13 Dec 2023, https://www.irishnews.com/news/uk/bibby-stockholm-asylum-barge-costing-taxpayers-22m-says-home-office-chief-IGO7JRVFAVLCJMZFHEO2ZSWWM4/

154 Aubrey Allegretti and Diane Taylor, 'First 50 people coming to Bibby Stockholm asylum barge despite safety worries', Guardian, 27 Jul 2023, https://www.theguardian.com/uk-news/2023/jul/27/first-50-people-coming-to-bibby-stockholm-asylum-barge-despite-safety-worries

155 Horatio Clare, 'A boat to stop the boats? Bibby Stockholm and the battle over asylum', FT, 22 Jul 2023, https://www.ft.com/content/ed6d313c-81f0-418e-89bd-c15c8c87761d

156 Catherine Nicholls and Sana Noor Haq, 'Asylum-seekers board UK's controversial 'deathtrap' housing barge', CNN, 8 Aug 2023, https://edition.cnn.com/2023/08/07/uk/bibby-stockholm-barge-asylum-seekers-intl-gbr/index.html

157 Aubrey Allegretti and Diane Taylor, 'First 50 people coming to Bibby Stockholm asylum barge despite safety worries', Guardian, 27 Jul 2023, https://www.theguardian.com/uk-news/2023/jul/27/first-50-people-coming-to-bibby-stockholm-asylum-barge-despite-safety-worries

158 Bibby Marine Limited, https://www.bibbymarine.com/bibby-stockholm/

159 Catherine Nicholls and Sana Noor Haq, 'Asylum-seekers board UK's controversial 'deathtrap' housing barge', CNN, 8 Aug 2023, https://edition.cnn.com/2023/08/07/uk/bibby-stockholm-barge-asylum-seekers-intl-gbr/index.html

160 Marie-Claire Alfonso, 'MP Richard Drax backs Attorney General Suella Braverman to become Johnson's successor', Dorset Echo, 10 Jul 2022, https://www.dorsetecho.co.uk/news/20268705.mp-richard-drax-backs-attorney-general-suella-braverman-become-johnsons-successor/

161 Nick Eardley and Oliver Snow, 'Asylum seeker barge plan could face legal challenge', BBC News, 4 Apr 2023, https://www.bbc.co.uk/news/uk-65172368

162 'Charborough House', Wikipedia, https://en.wikipedia.org/wiki/Charborough_House

163 Paul Lashmar and Jonathan Smith, 'He's the MP with the Downton Abbey lifestyle. But the shadow of slavery hangs over the gilded life of Richard Drax', The Guardian, 12 Dec 2020, https://www.theguardian.com/world/2020/dec/12/hes-the-mp-with-the-downton-abbey-lifestyle-but-the-shadow-of-slavery-hangs-over-the-gilded-life-of-richard-drax

164 Jonathan Smith and Paul Lashmar, 'Tory MP from slave-owning family set to gain £3m from sale of former plantation', The Guardian, 20 Apr 2024, https://www.theguardian.com/world/2024/apr/20/tory-mp-from-slave-owning-family-set-to-gain-3m-from-sale-of-former-plantation

165 'MP Richard Drax gives warning on immigration', Bournemouth Echo, 11 Sep 2012, https://www.bournemouthecho.co.uk/news/9921680.mp-richard-drax-gives-warning-on-immigration/

166 David Burke, 'Urgent warning issued as six migrants found cramped in one bedroom on Bibby Stockholm', Mirror, 2 Feb 2024, https://www.mirror.co.uk/news/politics/urgent-warning-issued-six-migrants-32028319

167 Marcus White and Mark Eaton, 'Bibby Stockholm: First asylum seekers board housing barge in Dorset', BBC News, 8 Aug 2023, https://www.bbc.co.uk/news/uk-england-dorset-66289857

168 Diane Taylor, 'Contractors told about legionella on day asylum seekers boarded barge', Guardian, 13 Aug 2023, https://www.theguardian.com/uk-news/2023/aug/13/home-office-was-told-about-legionella-on-refugees-barge-on-day-they-boarded

169 'Bibby Stockholm barge migrants moved after Legionella bacteria found', BBC News, 12 Aug 2023, https://www.bbc.com/news/uk-england-dorset-66476538

170 David Hughes and Dominic McGrath, 'Bibby Stockholm asylum barge costing taxpayers £22m, says Home Office chief', Irish News, 13 Dec 2023, https://www.irishnews.com/news/uk/bibby-stockholm-asylum-barge-costing-taxpayers-22m-says-home-office-chief-IGO7JRVFAVLCJMZFHEO2ZSWWM4/

171 Aletha Adu, Jessica Elgot and Kiran Stacey, 'Senior Conservatives hit out at Suella Braverman's 'racist rhetoric'', The Guardian, 13 Apr 2023 ,https://www.theguardian.com/world/2023/apr/13/senior-conservatives-hit-out-at-suella-bravermans-racist-rhetoric

172 Aletha Adu, Jessica Elgot and Kiran Stacey, 'Senior Conservatives hit out at Suella Braverman's 'racist rhetoric'', The Guardian, 13 Apr 2023, https://www.theguardian.com/world/2023/apr/13/senior-conservatives-hit-out-at-suella-bravermans-racist-rhetoric

173 Aletha Adu, Jessica Elgot and Kiran Stacey, 'Senior Conservatives hit out at Suella Braverman's 'racist rhetoric'', The Guardian, 13 Apr 2023, https://www.theguardian.com/world/2023/apr/13/senior-conservatives-hit-out-at-suella-bravermans-racist-rhetoric

174 'Cause of asylum seeker's death on board Bibby Stockholm barge revealed by coroner', Sky News, 21 Dec 2023, https://news.sky.com/story/cause-of-asylum-seekers-death-on-board-bibby-stockholm-barge-revealed-by-coroner-13035828

175 'Bibby Stockholm factsheet', Bibby Marine Limited, https://www.bibbymarine.com/wp-content/uploads/2023/05/Stockholm-Factsheet.pdf

176 Mikey Smith, 'Nigel Farage resigns as leader of Ukip, saying 'I want my life back'', Mirror, 4 Jul 2016, https://www.mirror.co.uk/news/uk-news/nigel-farage-resigns-leader-ukip-8344369

177 'Michael Gove: Boris Johnson wasn't up to the job', BBC News, 30 Jun 2016, https://www.youtube.com/watch?v=nfWYhJyGsPU

178 Matthew Champion, '9 Times Michael Gove Said He Didn't Want To Be Prime Minister', Buzzfeed News, 30 Jun 2016, https://www.buzzfeed.com/matthewchampion/should-i-stay-or-should-i-gove

179 George Parker, 'Michael Gove and Gisela Stuart to head Vote Leave group', Financial Times, 13 Mar 2016, https://www.ft.com/content/57b74004-e91d-11e5-bb79-2303682345c8

180 Anushka Asthana and Rowena Mason, 'Theresa May wins first round of voting in Tory leadership race', The Guardian, 5 Jul 2016, https://www.theguardian.com/politics/2016/jul/05/theresa-may-wins-first-round-of-voting-in-tory-leadership-race

181 Jessica Elgot, 'Theresa May calls for 'red, white and blue Brexit'', The Guardian, 6 Dec 2016, https://www.theguardian.com/politics/2016/dec/06/theresa-may-calls-for-red-white-and-blue-brexit

182 Mikey Smith, 'Boris Johnson dismissed £250,000 second job as 'chicken feed' in unearthed clip', Mirror, 13 Nov 2021, https://www.mirror.co.uk/news/politics/boris-johnson-dismissed-250000-second-25450261

183 Toby Helm, 'Brexit has completely failed for UK, say clear majority of Britons – poll', The Guardian, 30 Dec 2023, https://www.theguardian.com/politics/2023/dec/30/britons-brexit-bad-uk-poll-eu-finances-nhs

184 'UK abandons pledge for Brexit 'bonfire' of EU law by end of 2023', ITV News, 10 May 2023, https://www.itv.com/news/2023-05-10/uk-abandons-pledge-for-brexit-bonfire-of-eu-law-by-end-of-2023

185 Nick Sommerlad, 'Boris Johnson under fire as No10 staff shredded Partygate docs weeks before Covid inquiry', Mirror, 11 Jan 2023, https://www.mirror.co.uk/news/politics/boris-johnson-under-fire-no10-28932607

186 Christopher Hope, 'Tories to leave thousands of EU laws intact in latest Brexit betrayal', Telegraph, 27 Apr 2023, https://www.telegraph.co.uk/politics/2023/04/27/tories-scrap-one-in-five-redundant-eu-laws-brexit-betrayal/

187 Jacob Rees-Mogg, 'Brexit is being surrendered to the declinist Europhile establishment', Telegraph, 6 Jan 2023, https://www.telegraph.co.uk/news/2023/01/06/brexit-surrendered-declinist-europhile-establishment/

188 Christopher Hope, 'Tories to leave thousands of EU laws intact in latest Brexit betrayal', Telegraph, 27 Apr 2023, https://www.telegraph.co.uk/politics/2023/04/27/tories-scrap-one-in-five-redundant-eu-laws-brexit-betrayal/

189 Lisa O'Carroll, 'Bonfire of EU laws watered down to just 800 after meeting of Brexiter MPs', Guardian, 28 Apr 2023, https://www.theguardian.com/politics/2023/apr/28/bonfire-of-eu-laws-watered-down-to-just-800-after-meeting-of-brexit-mps

190 'UK abandons pledge for Brexit 'bonfire' of EU law by end of 2023', ITV News, 10 May 2023, https://www.itv.com/news/2023-05-10/uk-abandons-pledge-for-brexit-bonfire-of-eu-law-by-end-of-2023

191 Ben Wright, Laura Kuenssberg, 'Rishi Sunak to consult ethics adviser over Suella Braverman speeding claims', BBC News, 21 May 2023, https://www.bbc.co.uk/news/uk-politics-65659053

192 Ben Wright, Laura Kuenssberg, 'Rishi Sunak to consult ethics adviser over Suella Braverman speeding claims', BBC News, 21 May 2023, https://www.bbc.co.uk/news/uk-politics-65659053

193 James Gregory, 'MPs asked to repay driving fines claimed on expenses', BBC News, 28 May 2023, https://www.bbc.co.uk/news/uk-politics-65736601

194 Heather Stewart, 'Suella Braverman: what are the allegations over her speeding fine?', The Guardian, 21 May 2023, https://www.theguardian.com/politics/2023/may/21/suella-braverman-what-are-allegations-speeding-fine-explainer

195 Adam Forrest and Archie Mitchell, 'The battle for Boris's secret WhatsApps: Tory frustration as ex-PM 'drags down party'', Independent, 24 May 2023, https://www.independent.co.uk/news/uk/politics/boris-johnson-covid-whatsapp-sunak-braverman-b2345099.html

196 Adam Forrest, 'Tory MPs urge Sunak to sack Braverman if she broke rules over speeding offence', Independent, 22 May 2023, https://www.independent.co.uk/news/uk/politics/suella-braverman-speeding-sunak-sack-b2343624.html

197 'Marcus Fysh MP told to apologise after breaching code of conduct', BBC News, 7 Sept 2023, https://www.bbc.co.uk/news/uk-england-somerset-66739185

198 Rowena Mason, 'Steve Brine breached rules when lobbying ministers in pandemic, watchdog finds', The Guardian, 9 May 2023, https://www.theguardian.com/politics/2023/may/09/steve-brine-breached-rules-when-lobbying-ministers-in-pandemic-watchdog-finds

199 'Henry Smith ordered to apologise and repay public £1,763 for newsletter rule breach', Guido Fawkes, 8 Jun 2023, https://order-order.com/2023/06/08/henry-smith-ordered-to-apologise-and-repay-public-1763-for-newsletter-rule-breach/

200 'Conservative Party Chair Greg Hands says former prime minister Boris Johnson is 'campaigning asset'', Sky News, 22 Mar 2023, https://news.sky.com/video/boris-johnson-conservative-chair-greg-hands-says-the-former-prime-minister-is-still-a-campaigning-asset-12840384

201 Peter Walker, 'Boris Johnson records election clip inside moving car without seatbelt on', The Guardian, 5 May 2023, https://www.theguardian.com/politics/2023/may/05/boris-johnson-records-election-clip-inside-moving-car-without-seatbelt-on

202 'Conservative Party Chair Greg Hands says former prime minister Boris Johnson

is 'campaigning asset", Sky News, 22 Mar 2023, https://news.sky.com/video/boris-johnson-conservative-chair-greg-hands-says-the-former-prime-minister-is-still-a-campaigning-asset-12840384
203. Dave Burke, "Rogues' gallery' of 12 controversial candidates on ballot papers thanks to Tories", Mirror, 3 May 2023, https://www.mirror.co.uk/news/politics/rogues-gallery-12-controversial-candidates-29866531
204. Dave Burke, "Rogues' gallery' of 12 controversial candidates on ballot papers thanks to Tories", Mirror, 3 May 2023, https://www.mirror.co.uk/news/politics/rogues-gallery-12-controversial-candidates-29866531
205. Susan Newton, 'Wannabe Blackpool councillor suspended by Tories after civil service staff called 'pedos' in Facebook post', Lancs Live, 8 Feb 2023, https://www.lancs.live/news/lancashire-news/wannabe-blackpool-councillor-suspended-tories-26177320
206. 'Public Administration and Constitutional Affairs Committee', Parliament, 2021, https://committees.parliament.uk/writtenevidence/38405/html/
207. 'All the Tories embroiled in sexual misconduct allegations since 2019', ITV News, 4 Jul 2022, https://www.itv.com/news/2022-07-01/all-the-tories-embroiled-in-sexual-misconduct-allegations-since-2019
208. Peter Walker, 'Hundreds of thousands face exclusion over voter ID laws, UK watchdog says', The Guardian, 13 Sept 2023, https://www.theguardian.com/politics/2023/sep/13/uk-election-watchdog-issues-damning-verdict-on-voter-id-impact
209. 'Political attitudes by ethnicity', Ipsos, Nov 2023, https://www.ipsos.com/sites/default/files/ct/news/documents/2023-11/ipsos-uk-political-attitudes-by-ethnicity-2023.pdf
210. Peter Walker, 'Voter ID rule may have stopped 400,000 taking part in UK election, poll suggests', The Guardian, 8 Jul 2024, https://www.theguardian.com/politics/article/2024/jul/08/voter-id-rule-may-have-stopped-400000-taking-part-in-uk-election-poll-suggests
211. Doug Cowan, 'Voter ID is a 'gerrymandering scheme' suggests Jacob Rees-Mogg', Electoral Reform Society, 16 May 2023, https://www.electoral-reform.org.uk/voter-id-is-a-gerrymandering-scheme-admits-jacob-rees-mogg/
212. Farrukh [@implausibleblog], Twitter, 14 May 2023, https://twitter.com/implausibleblog/status/1657663668102868992
213. Rowena Mason, 'What do the disastrous Tory local election results mean for Rishi Sunak', The Guardian, 5 May 2023, https://www.theguardian.com/politics/2023/may/05/what-do-disastrous-tory-local-election-results-mean-for-rishi-sunak
214. Matthew Goodwin, 'Sunak's Tories have lost the Red Wall – and are destined for oblivion', The Telegraph, 6 May 2023, https://www.telegraph.co.uk/news/2023/05/06/tories-lost-the-red-wall-destined-for-oblivion/
215. Arj Singh, Hugo Gye, Jane Merric, "Rishi Sunak lied to us about Brexit': Angry Tories consider changing leader – again', iNews, 13 May 2023, https://inews.co.uk/news/politics/rishi-sunak-lied-to-us-about-brexit-angry-tories-consider-changing-leader-again-2337974
216. Hugo Gye, 'Conservative Democratic Organisation is 'front group' for bringing back Boris Johnson, Tory MPs fear', iNews, 20 Dec 2022, https://inews.co.uk/news/politics/conservative-democratic-organisation-boris-johnson-tory-mps-2039159
217. Aubrey Allegretti, 'Tory MP Daniel Kawczynski reprimanded but avoids suspension for conference talk alongside far-right figures', Sky News, 6 Feb 2020, https://news.sky.com/story/tory-mp-daniel-kawczynski-reprimanded-but-avoids-suspension-for-conference-talk-alongside-far-right-figures-11927858
218. Arj Singh, Hugo Gye, Jane Merric, "Rishi Sunak lied to us about Brexit': Angry Tories consider changing leader – again', iNews, 13 May 2023, https://inews.co.uk/news/

politics/rishi-sunak-lied-to-us-about-brexit-angry-tories-consider-changing-leader-again-2337974

219 Graeme Demianyk, "Marxism, Narcissism And Paganism' Among Tory Fears During Bizarre Gathering', Huffington Post, 15 May 2024, https://www.huffingtonpost.co.uk/entry/national-conservatism-conference-braverman-kruger-cates_uk_646251bbe4b03e16f1a4aa5d

220 Joshua Nevett, 'Sunak rejects Tory MP's claim about marriage between men and women', BBC News, 16 May 203, https://www.bbc.co.uk/news/uk-politics-65612836

221 'Rayne Kruger Obituary', The Telegraph, 9 Jan 2003, https://www.telegraph.co.uk/news/obituaries/1418279/Rayne-Kruger.html

222 Atul Singh, 'Do Rumors of Boris Johnson's Purported Twelfth Child Matter?', Fair Observer, 21 May 2022, https://www.fairobserver.com/politics/do-rumors-of-boris-johnsons-purported-twelfth-child-matter/

223 May Bulman, 'Questions over Boris Johnson's relationship with ex-model 'awarded £126,000 of public funds'', Independent, 22 Sep 2019 https://www.independent.co.uk/news/uk/home-news/boris-johnson-jennifer-arcuri-model-london-mayor-friendship-conflict-interest-a9115211.html

224 Janice Turner, 'Is Miriam Cates a mainstream Tory or a right-wing ideologue?', The Times, 29 Jun 2023, https://www.thetimes.co.uk/article/miriam-cates-interview-conservative-mp-politics-right-wing-abortion-gender-qcxrj6vdr

225 Miriam Cates, 'Our declining birth rate', miriamcates.org.uk, 15 May 2023, https://www.miriamcates.org.uk/news/our-declining-birth-rate

226 Eleanor Lawrie, 'Two-child benefit cap: 'Every month is a struggle'', BBC News, 31 Jan 2024, https://www.bbc.co.uk/news/uk-67999028

227 Dominic Penna, "Cultural Marxism' is destroying our children's souls, says Miriam Cates', The Telegraph, 15 May 2023, https://www.telegraph.co.uk/politics/2023/05/15/cultural-marxism-conservatism-miriam-cates-tory-mp/

228 David Wilcock, 'Tory MP suggests woke culture is 'systematically destroying our children's souls' and driving them to self-harm and suicide as she says tax system should encourage mums to have more babies to avert 'overarching threat to Western civilisation'', Daily Mail, 15 May 2023, https://www.dailymail.co.uk/news/article-12084755/Tory-MP-Miriam-Dates-suggests-woke-culture-driving-children-self-harm-suicide.html

229 Ross McGuinness, 'Anger after author says 'Germans mucked up twice' at conference attended by top Tories', Yahoo!News, 16 May 2023, https://uk.news.yahoo.com/anger-author-germans-mucked-up-twice-conservatism-conference-112949377.html

230 National Conservatism [@NatConTalk], Twitter, 16 May 2023, https://twitter.com/NatConTalk/status/1658460691974574082

231 'Unaddressed weaknesses of social care sector impacted the ability to respond to Covid', Nuffield Trust, 5 May 2023, https://www.nuffieldtrust.org.uk/news-item/unaddressed-weaknesses-of-social-care-sector-impacted-the-ability-to-respond-to-covid

232 Robert Booth, 'Government 'to cut £250m from social care workforce funding' in England', The Guardian, 17 May 2023, https://www.theguardian.com/society/2023/mar/17/government-to-cut-250m-from-social-care-workforce-funding-in-england-report-says

233 Neil Shaw, 'Animal testing for make-up restarts in UK after 25-year ban', Wales Online, 6 May 2023, https://www.walesonline.co.uk/news/uk-news/animal-testing-make-up-restarts-26858030

234 'Bank of England Greenlights 12th Consecutive Interest Rate Rise: What This Means for UK Business Owners', VosCap, May 2023, https://www.voscap.co.uk/

bank-of-england-greenlights-12th-consecutive-interest-rate-rise-what-this-means-for-uk-business-owners/
235 Haggis UK [@Haggis_UK], Twitter, 11 May 2023, https://twitter.com/Haggis_UK/status/1656553898579210241
236 Joshua Nevett, 'UKIP on brink of wipeout after losing all seats in local elections', BBC News, 9 May 2023, https://www.bbc.co.uk/news/uk-politics-65538114
237 Poppy Wood, 'Tory MP Adam Afriyie who repeatedly promoted vaping didn't declare wife's shares in vape retailer', iNews, 12 May 2023, https://inews.co.uk/news/tory-mp-adam-afriyie-promoted-vaping-wife-shares-firm-2337201
238 Oscar Edwards, 'Water pollution: Tory MP says he swam in sewage as a child', BBC News, 18 May 2023, https://www.bbc.co.uk/news/uk-wales-65615711
239 https://www.opendemocracy.net/en/dark-money-investigations/concerns-raised-over-dark-money-funding-anti-lockdown-mps/
240 Ben Quinn, 'Government defeats move to tighten UK foreign donations law', The Guardian, 3 May 2023, https://www.theguardian.com/politics/2023/may/03/government-defeats-move-to-tighten-uk-foreign-donations-law
241 Ben Quinn, 'Government defeats move to tighten UK foreign donations law', The Guardian, 3 May 2023, https://www.theguardian.com/politics/2023/may/03/government-defeats-move-to-tighten-uk-foreign-donations-law
242 Seth Thévoz, Martin Williams and Peter Geoghegan , 'Tories have accepted £2.6m from 'shadowy' donors since Boris Johnson became PM', Open Democracy, 8 Jul 2021, https://www.opendemocracy.net/en/dark-money-investigations/tories-have-accepted-26m-from-shadowy-donors-since-boris-johnson-became-pm/
243 'Revealed: The Tories are still receiving funds from Russia-linked donors', Good Law Project, 11 Apr 2023, https://goodlawproject.org/revealed-the-tories-are-still-receiving-funds-from-russia-linked-donors/
244 Ben Quinn, 'Government defeats move to tighten UK foreign donations law', The Guardian, 3 May 2023, https://www.theguardian.com/politics/2023/may/03/government-defeats-move-to-tighten-uk-foreign-donations-law
245 Aletha Adu, 'UK security minister defends new anti-protest laws before coronation', The Guardian, 3 May 2023, https://www.theguardian.com/uk-news/2023/may/03/uk-security-minister-defends-new-anti-protest-laws-coronation
246 Ben Quinn, Rajeev Syal and Vikram Dodd, 'Anti-monarchists receive 'intimidatory' Home Office letter on new protest laws', The Guardian, 2 May 2023, https://www.theguardian.com/politics/2023/may/02/anti-monarchists-receive-intimidatory-home-office-letter-on-new-protest-laws-coronation
247 'Nottinghamshire MP Lee Anderson tells anti-monarchy protestors to 'emigrate'', ITV News, 7 May 2023, https://www.itv.com/news/central/2023-05-07/tory-mp-lee-anderson-tells-anti-monarchy-protestors-to-emigrate
248 Young Conservative [@Young_Tories], Twitter, 12 Apr 2023, https://twitter.com/Young_Tories/status/1646134550974660608
249 'Penny Mordaunt replaces Priti Patel in cabinet reshuffle', BBC News, 9 Nov, 2017, https://www.bbc.co.uk/news/uk-politics-41931063
250 'Amber Rudd's resignation letter and Theresa May's response', BBC News, 30 Apr 2018, https://www.bbc.co.uk/news/uk-politics-43944710
251 'Defence Secretary Gavin Williamson sacked over Huawei leak', BBC News, 1 May 2019, https://www.bbc.co.uk/news/uk-politics-48126974
252 'Voting Intention: Con 25%, Lab 44% (30-31 May 2023)', YouGov, 7 Jun 2023 https://yougov.co.uk/politics/articles/45791-voting-intention-con-25-lab-44-30-31-may-2023
253 'Brexit stopped Ukraine invasion from succeeding, Jacob Rees-Mogg says', Sky News,

14 May 202, https://news.sky.com/story/brexit-stopped-ukraine-invasion-from-succeeding-jacob-rees-mogg-says-12880590

254 Adam Forrest, 'David Cameron: Don't criticise Braverman's Rwanda plan unless you've got better answer', Independent, 24 May 2023, https://www.independent.co.uk/news/uk/politics/braverman-rwanda-immigration-david-cameron-b2344718.html

255 'Irregular migration to the UK, year ending June 2023', Home Office, Nov 2023,https://www.gov.uk/government/statistics/irregular-migration-to-the-uk-year-ending-june-2023/irregular-migration-to-the-uk-year-ending-june-2023

256 Dan Bloom, 'Rwanda asylum seeker flight will cost hundreds of thousands of pounds - for seven people', Mirror, 14 Jun 2023, https://www.mirror.co.uk/news/politics/rwanda-asylum-seeker-flight-cost-27234328

257 'Rishi Sunak indicates he's no longer committed to manifesto pledge to bring net immigration below 2019 levels', The Guardian, 19 May 2018, https://www.theguardian.com/politics/live/2023/may/18/rishi-sunak-net-migration-conservatives-manifesto-g7-japan-keir-starmer-uk-politics-latest?page=with:block-6465d4a18f08293047a565b0#block-6465d4a18f08293047a565b0

258 Rowena Mason 'Rishi Sunak says he aims to bring immigration below level he 'inherited'', The Guardian, 19 May 2023, https://www.theguardian.com/uk-news/2023/may/19/rishi-sunak-says-he-aims-to-brings-immigration-below-level-he-inherited

259 Faye Brown, 'Net migration rises to new record calendar year figure of 606,000 in the 12 months to December 2022', Sky News, 25 May 2023, https://news.sky.com/story/net-migration-rises-to-new-record-figure-of-606-000-in-the-year-to-december-2022-12888478

260 Arj Singh, 'Rishi Sunak bids to reset his leadership with 'five pledges' to voters on economy, NHS and migration', iNews, 4 Jan 2023, https://inews.co.uk/news/politics/rishi-sunak-leadership-five-pledges-economy-nhs-migration-speech-2065010

261 Poppy Wood, 'How Rishi Sunak's five pledges are going, as underwhelming inflation drop casts doubt on PM's key promises', iNews, 24 May 2023, https://inews.co.uk/news/rishi-sunak-pledges-inflation-drop-doubt-pm-promises-2363229

262 'Economic and fiscal outlook – March 2023', OBR, 15 Mar 2023, https://obr.uk/efo/economic-and-fiscal-outlook-march-2023/

263 Richard Partington, 'UK tips into recession in blow to Rishi Sunak', The Guardian, 15 Feb 2024, https://www.theguardian.com/business/2024/feb/15/uk-recession-consumers-cut-spending-gdp

264 'TUC – UK families suffering "worst decline" in living standards in the G7', TUC, 9 Jan 2024, https://www.tuc.org.uk/news/tuc-uk-families-suffering-worst-decline-living-standards-g7

265 Valentina Romei, 'UK government debt surpasses GDP for first time in 62 years', FT, 21 Jun 2023, https://www.ft.com/content/f8eba4ca-2402-4932-bd4a-7f4534b374bd

266 Anna Wise, 'Bank of England set to raise interest rates for 12th time in a row', Independent, 10 Ma 2023, https://www.independent.co.uk/business/interest-rates-rise-bank-of-england-b2336421.html

267 'NHS waiting lists hit record high in England', BBC News, 13 Jul 2023, https://www.bbc.co.uk/news/health-66188529

268 Daniel Dunford, Ganesh Rao and Lauren Pinkne, 'NHS waiting list: Number of people waiting more than a year for treatment almost 200 times higher than pre-pandemic', Sky News, 24 May 2023 https://news.sky.com/story/nhs-waiting-list-number-of-people-waiting-more-than-a-year-for-treatment-almost-200-times-higher-than-pre-pandemic-12589790

269 'Minister wrong to claim small boat arrivals are down 20% in the first six months

of 2023', FullFact, 10 Jul 2023, https://fullfact.org/immigration/chris-philp-asylum-seekers/
270 Diane Taylor and Ben Quinn, 'Braverman plan to send asylum seekers to Rwanda unlawful, appeal court rules', The Guardian, 29 Jun 2023, https://www.theguardian.com/uk-news/2023/jun/29/plan-to-send-asylum-seekers-to-rwanda-is-unlawful-uk-appeal-court-rules
271 Katy Balls, "'Do you want to turn our party into a skip fire?': Tory MPs have had it with team Johnson', The Guardian, 25 May 2023, https://www.theguardian.com/commentisfree/2023/may/25/party-skip-fire-tory-mps-had-it-team-johnson
272 John Stevens, 'Boris Johnson's £840-a-roll gold wallpaper 'peeling off the walls of Downing Street flat''', Mirror, 24 Nov 2022, https://www.mirror.co.uk/news/politics/boris-johnsons-840-roll-gold-28574821
273 Emily White, 'Millions more people could qualify for legal aid as the scheme is expanded – here's what's changing', Money Saving Expert, 9 Jun 2023, https://www.moneysavingexpert.com/news/2023/06/legal-aid-eligibility-earning-threshold-expanding/
274 'Boris Johnson's partygate legal fees cost taxpayer £265,000', Sky News, 21 Jul 2023, https://news.sky.com/story/boris-johnsons-partygate-legal-fees-cost-taxpayer-265-000-12924534
275 Keir Mudie, 'Boris Johnson's sister Rachel flouts lockdown to stay at second home and play tennis', Mirror, 31 May 2020, https://www.mirror.co.uk/news/politics/boris-johnsons-sister-flouts-lockdown-22115003
276 Heather Stewart, 'Chillaxing at Chequers: how Boris Johnson used the PM's country house', The Guardian, 25 May 2023, https://www.theguardian.com/politics/2023/may/25/chillaxing-at-chequers-how-boris-johnson-used-the-pms-country-house
277 Heather Stewart, 'Chillaxing at Chequers: how Boris Johnson used the PM's country house', The Guardian, 25 May 2023, https://www.theguardian.com/politics/2023/may/25/chillaxing-at-chequers-how-boris-johnson-used-the-pms-country-house
278 Aubrey Allegretti, 'Boris Johnson cuts ties with government lawyers assisting him in Covid inquiry', The Guardian, 24 May 2023, https://www.theguardian.com/uk-news/2023/may/24/boris-johnson-cuts-ties-government-lawyers-assisting-him-covid-inquiry
279 Will Taylor, 'Boris 'threatens to sue Cabinet Office' over Covid 'stitch-up' after latest lockdown rule breaking claims', LBC, 23 May 2023, https://www.lbc.co.uk/news/boris-johnson-referred-police-lockdown-parties/
280 'I think that this report is in danger of making the House of Commons look foolish, says Jacob Rees-Mogg', Conservative Post, 15 Jun 2023, https://conservativepost.co.uk/i-think-that-this-report-is-in-danger-of-making-the-house-of-commons-look-foolish-says-jacob-rees-mogg/
281 'Jacob Rees-Mogg – 2022 Statement on EU Retained Law', UK Pol Political Speech Archive, 23 Jun 2022, https://www.ukpol.co.uk/jacob-rees-mogg-2022-statement-on-eu-retained-law/
282 Jacob Rees-Mogg, 'Parliament matters more than ever after Brexit', The Spectator, 13 Jan 2021, https://www.spectator.co.uk/article/why-parliament-matters/
283 Peter Walker, 'Partygate report: key findings of Commons privileges committee', The Guardian, 15 Jun 2023, https://www.theguardian.com/politics/2023/jun/15/partygate-report-key-findings-of-commons-privileges-committee-boris-johnson
284 'Resignation statement in full as Boris Johnson steps down', BBC News, 9 Jun 2023, https://www.bbc.co.uk/news/uk-politics-65863336
285 'Contributions for Boris Johnson', Hansard, https://hansard.parliament.uk/search/

MemberContributions?endDate=2022-11-15&memberId=1423&outputType=List&partial=False&searchTerm=uxbridge&startDate=2015-05-07&type=Spoken

286 Richard Vaughan, 'Boris Johnson has made £4m since leaving Downing Street but missed 187 Commons votes', iNews, 26 May 2023, https://inews.co.uk/news/politics/boris-johnson-made-since-leaving-downing-street-missed-commons-votes-2366555

287 Rowena Mason and Aubrey Allegretti, 'Boris Johnson resigns as MP with immediate effect over Partygate report', The Guardian, 9 Jun 2023, https://www.theguardian.com/politics/2023/jun/09/boris-johnson-resigns-as-mp-with-immediate-effect-over-partygate-report

288 Aubrey Allegretti, 'Rishi Sunak to miss Boris Johnson Partygate sanctions vote', The Guardian, 19 Jun 2023, https://www.theguardian.com/politics/2023/jun/19/rishi-sunak-to-miss-vote-sanctioning-boris-johnson-over-partygate

289 Alexandra Rogers, 'Boris Johnson denied special access to parliament as MPs endorse report which said he lied', Sky News, 20 Jun 2023, https://news.sky.com/story/boris-johnson-denied-special-access-to-parliament-as-mps-endorse-report-which-said-he-lied-12905498

290 'Boris Johnson signs '£1m' Daily Mail contract following damning partygate report', ITV News, 16 Jun 2023, https://www.itv.com/news/2023-06-16/boris-johnson-set-to-be-new-daily-mail-columnist-after-damning-partygate-report

291 Ben Quinn and Henry Dyer, 'Boris Johnson has breached rules in taking Daily Mail job, says watchdog', The Guardian, 16 Jun 2023, https://www.theguardian.com/politics/2023/jun/16/boris-johnson-fresh-questions-as-daily-mail-signs-ex-pm-as-columnist

292 Brian Wheeler and Chas Geiger, 'Boris Johnson breaks ministerial code with new Daily Mail job', BBC News, 17 Jun 2023, https://www.bbc.co.uk/news/uk-politics-65930008

293 Boris Johnson, 'The wonder drug I hoped would stop my 11.30pm fridge raids for cheddar and chorizo didn't work for me. But I still believe it could change the lives of millions', Daily Mail, 16 Jun 2023, https://www.dailymail.co.uk/news/article-12203407/BORIS-JOHNSON-Wonder-drug-hoped-stop-raids-cheddar-chorizo-didnt-work-me.html

294 Peter Walker, "Actions akin to mutiny': the Tories speaking out against Boris Johnson', The Guardian, 12 Jun 2023, https://www.theguardian.com/politics/2023/jun/12/actions-mutiny-tories-speaking-out-against-boris-johnson

295 The Independent [@independent], Twitter, 10 Jun 2023, https://twitter.com/Independent/status/1667584748275867650'

296 Aletha Adu, 'Sunak faces test as another Johnson ally quits triggering third byelection', The Guardian, 10 Jun 2023, https://www.theguardian.com/politics/2023/jun/10/rishi-sunak-faces-further-test-nigel-adams-johnson-ally-quits-parliament

297 Matt Chorley [@MattChorley], Twitter, 9 Jun 2023, https://twitter.com/MattChorley/status/1667183710561615880

298 Nadine Dorries [@NadineDorries], Twitter, 9 Jun 2023, https://twitter.com/NadineDorries/status/1667182498042740742

299 Press Association, "I have to remove myself': Nadine Dorries to step down as an MP', The Guardian, 9 Feb 2023, https://www.theguardian.com/politics/2023/feb/09/i-have-to-remove-myself-nadine-dorries-to-step-down-as-an-mp

300 Josiah Mortimer, 'Anger as Nadine Dorries' Year-Long Silence in Parliament is Deemed 'Within the Rules' By Standards Watchdog', Byline Times, 14 Aug 2023, https://bylinetimes.com/2023/08/14/anger-as-nadine-dorries-year-long-silence-in-parliament-is-deemed-within-the-rules-by-standards-watchdog/

301 Kate Devlin, 'Boris Johnson told 'months ago' peerage for Nadine Dorries had been

rejected', Independent, 14 June 2023, https://www.independent.co.uk/news/uk/politics/nadine-dorries-peerage-rejected-johnson-b2357191.html
302 Alexandra Rogers, 'Nadine Dorries claims 'sinister forces' were behind House of Lords snub', Sky News, 13 Jun 2023, https://news.sky.com/story/nadine-dorries-claims-sinister-forces-were-behind-house-of-lords-snub-12901468
303 'Resignation peerages', Gov.uk, 2023 https://assets.publishing.service.gov.uk/government/uploads/system/uploads/attachment_data/file/1165570/Resignation_Peerages_2023.pdf
304 Michael Savage, 'Honours row grows after claim Charlotte Owen 'worked as maternity cover'', The Guardian, 18 Jun 2023, https://www.theguardian.com/politics/2023/jun/18/honours-row-grows-after-claim-charlotte-owen-worked-as-maternity-cover
305 Alex Daniel, 'People are sharing Baroness Owen's official Parliament profile for this awkward reason', Indy100, 21 Dec 2023, https://www.indy100.com/politics/charlotte-owen-baroness-lords-boris
306 Catherine Neilan, 'Charlotte Owen's claim to have worked in George Osborne's Tatton office in tatters', Tortoise Media, 21 Jun 2023, https://www.tortoisemedia.com/2023/06/21/charlotte-owens-claim-to-have-worked-in-george-osbornes-tatton-office-in-tatters/
307 Becky Morton, 'Nadine Dorries and Jacob Rees-Mogg accused of interfering with Partygate probe', BBC News, 29 Jun 2023, https://www.bbc.co.uk/news/uk-66051280
308 'Andrea Jenkyns: Minister says she raised her middle finger because of a 'baying mob'', BBC News, 9 Jul 2022, https://www.bbc.co.uk/news/uk-politics-62105688
309 'Priti Patel: Bullying inquiry head quits as PM backs home secretary', BBC News, 20 Nov 2020, https://www.bbc.co.uk/news/uk-politics-55016076
310 'Priti Patel quits cabinet over Israel meetings row', BBC News, 8 Nov 2017, https://www.bbc.co.uk/news/uk-politics-41923007
311 Rob Merick, 'Migrants at risk of drowning if Priti Patel sends Navy warships to Channel, warns ex-home secretary', Independent, 8 Aug 2020, https://www.independent.co.uk/news/uk/politics/migrant-channel-crossings-france-navy-priti-patel-home-secretary-a9660846.html
312 Tim Shipman, 'Charlotte Owen and Ross Kempsell: the curious rise of Johnson's junior peers', The Sunday Times, 29 Jul 2023, https://www.thetimes.co.uk/article/charlotte-owen-boris-johnson-peer-house-lords-honours-l56qcm56f
313 Aletha Adu, 'Peer faces year's ban from Lords bars for bullying two people while drunk', The Guardian, 17 May 2024, https://www.theguardian.com/politics/article/2024/may/17/peer-kulveer-ranger-faces-years-ban-from-lords-bars-for-bullying-two-people-while-drunk
314 Anna Isaac and Stephanie Kirchgaessner, 'Washington Post publisher alleged to have advised Boris Johnson to 'clean up' phone during Partygate Covid scandal', The Guardian, 19 Jun 2024, https://www.theguardian.com/media/article/2024/jun/19/will-lewis-washington-post-publisher-boris-johnson-partygate
315 Brendan Clarke-Smith, '@Bren4Bassetlaw', Twitter, 19 Jun 2023, https://x.com/Bren4Bassetlaw/status/1670774891736449025
316 Aletha Adu, 'Dame Priti and Sir Jacob: the allies and aides in Johnson's honours list', The Guardian, 9 Jun 2023, https://www.theguardian.com/politics/2023/jun/09/dame-priti-and-sir-party-marty-the-aides-and-allies-in-boris-johnsons-honours-list
317 Daniel Angelini, 'Boris honours list 'full of sycophants and failures'', Swindon Advertiser, 13 Jun 2023, https://www.swindonadvertiser.co.uk/yoursay/swindonletters/23583218.boris-honours-list-full-sycophants-failures/
318 Kevin Schofield, 'Boris Johnson's New Spin Doctor Once Accused Him Of 'Digging His

Political Grave", Huffington Post, 6 Feb 2022, https://www.huffingtonpost.co.uk/entry/guto-harri-boris-johnson_uk_61ff6fa1e4b05004242e4d3b

319 Nathan Hyde, 'Teesside Freeport: Was valuable land sold to developers for just £1 per acre?', The Yorkshire Post, 12 May 2023 https://www.yorkshirepost.co.uk/news/politics/teesside-freeport-was-valuable-land-sold-to-developers-for-just-ps1-per-acre-4139474

320 Richard Partington, 'Gove refuses to set deadline for investigation into Tees freeport 'corruption'', The Guardian, 10 Jan 2024, https://www.theguardian.com/business/2024/jan/10/gove-refuses-to-set-deadline-for-investigation-into-tees-freeport-corruption

321 'Tees Valley Review' 23 Jan 2024, https://assets.publishing.service.gov.uk/media/65ba58ec3be8ad0010a081a9/Tees_Valley_Review_Report.pdf

322 Julia Mazza, 'Teesworks and Billingham: a tale of two fiascos', North East Bylines, 1 Apr 2024, https://northeastbylines.co.uk/region/teesside/teesworks-and-billingham-a-tale-of-two-fiascos/

323 'Labour Market Information', Middlesborough College, 2023, https://www.mbro.ac.uk/services-and-support/careers-advice/labour-market-information/

324 Richard Murphy, 'Freeports: a pathway to the end of government as we know it', The Moorlander, 25 Oct 2023, https://www.themoorlander.co.uk/news/politics/1329888/freeports-a-pathway-to-the-end-of-government-as-we-know-it.html

325 ITV News [@itvnews], ITV News, Twitter, 10 May 2024, https://twitter.com/itvnews/status/1788986874263957696

326 'Covid inquiry: What is it investigating and how does it work?', BBC News, 21 May 2023, https://www.bbc.co.uk/news/explainers-57085964

327 Detailed in The Decade In Tory by Russell Jones, pages 383–505 (Unbound, 2022).

328 Steve Barrett, 'Sunak's absurd decision to sue the Covid inquiry judge', The Spectator, 2 Jun 2023, https://www.spectator.co.uk/article/why-is-the-government-suing-its-own-judge/

329 Jon Craig, 'Rishi Sunak's costly COVID Inquiry legal challenge was doomed to failure - and has now been kicked into touch', Sky News, 6 Jul 2023, https://news.sky.com/story/sunaks-costly-covid-inquiry-legal-challenge-was-doomed-to-failure-and-has-now-been-kicked-into-touch-12916318

330 'Downing Street says some of Boris Johnson's WhatsApp messages not 'permanently stored'', The Guardian, 30 May 2023, https://www.theguardian.com/politics/live/2023/may/30/covid-inquiry-boris-johnson-government-messages-deadline-rishi-sunak-conservatives-labour-uk-politics-latest?CMP=share_btn_url&page=with:block-6475df3a8f08664f2ff42422#block-6475df3a8f08664f2ff42422

331 Tim Baker and Alexandra Rogers, 'COVID inquiry: Government seeks judicial review over order to hand over Boris Johnson WhatsApp messages', Sky News, 1 Jun 2023, https://news.sky.com/story/covid-inquiry-government-seeks-judicial-review-over-order-to-hand-over-johnson-whatsapp-messages-12892475

332 Harroon Saddique, 'Why does the government want to reform judicial review?', The Guardian, 7 Aug 2023, https://www.theguardian.com/law/2022/aug/07/why-does-the-government-want-to-reform-judicial-review

333 Josiah Mortimer, 'Government Forced to Reveal Cost of Failed Legal Challenge Over Release of Covid-Era WhatsApp Messages from Johnson and Sunak', Byline Times, 12 Dec 2023, https://bylinetimes.com/2023/12/12/government-forced-to-reveal-cost-of-failed-legal-challenge-over-release-of-covid-era-whatsapp-messages-from-johnson-and-sunak/

334 Pippa Crerar, 'Sunak fails to hand WhatsApp messages from time as chancellor to Covid inquiry', The Guardian, 2 Oct 2023, https://www.theguardian.com/uk-news/2023/oct/02/sunak-fails-to-hand-whatsapp-messages-from-time-as-chancellor-to-covid-inquiry

335 Aletha Adu, 'Boris Johnson 'has forgotten' passcode for phone wanted by Covid inquiry', The Guardian, 23 Jul 2023, https://www.theguardian.com/uk-news/2023/jul/13/boris-johnson-has-forgotten-passcode-for-phone-wanted-by-covid-inquiry

336 Holly Bancroft, 'Suella Braverman arrives at Manston migrant centre by Chinook helicopter', Independent, 3 Nov 2022, https://www.independent.co.uk/news/uk/home-news/suella-braverman-dover-manston-immigration-chinook-b2217000.html

337 Mark Townsend, 'Revealed: scores of child asylum seekers kidnapped from Home Office hotel', The Guardian, 21 Jan 2023, https://www.theguardian.com/uk-news/2023/jan/21/revealed-scores-of-child-asylum-seekers-kidnapped-from-home-office-hotel

338 Mark Townsend, 'Revealed: scores of child asylum seekers kidnapped from Home Office hotel', The Guardian, 21 Jan 2023, https://www.theguardian.com/uk-news/2023/jan/21/revealed-scores-of-child-asylum-seekers-kidnapped-from-home-office-hotel

339 'Local government finances: Impact on communities', House of Lords Library, 14 Mar 2024, https://lordslibrary.parliament.uk/local-government-finances-impact-on-communities/

340 'How Much Has Homelessness Increased In The UK', Greater Change, 8 Jun 2022, https://www.greaterchange.co.uk/post/how-much-has-homelessness-increased-in-the-uk

341 Thomas Brown, 'Child poverty: Statistics, causes and the UK's policy response', House of Lords Library, 13 Apr 2024, https://lordslibrary.parliament.uk/child-poverty-statistics-causes-and-the-uks-policy-response/

342 'More adults living with their parents', ONS, 10 May 2023, https://www.ons.gov.uk/peoplepopulationandcommunity/populationandmigration/populationestimates/articles/moreadultslivingwiththeirparents/2023-05-10

343 Michael Goodier, Carmen Aguilar García and Richard Partington, 'How a decade of austerity has squeezed council budgets in England', The Guardian, 29 Jan 2024, https://www.theguardian.com/uk-news/2024/jan/29/how-a-decade-of-austerity-has-squeezed-council-budgets-in-england

344 'Why do councils go bust and what happens when they do?', BBC News, 5 Mar 2024, https://www.bbc.co.uk/news/uk-politics-66878229

345 Peter Henshaw, 'Councils lose 96% of SEND tribunals – at a cost of £60m', Headteacher Update, 27 Sep 2023, https://www.headteacher-update.com/content/news/councils-lose-96-of-send-tribunals-at-a-cost-of-60m/

346 'SEND system is 'lose, lose, lose', admits Keegan', Schools Week, 19 Oct 2023, https://schoolsweek.co.uk/send-system-is-lose-lose-lose-admits-keegan/

347 Matt Keer, 'SEND Tribunal 2023: When will councils stop wasting public funds defending SEND appeals when they fail almost all the time?', Special Needs Jungle, 15 Dec 2023, https://www.specialneedsjungle.com/send-tribunal-2023-councils-stop-wasting-public-funds-send-appeals-fail-almost-all-time/

348 Sarah Calkin, 'Gove: Send services need 'reform'', Local Government Chronical, 21 Nov 2023, https://www.lgcplus.com/services/children/gove-send-services-need-reform-21-11-2023/

349 Rajeev Syal, 'Rwanda plan to cost UK £1.8m for each asylum seeker, figures show', The Guardian, 1 Mar 2024, https://www.theguardian.com/uk-news/2024/mar/01/rwanda-plan-uk-asylum-seeker-cost-figures

350 Diane Taylor and Ben Quinn, 'Braverman plan to send asylum seekers to Rwanda unlawful, appeal court rules', The Guardian, 29 Jun 2023, https://www.theguardian.com/uk-news/2023/jun/29/plan-to-send-asylum-seekers-to-rwanda-is-unlawful-uk-appeal-court-rules

July to December 2023

1. Arj Singh, Joe Duggan, 'Home Office staff 'refusing minister's order' to paint over Mickey Mouse art for children at asylum centre', iNews, 5 Jul 2023, https://inews.co.uk/news/politics/home-office-staff-refusing-ministers-order-to-paint-over-art-for-children-at-asylum-centre-2457066
2. Adam Forrest, 'Fresh Tory infighting sparked by right-wing group's radical immigration plan: "The last thing we need"', Independent, 4 Jul 2023, https://www.independent.co.uk/news/uk/politics/sunak-immigration-braverman-tories-lee-anderson-b2368646.html
3. 'Female Doctor Who robs boys of role models, claims Tory MP', BBC News, 25 Nov 2021, https://www.bbc.co.uk/news/uk-politics-59421259
4. Joshua Nevett, 'Tory MPs issue plan for Rishi Sunak to slash migration', BBC News, 3 Jul 2023, https://www.bbc.co.uk/news/uk-politics-66084962
5. Joshua Nevett, 'Tory MPs issue plan for Rishi Sunak to slash migration', BBC News, 3 Jul 2023, https://www.bbc.co.uk/news/uk-politics-66084962
6. Ammar Kalia, "It is devastating': the millennials who would love to have kids – but can't afford a family', The Guardian, 13 Oct 2021, https://www.theguardian.com/lifeandstyle/2021/oct/13/it-is-devastating-the-millennials-who-would-love-to-have-kids-but-cant-afford-a-family
7. Tim Wallace, 'Why baby boomers are the luckiest generation in history', The Telegraph, 10 Apr 2024, https://www.telegraph.co.uk/business/2024/04/10/pensioners-luckiest-generation-in-history-charts/
8. 'UK Public Opinion toward Immigration: Overall Attitudes and Level of Concern', Migration Observatory, 28 Sep 2023, https://migrationobservatory.ox.ac.uk/resources/briefings/uk-public-opinion-toward-immigration-overall-attitudes-and-level-of-concern/
9. Kate Nicholson, 'There's A Budding Conversation About 'Breeding For Britain' At The Tory Party Conference', Huffington Post, 30 Sep 2024, https://www.huffingtonpost.co.uk/entry/theres-a-budding-conversation-about-breeding-for-britain-at-the-tory-party-conference_uk_66faa6e8e4b0a61d19be906f
10. Joshua Nevett, 'Tory MPs issue plan for Rishi Sunak to slash migration', BBC News, 3 Jul 2023, https://www.bbc.co.uk/news/uk-politics-66084962
11. Josh Salisbury, 'Half of British workers do not earn new family visa salary threshold, data suggests', Evening Standard, 3 Feb 2024, https://www.standard.co.uk/news/uk/visa-uk-family-salary-home-office-threshold-changes-study-b1136470.html
12. 'Number of people receiving emergency food parcels from Trussell Trust foodbanks in the United Kingdom from 2008/09 to 2022/23', Statista, 2023, https://www.statista.com/statistics/382695/uk-foodbank-users/
13. Deborah Haynes, Sophia McBride, 'Revealed: The military personnel turning to food banks as cost of living crisis hits', Sky News, 12 Jun 2023, https://news.sky.com/story/some-military-personnel-forced-to-use-food-banks-as-inflation-tips-members-of-armed-forces-into-crisis-12900704
14. Aubrey Allegretti, 'Food bank use a 'personal decision', says veterans minister', The Guardian, 4 Jul 2023, https://www.theguardian.com/society/2023/jul/04/food-bank-use-uk-military-poverty-personal-budgeting-johnny-mercer
15. Patrick Butler, 'UK benefits fall short of minimum living cost by £140 a month, charities say', The Guardian, 26 Feb 2023, https://www.theguardian.com/society/2023/feb/26/uk-benefits-fall-short-of-minimum-living-cost-by-140-a-month-charities-say
16. Jo Faragher, 'Fifth of food bank users are from working households', Personnel Today, 10 Nov 2022, https://www.personneltoday.com/hr/cost-of-living-food-banks/

17 Miranda Bryant, 'Half of NHS trusts providing or planning food banks for staff', The Guardian, 8 Jan 2023, https://www.theguardian.com/business/2023/jan/08/nhs-trusts-hospitals-food-banks-for-staff-nurses
18 'MP Simon Clarke's nurses-using-food banks remarks criticised by RCN', BBC News, 18 Jan 2023, https://www.bbc.co.uk/news/uk-england-tees-64317593
19 Adam Forest, 'Liz Truss mini-Budget 'left homeowners £300bn worse off'', Independent, 16 Sep 203, https://www.independent.co.uk/news/uk/politics/truss-mini-budget-house-prices-b2412878.html
20 Phil Kemp, 'UK to keep EU safety mark in post-Brexit climbdown', BBC News, 1 Aug 2023, https://www.bbc.co.uk/news/uk-politics-66375185
21 Steven McIntosh, 'GB News: Politicians' shows under scrutiny in new Ofcom investigations', BBC News, 7 Aug 2023, https://www.bbc.co.uk/news/entertainment-arts-66426544
22 Lee Anderson [@LeeAndersonMP_], Twitter, 3 Jul 2023, https://twitter.com/LeeAndersonMP_/status/1675861641026478080
23 Jon Stone, 'Tory deputy chair Lee Anderson tries to make guest eat cat food on new TV show', Independent, 3 Jul 2023, https://www.independent.co.uk/news/uk/politics/lee-anderson-eat-cat-food-tories-b2368362.html
24 Adam Forrest, 'MPs' £86,000 salary should be doubled, says senior Tory Sajid Javid', Independent, 3 Jul 2023, https://www.independent.co.uk/news/uk/politics/sajid-javid-mps-salary-pay-b2368677.html
25 Oliver Pritchard-Jones, 'Tories write out Boris and party as election leaflet fails to mention either in ex-PM's former constituency', Independent, 6 Jul 2023, https://www.independent.co.uk/news/uk/politics/boris-johnson-tories-by-election-uxbridge-b2368502.html
26 Susan Hall [@Councillorsuzie], Twitter, 23 Jan 2023, https://twitter.com/Councillorsuzie/status/1617606744762650626
27 'Mayor confirms world's first Ultra Low Emission Zone', Mayor of London, 26 Mar 2015, https://www.london.gov.uk/press-releases/mayoral/ultra-low-emission-zone
28 'Tory councils wasted £1m on High Court challenge to ULEZ ', Inside Croydon, 28 Jul 2023, https://insidecroydon.com/2023/07/28/tory-councils-wasted-1m-on-high-court-challenge-to-ulez/
29 Alexandra Rodgers, 'Boris Johnson hits out at 'bone-headed' ULEZ - despite it being his idea', Sky News, 7 Jul 2023, https://news.sky.com/story/boris-johnson-hits-out-at-bone-headed-ulez-despite-setting-up-the-scheme-while-he-was-london-mayor-12916924
30 Shanti Das and Jon Ungoed-Thomas, 'Tory staff running network of anti-Ulez Facebook groups riddled with racism and abuse', The Guardian, 27 Apr 2024, https://www.theguardian.com/politics/2024/apr/27/tory-staff-running-network-of-anti-ulez-facebook-groups-riddled-with-racism-and-abuse
31 Becky Morton, 'Big defeats for Tories but party holds on to Uxbridge', BBC News, 21 Jul 2023, https://www.bbc.co.uk/news/uk-politics-66264317
32 Yasmin Rufo, 'Residents of Uxbridge react to narrow Tory by-election victory', BBC News,21 Jul 2023, https://www.bbc.co.uk/news/uk-politics-66264317
33 Pete Saull, Kate Whannel & Paul Seddon, 'MPs' severance pay to double at next general election', BBC News, 25 Aug 2023, https://www.bbc.co.uk/news/uk-politics-66612463
34 Chris Smyth, 'Liz Truss debacle cost taxpayer £3m in severance fees', The Times, 21 Jul 2023, https://www.thetimes.co.uk/article/liz-truss-prime-minister-cost-taxpayer-uk-2023-hd9gqqjjb
35 Sam Francis, 'Migration Bill: Lords reinsert child detention limits', BBC News, 13 Jul

2023, https://www.bbc.co.uk/news/uk-politics-66180897

36. Nick Edser, 'CPTPP trade deal will benefit UK if we use it, says Kemi Badenoch', BBC News, 16 Jul 2023,. https://www.bbc.co.uk/news/business-66214927
37. 'How are our Brexit trade forecast assumptions performing?', OBR, Mar 2024, https://obr.uk/box/how-are-our-brexit-trade-forecast-assumptions-performing/
38. Kate Devlin, 'Flagship post-Brexit trade deal worth even less than ministers claimed, official estimates show', Independent, 25 Nov 2023, https://www.independent.co.uk/news/uk/politics/brexit-trade-deal-less-cptpp-b2453423.html
39. 'Vote Leave head Matthew Elliott: "The Brexiteers won the battle but we could lose the war"', The New Statesman, 5 Sep 2018, https://www.newstatesman.com/encounter/2018/09/vote-leave-head-matthew-elliott-brexiteers-won-battle-we-could-lose-war
40. Nick Robinson, 'Eleven gambles that went wrong for Liz Truss', BBC News, 4 Dec 2022, https://www.bbc.co.uk/news/uk-63838387
41. Graham Hiscott, 'Liz Truss chaos helped drive over 300,000 people into poverty, bombshell study finds', Mirror, 25 Jul 2024, https://www.mirror.co.uk/news/politics/liz-truss-chaos-helped-drive-33317838
42. Matt Dathan, 'Liz Truss hands out one gong for every four days she was in No 10', The Times, 6 Aug 2023, https://www.thetimes.co.uk/article/truss-pm-honours-list-one-gong-for-every-four-days-in-no-10-902jx9zqz
43. Joshua Nevett and Damian Grammaticas, 'Rishi Sunak's wife holds shares in childcare firm given Budget boost', BBC News, 29 Mar 2023, https://www.bbc.co.uk/news/uk-politics-65115204
44. Damian Grammaticas and Kate Whannel, 'Rishi Sunak inadvertently failed to declare childcare interest, rules MPs watchdog', BBC News, 24 Aug 2023, https://www.bbc.co.uk/news/uk-politics-66596319
45. Chas Geiger, 'Rishi Sunak inadvertently broke code of conduct in wife's shares probe', BBC News, 14 Sep 2023, https://www.bbc.co.uk/news/uk-politics-66808084
46. Joshua Nevett, 'Rishi Sunak most frequent UK flyer among recent PMs', BBC News, 11 Aug 2023, https://www.bbc.co.uk/news/uk-politics-66434605
47. 'Rishi Sunak says approving new licences for oil and gas drilling 'entirely consistent' with net zero plan', The Guardian, 31 Jul 2023, https://www.theguardian.com/politics/live/2023/jul/31/rishi-sunak-oil-gas-north-sea-tories-labour-uk-politics-live?page=with:block-64c791a98f08db2904abd22b#block-64c791a98f08db2904abd22b
48. Alex Lawson and Jillian Ambrose, 'North Sea oil and gas: what is the new licensing scheme, and will it cut bills?', The Guardian, 7 Nov 2023, https://www.theguardian.com/business/2023/nov/07/north-sea-oil-gas-licensing-scheme-rishi-sunak-kings-speech-bills
49. 'Rishi Sunak defends granting new North Sea oil and gas licences', BBC News, 31 Jul 2023, https://www.bbc.co.uk/news/uk-scotland-66354478
50. 'World's biggest machine capturing carbon from air turned on in Iceland', The Guardian, 9 Sep 2021, https://www.theguardian.com/environment/2021/sep/09/worlds-biggest-plant-to-turn-carbon-dioxide-into-rock-opens-in-iceland-orca
51. 'Measuring UK greenhouse gas emissions', ONS, 2 May 2024, https://www.ons.gov.uk/economy/environmentalaccounts/methodologies/measuringukgreenhousegasemissions
52. Damian Carrington, 'Sunak's new oil and gas licences are 'moral and economic madness'', The Guardian, 31 Jul 2023, https://www.theguardian.com/environment/2023/jul/31/new-oil-gas-licences-rishi-sunak-un-climate-crisis
53. Eleanor Langford, 'Rishi Sunak is on the 'wrong side of history' over fresh North Sea

drilling, says former Tory minister', iNews, 31 Jul 2023, https://inews.co.uk/news/politics/north-sea-oil-drilling-rishi-sunak-wrong-side-histor-2515800

54 Helena Horton, 'Zac Goldsmith: Michael Gove must be a monster to attack green policies', The Guardian, 26 Jul 2023, https://www.theguardian.com/politics/2023/jul/26/zac-goldsmith-interview-michael-gove-monster-green-policies-climate-crisis

55 Paul Seddon, 'Sunaks' wealth rises to £651m in latest Sunday Times Rich List', BBC News, 28 May 2023, https://www.bbc.co.uk/news/uk-politics-69027955

56 Jack Peat, 'Sunak's family firm signed a billion-dollar deal with BP before PM opened new North Sea licences', The London Economic, 1 Aug 2023, https://www.thelondoneconomic.com/politics/sunaks-family-firm-signed-a-billion-dollar-deal-with-bp-before-pm-opened-new-north-sea-licences-353690/

57 'Theresa Villiers: Ex-environment secretary failed to declare Shell shares', BBC News, 11 Aug 2023, https://www.bbc.co.uk/news/uk-politics-66469317

58 'Concern Over Corruption Red Flags In 20% Of UK's PPE Procurement', Transparency International, 21 Apr 2021, https://www.transparency.org.uk/track-and-trace-uk-PPE-procurement-corruption-risk-VIP-lane

59 Mikey Smith, 'NHS-owned PPE worth £225 million burned in China pumping out 6,000 tonnes of CO2', Mirror, 29 Jul 2023, https://www.mirror.co.uk/news/politics/nhs-owned-ppe-worth-225-30584523

60 'Timeline: Policy and legislative changes affecting migration to the UK', GOV.UK, https://assets.publishing.service.gov.uk/media/6744490d4a89e48361cb351b/user-guide-policy-changes-sep-24.ods

61 Diane Taylor, 'Contractors told about legionella on day asylum seekers boarded barge', Guardian, 13 Aug 2023, https://www.theguardian.com/uk-news/2023/aug/13/home-office-was-told-about-legionella-on-refugees-barge-on-day-they-boarded

62 Kevin Schofield, 'Cabinet Minister Backs Lee Anderson Over 'F*** Off Back To France' Migrants Jibe', HuffPost, 8 Aug 2023, https://www.huffingtonpost.co.uk/entry/cabinet-minister-backs-lee-anderson-over-f-off-back-to-france-migrants-jibe_uk_64d1f036e4b05c10fd6bfd9c

63 Kate Devlin, 'Tory rift after Rishi Sunak backs Lee Anderson over migrant f-word slur', Independent, 9 Aug 2023, https://www.independent.co.uk/news/uk/politics/rishi-sunak-lee-anderson-fword-migrants-b2390392.html

64 Luke Whelan, 'https://www.express.co.uk/news/uk/1800025/carole-volderman-lee-anderson-row-migrants-bibby-stockholm', Express, 8 Aug 2023, https://www.express.co.uk/news/uk/1800025/carole-volderman-lee-anderson-row-migrants-bibby-stockholm

65 Kevin Rawlinson, 'Ministers accused of 'lawyer-bashing' to distract from asylum policy failures', The Guardian, 8 Aug 2023, https://www.theguardian.com/uk-news/2023/aug/08/ministers-accused-of-lawyer-bashing-to-distract-from-asylum-policy-failures

66 Haroon Siddique, 'Conservative HQ criticised for 'targeted campaign' against immigration lawyer', The Guardian, 9 Aug 2023, https://www.theguardian.com/uk-news/2023/aug/09/jacqueline-mckenzie-conservative-hq-criticised-targeted-campaign-against-immigration-lawyer

67 Miles Ellingham, 'Conservative attacks on 'lefty lawyers' fuel hate mail and racist abuse', Financial Times, 28 Aug 2023, https://www.ft.com/content/7a98b644-7257-43b7-aa99-fabe618fa894

68 Will Taylor, 'Organised crime gang steals hard drive containing vital evidence against Channel people smugglers from UK base', LBC, 11 Aug 2023, https://www.lbc.co.uk/news/gang-steals-evidence-migrant-crossings/

69 'The Observer view: 'small boats week' chaos reveals a bankrupt strategy', The

Observer, 12 Aug 2023, https://www.theguardian.com/commentisfree/2023/aug/12/uk-migration-policy-small-boats-week-chaos-reveals-bankrupt-strategy

70. Mark Townsend, 'How the 'small boats week' unravelled', The Guardian, 13 Aug 2023, https://www.theguardian.com/uk-news/2023/aug/13/how-the-small-boats-week-unravelled

71. Nick Eardley, 'Tories could campaign to leave European human rights treaty if Rwanda flights blocked', BBC News, 9 Aug 2023, https://www.bbc.co.uk/news/uk-politics-66438422

72. George Parker, William Wallis, 'Rishi Sunak warned of Tory backlash if he tries to take UK out of ECHR', Financial Times, 5 Feb 2023, https://www.ft.com/content/2117480f-a9e5-4768-b365-1eedc666bc40

73. Toby Helm, 'Government's 'small boats week' backfires as Labour lead on immigration rises', The Guardian, 19 Aug 2023, https://www.theguardian.com/world/2023/aug/19/governments-small-boats-week-backfires-as-labour-lead-on-immigration-rises

74. 'Channel crossings: Social media giants to crack down on posts encouraging migrants to make journey', Sky News, 6 Aug 2023, https://news.sky.com/story/channel-crossings-facebook-and-tiktok-team-up-with-police-to-crack-down-on-people-smugglers-12934429

75. Nina Lloyd, 'Bibby Stockholm: Home Office under fresh scrutiny over migrant barge 'incompetence'', Independent, 12 Aug 2023, https://www.independent.co.uk/news/uk/home-news/bibby-stockholm-legionnaires-migrant-barge-b2391967.html

76. Ben Bloch, 'Dame Priti Patel takes aim at government's 'alarming and staggering lack of clarity' over plans to house asylum seekers at Essex RAF base', Sky News, 14 Aug 2023, https://news.sky.com/story/dame-priti-patel-takes-aim-at-governments-alarming-and-staggering-lack-of-clarity-over-plans-to-house-asylum-seekers-at-essex-raf-base-12940218

77. Polly Curtis, 'School building programme scrapped in latest round of cuts', The Guardian, 5 Jul 2010, https://www.theguardian.com/education/2010/jul/05/school-building-programme-budget-cuts

78. 'NEWS: School cuts data reveals 70% real-term cuts', Executive Education, 27 Feb 2024, https://edexec.co.uk/news-school-cuts-data-reveals-70-real-term-cuts/

79. 'Jeremy Hunt says government will 'spend what it takes' to make schools safe', BBC News, 3 Sep 2023, https://www.bbc.co.uk/news/uk-66700026

80. Mabel Banfield-Nwachi, 'What is Raac and why is it forcing schools to shut buildings?', The Guardian, 31 Aug 2023, https://www.theguardian.com/education/2023/aug/31/what-is-raac-reinforced-autoclaved-aerated-concrete-schools-buildings-england-close

81. Sally Weale, 'English pupil funding at same level as when Tories took power, study finds', The Guardian, 4 Jun 2024, https://www.theguardian.com/education/article/2024/jun/04/english-pupil-funding-at-same-level-as-when-tories-took-power-study-finds

82. Anna Fazackerley, 'Cold, damp, unsafe: record number of UK schools refused funding for repairs', The Guardian, 31 Mar 2024, https://www.theguardian.com/education/2024/mar/31/cold-damp-unsafe-record-number-of-uk-schools-refused-funding-for-repairs

83. Sally Weale, 'Teachers in England and Wales report vermin and pests in schools', The Guardian, 6 Apr 2024, https://www.theguardian.com/education/2024/apr/06/teachers-england-wales-schools-vermin-sewage-mould-survey

84. Mikey Smith, 'Rishi Sunak helped fund £40million pool at old private school while slashing state school budgets', Mirror, 15 Jun 2024, https://www.mirror.co.uk/news/politics/rishi-sunak-helped-fund-40million-33038982

85. Joshua Nevett, 'Rishi Sunak refuses to say if he uses private GP', BBC News, 8 Jan 2023, https://www.bbc.co.uk/news/uk-politics-64202855

86 Rupert Neate, 'Call for wealth tax as UK billionaire numbers up by 20% since pandemic', The Guardian, 9 Dec 2022, https://www.theguardian.com/news/2022/dec/19/call-for-wealth-tax-as-uk-billionaire-numbers-up-by-20-since-pandemic

87 Hazel Sheffield and Larry Elliott, 'Low wages under Tories have pushed 900,000 UK children into poverty, report finds', The Guardian, 25 Jun 2024, https://www.theguardian.com/society/article/2024/jun/25/low-wages-under-tories-have-pushed-900000-uk-children-into-poverty-report-finds

88 Sally Weale, 'Eight in 10 primary teachers in England spending own money to help pupils', The Guardian, 5 Jun 2024, https://www.theguardian.com/education/article/2024/jun/05/eight-in-10-primary-teachers-in-england-spending-own-money-to-help-pupils

89 'Labour move to force school funding documents fails', BBC News, 6 Sep 2023, https://www.bbc.co.uk/news/uk-politics-66669998

90 'Counting the cost of the RAAC crisis', BCIS, 13 Sep 2023, https://bcis.co.uk/news/counting-the-cost-of-the-raac-crisis/

91 'What we're doing to permanently remove RAAC from schools and colleges', Gov, 8 Feb 2023, https://educationhub.blog.gov.uk/2024/02/08/new-guidance-on-raac-in-education-settings/

92 'Hospitals, courts and a shopping centre: Which other buildings are at risk of concrete collapse?', Sky News, 6 Sep 2023, https://news.sky.com/story/hospitals-courts-and-a-shopping-centre-which-other-buildings-are-at-risk-of-concrete-collapse-12952243

93 'RAAC found at five prisons, minister reveals', Civil Service World, 5 Apr 2024, https://www.civilserviceworld.com/professions/article/raac-found-at-five-prisons-minister-reveals

94 'Sunday Times Rich List reveals biggest decrease in UK billionaires ever recorded', International Adviser, 17 May 2024, https://international-adviser.com/sunday-times-rich-list-reveals-biggest-decrease-in-uk-billionaires-ever-recorded

95 Matt Honeycombe-Foster, 'Crumbling schools? UK's sweary education chief wants praise for 'f**king good job'', Politico, 4 Sept 2023, https://www.politico.eu/article/crumbling-school-uk-sweary-education-chief-gillian-keegan-praise-fucking-good-job/

96 Joshua Nevett, 'Gavin Williamson ordered to apologise over bullying texts to Wendy Morton', BBC News, 4 Sept 2023, https://www.bbc.co.uk/news/uk-politics-66706287

97 Jim Waterson, 'Cads' Corner and Mark Francois holding court: inside the Carlton Club', The Guardian, 1 Jul 2022, https://www.theguardian.com/politics/2022/jul/01/cads-corner-and-mark-francois-holding-court-inside-the-carlton-club

98 Andy Giddings, 'MP Chris Pincher quits after losing groping appeal', BBC News, 7 Sep 2023, https://www.bbc.co.uk/news/uk-england-stoke-staffordshire-66739410

99 'Marcus Fysh MP told to apologise after breaching code of conduct', BBC News, 7 Sep 2023, https://www.bbc.co.uk/news/uk-england-somerset-66739185

100 Nick Eardley, 'Tory MP Ellwood quits Commons post after Afghanistan row', BBC News, 13 Sep 2023, https://www.bbc.co.uk/news/uk-politics-66797794

101 Chas Geiger, 'Rishi Sunak inadvertently broke code of conduct in wife's shares probe', BBC News, 14 Sep 2023, https://www.bbc.co.uk/news/uk-politics-66808084

102 Adam Forrest, 'Being gay or a woman isn't enough to claim asylum, says Suella Braverman', Independent, 26 Sep 2023, https://www.independent.co.uk/news/uk/politics/suella-braverman-un-refugee-convention-b2418275.html

103 'Map of Jurisdictions that Criminalise LGBT People', Human Dignity Trust, 2023, https://www.humandignitytrust.org/lgbt-the-law/map-of-criminalisation/

104 Tom Peck, 'The moment Suella Braverman became a global laughing stock', Independent, 26 Sep 2023, https://www.independent.co.uk/voices/suella-braverman-migration-immigration-washington-b2418891.html

105 Adam Forrest, 'Braverman accused of 'dog whistle' leadership bid as migrant speech sparks outrage from gay community', Independent, 26 Sep 2023, https://www.independent.co.uk/news/uk/politics/suella-braverman-asylum-speech-gay-b2418678.html

106 Matt Dathan, 'Gay Tories complain to whips over Suella Braverman speech', The Times, 29 Sep 2023, https://www.thetimes.com/uk/law/article/gay-tories-condemn-suella-braverman-over-poisonous-anti-migrant-speech-xqd0d7pvr

107 Ramzy Alwakeel, Adam Bychawski, 'Braverman had no evidence for 'fake gay asylum seekers' claim', OpenDemocracy, 15 Nov 2023, https://www.opendemocracy.net/en/suella-braverman-fake-gay-asylum-seekers-home-office-rwanda-refugees/

108 Xander Elliards, 'Suella Braverman: 'People pretend to be gay to get special treatment'', The National, 27 Sep 2023, https://www.thenational.scot/news/23818409.suella-braverman-people-pretend-gay-get-special-treatment/

109 'Braverman out of Conservative Party leadership contest', BBC News, 14 Jul 2023, https://www.bbc.co.uk/news/av/uk-politics-62164014

110 Adam Payne, 'These are the most left and right-wing cities in Britain — did yours make the list?', Business Insider, 18 Sep 2016, https://www.businessinsider.com/britain-labour-conservative-jeremy-corbyn-theresa-may-2016-9

111 Polly Toynbee, 'The Tories are running scared, but we should all fear what they may become', The Guardian, 2 Oct 2023, https://www.theguardian.com/commentisfree/2023/oct/02/tories-right-centrists-conservative-party-conference

112 Noah Vickers, "'It's trash': Senior London Tory removed from party conference for heckling Suella Braverman', The Standard, 3 Oct 2023, https://www.standard.co.uk/news/politics/andrew-boff-suella-braverman-conservative-conference-speech-heckling-gender-ideology-homophobic-rant-b1111143.html

113 James W Kelly, 'London Assembly chair ejected during Braverman speech', BBC News, 3 Oct 2023, https://www.bbc.co.uk/news/uk-england-london-66993794

114 Emilia Kettle, 'Suella Braverman stands on Guide dogs tail at Tory party conference', Daily Echo, 3 Oct 2023, https://www.bournemouthecho.co.uk/news/national/uk-today/23831660.suella-braverman-stands-guide-dogs-tail-tory-party-conference/

115 'Who are the 100 million displaced people Suella Braverman said could qualify for UK protection?', FullFact, 8 Mar 2023, https://fullfact.org/immigration/suella-braverman-100-million-claim/

116 Peter Walker and Helena Horton, 'Sunak refuses to rule out welcoming Farage back into Tory party', The Guardian, 3 Oct 2023, https://www.theguardian.com/politics/2023/oct/03/sunak-refuses-to-rule-out-welcoming-farage-back-into-tory-party

117 Tom Goodenough, 'Is this year's Tory conference slogan the worst ever?' The Spectator, 2 Oct 2023, https://www.spectator.co.uk/article/is-this-years-tory-conference-slogan-the-worst-ever/

118 David Connett, 'HS2 rail link might not reach London Euston until 2040, Transport Secretary admits', iNews, 19 Apr 2023, https://inews.co.uk/news/business/hs2-rail-not-reach-london-euston-2040-transport-secretary-mark-harper-2284039

119 Katy Austin, 'HS2 to Birmingham may cost £65bn, railway boss says', BBC News, 11 Jan 2024, https://www.bbc.co.uk/news/business-67932247

120 Katy Austin, 'Fewer HS2 seats could force passengers not to travel', BBC News, 23 Jul 2024, https://www.bbc.co.uk/news/articles/c725k6ynw7go

121 Michael Savage, 'Government still buying properties along HS2 route – despite scrapping scheme', The Guardian, 13 Apr 2024, https://www.theguardian.com/uk-news/2024/apr/13/hs2-route-government-buying-properties

122 'New warning on soaring costs of HS2 Euston', RailNews, 27 Mar 2023, https://www.railnews.co.uk/news/2023/03/27-new-warning-on-soaring-costs.html

123 'Royal opening for Extremadura HSL', Railway Pro, 21 Jul 2022. https://www.railwaypro.com/wp/royal-opening-for-extremadura-hsl/
124 Heather Carrick, 'HS2: more than £280 million spent on consultants in past seven years for 'runaway gravy train' rail link', Banbury Guardian, 29 Sep 2023.,https://www.banburyguardian.co.uk/read-this/hs2-280m-spent-consultants-seven-years-runaway-gravy-train-4353822
125 Emma Norris, Gemma Tatlow, 'HS2 is a fiasco of change and churn ', Institute for Government, 5 Oct 2023, https://www.instituteforgovernment.org.uk/comment/hs2-fiasco-change-churn
126 Richard Vaughan, 'HS2 trains too high for station platforms – leaving taxpayers with £200m bill', iNews, 23 Aug 2024, https://inews.co.uk/news/politics/hs2-trains-too-high-station-platforms-taxpayers-bill-3240475
127 Rob Davies, 'HS2 reveals £2bn in costs linked to Sunak's downgrade of line', The Guardian, 29 Jul 2024, https://www.theguardian.com/uk-news/article/2024/jul/29/hs2-costs-rishi-sunak-chief-executive
128 Pippa Crerar, 'Sunak to tell Tories of Britain's broken politics amid chaotic conference', The Guardian, 3 Oct 2023, https://www.theguardian.com/politics/2023/oct/03/sunak-to-tell-tories-of-britains-broken-politics-amid-chaotic-conference
129 Richard Vaughan, 'Birmingham's £460m station to sit largely unused after HS2 northern leg scrapped', iNews, 23 Jul 2024, https://inews.co.uk/news/politics/hs2-waste-new-birmingham-station-unused-3184804
130 Emma Norris, Gemma Tatlow, 'HS2 is a fiasco of change and churn ', Institute for Government, 5 Oct 2023, https://www.instituteforgovernment.org.uk/comment/hs2-fiasco-change-churn
131 'HS2: Johnson warns against 'mutilated' version of rail link', BBC News, 24 Sep 2024, https://www.bbc.co.uk/news/business-66895425
132 Ben Gartside, '200 staff employed on full pay for Government rail body… that doesn't exist', iNews, 25 Feb 2024, https://inews.co.uk/news/politics/staff-full-pay-government-rail-doesnt-exist-2922221
133 Ben Quinn, 'HS2: announced transport projects were just 'examples', says minister', The Guardian, 8Oct 2023, https://www.theguardian.com/uk-news/2023/oct/08/hs2-announced-transport-project-were-just-examples-says-minister
134 Savanta UK [@Savanta_UK], Twitter, 3 Oct 2023, https://twitter.com/Savanta_UK/status/1709152255675334796
135 Greg Hurst, 'The MPs who can't stop talking', The Times, 27 Feb 2006, https://www.thetimes.com/article/the-mps-who-cant-stop-talking-l2qv97hs33z
136 Sam Coates, 'Tory MPs' use of staff budgets to pay for PR advice 'against rules'', The Times, 17 Jul 2017, https://www.thetimes.com/article/tory-mps-use-of-staff-budgets-to-pay-for-pr-advice-against-rules-zfdkk5krt9r
137 Jason Beattie, 'Tories bid to wreck minimum wage', Mirror, 13 May 2009, https://www.mirror.co.uk/news/uk-news/tories-bid-to-wreck-minimum-wage-393724
138 Peter Bone [@PeterBoneUK], Twitter, 17 Jun 2018, https://x.com/PeterBoneUK/status/1008473046611562496
139 Hannah Miller and Phil Kemp, 'Peter Bone: Abuse by MP left me broken, former aide says', BBC News, 25 Oct 2023, https://www.bbc.co.uk/news/uk-politics-67203602
140 Kiran Stacey, 'Tory MP Peter Bone hit and abused staff member, watchdog says', The Guardian, 16 Oct 2023, https://www.theguardian.com/politics/2023/oct/16/tory-mp-peter-bone-hit-and-abused-staff-member-watchdog-says
141 Archie Mitchell, 'Brexiteer Tory MP who 'exposed himself to staff member and trapped him in hotel bathroom' facing suspension', Independent, 18 Oct 2023, https://

www.independent.co.uk/news/uk/politics/peter-bone-bullying-sexual-tory-mp-byelection-b2430361.html

142 Peter Bone [@PeterBoneUK], Twitter, 19 Dec 2023, https://x.com/PeterBoneUK/status/1737208755895291977

143 John Stevens, 'Blundering Tories give flasher ex-MP Peter Bone £5,600 of taxpayer cash by mistake', Mirror, 21 Jan 2024, https://www.mirror.co.uk/news/politics/blundering-tories-give-flasher-ex-31932988

144 Alethu Adi, 'Labour vows to reform ministerial severance pay after Tories handed £1m last year', The Guardian, 26 Jan 2023, https://www.theguardian.com/politics/2024/jan/26/labour-reform-ministerial-severance-pay-tories

145 Sammy Gecsloyer, 'Labour overturns 18,000 Tory majority to win Wellingborough byelection', BBC News, 16 Feb 2023, https://www.theguardian.com/politics/2024/feb/16/labour-wins-wellingborough-byelection-gen-kitchen

146 Aletha Adu, 'Tory candidate shared post using foul language towards struggling parents', The Guardian, 18 Oct 2023, https://www.theguardian.com/politics/2023/oct/18/tory-candidate-andrew-cooper-foulmouthed-outburst-at-jobless-parents

147 Sam Blewett, 'Labour wins Mid Bedfordshire in historic by-election result', Independent, 20 Oct 2023, https://www.independent.co.uk/news/uk/labour-conservative-conservatives-prime-minister-lib-dems-b2432922.html

148 Aubrey Allegretti, 'Rishi Sunak's efforts to hold his party together look increasingly futile'. The Guardian, 23 Oct 2023, https://www.theguardian.com/politics/2023/oct/23/rishi-sunaks-efforts-to-hold-his-party-together-look-increasingly-futile

149 Adam Forrest, "Architects of disaster': Boris, Truss and Tory right accused of leading party into electoral wilderness', Independent, 20 Oct 2023, https://www.independent.co.uk/news/uk/politics/byelections-tories-sunak-boris-truss-b2433195.html

150 Chas Geiger, 'Fines to be issued for Covid Christmas party at Tory HQ', BBC News, 13 Oct 2023, https://www.bbc.co.uk/news/uk-politics-67106804

151 The Decade In Tory, by Russell Jones, 2022, pages 314 to 500.

152 Paul Seddon, 'Simon Case: Top official thought Johnson couldn't lead on Covid', BBC News, 30 Oct 2023, https://www.bbc.co.uk/news/uk-politics-67262984

153 Matthew Weaver, "Nature's way of dealing with old people': the damning messages revealed to Covid inquiry', The Guardian, 31 Oct 2023, https://www.theguardian.com/uk-news/2023/oct/31/natures-way-of-dealing-with-old-people-the-damning-messages-revealed-to-covid-inquiry

154 Pippa Crerar, Aletha Adu, Rachel Hall and Emily Dugan, 'Dead cats and hairdryers: Dominic Cummings' evidence to Covid inquiry', The Guardian, 1 Nov 2023, https://www.theguardian.com/uk-news/2023/nov/01/dead-cats-and-hairdryers-dominic-cummings-evidence-to-covid-inquiry

155 Andrew MacAskill, 'UK PM Sunak reportedly said 'just let people die', COVID inquiry hears', Reuters, 21 Nov 2023, https://www.reuters.com/world/uk/uk-pm-sunak-reportedly-said-just-let-people-die-covid-inquiry-hears-2023-11-20/

156 Pippa Crerar, Aletha Adu, Rachel Hall and Emily Dugan, 'Dead cats and hairdryers: Dominic Cummings' evidence to Covid inquiry', The Guardian, 1 Nov 2023, https://www.theguardian.com/uk-news/2023/nov/01/dead-cats-and-hairdryers-dominic-cummings-evidence-to-covid-inquiry

157 Matt Honeycombe-Foster, 'Boris Johnson's COVID inquiry grilling: All the bombshell moments', Politico, 7 Dev 2023, https://www.politico.eu/article/boris-johnson-covid-19-inquiry-hearing-grilling-big-moments-pandemic/

158 Andrew Fisher [@FisherAndrew79], Twitter, 31 Oct 2023, https://twitter.com/FisherAndrew79/status/1719408935231193498

159 Jim Dunton, 'Covid Inquiry: Cummings lets rip at 'dumpster fire' Cabinet Office', Civil Service World, 1 Nov 2023, https://www.civilserviceworld.com/professions/article/covid-inquiry-dominic-cummings-dumpster-fire-cabinet-office-mark-sedwill
160 Annabel Rackham & Becky Morton, 'Boris Johnson: Former prime minister to host GB News show', BBC News, 27 Oct 2023, https://www.bbc.co.uk/news/entertainment-arts-67242822
161 'Conservative MP Bob Stewart guilty of racially aggravated public order offence', BBC News, 4 Nov 2023, https://www.bbc.co.uk/news/uk-england-london-67310954
162 Sam Francis, 'MP Crispin Blunt arrested on suspicion of rape', BBC News 26 Oct 2023, https://www.bbc.co.uk/news/uk-politics-67233090
163 Kete Devlin and Adam Forrest, 'Human extinction risk from AI on same scale as pandemics or nuclear war, Sunak warns', Independent, 26 Oct 2023, https://www.independent.co.uk/news/uk/politics/ai-sunak-weapon-war-uk-b2436000.html
164 Anna Gross, 'Rishi Sunak says he will 'not rush to regulate' AI', FT, 26 Oct 2023, https://www.ft.com/content/509012f9-4e08-414c-a97f-dd733b9de6ef
165 Zoe Kleinman and Sean Seddon, 'Elon Musk tells Rishi Sunak AI will put an end to work', BBC News, 3 Nov 2023, https://www.bbc.co.uk/news/uk-67302048
166 Dan Milmo, 'Elon Musk unveils Grok, an AI chatbot with a 'rebellious streak'', The Guardian, 5 Nov 2023, https://www.theguardian.com/technology/2023/nov/05/elon-musk-unveils-grok-an-ai-chatbot-with-a-rebellious-streak
167 Sam Coates [@SamCoatesSky], Twitter, 2 Nov 2023, https://x.com/SamCoatesSky/status/1720189979660353696
168 Michael Savage, 'Tory MPs blast 'out of touch' Sunak as he woos homeowners in king's speech', The Observer, 4 Nov 2023, https://www.theguardian.com/politics/2023/nov/04/tory-mps-blast-out-of-touch-sunak-as-he-woos-homeowners-in-kings-speech
169 Rowena Mason, 'Tory MP investigated over payments for chairing group that lobbied PM', The Guardian, 25 Oct 2023, https://www.theguardian.com/politics/2023/oct/25/conservative-mp-bim-afolami-investigated-lobbying-payments
170 Rowena Mason, 'Former Tory chair takes six-figure job at firm part-owned by sanctioned Russians', The Guardian, 25 Oct 2023, https://www.theguardian.com/politics/2023/oct/25/former-tory-chair-brandon-lewis-takes-six-figure-job-at-firm-part-owned-by-sanctioned-russians
171 Glen Owen, 'Tory Party covered up for 'serial rapist' MP: Devastating letter to police from top official claims party did little to stop attacker - but paid for victim to get treatment', Daily Mail, 3 Nov 2023, https://www.dailymail.co.uk/news/article-12711069/Tory-Party-covered-serial-rapist-MP-official-claims.html
172 'Rishi Sunak's communications chief Amber de Botton leaves No 10', BBC News, 1 Sep 2023, https://www.bbc.co.uk/news/uk-politics-66686099
173 Alan Smith, Anna Gross, Rafe Uddin and Eri Sugiura, 'Is this the age of churn in UK politics?', FT, 13 Nov 2023, https://www.ft.com/content/0d515136-5040-4b9e-aaf8-380c33b16fb8
174 James Hockaday, 'The five jobs Grant Shapps has had in less than a year', Yahoo! News, 31 Aug 2023, https://uk.news.yahoo.com/the-five-jobs-grant-shapps-has-had-in-less-than-a-year-135712193.html
175 Sarah Young, 'Seven turbulent years: British ministerial churn since the Brexit vote', Reuters, 13 Nov 2023, https://www.reuters.com/world/uk/seven-turbulent-years-british-ministerial-churn-since-brexit-vote-2023-11-13/
176 Archie Mitchell, 'Revealed: The four promises Sunak made to Braverman in 'secret migration deal'', Independent, 27 Nov 2023, https://www.independent.co.uk/news/uk/politics/rishi-sunak-suella-braverman-migration-b2453995.html

177 'Voting Intention: Con 22%, Lab 44% (12-13 Dec 2023)', YouGov, 14 Dec 2023, https://yougov.co.uk/politics/articles/48175-voting-intention-con-22-lab-44-12-13-dec-2023

178 Claire Duffin, 'Woke critics won't stop me from tackling grooming gangs, pledges Suella Braverman as she rolls out plans for a new taskforce', Daily Mail, 3 Apr 2023, https://www.dailymail.co.uk/news/article-11934805/Woke-critics-wont-stop-tackling-grooming-gangs-pledges-Suella-Braverman.html

179 Elisa Menendez, 'A timeline of Suella Braverman's most controversial moments as home secretary', ITV News, 13 Nov 2023, https://www.itv.com/news/2023-11-10/a-timeline-of-suella-bravermans-most-controversial-moments-as-home-secretary

180 'Attack on UK immigration centre 'terrorist' incident, police say', Al Jazeera, 5 Nov 2022, https://www.aljazeera.com/news/2022/11/5/attack-on-uk-immigration-centre-terrorist-incident-police

181 'Suella Braverman faces criticism for Channel migrant 'invasion' claim', ITV News, 1 Nov 2022, https://www.itv.com/news/2022-10-31/braverman-deflects-blame-for-manston-migrant-saga-as-she-denies-blocking-hotels

182 Jessica Parker, 'Tory MPs complain to chief whip about Suella Braverman's asylum speech', BBC News, 29 Sep 2023, https://www.bbc.co.uk/news/uk-politics-66964607

183 Jedidajah Otte, 'Suella Braverman says rough sleeping is 'lifestyle choice'', The Guardian, 4 Nov 2023, https://www.theguardian.com/society/2023/nov/04/suella-braverman-says-rough-sleeping-is-lifestyle-choice

184 'Rough sleeping in the UK: 2002 to 2021', ONS Census 2021, 2021 https://www.ons.gov.uk/peoplepopulationandcommunity/housing/articles/roughsleepingintheuk/2002to2021

185 'Tommy Robinson 'racist invective' led to far-right targeting family, court hears', Press Association, 12 Mar 2020, https://www.theguardian.com/uk-news/2020/mar/12/tommy-robinson-racist-invective-led-to-far-right-targeting-family-court-hears

186 Dominic Casciani, 'Tommy Robinson leaves UK on eve of court case', BBC News, 29 Jul 2024, https://www.bbc.co.uk/news/articles/cjerxd00rlxo

187 Níall Feiritear, 'Far right activist Tommy Robinson is an Irish citizen, leaked documents show', Sunday World, 29 Jun 2024, https://www.sundayworld.com/crime/irish-crime/far-right-activist-tommy-robinson-is-an-irish-citizen-leaked-documents-show/a486535645.html

188 Sam Courtney-Guy, 'Tommy Robinson 'flees UK' hours before he was due in High Court', Metro, 29 Jul 2024, https://metro.co.uk/2024/07/29/tommy-robinson-leaves-uk-skips-high-court-hearing-21318028/

189 Elisa Menendez, 'A timeline of Suella Braverman's most controversial moments as home secretary', ITV News, 13 November 2023, https://www.itv.com/news/2023-11-10/a-timeline-of-suella-bravermans-most-controversial-moments-as-home-secretary

190 Ben Bloch, 'Suella Braverman accuses Met of 'double standards' over pro-Palestinian protests', Sky News, 9 Nov 2023, https://news.sky.com/story/suella-braverman-accuses-met-of-double-standards-over-pro-palestinian-protests-13003714

191 Rajeev Syal and Rowena Mason, 'Is Braverman trying to get sacked? Some Tory insiders think so', The Guardian, 8 Nov 2023, https://www.theguardian.com/politics/2023/nov/08/tory-insiders-suggest-suella-braverman-trying-to-get-sacked

192 Adam Forrest, 'Braverman defies No 10's order to take out inflammatory element of police attack article', Independent, 9 Nov 2023, https://www.independent.co.uk/news/uk/politics/braverman-sunak-palestine-march-police-b2444331.html

193 'News from Siân Berry: After long delay, Met publishes 2020 protest arrest figures', London.Gov, 21 Mar 2021, https://www.london.gov.uk/press-releases/assembly/sian-berry/met-publishes-2020-protest-arrest-figures

194 Jenny Medlicott, 'Met police make 92 arrests as counter-protesters try to reach Palestine march after clash with officers', LBC, 11 Nov 2023., https://www.lbc.co.uk/news/met-police-make-82-arrests-pro-palestine-protests-london/
195 Tobi Thomas and Rajeev Syal, 'Suella Braverman accused of fuelling far-right violence near Cenotaph', The Guardian, 11 Nov 2023, https://www.theguardian.com/politics/2023/nov/11/suella-braverman-accused-of-fuelling-far-right-violence-near-cenotaph
196 '300,000 attend pro-Palestinian march as about 100 counter-protesters arrested', BBC News, 11 Nov 2023, https://www.bbc.co.uk/news/live/uk-67390343
197 Simon Childs, 'The Far-Right Observed Remembrance Day by Fighting the Police', Novora Media, 11 Nov 2023, https://novaramedia.com/2023/11/11/the-far-right-observed-remembrance-day-by-fighting-the-police/
198 'Rishi Sunak: Far-Right thugs and Hamas sympathisers disrespect our heroes', Telegraph, 12 Nov 2023, https://www.telegraph.co.uk/news/2023/11/11/pro-palestine-rally-protest-armistice-day-london-police/
199 Vikram Dodd and Heather Stewart, 'Police say Suella Braverman's claims of force's bias 'a factor' in attacks on them', The Guardian, 12 Nov 2023, https://www.theguardian.com/politics/2023/nov/12/police-say-suella-bravermans-claims-of-forces-bias-a-factor-in-attacks-on-them
200 Mark Townsend, 'Far-right 'defends' the Cenotaph to the echo of home secretary's words', The Observer, 11 Nov 2023, https://www.theguardian.com/uk-news/2023/nov/11/far-right-defends-cenotaph-home-secretary-gaza-armistice-day-london
201 Matt Dathan, 'Two Tories threaten to quit if Suella Braverman is sacked', The Times, 10 Nov 2023, https://www.thetimes.com/uk/law/article/suella-braverman-home-secretary-sacked-tories-times-article-scrlcrdq7
202 Peter Walker and Ben Quinn, 'Rightwing Tories meet in wake of Suella Braverman's sacking', The Guardian, 13 Nov 2023, https://www.theguardian.com/politics/2023/nov/13/suella-braverman-sacked-home-secretary
203 Ashley Cowburn, 'Rishi Sunak faces revolt as Tory MP delivers brutal warning in letter of no confidence', Mirror, 13 Nov 2023, https://www.mirror.co.uk/news/politics/rishi-sunak-faces-revolt-tory-31430450
204 Arj Singh and Richard Vaughan, 'Suella Braverman: Tory anger at 'narcissistic crap' after scathing attack on Rishi Sunak', iNews, 24 Nov 2024, https://inews.co.uk/news/suella-braverman-tory-anger-narcissistic-crap-attack-rishi-sunak-2755367
205 Andrew McDonald, 'Rishi Sunak tries to distance himself from 13 years of the Tories in conference speech', Politico, 4 Oct 2023, https://www.politico.eu/article/prime-minister-rishi-sunak-distance-himself-13-years-tory-party-government-conference-speech/
206 George Wright and Kate Whannel, 'David Cameron returns to cabinet table after seven years', BBC News, 14 Oct 2024, https://www.bbc.co.uk/news/uk-politics-67411550
207 'Steve Barclay: PM's new chief of staff pledges smaller state', BBC News, 13 Feb 2022, https://www.bbc.co.uk/news/uk-politics-60366086
208 Alastair McLellan, 'Steve Barclay is NHS leadership's worst 'nightmare'', HSJ, 6 Jul 2022, https://www.hsj.co.uk/comment/steve-barclay-is-nhs-leaderships-worst-nightmare/7032754.article
209 Mikey Smith, 'Health Secretary Steve Barclay faces questions over meetings with nightclub owners', Mirror, 8 Apr 2023, https://www.mirror.co.uk/news/politics/health-secretary-steve-barclay-faces-29663525
210 Max Warner, 'IFS response to new NHS waiting times figures', IFS, 11 Aug 2022, https://ifs.org.uk/news/ifs-response-new-nhs-waiting-times-figures

211 Nick Triggle, 'One million people on more than one waiting list as NHS backlog grows', BBC News, 9 Nov 2023, https://www.bbc.co.uk/news/health-67367311

212 Sandra Laville, 'Alarm raised over water firm job of new environment secretary's wife', The Guardian, 14 Nov 2023, https://www.theguardian.com/politics/2023/nov/14/possible-conflict-of-interest-for-new-environment-secretary-steve-barclay-anglian-water-sewage

213 Tim Dale, 'Health Secretary Victoria Atkins says husband's sugar job no conflict', BBC News, 17 Nov 2023, https://www.bbc.co.uk/news/uk-england-lincolnshire-67448520

214 Andrew Gilligan, 'Drug minister Victoria Atkins's husband oversees cannabis farm', The Sunday Times, 13 May 2018, https://www.thetimes.com/uk/society/article/drug-minister-victoria-atkinss-husband-oversees-cannabis-farm-hv5q25pqr

215 'James Cleverly does not deny privately ridiculing Rwanda policy', BBC News, 16 Nov 2023, https://www.bbc.co.uk/news/av/uk-politics-67440137

216 Young Conservative Network [@YoungConNetwork], Twitter, 20 Nov 2023, https://x.com/YoungConNetwork/status/1726572805196771524

217 Rowena Mason, 'Young Tories urge party to broaden appeal after rise in voter 'crossover' age', The Guardian, 15 Aug 2024, https://www.theguardian.com/politics/article/2024/aug/15/young-tories-urge-party-to-broaden-appeal-after-rise-in-voter-crossover-age

218 'UK has highest housing costs in the English-speaking world', Social Market Foundation, 12 Mar 2024, https://www.smf.co.uk/uk-has-highest-housing-costs-in-the-english-speaking-world/

219 '3 million pensioner millionaires', Intergenerational Foundation, 2022, https://www.if.org.uk/wp-content/uploads/2022/06/pensioner_millionaires_FINAL.pdf

220 Polly Toynbee, 'Pensioner poverty is at a new high – so why are older people still voting Tory?', The Guardian, 18 Mar 2022, https://www.theguardian.com/commentisfree/2022/mar/18/pensioner-poverty-tory-crisis-wealth-rich-pensioners

221 Time Wallace, 'https://www.telegraph.co.uk/business/2024/03/13/halfmillion-pensioners-on-course-lose-1800-under-tories/', The Telegraph, 13 Mar 2024, https://www.telegraph.co.uk/business/2024/03/13/halfmillion-pensioners-on-course-lose-1800-under-tories/

222 'Supreme Court rules Rwanda asylum policy unlawful', BBC News, 15 Nov 2023, https://www.bbc.co.uk/news/uk-67423745

223 David Williamson, 'Warning left-wing 'Blob' will plot to ruin chances of sending migrants to Rwanda', Express, 19 Nov 2023, https://www.express.co.uk/news/politics/1836743/left-wing-whitehall-rwanda

224 Graeme Demianyk, 'Nadine Dorries Makes Confusing Claims About Tech Bosses With Their 'Big Dials'', Huffington Post, 24, Oct 2023, https://www.huffingtonpost.co.uk/entry/nadine-dorries-big-dials-google_uk_65380e0be4b0689b3fbe4ed2

225 Nina Lloyd, 'Lee Anderson says Govt should 'ignore the law' and start sending asylum seekers to Rwanda', The London Economic, 15 Nov 2023, https://www.thelondoneconomic.com/politics/lee-anderson-says-govt-should-ignore-the-law-and-start-sending-asylum-seekers-to-rwanda-363162/

226 Isabel Hardman, 'Labour and the Tories are strikingly similar on the NHS – just look at their embrace of the private sector', iNews, 26 May 2023, https://inews.co.uk/opinion/labour-nhs-plan-tories-private-sector-2365499

227 Rishi Sunak, '"I will not allow a foreign court to block these flights." Sunak's Rwanda statement. Full text.', Conservative Home, 16 Nov 2023, https://conservativehome.com/2023/11/16/i-will-not-allow-a-foreign-court-to-block-these-flights-sunaks-rwanda-statement-full-text/

228 Rajeev Syal, 'Supreme court rejects Rishi Sunak's plan to send asylum seekers to Rwanda', The Guardian, 15 Nov 2023, https://www.theguardian.com/uk-news/2023/nov/15/supreme-court-rejects-rishi-sunak-plan-to-deport-asylum-seekers-to-rwanda

229 Tim Baker, 'Blocked Rwanda scheme 'already having effect' - home secretary claims', Sky News, 16 Nov 2023, https://news.sky.com/story/blocked-rwanda-scheme-already-having-effect-home-secretary-claims-13009345

230 'Who is Esther McVey and what is her new role as 'common sense minister' in government?', ITV News, 14 Nov 2023, https://www.itv.com/news/granada/2023-11-14/who-is-the-minister-for-common-sense-and-what-will-they-do

231 Harry Cole, 'Jacob Rees-Mogg blasts 'ridiculously tokenistic' appointment of anti-woke minister Esther McVey', The Sun, 15 Nov 2023, https://www.thesun.co.uk/news/24739763/jacob-rees-mogg-esther-mcvey-anti-woke-minister/

232 Lottie Elton, 'Nobody knows what Esther McVey's new 'anti-woke' cabinet job means – except for even more culture wars', Big Issue, 15 Nov 2023, https://www.bigissue.com/news/politics/esther-mcvey-cabinet-reshuffle-common-sense-minister-woke/

233 Esther McVey, 'Esther reflects on the policies that are important to her and her bid for the leadership', 27 Jun 2019, https://www.esthermcvey.com/news/esther-reflects-policies-are-important-her-and-her-bid-leadership

234 GB News, https://www.gbnews.com/authors/philip-davies

235 Esther McVey, 'Esther McVey: Hunt's tax rises were socialist measures. We're punishing Conservative voters – who, come the next election, are now set to punish us', Conservative Home, 22 Nov 2022, https://conservativehome.com/2022/11/22/esther-mcvey-hunts-tax-rises-were-socialist-measures-were-punishing-conservative-voters-who-come-the-next-election-are-now-set-to-punish-us/

236 Esther McVey, 'It's out with the old political correctness... and in with a blast of common sense', Daily Mail, 17 Dec 2023, https://www.dailymail.co.uk/debate/article-12874835/esther-mcvey-mail-political-correctness.html

237 Simon Murphy, 'Esther McVey claimed £8,750 in expenses for personal photographer', The Guardian, 21 Jun 2019, https://www.theguardian.com/politics/2019/jun/12/esther-mcvey-expensed-thousands-of-pounds-for-personal-photographer

238 Eleni Courea, 'Esther McVey claims expenses to rent flat while husband lets out nearby home', The Guardian, 21 Mar 2024, https://www.theguardian.com/politics/2024/mar/21/esther-mcvey-expenses-flat-philip-davies

239 Richard Partington, 'The mini-budget that broke Britain – and Liz Truss', The Guardian, 20 Oct 2022, https://www.theguardian.com/business/2022/oct/20/the-mini-budget-that-broke-britain-and-liz-truss

240 Nadheem Badshah, 'Labour says 'Tory mortgage penalty' costs homeowners extra £7,000 a year', The Guardian, 10 Jun 2023, https://www.theguardian.com/money/2023/jun/10/labour-says-tory-mortgage-penalty-costs-homeowners-extra-7000

241 Marian Issimdar, Press Association, 'George Freeman quit as minister as he 'couldn't afford' mortgage', BBC News, 29 Jan 2024, https://www.bbc.co.uk/news/uk-england-norfolk-68133873

242 'Watch: The clip where Labour MP says Cleverly swore in Commons', BBC News, 23 Nov 2023, https://www.bbc.co.uk/news/av/uk-politics-67510795

243 Rajeev Syal, Rowena Mason and Aletha Adu, 'Home Office ordered to give full cost of Rwanda deportation plan', The Guardian, 8 Dec 2023, https://www.theguardian.com/uk-news/2023/dec/08/sunak-didnt-mislead-mps-over-costs-of-rwanda-deportation-plan-says-no-10

244 Rajeev Syal and Kiran Stacey, 'Robert Jenrick quits frontbench over Rwanda bill, piling pressure on Sunak', The Guardian, 6 Dec 2023, https://www.theguardian.com/

politics/2023/dec/06/robert-jenrick-quits-as-immigration-minister-after-rwanda-bill-published

245 Pippa Crerar [@PippaCrerar], Twitter, 6 Dec 2023, https://x.com/PippaCrerar/status/1732477443200499828

246 Zoe Grunewald, 'How mild-mannered 'Robert Generic' turned into a ruthless right-wing wannabe Tory leader', Independent, 23 Jan 2024, https://www.independent.co.uk/news/uk/politics/robert-jenrick-right-wing-conservative-leader-b2483172.html

247 'Membership of UK Political Parties', House of Commons Library, 2022, https://commonslibrary.parliament.uk/research-briefings/sn05125/

248 'Daily Mail: The average age of a Conservative party member is 72, according to a 2017 study by The Bow Group', Bow Group, 12 Mar 2019, https://www.bowgroup.org/daily-mail-the-average-age-of-a-conservative-party-member-is-72-according-to-a-2017-study-by-the-bow-group/

249 Pippa Crerar, 'Kemi Badenoch accused of 'bullying and traumatising' staff', The Guardian, 30 Jul 2024, https://www.theguardian.com/politics/article/2024/jul/30/kemi-badenoch-accused-of-bullying-and-traumatising-staff

250 Andrew Sparrow, 'UK politics live: Robert Jenrick resigns over immigration policy – as it happened', The Guardian, 6 Dec 2023, https://www.theguardian.com/politics/live/2023/dec/06/boris-johnson-covid-inquiry-pmqs-conservatives-labour-uk-politics-latest?page=with:block-6570c9c18f08807d1ae12306#block-6570c9c18f08807d1ae12306

251 Kate McCann [@KateEMcCann], Twitter, 6 Dec 2023, https://x.com/KateEMcCann/status/1732475486301831175

252 Thomas Harding, 'Airlines refuse planes for UK's Rwanda deportation flights plan', The National, 27 Dec 2023, https://www.thenationalnews.com/world/uk-news/2023/12/17/airlines-refuse-planes-for-uks-rwanda-deportation-flights-plan/

253 Joshua Nevett, 'Get behind my Rwanda asylum plan, Rishi Sunak tells Tories', BBC News, 7 Dec 2023, https://www.bbc.co.uk/news/uk-politics-67649447

254 Holly Patrick, 'Rishi Sunak locked outside No 10 with Mark Rutte in awkward moment', Independent, 10 Dec 2023, https://www.independent.co.uk/tv/news/rishi-sunak-downing-street-mark-rutte-b2461020.html

255 Isabel Hardman, 'If the Tories needed proof that Rishi Sunak is a loser, they found it in a game of marbles', The Guardian, 3 Dec 2023, https://www.theguardian.com/commentisfree/2023/dec/03/parthenon-sculptures-if-tories-needed-proof-rishi-sunak-loser-found-in-game-of-marbles?CMP=share_btn_tw

256 Pippa Crerar, Ben Quinn and Peter Walker, 'Relief for Rishi Sunak as Rwanda bill passes first vote in Commons', The Guardian, 12 Dec 2024, https://www.theguardian.com/uk-news/2023/dec/12/rishi-sunak-survives-rwanda-bill-commons-vote

257 Nadeem Badshah, 'James Cleverly apologises for 'appalling' date rape drug joke at No 10 event', The Observer, 23 Dec 2023, https://www.theguardian.com/politics/2023/dec/23/james-cleverly-apologises-for-appalling-date-drug-joke-at-no-10-event

258 'Are you in business?, Rishi Sunak asks homeless man during shelter visit', BBC News, 24 Dec 2024, https://www.bbc.co.uk/news/av/uk-64087160

Part 2
January to May, 2024
1. Larry Elliot, 'British recessions: a short history', The Guardian, 7 Dec 2012, https://www.theguardian.com/business/2012/dec/07/britain-recessions-history
2. 'Post Office / Horizon scandal', Criminal Cases Review Commission, 2024, https://ccrc.gov.uk/post-office/
3. Julia Banim, 'Post Office scandal victims now - 250 dead, four 'suicides' and pregnant mum behind bars', Mirror, 9 Apr 2024, https://www.mirror.co.uk/news/uk-news/post-office-scandal-victims-now-32543738
4. Rowena Mason, 'Kemi Badenoch failed to raise Horizon scandal when she met Fujitsu at Davos', The Guardian, 11 Feb 2024, https://www.theguardian.com/uk-news/2024/feb/11/kemi-badenoch-failed-to-raise-horizon-scandal-when-she-met-fujitsu-at-davos
5. 'Mr Bates vs The Post Office hits 13.5m', The Knowledge, 5 Feb 2024, https://www.theknowledgeonline.com/news/mr-bates-vs-post-office-hits-whopping-13-5m
6. Oliver Shah, 'Post Office boss: I was told to stall compensation to help Tories', The Sunday Times, 18 Feb 2024, https://www.thetimes.com/uk/article/post-office-chairman-interview-henry-staunton-ws5k6sh9p
7. Oliver Shah, 'Post Office boss: I was told to stall compensation to help Tories', The Sunday Times, 18 Feb 2024, https://www.thetimes.com/uk/article/post-office-chairman-interview-henry-staunton-ws5k6sh9p
8. 'Post Office Management Culture', Hansard, 8 Feb2024, https://hansard.parliament.uk/Commons/2024-02-08/debates/624B138D-B8A1-46A6-8D12-77C754ED6191/PostOfficeManagementCulture
9. Jane Croft, 'Hundreds of Post Office victims to get access to new compensation scheme', The Guardian, 30 Jul 2024, https://www.theguardian.com/uk-news/article/2024/jul/30/victims-of-post-office-horizon-scandal-compensation-scheme
10. 'Statistics watchdog to examine government asylum backlog claims', BBC News, 3 Jan 2024, https://www.bbc.co.uk/news/uk-politics-67876860
11. Nick Eardley and Paul Seddon, 'Rishi Sunak rebuked by stats watchdog over asylum backlog claim', BBC News, 18 Jan 2024, https://www.bbc.co.uk/news/uk-politics-68017887
12. Anthony Reuben, 'Rishi Sunak asked to correct asylum figures error', , BBC News 4 par 2023, https://www.bbc.co.uk/news/65179974
13. Anne Morris, 'Immigration & Societal Contributions', Davidson Morris, 15 Apr 2024, https://www.davidsonmorris.com/immigration-societal-contributions/
14. 'What does the government spend money on?', IFS, 2022/2023, https://ifs.org.uk/taxlab/taxlab-key-questions/what-does-government-spend-money
15. 1 July 2024, 'Asylum and refugee resettlement in the UK', Migration Observatory, https://migrationobservatory.ox.ac.uk/resources/briefings/migration-to-the-uk-asylum/
16. 1 July 2024, 'Asylum and refugee resettlement in the UK', Migration Observatory, https://migrationobservatory.ox.ac.uk/resources/briefings/migration-to-the-uk-asylum/
17. Daniel Waldron, 'UK immigration budget slashed by £40 million', Work Permit, 8 Aug 2021, https://workpermit.com/news/uk-immigration-budget-slashed-ps40-million-20211008
18. Tom Sasse, Rhys Clyne, Sachin Savur, 'Asylum backlog', Institute for Government, 24 Feb 2023, https://www.instituteforgovernment.org.uk/article/explainer/asylum-backlog
19. Tom Sasse, Rhys Clyne, Sachin Savur, 'Asylum backlog', Institute for Government, 24 Feb 2023, https://www.instituteforgovernment.org.uk/article/explainer/asylum-backlog

20 Lindsey Kennedy and Nathan Paul Southern, 'Rwanda Creates Nearly a Million Refugees Since Signing Asylum Deal with UK Government', Byline Times, 19 Feb 2024, https://bylinetimes.com/2024/02/19/rwanda-creates-nearly-a-million-refugees-since-signing-asylum-deal-with-uk-government/

21 'UK grants asylum to 15 Rwandans despite "Safe Country" claims', Bloomberg, 29 Feb 2024, https://www.bloomberg.com/news/articles/2024-02-29/uk-grants-asylum-to-15-rwandans-despite-safe-country-claims

22 David Burke, 'Dossier claims torture 'rampant' in Rwanda and officials turn blind eye to executions', Mirror, 16 Jan 2024, https://www.mirror.co.uk/news/politics/dossier-claims-torture-rampant-rwanda-31894224

23 'Who are the 'five families' of the Tory party in Westminster?', Independent, 1 Jan 20224, https://www.independent.co.uk/news/uk/politics/politics-explained/tory-new-conservatives-factions-erg-b2479437.html

24 Dame Andrea Jenkyns, '@andreajenkyns', Twitter, 15 Jan 2024, https://x.com/andreajenkyns/status/1746973007740870755

25 'Lee Anderson and Brendan Clarke-Smith resign over Rwanda vote', BBC News, 16 Jan 2024, https://www.bbc.co.uk/news/live/uk-politics-67998491

26 Adam Payne, 'Tory Rebellion Falls Flat As Rwanda Bill Clears House Of Commons Hurdle', PoliticsHome, 17 Jan 2024, https://www.politicshome.com/news/article/rwanda-bill-comfortably-clears-commons-tory-rebellion-falls-flat

27 Adam Forrest, 'Lee Anderson says he would like his old job back and regrets Rwanda revolt', Independent, 25 Jan 2024, https://www.independent.co.uk/news/uk/politics/lee-anderson-tories-sunak-rwanda-b2484236.html

28 Adam Forrest, 'Voters turn on 'spineless' Sunak as dire poll results and Rwanda row spark fresh leadership crisis', Independent, 16 Jan 2024, https://www.independent.co.uk/news/uk/politics/sunak-general-election-poll-rwanda-bill-tories-b2478999.html

29 Archie Michell, 'Home Office using dummy plane to practice forcing migrants onto Rwanda flights', Independent, 19 Jan 2024, https://www.independent.co.uk/news/uk/politics/rwanda-asylum-deportation-rishi-suank-home-office-b2481340.html

30 Matt Dathan, 'Home Office has no plane for Rwanda flights amid 'migration emergency'', The Times, 21 Mar 2024, https://www.thetimes.com/uk/politics/article/english-channel-crossing-rwanda-plane-migration-emergency-514-record-zxlxxnr25

31 'The uncertain financial implications of the UK's Rwanda policy', Migration Observatory, 26 Apr 2024, https://migrationobservatory.ox.ac.uk/resources/commentaries/the-uncertain-financial-implications-of-the-uks-rwanda-policy/

32 Dave Burke, 'Bungling Tories admit 5,598 asylum seekers have gone missing in immigration farce', Mirror, 18 Jan 2024, https://www.mirror.co.uk/news/politics/bungling-tories-admit-5598-asylum-31911413

33 'Parliamentary Under Secretary of State (Minister for Safe and Legal Migration)', Home Office, Gov.uk https://www.gov.uk/government/ministers/parliamentary-under-secretary-of-state-minister-for-future-borders-and-immigration

34 'Secretary of State for the Home Department', Home Office, Gov.uk, https://www.gov.uk/government/ministers/secretary-of-state-for-the-home-department

35 Lizzie Dearden, 'Revealed: Conservatives spent £134m on never-used IT systems for failed Rwanda scheme', The Guardian, 18 Jan 2025, https://www.theguardian.com/world/2025/jan/18/revealed-conservatives-spent-134m-on-never-used-it-systems-for-failed-rwanda-scheme

36 Steven Rigley, 'Rwanda deportation scheme cost £700m and saw just four volunteers sent to Africa, Home Secretary reveals', LBC, 22 Jul 2024, https://www.lbc.co.uk/news/rwanda-deportation-scheme-cost-700m-and-saw-just-four-volunteers-sent-to-africa/

37 Zia Qureshi, 'Rising inequality: A major issue of our time', Brookings Institute, May 16 2023, https://www.brookings.edu/articles/rising-inequality-a-major-issue-of-our-time/
38 'List of ongoing armed conflicts', Wikipedia, 2024 https://en.wikipedia.org/wiki/List_of_ongoing_armed_conflicts
39 Anthony Selden, "Frivolous to his very core": Boris Johnson was the worst prime minister in history', Independent, 20 Jun 2023, https://www.independent.co.uk/voices/boris-johnson-worst-prime-minister-history-b2361061.html
40 'BORIS JOHNSON: Would I sign up to fight for King and country?', Daily Mail, 26 Jan 2024, https://www.dailymail.co.uk/debate/article-13010871/BORIS-JOHNSON-fight-King-country.html
41 Heather Stewart, 'Boris Johnson 'hides in a fridge' to avoid Piers Morgan interview', The Guardian, 11 Dec 2019, https://www.theguardian.com/politics/2019/dec/11/boris-johnson-hides-in-fridge-to-avoid-piers-morgan-interview
42 'Boris Johnson: 'The boy who wanted to be world king'', BBC News, 24 Jul 2019, https://www.bbc.co.uk/news/av/uk-politics-49088773
43 Mark Townsend, 'Fresh revelations about Jennifer Arcuri affair threaten to damage Boris Johnson', The Guardian, 29 Jan 2022, https://www.theguardian.com/politics/2022/jan/29/fresh-revelations-about-jennifer-arcuri-affair-threaten-to-damage-boris-johnson
44 Martin Fletcher, 'Liz Truss has proved to be the worst Tory prime minister yet', The New Statesman, 20 Oct 2022, https://www.newstatesman.com/comment/2022/10/liz-truss-worst-conservative-prime-minister
45 Tristran Fielder, 'Liz Truss now the least-popular UK prime minister in the history of polling' Politico, 18 Oct 2022, https://www.politico.eu/article/uk-liz-truss-tories-least-popular-pm/
46 Adam Forrest, 'Liz Truss 'PopCons' comeback bid hit by chaos as key Tory allies drop out', Independent, 6 Feb 2024, https://www.independent.co.uk/news/uk/politics/liz-truss-popular-conservatism-farage-lee-anderson-b2491427.html
47 Simon Clarke, 'Replace Sunak as PM or face decade of decline under Starmer', The Telegraph, 23 Jan 2024, https://www.telegraph.co.uk/politics/2024/01/23/replace-sunak-pm-face-decade-decline-starmer-simon-clarke/
48 'Three-Quarters Of British Voters Want A General Election By Next Spring', Huffington Post, 22 Oct 2023, https://www.huffingtonpost.co.uk/entry/three-quarters-of-british-voters-want-a-general-election-by-next-spring_uk_6535467ae4b011a9cf79ec91
49 The News Agents [@TheNewsAgents], Twitter, 24 Jan 2024, https://x.com/TheNewsAgents/status/1750183888100487425
50 Dominic Penna, 'Senior Tories condemn Sir Simon Clarke's 'dangerous, reckless, selfish' call to oust Sunak', The Telegraph, 24 Jan 2024, https://www.telegraph.co.uk/politics/2024/01/24/sir-simon-clarke-senior-tories-rebuke-rishi-sunak-resign/
51 Politics UK [@PolitlcsUK], Twitter, 23 Jan 2024, https://x.com/PolitlcsUK/status/1749932326576861367
52 Aletha Adu, 'Simon Clarke advised to lie down by Tory MP after calling for Sunak to quit', The Guardian, 24 Jan 2024, https://www.theguardian.com/politics/2024/jan/24/simon-clarke-tory-backlash-after-calling-rishi-sunak-resign
53 "'I've just completely messed up': Nadine Dorries struggles with autocue on Piers Morgan's TalkTV show', Independent, 26 Oct 2022, https://www.independent.co.uk/tv/news/piers-morgan-nadine-dorries-talktv-b2210754.html
54 Scott Bryan [@scottygb], Twitter, 25 Oct 2022, https://x.com/scottygb/status/1584853529864175616
55 John Stevens, 'Nadine Dorries' Friday night Talk TV show axed after less than a year

on air', Mirror, 24 Jan 2024, https://www.mirror.co.uk/news/politics/nadine-dorries-friday-night-talk-31959924

56 Anita Singh, 'Culture Secretary accuses BBC of bias', The Telegraph, 22 Jan 2024, https://www.telegraph.co.uk/news/2024/01/22/culture-secretary-lucy-frazer-accuses-bbc-political-bias/

57 Haggis UK [@Haggis_UK], Twitter, 22 Jan 2024, https://x.com/Haggis_UK/status/1749338326656561581

58 Holly Patrick, 'Tory minister mistakes Art Attack presenter for BBC journalist in bias debate', Independent, 23 Jan 2024, https://www.independent.co.uk/tv/news/bbc-huw-merriman-neil-buchanan-art-attack-b2483419.html

59 'The Conservative manifesto at a glance', The Guardian, 13 Apr 2010, https://www.theguardian.com/politics/2010/apr/13/conservative-manifesto-at-a-glance

60 Larry Elliot, 'Tory austerity 'has cost UK half a trillion pounds of public spending since 2010'', The Guardian, 3 Mar 2023, https://www.theguardian.com/business/2023/mar/03/tory-austerity-has-cost-uk-half-a-trillion-pounds-of-public-spending-since-2010

61 Peter May, 'The National Debt doesn't add up', Progressive Pulse, 12 Feb 2024, https://www.progressivepulse.org/economics/the-national-debt-doesnt-add-up

62 'UK health system is top on 'efficiency', says report ', BBC News, 23 Jun 2010, https://www.bbc.co.uk/news/10375877

63 Kathryn Marszalek, 'Ups and downs: what's next for the NHS waiting list?', The Health Foundation, 18 Apr 2024, https://www.health.org.uk/news-and-comment/blogs/ups-and-downs-whats-next-for-the-nhs-waiting-list

64 Jon Craig, 'Rishi Sunak stuck to his new slogan relentlessly - but some MPs believe it backfired spectacularly', Sky News, 18 Jan 2024, https://news.sky.com/story/rishi-sunak-stuck-to-his-new-slogan-relentlessly-but-some-mps-believe-it-backfired-spectacularly-13051068

65 Ned Simons, 'Brits Suffering 'Grim' Victorian Diseases Due To Poverty, Says Public Health Expert', LBC, 23 Jan 2024, https://www.huffingtonpost.co.uk/entry/brits-suffering-grim-victorian-diseases-due-to-poverty-says-public-health-expert_uk_65af7d66e4b09e7f5b9cf415

66 'Gini coefficient of the United Kingdom from 1977 to 2021', Statista, 2023, https://www.statista.com/statistics/872472/gini-index-of-the-united-kingdom/

67 Anna Fleck, 'The UK's rich are getting richer', Statista/Sunday Times, 23 May 2022, https://www.statista.com/chart/27505/uks-richest-are-getting-richer/

68 'The Scale of Economic Inequality in the UK', The Equality Trust, https://www.equalitytrust.org.uk/scale-economic-inequality-uk

69 Clifford Singer, '8 reasons to share the wealth', New Economics Foundation, 15 Dec 2022, https://neweconomics.org/2022/12/8-reasons-to-share-the-wealth

70 George Easton, '"This country doesn't invest in its own future": Torsten Bell on why the UK is being hit hardest', New Statesman, 4 Jan 2023, https://www.newstatesman.com/encounter/2023/01/britain-invest-own-future-torsten-bell-uk-fell-rivals

71 'Biggest economies in 2021 by gross domestic product', World Data, https://www.worlddata.info/largest-economies.php

72 'The next government will face some of the toughest choices in generations', IFS, 25 Jan 2024, https://ifs.org.uk/news/next-government-will-face-some-toughest-choices-generations

73 Edward Siddons, 'HMRC has not charged a single company over tax evasion under landmark legislation', The Guardian, 20 Jan 2024, https://www.theguardian.com/politics/2024/jan/20/hmrc-has-not-charged-a-single-company-over-tax-evasion-under-landmark-legislation

74 'UK's tax burden highest on record despite recent national insurance cut', ITV, 11 Dec 2023, https://www.itv.com/news/2023-12-11/uks-tax-burden-highest-on-record-despite-recent-national-insurance-cut

75 Rowena Mason, 'Rishi Sunak paid effective tax rate of 23% on £2.2m income last year', The Guardian, 9 Feb 2024, https://www.theguardian.com/politics/2024/feb/09/rishi-sunak-paid-effective-tax-rate-of-23-on-22m-income-last-year

76 'Rishi Sunak registers lowest favourability scores as Prime Minister', Ipsos, 22 Feb 2024, https://www.ipsos.com/en-uk/rishi-sunak-registers-lowest-favourability-scores-prime-minister

77 'Rishi Sunak registers lowest favourability scores as Prime Minister', Ipsos, 22 Feb 2024, https://www.ipsos.com/en-uk/rishi-sunak-registers-lowest-favourability-scores-prime-minister

78 George Parker, Lucy Fisher and Peter Campbell, 'Canada contradicts Kemi Badenoch claims on 'ongoing' trade talks', FT, 20 Feb 2024, https://www.ft.com/content/373b7ab9-2a51-4db3-a0f5-2d021155c778

79 Hannah Brenton, 'Brexit's latest twist: Britain pushes the EU to increase red tape', Politico, 20 Feb 2024, https://www.politico.eu/article/brexits-latest-twist-its-the-uk-now-pushing-eu-to-increase-red-tape/

80 Adam Forrest, Joe Middleton, 'The Brexit bill: £100bn hit to UK exports as toy, medical kit and jewellery sales slump', Independent, 11 Feb 2024, https://www.independent.co.uk/news/uk/politics/brexit-uk-economy-cost-damage-b2491585.html

81 Rupert Carey, Anthony Reuben and Gerry Georgieva, 'Laura Trott interview: Fact-checking Treasury minister's claim on debt', BBC News, 9 Feb 2024, https://www.bbc.co.uk/news/uk-politics-68250020

82 Vanessa Allen, 'Universities on the brink of collapse amid funding crisis with some forced to make cuts to avoid being shut down', Daily Mail, 17 May 2024, https://www.dailymail.co.uk/news/article-13428297/Universities-brink-collapse-amid-funding-crisis-forced-make-cuts-avoid-shut-down.html

83 Rajeev Syal, 'Braverman announces new limits on overseas students bringing family to UK', The Guardian, 23 May 2023, https://www.theguardian.com/politics/2023/may/23/suella-braverman-restrictions-overseas-international-students-family

84 Carmen Aguilar García, Sally Weale, Lucy Swan and Harvey Symons, 'Fifth of UK universities' income comes from overseas students, figures show', The Guardian, 14 Jul 2024, https://www.theguardian.com/education/2023/jul/14/overseas-students-uk-universities-income

85 Ian Sample, 'Top scientists turning down UK jobs over 'tax on talent', says Wellcome boss', The Guardian, 29 Jun 2024, https://www.theguardian.com/education/article/2024/jun/29/top-scientists-turning-down-uk-jobs-over-tax-on-talent-says-wellcome-boss

86 Archie Mitchell, 'Fury over foreign aid budget being used to train Russia's future leaders at British universities', Independent, 26 Feb 2024, https://www.independent.co.uk/news/uk/politics/russia-students-university-funding-chevening-uk-putin-b2500743.html

87 Ben Clatworthy, 'Borders chief sacked for revealing security threat from private jet passengers', The Times, 20 Feb 2024, https://www.thetimes.com/article/0724ffb7-d638-4e10-9388-500f02f09d83?shareToken=d0f2a1b5721e8c8cef570447bc643b67

88 Matt Dathan, 'Security failings 'let high-risk private jet passengers into UK'', The Times, 20 Feb 2024, https://www.thetimes.com/uk/article/security-failings-let-high-risk-private-jet-passengers-into-uk-xknxdn2qw

89 Lizzie Dearden, 'Home Office likely to escape critical Rwanda report after sacking

watchdog boss', iNews, 21 Feb 2024, https://inews.co.uk/news/politics/home-office-escape-critical-rwanda-report-after-sacking-watchdog-2918778

90 'Understanding modern slavery – and how to spot the signs', Crimestoppers, https://crimestoppers-uk.org/keeping-safe/community-family/modern-slavery

91 Michael Spicer [@MrMichaelSpicer], Twitter, 23 Feb 2024, https://x.com/MrMichaelSpicer/status/1761084628478136331

92 Rozina Sabur, "Weak' Biden is 'asleep at the wheel', Liz Truss tells conservative conference', The Telegraph, 22 Feb 2024, https://www.telegraph.co.uk/world-news/2024/02/22/weak-biden-asleep-at-wheel-liz-truss-cpac/

93 Poppy Wood, 'Liz Truss blames 'deep state' for failed premiership in Fox News article', iNews, 21 Feb 2024, https://inews.co.uk/news/politics/liz-truss-blames-deep-state-fox-news-2917840

94 Jim Waterson, 'Liz Truss book enters bestseller list in 70th place with 2,228 copies sold', The Guardian, 26 Apr 2024, https://www.theguardian.com/politics/2024/apr/26/liz-truss-book-first-week-sales-bestseller-list

95 Brian Stelter, 'This infamous Steve Bannon quote is key to understanding America's crazy politics', CNN, 16 Nov 2021, https://edition.cnn.com/2021/11/16/media/steve-bannon-reliable-sources/index.html

96 Gary Kasparov, Good Reads, https://www.goodreads.com/quotes/8220792-the-point-of-modern-propaganda-isn-t-only-to-misinform-or

97 Lindsay Fortado, 'Sir Paul Marshall, co-founder Marshall Wace, backing Brexit', FT, 23 Apr 2017, https://www.ft.com/content/5ab5fb78-2437-11e7-8691-d5f7e0cd0a16

98 Hannah Goff, 'Lib Dem 'lurch to right' warning', BBC News, 21 Sep 2004, http://news.bbc.co.uk/1/hi/uk_politics/3677838.stm

99 Samuel Earle, 'Loud and uncowed: how UnHerd owner Paul Marshall became Britain's newest media mogul', The Guardian, 28 Oct 2023, https://www.theguardian.com/media/2023/oct/28/loud-and-uncowed-how-unherd-owner-paul-marshall-became-britains-newest-media-mogul

100 Samuel Earle, 'Loud and uncowed: how UnHerd owner Paul Marshall became Britain's newest media mogul', The Guardian, 28 Oct 2023, https://www.theguardian.com/media/2023/oct/28/loud-and-uncowed-how-unherd-owner-paul-marshall-became-britains-newest-media-mogul

101 Lindsay Fortado, 'Sir Paul Marshall, co-founder Marshall Wace, backing Brexit', FT, 23 Apr 2017, https://www.ft.com/content/5ab5fb78-2437-11e7-8691-d5f7e0cd0a16

102 'Areopagitica', Wikipedia, https://en.wikipedia.org/wiki/Areopagitica

103 Gregory Davis, 'Revealed: The Shocking Tweets of GB News Co-owner Sir Paul Marshall', Hope Not Hate, 22 Feb 2024, https://hopenothate.org.uk/2024/02/22/revealed-the-shocking-tweets-of-gb-news-co-owner-sir-paul-marshall/

104 Christopher Hope, 'Boycott Channel 4 News, over Jon Snow's Labour 'bias', former Tory minister tells Conservative MPs', Telegraph, 30 Jun 2017, https://www.telegraph.co.uk/news/2017/06/30/boycott-channel-4-news-jon-snows-labour-bias-former-tory-minister/

105 Silvia Pellegrino, 'Who are GB News' presenters? Everything you need to know', Press Gazette, 10 Apr 2023, https://pressgazette.co.uk/publishers/broadcast/gb-news-presenters-shows/

106 Jane Kanter, 'GB News Has Tested British TV Rules To Breaking Point — Will 2024 Be Its Year Of Reckoning', Deadline, 8 Jan 2024, https://deadline.com/2024/01/gb-news-potential-sanctions-ofcom-tv-rules-1235695900/

107 Jim Waterson, 'No rule to stop Tory MP interviewing minister on GB News, says Ofcom boss', Guardian, 28 Sep 2023, https://www.theguardian.com/media/2023/

sep/28/no-rule-to-stop-tory-mp-interviewing-minister-on-gb-news-says-ofcom-boss
108 'https://www.bbc.co.uk/news/business-68480543', BBC News, 5 Mar 2024, https://www.bbc.co.uk/news/business-68480543
109 'Comparing Democrats and Republicans on Intrinsic and Extrinsic Values', Journal of Applied Psychologists, 23 Feb 2009, https://onlinelibrary.wiley.com/doi/abs/10.1111/j.1559-1816.2009.00452.x
110 Harriet Sherwood, 'Huge rise in antisemitic abuse in UK since Hamas attack, says charity', The Guardian, 15 Feb 2024, https://www.theguardian.com/news/2024/feb/15/huge-rise-in-antisemitic-abuse-in-uk-since-hamas-attack-says-charity
111 'Number of police recorded racial hate crimes in England and Wales from 2011/12 to 2022/23', Statista, 11 Oct 2023, https://www.statista.com/statistics/624093/racist-incidents-in-england-and-wales/
112 Lucy Fisher, 'MPs clock off early as length of Commons work day hits record low', FT, 14 Mar 2024, https://www.ft.com/content/fef202b8-576d-429d-8136-cbb6db52f0f0
113 Matt Payton, 'Racist hate crimes increase five-fold in week after Brexit vote', Independent, 1 Jul 2016, https://www.independent.co.uk/news/uk/crime/racism-hate-crimes-increase-brexit-eu-referendum-a7113091.html
114 'Brexit referendum vote caused an increase in hate crime', IZA Newsroom, 14 Dec 2020, https://newsroom.iza.org/en/archive/research/brexit-referendum-vote-caused-an-increase-in-hate-crime/
115 John Stevens, 'Tory hypocrite Lee Anderson earns same as weekly family food shop every minute on GB News', Mirror, 10 Aug 2023, https://www.mirror.co.uk/news/politics/tory-hypocrite-lee-anderson-earns-30673057
116 John Stevens, 'Tory hypocrite Lee Anderson earns same as weekly family food shop every minute on GB News', Mirror, 10 Aug 2023, https://www.mirror.co.uk/news/politics/tory-hypocrite-lee-anderson-earns-30673057
117 Patrick Maguire, 'Who is Lee Anderson, the pro-death penalty Tory deputy chairman?', The Times, 10 Feb 2023, https://www.thetimes.co.uk/article/who-is-lee-anderson-mp-tory-deputy-chairman-kxhlm9lvb
118 Katie Boyden, 'What did Lee Anderson say to Sadiq Khan on GB News?', Metro, 25 Feb 2024, https://metro.co.uk/2024/02/25/lee-anderson-say-sadiq-khan-gb-news-20342608/
119 'Conservative MP Lee Anderson claims he was 'guaranteed' job to defect', BBC News, 26 Nov 2023, https://www.bbc.co.uk/news/uk-politics-67536235
120 Katie Boyden, 'What did Lee Anderson say to Sadiq Khan on GB News?', Metro, 25 Feb 2024, https://metro.co.uk/2024/02/25/lee-anderson-say-sadiq-khan-gb-news-20342608/
121 Suella Braverman, 'Islamists are bullying Britain into submission', The Telegraph, 22 Feb 2022, https://www.telegraph.co.uk/news/2024/02/22/islamists-are-bullying-britain-into-submission/
122 Peter Walker, 'Conservatives under fire for failing to tackle party's Islamophobia', The Guardian, 31 May 2018, https://www.theguardian.com/politics/2018/may/31/muslim-council-calls-for-inquiry-into-conservative-party-islamophobia
123 Zoe Grunewald, 'Sunak says Lee Anderson comments were wrong but denies Conservative party has 'Islamophobic tendencies'', Independent, 26 Feb 2024, https://www.independent.co.uk/news/uk/politics/rishi-sunak-lee-anderson-islamophobia-b2502425.html
124 Richard Vaughan, 'Baroness Warsi: Conservative Party 'poisoned by Islamophobia at every level', iNews, 11 Jun 2018, https://inews.co.uk/news/politics/baroness-warsi-tory-party-poisoned-islamophobia-every-level-163593

125 Hugh Muir, 'Lynton Crosby: the 'evil genius' taking Cameron into bare-knuckle politics', The Guardian, 23 Nov 2012, https://www.theguardian.com/politics/2012/nov/23/guardian-profile-lynton-crosby

126 Judith Brown (ed) et al, 'The Oxford History of the British Empire: Volume IV: The Twentieth Century', Oxford Academic, 1999, https://academic.oup.com/book/8180/chapter-abstract/153706812

127 Frances Perraudin, 'Boris Johnson claimed Islam put Muslim world 'centuries behind'', The Guardian, 15 Jul 1019, https://www.theguardian.com/politics/2019/jul/15/boris-johnson-islam-muslim-world-centuries-behind-2007-essay

128 Adam Bienkov, 'Boris Johnson said that Islamophobia is a 'natural reaction' to Islam and that 'Islam is the problem'', Business Insider, 27 Nov 2019, https://www.businessinsider.com/boris-johnson-islam-is-the-problem-and-islamophobia-is-a-natural-reaction-2018-8

129 Greg Heffer, 'Tory Islamophobia inquiry: Boris Johnson says he would not use 'offending language' again now he's PM', Sky News, 25 May 2021, https://news.sky.com/story/tory-islamophobia-inquiry-boris-johnson-says-he-would-not-use-offending-language-again-now-hes-pm-12316699

130 Nazia Parveen, 'Boris Johnson's burqa comments 'led to surge in anti-Muslim attacks'', The Guardian, 2 Sep 2019, https://www.theguardian.com/politics/2019/sep/02/boris-johnsons-burqa-comments-led-to-surge-in-anti-muslim-attacks

131 Stephen Colegrave, '40% of the Cabinet: Shocking Levels of Islamophobia Found in the Conservative Party', Byline Times, 28 Nov 2019 https://bylinetimes.com/2019/11/28/40-of-the-cabinet-shocking-levels-of-islamophobia-found-in-the-conservative-party/

132 Greg Heffer, 'Tory Islamophobia inquiry: Anti-Muslim sentiment 'remains a problem' within Conservative Party, report finds', Sky News, 25 May 2021, https://news.sky.com/story/tory-islamophobia-anti-muslim-sentiment-remains-a-problem-within-conservative-party-report-finds-12316516

133 Best for Britain [@BestForBritain], Twitter, 27 Feb 2024, https://twitter.com/BestForBritain/status/1762398839208624372

134 Archie Mitchell, 'Rishi Sunak's popularity plunges to record low among Tory members', Independent, 4 Dec 2023, https://www.independent.co.uk/news/uk/politics/rishi-sunak-conservative-labour-general-election-b2457888.html

135 Ollie Corfe, 'The graphs that show why this year's Tory leadership race is a complete mess', The Telegraph, 8 Oct 2024, https://www.telegraph.co.uk/politics/2024/10/08/polling-shows-the-tory-leadership-contest-an-unusual-mess/

136 'To what extent do you support or oppose the government's proposed policy to send some asylum seekers to Rwanda?', YouGov, 30 Jun 2023, https://yougov.co.uk/topics/politics/survey-results/daily/2023/06/30/726e7/1

137 Kiran Stacey, 'More than half of Tory members in poll say Islam a threat to British way of life', The Guardian, 28 Feb 2024, https://www.theguardian.com/politics/2024/feb/28/more-than-half-of-tory-members-in-poll-say-islam-a-threat-to-british-way-of-life

138 Phillip Inman and Larry Elliot, 'Head of OBR says lack of budget details led to 'work of fiction' forecasts last year', The Guardian, 23 Jan 2024, https://www.theguardian.com/politics/2024/jan/23/head-of-obr-says-lack-of-budget-details-led-to-work-of-fiction-forecasts-last-year

139 Phillip Inman, 'How bad are Britain's finances? Key questions and answers on the state of the economy', The Observer, 27 Jul 2024, https://www.theguardian.com/politics/article/2024/jul/27/britain-finances-key-questions-answers-state-economy-labour-government

140 Steven Swinford, Oliver Wright, 'Tory MPs fear Jeremy Hunt's national insurance gamble will backfire', The Times, 8 Mar 2024, https://www.thetimes.com/uk/politics/article/jeremy-hunt-budget-national-insurance-gamble-backfire-tory-mps-hhk32hc7p

141 Zoe Grunwald, 'Blow for Sunak's budget plan as fewer than 1 in 5 Tory voters want tax cuts if it means public spending cuts', Independent, 23 Feb 2024, https://www.independent.co.uk/news/uk/politics/tory-voters-tax-cuts-jeremy-hunt-public-spending-b2500578.html

142 Richard Partington, Aletha Adu and Kevin Rawlinson, 'Budget plans risk 'second lost decade' of living standards, Jeremy Hunt told', The Guardian, 4 Mar 2024, https://www.theguardian.com/uk-news/2024/mar/04/budget-plans-risk-second-lost-decade-of-living-standards-jeremy-hunt-told

143 Phillip Inman, 'Treasury may have broken law by failing to reveal £9.5bn spend in Tory budget, MPs told', The Guardian, 5 Nov 2024, https://www.theguardian.com/business/2024/nov/05/treasury-may-have-broken-law-failing-reveal-budget-plan-mps-told

144 Peter Walker, Kalyeena Makortoff, Graeme Wearden, Jessica Elgot and Rupert Neate, 'Akshata Murty may have avoided up to £20m in tax with non-dom status', The Guardian, 7 Apr 2022, https://www.theguardian.com/politics/2022/apr/07/rishi-sunaks-wife-says-its-not-relevant-to-say-where-she-pays-tax-overseas

145 Paul Seddon, 'Budget 2024: Jeremy Hunt cuts National Insurance again as election looms', BBC News, 7 Mar 2024, https://www.bbc.co.uk/news/uk-politics-68488467

146 Steven Swinford, 'Budget 2024: how Tories have been left clutching at straws', The Times, 2 Mar 2024, https://www.thetimes.com/uk/politics/article/jeremy-hunt-spring-budget-missteps-tories-mbl059wh6

147 Aletha Adu, 'Jeremy Hunt has given over £100,000 to local Tory party in bid to retain seat', The Guardian, 3 Mar 2024, https://www.theguardian.com/politics/2024/mar/03/jeremy-hunt-personal-donations-local-conservative-association-godalming-ash-seat

148 'The Conservatives and the Economy, 2010–24', IFS, 3 Jun 2024, https://ifs.org.uk/publications/conservatives-and-economy-2010-24

149 ' Nationwide Average House Prices Adjusted for Inflation: 'Real House Prices'', House Price Crash, 2024, https://www.housepricecrash.co.uk/indices-nationwide-national-inflation/#google_vignette

150 'The Conservatives and the Economy, 2010–24', IFS, 3 Jun 2024, https://ifs.org.uk/publications/conservatives-and-economy-2010-24

151 Kiran Stacey, 'Corporate UK tax breaks to cost £20bn more than they generate, study finds', The Guardian, 22 Sep 2024, https://www.theguardian.com/politics/2024/sep/22/corporate-uk-tax-breaks-to-cost-20bn-more-than-they-generate-study-finds

152 BrainyQuote, https://www.brainyquote.com/quotes/henry_kissinger_100085

153 Aubrey Allegretti, 'Honeytrap sext scandal MP William Wragg will keep Tory whip', The Times, 5 Apr 2024, https://www.thetimes.co.uk/article/william-wragg-tory-mp-honeytrap-sext-scandal-photo-whatsapps-63zqb3bd9

154 Jane Dalton, '"Honeytrap" MP William Wragg accidentally reveals WiFi password during photoshoot', Independent, 11 Apr 2024, https://www.independent.co.uk/news/uk/home-news/william-wragg-honeytrap-mp-wifi-password-b2526702.html

155 Faye Brown, 'Who is William Wragg? The MP at centre of sexting scam scandal', Sky News, 10 Apr 2024, https://news.sky.com/story/who-is-william-wragg-the-tory-mp-at-centre-of-sexting-scam-scandal-13108497

156 Chloe Chaplain, '"Worst I've seen": Tory activists' despair at party readiness for election campaign', iNews, 4 Apr 2024, https://inews.co.uk/news/politics/tory-activist-despair-party-readiness-election-campaign-2989183

157 Steven Swinford, 'Forget the election — Rishi Sunak's allies wonder if he'll get that far', The Times, 29 Mar 2024, https://www.thetimes.co.uk/article/forget-the-election-rishi-sunaks-allies-wonder-if-hell-get-that-far-t5zxtxtqh

158 Laura Webster, 'Tory MP Richard Holden demands police probe Keir Starmer's Durham beer clip', The National, 23 Apr 2022, https://www.thenational.scot/news/20089267.tory-mp-richard-holden-demands-police-probe-keir-starmers-durham-beer-clip/

159 Zoe Grunewald, Archie Mitchell, 'Keir Starmer accuses Rishi Sunak of 'smears' over Angela Rayner tax row', Independent, 17 Apr 2024, https://www.independent.co.uk/news/uk/politics/angela-rayner-conservative-tax-police-investigation-b2530065.html

160 Sky News [@SkyNews], Twitter, 17 Apr 2024, https://twitter.com/SkyNews/status/1780567186836246565

161 Paul Byrne, 'Angela Rayner's old neighbours brand police probe 'witch hunt' and 'waste of money'', Mirror, 17 Apr 2024, https://www.mirror.co.uk/news/politics/angela-rayners-old-neighbours-brand-32610841

162 Peter Walker and Vikram Dodd, 'Angela Rayner cleared of criminal wrongdoing over sale of home', The Guardian, 28 May 2024, https://www.theguardian.com/politics/article/2024/may/28/angela-rayner-cleared-of-criminal-wrongdoing-over-sale-of-home

163 Will Bolton, 'Angela Rayner's ex-husband 'made £134,000 from council house sale'', The Telegraph, 22 Apr 2024, https://www.telegraph.co.uk/news/2024/04/22/angela-rayner-ex-husband-mark-134000-council-house-sale/

164 Nick Sommerlad, 'Four Tory MPs who made £5.4million selling taxpayer-funded second homes won't say if they paid tax', Mirror, 24 May 2024, https://www.mirror.co.uk/news/politics/four-tory-mps-who-made-32793408

165 Anna Isaac, 'Tory donors from JCB empire could face £500m bill to settle tax inquiry', The Guardian, 22 Oct 2023, https://www.theguardian.com/politics/2023/oct/22/tory-donors-anthony-mark-bamford-jcb-empire-could-face-500m-bill-to-settle-tax-inquiry

166 Polly Toynbee, 'Without state funding, Britain's politics will always stink', The Guardian, 15 Feb 2022, https://www.theguardian.com/commentisfree/2022/feb/15/state-funding-british-politics-donors-tory-funds

167 'TPP Part of PM's trade mission to India', [Web Archive] TPP, 18 Jan 2014, https://web.archive.org/web/20170804173833/http://www.tpp-uk.com/latest-news-stories/tpp-part-of-prime-ministers-trade-mission-to-india

168 'Government gives Tory donor £137m in hidden payments', Good Law Project, 20 Sep 2023, https://goodlawproject.org/government-gives-tory-donor-137m-in-hidden-payments/

169 Rowena Mason, "'Nope, no way': can the Tories afford to give Frank Hester's money back?', The Guardian, 15 Mar 2024, https://www.theguardian.com/business/2024/mar/15/frank-hester-tory-donation-finances

170 Kiran Stacey, 'From 'move on' to 'racist and wrong': how the Tory line on Frank Hester shifted', The Guardian, 13 Mar 2024, https://www.theguardian.com/politics/2024/mar/13/tory-line-frank-hester-changing-rishi-sunak

171 Rowena Mason, 'Tory donor's comments about Diane Abbott 'racist and wrong', No 10 say', The Guardian, 12 Mar 2024, https://www.theguardian.com/politics/2024/mar/12/conservative-donor-frank-hester-comments-diane-abbott-racist-wrong-no-10-rishi-sunak

172 Rowena Mason, 'Tory donor's comments about Diane Abbott 'racist and wrong', No 10 say', The Guardian, 12 Mar 2024, https://www.theguardian.com/politics/2024/mar/12/conservative-donor-frank-hester-comments-diane-abbott-racist-wrong-no-10-rishi-sunak

173 Rowena Mason, "Nope, no way': can the Tories afford to give Frank Hester's money back?', The Guardian, 15 Mar 2024, https://www.theguardian.com/business/2024/mar/15/frank-hester-tory-donation-finances

174 Henry Dyer and Rowena Mason, 'Frank Hester donated further £5m to Tories in January, figures show', The Guardian, 6 Jun 2024, https://www.theguardian.com/business/article/2024/jun/06/frank-hester-donated-further-5m-to-tories-in-january-figures-show

175 Billy Kenber, 'Revealed: Tory MP demanded campaign cash to pay 'bad people'', The Times, 17 Apr 2024, https://www.thetimes.co.uk/article/28f948c4-70b5-4b29-a094-ea5ccfc2a53b

176 'Mark Menzies MP quits as aide over newspaper allegations', BBC News, 30 Mar 2014, https://www.bbc.co.uk/news/uk-politics-26806715

177 Benjamin Kentish, 'Tory MP Mark Menzies interviewed by police over claims he got dog drunk and started brawl with friend', Independent, 29 May 2017, https://www.independent.co.uk/news/uk/politics/conservative-mp-mark-menzies-got-dog-drunk-street-brawl-fylde-thames-valley-police-a7761486.html

178 Billy Kenber, 'Revealed: Tory MP demanded campaign cash to pay 'bad people'', The Times, 17 Apr 2024, https://www.thetimes.co.uk/article/28f948c4-70b5-4b29-a094-ea5ccfc2a53b

179 Billy Kenber, 'Tories 'didn't report Mark Menzies fraud claim as cash came from donors'', The Times, 19 Apr 2024, https://www.thetimes.co.uk/article/mark-menzies-fraud-claim-tories-money-donors-whistleblower-hmcv62n2c

180 Baul Byrne, 'Mark Menzies MP: Tory volunteer, 78, breaks silence over 'life or death' 3am cash demand', Mirror, 18 Apr 2024, https://www.mirror.co.uk/news/politics/mark-menzies-mp-tory-volunteer-32618031

181 Kiran Stacey, 'Tory activist 'appalled' by party's response to Mark Menzies claims', The Guardian, 19 Apr 2024 https://www.theguardian.com/politics/2024/apr/19/tory-activist-katie-fieldhouse-appalled-response-mark-menzies-claims

182 Rob Davies and Michael Goodier, 'At least 12 Tory MPs set up consultancy firms as election defeat loomed', The Guardian, 29 Jul 2024, https://www.theguardian.com/business/article/2024/jul/29/tory-mps-consultancy-firms-election

183 Adam Payne, 'Senior Tory Advisers Are "Jumping Before They Are Pushed"', PoliticsHome, 20 Apr 2024, https://www.politicshome.com/news/article/senior-tory-advisers-standing-down-general-election-conservative-doom

184 'The Guardian view on Tory decline: splits, sleaze and a rush for the exit', The Guardian, 18 Apr 2024, https://www.theguardian.com/commentisfree/2024/apr/18/the-guardian-view-on-tory-decline-splits-sleaze-and-a-rush-for-the-exit

185 Mikey Smith, 'Suspended MPs set to pocket at least £29,000 each for hanging on until General Election', Mirror, 28 Apr 2024, https://www.mirror.co.uk/news/politics/suspended-mps-set-pocket-up-32686225

186 Michael Savage, "You can't rule out a complete panicked meltdown': Tories fear wipeout after another disastrous week', The Guardian, 20 Apr 2024, https://www.theguardian.com/politics/2024/apr/20/you-cant-rule-out-a-complete-panicked-meltdown-tories-fear-wipeout-after-another-disastrous-week

187 Adam Bienkov [@AdamBienkov], Twitter, 18 Apr 2024, https://twitter.com/AdamBienkov/status/1780854969874235571

188 Michael Savage, "You can't rule out a complete panicked meltdown': Tories fear wipeout after another disastrous week', The Guardian, 20 Apr 2024, https://www.theguardian.com/politics/2024/apr/20/you-cant-rule-out-a-complete-panicked-meltdown-tories-fear-wipeout-after-another-disastrous-week

189 Steven Swinford, Oliver Wright and Chris Smyth, 'Rishi Sunak tempted to go for broke with a summer general election', The Times, 19 Apr 2024, https://www.thetimes.co.uk/article/sunak-tempted-to-go-for-broke-with-a-summer-election-fzkdnx5j3

190 Nadeem Badshah, 'Who were the prominent Tory MPs to oppose Sunak's smoking ban?', The Guardian, 16 Apr 2024, https://www.theguardian.com/society/2024/apr/16/who-were-the-prominent-tory-mps-to-oppose-sunaks-smoking-ban

191 Ethan Croft, 'Ocado deliveries, Nigel Farage's birthday and the Queen's final advice: key revelations from Liz Truss's book', Standard, 15 Apr 2024, https://www.standard.co.uk/lifestyle/liz-truss-book-advance-ten-years-to-save-the-west-b1151482.html

192 Gabriel Pogrund and Matt Chorley, '"Dishonest" MP Bridgen "lied" about conduct in family dispute', The Times, 17 Apr 2022, https://www.thetimes.co.uk/article/12ba7432-bdb8-11ec-84c4-70cc6ae427fb

193 Stuart Jeffries, 'Ten Years to Save the West by Liz Truss review – shamelessly unrepentant', The Guardian, 17 Apr 2024, https://www.theguardian.com/books/2024/apr/17/ten-years-to-save-the-west-by-liz-truss-review-shamelessly-unrepentant

194 Emily Atkinson, 'Liz Truss thought 'why me, why now?' after Queen's death', BBC News, 13 Apr 2024, https://www.bbc.co.uk/news/uk-68803610

195 Tim Baker, 'Liz Truss's book Ten Years To Save The West in breach of rules in place on minister's memoirs', Sky News, 18 Apr 2024, https://news.sky.com/story/liz-trusss-book-ten-years-to-save-the-west-in-breach-of-rules-in-place-on-ministers-memoirs-13118151

196 Tom Peck, 'If you think Liz Truss's book is deluded, the TV interviews are even worse', The Times, 18 Apr 2024, https://www.thetimes.co.uk/article/if-you-think-liz-trusss-book-is-deluded-the-tv-interviews-are-even-worse-7hcnxmv8j

197 Kiran Stacey, 'Liz Truss considered cutting NHS cancer care to pay for tax cuts, claims new book', The Guardian, 27 Aug 2024, https://www.theguardian.com/politics/article/2024/aug/27/liz-truss-considered-cutting-nhs-cancer-care-to-pay-for-tax-cuts-claims-new-book

198 Bill Grueskin [@BGrueskin], Twitter, 16 Apr 2024, https://twitter.com/BGrueskin/status/1780213620720251029

199 Dave Burke, 'Deputy PM Oliver Dowden makes bizarre defence of Liz Truss in Tommy Robinson 'hero' row', Mirror, 25 Feb 2024, https://www.mirror.co.uk/news/politics/deputy-pm-oliver-dowden-makes-32207494

200 Lizzie Dearden, 'Tommy Robinson could have caused Huddersfield grooming trials to collapse and child rapists go free', Independent, 20 Oct 2018, https://www.independent.co.uk/news/uk/crime/tommy-robinson-prison-jail-grooming-gangs-huddersfield-leeds-contempt-court-facebook-video-a8592871.html

201 Jabed Ahmed, 'Liz Truss, lettuce and the Deep State: Seven car crash moments from former PM's book tour', Independent, 18 Apr 2024, https://www.independent.co.uk/news/uk/politics/liz-truss-memoir-book-save-west-b2530221.html

202 Simon Marks, '"They've heard it all before': Truss's struggles to sell her book to Maga movement', iNews, 18 Apr 2024, https://inews.co.uk/news/world/us-right-truss-limited-venue-declines-book-tour-3012057

203 Steven Swinford, Oliver Wright, Chris Smyth, 'Rishi Sunak tempted to go for broke with a summer general election', The Times, 19 Apr 2024, https://www.thetimes.co.uk/article/sunak-tempted-to-go-for-broke-with-a-summer-election-fzkdnx5j3

204 Gabrial Pogrund, Matthew Campbell, 'Boris Johnson paid by hedge fund — and met Maduro with its boss', The Sunday Times, 16 Mar 2024. https://www.thetimes.co.uk/article/oris-johnson-consultant-hedge-fund-venezuela-jgzsz6ll2

205 Associated Press, 'Exiled Jurists Symbolically Sentence Maduro to 18 Years', 15 Aug

2018, https://www.voanews.com/a/exiled-jurists-symbolically-sentence-nicolas-maduro/4530783.html
206 Henry Dyer, 'Boris Johnson 'refused to be open' with watchdog about hedge fund role', The Guardian, 19 Apr 2024, https://www.theguardian.com/politics/2024/apr/19/boris-johnson-refused-to-be-open-with-watchdog-about-hedge-fund-role
207 Haggis UK [@Haggis_UK], Twitter, 18 Apr 2024, https://twitter.com/Haggis_UK/status/1781030964782580117
208 'General Terms and Conditions of Membership of the Conservative Party', Conservatives.com, https://public.conservatives.com/static/documents/General_Terms_and_Conditions_of_Membership_2020.pdf
209 Chas Geiger, 'Tory MP Nick Fletcher appears to back Reform UK's Lee Anderson in election', BBC News, 11 Apr 2024, https://www.bbc.co.uk/news/uk-politics-68787921
210 Tobi Thomas, 'Almost 10 million people in England could be on NHS waiting list', The Guardian, 3 Apr 2024, https://www.theguardian.com/society/2024/apr/03/almost-10-million-people-in-england-could-be-on-nhs-waiting-list
211 'Fighting Fraud in the Welfare System', Gov.uk, 13 May 2024, https://www.gov.uk/government/publications/fighting-fraud-in-the-welfare-system/fighting-fraud-in-the-welfare-system--2
212 Richard Partington, 'Tax lost in UK amounts to £35bn – almost half, say campaigners, due to fraud', The Guardian, 16 Sep 2021, https://www.theguardian.com/politics/2021/sep/16/tax-lost-in-uk-amounts-to-35bn-almost-half-say-campaigners-due-to
213 Anoosh Chakelian, 'New: You're 23 times more likely to be prosecuted for benefit fraud than tax fraud in the UK', New Statesman, 19 Feb 2021, https://www.newstatesman.com/politics/welfare/2021/02/new-you-re-23-times-more-likely-be-prosecuted-benefit-fraud-tax-fraud-uk
214 Edward Siddons and Jon Ungoed-Thomas, 'HMRC has failed to fine a single 'enabler' of offshore tax fraud in five years', The Guardian, 16 Jun 2024, https://www.theguardian.com/politics/article/2024/jun/16/hmrc-has-failed-to-fine-a-single-enabler-of-offshore-tax-in-five-years
215 Zoe Crowther, 'Quarter Of Tory Councillors Think Adult Social Care Is Underfunded In Their Area', PoliticsHome, 19 Apr 2024, https://www.politicshome.com/news/article/quarter-tory-councillors-think-adult-social-care-underfunded-local-authority
216 Steven Davies, 'Good riddance to the worst Parliament in history', Telegraph, 30 May 2024, https://www.telegraph.co.uk/news/2024/05/30/good-riddance-to-the-worst-parliament-in-history/
217 'Matt Hancock quits as health secretary after breaking social distance guidance', BBC News, 27 Jun 2021, https://www.bbc.co.uk/news/uk-57625508
218 Adam Forrest, 'What did Owen Paterson do? Everything you need to know about Tory lobbying scandal', Independent, 23 Nov 2022, https://www.independent.co.uk/news/uk/politics/what-did-owen-paterson-do-b1952077.html
219 Ione Wells and Catrin Haf Jones, 'Delyn MP Rob Roberts invited intern to 'fool around' with him', BBC News, 1 Jul 2020, https://www.bbc.co.uk/news/uk-wales-politics-53472289
220 Gabriel Pogrund, 'The story that exposed Tory MP David Warburton', The Sunday Times, 3 Apr 2022, https://www.thetimes.co.uk/article/tory-mp-david-warburton-suspended-after-sex-and-drugs-allegations-h3t8ghj0q
221 David Conn, 'Revealed: Tory peer Michelle Mone secretly received £29m from 'VIP lane' PPE firm', The Guardian, 23 Nov 2022, https://www.theguardian.com/uk-news/2023/nov/06/michelle-mone-admits-involvement-with-vip-lane-ppe-company

222 'Greensill: What is the David Cameron lobbying row about?', BBC News, 9 Aug 2021, https://www.bbc.co.uk/news/uk-politics-56578838

223 Kathryn Snowdon & Paul Seddon, 'Chris Pincher: New claims emerge against former Tory MP', BBC News, 3 Jul 2022, https://www.bbc.co.uk/news/uk-politics-62025612

224 Archie Mitchell, 'Tractor porn MP Neil Parish says other MPs behaved 'much worse'', Independent, 1 Nov 2023, https://www.independent.co.uk/news/uk/politics/neil-parish-banged-up-tractor-porn-b2439583.html

225 Esther Webber, 'Senior MP Julian Knight accused of sexually harassing young women', Politico, 10 Jul 2023 https://www.politico.eu/article/uk-senior-mp-julian-knight-accused-of-sexually-harassing-young-women/

226 Pippa Crerar, 'Michelle Donelan used £34,000 of taxpayer funds to cover libel costs', The Guardian, 11 Apr 2024, https://www.theguardian.com/politics/2024/apr/11/michelle-donelan-used-34000-of-taxpayer-funds-to-cover-libel-costs

227 Stephen Davies, 'Good riddance to the worst Parliament in history', The Telegraph, 30 May 2024, https://www.telegraph.co.uk/news/2024/05/30/good-riddance-to-the-worst-parliament-in-history/

228 Anna Isaac, 'Operation Save Big Dog: Boris Johnson draws up plan for officials to quit over partygate so he can keep job', Independent, 14 Jan 2022, https://www.independent.co.uk/news/uk/politics/boris-johnson-downing-street-partygate-b1993433.html

229 Alex Wickham, "Operation Save Rishi' Aims to Get Leader Through Key Vote', Bloomberg, 27 Apr 2024, https://www.bloomberg.com/news/articles/2024-04-27/-operation-save-rishi-aims-to-get-uk-premier-through-key-vote

230 Beth Rigby, 'Rishi Sunak will feel 'reset week' was job well done - but a horrible reality check awaits', Sky News, 27 Apr 2024, https://news.sky.com/story/rishi-sunak-will-feel-reset-week-was-job-well-done-but-a-horrible-reality-check-awaits-13122847

231 Toby Helm, 'Top Tory MP defects to Labour in fury at NHS crisis', The Observer, 27 Apr 2024, https://www.theguardian.com/politics/2024/apr/27/top-tory-mp-defects-to-labour-in-fury-at-nhs-crisis

232 John Stevens, 'David Cameron accused of acting 'like a Kardashian sister' as he hires £42million VIP plane', Mirror, 28 Apr 2024, https://www.mirror.co.uk/news/politics/david-cameron-accused-acting-like-32688296

233 Alan Rusbridger, 'The public is way ahead of politicians when it comes to paying more tax', Independent, 5 Apr 2024, https://www.independent.co.uk/voices/higher-taxes-public-sepending-hmrc-mps-b2523808.html

234 'Foreign Secretary travels to Central Asia and Mongolia in landmark visit to region', Gov.UK, 22 Apr 2024, https://www.gov.uk/government/news/foreign-secretary-travels-to-central-asia-and-mongolia-in-landmark-visit-to-region

235 Sian Elvin, 'Is the Union Flag upside down on Boris Johnson's £900,000 plane?', Metro, 26 Jun 2020, https://metro.co.uk/2020/06/26/union-flag-upside-boris-johnsons-900000-plane-12905817/

236 Holly Hales, 'Boris Johnson spent £800,000 in taxpayers' cash to get Union Jack painted on plane', Independent, 9 Jul 2023, https://www.independent.co.uk/news/uk/home-news/boris-johnson-plane-union-jack-flag-b2371961.html

237 Kara Godfrey, 'Flight secrets reveal how much your in-flight meal REALLY costs you', Express, 24 Nov 2017, https://www.express.co.uk/travel/articles/883867/flight-secrets-plane-inflight-meal-cost

238 Zoe Grunewald, 'Liz Truss spent more than £15,000 of taxpayer money on catering during Australia flight', Independent, 7 Mar 2024, https://www.independent.co.uk/news/uk/politics/liz-truss-flight-catering-australia-taxpayer-b2508916.html

239 Kiran Stacey, Eleni Courea and Patrick Wintour, 'First deportation flight to Rwanda

will not leave till summer, admits Sunak', The Guardian, 22 Apr 2024, https://www.theguardian.com/uk-news/2024/apr/22/first-deportation-flight-to-rwanda-will-not-leave-until-july-admits-sunak
240 Rajeev Syal, 'Home Office department processing Rwanda deportations told to cut jobs', The Guardian, 14 May 2024, https://www.theguardian.com/uk-news/article/2024/may/14/home-office-department-processing-rwanda-deportations-told-to-cut-jobs
241 Donna Ferguson, 'Minister for London Paul Scully fails to make Tory shortlist to run for city mayor', The Guardian, 11 Jun 2023, https://www.theguardian.com/uk-news/2023/jun/11/minister-for-london-paul-scully-fails-to-make-tory-shortlist-to-run-for-city-mayor
242 Sammy Gecsoyler, 'Tory hopeful for London mayor accused of groping TV producer Daisy Goodwin', The Guardian, 27 Jun 2023, https://www.theguardian.com/politics/2023/jun/27/tory-hopeful-for-london-mayor-accused-of-groping-tv-producer
243 Kate Devlin, Archie Mitchell, 'Tory party 'knew about groping claims against Daniel Korski' but put him on London mayor shortlist anyway', Independent, 28 Jun 2023, https://www.independent.co.uk/news/uk/politics/daniel-korski-daisy-goodwin-tory-probe-b2364885.html
244 Jess Warren, 'Tory mayoral candidate liked Enoch Powell posts', BBC News, 15 Sep 2023, https://www.bbc.co.uk/news/uk-england-london-66820979
245 Helena Horton, 'Tory hopeful for London mayor joins anti-Ulez Facebook group rife with Islamophobia', The Guardian, 1 May 2024, https://www.theguardian.com/politics/2024/may/01/tory-hopeful-for-london-mayor-joins-anti-ulez-facebook-group-rife-with-islamophobia
246 Ellie O'Donnell, 'Tory mayoral candidate Hall joins another anti-Ulez Facebook group hosting Islamophobia and threats', Unearthed, 1 May 2024, https://unearthed.greenpeace.org/2024/05/01/tory-susan-hall-anti-ulez-facebook-group-islamophobia-racism/
247 'Evening Standard front page of mayoral candidate a mockery, say Tories', BBC News, 19 Jul 2023, https://www.bbc.co.uk/news/uk-england-london-66250844
248 Noah Vickers, "Proud' Susan Hall says she 'so nearly' defeated Sadiq Khan despite losing by record margin', The Standard, 8 May 2024, https://www.standard.co.uk/news/london/susan-hall-tory-london-mayoral-election-sadiq-khan-message-conservative-b1156457.html
249 Anoosh Chakalian, 'Britain's worklessness crisis is getting worse', The New Statesman, 22 Apr 2024, https://www.newstatesman.com/comment/2024/04/britain-worklessness-crisis-is-getting-worse
250 Ben Riley-Smith, 'Disability benefits could be vouchers, not cash, in Sunak crackdown', Telegraph, 28 Apr 2024, https://www.telegraph.co.uk/politics/2024/04/28/disabled-people-benefits-clampdown-rishi-sunak/
251 Rowena Mason and Patrick Butler, 'Sunak accused of launching 'full-on assault on disabled people'', The Guardian, 19 Apr 2024, https://www.theguardian.com/politics/2024/apr/19/sunak-disability-benefit-curbs-sicknote-culture-pip
252 Joshua Askew, 'This country has the worst unemployment benefits in northern Europe', EuroNews, 3 Aug 2023, https://www.euronews.com/business/2023/08/03/this-country-has-the-worst-unemployment-benefits-in-northern-europe
253 'New figures lay bare the consequences of years of underinvestment in the NHS', The Heath Foundation, 12 Sep 2024, https://www.health.org.uk/news-and-comment/news/new-figures-lay-bare-the-consequences-of-years-of-underinvestment-in-the-nhs
254 Tobi Thomas, 'Almost 10 million people in England could be on NHS waiting list', The Guardian, 3 Apr 2024, https://www.theguardian.com/society/2024/apr/03/almost-10-

million-people-in-england-could-be-on-nhs-waiting-list
255 'NHS backlog data analysis', BMA, 10 Oct 2024, https://www.bma.org.uk/advice-and-support/nhs-delivery-and-workforce/pressures/nhs-backlog-data-analysis
256 'Coronavirus: Long covid', House of Commons Library, 31 Oct 2024, https://commonslibrary.parliament.uk/research-briefings/cbp-9112/
257 Detailed in The Decade In Tory, by Russell Jones, 2022, pages 383 to 501.
258 https://bylinetimes.com/2020/04/11/a-national-scandal-a-timeline-of-the-uk-governments-woeful-response-to-the-coronavirus-crisis/
259 'UK Covid deaths among worst of big European economies', BBC News, 22 Jun 2023, https://www.bbc.co.uk/news/health-65975154
260 Ian Sinclair and Rupert Read, "A National Scandal': A Timeline of the UK Government's Woeful Response to the Coronavirus Crisis', Byline Times, 11 Apr 2020, https://bylinetimes.com/2020/04/11/a-national-scandal-a-timeline-of-the-uk-governments-woeful-response-to-the-coronavirus-crisis/
261 'Covid: Discharging untested patients to care homes 'unlawful'', BBC News, 27 Apr 2022, https://www.bbc.co.uk/news/uk-england-61227709
262 'Deaths involving COVID-19 in the care sector, England and Wales: deaths registered between week ending 20 March 2020 and week ending 21 January 2022', ONS, 28 Feb 2022, https://www.ons.gov.uk/peoplepopulationandcommunity/birthsdeathsandmarriages/deaths/articles/deathsinvolvingcovid19inthecaresectorenglandandwales/deathsregisteredbetweenweekending20march2020andweekending21january2022
263 George Martin, 'How has South Korea avoided any coronavirus care home deaths?', Yahoo News, 19 May 2020, https://uk.news.yahoo.com/south-korea-avoids-care-home-deaths-135918520.html
264 'Three Years On, Brexit Casts a Long Shadow Over the UK Economy', Tony Blair Institute for Global Change, 3 Feb 2023, https://institute.global/insights/geopolitics-and-security/three-years-brexit-casts-long-shadow-over-uk-economy
265 'Brexit Explains 80% of U.K. Inflation, Former BOE Official Says", Bloomberg, 27 Apr 2024, https://www.bloomberg.com/news/articles/2022-04-27/brexit-explains-80-of-u-k-inflation-former-boe-official-says
266 Jack Peat, 'Sunak in the spotlight amid accusations that he profited from the financial crash', The London Economic, 30 Apr 2024, https://www.thelondoneconomic.com/business-economics/economics/sunak-in-the-spotlight-amid-accusations-that-he-profited-from-the-financial-crash-376058/
267 'Richest 1% grab nearly twice as much new wealth as rest of the world put together', Oxfam, 16 Jan 2023, https://www.oxfam.org.uk/media/press-releases/richest-1-grab-nearly-twice-as-much-new-wealth-as-rest-of-the-world-put-together/
268 Kiran Stacey, 'Rishi Sunak: UK is facing some of the most dangerous years in its history', The Guardian, 12 May 2024, https://www.theguardian.com/politics/article/2024/may/12/rishi-sunak-britain-facing-some-most-dangerous-few-years-history
269 'RAAC in the NHS - media fact sheet', Department of Health and Social Care, 29 Feb 2024, https://healthmedia.blog.gov.uk/2023/09/01/media-fact-sheet-raac-in-the-nhs/
270 Alain Tolhurst, 'Tory MP Says BNP Is A Better Fit For Natalie Elphicke Than Labour', PoliticsHome, 10 May 2024, https://www.politicshome.com/news/article/natalie-elphicke-defecting-bnp-reform-labour-garnier
271 'Ex-MP Charlie Elphicke 'groped woman and sang about it'', BBC News, 6 Jul 2020, https://www.bbc.co.uk/news/uk-england-kent-53309404
272 'Charlie Elphicke: Ex-MP jailed for sex assaults on women', BBC News, 15 Sep 2020,

https://www.bbc.co.uk/news/uk-england-kent-54161766
273 Best for Britain [@BestForBritain], Twitter, 10 May 2024, https://twitter.com/BestForBritain/status/1788930583571079425
274 Jessica Elgot, 'Esther McVey planning crackdown on civil service diversity initiatives', The Guardian, 13 May 2024, https://www.theguardian.com/politics/article/2024/may/13/esther-mcvey-crack-down-diversity-initiatives-civil-service
275 Channel 4 News [@Channel4News], Twitter, 15 May 2024, https://twitter.com/Channel4News/status/1790751232211988520
276 Henry Riley [@HenryRiley1], Twitter, 14 May 2024, https://twitter.com/HenryRiley1/status/1790422948718715289
277 'PR 250: Government Launch Emergency Prison Release Scheme', Prison Officers Association, https://www.poauk.org.uk/news-events/news-room/posts/2023/october/pr-250-government-launch-emergency-prison-release-scheme/
278 Kevin Rawlinson, 'Inmates dug through Winchester prison walls with plastic cutlery, report finds', The Guardian, 22 May 2024, https://www.theguardian.com/society/article/2024/may/22/inmates-dug-through-winchester-prison-walls-with-plastic-cutlery-report-finds
279 Michael Knowles, 'Protest organisers should be forced to pay for policing them, Michael Gove declares', Express, 21 May 2024, https://www.express.co.uk/news/politics/1901778/Michael-Gove-protests-crackdown-costs
280 Laura Kuenssberg and Jennifer McKiernan, 'Michael Gove steps down in mass exodus of MPs before election', BBC News, 24 May 2024, https://www.bbc.co.uk/news/articles/cv22pk094780
281 Damien Gayle, Rajeev Syal and Daniel Boffey, '"Close to a police state": campaign groups condemn UK report into protests', The Guardian, 21 May 2024, https://www.theguardian.com/world/article/2024/may/21/close-to-a-police-state-campaign-groups-condemn-uk-report-into-protests
282 Sophie Wingate, 'Police told to arrest fewer people to ease prison overcrowding', Independent, 22 May 2024, https://www.independent.co.uk/news/uk/home-news/prison-overcrowding-arrests-operation-early-dawn-b2549189.html
283 Kitty Donaldson and Joe Mayes, 'Rishi Sunak Drops Promise of Rwanda Deportation Flights in the Spring', Yahoo News, 22 Apr 2024, https://www.yahoo.com/news/rishi-sunak-drops-promise-rwanda-110846384.html
284 David Gritten, 'Ebrahim Raisi: The hardline cleric who became Iran president', BBC News, 20 May 2024, https://www.bbc.co.uk/news/world-middle-east-57421235
285 Michael Fabricant , [@Mike_Fabricant], Twitter, 18 May 2024, https://twitter.com/Mike_Fabricant/status/1792198466661433784

Part 3
The General Election of 2024

1. 'Chancellor George Osborne downgrades growth forecast for UK', Daily Echo, 29 Nov 2011, https://www.dailyecho.co.uk/news/9390753.chancellor-george-osborne-downgrades-growth-forecast-for-uk
2. Simon Rocker, 'Daily Mail accused of antisemitism over Miliband story', The Jewish Chronicle, 3 Oct 2013, https://www.thejc.com/news/daily-mail-accused-of-antisemitism-over-miliband-story-htssfgn6
3. Jim Pickard, 'David Cameron falls silent on 'long-term economic plan'', FT, 28 Dec 2015, https://www.ft.com/content/dfea715e-a5ab-11e5-a91e-162b86790c58
4. Professor Hannah Fry [@frysquared], TikTok, https://www.tiktok.com/@fryrsquared/video/7326976812322393377
5. 'Brexit Explains 80% of U.K. Inflation, Former BOE Official Says'', Bloomberg, 27 Apr 2024, https://www.bloomberg.com/news/articles/2022-04-27/brexit-explains-80-of-u-k-inflation-former-boe-official-says
6. 'Brexit is costing the UK £100 billion a year in lost output', Bloomberg, 31 Jan 2023, https://www.bloomberg.com/news/articles/2023-01-31/brexit-is-costing-the-uk-100-billion-a-year-in-lost-output
7. Rob Davies, 'RBS pays its first dividend since £45.5bn bailout 10 years ago', The Guardian, 12 Oct 2019, https://www.theguardian.com/business/2018/oct/12/rbs-pays-its-first-dividend-since-bailout-10-years-ago
8. Fiona Jones, 'EU gave us 'very funny numbers': Rees-Mogg on new post-Brexit laws', LBC, 24 Jun 2022, https://www.lbc.co.uk/hot-topics/brexit/eu-post-brexit-jacob-rees-mogg/
9. Steven Poole, "Strong and stable leadership!' Could Theresa May's rhetorical carpet-bombing backfire?', The Guardian, 10 May 2017, https://www.theguardian.com/politics/2017/may/10/strong-and-stable-leadership-could-theresa-mays-rhetorical-carpet-bombing-backfire
10. 'Boris Johnson takes ITV reporter's phone after refusing to look at photo of boy on hospital floor', ITV News, 9 Dec 2019, https://www.itv.com/news/calendar/2019-12-09/boris-johnson-takes-itv-reporter-s-phone-after-refusing-to-look-at-photo-of-boy-on-hospital-floor
11. Heather Stewart and Aamna Mohdin, 'Boris Johnson 'hides in a fridge' to avoid Piers Morgan interview', The Guardian, 11 Dec 2019, https://www.theguardian.com/politics/2019/dec/11/boris-johnson-hides-in-fridge-to-avoid-piers-morgan-interview
12. Alan Tolhurst, 'Twitter warns Tories after they rebrand official account as 'FactcheckUK' during leaders' debate', PoliticsHome, 9 Nov 2019, https://www.politicshome.com/news/article/twitter-warns-tories-after-they-rebrand-official-account-as-factcheckuk-during-leaders-debate
13. Rowena Mason, "This is going to be a disaster': inside the Tories' chaotic election campaign', The Guardian, 6 Jul 2024, https://www.theguardian.com/politics/article/2024/jul/06/this-is-going-to-be-a-disaster-inside-the-tories-chaotic-election-campaign
14. 'The Guardian view on the local elections: an anti-Tory landslide points to the end of an era', The Guardian, 6 May 2024, https://www.theguardian.com/commentisfree/article/2024/may/06/the-guardian-view-on-the-local-elections-an-anti-tory-landslide-points-to-the-end-of-an-era
15. Eleni Courea, 'Rishi Sunak rules out holding general election on 2 May', The Guardian, 14 Mar 20224, https://www.theguardian.com/politics/2024/mar/14/rishi-sunak-rules-out-general-election-may-local-elections

16 Alix Culbertson, 'Britons should have three days' worth of tinned food and water, government says', Sky News, 22 May 2024, https://news.sky.com/story/britons-should-have-three-days-worth-of-tinned-food-and-water-government-says-13141114
17 'Bedroom Tax', Disability Rights UK, 6 Apr 2024, https://www.disabilityrightsuk.org/resources/bedroom-tax
18 Chris Dorrell, 'Sunak: 'The plan is working'... But what is the plan?', CityAM, 6 Jul 2024, https://www.cityam.com/sunak-the-plan-is-working-but-what-is-the-plan/
19 Aubrey Allegretti, 'First pictures released of Boris Johnson's new £2.6m briefing room', The Guardian, 14 Mar 2021, https://www.theguardian.com/politics/2021/mar/15/no-10-offers-first-sight-of-26m-white-house-style-briefing-room
20 Sam Gegsoyler, 'Things can only get wetter: D:Ream song drowns out Sunak's damp election announcement', The Guardian, 22 May 2024, https://www.theguardian.com/politics/article/2024/may/22/things-can-only-get-wetter-rishi-sunak-calls-general-election-in-the-rain
21 'Politics latest', Sky News, 23 May 2024 https://news.sky.com/story/politics-latest-sunak-starmer-davey-tories-labour-lib-dems-general-election-12593360?postid=7717157#liveblog-body
22 Arj Singh, Hugo Gye, Eleanor Langford, Richard Vaughan, Jane Merrick , "It was sh*te': Tories lament campaign start but still think they can beat Labour', iNews, 25 May 2024, https://inews.co.uk/news/politics/it-was-shte-tories-lament-campaign-start-but-still-think-they-can-beat-labour-3073564
23 Archie Bland, 'Thursday briefing: How a day of fevered general election speculation unfolded', The Guardian, 23 May 2024, https://www.theguardian.com/world/article/2024/may/23/first-edition-rishi-sunak-general-election
24 Pippa Crerar, 'Tory MPs mull over their fate after Rishi Sunak's election call', The Guardian, 24 May 2024, https://www.theguardian.com/politics/article/2024/may/24/tory-mps-mull-over-their-fate-after-rishi-sunaks-election-call
25 Adam Bienkov, 'Rishi Sunak Takes Staged Election Questions from Conservative Councillors Posing as Ordinary Voters', Byline Times, 23 May 2024, https://bylinetimes.com/2024/05/23/rishi-sunak-staged-election-question-from-conservative-councillor-posing-as-ordinary-voter/
26 ITV Politics [@ITVNewsPolitics], Twitter, 23 May 2024, https://x.com/ITVNewsPolitics/status/1793628105250402676
27 Andrew Sparrow, 'Labour says early general election leaves many government commitments 'in the bin' – as it happened', The Guardian, 23 May 2024, https://www.theguardian.com/politics/live/2024/may/23/uk-general-election-2024-rishi-sunak-keir-starmer-conservatives-labour-lib-dems-live-latest-news-updates?page=with:block-664f20b98f0862e793aa0714#block-664f20b98f0862e793aa0714
28 Rowena Mason, 'Tory donors pour cash into seats held by big names at risk of losing', The Guardian, 24 May 2024, https://www.theguardian.com/politics/article/2024/may/24/tory-donors-pour-cash-seats-big-names-risk-losing-gove-mordaunt
29 Michael Gove [@michaelgove], Twitter, 24 May 2024, https://x.com/michaelgove/status/1794066234406768881?t=sRU-i_jgbMp0yr5m890TNA&s=19
30 'Rishi Sunak confirms July election; 'Who do you trust?' he asks voters', Proactive Investors, 22 May 2024, https://www.proactiveinvestors.co.uk/companies/news/1048221/rishi-sunak-confirms-july-election-who-do-you-trust-he-asks-voters-1048221.html
31 David Maddox, 'Tory MPs snub Rishi Sunak's election rally to drown their sorrows in parliament's 'Strangers' bar', Independent, 23 May 2024, https://www.independent.co.uk/news/uk/politics/general-election-rishi-sunak-tory-mp-strangers-bar-b2550286.html

32 Liam Geraghty, 'What is the Renters' Rights Bill? All you need to know about Labour's plan to end no-fault evictions?', Big Issue, 11 Sep 2024, https://www.bigissue.com/news/housing/renters-rights-bill-labour-no-fault-evictions/

33 Holly Bancroft, 'Rishi Sunak accused of letting renters down after no-fault eviction bill dropped before election', Independent, 24 May 2024, https://www.independent.co.uk/news/uk/politics/rent-landlords-bill-section-21-no-fault-eviction-b2550862.html

34 Eleni Courea, 'Smoking ban in doubt after exclusion from Commons schedule', The Guardian, 23 May 2024, https://www.theguardian.com/society/article/2024/may/23/uk-election-tobacco-vapes-bill-smoking-commons-parliament

35 Sophie Wingate, 'Rishi Sunak 'disappointed' Bill to ban smoking shelved before election', Independent, 24 May 2024, https://www.independent.co.uk/news/uk/rishi-sunak-bill-prime-minister-parliament-mps-b2550924.html

36 Kiran Stacey, 'Sunak to take a day at home after hapless election campaign start', The Guardian, 24 May 2024, https://www.theguardian.com/politics/article/2024/may/24/sunak-to-take-a-day-at-home-after-hapless-election-campaign-start

37 Zoe Kleinman and Sean Seddon , 'Elon Musk tells Rishi Sunak AI will put an end to work', BBC News, 3 Nov 2023, https://www.bbc.co.uk/news/uk-67302048

38 Tim Sigsworth, 'Ed Davey falls into lake five times while campaigning from paddleboard', The Telegraph, 28 May 2024, https://www.telegraph.co.uk/politics/2024/05/28/ed-davey-falls-into-lake-five-times-while-paddleboarding-on/

39 Tim Scotson, 'Conservatives Are Struggling To Rally Activists On The Campaign Trail', PoliticsHome, 1 Jun 2024, https://www.politicshome.com/news/article/general-election-conservative-campaign-unmotivated-activists-young-tories-rishi-sunak

40 Michael Savage, 'Sunak promises to bring back national service for 18-year-olds', The Observer, 25 May 2024, https://www.theguardian.com/politics/article/2024/may/25/sunak-promises-to-bring-back-national-service-for-18-year-olds

41 Josiah Mortimer, 'Anger as Nadine Dorries' Year-Long Silence in Parliament is Deemed 'Within the Rules' By Standards Watchdog', Byline Times, 14 Aug 2023, https://bylinetimes.com/2023/08/14/anger-as-nadine-dorries-year-long-silence-in-parliament-is-deemed-within-the-rules-by-standards-watchdog/

42 Mark Honigsbaum, "It is shameful': why the return of Victorian-era diseases to the UK alarms health experts', The Observer, 18 Feb 2024, https://www.theguardian.com/society/2024/feb/18/return-of-victorian-era-diseases-to-the-uk-scabies-measles-rickets-scurvy

43 Amy Gibbons, 'Prince George, Princess Charlotte and Prince Louis 'would not be exempt from National Service'', The Telegraph, 26 May 2024, https://www.telegraph.co.uk/politics/2024/05/26/young-royals-face-national-service-rish-sunak-plans/

44 Eleni Courea and Aletha Adu, 'Rishi Sunak's national service pledge is 'bonkers', says ex-military chief', The Guardian, 26 May 2024, https://www.theguardian.com/politics/article/2024/may/26/rishi-sunaks-national-service-pledge-is-bonkers-says-ex-military-chief

45 Lucy Fisher and George Parker, 'Rishi Sunak's national service pledge rejected by defence minister days ago', FT, 26 May 2024, https://www.ft.com/content/56c7a24f-06b7-472a-921c-248b58cfd1b2

46 Jane Merrick, 'Day-to-day defence spending cut by nearly £10bn since 2010, new figures show', iNews, 6 May 2024, https://inews.co.uk/news/politics/day-to-day-defence-spending-cut-by-nearly-10bn-since-2010-new-figures-show-3043364

47 '£2.5 billion: The price tag for Rishi Sunak's national service plans for 18-year-olds', Forces News, 26 May 2024, https://www.forcesnews.com/news/ps25-billion-price-tag-rishi-sunaks-national-service-plans

48 Dominic Penna, 'Parents 'could be fined if children refuse to do national service'', The Telegraph, 27 May 2024, https://www.telegraph.co.uk/politics/2024/05/27/parents-could-be-fined-children-refuse-national-service/

49 Eleni Courea and Vikram Dodd, "No one going to jail' for avoiding UK national service, says Cleverly", The Guardian, 26 May 2024, https://www.theguardian.com/politics/article/2024/may/26/no-one-going-to-jail-for-avoiding-uk-national-service-says-cleverly

50 Anna Isaac, 'Nadhim Zahawi 'agreed on penalty' to settle tax bill worth millions', The Guardian, 20 Jan 2023, https://www.theguardian.com/uk-news/2023/jan/20/nadhim-zahawi-agreed-on-penalty-to-settle-tax-bill-worth-millions

51 David Maddox, 'Tories scramble to find almost 200 election candidates as Gove leads exodus', Independent, 24 May 2024, https://www.independent.co.uk/news/uk/politics/tory-party-election-candidate-mp-b2551163.html

52 Tim Baker, 'Former Tory MP Bob Stewart has racist abuse conviction overturned', Sky News, 23 Feb 2024, https://news.sky.com/story/former-tory-mp-bob-stewart-has-racist-abuse-conviction-overturned-13079381

53 Jacob Freedland, 'Decision to restore Tory whip to Bob Stewart branded 'shameful'', Independent, 24 May 2024, https://www.independent.co.uk/news/uk/bob-stewart-westminster-london-beckenham-southwark-crown-court-b2551192.html

54 Kate Nicholson, 'Why Did Matt Hancock Just Get The Tory Whip Back?', Huffington Post, 24 May 2024, https://www.huffingtonpost.co.uk/entry/why-did-matt-hancock-just-get-the-tory-whip-back_uk_66505172e4b042129b8a5acd

55 'MP suspended after endorsing Reform UK candidate', BBC News, 27 May 2024, https://www.bbc.co.uk/news/articles/c0kkzv12wndo

56 'Nigel Farage to replace Richard Tice as Reform UK leader ahead of General Election', ITV News, 3 Jun 2024, https://www.itv.com/news/2024-06-03/general-election-nigel-farage-to-replace-richard-tice-as-reform-uk-leader

57 Rowena Mason and Ben Quinn, 'Conservative Mark Logan defects to Labour in fresh blow to Rishi Sunak', The Guardian, 30 May 2024, https://www.theguardian.com/politics/article/2024/may/30/conservative-mark-logan-defects-to-labour-in-fresh-blow-to-rishi-sunak

58 Kate Nicholson, 'A Minister Has Gone On Holiday Days Into Rishi Sunak's Struggling Election Campaign', Huffington Post, 28 May 2024, https://www.huffingtonpost.co.uk/entry/minister-jets-off-on-holiday-days-into-election-campaign_uk_665583d8e4b022987c3153d7

59 Alexander Butler, "'Skydiving, catamarans': MP Steve Baker's extraordinary response when asked what he will do if loses election", Independent, 24 May 2024, https://www.independent.co.uk/news/uk/politics/uk-general-election-steve-baker-wycombe-b2550954.html

60 Robert Largan [@robertlargan] Twitter, 1 Jun 2024, https://x.com/robertlargan/status/1796819961194627547

61 SMR Rejoin [@SMRRejoinRadio], Twitter, 1 Jun 2024, https://x.com/SMRRejoinRadio/status/1796854581596389854

62 Max Colbert, 'Conservatives Accused of 'Camouflage' Campaign Tactics After Imitating Green Party Leaflets', Byline Times, 13 Jan 2023, https://bylinetimes.com/2023/01/13/conservatives-accused-of-camouflage-campaign-tactics-after-imitating-green-party-leaflets/

63 Barney Davis, 'Police probe Tory candidate after using Labour and Reform-style poster', Independent, 2 Jun 2024, https://www.independent.co.uk/news/uk/politics/tory-labour-poster-election-b2555230.html

64 Cameron Roy, 'Jacob Rees-Mogg takes to the campaign trail: Double-breasted Tory MP reveals what he wears when it is too hot for his suit, how he hates bananas and why Nigel Farage should be welcomed back into the Conservative party', Daily Mail, 1 Jun 2024, https://www.dailymail.co.uk/news/article-13483671/Jacob-Rees-Mogg-takes-campaign-trail-nigel-farage.html

65 Lucy Clark-Billings and Sam Francis, 'Penny Mordaunt says Rishi Sunak leaving D-Day event was 'wrong'', BBC News, 7 Jun 2024, https://www.bbc.co.uk/news/articles/cg33x0907nro

66 Steven Swinford, Chris Smyth, Aubrey Allegretti, 'How Sunak's D-Day disappearance blindsided No 10', The Times, 7 Jun 2024, https://www.thetimes.com/uk/politics/article/how-sunaks-d-day-disappearance-left-staff-rattled-339hffdq3

67 Peter Walker, Rowena Mason and Aletha Adu, 'Furious Tories turn on Rishi Sunak over D-day commemorations snub', The Guardian, 7 Jun 2024 https://www.theguardian.com/politics/article/2024/jun/07/he-lets-the-country-down-sunak-provokes-tory-grassroots-fury-for-skipping-d-day-commemorations

68 Archie Mitchell, 'Rishi Sunak accused of being 'in hiding' after disastrous D-Day gaffe', Independent, 9 June 2024, https://www.independent.co.uk/news/uk/politics/rishi-sunak-general-election-conservative-d-day-b2559471.html

69 Becky Morton, 'Farage enters election race as Reform UK candidate', BBC News, 3 Jun 2024, https://www.bbc.co.uk/news/articles/c3gg66pm8ylo

70 'Brexit: Nigel Farage only turned up to one of 42 EU fisheries committee meetings', The Descrier, 16 Jun 2016, https://descrier.co.uk/politics/brexit-nigel-farage-turned-one-42-eu-fisheries-committee-meetings/

71 Alix Culbertson, 'Reform's Nigel Farage backtracks on claim parliament's security team told him not to hold in-person surgeries in Clacton', Sky News, 7 Oct 2024, https://news.sky.com/story/reforms-nigel-farage-backtracks-on-claim-parliaments-security-team-told-him-not-to-hold-in-person-surgeries-in-clacton-13229883

72 Sian Baldwin, 'Nigel Farage's nine jobs revealed: Reform UK leader reports £571,000 on top of MP's salary', The Standard, 14 Jan 2025, https://www.standard.co.uk/news/uk/nigel-farage-mp-nine-jobs-earnings-b1204456.html

73 'Farage earns more than £1m a year for non-MP work', BBC News, 17 Aug 2024, https://www.bbc.co.uk/news/articles/c9wjgkr1750o

74 Rowena Mason, 'Nigel Farage paid £189,000 last year by gold company to work part-time', The Guardian, 7 Jan 2025, https://www.theguardian.com/politics/2025/jan/07/nigel-farage-paid-189000-last-year-by-gold-dealer-to-work-four-hours-a-month

75 Steerpike, 'Full list: every controversial Reform candidate', The Spectator, 28 Jun 2024, https://www.spectator.co.uk/article/full-list-every-controversial-reform-candidate/

76 Becky Morton, 'Reform drops three candidates over offensive comments', BBC News, 29 Jun 2024, https://www.bbc.co.uk/news/articles/c727xz2kkgjo

77 Serena Barker-Singh, 'James McMurdock: Reform MP previously jailed for repeatedly kicking girlfriend questioned by Sky News at party conference', Sky News, 4 Jan 2025, https://news.sky.com/story/james-mcmurdock-reform-mp-previously-jailed-for-repeatedly-kicking-girlfriend-challenged-at-party-conference-13283691

78 Sinead Butler, 'Rishi Sunak scores another own goal by visiting Titanic site', Indy100, 26 May 2024, https://www.indy100.com/politics/rishi-sunak-titanic-general-election

79 James Martin McCarthy, 'Captaining a sinking ship - Inside Prime Minister Rishi Sunak's shambolic visit to Northern Ireland', Belfast Live, 24 May 2024, https://www.belfastlive.co.uk/news/news-opinion/captaining-sinking-ship-prime-ministers-29233530

80 Jessica Rawnsley, Geraldine Scott, Peter Chappell, Max Kendix, Ed Halford, Oliver

Wright, 'Sunak pledges £17 billion in tax cuts as he launches Tory manifesto — as it happened', The Times, 11 Jun 2024, https://www.thetimes.com/uk/politics/article/general-election-2024-latest-news-conservative-manifesto-rishi-sunak-5tjbkg62t

81 'A third of children now living in poverty in the UK as cost of living crisis continues to hit hard', British Association of Social Workers, 2 Apr 2024, https://basw.co.uk/about-social-work/psw-magazine/articles/third-children-now-living-poverty-uk-cost-living-crisis

82 Patrick Butler, 'Families affected by two-child benefit limit 'more likely to skip meals'', The Guardian, 25 Jul 2024, https://www.theguardian.com/society/article/2024/jul/25/families-affected-by-two-child-benefit-limit-more-likely-to-skip-meals

83 Zoe Williams, 'This should be the climate election. Instead we are in a frustrating, Farage-obsessed fantasyland', The Guardian, 18 Jun 2024, https://www.theguardian.com/commentisfree/article/2024/jun/18/sane-world-sandi-toksvig-politician-nigel-farage-entertainer

84 'The Conservative manifesto: an initial response', IFS, 11 Jun 2024, https://ifs.org.uk/articles/conservative-manifesto-initial-response

85 Paul Johnson, 'The £22bn 'black hole' was obvious to anyone who dared to look', IFS, 5 ug 2024, https://ifs.org.uk/articles/ps22bn-black-hole-was-obvious-anyone-who-dared-look

86 Rishi Sunak [@RishiSunak], Twitter, 4 Oct 2023, https://twitter.com/RishiSunak/status/1709521604571529672

87 Jeremy Hunt [@Jeremy_Hunt], Twitter, 3 Jul 2024, https://x.com/Jeremy_Hunt/status/1808543366725898350

88 Jessica Rawnsley, Geraldine Scott, Peter Chappell, Max Kendix, Ed Halford, Oliver Wright, 'Sunak pledges £17 billion in tax cuts as he launches Tory manifesto — as it happened', The Times, 11 Jun 2024, https://www.thetimes.com/uk/politics/article/general-election-2024-latest-news-conservative-manifesto-rishi-sunak-5tjbkg62t

89 Richard Murphy, '19% of all people at work in the UK don't make enough to pay tax', Tax Research, 2 May 2017, https://www.taxresearch.org.uk/Blog/2017/05/02/19-of-all-people-at-work-in-the-uk-dont-make-enough-to-pay-tax/

90 Pippa Crerar, Ben Quinn, Eleni Courea and Jessica Elgot, 'Rightwing Tories plan 'rebel manifesto' if Sunak's policy launch falls flat', The Guardian, 10 Jun 2024, https://www.theguardian.com/politics/article/2024/jun/10/tory-right-plans-to-present-sunak-with-set-of-demands-if-manifesto-falls-flat

91 'MPs who stood down at the 2024 general election', Institute for Government, 7 Jun 2024, https://www.instituteforgovernment.org.uk/explainer/mps-who-stood-down-general-election-2024

92 Tali Fraser, 'Tory Chair Faces Calls To Resign Over "Arrogant" Chicken Run', PoliticsHome, 15 Jun 2024, https://www.politicshome.com/news/article/ric-holden-pressure

93 Tali Fraser, 'Tory Chair Faces Calls To Resign Over "Arrogant" Chicken Run', PoliticsHome, 15 Jun 2024, https://www.politicshome.com/news/article/ric-holden-pressure

94 Jessica Parker, 'Tory chairman's leaflets sent to wrong constituency', BBC News, 25 Jun 2024, https://www.bbc.co.uk/news/articles/clllle746l8o

95 Simon Murphy, 'Tory election candidate quits after sharing inappropriate photos from club nights for kids', Mirror, 7 Jun 2024, https://www.mirror.co.uk/news/politics/tory-election-candidate-quits-after-32984139

96 Brian Wheeler, 'Johnson help will make a difference, says Sunak', BBC News, 18 Jun 2024, https://www.bbc.co.uk/news/articles/cg33wjljyd9o

97 Kate Devlin, 'Boris Johnson to go on second holiday instead of joining Tory election campaign trail', Independent, 19 Jun 2024, https://www.independent.co.uk/news/uk/politics/boris-johnson-holiday-tory-election-campaign-b2565198.html
98 Alice Hopkin [@AliceMHopkin], Twitter, 7 Jun 2024, https://x.com/AliceMHopkin/status/1802789336343035953
99 Pippa Crerar, 'Former Tory minister vows to vote Labour over party's climate failures', The Guardian, 20 Jun 2024, https://www.theguardian.com/politics/article/2024/jun/20/former-tory-minister-vows-to-vote-labour-over-tories-climate-failures
100 Tom Peck, 'Zac Goldsmith 'defecting to Labour' will send chills through the party (the Labour Party), Independent, 10 Aug 2023, https://www.independent.co.uk/voices/zac-goldsmith-defecting-labour-tories-b2390989.html
101 Josiah Mortimer, 'Why Have the Conservatives Suspended Their Digital Campaign?', Byline Supplement, 7 Jun 2024, https://www.bylinesupplement.com/p/why-have-the-conservatives-suspended
102 Sir Bill Cash [@SirBillCash], Twitter, 16 Jun 2024, https://x.com/SirBillCash/status/1802266075536486830
103 The Sunday Sport [@thesundaysport], Twitter, 16 Jun 2024, https://x.com/thesundaysport/status/1802328840519241855
104 Sam Francis, 'Sunak 'incredibly angry' over alleged election betting', BBC News, 20 Jun 2024, https://www.bbc.co.uk/news/articles/c844je9nq89o
105 Dominic Penna, 'MPs should be banned from gambling, suggests Cabinet minister', The Telegraph, 26 Jun 2024, https://www.telegraph.co.uk/politics/2024/06/26/mps-should-be-banned-from-gambling-mel-stride-suggests/
106 Michael Savage, 'Tory minister who placed three bets on election date in line for Sunak peerage', The Guardian, 29 Jun 2024, https://www.theguardian.com/politics/article/2024/jun/29/tory-minister-who-placed-three-bets-on-election-date-in-line-for-sunak-peerage
107 Dominic Penna, 'MPs should be banned from gambling, suggests Cabinet minister', The Telegraph, 26 Jun 2024, https://www.telegraph.co.uk/politics/2024/06/26/mps-should-be-banned-from-gambling-mel-stride-suggests/
108 Rowena Mason and Vikram Dodd, 'Election betting: Tories drop two candidates in major U-turn', The Guardian, 25 Jun 2024, https://www.theguardian.com/politics/article/2024/jun/25/election-betting-conservatives-drop-two-candidates-craig-williams-laura-saunders
109 Kate Whannel, 'PM 'not aware' of other Tory candidates linked to betting inquiry', BBC News, 24 Jun 2024, https://www.bbc.co.uk/news/articles/crgggj5r005o
110 Becky Morton, 'Farage defends claim PM 'doesn't understand our culture'', BBC News 9 Jun 2024, https://www.bbc.co.uk/news/articles/cx005vdgg5yo
111 Politics UK [@PolitlcsUK], Twitter, 27 Jun 2024, https://x.com/PolitlcsUK/status/1806320693828542486
112 Alisha Rahaman Sarkar, 'Sir Philip Davies latest Tory caught up in gambling row 'after betting £8,000 against himself'', Independent, 27 Jun 2024, https://www.independent.co.uk/news/uk/politics/elections-tory-philip-davies-gambling-b2569698.html
113 'Philip Davies MP, Shipley', The Public Whip, https://www.publicwhip.org.uk/mp.php?mpn=Philip_Davies&mpc=Shipley&house=commons
114 David Maddox, 'Tory director of campaigning takes 'leave of absence' as election betting scandal grows', Independent, 20 Jun 2024, https://www.independent.co.uk/news/uk/politics/tories-betting-scandal-general-election-b2565814.html
115 Shiler Mahmoudi, 'Tory insider admits party 'running out of cash' as it airs cheap election broadcast', Mirror, 20 Jun 2024, https://www.mirror.co.uk/news/politics/tory-

party-running-out-cash-33070784

116 Daniel Boffey, 'Frank Hester racism row: how key figures reacted to remarks about Diane Abbott', The Guardian, 15 Mar 2024, https://www.theguardian.com/business/2024/mar/15/frank-hester-racism-row-how-key-figures-reacted-to-diane-abbott-remarks

117 https://inews.co.uk/news/sunak-campaign-trail-abandoned-marginals-safe-seats-d-day-3100228

118 Peter Walker, 'Rishi Sunak floats sanctions on young people for refusing national service', The Guardian, 20 Jun 2024, https://www.theguardian.com/politics/article/2024/jun/20/rishi-sunak-floats-sanctions-on-young-people-for-refusing-national-service

119 Andrew Sparrow 'Rishi Sunak says he is 'incredibly angry' about betting allegations in BBC Question Time election special – as it happened', The Guardian, 20 Jun 2024, https://www.theguardian.com/politics/live/2024/jun/20/bbc-question-time-leaders-debate-conservatives-labour-lib-dem-snp-latest-updates

120 Rajeev Syal, Peter Walker, Rowena Mason and Ben Quinn, 'Rishi Sunak to bring in emergency law after supreme court's Rwanda ruling', The Guardian, 15 Nov 2023, https://www.theguardian.com/uk-news/2023/nov/15/rishi-sunak-to-bring-in-emergency-law-after-courts-rwanda-ruling

121 Andrew Sparrow 'Rishi Sunak says he is 'incredibly angry' about betting allegations in BBC Question Time election special – as it happened', The Guardian, 20 Jun 2024, https://www.theguardian.com/politics/live/2024/jun/20/bbc-question-time-leaders-debate-conservatives-labour-lib-dem-snp-latest-updates?page=with:block-667498358f08035ce49e7a17#block-667498358f08035ce49e7a17

122 Jessica Elgot, 'Tory MPs paid £100,000 of public funds to party's in-house web designers', The Guardian, 23 Jun 2024, https://www.theguardian.com/politics/article/2024/jun/23/tory-mps-paid-100000-of-public-funds-to-partys-in-house-web-designers

123 Faye Brown, 'Jeremy Hunt donates £32,000 of own money to local party amid 'neck and neck' fight to keep seat', Sky News, 27 Jun 2024, https://news.sky.com/story/jeremy-hunt-donates-32-000-of-own-money-to-local-party-amid-neck-and-neck-fight-to-keep-seat-13159487

124 Anders Anglesey, 'Bungling Tory Chancellor Jeremy Hunt deletes photo of wife voting amid claims it could break voting rules', Mirror, 24 Jun 2024, https://www.mirror.co.uk/news/politics/bungling-tory-chancellor-jeremy-hunt-33096466

125 Paul McNamara, 'Jeremy Hunt forgets nationality of his own wife', Channel 4 News, 30 Jul 2018, https://www.channel4.com/news/jeremy-hunt-forgets-nationality-of-his-own-wife

126 Denis Campbell, 'Tory minister accused of cronyism after associate's firm hired as adviser', The Guardian, 24 Jun 2024, https://www.theguardian.com/politics/article/2024/jun/24/tory-minister-accused-of-cronyism-after-associates-firm-hired-as-adviser

127 'The government has given six hospitals money to upgrade buildings', FullFact, 3 Oct 2019, https://fullfact.org/health/six-hospitals-not-forty/

128 Denis Campbell, 'Tory minister accused of cronyism after associate's firm hired as adviser', The Guardian, 24 Jun 2024, https://www.theguardian.com/politics/article/2024/jun/24/tory-minister-accused-of-cronyism-after-associates-firm-hired-as-adviser

129 Simon Hattenstone and Jessica Elgot, 'Tories are a 'shower of shit', says Conservative candidate James Cracknell', The Guardian, 24 Jun 2024, https://www.theguardian.com/

politics/article/2024/jun/24/tories-are-a-shower-of-shit-says-conservative-candidate-james-cracknell
130. Isabel Hardman, 'Why is Mel Stride always doing the broadcast round?', The Spectator, 26 Jun 2024, https://www.spectator.co.uk/article/why-is-mel-stride-always-doing-the-broadcast-round/
131. Sophie Huskisson, 'Cringe live interview as wannabe Tory leader makes bizarre brag', Mirror, 4 Aug 2024, https://www.mirror.co.uk/news/politics/tory-leadership-hopeful-who-25-33391907
132. John Stevens, 'Rishi Sunak's pal fails to put word 'Conservative' on election leaflet - even in small print', Mirror, 1 Jul 2024, https://www.mirror.co.uk/news/politics/rishi-sunaks-pal-fails-put-33143882
133. John Stevens, 'Ex-Tory chairman fails to mention party anywhere on election leaflet', Mirror, 2 Jul 2024, https://www.mirror.co.uk/news/politics/ex-tory-chairman-fails-mention-33145830
134. Cara Simmonds, 'Conservative Laura Trott and Reform UK's James Milmine replaced with toy squirrel and pinecone at Sevenoaks hustings', Kent Online, 24 Jun 2024, https://www.kentonline.co.uk/sevenoaks/news/tory-candidate-replaced-with-toy-squirrel-after-debate-no-sh-308756/
135. Faye Brown, 'Laura Trott accused of not knowing 'basic facts of her job' after questions over debt', Sky News, 9 Feb 2024, https://news.sky.com/story/laura-trott-accused-of-not-knowing-basic-facts-of-her-job-after-questions-over-debt-13067047
136. Max Kendix and Geraldine Scott, 'Leadership campaign websites registered for senior Tories', The Times, 30 Jun 2024, https://www.thetimes.com/uk/politics/article/senior-tories-register-leadership-campaign-websites-0p09h9prj
137. Max Kendix and Geraldine Scott, 'Leadership campaign websites registered for senior Tories', The Times, 30 Jun 2024, https://www.thetimes.com/uk/politics/article/senior-tories-register-leadership-campaign-websites-0p09h9prj
138. Christy Cooney, 'Tory student group condemned after video shows them 'singing to Nazi song'', The Guardian, 30 Jun 2024, https://www.theguardian.com/education/article/2024/jun/30/tory-student-group-condemned-over-video-shows-them-singing-to-nazi-song
139. 'Wage progression and the gender wage gap: the causal impact of hours of work', IFS, 5 Feb 2018, https://ifs.org.uk/publications/wage-progression-and-gender-wage-gap-causal-impact-hours-work
140. '1980s: A decade of state-sanctioned homophobia', Peter Tatchell Foundation, 7 Nov 2012, https://www.petertatchellfoundation.org/1980s-a-decade-of-state-sanctioned-homophobia/
141. Joshua Stein, 'Nigel Farage 'dismayed' after Reform UK campaigner calls Sunak a 'f**king P**i'', iNews, 27 Jun 2024, https://inews.co.uk/news/nigel-farage-dismayed-after-reform-uk-campaigner-calls-sunak-a-fking-pi-3136526
142. Joshua Stein, 'Nigel Farage 'dismayed' after Reform UK campaigner calls Sunak a 'f**king P**i'', iNews, 27 Jun 2024, https://inews.co.uk/news/nigel-farage-dismayed-after-reform-uk-campaigner-calls-sunak-a-fking-pi-3136526
143. David Parsley, Hugo Gye, 'Inside Reform's meltdown as racism and homophobia row engulfs party', iNews, 28 Jun 2024, https://inews.co.uk/news/inside-reform-meltdown-race-sexism-row-election-3138213
144. Rebecca Jones, 'Nigel Farage's defence of racist campaigner ridiculed by Loose Women in fiery clash', Express, 28 Jun 2024, https://www.express.co.uk/showbiz/tv-radio/1916719/Nigel-Farage-racist-homophob
145. Joe Middleton, David Maddox, Kate Devlin, 'Sunak reveals anger as daughters

forced to hear Reform activist call him racist slur', Independent, 28 Jun 2024, https://www.independent.co.uk/news/uk/politics/rishi-sunak-nigel-farage-reform-racism-b2570633.html
146 Peter Walker, 'Sunak says public should accept Frank Hester's apology for Abbott remarks', The Guardian, 13 Mar 2024, https://www.theguardian.com/politics/2024/mar/13/sunak-says-public-should-accept-frank-hesters-apology-for-abbott-remarks
147 Henry Dyer and Rowena Mason, 'Frank Hester donated further £5m to Tories in January, figures show', The Guardian, 6 Jun 2024, https://www.theguardian.com/business/article/2024/jun/06/frank-hester-donated-further-5m-to-tories-in-january-figures-show
148 Peter Walker, 'Sunak says no Islamophobia issues in Tory party despite Anderson remarks', The Guardian, 26 Feb 2024, https://www.theguardian.com/politics/2024/feb/26/lee-anderson-sadiq-khan-tory-london-mayor
149 Noah Keate, 'Nigel Farage suffers new blow as bigotry storm engulfs his party just before UK election', Politico, 2 Jul 2024, https://www.politico.eu/article/nigel-farages-party-accused-racism-misogyny-by-former-election-candidate/
150 Holly Patrick, 'Nigel Farage claims he's 'done more to drive far-right out of British politics than anyone alive'', Independent, 28 Jun 2024, https://www.independent.co.uk/tv/news/bbc-question-time-farage-reform-racist-b2570911.html
151 Nigel Farage [@Nigel_Farage], Twitter, 29 Jun 2024, https://x.com/Nigel_Farage/status/1807024727283675211
152 Joe Kasper, 'BEEB BAN Nigel Farage vows to boycott the BBC after accusing it of treating him like a 'war criminal'', The Sun, 13 Sep 2019, https://www.thesun.co.uk/news/9925400/nigel-farage-boycott-bbc-war-criminal/
153 Tim Shipman, 'The Shippers Awards 2010-2020: a crazy decade in politics', The Times, 5 Jan 2020, https://www.thetimes.com/article/the-shippers-awards-2010-2020-a-crazy-decade-in-politics-xn5vs355f
154 Rowena Mason and Kiran Stacey, 'Senior Tory criticises 'worst campaign in my lifetime' as frustration grows', The Guardian, 2 Jul 2024, https://www.theguardian.com/politics/article/2024/jul/02/senior-tory-criticises-worst-campaign-in-my-lifetime-as-frustration-grows
155 Ryan Coogan, 'Just when you thought it couldn't get any worse for Rishi Sunak... he goes on This Morning', Independent, 3 Jul 2024, https://www.independent.co.uk/voices/rishi-sunak-this-morning-tattoo-sandwich-b2573344.html
156 Simon Dedman, 'I'm happy with my unique lunch choices, says Badenoch', BBC News, 13 Dec 2024, https://www.bbc.co.uk/news/articles/cewxd1y99ryo
157 Jacob Phillips, 'General election polling: Quarter of Conservative 2019 voters think party deserves to win no seats', The Standard, 13 Jun 2024, https://www.standard.co.uk/news/politics/general-election-polling-conservative-labour-voters-mps-ipsos-yougov-b1164066.html https://x.com/BestForBritain/status/1800868173861826690
158 Christopher Hope [@christopherhope], Twitter, 26 Jun 2024, https://twitter.com/christopherhope/status/1805947193313894568
159 David Maddox, 'Tory blame game already begins with a week to go before polling day', Independent, 27 Jun 2024, https://www.independent.co.uk/news/uk/politics/tory-blame-game-election-defeat-b2568885.html
160 Ian Jones, 'General Election in numbers: Records broken and historic milestones', Independent, 6 Jul 2024, https://www.independent.co.uk/news/uk/labour-mps-conservatives-snp-aldershot-b2575312.html
161 'General election 2024 in maps and charts', BBC News, 4 Jul 2024, https://www.bbc.co.uk/news/articles/c4nglegege1o

162 The Decade In Tory, 2022, and Four Chancellors and a Funeral, 2023.
163 Toby Helm, 'UK growth since 2010 has been lacklustre and largely driven by immigration, says report', The Observer, 9 Jun 20210, https://www.theguardian.com/business/article/2024/jun/09/uk-growth-since-2010-has-been-lacklustre-and-largely-driven-by-immigration-says-report
164 Philip Aldrick, 'A Dismal Inheritance Awaits Labour's Return in the UK', Bloomberg, 2 Jul 2024, https://www.bloomberg.com/news/newsletters/2024-07-02/uk-elections-a-dismal-inheritance-awaits-labour-s-return-to-power
165 Ros Atkins, 'The Liz Truss moment: What it was like to be in the room', BBC News, 8 Jul 2024., https://www.bbc.co.uk/news/articles/crgrz2d77lgo
166 Rebecca Perring, 'Bungling Tory MP vows to 'level' Stoke and spells his OWN name wrong in leadership gaff', Express, 15 Jul 2022, https://www.express.co.uk/news/politics/1641159/Tory-mp-leader-race-penny-mordaunt-Jack-Brereton
167 Edward Malnick, 'Ex-minister Stephen Crabb becomes first Tory MP investigated under party's new code', Telegraph, 4 Nov 2017, https://www.telegraph.co.uk/news/2017/11/04/ex-minister-stephen-crabb-becomes-first-tory-mp-investigated/
168 Samantha Booth, 'Education secretary Michelle Donelan resigns after less than two days', Schools Week, 7 Jul 2022, https://schoolsweek.co.uk/education-secretary-michelle-donelan-resigns-after-less-than-two-days/
169 Megan White, 'MP Andrea Jenkyns left with whiplash and concussion after falling off chair in a meeting', The Standard, 30 Jul 2019, https://www.standard.co.uk/news/politics/mp-andrea-jenkyns-left-with-whiplash-and-concussion-after-falling-off-chair-in-a-meeting-a4201826.html
170 Paul Lashmar and Jonathan Smith, 'He's the MP with the Downton Abbey lifestyle. But the shadow of slavery hangs over the gilded life of Richard Drax', The Guardian, 12 Dec 2020, https://www.theguardian.com/world/2020/dec/12/hes-the-mp-with-the-downton-abbey-lifestyle-but-the-shadow-of-slavery-hangs-over-the-gilded-life-of-richard-drax
171 Amelia Hill and Owen Bowcott, "It's completely wrong': falsely accused Tory MP attacks legal aid cuts', The Guardian, 27 Dec 2018, https://www.theguardian.com/law/2018/dec/27/its-completely-wrong-falsely-accused-tory-mp-attacks-legal-aid-cuts
172 Basit Mahmood, 'Former Tory MP Jonathan Gullis complains he still can't find a job after voters dumped him', Left Foot Forward, 2 Jan 2025, https://leftfootforward.org/2025/01/former-tory-mp-jonathan-gullis-complains-he-still-cant-find-a-job-after-voters-dumped-him/
173 Sue Austin, 'Shrewsbury MP Daniel Kawczynski defends taxpayer-funded Polish lessons', Shropshire Star, 3 Jan 2022, https://www.shropshirestar.com/news/politics/2022/01/04/shrewsbury-mp-daniel-kawczynski-defends-claiming-expenses-for-polish-lessons/
174 Tim Scunthorpe, 'Daniel Kawczynski becomes the THIRD Tory MP referred to a disciplinary committee after he is accused of pressuring young researcher to go on a date with a wealthy businessman who was 'older than her father'", Daily Mail, 4 Nov 2017, https://www.dailymail.co.uk/news/article-5050291/David-Cameron-adviser-named-Westminster-sleaze-scandal.html
175 Daniel Bond, 'Class of 2019: Meet the new MPs', PoliticsHome, 16 Dec 2019, https://www.politicshome.com/thehouse/article/class-of-2019-meet-the-new-mps
176 'Suella Braverman', Global Player, https://www.globalplayer.com/catchup/lbc/uk/b8FPjgv/
177 Adam Bienkov [BlueSky], 2 Jan 2025, https://bsky.app/profile/adambienkov.bsky.social/post/3ler2pke3zs2a

178 https://www.bbc.co.uk/news/articles/ckg1ljn80geo
179 Luke Buckmaster, 'The Office Australia review – an edgeless reboot doomed for the shredder', The Guardian, 16 Oct 2024, https://www.theguardian.com/tv-and-radio/2024/oct/16/the-office-australia-review-an-edgeless-reboot-doomed-for-the-shredder
180 https://variety.com/2023/film/news/russel-crowe-gladiator-script-rubbish-turned-film-down-1235592393/
181 https://www.abc.net.au/news/2024-01-01/hollywood-is-obsessed-with-remakes-and-reboots-but-so-are-audien/103220136
182 'Jenna Ortega Answers the Web's Most Searched Questions', YouTube, https://www.youtube.com/watch?v=xXvgT-AgLAo
183 Rebecca Strassberg, '13 Famous Actors Who Learned New Skills for a Role', Backstage, 21 Mar 2023, https://www.backstage.com/magazine/article/famous-actors-learned-new-skills-films-8103/
184 'Kate Winslet reveals the biggest challenge she faced making Avatar: The Way of Water – and it wasn't holding her breath', Games Radar, 13 Dec 2022, https://www.gamesradar.com/kate-winslet-interview-avatar-way-of-water/
185 Alex Hern, 'Bafflement over Tory MP's admission she hacked Harriet Harman's website', The Guardian, 9 Apr 2018, https://www.theguardian.com/technology/2018/apr/09/bafflement-over-tory-mps-admission-she-hacked-harriet-harmans-website
186 'Suella Braverman will not run in Tory leadership race', Sky News, 29 Jul 2024, https://news.sky.com/story/suella-braverman-will-not-run-in-tory-leadership-race-13186430
187 Jack Pannell, '2024 Conservative Party leadership contest', Institute for Government, 8 Oct 2024, https://www.instituteforgovernment.org.uk/explainer/2024-conservative-party-leadership-contest
188 https://news.sky.com/story/tory-leadership-contender-robert-jenrick-took-weight-loss-drug-ozempic-but-didnt-enjoy-it-13200301
189 Pippa Crerar [@PippaCrerar], Twitter, 9 Oct 2024, https://x.com/PippaCrerar/status/1844024791759749594
190 Daniel Martin, 'Cleverly out of Tory race 'after tactical voting backfires'', The Telegraph, 9 Oct 2024, https://www.telegraph.co.uk/politics/2024/10/09/james-cleverly-out-of-tory-race-tactical-voting/
191 James Tapfield, 'James Cleverly says he WON'T serve on Tory front bench under new leader... with Jeremy Hunt and ex-deputy PM Oliver Dowden also stepping aside', Daily Mail, 2 Nov 2024, https://www.dailymail.co.uk/news/article-14032447/James-Cleverly-Tory-leader-Jeremy-Hunt-Oliver-Dowden-Rishi-Sunak.html
192 Peter Walker, 'Kemi Badenoch wins Tory leadership election', The Guardian, 2 Nov 2024, https://www.theguardian.com/politics/2024/nov/02/kemi-badenoch-wins-tory-leadership-election
193 'Estimated membership numbers of political parties in the United Kingdom in 2022', Statista, 2022, https://www.statista.com/statistics/871460/political-party-membership-in-the-uk/
194 Andrew Sparrow, 'Kemi Badenoch elected new Conservative leader – as it happened', 2 Nov 2024, https://www.theguardian.com/politics/live/2024/nov/02/tory-leadership-election-results-live-kemi-badenoch-robert-jenrick-new-conservative-leader?page=with:block-6725ec158f080a1fc5f94e3c#block-6725ec158f080a1fc5f94e3c
195 David Maddox, 'Tory plotting already underway to replace Kemi Badenoch as leader after local elections disaster', Independent, 3 May 2025, https://www.independent.co.uk/news/uk/politics/kemi-badenoch-tory-local-elections-jenrick-b2743870.html

196 Rowena Mason, 'Conservative party is fighting for its life, says former Tory cabinet minister', The Guardian, 9 May 2025, https://www.theguardian.com/politics/2025/may/09/conservative-party-is-fighting-for-its-life-says-uk-ex-cabinet-minister

Repeating the Error
197 Paul Seddon, 'Reform UK makes big gains in English local elections', BBC News, 2 May 2025, https://www.bbc.co.uk/news/articles/cd6j8e38p79o
1 'Police 'overwhelmed' by riots in Manchester and Salford', BBC News, 10 Aug 2011, https://www.bbc.co.uk/news/uk-england-manchester-14467588
2 'Hundreds join Manchester clean-up after riots', BBC News, 10 Aug 2011, https://www.bbc.co.uk/news/uk-england-manchester-14478902
3 'Keir Starmer's Government Should Stop the Austerity Denial About These Cuts', Byline Times, 26 Mar 2025, https://bylinetimes.com/2025/03/26/spring-statement-rachel-reeves-keir-starmer-austerity-cuts-budget/
4 Anoosh Chakelian, 'Britain's richest 10% don't think they're wealthy – and that's disastrous in the fight against inequality', The Guardian, 24 Jan 2024, https://www.theguardian.com/commentisfree/2024/jan/24/britain-richest-10-per-cent-wealthy-inequality-labour-private-schools
5 Don Young, 'Having Their Cake', https://www.havingtheircake.com/content/Society/How%20to%20make%20the%20super-rich%20contribute%20to%20the%20health%20of%20the%20wider%20society.php
6 Anna Fleck, 'The UK'S Rich Are Getting Richer', Statista, 23 May 2022, https://www.statista.com/chart/27505/uks-richest-are-getting-richer/
7 'Child poverty in working households has increased by over 1,300 a week since 2010', TUC, 15 Jun 2024, https://www.tuc.org.uk/news/child-poverty-working-households-has-increased-over-1300-week-2010
8 Anoosh Chakelian, 'Replacing lost Sure Start centres is a tacit admission of austerity's failure', The New Statesman, 10 Feb 2023, https://www.newstatesman.com/thestaggers/2023/02/replacing-lost-sure-start-centres-is-a-tacit-admission-of-austeritys-failure
9 Gurpreet Narwan, 'Reform UK's tax plans disproportionately benefit high earners, analysis shows', Sky News, 22 Jun 2024, https://news.sky.com/story/reform-uks-tax-plans-disproportionately-benefit-high-earners-analysis-shows-13156776
10 Eliza Parr, 'Reform UK pledges private GP for patients left waiting for appointment', Pulse, 18 Jun 2024, https://www.pulsetoday.co.uk/news/politics/reform-uk-pledges-private-gp-for-patients-left-waiting-for-appointment/
11 Jim Dunton, 'Farage floats plans to slash £50bn from departments and cut taxes', Civil Service World, 18 Jun 2024, https://www.civilserviceworld.com/professions/article/farage-floats-plans-to-slash-50bn-from-departments-and-cut-taxes
12 Steph Spyro, 'Nigel Farage blasts Labour's VAT raid on private schools: 'Not morally right!'', Express, 30 May 2024, https://www.express.co.uk/news/politics/1905599/nigel-farage-vat-private-schools-labour-piers-morgan
13 'Sir Keir Starmer: bureaucrat first, politician second', The Economist, 21 Feb 2024, https://www.economist.com/britain/2024/02/21/sir-keir-starmer-bureaucrat-first-politician-second
14 Rowena Mason, 'Film shows Nigel Farage calling for move away from state-funded NHS', The Guardian, 12 Nov 2014, https://www.theguardian.com/politics/2014/nov/12/film-nigel-farage-insurance-based-nhs-private-companies
15 'Mussolini on the Corporate State', Political Research Associates, 12 Jan 2005, https://politicalresearch.org/2005/01/12/mussolini-corporate-state

16 'Elon Musk's net worth sees a new record, wealth is more than GDP of over 140 countries. Here's how he built his venture', The Economic Times, 18 Dec 2024, https://economictimes.indiatimes.com/news/international/global-trends/elon-musks-net-worth-500-billion-reaches-new-high-first-ever-person-to-achieve-this-feat-check-wealth-and-how-he-built-his-venture/articleshow/116427332.cms

17 Julia Ingram, 'Elon Musk spends $277 million to back Trump and Republican candidates', CBS News, 6 Dec 2024, https://www.cbsnews.com/news/elon-musk-277-million-trump-republican-candidates-donations/

18 'Sir James Dyson fifth wealthiest in Sunday Times Rich List with £23 billion fortune', ITV News, 21 May 2023, https://www.itv.com/news/westcountry/2023-05-21/richest-person-in-the-west-country-revealed-with-23-billion-fortune

19 Pieter Snepvangers , 'How farmers can dodge Labour's inheritance tax raid', The Telegraph, 19 Nov 2024, https://www.telegraph.co.uk/money/tax/inheritance/how-farmers-dodge-labour-inheritance-tax-raid/

20 'Britain's most powerful people 5 times more likely to go to private school', Sutton Trust, 24 Jun 2019, https://www.suttontrust.com/news-opinion/all-news-opinion/elitist-britain-five-times-more-likely-to-go-to-private-school/

21 'School Cuts', 2024, https://schoolcuts.org.uk/

22 ' Teachers Spending Hundreds of their Own Money on Supplies', ERA Group, https://adria.eragroup.com/news/teachers-spend-money-supplies/

23 Sian Hopkins, 'Increase in teachers providing food for hungry pupils', Children and Young People Now, 29 Aug 2024, https://www.cypnow.co.uk/content/news/increase-in-teachers-providing-food-for-hungry-pupils/

24 Alix Culbertson, 'Row over how many farms will be affected by inheritance tax policy - as PM doubles down ahead of farmers protest', Sky News, 19 Nov 2024, https://news.sky.com/story/row-over-how-many-farms-will-be-affected-by-inheritance-tax-policy-as-pm-doubles-down-ahead-of-farmers-protest-13256273

25 Hannah McGreevy, 'Jeremy Clarkson's staggering net worth after crippling farm loss and Grand Tour payout', Mirror, 12 Sep 2024, https://www.mirror.co.uk/tv/tv-news/jeremy-clarksons-staggering-net-worth-33657733

26 Jack Peat, 'Jeremy Clarkson is furious about the Budget and people think they know why', The London Economic, 1 Nov 2024, https://www.thelondoneconomic.com/news/jeremy-clarkson-is-furious-about-the-budget-and-people-think-they-know-why-385001/

27 Teagan Goddard, 'It's the Economy Stupid', Political Dictionary, https://politicaldictionary.com/words/its-the-economy-stupid/

28 Derek Saul, 'How The Economy Really Fared Under Biden/Harris And Trump—From Jobs To Inflation (Final Update)', Forbes, 1 Nov 2024, https://www.forbes.com/sites/dereksaul/2024/11/01/how-the-economy-really-fared-under-bidenharris-and-trump-from-jobs-to-inflation-final-update/

29 'As Election Nears, Kelly Warns Trump Would Rule Like a Dictator', New York Times, 22 Oct 2024, https://www.nytimes.com/2024/10/22/us/politics/john-kelly-trump-fitness-character.html

30 Jordan Valinsky, 'The world's 10 richest people got a record $64 billion richer from Trump's reelection', CNN Business, 7 Nov 2024, https://edition.cnn.com/2024/11/07/investing/billionaires-net-worth-trump-win/index.html

31 'Richest 1% grab nearly twice as much new wealth as rest of the world put together', Oxfam, 16 Jan 2023, https://www.oxfam.org.uk/media/press-releases/richest-1-grab-nearly-twice-as-much-new-wealth-as-rest-of-the-world-put-together/

32 David Hughes, 'Reform UK lines up billionaires to fund 'political disruption'', The

Standard, 22 Dec 2024, https://www.standard.co.uk/news/politics/elon-musk-nigel-farage-nick-candy-reform-uk-party-b1201460.html

33 Joshua Nevett, 'Starmer faces growing rebellion over welfare cuts', BBC News, 8 May 2025, https://www.bbc.co.uk/news/articles/c9q0g43exg4o

34 Rajeev Syal, 'Starmer accused of echoing far right with 'island of strangers' speech', The Guardian, 12 May 2025, https://www.theguardian.com/politics/2025/may/12/keir-starmer-defends-plans-to-curb-net-migration

35 'This Labour budget is austerity by another name', The Guardian, 31 Oct 2024, https://www.theguardian.com/uk-news/2024/oct/31/this-labour-budget-is-austerity-by-another-name

36 Good Reads, 'Aristotle Quotes' https://www.goodreads.com/quotes/1485252-in-a-democracy-the-poor-will-have-more-power-than

Supporters

Vij A
Matthew Abercrombie
Joe Abley
ACH
Lesley Adams
Mark Adams
James Afford
Zoe Alderman
Zoë Alderman
Rachel Ali
Syeda Ali
Richard Allard
Jenni Allen
Michael Allison
Nicola Alloway
Kevin Allsop
AMD
Steve Amos
Tracy Ampah
Michael Anders
Carolyn B Anderson
Keith Anderson
Igor Andronov
Lee Ankrett
Kirk Annett
Mark Appleton
Ana Araujo

Frances Armstrong
Johnny Armstrong
Malc Arnold
Tim C. Ashcroft
Nicola Ashdown
Hilary Ashton
Penny Asquith-Evans
Helen Astley
Richard Atkin
Janice Bailey
Matthew Bailey
Suzan & Dominic Baker
Paul Balbi
Bernie Baldwin
Kate Ball
Haydon Bambury
Aidan Bannon
Howard Bargroff
Matthew J. Barker
Moo Barman
Andrew Barrett
Lucy Barrett
Felix Bartle
Andrew Batchelor
Kaye Batchelor
Ryan Bate
Barbara Bayliss

TORIES: THE END OF AN ERROR

Tracy Bayly
Samantha Beavis
Chris Beddoes
Dave Beech
Grahame Bell
Richard Bellinger
Andrew Belton
Mark Bennett
Michael Bennett
Phillip Bennett-Richards
Shaun Bent
Christopher Berry
Anthony Betts
Simon Binks
Chris Binner
Alan Birse
Dorothy Bishop
Stuart Bishop
Richard Black
Simon Blackham
Graham Blenkin
Patrick Bolger
Catherine Bolt
Hannah Bolton
Martin Booth
Nic Boothby
David Boughton
James Bourke
Mike Bowker
Graham Brack
Carolina Bracken
Elizabeth Bradley
Lisa Bradley
Neil Bradley
Simon Bradley
Tina Bradley
Maryam Brady
Caroline Braithwaite
Adrienne Briarshade
Richard J Bridgwater
Michael Brockbanks

The Brollinsons
Jim Brookbank
Amy Brooke
Adrian Brooks
Brad Brooks
Bill Brown
Graham Brown
Julia Brown
Robert Brown
Sara Brown
Brian Browne
Lesley Bruce
Danny Buchanan
Louise Buchanan
Yvonne Budden
Lia Buddle
Alison Bunce
John Burdall
Andrea Burden
Rob Burney
Christine Burns
Lisa Burrell
Keith Burton
Lisa Butler
Morris Butler
Stephen Buxton
Kit & Shellie Byatt
Tom Cadmore
Tony Cameron
Donatella Campbell
Kirsty Campbell
Deborah Canavan
Ian Cannings
Janet Carberry
David Carlill
Ann Carrier
Claire Carroll
Charles Carsberg
Amanda Carter
John Carter
Peter Cash

SUPPORTERS

Keith Cass
Andrew Cattanach
Matthew Catterall
William Cave
Lucy Cavell
Louise Cawte
Jim Cessford
Elaine Chadwick
Marie Chadwick
Jenni Chambers
Jessica Chambers
Shelley Chambers
Colin Chapman
Richard Chapman
James Chiles
Fiona Chow
Jamie Christie
Debby Claber
Doug Clark
Ian Clarke
Mick Clarke
Si Clarke
Chris Clegg
Ian Clements
Richmond Clements
Andrew Cogan
Genevieve Cogman
Chris Coldwell
Lucy Rose Coleman
Henry Collet
Lesley Collett
Ian Collier
Alan Collins
Brendan Collins
Katie Collins
ML Collinson
Denny Conway
George A.J. Cook
David Cooke
Chris Cooper
Jane Cooper

Suzanne Cordier
Lisa Corkerry
Nick Corlett
Rosie Corlett
Charlotte Covell
Katharine Cowley
Nick Craggs
Fiona Craig
Malcolm Craik
Hazel Crane
Neil Crane
John Crawford
Jon Crawford
Adam Crawte
David Creasey-Benjamin
Tamsin Cromwell
Phil Crookall
Robert Cross
Sorcha Cross
Susan Cross
Dan Crouch
Steven Culliford
Graham Cumming
Brian Cunningham
Ian Cunningham
Sam Curran
Robert Currie
Jon Curwen
Renata Czinkotai
William Dale
Eleanor Dalglish
John Dallimore
Kieron Darcy
Chris Davenport
Elizabeth Davidson
Barry Davies
Jonathan Davies
Kathryn Davies
Nigel Davies
Philippa Davies
Sally Davies

Sian Davies
Sophie Davies
Sue Davies
Stephen Boyd Davis
Alexandra Dawe
Darren Dawson
Pat Dawson
Martin Dean
Dino Deasha
Nick Dempsey
Alison Denham
Calum Dennehy
Ian Dennis
Mark Dennison
Anna Denny
Zoe Dickinson
Ian Diddams
Lisa Diver
DJG
Sally Dodd
Adrian Doggett
Katherine Doggrell
Keith Donela
Lisa Donovan
Paul Drage
Gaynor Drake
Nigel Draper
Vikki Drummond
Miranda Dubner
E Dumergue
Mhairi Duncan
Pam Dunn
Peter Durbin
Simon Dutton
Dave Eagle
Richard Earney
Lynne Maria East
Adam Edge
Andrew Edmonstone
Michael Edmunds
David John Edmundson

Mark Edwards
Paul Edwards
Sarah Ellingworth
Chris Elliott
Graham Elliott
Richard Ellis
Todd Ellner
Lesley Elrick
Brad Emerson
Andrew Engel
Charl Engela
Jeannie Engela
J M Esq
Simon Everett
Stephen Eyre
Lisa Fairbairn
Andrea Fairhurst
Mike Fallbrown
Colin Farquhar
Melanie Farquhar
Louise Farquharson
David Faulkes
Craig Faulkner
Ron Faulkner
Tony Fenn
Mark Ferguson
Jakob Fey
Mimi Findlay
Paula Finn
Aaron Fisher
Nick Fitzsimons
Alastair Fleck
Chris Forrest
G Foskett
Brian Foster
Rob Foster
Joanne Foxton
Frances
Alastair Fraser
Lyndsey Fraser
Stuart Fraser

SUPPORTERS

Peta Free
Harry French
David Frew
Penelope Friday
David J Fry
Rhys Fullerton
Dave Furlong
Callum Furner
Myles Furr
Nick Gage
Marjorie Galloway
Lukas Gamble
Mark Gamble
Paul Gardiner
Alison Garner
Richard Garner
Helen Gateley
Stuart Gaunr
Marcus Gearini
Amanda George
Caroline Gerrard
Maggie Gibbs
Claire Gibson
Jane Gidman
Julie Giles
Ben Gill
Christine Gill
Matthew Gill
Roy Gillett
Giuseppe
Andrew Gledhill
David Glennie
Ryan Gliddon
Tony Glover
Matt Goddard
Roger Godfrey
Chris Goff
Natalie Goldspink
Sophie Goldspink
Mercedes Gonzalez
Laurence Good

Mx Goodall
Annette Goosey
Nicola Gordon-Thaxter
Frank Gorman
Will Gormley
Evelyn Gothard
Fred Gough
Richard Gough
Paul Grave
Catherine Greaves-Lord
Anne Green
Jen Green
Ste Greenall
Wayne Greenfield
Andrew Gregg
Louise Gregory
Phil Gregson
William Griffiths
James Grizzell-Jones
Julie Groom
Christine Grove
Ann Hadlow
Geoff Haederle
Ros Haigh
Alan Hall
Neil Hallam
Robert Hallett
Dave Hallwood
Ian Hammond
Tim Handley
Jo Harnett
Andrew Harper
Paul Harper
Alex Harrington
Jacqueline Harrington
Denise Harris
Steve Harris
Chris Harrison
Dr J Harrison
Chris Grace Hartness
Graham Harvey

Jon Harvey
Jo Haswell
Martine Van Haute
Rob Hawes
Judith Hawkins
David Hawksworth
Martin Hay
Peter Haydon
John Haynes
Mark Heafield
Damien Healey
Joyce Heard
Heini
William Hendry
Adam Henley
Elizabeth Henwood
Sarah Herring
Lee Herron
Alison Hesketh
Neil Heyes
Colin Hicks
Gary Hicks
Stephen Higginson
David Hilary
Richard Hildyard
Suzanne Hillman
Thomas Hind
Charles Hindle
Jennifer Hirst
Martin Hobbs
Steven Hodges
Kathryn Hodgson
Diane Holden
Adam Holmes
Steve Holmes
Joe Holsman
Katherine Honan
Antonia Honeywell
Simon Horbury
Rich Horsfall
Matthew Hothersall

Gary Houghton
Jon Hourihan
Phil Howard
Dan Howarth
David Howker
Tony Howse
Karen Hubbard
Andrew Hughes
Ben Hughes
Peter Hughes
Sheila Hughes
Chris Hulbert
Andrew Hulme
Jay Humphrey
Alan Hunt
Gordon Hunt
Paul Hunt-Terry
Chris R Hurst
Martin Hussey
Dan Hutson
Mark Hymers
Mark Iliff
Maggie Innes
Niall Innes
John Ireland
Adam Irvine
Graham Ives
Adam Jackson
Amy Jackson
Carole Jackson
Dr. Ian Jackson
Judith Jackson
Mike Jackson
Alexandra Jeffries
Rigby Jerram
Tom Jin
Andrea Johnson
Edward Johnson
Philip Johnson
Christopher GW Jones
Heather Jones

SUPPORTERS

Jim Jones
Lee Jones
Matthew Jones
Phil Jones
Tim and Clare Jones
Ronan Jouffe
Kevin Joynes
Nick Kaijaks
Maxwell Kates
Lesley Kazan-Pinfield
Helen Keay
Chris Keen
Andy Kelly
Catherine Kelly
Christopher Kelly
Jo Kennedy
Stephen Kent
Duncan Kerr
Neil Kerr
Helen Kershaw
Rob Kevan
Mike Khan
David Kiernan
David King
Ian Kirby
Richard Kirk
Tim Kirk
Jackie Kirkham
Tony Kitson
Ashley Knight
Terry Knipe
Daniel Krämer
Kenneth Kwek
Nick Lacey
Robert Laedlein
Nigel Lake
Ben Lambert
Steve Lambley
Ian Langmead
James Larner
Liz Lavelle

Leigh Lawrence
Nathan Lawrence
Dean Lea
Jo Leatham
Marcel LeCocq
Diane Lee
Mark Lee
Emma Leech
Kate Leimer
David Leonard
Helen Lester
Paul Lewis
Philip Lewis
Steven Linnington
Michael Linskey
Adrian Littlejohn
Flora Logan
Gareth Logue
Christina Lomas
JP Lomas
Lori
Craig Lowe
Pat Lowe
Peter Lowe
Sebastian Lucas
Maureen Luff
Min Luk
Andy Lulham
Sally Luxmoore
Dion Luyk
Chris Lydon
Jonathan and Clare Lynas
Ciaron Lynch
Paul Lynch
Hannawin Lynn
Gerard Lyons
L M
Elizabeth Macaulay
Cass Macdonald
Liz Mace
Shaun MacFarlane

Steve Mack
Iain Mackenzie
John Mackenzie
Justin Mackenzie
Mhairi Maclennan
David Male
David Maloney
Wendy Maloney
Dale Maltby
Marie Man
Deborah Manzoori
John Mapley
Hayleigh Marks
Andrew Marmot
Joseph Marshall
Peter Marshall
Jacqueline Mason
Dan Masters
Mat
David Matkins
Ben Matthews
Julie Matthews
Matthew Maude
Indigo Maughn
Max
Tim May
LaToyah McAllister-Jones
Joanne McBride
Remy McCabe
Stephen McClay
Selina McClure
John McCubbin
Ian McDougall
Michael McFarlane
Mitch McGregor
Kathleen McGurl
Bernie McIlvenny
Bryan McIlvenny
Gavin McKeown
Andrew McKeown-Henshall
Andrew McLachlan

Chris McLoughlin
Kerry McMahon
Graham McNeill
Hugo McNestry
Esther McQuillan
Andrew & Fiona McRait
Kay Melmoth-McKay
Angela Melton
Simon Melton
Kay Melville
Emma Menhinnitt
Edward Mercer
Nicholas Mew
Christine Midgley
Birgit Mikus
Philippa Milbourne
Eleanor Miller
John Miller
Tony Miller
Alex Milne
Brian Milne
Carolyn Moir
Paul Monks
Brigid Moore
C Moore
Harriett Moore-Boyd
Mike Moran
Terry Morgan
Dorita Morito
Sarah Morrison
David Moss
Hilary Moules
Tanya Anstey Mudd
Shane Mullally
Alan Mullett
Graeme Mulvey
Colin Murphy
Hannah Mycock-Overell
Malcolm Myles-Hook
Antony Nelson
Lisa Newby

SUPPORTERS

Rob Newby
Steve Nicholson
Gary Nicol
Niels Aagaard Nielsen
Linda Norman
Chris Novakovic
Andy O'Brien
Michael J. O'Neil
Sean O'Neill
Ann O'Shaughnessy
Jonathan Oldfield
Susan Olney
Paul Oneill
Daniel Opitz
Neil Orford
Lewis Orrow
Karen Osborne
Tim Owen
Donna P
Rob P
Anita Padwagga
Tara Palmer
David Pannette
Emma Papanikitas
Stephen Parker
Steven Parker
Andy Parsons
Jeni Parsons
Pratik Patel
Jane Paterson
Adam Ross Patterson
Bonnie Patterson
Cath Payne
Russell Peaker
Debbie Pearce
Cathy Pearse
Richard Pemberton
Louise Pengelly
Chris Pennell
Monika Peretz
Alex Phennah

Jonathan Phillips
Nigel Phillips
Daniel Piddock
Clay Pilfold
Seb Pillon
Colin Pink
Steve Pont
Mark Pope
Colin Powers
Jane Pratt
Rowan N Piper Preskey
Amber Prestidge
Sarah Price
Tom Priddle
Simon Proctor
Maureen Prowse
Tim Pugh
Joris Quaatbloet
Melissa Quilter
Robert Quinn
Adam Radcliffe
Susan Radford
Catherine Radley
Sarah Ramage
Rowan Ramsey
Edward Ratnam
Maggie Rawlings
Rauf Rawson
Wendy Rayner
Colette Reap
Simon Reap
Lyndsey Redpath
Freya Rennie
Alistair Renwick
Josh Reynolds
Tina Reynolds
Sarah Rhodes
Andy Richbell
Tracy Rimmer
Huw Ringer
Hazel Roberts

Martin R Roberts
Nick Roberts
Douglas Robertson
Adam Robinson
Bobby Lee Robinson
Phil Robinson
Andreas Hjorth Røen
Jay Roff
Geraint Rogers
Lisa Ronan
Sarah Rooke
Helen Rose
Sonny Ross
Anna Route
Nicholas Rowles
Sally Ruffer
Lisa Rull
Jon Rumfitt
Amanda Rutter
Bruce Ryan
Sarah-Jane Ryan
Paul Sabourin
Sally #FBPPR
Dave Sample
Jayne Samuel-Walker
Shreya Sawhney
David Saxon
Andrea Schauenburg
Thierry Schmidlin
Devin Scobie
Gemma Scott
Roger Scott
Neil Sellers
Karen Selley
Roland Serjeant
Mark Seton
Daniel Sewell
Bryan Sexton
James Sharp
Graham Shaw
Siobhan Shea

Rob Shelton
David Shepherd
Su Sheppard
Ian Shipley
Kate Shipway
Paul Shodimu
Tracey Sibun
Ronnie Sievewright
Andrea Sim
Jeremy Simmonds
Bryan Simon
Katie Singer
Gurdial Singh
Guru Singh
Deborah Sippitt
Mark Skinner
Ruth Slavin
Adrian Smith
Alan C Smith
Andrea Smith
Gavin Smith
Jacky Smith
Jane Smith
Jane Heron Smith
Leigh Smith
Ron Smith
Stuart Smith
Tom Smith
Jamie Snashall
Solvester
Ian Sorensen
Carrie Spacey
Chris Spear
James Spibey
Breda Spillane
Harald Sprengel
Dave Spring
Siobhan Spurle
Louise Squire
Simon Stacey
Susan Stainer

SUPPORTERS

Catherine Stalker
Marios Stavridis
Ben Stephen
Chris Storer
Bekah Stott
Marin Stoychev
Charles Strange
Jim Strange
Michael Stringer
David Stuart
Mike Sum
Zoie Sutherland
Uma Suthersanen
Pauline Swales
Anthony Swan
Luke Sweeney
Helen Szewczyk
Tim T
Anne Tait
Oliver Tate
Brian Taylor
Kev Taylor
Leanne Taylor
Wayne Taylor
Judith Thomas
Nigel Thomas
Stella-Maria Thomas
Ian Thompson
Lynn Thompson
John Thomson
Charlie Thwaites
Alex Tischer
Mike Tobyn
Giles Todd
Nyssa Toghill
Stu Tomlinson
Jo Toon
Ian Travis
Scott Treacy
Gareth Tregidon
Vicki Trowler

Christian Turner
Richard Turner
Sarah Thompson Turvey
Ben Twemlow
David Spinolli Tyler
Mike Tynan
Andrew van Doorn
Caroline Vanzie
Dominic Varley
Susan Vass
Paul Vaughan
Zoe Veal
Mark Vent
Paul Verbinnen
Sue Vickers-Thompson
Victor
Anna Vissens
Salim Vohra
Marcel Volker
Simon Wailling
John Wainwright
Nicola Wake
David Wakely
Bridget Walker
Natalie Walker
Zoe Walker
Andy Wallace
David Walton
Geoffrey Walton
Kellie Walton
Carole-Ann Warburton
Charlie Wardrop
Adam Watkins
Christine Watson
James Watts
Revd. Matthew Watts
Artur Wawrowski
Amy Webber
Ben Webster
Jennifer Welch
Nigel Welham

Jonathan Westwood
Nigel White
Steven White
Kirsten Whitehead
Steve Wiffin
Eve Wigham
Patricia Wightman
Ian Wilkins
Rachel Wilkinson
Sam Wilkinson
Suzanne Wilkinson
Christopher Williams
David Williams
Gareth Williams
Ian Williams
Judi Williams
Paul Williams
Mark Willis
Kerry Wilson
Nigel Wilson
Robin Wilton
Jez Wingham
M F Winiberg

Roger Winter
Stephan Wolf
mark wood
Melanie Wood
Tom Wood
Andrew Woodall
Mark Woodfield
Mick Woolley
Graham Wright
Jo Wright
Neil Wright
Solveig Wright
Curly Wyer
Mike Yorwerth
Happy 60th, Mr Alan Young
Jenn Young
Tom Young
Erica Youngman
Frances Yule
Rachel Yule
Andrey Zaytsev
Eckhard Zemp
Maik Zumstrull

Past Examination
Sugg

Constitutional Law

LLB

University of London
External Examinations

HLT Publications

HLT PUBLICATIONS
200 Greyhound Road, London W14 9RY

Examination Questions
© The University of London 1985, 1986, 1987, 1988, 1989, 1990
Solutions © The HLT Group Ltd 1993

All HLT publications enjoy copyright protection and the copyright belongs to The HLT Group Ltd.

All rights reserved. No part of this publication may be reproduced or transmitted in any form or by any means, electronic, mechanical, photocopying, recording or otherwise, or stored in any retrieval system of any nature without either the written permission of the copyright holder, application for which should be made to The HLT Group Ltd, or a licence permitting restricted copying in the United Kingdom issued by the Copyright Licensing Agency.

Any person who infringes the above in relation to this publication may be liable to criminal prosecution and civil claims for damages.

ISBN 0 7510 0380 8

British Library Cataloguing-in-Publication.

A CIP Catalogue record for this book is available from the British Library.

Printed and bound in Great Britain.

CONTENTS

Acknowledgement   page v

Introduction   vii

Questions and Suggested Solutions

    1985   1

    1986   39

    1987   71

    1988   105

    1989   135

    1990   163

ACKNOWLEDGEMENT

The questions used are taken from past University of London LLB (External) Degree examination papers and our thanks are extended to the University of London for the kind permission which has been given to us to use and publish the questions.

Caveat:

The answers given are not approved or sanctioned by the University of London and are entirely our responsibility.

They are not intended as 'Model Answers', but rather as Suggested Solutions.

The answers have two fundamental purposes, namely:

1. To provide a detailed example of a suggested solution to examination questions, and
2. To assist students with their research into the subject and to further their understanding and appreciation of the subject of Laws.

Note:

Please note that the solutions in this book were written in the year of the examination for each paper. They were appropriate solutions at the time of preparation, but students must note that certain caselaw and statutes may subsequently have changed.

INTRODUCTION

Why choose HLT publications

Holborn College has earned an International reputation over the past ten years for the outstanding quality of its teaching, Textbooks, Casebooks and Suggested Solutions to past examination papers set by the various examining bodies.

Our expertise is reflected in the outstanding results achieved by our students in the examinations conducted by the University of London, the Law Society, the Council of Legal Education and the Associated Examining Board.

The object of Suggested Solutions

The Suggested Solutions have been prepared by College lecturers experienced in teaching to this specific syllabus and are intended to be an example of a full answer to the problems posed by the examiner.

They are not 'model answers', for at this level there almost certainly is not just one answer to a problem, nor are the answers written to strict examination time limits.

The opportunity has been taken, where appropriate, to develop themes, suggest alternatives and set out additional material to an extent not possible by the examinee in the examination room.

We feel that in writing full opinion answers to the questions that we can assist you with your research into the subject and can further your understanding and appreciation of the law.

Notes on examination technique

Although the SUBSTANCE and SLANT of the answer changes according to the subject-matter of the question, the examining body and syllabus concerned, the TECHNIQUE of answering examination questions does not change.

You will not pass an examination if you do not know the substance of a course. You may pass if you do not know how to go about answering a question although this is doubtful. To do well and to guarantee success, however, it is necessary to learn the technique of answering problems properly. The following is a guide to acquiring that technique.

Time

All examinations permit only a limited time for papers to be completed. All papers require you to answer a certain number of questions in that time, and the questions, with some exceptions carry equal marks.

It follows from this that you should never spend a disproportionate amount of time on any question. When you have used up the amount of time allowed for any one question STOP and go on to the next question after an abrupt conclusion, if necessary. If you feel that you are running out of time, then complete your answer in note form. A useful way of ensuring that you do not over-run is to write down on a piece of scrap paper the time at which you should be starting each part of the paper. This can be done in the few minutes before the examination begins and it will help you to calm any nerves you may have.

Reading the question

It will not be often that you will be able to answer every question on an examination paper. Inevitably, there will be some areas in which you feel better prepared than others. You will prefer to answer the questions which deal with those areas, but you will never know how good the questions are unless you read the whole examination paper.

You should spend at least 10 MINUTES at the beginning of the examination reading the questions. Preferably, you should read them more than once. As you go through each question, make a brief note on the examination paper of any relevant cases and/or statutes that occur to you even if you think you may not answer that question: you may well be grateful for this note towards the end of the examination when you are tired and your memory begins to fail.

Re-reading the answers

Ideally, you should allow time to re-read your answers. This is rarely a pleasant process, but will ensure that you do not make any silly mistakes such as leaving out a 'not' when the negative is vital.

The structure of the answer

Almost all examination problems raise more than one legal issue that you are required to deal with. Your answer should include the following:

Identify the issues raised by the question

This is of crucial importance and gives shape to the whole answer. It indicates to the examiner that you appreciate what he is asking you about.

This is at least as important as actually answering the questions of law raised by that issue.

The issues should be identified in the first paragraph of the answer.

Deal with those issues one by one as they arise in the course of the problem

This, of course, is the substance of the answer and where study and revision pays off.

If the answer to an issue turns on a provision of a statute, CITE that provision briefly, but do not quote it from any statute you may be permitted to bring into the examination hall.

Having cited the provision, show how it is relevant to the question.

If there is no statute, or the meaning of the statute has been interpreted by the courts, CITE the relevant cases

'Citing cases' does not mean writing down the nature of every case that happens to deal with the general topic with which you are concerned and then detailing all the facts you can think of.

You should cite only the most relevant cases – there may perhaps only be one. No more facts should be stated than are absolutely essential to establish the relevance of the case. If there is a relevant case, but you cannot remember its name, it is sufficient to refer to it as 'one decided case'.

Whenever a statute or case is cited, the title of statute or the name of the case should be underlined

This makes the examiner's job much easier because he can see at a glance whether the relevant material has been dealt with, and it will make him more disposed in your favour.

Having dealt with the relevant issues, summarise your conclusions in such a way that you answer the question

A question will often say at the end simply 'Advise A', or B, or C, etc. The advice will usually turn on the individual answers to a number of issues. The point made here is that the final paragraph should pull those individual answers together and actually give the advice required. For example, it may begin something like: 'The effect of the answer to the issues raised by this question is that one's advice to A is that ...'

Related to the previous paragraph, make sure at the end that you have answered the question

For example, if the question says 'Advise A', make sure that is what your answer does. If you are required to advise more than one party, make sure that you have dealt with all the parties that you are required to and no more.

Some general points

You should always try to get the examiner on your side. One method has already been mentioned – the underlining of case names, etc. There are also other ways as well.

Always write as neatly as you can. This is more easily done with ink than with a ball-point.

Avoid the use of violently coloured ink eg turquoise; this makes a paper difficult to read.

Space out your answers sensibly: leave a line between paragraphs. You can always get more paper. At the same time, try not to use so much paper that your answer book looks too formidable to mark. This is a question of personal judgment.

NEVER put in irrelevant material simply to show that you are clever. Irrelevance is not a virtue and time spent on it is time lost for other, relevant, answers.

UNIVERSITY OF LONDON
INTERMEDIATE EXAMINATION IN LAWS 1985
for External Students

CONSTITUTIONAL LAW

Wednesday, 19 June: 10.00 am to 1.00 pm

Answer *FIVE* of the following NINE questions

1. Describe the constitutional structure of the Commonwealth.

2. Argue the case for and against codification in a legal form, of the conventions of the British constitution.

3. Outline the constitutional problems and benefits, if any, that would arise if the House of Lords were abolished.

4. 'The two Houses justify the special rights, powers and immunities conferred by parliamentary privilege as being necessary for the welfare of the nation. Citizens denied legal redress against MPs or judged by the House of Commons to have committed a high contempt and a breach of its privileges, tend to be less impressed by these claims.' (de Smith)

5. 'I do not relish the prospect of the judiciary being invested with the ultimate power to declare invalid the laws emanating from the will of Parliament on any subject to all and certainly not on human rights ... I would prefer it should not be given tasks beyond its scope which are more properly left to other organs of the constitution.' (Lord Lloyd of Hampstead)
   Discuss.

6. 'Judicial review is concerned, not with the decisions, but with the decision making process.' (*Chief Constable of North Wales Police* v *Evans* [1982] 1 WLR 1155 per Lord Brightman 1174)
   Discuss.

7. The Peace in Britain campaign organises a march to a Royal Air Force base. The marchers surround the base and in doing so block all the roads to the vicinity. They refuse to move when asked to do so by the police. Travellers, angry at the disruption to traffic, threaten to attack the marchers and to run them down.
   Advise the local Chief Constable as to his powers and duties.

8 To what extent is it true to say today that the remedy for abuse of the prerogative lies in the political and not in the judicial field?

9 Two detective constables, Able and Bell, are investigating a burglary at Cringes, a firm of solicitors. They are informed that Nancy, a typist employed by a rival firm of solicitors, may have been involved, and, after questioning her, search the offices where she works, and investigate the contents of her handbag. She agrees to accompany them to the police station, having been told that she will only be kept a few minutes. On the way to the police station Able, Bell and Nancy drive past the house where Nancy lives with her boyfriend. Nancy asks if she can collect her coat; Able and Bell agree to accompany her to the house, and see a pile of legal textbooks, which they believe have been stolen from Cringes. Nancy says that they belong to her boyfriend, who is a law student. Able and Bell disbelieve her, and take the books to the police station, where Nancy is questioned for forty-eight hours; she is given cups of tea and biscuits but no proper meals, neither is she allowed to smoke. She is not allowed to phone her employers or her boyfriend. After the interrogation is over, she is released and told that no charges will be brought.
Discuss.

QUESTION 1

General Comment

A relatively straightforward question on the constitutional structure of the Commonwealth. Students should stress the lack of any formal Commonwealth constitutional structure and the reasons why this should be so ie the ad hoc nature of its development, the need for flexibility and informality in Commonwealth affairs and the fact that legal rules may lead to conflict through their inflexibility. Students should then deal with the main constitutional organs of the Commonwealth which do exist: the Head of the Commonwealth; the Heads of Commonwealth Governments Meetings and the Commonwealth Secretariat. Remember, when answering questions on the Commonwealth do not treat it as a general excuse for writing everything you know about the topic. Do not simply produce a potted history of the Empire.

Skeleton Solution

General introduction – what is the Commonwealth?

The ad hoc nature of the Commonwealth; the lack of any formal legal structure.

Rules of convention and the Commonwealth; their advantages over a formal legal structure.

The Head of the Commonwealth, the Heads of Commonwealth Governments Meetings and the Commonwealth Secretariat and Secretary General.

Suggested Solution

The Commonwealth (1) is an association of states comprising the United Kingdom and those territories which were once a part of the British Empire but which are now independent states. The modern Commonwealth dates effectively from India's independence in 1947. Since then as Britain's colonial territories in Africa, Asia, the Caribbean, Pacific and Mediterranean have gained independence, it has expanded to include 49 member states. Today it comprises one quarter of the world's population; some 1,000 million people of many races, religions and languages, from all parts of the globe (2). In 1971, the Heads of Commonwealth Governments described the Commonwealth as a voluntary association of independent sovereign states, each responsible for its own policies, consulting and co-operating in the common interests of their peoples and in the promotion of international understanding and world peace (3).

The Commonwealth has no constitutional structure in the accepted sense, mainly because it wasn't deliberately created but simply evolved without legal formality to provide a loose framework for continued international association between its former territories of the British Empire. The unique feature of the Commonwealth therefore is that unlike other international or regional organisations, such as the United Nations Organisation or the European Economic Community, it has no written charter, treaty or other formal instrument which lays down its constitution or formulates the legal rules governing the relationshp between the various member states. Indeed, there is an almost complete absence of any constitutional law governing the organisation and its workings, and this in turn is partly due to the fact that the Commonwealth possesses no real legislative, executive or judicial organs.

The few rules which do exist are almost exclusively concerned with the acquisition and discontinuance of membership of the Commonwealth and might more properly be regarded as conventions rather than law, in that they are not rules which are justicable in any international court, but simply rules of practice which have been evolved as and when necessary to meet any new developments which have called for regulations. These rules of convention can be adopted or discarded as and when it appears necessary, and thus ensure maximum flexibility, which is essential for a body such as the Commonwealth because of the divergent racial, religious, cultural, social, economic and political backgrounds of its member states.

The constitutional Head of the Commonwealth is the British sovereign who, prior to 1947, was also the Head of State of each Commonwealth country. However in 1947, on achieving independence, India chose to become a republic and ceased to recognise the former King Emperor as Head of State. In 1949, the Declaration of London accepted that India could become a republic and still remain a member of the Commonwealth provided that it recognised the King as Head of the Commonwealth. This practice continues to the present day with many colonial territories opting to become republics on achieving independence but continuing to recognise the Queen as Head of the Commonwealth. However 'Head of the Commonwealth' is not an hereditary title, but one which was conferred upon the Queen with the agreement of the Commonwealth states at the beginning of her reign. It will not automatically pass to the heir of the throne. The actual functions of the Head of the Commonwealth are nowhere defined and it has been largely left to the Queen to carve out her own role within the Commonwealth.

The main constitutional organ of the Commonwealth is the Heads of Commonwealth Governments Meeting, which is about as near to a legislature as the organisation gets. The Heads of Commonwealth Governments Meetings had their origins in the old Imperial Conferences. Today they are hosted in a different member state every two years and although they have become more concerned with the role of the Commonwealth in international affairs they also, when necessary, formulate rules to regulate the organisation. However, as the 1965 Meeting declared:

> 'The Commonwealth is not a formal organisation. It does not encroach on the sovereignty of individual members, nor does it require its members to seek to reach collective decisions or take united action.'

Certainly, because of the great disparity between the various member states it is not always possible to reach agreement on specific policies. The meetings therefore tend to work on the basis of broad principles, leaving it to the individual member states to interpret their 'obligations' as they think fit, an example being the Declaration of Commonwealth Principles agreed by Commonwealth leaders in 1971, and to which all member states must subscribe. The Declaration expresses in very broad terms the commitment to world peace and order, equal rights for all citizens, the liberty of the individual, opposition to colonial domination and racial oppression and a resolve to achieve a fairer society.

The main subsidiary organ of the Commonwealth is the Secretariat which was established under an Agreed Memorandum issued at the 1965 Heads of Commonwealth Governments Meeting (4). However it was expressly provided that the Secretariat and its Secretary General should have no executive functions. The Memorandum noted that both the Secretary General and his staff should be seen to be the servants of the Commonwealth countries collectively. The Secretariat should not arrogate to itself executive functions and it should operate initially on a modest footing and its staff and functions should be left to expand pragmatically in the light of experience subject always to the approval of governments. Today the Secretariat is mainly responsible for servicing

Commonwealth Meetings, circulating factual information and helping consultations between members on international affairs and on economic matters.

References

1) See, generally, de Smith, *The New Commonwealth and Its Constitutions* (1964); Roberts-Wray *Commonwealth and Colonial Law* (1966).
2) *Year Book of the Commonwealth* (1984) (HMSO).
3) Commonwealth Declaration, 22 January 1971 (*Yearbook of the Commonwealth*, 1973, p35).
4) Commonwealth Secretariat: Cmnd 2713 (1965); Commonwealth Secretariat Act 1966.

QUESTION 2

General Comment

This is a very straightforward question involving discussion of conventions of the constitution, the differences between law and convention and the arguments for and against the codification of conventions in a legal form. Students should remember to stick to the specific points raised in the question. Don't write everything you know about conventions and don't simply produce a list of conventions.

Skeleton Solution

Introduction – what are conventions; why are they obeyed?

Distinction between law and convention. Dicey's views contrasted with those of Jennings.

Why maintain a distinction between law and convention?

The advantages of codification of conventions in legal form: clarification of the present vague and undefined rules of conventions; the provision of a clear legal definition of unconstitutional behaviour; certainty.

The advantages of retaining conventions: helps to bring about constitutional change without formal change in the law: flexibility helps to keep the judiciary out of political controversy.

Suggested Solution

A great many rules of the British constitution, which are observed by the sovereign, the Prime Minister, ministers, members of Parliament, the judiciary and civil servants, are not contained in Acts of Parliament or judicial decisions, but are to be found in those rules of conduct called constitutional conventions. These have been described as 'rules of constitutional behaviour which are considered to be binding by and upon those who operate the constitution but which are not enforced by the law courts ... nor by the presiding officers in the Houses of Parliament' (1). These conventions of the constitution are obeyed by those to whom they apply not because of the threat of any legal sanction in case of breach, but because of the political difficulties which may follow if they are not obeyed (2).

Conventions therefore differ from laws in that unlike laws they are not enforced by the courts. According to Dicey (3), conventions are not 'laws in the true sense of the word, for if any or all of them were broken, no court would take notice of their violation'. Laws are rules enforced and recognised by the courts whereas conventions are 'a body not of laws but of constitutional or political ethics – the constitutional morality of the day, not enforced or recognised by the courts'. However, this approach is too simplistic. Conventions of the constitution are sometimes recognised by the courts. For example in *Carltona Ltd* v *Commissioners of Works* (4), the court recognised the convention of ministerial responsibility. Also some rules of strict law may be non-justicable. According to Jennings (5), the real distinction between law and convention lies in the fact that legal rules are either formally expressed, or illustrated by a decision of a court, whereas conventions arise out of practice. Law and convention are however closely interlocked. Conventions, it is said, 'provide the flesh which clothes the dry bones of the law; they make the legal constitution work; they keep it in touch with the growth of ideas'.

The question therefore arises, why maintain the distinctions between strict law and convention? Why not codify conventions of the constitution in a legal form? In theory, all the conventional rules of the constitution could be enacted in legal form by one or more Acts of Parliament. Indeed, this has been achieved under several Commonwealth constitutions. Such a step would have distinct advantages. Codification would for example clarify certain constitutional rules which are at present vague and undefined. It is unsatisfactory that major rules of the constitution remain indeterminate. For instance, under what circumstances may the Queen dismiss her Prime Minister? If the Queen were to dismiss or to refuse to dismiss the Prime Minister under certain circumstances this would undoubtedly provoke controversy, because of the uncertainty surrounding the Queen's power of dismissal. This controversy would be avoided if the circumstances in which the Queen can and must dismiss her Prime Minister were set out in legal form. Also, where the rules of the constitution are in legal form, legislative or executive acts which conflict with the constitution may be held to be unconstitutional and therefore illegal. In the United Kingdom the absence of any fully legal constitutional code means that 'unconstitutional' has no definition. It is not always easy to determine whether the boundary between constitutional and unconstitutional behaviour has been crossed.

However, while codification may have the advantage of clarifying particular rules the disadvantages of such a step are considerable. Conventions cover such a diverse area and they differ so much in character that they cannot logically be included within a single code. Even if such an attempt were made it would be impossible to stop the process by which formal rules are gradually modified by non-legal rules from starting all over again.

Conventions also have several distinct advantages over legal rules in the context of constitutional law. Firstly they provide a means of bringing about constitutional change without the need for a formal change in the law. For example, many conventions concern the powers of the sovereign. They allow the legal powers of the Queen to remain intact, thus lending dignity to the affairs of state, while at the same time allowing the democratically elected Government to actually exercise those powers. It may also be difficult or even harmful to define some important constitutional conventions. Codification may bring certainty, but only at the expense of flexibility. Law is rigid and may be difficult to change. Conventions on the other hand allow the constitution to evolve and keep up to date with changing circumstances without the need for formal enactment or repeal of law. Law must also be followed in every case. Conventions, being flexible and unenforceable by the courts, allow discretion to be exercised and can be waived if the particular circumstances make this desirable. Most conventions also concern matters of a political nature. Their non-legal nature thus helps keep the judiciary and the courts out of politics and political controversy. Experience in the Commonwealth has illustrated the difficulty that can arise when the courts become involved in politically sensitive situations.

Therefore, so long as conventions are obeyed there is no need for legal codification. Nevertheless, if a particular convention is disregarded then it can, if necessary, be formally enacted and given legal status. For example, in 1909 the House of Lords ignored the convention that they must defer to the will of the House of Commons. The result was the enactment of the Parliament Act 1911 defining the relationship between the two Houses on a statutory basis.

References

1) Marshall & Moodie, *Some Problems of the Constitution*, 5th edition (1971) pp22–23.
2) See Jennings, *The Law and the Constitution*, 5th edition (1959) p134.

References (continued)
3) Dicey, *The Law of the Constitution*, 10th edition (1959).
4) *Carltona Ltd* v *Commissioners of Works* [1943] 2 All ER 560.
5) Jennings, op cit.

QUESTION 3

General Comment

This question involves discussion of the role of the House of Lords as the second chamber in our bicameral parliamentary system and the constitutional problems and benefits which would arise if the Lords were abolished in favour of an unicameral parliamentary system. Don't write everything you know about the House of Lords and don't be tempted to simply turn out the traditional (and now largely discredited) criticisms of Lords on justification for their abolition. Remember, the House of Lords plays a vital function as a revision chamber and helps relieve the pressure of work on the already overburdened House of Commons. Recent events have also shown that the House of Lords is the only effective check on a Government which dominates the House of Commons. It is doubtful whether any real benefits would arise from the abolition of the House of Lords. Reform yes, abolition no.

Skeleton Solution

Introduction: arguments for reform/abolition of the House of Lords.

The problems caused by adopting a unicameral parliamentary system. The position of the Judicial Comminttee; role of the House as a revision chamber for public Bills; inability of Commons to deal adequately with all Bills passed; need for fundamental change in House of Commons procedure; role of Lords as a check on the Executive; need for written constitution/Bill of Rights.

Benefits of abolition: saving of costs; space; forcing of change and reform of House of Commons procedures.

Suggested Solution

For many years there has been opposition of some sort or another to the continued existence of the House of Lords as the second chamber in our present bicameral parliamentary system. The argument is that as presently constituted the House of Lords is undemocratic, outdated and unsuitable in a modern society. Some therefore favour reform, so that for example its composition becomes more democratic and its powers perhaps increased so that it can act as a more effective check on the House of Commons (and thus, in reality, on the government of the day) than it does at present. Others, however, wish to go further still and see the total abolition of the second chamber altogether in favour of a unicameral parliamentary system.

If the House of Lords were abolished in favour of a unicameral parliamentary system certain constitutional problems would undoubtedly result. Whether these problems would be insuperable is a matter of opinion. What cannot be denied, however, is that despite the problems regarding its composition, the fact remains that the House of Lords does perform a valuable service within the present parliamentary system and if abolished many of its functions would still have to be performed by some other body, presumably the House of Commons. In 1965, the Government White Paper 'House of Lords Reform' referred to seven functions of the House of Lords. An examination of each of these functions serves to illustrate some of the problems that might result from abolition.

Firstly the House of Lords acts as the final court of appeal for the whole of the United Kingdom in civil cases and for England, Wales and Northern Ireland in criminal cases. If the House were abolished therefore a new 'supreme' court would have to be established to take its place, unless of course the Court of Appeal were to become the final appeal court for England and Wales. However, as the judicial work of the House is separate from its other functions and only involves the Judicial Committee, drawn from the Lord High Chancellor, the Lords of Appeal in Ordinary and Lords who hold or have held high judicial office, the separation of the Judicial Committee from the rest of the House of Lords or its replacement by some new body would not perhaps cause too great a constitutional problem.

Secondly, the House provides a forum for free debate on matters of public interest, Wednesday in particular being traditionally set aside for special debate on a wide range of subjects. Apart from the fact that these debates are usually of a very high standard, a standard that would perhaps never be reached in the Commons, even if the time were available, this loss would not pose any great constitutional problem.

Thirdly, and perhaps most importantly, the House acts as a revising chamber for public Bills brought from the House of Commons. About one half of the time of the House of Lords is devoted to the consideration of public Bills. The majority of this time is spent on revising Bills which have already passed the

Commons, where the great majority of goverment legislation is introduced. The House of Commons does not have the time to fully debate all the legislation it has to pass each session and the use of procedures for the curtailment of debate, such as the guillotine, often means that Bills are passed by the Commons without really being considered at all. A second chamber is therefore required to examine and revise such Bills. If the second chamber is abolished then the procedures of the House of Commons for enacting legislation will have to be changed if the present standard and volume of legislation is to be maintained. This could be achieved by membership of the House of Commons becoming full-time and by making even more use of committees. However, even then the volume of legislation may still prove to be too great, necessitating either a shortening of the procedure by which a Bill is enacted or making more use of subordinate legislation, which some would argue is already over used as it is. Certainly some fundamental changes would have to be made to the proceedings of the House of Commons and these may prove unacceptable to many of the present MPs.

Also it must be remembered that the House of Commons, because of the distortion produced by our electoral system, is largely controlled by a government which does not represent even 50 per cent of the electorate. A second chamber is thus required to at least delay substantially controversial legislation which may be unpopular with the majority of the people of the country. If the second chamber is abolished then the only way to control a government with an absolute majority in the House of Commons may be to have either a written constitution or a Bill of Rights containing entrenched clauses, perhaps requiring a referendum for amendment.

The House of Lords also initiates public Bills. While the more important and controversial Bills almost invariably begin in the House of Commons, Bills which are relatively uncontroversial in party political terms are regularly introduced in the House of Lords. If abolished, these Bills will have to be dealt with by the Commons thus adding to its already overburdened workload. Similarly, the subordinate legislation and the private legislation at present dealt with by the House of Lords would also fall to be wholly dealt with by the Commons if the second chamber were abolished.

The arguments in favour of a unicameral Parliament are mainly political and it is doubtful whether any real practical benefit would result from the abolition of the House of Lords. Certainly it is doubtful that the loss of the Lords could ever be compensated for. However, there are benefits of sorts which would flow from abolition, such as the saving of money and the making available of more space in the Palace of Westminster. Abolition would also have to result in the widespread reform of the House of Commons if any semblance of a parliamentary democracy is to be maintained. Such reform may be viewed as a substantial benefit. However, the main fear, and indeed the most likely consequence of the abolition of the House of Lords is that it will simply serve to strengthen the executive control of the legislature.

QUESTION 4

General Comment

A relatively simple question on parliamentary prestige dealing with two main criticisms of the doctrine from the point of view of the aggrieved individual. There are two issues to be considered: (i) the case of citizens denied legal redress where the MP hides behind his privileges; and (ii) the case of those adjudged to have committed a breach of privilege who are usually found 'guilty' following a procedure which breaches the rules of natural justice. Remember that the question is fairly specific. There is no need to go into detail regarding the various privileges. Freedom of speech in debate is the most relevant.

Skeleton Solution

Introduction: definition of parliamentary privilege; the justification for the privilege; examples of privileges.

Cases of abuse where the Member hides behind privilege; example of freedom of speech in debate and the law of defamation.

Procedure for determining breaches of privilege: punishments available to those found guilty of contempt or breach of privilege; procedure for dealing with complaints – breaches of the rules of natural justice; recommendations of the 1967 Select Committee on Parliamentary Privilege.

General conclusion: breach of the rule of law; breach of natural justice.

Suggested Solution

Parliamentary privilege forms part of the law and custom of Parliament evolved by the two Houses in order to protect their freedom to conduct their proceedings without improper interference by the sovereign, the courts, or other bodies or persons outside Parliament. It is defined by Erskine May as 'the sum of the peculiar rights enjoyed by each House collectively as a constitutional part of the High Court of Parliament and by members of each House individually, without which they could not discharge their functions, and which exceed those possessed by other bodies or individuals' (1).

The privileges enjoyed by the House of Commons include those 'ancient and undoubted privileges' claimed by the Speaker at the beginning of each new Parliament such as freedom of speech in debate, freedom from civil arrest, freedom of access via the Speaker to the sovereign and that the most favourable construction should be placed upon all their proceedings. There are also more privileges enjoyed by the House in its corporate capacity such as the right to regulate its own composition, the right to take exclusive cognisance of matters arising within the precincts of the House and the right to punish both members and non-members for breach of privilege and contempt. Similar provisions apply in respect of the House of Lords. These special rights, powers and immunities conferred by parliamentary privilege are justified as being essential for the conduct of the business and the maintenance of the authority of the House.

There is no doubt, however, that while parliamentary privilege may be considered necessary for the welfare of the nation, there is wide scope for abuse by MPs especially as regards freedom of speech. Article 9 of the Bill of Rights 1689 provides that the freedom of speech, and debates or proceedings in Parliament ought not to be imposed or questioned in any court or place out of Parliament. Therefore no action or prosecution can be brought against a member for any words used in the course of parliamentary proceedings (2). If a member were to be sued for libel or slander in respect of words used in Paliament in the course of 'proceedings in Parliament', the writ should be struck out as disclosing no cause of action. If the case were to come to trial the court would hold that the member was protected by absolute privilege in the law of defamation (3). Thus, an MP may make defamatory statements regarding an individual, in the course of proceedings in Parliament, knowing that even if there is no basis to his allegations he is protected from a civil action for damages in tort. No action would be against him even if his remarks were shown to be defamatory, untrue, malicious and unfair, no matter how much damage is caused to the individual as a result.

Further, the House still reserves to itself the right to treat the institution of legal proceedings against a member in respect of a matter covered, in its opinion, by parliamentary privilege, as a breach of its own privilege and may punish the individual concerned for breach of privilege or contempt (4). Of course, a member who abuses his privilege of freedom of speech may be subject to disciplinary sanctions by the House, but this is no great deterrent. The fact remains that every year innocent individuals are defamed by ill-informed, careless or even malicious MPs and suffer considerable damage to their reputation as a result, but are nevertheless denied any legal redress because the MP concerned hides behind his parliamentary privilege.

Those individuals adjudged by the House to have committed a high contempt and a breach of its privileges are also treated in a manner which is open to considerable criticism. Parliamentary privileges are part of the common law in so far as their existence and validity are recognised by the courts. But they are enforced not by the courts but exclusively by Parliament.

By virtue of its inherent right to control its own proceedings and maintain its dignity, the House of Commons in protecting its privileges may punish those who violate them or commit contempt of the House. Breach of privilege consists of either an abuse of a particular privilege by a member, or any conduct which interferes with one of the privileges of Parliament. Contempt is a much wider concept and consists of any conduct which tends to bring the House into disrepute or detract from its dignity (5). No matter whether the offence is styled a breach of privilege or a contempt, or both, the penal powers of the House are the same. Offenders may be reprimanded or admonished by the Speaker. Members may be suspended or expelled. Officials of the House may be dismissed and any Member or stranger may be committed to prison for the duration of the parliamentary session. However, it is the procedure by which complaints of breach of privilege are dealt with which is open to most criticism.

Complaints of breach of privilege may be raised by a member or in the House by the Speaker. If the Speaker rules that a prima facie case has been made out a motion is proposed that the matter be referred to the Committee of Privileges. The motion may then be debated and voted upon. The Committee, comprising the fifteen most senior members of the parties in the House is the master of its own proceedings. It can compel the attendance of witnesses and the production of documents, failure to comply being a contempt. There is no requirement of legal representation, indeed the 'defendant' may not be given any hearing at all. At the conclusion of its investigation the Committee reports its findings to the House and may recommend the action that the House should take. The House need not accept the Committee's findings nor recommendations, but it almost always does. This procedure has been criticised. The Select Committee on Parliamentary Privilege in 1967 (6) recommended that persons directly concerned in the Committee's investigations should have the right to attend its hearings, make submissions, call, examine and cross-examine witnesses and, with leave of the Committee, be legally represented and apply for legal aid. These recommendations have however never been adopted.

It can be seen therefore that whatever the justification for parliamentary privilege may be, it is open to abuse by the less responsible members of the House, it is a breach of the rule of law, and the procedures for dealing with allegations of breach of privilege and contempt invariably breach the rules of natural justice. It is therefore an area ripe for reform.

References
1) Erskine May, *Parliamentary Practice*.
2) See *Eliot's Case* 3 St Tr 294; case of Duncan Sandys (1938).
3) See *Dillon* v *Balfour* (1887) 29 IR LR 600.
4) See generally, case of Strauss (1957–8).
5) For examples of contempts see Erskine May, op cit.
6) HC 34 (1967–68), xiv–x/vii.

QUESTION 5

General Comment

A very difficult question which seems to encompass inter alia the doctrine of parliamentary supremacy, the question of a Bill of Rights for the United Kingdom, and the role of the judiciary in enforcing such a Bill of Rights as against inconsistent legislation. Like all such essay questions students may find difficulty in identifying the relevant issues and covering all the possible points raised in the time available. Therefore, unless you are absolutely sure that you know the specific area concerned and have sufficient information to write without straying from the point, such questions are best avoided.

Skeleton Solution

Introduction: supremacy of Parliament; residual nature of civil liberties in the United Kingdom and the role of the common law in protecting individual liberty.

Proposals for a Bill of Rights: difficulty of entrenchment. Incorporation of the European Convention of Human Rights into United Kingdom law.

Role of the judiciary in enforcing a Bill of Rights: objections and practical difficulties likely to result from judiciary declaring Acts of Parliament invalid.

Role of the legislature in checking breaches of human rights by Executive policy.

Suggested Solution

Two fundamental features of the unwritten constitution of the United Kingdom are the legislative supremacy of Parliament and the role played by the common law, particularly in the field of protecting individual freedoms. In the United Kingdom individual freedoms are not guaranteed in any formal document, they are residual; the individual being free to do as he wishes provided that he does not commit any civil wrong or any criminal offence. Further, under the principle ubi jus ibi remedium, for every wrongful encroachment upon the liberty of an individual there is a legal remedy available before an independent court of justice.

Therefore in the United Kingdom, individual liberty is largely protected by the ordinary courts of law applying the common law. However, the protection afforded by the courts in this way is necessarily limited because of the operation of the doctrine of parliamentary supremacy, under which there is no legal limitation upon the legislative competence of Parliament. The Queen in Parliament may legislate upon any subject. No Parliament can bind its successors or be bound by its predecessors, and once Parliament has legislated no court or other person can pass judgment upon the validity of the legislation. In the field of individual liberty therefore, Parliament, by enacting legislation can take away, suspend or alter the fundamental freedoms hitherto enjoyed by the individual citizen and the courts will be bound to give effect to that legislation, no matter how repugnant it may seem to traditional English values.

Since the early 1970s there has been growing disenchantment with this typically British approach to safeguarding individual liberty, and much discussion has taken place regarding the possibility of enacting some form of Bill of Rights to protect the fundamental freedoms of the individual from executive encroachment. In particular, Lord Scarman, in his Hamlyn lectures in 1974 (1), called for the enactment of entrenched and fundamental laws protected by a Bill of Rights, 'a constitutional law which it is the duty of the courts to protect even against the power of Parliament'. But, of course, such a measure, even if desirable, is easier said than done.

Under the present constitutional system of the United Kingdom, it is impossible to entrench legislation in the face of a supreme Parliament which cannot bind its successors or be bound by its predecessors. Whatever 'Bill of Rights' one Parliament enacts, another Parliament can amend or repeal. However, ignoring the largely sterile academic argument as to whether or not entrenchment is possible in the United Kingdom, various practical propositions have been put forward for enacting a new Bill of Rights in the United Kingdom. The Canadian Bill of Rights 1960 (2), illustrates that it is possible to have a Bill of Rights enacted as an ordinary statute. Under the Canadian Bill Federal legislation was to be so construed and applied as to conform to the Bill except in an emergency or unless an Act expressly stated that it was to take effect notwithstanding the Bill of Rights (3). Further, the United Kingdom is a party to the European Convention of Human Rights and Fundamental Freedoms (4). It has been widely canvassed that the convention should be assimilated into English law, for example under a similar arrangement to that by which

EEC law was assimilated by the European Communities Act 1972. Professor Wade has even proposed that the judges' oath of office should be amended, so that they swear allegiance to a Bill of Rights and would be expected to follow it.

However, the crucial question with regard to any Bill of Rights, however enacted, is how much power to strike down legislation in conflict with a Bill of Rights would Parliament be prepared to give the judiciary, and in any case, as Lord Lloyd argues, is this a proper task for the judiciary to perform. As de Smith points out, a Bill of Rights could, especially if difficult to amend, lead to government by judges. Governments, frustrated by judicial intransigence, could start to make political appointments to the bench thus causing public confidence in the impartial administration of justice to dwindle. The very independence of the judiciary would thus be threatened and conflict created between the organs of government. Delay and uncertainty in the law would also follow, because the politicians will not be sure what they are entitled to do until the judges have told them. There would be an increase in litigation. Many critics also adopt Dicey's (5) view and see a Bill of Rights as something alien to the British constitution. Such Bills may be all right for foreigners, but in the United Kingdom, with our long history of responsible governments, the rule of law, an independent judiciary, the safeguards of the common law and the residual nature of our freedoms, they are unnecessary and irreconcilable with our ancient traditions.

Therefore, while some of the more adventurous judges would not perhaps share Lord Lloyd's reticence, his objection to the courts being given the task of challenging Executive policy as expressed through legislation, does have a degree of merit, especially as the controversy surrounding human rights is almost certainly going to give rise to confrontation and possible conflict between the judiciary and the Executive. His Lordship supports the traditional role of the judiciary vis-à-vis statute, ie if the statute is duly enacted by the Queen in Parliament it cannot be questioned by the courts. The only power the courts have in respect of validly enacted Acts of Parliament is one of statutory interpretation in cases where the wording of the Act is ambiguous or uncertain. Lord Lloyd also makes the valid point that any check on Executive encroachment or breach in the field of human rights is the task of the other organs of the constitution, ie the legislature. If the House of Commons were reformed so as to reassert its independence and remove the government's dominance and control, or if the House of Lords were reformed and perhaps given more powers to block legislation, then there would be no need for a Bill of Rights or the involvement of the judiciary in declaring statutes to be invalid. The check on Executive policy implementations would take place in the proper constitutional forum, ie Parliament itself.

References
1) Sir Leslie Scarman, *English Law – the new dimension* (1974).
2) See WS Tarnopolsky, *The Canadian Bill of Rights* (1975).
3) See *R v Drybones* (1970) SCR 282.
4) See AH Robertson, *Human Rights in Europe*.
5) AV Dicey, *Introduction to the Study of the Law of the Constitution* (10th edition) p198.

QUESTION 6

General Comment

Another relatively straightforward question, concerning judicial review of administrative action. Students should generally argue that Lord Brightman is correct in his statement and support the argument that judicial review is concerned not with the decisions, but with the decision making process, with appropriate examples drawn from the doctrine of ultra vires and the rules of natural justice. The distinction between appeals and judicial review must also be stressed, together with the effects of the public law remedies available under judicial review, in particular that of certiorari.

Skeleton Solution

Introduction: nature of administrative law; purpose of judicial review.

The distinction between an appeal and judicial review.

Examples to illustrate that judicial review is concerned with the decision making process: ultra vires – substantive and procedural; natural justice – procedural nature of audi alteram partem and nemo judex in causa sua.

Public law remedies as an illustration of judicial review being concerned with the decision making process: the effect of an order of certiorari.

Conclusion.

Suggested Solution

Administrative law is the law relating to the control of governmental power, and in particular with the legal controls upon the exercise of those powers by subordinate administrative authorities. Judicial review (1) is the means whereby the courts achieve this control, and as Lord Brightman points out, in reviewing administrative action the court is not so much concerned with the merits of an actual decision, but rather with the process by which that decision was reached.

Judicial review must therefore be distinguished from an appeal. An appeal is concerned with the merits of a decision. A superior court is thus called upon to determine whether the decision of a lower court is right or wrong. With judicial review, however, the Divisional Court of the Queen's Bench Division is called upon to consider the legality of an act or order of a subordinate body. It must determine whether that act or order is lawful or unlawful. Instead of substituting its own decision for that of some other body, as on appeal, the court on review is concerned only with the question whether the act or order under attack should be allowed to stand or not.

The grounds upon which judicial review will lie illustrate the fact that it is the decision making process rather than the actual decision which is the subject of the review. Ultra vires for example is based upon the fundamental principle of English law that no person or body should be permitted to exceed its lawful powers. When considering the question of ultra vires therefore the courts are not concerned with the merits of a particular decision, but rather with discovering whether or not the administrative authority in question has acted in excess of its statutory powers (2) or acted in excess of its jurisdiction (3), or whether or not the authority in the performance of its functions has followed the procedures prescribed by the parent Act (4). The point is illustrated by the power of the court to declare an excess of jurisdiction on the part of an administrative authority to be ultra vires. All administrative authorities have limited jurisdiction. Where an authority acts in excess of its jurisdiction as laid down in the parent Act, its acts will be ultra vires and void. But where an authority makes a mistake, the traditional view (5) has been that so long as the authority is acting within its jurisdiction to hear an applicant, it does not lose its jurisdiction and thereby act ultra vires, by coming to a wrong conclusion, whether it was wrong in law or in fact. Therefore the fact that an administrative authority makes a mistake in the exercise of a power does not necessarily render its decision ultra vires, and thereby subject to judicial review, so long as the error was committed within its jurisdiction.

Similarly with procedural ultra vires, when, for example, the courts are determining whether or not there has been an unreasonable use of a discretion the courts are concerned with the legality of the process by which the discretion was exercised and not with its merits. The requirements of reasonableness summarised by Lord Greene in *Associated Provincial Picture Houses v Wednesbury Corporation* (6) illustrates this by being wholly and exclusively concerned with the decision making process viz has the person entrusted with a discretion directed himself properly in law, called to his attention those matters which he is bound to consider and excluded from his consideration matters which are irrelevant. So long as these procedural requirements have been satisfied the decision reached will stand and will not be subject to review.

The requirements of natural justice also illustrate the point that judicial review is concerned solely with the decision making process. The right to a fair hearing, audi alteram partem, in practice means that a person or body taking a decision must consider both sides of the case before taking that decision. No man is to be condemned without a hearing. Where a decision is one to which natural justice applies, or where the decision involves the duty to act fairly, then the person or body taking that decision must observe certain procedural requirements (7). Basically, the right to a fair hearing requires that a person who stands to be affected by the decision of an administrative authority should be given notice of the case he has to meet and a fair opportunity to answer the case against him and to present his own side of the case. The risk against bias, nemo judex in causa sua, is also purely procedural in providing that no man should be a judge in his own cause (8) ie justice must be seen to be done.

The public law remedies available under an application for judicial review also illustrate the fact that judicial review is concerned not with the decisions but with the decision making process. The effect of an order of certiorari for example is to quash the decision of an inferior body, thus rendering it null and void. However, in quashing a decision by way of certiorari the reviewing court does not substitute its own decision for that of the inferior body, but usually simply refers the case back to the authority concerned to decide against this time observing the rules of natural justice or acting intra vires.

The aim of judicial review therefore is to ensure that public bodies act within the law. It is not aimed at compensating the individual for what he has lost because of the ultra vires in question: *Dunlop v Woollahra Municipal Council* (9). Consequently the courts are only concerned with the legality of a decision, not with its merits. The court is not there to substitute its own value judgments for those of the inferior body. Judicial review must therefore be contrasted with a statutory right of appeal where a decision can be overruled and a new decision taken on the merits of the case. With judicial review a decision may simply be quashed and remitted to the inferior body to take again. By exercising their powers of judicial review the courts hope to indicate to administrative bodies the way in which they should act in future, and through this the courts can provide fairer and more efficient administrative practices.

References

1) See de Smith *Judicial Review of Administrative Action* (1980).
2) For example see *A-G v Fulham Corporation* [1921] 1 Ch 440.
3) See *Anisminic v Foreign Compensation Commission* [1969] 2 AC 147.
4) For example see *Grunwick Processing Laboratories Ltd v ACAS* [1978] AC 655.
5) See *R v Fulham, Hammersmith and Kensington Rent Tribunal, ex parte Zerek* [1951] 2 KB 1.
6) *Associated Provincial Picture Houses Ltd v Wednesbury Corporation* [1948] 1 KB 223.
7) See generally *Selvarajan v Race Relations Board* [1976] 1 All ER 12.
8) See *Dimes v Grand Junction Canal Proprietors* (1852) 3 HL Cas 759; *Metropolitan Properties Ltd v Lannon* [1969] 1 QB 577.
9) *Dunlop v Woollahra Municipal Council* [1981] 2 WLR 693.

QUESTION 7

General Comment

This question deals with the restrictions upon the freedom of association and expression. Students are asked to advise the local chief constable as to his powers and duties in respect of the march to the Royal Air Force base and the resulting obstruction of the highway, and also the threats by the travellers to attack the marchers. This will mainly involve a discussion of s137(1) Highways Act 1980, breach of the peace, s5 Public Order Act 1936, the *Beatty* v *Gilbanks* principle, and mention should also be made of the Official Secrets Act 1911. Students are reminded to keep to the constitutional law implications of the question and not to get involved in discussion of the criminal law generally.

Skeleton Solution

Introduction: the basic rule of freedom to demonstrate.

Duty of the chief constable to keep the highway free for passage; powers available to achieve this object.

Duty of the chief constable to keep the peace; possible public order offences committed by the travellers; powers available to deal with threats to breach public order.

The possible application of the *Beatty* v *Gilbanks* principle and the exceptions to it which might apply in the present case.

Discussion of possible breach of s1(1)(a) of the Official Secrets Act 1911.

Suggested Solution

The basic rule is that anyone is free to assemble for the purposes of demonstrating provided that no law is breached. The law in this area consists in essence of the restrictions that Parliament and the courts have felt necessary over the years to impose on the freedom to assemble in public, in the interests of maintaining order.

The first duty of the chief constable is to keep the highway free for lawful passage. The march to the Royal Air Force base will generally be lawful provided the marchers keep to the public highway and do not cause any obstruction. When the marchers surround the base, however, and block all the roads in the vicinity, their actions become unlawful. Under the Highways Act 1980 s137(1) it is a criminal offence wilfully to obstruct the free passage along a highway. If the highway is obstructed then a constable can arrest those causing the obstruction. Obstruction in this context is a very flexible term. In *Horner* v *Codman* (1) it was held that it is no defence to show that there was a way around the obstruction. In *Arrowsmith* v *Jenkins* (2), Arrowsmith was arrested for obstructing the highway under s121 of the Highways Act 1959. She argued that the prosecution had to show that she had an intention to obstruct the highway. The court rejected this argument, holding that if a person does an act according to her free will which results in an obstruction, it will be sufficient for the offence of obstruction.

The marchers therefore are committing an obstruction of the highway and when asked to move on by the police they refuse to do so. In these circumstances the chief constable has the power to order the arrest of those persons committing the obstruction, under the Highways Act 1980, or they may be charged with wilfully obstructing a police officer in the execution of his duty, under s51(3) of the Police Act 1964.

The reaction of the travellers to the obstruction caused by the marchers raises the prospects of public order offences being committed. The travellers threaten to attack the marchers and run them down. A breach of the peace therefore seems likely. The travellers may also under these circumstances be committing an unlawful assembly and also breaching s5 of the Public Order Act 1936, which makes it an offence to use threatening, abusive or insulting words or behaviour in a public place or meeting with intent to provoke a breach of the peace or whereby a breach of the peace is likely to be occasioned. The chief constable, like all citizens, has a duty to commission law to prevent breaches of the peace occurring. While breach of the peace is not in England a criminal offence it does form the basis of important police powers. If the police reasonably apprehend an imminent breach of the peace they may take any action which is necessary to control or prevent it, including arresting those travellers who are responsible.

The threat to the peace comes not from the marchers but from the travellers. The question arises therefore whether the chief constable can, as a preventative measure, disperse the marchers if they themselves are committing no threat to the peace. Under the principle stated in *Beatty* v *Gilbanks* (3) a lawful act does not become unlawful merely because other persons decide to offer unlawful reaction to it. But while the principle in *Beatty* v *Gilbanks* still stands today, its operation has been modified. While the police have no power to stop meetings (as opposed to marches which can be banned under s3 of the Public Order Act 1936) there may be situations of actual disorder where, if order is to be restored swiftly, the police are entitled to stop someone doing what he would otherwise be entitled to do. For example, in *O'Kelly* v *Harvey* (4) a magistrate was held to be entitled to disperse a lawful meeting since he had reasonable grounds for supposing that those opposed to the meeting would use violence and that there was no other way in which the peace could be preserved.

Therefore, if the *Beatty* v *Gilbanks* principle applies, the threat of the travellers will not justify the disposal of the marchers. But, if a breach of the peace is threatened and no other way of preventing such a breach exists, the police may dispose of marchers, as in *O'Kelly* v *Harvey*. In any case it is doubtful that the *Beatty* v *Gilbanks* principle will apply in this case beacuse the marchers have directly provoked the travellers by their own illegality in obstructing the highway. If the police did decide to disperse the marchers because they reasonably apprehended a breach of the peace, and if the marchers refuse to co-operate with the police, then, as in *Duncan* v *Jones*, they may be charged with the wilful obstruction of a police officer in the execution of his duty under s51(3) of the Police Act 1964.

If the marchers intend to act for any purpose prejudicial to the safety or interests of the state while in the vicinity of the Royal Air Force base this also raises the possibility of a breach of s1 of the Official Secrets Act 1911. Under s1(1)(a) of the Act it is an offence, punishable with 14 years' imprisonment, if any person for any purpose prejudicial to the safety or interests of the state, approaches, inspects, passes over or is in the neighbourhood of, or enters any prohibited place within the meaning of the Act. For example, in *Chandler* v *DPP* (5), anti-nuclear demonstrators sought to enter an RAF base and sit on the runway in order to prevent nuclear bombers taking off. As they approached the base they were arrested and charged with conspiracy to enter a prohibited place for a purpose prejudicial to the safety or interests of the state, contrary to s1 of the 1911 Act. The House of Lords unanimously upheld the conviction. Thus the 1911 Act is not restricted to spying but includes acts of sabotage and other acts of physical interference. However, it is unlikely that the chief constable will be able to rely on this offence in respect of the marchers from the Peace in Britain campaign. If their intention is merely to hold a protest meeting outside the Air base it may be difficult to establish that this in itself constitutes an act which is prejudicial to the safety or interests of the state.

References

1) *Hormer* v *Codman* (1886) 55 LJMC 110.
2) *Arrowsmith* v *Jenkins* [1963] 2 QB 561.
3) *Beatty* v *Gilbanks* (1882) 9 QBD 308.
4) *O'Kelly* v *Harvey* (1883) 15 Cox CC 435.
5) *Chandler* v *DPP* ([1964] AC 763.

QUESTION 8

General Comment

This question is based upon the recent decision of the House of Lords in *Council for Civil Service Unions* v *Minister for the Civil Service* (GCHQ case) and concerns the powers of the courts to review the prerogative Acts of the Crown. Students should state the traditional role of the courts in relation to the royal prerogative and then consider the implications of the GCHQ case. This is a very straightforward and relatively easy prerogative question, but knowledge of the GCHQ case is vital, thus showing the need to keep well up to date with case law developments. The approach of the House of Lords in the GCHQ case can be seen as another attempt by the judiciary to bring the Executive within the rule of law.

Skeleton Solution

Introduction: definition and examples of the prerogative.

The traditional role of the courts in relation to the prerogative: the existence of the prerogative, its extent, who is entitled to its benefit, the effect of statute upon the prerogative; non justicability of a validly exercised prerogative.

The implications of *Council for Civil Service Unions* v *Minister for the Civil Service*: situations in which the House of Lords may be prepared to review a prerogative act.

Suggested Solution

According to Blackstone the prerogative is 'that special preeminence which the King has, over and above all other person, and out of the ordinary course of the common law, in right of his royal dignity' (1). Today the prerogative consists mainly of a miscellaneous collection of residual executive governmental powers which are considered to be necessary to enable the government to function. These are powers enjoyed by the Crown but not by the subjects of the Crown and include, for example, the power to conduct foreign relations, to declare war and make peace, to regulate the disposition of the armed forces, to appoint and dismiss ministers, to dissolve Parliament, to assent to Bills, to grant honours, etc. The prerogative also includes certain immunities and privileges, such as the Queen's personal immunity from suit or prosecution.

The traditional view has been that where the Crown purports to act under the prerogative and in so doing directly affects the rights of an individual, the courts' power is limited to determining the existence of the claimed prerogative and, if it is found to exist, its extent. Once it is established that the conduct complained of is an exercise of the prerogative, the courts cannot challenge its use. The only 'remedy' the aggrieved individual has is a political remedy, for example by trying to have the matter raised in Parliament.

The role of the judiciary in relation to the prerogative has therefore largely been limited to the consideration of preliminary issues. With regard to the existence of a purported prerogative act the courts' main task is to ensure that no new prerogatives are created. Only those prerogatives already recognised at common law will be upheld. As Diplock LJ said in *BBC v Johns* (2): 'It is 350 years and a civil war too late for the Queen's courts to broaden the prerogative. The limits within which the executive government may impose obligations or restraints on citizens of the United Kingdom without any statutory authority are now well settled and incapable of extension'. If the prerogative claimed is found to exist the court will next consider its extent. Problems may arise in the purported application of ancient prerogative powers in modern situations. For example, under the prerogative the Crown has the right to intercept postal communications. In *Malone v Metropolitan Police Commissioner* (3) the question arose as to whether this prerogative also justified the tapping of telephones. In such cases the courts must distinguish between the application of an established prerogative to new circumstances and the creation of an entirely new prerogative, which of course the courts will not allow.

Once it is established that the act complained of is an exercise of the prerogative the traditional view was that the courts cannot challenge its use. They can, however, seek to contain its exercise in accordance with common law principles. For example the courts can consider whether the body or person purporting to act under the prerogative is entitled to the benefit of the prerogative. To be entitled to the benefit of the prerogative the person or body concerned must be entitled to statute or otherwise to benefit from the privileges, rights or immunities of the Crown. The court must also consider whether existence or exercise of the prerogative power has been affected by statute. Parliament is supreme. A prerogative can therefore be expressly abolished or restricted by statute. For example the Crown Proceedings Act 1947 abolishes the immunity of the Crown from being sued in contract and tort, while leaving the personal immunity of the sovereign intact. The prerogative may not, however, be impliedly abolished by statute. In such cases the prerogative is merely placed in abeyance and if the statute is repealed the prerogative will be revived. If a statute does conflict with a prerogative without expressly abolishing the prerogative, the courts must give effect to the statute and treat the prerogative as being in abeyance – see *Attorney-General* v *De Keyser's Royal Hotel* (4). However, a statute which conflicts with a prerogative may expressly provide that the prerogative be left intact. For example, s33(5) of the Immigration Act 1971 provided that the powers conferred under the Act should be additional to any prerogative power. Finally, the courts must consider whether the prerogative imposes a duty on the Crown to compensate the subject for damage caused by its exercise, as for example was the case in *Burmah Oil* v *Lord Advocate* (5).

But while the courts were prepared to consider the existence and the extent of a purported prerogative power they traditionally declined to go any further and review the merits of the actual exercise of the prerogative. However, recent cases indicate a shift in favour of granting judicial review in respect of the exercise of the prerogative in certain circumstances. This view, first expressed by Lord Denning MR in *Laker Airways Ltd* v *Department of Trade* (6), that the courts can intervene where a prerogative discretion is exercised improperly, was recently considered by the House of Lords in *Council for Civil Service Unions* v *Minister for the Civil Service* (7), where their Lordships were called upon to consider whether the courts had the power to review, on the grounds of procedural irregularity, an instruction made in the exercise of a power conferred under the royal prerogative. Their Lordships were of the opinion that simply because a decision making power was derived from a common law and not a statutory source it should not, for that reason only, be immune from judicial review.

However, Lord Roskill thought that the right of challenge could not be unqualified. It must depend on the subject matter of the prerogative power that was exercised. Prerogative powers such as those relating to the making of treaties, the defence of the realm, the prerogative of mercy, the grant of honours, the dissolution of Parliament and the appointment of ministers, as well as others, were not, he thought, susceptible to judicial review because their nature and subject matter was such as not to be amenable to the judicial process. It was also pointed out that prerogative decisions would usually involve the application of government policy of which the courts were not the appropriate arbiters.

Their Lordships agreed, therefore, that executive action based on common law or the use of a prerogative power was not necessarily immune from review. This was especially so in the present case where the prerogative derived from an Order in Council which was virtually indistinguishable from an order deriving from statute. In such case the decision might be reviewed by the courts just as it would have been if it had rested on statutory powers.

Therefore while today it may still be true that the remedy for abuse of the prerogative will usually lie in the political and not in the judicial field, nevertheless there may be cases where the courts are prepared to question the exercise of the prerogative where its nature and subject matter are considered to be susceptible to judicial review. This trend may be seen as another attempt by the courts to bring the Executive within the rule of law.

References
1) Blackstone, *Commentaries on the Laws of England.*
2) *BBC v Johns* [1965] Ch 32 at 79.
3) *Malone v Metropolitan Police Commissioner* [1979] Ch 344.
4) *Attorney-General v De Keyser's Royal Hotel* [1920] AC 508.
5) *Burmah Oil Company v Lord Advocate* [1965] AC 75.
6) *Laker Airways Ltd v Department of Trade* [1977] 2 All ER 182.
7) *Council for Civil Service Unions v Minister for the Civil Service* [1984] 3 WLR 1174.

QUESTION 9

General Comment

A relatively simple and straightforward problem question on police powers. Students should simply identify the issues and then work through the problem logically discussing each point in the light of the relevant authorities. The main issues involved in this particular problem are: (i) the search of Nancy's handbag and employer's offices; (ii) the seizure of the textbooks from Nancy's house; and (iii) Nancy's subsequent detention. Remember that when answering this sort of problem question you should avoid the temptation to put down everything you know and leave it to the examiner to sort out what is relevant. Also remember that the whole of this area of the law undergoes change with effect from 1 January 1986 when the relevant provisions of the Police and Criminal Evidence Act 1984 come into force.

Skeleton Solution

The position regarding the search of Nancy's handbag and her employer's offices by detective constables Able and Bell.

The seizure of the textbooks from Nancy's house: the right of the police to enter private premises; the power of the police when lawfully on premises to search and seize property; the principles in *Ghani* v *Jones*; the effect of any illegality upon the probative value of evidence obtained.

The detention of Nancy: general rule of no detention without lawful arrest; procedures following detention; right to bail, right to a telephone call; the judges' rules.

Suggested Solution

When the two detective constables, Able and Bell, question Nancy in the office of her employer, presumably they are there at her invitation and not in the execution of any arrest or search warrant. In these circumstances, Able and Bell may only remain on the premises so long as the invitation to be there stands, and may ask Nancy questions, which of course she is not obliged to answer. They cannot, however, in the absence of a valid search warrant, or a lawful arrest on the premises, or some specific statutory power, search either the offices or Nancy's handbag unless they have permission to do so. While Nancy may consent to her bag being searched she cannot authorise the search of her employer's offices. As there appears to be no search warrant, arrest or statutory power to search, prima facie the search of the offices is unlawful and the searching of Nancy's handbag, in the absence of her permission, is also unlawful (1). If Able and Bell wish to search in these circumstances then they must either obtain a search warrant or arrest Nancy, in which case they can search the premises on which she is arrested (the offices) and anything in her possession (the handbag).

Regarding the seizure of the books, Able and Bell seem to have no legal right to enter Nancy's house. The general rule is that the police may only enter private premises where they have some lawful authority to do so, ie for the purpose of preventing or stopping a reasonably apprehended breach of the peace, or for the execution of a search or arrest warrant, or for effecting an arrest for certain offences under s2(6) of the Criminal Law Act 1967. It was held in *Davis v Lisle* (2) that in the absence of such authority a constable cannot force an entry or demand to remain on premises to make inquiries. He can only enter the premises with the permission of the occupier and must leave when such permission is withdrawn by the occupier or by some person acting with his authority. If the constable does not leave within a reasonable time he becomes a trespasser and can be required to leave, by reasonable force if necessary (3). Able and Bell therefore appear to have no legal authority to enter Nancy's house and may therefore only enter if Nancy invites them in, which she appears to do; or at least she doesn't seem to object to their presence. If they are there with Nancy's approval, albeit implied, they will be lawfully on the premises and will remain so until such time, if any, as Nancy asks them to leave.

Given the apparent lawful presence of Able and Bell on the premises it would appear that the seizure of the books may be lawful. The general powers of a police constable to search for and seize property following a lawful entry, albeit not in the execution of a warrant or to effect an arrest, were set out by Lord Denning MR in the case of *Ghani v Jones* (4). Lord Denning said that in order to justify the taking of an article, when no man has been arrested or charged, the following requirements must be satisfied. First, the police officers must have reasonable grounds for believing that a serious offence has been committed – so serious that it is of the first importance that the offenders should be caught and brought to justice. Second, the police officers must have reasonable grounds for believing that the article in question is either the fruit of the crime, or is the instrument by which the crime was committed or is material evidence to prove the commission of the crime. Third, the police officers must have reasonable grounds to believe that the person in possession of it has himself committed the crime, or is implicated in it, or is accessory to it, or at any rate his refusal must be quite unreasonable. Fourth, the police must not keep the article nor prevent its removal, for any longer than is reasonably necessary to complete their investigations or preserve it for evidence. Finally, the lawfulness of the conduct of the police must be judged at the time and not by what happens.

Therefore, depending upon the interpretation of 'serious offence' in relation to the burglary at Cringes, it may be that Able and Bell are legally justified in seizing the textbooks, even though they apparently belong to Nancy's boyfriend, for even if Nancy hasn't committed the crime her refusal to allow the police officers to take the books may be considered to be 'quite unreasonable'. If, however, Able and Bell have no lawful right to be in Nancy's house or if their conduct falls outside the rules in *Ghani* v *Jones* then any search and the subsequent seizure of the books may be regarded as illegal. However, even if Able and Bell do act illegally, this does not mean that any evidence obtained will be inadmissible in later proceedings (5). It is a question for the court to decide by balancing the probative value of the evidence against the prejudice to the accused in admitting it. Cases such as *R* v *Sang* (6) and *Kuruma* v *R* (7) illustrate the attitude of the courts that it is no concern of theirs how the evidence was obtained: if it is relevant, it is admissible.

With regard to Nancy's subsequent detention, this is undoubtedly unlawful. The general rule is that a person may not be detained unless he has been lawfully arrested and there is nothing to show that Nancy has been lawfully arrested. She is simply helping the police with their enquiries and unless lawfully arrested is entitled to leave the police station whenever she wishes (8), (unless a particular statute authorises her detention without arrest, which is unlikely). If she is detained against her will without being lawfully arrested then this amounts to false imprisonment for which she can bring an action in tort. Even if she had been lawfully arrested the subsequent detention is certainly in breach of the judges' rules and may also be unlawful. Under s43 of the Magistrates Courts Act 1980, a police officer must bring a person who is arrested without a warrant before a magistrate as soon as practicable. If it is not practicable to do so within twenty-four hours a senior police officer must consider granting bail to the accused. Nancy has in fact been held for 48 hours. Under s62 of the Criminal Law Act 1977 Nancy is also given the statutory right to have her presence at the police station notified to someone, unless it would be prejudicial to the police investigations. In fact she has been refused permission to telephone either her employer or her boyfriend. The judges' rules also provide that she is entitled to consult with a solicitor unless it would prejudice the investigation, and she must receive adequate refreshment, which doesn't seem to have been the case.

References
1) See *Entick* v *Carrington* (1765) 19 St Tr 1030.
2) *Davis* v *Lisle* [1936] 2 KB 434.
3) See *McArdle* v *Wallace (No 2)* (1964) 108 Sol J 483; *Robson* v *Hallett* [1967] 2 QB 939.
4) *Ghani* v *Jones* [1970] 1 QB 693.
5) See *Jeffrey* v *Black* [1978] QB 490.
6) *R* v *Sang* [1980] AC 402.
7) *Kuruma* v *R* [1955] AC 197.
8) *R* v *Lemsatef* [1972] 2 All ER 835.

UNIVERSITY OF LONDON
INTERMEDIATE EXAMINATION IN LAWS 1986
for External Students

CONSTITUTIONAL LAW

Wednesday, 18 June: 10.00 am to 1.00 pm

Answer *FIVE* of the following NINE questions

1. 'It is difficult to imagine a bigger contrast of legal and constitutional styles than that between the EEC and the Commonwealth.' (Wade and Bradley).
   Discuss.

2. 'A Written Constitution for the United Kingdom would preserve the best of the existing constitutional practices and would remove the major defects.'
   Discuss.

3. In July 1984 Parliament passed the Puffins Act: s1 provides that it shall be a criminal offence to kill a puffin; s2 provides that no Bill to repeal the Puffins Act shall be laid before Parliament unless the consent of the Birds Council has previously been obtained.
   In 1985 a Bill repealing the Puffins Act is laid before Parliament, without the consent of the Birds Council having been previously obtained, and this is subsequently enacted as the Puffins Repeal Act 1985.
   Advise the Birds Council whether they can challenge the 1985 Act and still bring a prosection against Mr. Toad who killed a puffin in 1986.
   How, if at all, would your advice differ if the European Commission had made a regulation in October 1984 providing that puffins were vermin and that a cash premium would be paid in respect of each puffin killed?

4. 'While a second chamber is needed to serve a number of legislative purposes the present House of Lords is restricted by its composition from exercising its powers effectively.' (Wade and Bradley).
   Discuss.

5 'The parliamentary function of legislation has effectively passed to the Cabinet.'
   Discuss.

6 To what extent, if at all, is it true to say that the conventions of individual and collective ministerial responsibility are twins and yet incompatible?

7 'The fact that the source of Executive power is the prerogative and not statute should not deprive the citizen today of the right of challenge to the manner of its exercise.'
   Discuss.

8 The Rural Mini-Buses Act 1986 provides that each District Council shall have the duty to subsidise such mini-bus services within its area as it shall consider necessary in the interests of the community.
   The Redvale District Council decides to subsidise:
   a) a mini-bus service running from Redvale to Blacktown (which is outside Redvale District);
   b) a daily coach service within Redvale provided by Henry, the brother of Ivan, the Chairman of the Council;
   c) a weekly mini-bus service to a shopping centre in Redvale which is used almost exclusively by old age pensioners who are Ivan's constituents.

   John, a mini-bus owner and Redvale ratepayer, has offered to provide a cheaper mini-bus service within Redvale (see (b) above) but his offer was rejected without reasons being given. He wishes to attack the legality of the decisions in (a), (b) and (c) above, and seeks your advice.

9 Argue the case for and against the adoption of the European Convention on Human Rights and its protocols as a Bill of Rights for the United Kingdom.

QUESTION 1

General Comment

A relatively straightforward question comparing the legal and constitutional structure of the Commonwealth with that of the European Economic Community. Students should stress the lack of any formal Commonwealth constitutional structure and the reasons why this should be so, ie the ad hoc nature of its development, the need for flexibility and informality in Commonwealth affairs and the fact that legal rules may lead to conflict through their inflexibility. Students should then deal with the legal and constitutional structure of the European Economic Community mentioning in particular the community treaties and the organisation and functions of the executive, legislative and judicial organs of the Community.

Skeleton Solution

What is the Commonwealth?

The ad hoc nature of the Commonwealth; the lack of any formal legal or constitutional structure.

Rules of convention and the Commonwealth; their advantages over a formal legal structure.

What is the European Economic Community? Article 3 of the 1957 Treaty.

The legal and constitutional structure of the Community; the Council of Ministers, Commission, Parliament and Court of Justice.

Suggested Solution

The Commonwealth (1) is an association of states comprising the United Kingdom and those territories which were once a part of the British Empire but which are now independent states. The modern Commonwealth dates effectively from India's independence in 1947. Since then, as Britain's colonial territories in Africa, Asia, the Caribbean, Pacific and Mediterranean have gained independence, it has expanded to include 49 member states. Today it comprises one quarter of the world's population; some 1,000 million people of many races, religions and languages, from all parts of the globe (2). In 1971, the Heads of Commonwealth Governments described the Commonwealth as a voluntary association of independent sovereign states, each responsible for its own policies, consulting and co-operating in the common interests of their peoples and in the promotion of international understanding and world peace (3).

The Commonwealth has no constitutional structure in the accepted sense, mainly because it was not deliberately created but simply evolved without legal formality to provide a loose framework for continued international association between the former territories of the British Empire. The unique feature of the Commonwealth therefore is that unlike other international or regional organisations, such as the United Nations or the European Economic Community, it has no written charter, treaty or other formal instrument which lays down its constitution or formulates the legal rules governing the relationship between the various member states. Indeed, there is an almost complete absence of any constitutional law governing the organisation and its workings, and this in turn is partly due to the fact that the Commonwealth possesses no real legislative, executive or judicial organs.

The few rules that do exist are almost exclusively concerned with the acquisition and discontinuance of membership of the Commonwealth and might more properly be regarded as conventions rather than law, in that they are not rules which are justicable in any international court, but simply rules of practice which have been evolved as and when necessary to meet any new developments which have called for regulations. These rules of convention can be adopted or discarded as and when it appears necessary, and thus ensure maximum flexibility, which is essential for a body such as the commonwealth because of the divergent racial, religious, cultural, social, economic and political backgrounds of its member states.

By contrast the European Economic Community (4) derives its existence from treaties entered into by its twelve Western European member states (5). It was created specifically for the purposes stated in these treaties, primarily to establish a common market and approximate the economic policies of the member states. The objectives of the community, set out in Article 3 of the EEC Treaty 1957 (6), include the elimination of customs duties and quantitative restrictions on imports and exports between the states members; the establishment of a common customs tariff and common commercial policies towards non-member states; the abolition of obstacles to freedom of movement of workers, services and capital within member states; the creation of procedures to ensure that competition within the Community is not distorted; such approximation of the laws of member states as is necessary for the proper functioning of the common market and the establishment of common policies in such matters as agriculture and transport.

Responsibilty for achieving the aims of the Community lies with four institutions exercising legislative, executive and judicial functions. The Council of Ministers is the community's principal decision making body. Its function is to make policy decisions and to issue regulations and directives on the basis of proposals from the Commission. The government of each nation in the community has a seat on the Council, and the Presidency of the Council rotates between the member governments at six monthly intervals. The Commission, an independent body with executive powers and responsibility, has seventeen members chosen for their all round capability by agreement between the governments of the member states and it is the guardian of the treaties setting up the European Community, responsible for seeing that the treaties are implemented. The Commission therefore is the initiator of community policy and exponent of the Community interest in the Council, and is the executive arm of the Community responsible for its administration.

Since 1979 there has also been an elected Parliament for the Community which exercises limited but growing supervisory powers. In particular the Parliament advises the Council of Ministers on Commission proposals; with the Council of Ministers determines the budget for the Community and exerts some political control over the Council and the Commission. The Members of the Parliament who represent the citizens of the community are directly elected and serve for a period of five years. Although decisions made by the Parliament are not binding, they do influence the Council of Ministers and direct elections have given Parliament greater political authority and new prestige both inside and outside the community.

The judicial organ of the community is the Court of Justice of the European Communities which is the Community's supreme judicial authority consisting of thirteen judges assisted by six Advocates-General. There is no appeal against its rulings. Each of the treaties establishing the European Communities uses the same broad terms to define the specific responsibilities of the Court of Justice, which is to 'ensure that in the interpretation and application of this treaty the law is observed'. The Court therefore interprets and applies the whole corpus of Community law from the basic treaties to the various implementing regulations, directives and decisions issued by the Council and the

Commission. Certain rules of Community law contained in both the treaties and in the regulations made by the Council or the Commission are directly applicable in that, of their own force, they create legal rights and duties enforceable in municipal courts. Community law also forms part of the national law of every member state and prevails over national law to the extent that they are inconsistent with one another.

This formal organisational and legal structure of the European Economic Community, which has no counterpart in the Commonwealth, illustrates that it is certainly very difficult to imagine a bigger contrast of legal and constitutional styles than that which exists between these two organisations.

References

1) See generally de Smith, *The New Commonwealth and its Constitutions* (1964); Roberts-Wray *Commonwealth and Colonial Law* (1966).
2) *Year Book of the Commonwealth* (1985) (HMSO).
3) Commonwealth Declaration, 22 January 1971 (*Year Book of the Commonwealth* (1973) p351).
4) See generally Lipstein, *The Law of the European Communities*.
5) Belgium, Denmark, France, Federal Republic of Germany, Greece, Italy, Luxemburg, Republic of Ireland, Netherlands, Portugal, Spain and the United Kingdom.
6) EEC Treaty 1957 (Cmnd 5179–11, 1972).

QUESTION 2

General Comment

A difficult question which should only be attempted as a last resort.

Skeleton Solution

Introduction: What is a constitution? The unwritten nature of the United Kingdom constitution.

The defects of our constitutional system: the absence of a higher form of law; the sovereignty of Parliament.

The benefits of our constitutional system: the flexible nature of the constitution; the process of evolution.

Conclusion: adoption of a written constitution need not result in rigidity but even if desirable is change necessary.

Suggested Solution

The constitution of a state may be defined as the body of rules relating to the structure, functions and powers of the organs of state, their relationship to one another, and to the private citizen. The word 'constitution' is also used to refer to a document having a special legal sanctity which sets out the framework and the principal functions of the organs of government within the state, and declares the principles by which those organs must operate. This document has usually been enacted by the legislature or adopted by some other constituent body, for example a Constituent Assembly. In this sense of the word, as de Tocqueville observed, the United Kingdom has no constitution. There is no single document from which is derived the authority of the main organs of government, such as the Crown, the Cabinet, Parliament and the courts of law. No single document lays down the relationship of the primary organs of goverment one with another, or with the people.

Within the United Kingdom therefore there is no written constitution which can serve as fundamental law. This can create certain difficulties. In most states the constitution is a higher form of law in the sense that other laws must conform with it. The constitution imposes limits on what may be done by ordinary legislation and the courts may declare certain legislative acts void. But in the United Kingdom, in the absence of a written constitution to serve as the foundation of the legal system, the vacuum is filled by the legal doctrine of the legislative supremacy of Parliament. The result is that formal restraints upon the exercise of power which exist in other states do not exist in the United Kingdom. Parliament may make or unmake any law. There is no limit to its competence to legislate. No Parliament may bind its successors or be bound by its predecessors and the courts cannot question the validity of an Act of Parliament.

A major defect therefore of the United Kingdom constitution is that the absence of any higher form of law makes it virtually impossible to ensure that the rights of minorities and individual citizens are protected against legislative infringement by Parliament. Moreover, the absence of a written constitution means that there is no special procedure prescribed for legislation and constitutional importance. For example, before the Republic of Ireland could join the EEC, a constitutional amendment to the Irish constitution had to be approved by referendum of the people. In the United Kingdom, however, while the European Communities Act 1972 was debated at length in Parliament, the Act was passed by essentially the same procedure as would apply to any legislation of purely domestic concern. This absence of a written constitution means that in practice the British constitution depends far less on legal rules and safeguards and relies much more upon political and democratic principles. But can the politicians be trusted to observe these informal restraints on their power?

These problems could, it is argued, be overcome if the United Kingdom adopted a formal written constitution which defined the scope, and set out the legal limitations on, the functions and powers of the organs of government. But it must be remembered that no written document alone can ensure the smooth working of a system of government. A written document has no greater force than that which persons in authority are willing to attribute to it. Also our present unwritten constitution founded as it is partly on Acts of Parliament and judicial decisions, partly upon political practice, and partly upon detailed procedures established by the various organs of government for carrying their own tasks, provides a complex and comprehensive system of government which has served the United Kingdom well. In particular, as all law in the United Kingdom, including laws relating to the constitution, may be enacted, repealed or amended by the Queen in Parliament using the same legislative procedure, our constitution is highly flexible and can adapt to meet changes in social, moral and political circumstances. Indeed this facility for gradual evolution has been one of the major contributions to the political and social stability of the United Kingdom.

But the adoption of a written constitution need not necessarily destroy this flexibility altogether. A written constitution cannot contain all the detailed rules upon which government depends and accordingly a written constitution usually evolves a wide variety of customary rules and practices which attune the operation of the constitution to changing conditions. These customary rules and practices will usually be more easily changed than the constitution itself and their constant evolution will reduce the need for formal amendment of the written constitution. For example the rules for electing the legislature are usually found not in the written constitution but in ordinary statutes enacted by the legislature within the limits laid down by the constitution. Such statutes can when necessary be amended by the ordinary process of legislation whereas amendments to the constitution may require a more elaborated process, such as a special majority in the legislature or approval by a referendum.

Therefore it may well be the case that a written constitution for the United Kingdom would preserve the best of the existing constitutional practices and would remove the major defects. But, in spite of the defects, so long as our present constitutional system works so well, why change?

QUESTION 3

General Comment

A relatively simple question on the sovereignty of Parliament and the effects of membership of the European Communities. As regards the first part of the question, after stating the content of the doctrine of parliamentary supremacy, students should argue as best they can the likely effect of the Puffins Repeal Act. There is no answer; just state the likely alternatives. The second part of the question is more straightforward as the supremacy of communtity law over national rules is now firmly established in situations such as the one in the problem.

Skeleton Solution

Introduction: the content of the doctrine of parliamentary sovereignty.

The Puffins Repeal Act 1985: the application of the doctrine of parliamentary sovereignty to the Act; the effects of s2 of the Act on the traditional doctrine.

The European Communities Act 1972 s2(4); the supremacy of Community law over national laws.

Suggested Solution

Under the doctrine of the sovereignty of Parliament there exists no legal limitation upon the legislative competence of the United Kingdom Parliament. This absence of legal restraint has three aspects: Parliament is legally competent to legislate upon any subject matter, no Parliament can bind its successors or be bound by its predecessors, and, once Parliament has legislated, no court or other person can pass judgment upon the validity of the legislation.

This rule that Parliament may not bind its successsors (and that no Parliament is bound by Acts of its predecessors) is often cited both as a limitation upon legislative supremacy and as an example of it. As Dicey says, 'The logical reason why Parliament has failed in its endeavours to enact unchangeable enactments is that a sovereign power cannnot, while retaining its sovereign character, restrict its own powers by any parliamentary enactment' (1). It is inherent in the nature of a legislature that it should continue to be free to make new laws and, within the United Kingdom legal system therefore, all statutes that have been enacted by the Queen in Parliament remain in force until they are repealed or amended. An Act can be repealed either expressly or impliedly (2). In the latter case if Parliament passes an Act which is contrary to a previous statute (or certain provisions of the earlier statute) the earlier statute (or those particular provisions) are held to have been repealed.

The doctrine therefore consists in essence, of a rule which governs the legal relationship between the courts and the legislature, namely that the courts are under a duty to apply the legislation made by Parliament and may not hold an Act of Parliament to be invalid or unconstitutional.

Regarding the problem for consideration, in July 1984 Parliament passed the Puffins Act: s1 provides that it shall be a criminal offence to kill a puffin; s2 provides that no Bill to repeal the Puffins Act shall be laid before Parliament unless the consent of the Birds Council has previously been obtained. In 1985 a Bill repealing the Pufffins Act is laid before Parliament, without the consent of the Birds Council having been previously obtained, and this is subsequently enacted as the Puffins Repeal Act 1985.

In order for the Birds Council to challenge the Puffins Repeal Act 1985 and prosecute Mr Toad the Council will have to satisfy the courts that the Act is invalid due to the failure to comply with the consultation provisions of the 1984 Act. Normally of course, under the doctrine of parliamentary supremacy, there will be no problem. The courts will consider the 1985 Act to have expressly repealed the 1984 Act. But in the present case, what is the effect of s2? The principle that the Parliament which passed the 1984 Act cannot bind the Parliament which purports to enact the 1985 Repeal Act may mean simply that, notwithstanding s2, the repeal is valid and the courts will be bound to give effect to the express wishes of the legislature. However it can also be argued that s2 creates a provision as to the manner by which repeal of the 1984 Act must be achieved and that this will be binding upon future Parliaments until s2 itself is expressly repealed. Therefore any attempt to repeal the whole Act without first removing s2 will be invalid. Of course it may also be argued that by expressly repealing the whole of the 1984 Act Parliament is in any case impliedly repealing the consultation provisions of s2.

The situation concerning the effect of the purported repeal is therefore somewhat uncertain. No uncertainty would exist however had the European Commission made a regulation in October 1984 providing that puffins were vermin and that a cash premium would be paid in respect of each puffin killed. Section

2(4) of the European Communities Act 1972 provides in effect that United Kingdom Acts of Parliament shall be construed and have effect subject to directly applicable Community law. Under Article 189 of the Treaty of Rome regulations have direct applicability and are binding in all member states without requiring implementation or adoption by national law. Therefore any regulation made by the European Commission in October 1984 would have supremacy over national laws and take effect notwithstanding the conflict with the then already existing Puffins Act 1984. In this respect it is both clear from the treaty and from statements made by the European Court of Justice (3) that Community law should prevail over national law in all circumstances and therefore any United Kingdom constitutional law doctrine of the legislative supremacy of Parliament is irrelevant.

Of course the approach taken by the European Court of Justice indicated above runs completly contrary to the traditional doctrine of the sovereignty of Parliament. This has resulted in controversy, with some arguing that, while the doctrine of implied repeal has been abandoned so far as Community law is concerned, the doctrine of express repeal of earlier law, including Community law, is nevertheless retained. However it is yet to be seen how the United Kingdom courts would act if faced by a United Kindom Act of Parliament expressing an intention of Parliament to legislate contrary to Community law. Such a situation is, perhaps, unlikely to arise since it would amount to a blatant repudiation by the United Kingdom of its international obligations under the European Community treaties. But, in the absence of such express repeal of Community law by our Parliament it is clear that as in *Macarthys Ltd v Wendy Smith* (4), where a conflict does exist between United Kingdom legislation and Community law the latter will prevail and accordingly, notwithstanding the Puffins Act 1984 and its provisions, the Community regulation of October 1984 will bind our courts.

References
1) Dicey, *The Law of the Constitution*, 10th edn, 1959, p68.
2) See *Ellen Street Estates Ltd v Minister of Health* [1934] 1 KB 590.
3) See *Costa v ENEL* [1964] CMLR 425.
4) *Macarthys Ltd v Wendy Smith* [1979] 3 All ER 325.

QUESTION 4

General Comment

The usual House of Lords question. As always don't write everything you know about the House of Lords and don't be tempted to simply turn out the traditional (and now largely discredited) criticisms of the Lords. Remember that while the undemocratic nature of its compostion is a major criticism of the House, it is also one of its greatest assets.

Skeleton Solution

Introduction: the need for a second chamber.

The criticisms of the hereditary and life peerage systems.

The advantages which flow from the undemocratic nature of the composition of the House of Lords.

The factors limiting the effective exercise of the powers of the House.

Suggested Solution

For many years there has been opposition to the continued existence of the House of Lords as the second chamber in our present bicameral parliamentary system. Nevertheless the fact remains that a second chamber is needed to assist in the legislative process and the House of Lords performs the functions of a second chamber extremely well.

However, despite the success of the House of Lords in performing its functions it can be argued that the House is nevertheless restricted by its aristocratic and unrepresentative composition from exercising its powers effectively. In a democracy, it may be argued all legislators should be directly accountable to the people at elections or at least accountable indirectly, for example, by election by the House of Commons. Their Lordships, however, take their seats in the legislature either because they are hereditary peers or because they have been created life peers under the Life Peerage Act 1958. The former are criticised on the grounds that high office should be awarded to those who earn it on merit and not by accident of birth, and as most hereditary peers are

Conservative this leads to a permanent Conservative majority in the House. The life peers are criticised because of the considerable powers of patronage it leaves in the hands of the Prime Minister to reward party loyalists and retiring ministers with seats in the Upper Chamber. It is also thought by some that since the members of the House of Lords do not represent any body of constituents they speak for a small, privileged section of the community.

But criticism of the composition of the House of Lords is often illfounded and uninformed. It can be argued that the composition of the House does not directly affect the effectiveness of the chamber - quite the opposite. The quality of members and speeches is often very high. Debates are well informed. Those upon whom peerages are conferred are usually persons with considerable experience of politics, public service or industry, or who have otherwise made their mark in public or intellectual life. They bring to the House a wide range of expertise. The hereditary element also provides many young peers and because the Lords do not have any constituencies to consider they can devote more time to their parliamentary duties and do not have to worry about reselection or re-election. In many respects therefore the membership of the House of Lords is far superior to that of the House of Commons. The only difficulty is the undemocratic nature of their appointment.

It is the consciousness of their undemocratic nature of appointment which is the major impediment to the effectiveness of the House. While the 1911 and 1949 Parliament Acts did have a direct effect on the effectiveness of the House of Lords, for example, the House no longer has power over money matters and governments no longer depend on the favour of the Lords for their continuation in office, nevertheless under the Parliament Acts their Lordships do retain the power to amend non-money Bills and although the House cannot impose its will on the Commons in legislation, it can effectively delay government Bills for one year. But the Lords are reluctant to exercise their suspensory powers over legislation which they still retain. If they interfere with government business they may lay themselves open to allegations of seeking to frustrate the wishes of the people as expressed through their democratically elected government.

This makes the House of Lords extremely vulnerable. How can they act as a check on the House of Commons in such circumstances? The government can brush aside opposition in the House of Lords 'because they don't represent the people', and the threat of abolition or reform is always present. Their Lordships are well aware of this. This is perhaps one reason why in spite of their inbuilt Conservative majority they have always shown restraint when dealing with Labour government legislation. Recent events have shown however that the reports of the impotence of the House of Lords have been exaggerated and that given the right cirumstances its effectiveness and efficiency is not altogether impaired by these legislative and political constraints.

When the threat of abolition is lifted, as it ususally is under a Conservative government, their Lordships can be very effective in carrying out their constitutional functions. The Lords retain a high degree of political independence inherent in their undemocratic character. They do not have to rely upon the continued support of a political party for their seats in the legislature and while the majority of hereditary peers may be Conservative, a Conservative government is not guaranteed a majority in the House. They vote according to their conscience, not the demands of the whips. Where the government has a heavy legislative programme, amendment or delay in the Lords can seriously threaten the legislative timetable for that particular session and the government will be forced to take notice and attempt a compromise with the Lords. If compromise fails and the government implements the procedure under the Parliament Acts, even a one year delay may prove fatal to the government's plans.

But such opposition is possible only where the House of Lords retains popular support for its action; where, for example, the government is acting unconstitutionally or outside the terms of its mandate, or as in the present parliamentary situation where the government majority in the House of Commons is such that there is no effective and efficient opposition in the Commons. In other situations their Lordships may be reluctant to seriously oppose the government's wishes. The fear of abolition or public censure would be decisive.

Therefore while the effectiveness of the House of Lords in respect of its legislative functions and powers is relatively unimpeded and in many respects enhanced by the anachronistic and undemocratic nature of its composition, its effectiveness as a check upon the House of Commons, and thus in reality upon the government of the day, may in some situations be seriously affected by a lack of political confidence directly attributable to the undemocratic nature of its composition.

QUESTION 5

General Comment

This question revolves around the old argument as to whether Parliament legislates or merely legitimates executive policy. As well as examining the role of the backbench MP and the House of Lords in the legislative process, students should also consider whether in fact today legislation is not so much decided by the Cabinet as the Prime Minister.

Skeleton Solution

Introduction: the enactment of legislation by the Queen of Parliament.

The House of Commons: does it legislate or merely legitimate; the control of the Commons by the Executive.

The role of the House of Lords: the ability of the Lords to check the Executive.

The role of the back-bench MP: private members Bills.

Conclusion: Cabinet legislation or prime ministerial legislation.

Suggested Solution

For purposes of constitutional analysis, the functions of government have often been divided into three broad classes – legislative, executive and judicial. The legislative function involves the enactment of general rules determining the structure and powers of public authorities and regulating the conduct of citizens and private organisations. In the United Kingdom, legislative authority is vested in the Queen in Parliament: new law being enacted when it has been approved by Commons and Lords and has received the royal assent.

The passing of legislation therefore is one of the primary functions of Parliament. Bills, which may be either public or private, cannot become law until they have been passed by Parliament and received the royal assent. However many consider that Parliament no longer legislates but rather that it merely legitimates proposed legislation already decided upon by the executive. Certainly, the great majority of public Bills are prepared for Parliament by the government, which is also responsible for supervising their passage through each House. The executive therefore participates actively in the process of legislation. Party domination of the House of Commons and the use of the whip system ensures that, generally speaking, when the government has a working majority in the commons, no new legislation can be enacted by Parliament which is not approved also by the government and that those Bills which are approved are passed.

There are however occasions when in spite of the government's control of the Commons its Members may exert their independence and refuse to act as a mere rubber stamp for Executive policy. For example the Commons effectively blocked attempts by the Labour government to reform the House of Lords in 1968 and recently attempts by Mrs Thatcher to reform the law on Sunday trading were defeated following a backbench Conservative revolt in the Commons. One must also remember that Parliament also includes the House of Lords and that although the legislative powers of the Lords have been severely curtailed under the Parliament Acts of 1911 and 1949 the chamber, retaining as it does a large degree of political independence, may still act as an effective check on government Bills.

Although the House of Lords no longer has power over money matters, under the Parliament Acts their Lordships do retain the power to amend non-money Bills and although the House cannot impose its will on the Commons in legislation, it can effectively delay government Bills for one year. In practice therefore where the government has a heavy legislative programme, amendment or delay in the Lords can seriously threaten the legislative timetable for that particular session and the government will be forced to take notice and attempt a compromise with the Lords. If compromise fails and the government implements the procedure under the Parliament Acts, even a one year delay may prove fatal to the government's plans. Recent events have illustrated just how effective the House of Lords can be in exerting its independence and challenging government legislation. It is certainly no rubber stamp. Mrs Thatcher's first administration sustained 45 defeats in their Lordships' Chamber.

It must also be remembered that not all public Bills are initiated by the executive. Although the bulk of the legislative programme of Parliament is taken up by government Bills, a small but significant part of the programme consists of Bills introduced by backbench MPs. Although the scope for legislative initiative by individual MPs is severely limited, both because of restricted parliamentary time and of the tight hold which the government maintains over departmental responsibilities, standing orders, while generally giving precedence to government business, nevertheless set aside ten Fridays in each session on which private members' Bills have priority. The fact that not many of these Bills reach the statute book does not detract from their value as expressions of the independent legislative function of Parliament.

However, in spite of the opportunities for private members to introduce their Bills, the independence of the House of Lords and the occasional rebellion amongst backbench members of the government party in the House of Commons, it is probably true to say that in the main the parliamentary function of legislation has effectively passed to the Cabinet, at least in the sense that the Cabinet is the core of collective responsibility.

Traditionally it is in the Cabinet where government policy is thrashed out before being put to Parliament for what has largely become the formality of approval. However this may not necessarily be the case today. We are experiencing a period of prime ministerial government where policy decisions are made by the Prime Minister and her small inner Cabinet based largely upon the advice of Cabinet committees and the Prime Minister's own policy unit. The full Cabinet, if consulted at all, merely approves whatever is put before it. It may therefore, at least for the time being, be more accurate to say that the parliamentary function of legislation has effectively passed to the Prime Minister.

QUESTION 6

General Comment

This question involves discussion of the conventions of collective and individual responsibility and comment upon the inter-relationship between them, in particular the overlaps which seem to exist in their application.

Skeleton Solution

Introduction – the doctrine of responsible government.

Collective responsibility; the content and application of, and the justification for, the convention.

Individual responsibilty; the content and application of, and the justification for, the convention.

The possibility for conflict in the application of collective and individual responsibility.

Suggested Solution

Democracy requires that those who govern should be responsible to those whom they govern. The convention of ministerial responsibility seeks to achieve this aim. It has two aspects. Firstly, the collective responsibilty of the government as a whole to Parliament and, secondly the individual responsibility of ministers to Parliament for decisions, taken in their departments, whether by themselves or by their civil servants.

The doctrine of collective responsibilty involves two rules. Firstly, it is accepted that the government must resign if it loses the support of the House of Commons. The Prime Minister and her ministers are collectively responsible to Parliament for the conduct of national affairs. If the Prime Minister loses support in Parliament she must resign or seek a dissolution of Parliament. The rule does not mean that the government must resign whenever it is defeated on any issue. There has to be a clear-cut defeat for the government on a matter of policy.

Secondly, the doctrine of collective responsibility involves the rule that the government must speak with one voice. All members of the government share in the collective responsibility of the government, and ministers may not publicly criticise or dissociate themselves from government policy. The essence of collective responsibility is that the Cabinet should be seen to be in agreement; a cabinet minister who feels unable to agree with his colleagues should resign. The constitutional justification for the rule is that the answerability of the government to Parliament would be severely impaired if individual ministers were able to say that they personally did not agree with decisions taken in Cabinet. Ministers, including non-Cabinet members, are normally bound therefore not to differ publicly from Cabinet decisions nor to speak or vote against the government in Parliament. The rule increases party discipline and unity within the government, strengthens the government in Parliament and reinforces the secrecy of decision making within the Cabinet, thereby minimising public disagreement between both ministers and departments of state. It also serves to strengthen the authority of the Prime Minister in relation to her colleagues.

The convention of individual responsibility requires that ministers are responsible to Parliament for their own actions, omissions and mistakes as well as for those of the officials in their departments. This principle is said to help preserve the anonymity and therefore the objectivity and efficiency of the civil service. Thus, Government Bills are introduced into Parliament by the departmental ministers, who are responsible for the proposals they contain. In debates concerning the work of individual departments, the minister concerned is expected to reply to the criticisms raised and usually seeks to defend the department. Ministers are also expected to meet the reasonable requests of members for information concerning their departments and answer questions relating to their departments at question time.

It can be seen therefore that in many respects the relationship between individual and collective responsibility is very close and to this extent they may be viewed as twins. However, there is also in some respects a high degree of incompatibility between the two. For instance, if responsibility for the making of policy decisions lies collectively with the whole government, isn't it inconsistent to hold the departmental minister individually responsible for the implementation of that policy? Many of the decisions announced by a minister will have been taken or approved in Cabinet or by Cabinet committees and to this extent the doctrine of collective responsibility will attach to them. Similarly, while a departmental minister may have the authority to make decisions relating exclusively to the sphere for which he is responsible, on many matters he may have to consult with other departments, for example the Treasury. Should that minister then be held responsible for the consequences? Conversely, if a minister is facing censure in Parliament as a result of his departmental policies, he may be individually responsible and accountable to Parliament, but he can nevertheless expect to receive the support of his governmental colleagues by bringing collective responsibility into play.

Of course, both individual and collective responsibility are rules of convention governed largely by political expediency and in consequence their practice may bear little relation to their theory. While their theory therefore may give an impression of imcompatibility, the practical application of these conventions, looked at in their individual context and judged on their particular facts, may display a close distinction dictating which is to prevail.

QUESTION 7

General Comment

This is a very straightforward and relatively easy prerogative question based upon the recent decision of the House of Lords in *Council for Civil Service Unions* v *Minister for the Civil Service* (GCHQ Case), which concerns the powers of the courts to review the prerogative acts of the Executive. Students should state the traditional role of the courts in relation to the royal prerogative and then consider the implications of the GCHQ case.

Skeleton Solution

Introdution: definition and examples of the prerogative.

Difference in the role of the courts when dealing with prerogative as opposed to statutory Executive powers.

The traditional role of the courts in relation to the prerogative.

The implications of *Council for Civil Service Unions* v *Minister for the Civil Service*.

Suggested Solution

Generally, the Executive derives its powers from two legal sources, statute and the royal prerogative. According to Blackstone the prerogative is 'that special pre-eminence which the King has, over and above all other persons, and out of the ordinary course of the common law, in right of his royal dignity' (1). Today the prerogative consists mainly of a miscellaneous collection of residual executive governmental powers which are considered to be necessary to enable the government to function. These are powers enjoyed by the Crown but not by the subjects of the Crown and include, for example, the power to conduct foreign relations, to declare war and make peace, to regulate the disposition of the armed forces, to appoint and dismiss ministers, to dissolve Parliament, to assent to Bills, to grant honours etc. The prerogative also includes certain immunities and privileges, such as the Queen's personal immunity from suit or prosecution.

Where the Executive purports to act under powers conferred by statute, then, in the absence of any effective ouster clause, the courts may review the action taken, and where necessary declare it void on the grounds of ultra vires or breach of natural justice. However where the executive purports to act under the prerogative, and in so doing directly affects the rights of an individual, then traditionally the courts' power is limited to the consideration of preliminary issues, namely the determination of the existence of the claimed prerogative and, if it is found to exist, its extent (2). Once it is established that the conduct complained of is an exercise of the prerogative, the courts cannot challenge its use. The only 'remedy' the aggrieved individual has is a political remedy, for example by trying to have the matter raised in Parliament.

So while the courts were prepared to consider the existence and the extent of a purported prerogative power they traditionally declined to go any further and review the merits or manner of the actual exercise of the prerogative. However, recent cases indicate a shift in favour of granting judicial review in respect of the exercise of the prerogative in certain circumstances. This view, first expressed by Lord Denning MR in *Laker Airways Ltd* v *Department of Trade* (3), that the courts can intervene where prerogative discretion is exercised improperly was recently considered by the House of Lords in *Council for Civil Service Unions* v *Minister for the Civil Service* (4), where their Lordships were called upon to consider whether the courts had the power to review, on the grounds of procedural irregularity, an instruction made in the exercise of a power conferred under the royal prerogative. Their Lordships were of the opinion that simply because a decision making power was derived fom a common law and not a statutory source it should, for that reason only, be immune from judicial review.

According to Lord Diplock, judicial review has developed to a stage where one could classify under three heads the grounds on which administrative action was subject to control by judicial review: 'illegality, irrationality, and procedural impropriety'. As regards procedural impropriety, his Lordship saw no reason why it should not be a ground for judicial review of a decision made under powers of which the ultimate source was the prerogative.

However, Lord Roskill thought that the right of challenge could not be unqualified. It must depend on the subject matter of the prerogative power that was exercised. Prerogative powers such as those relating to the making of treaties, the defence of the realm, the prerogative of mercy, the granting of honours, the dissolution of Parliament and the appointment of ministers, as well as others, were not, he thought, susceptible to judicial review because their nature and subject matter was such as not to be amenable to the judicial process. It was also pointed out that prerogative decisions would usually involve the application of government policy of which the courts were not the appropriate arbiters.

Their Lordships agreed therefore that executive action based on common law or the use of a prerogative power was not necessarily immune from review. This was especially so in the present case where the prerogative derived from an Order in Council, which was virtually indistinguishable from an order deriving from statute. In such cases the decision might be reviewed by the courts just as it would have been if it had rested on statutory powers.

Therefore while today it may still be true that the remedy for abuse of the prerogative will still lie in the political and not the judicial field, nevertheless the fact that the source of executive power is the prerogative and not statute will not necessarily deprive the citizen of the right of challenge as to the manner of its exercise, providing that the nature and subject matter of the particular prerogative in question are considered by the courts to be susceptible to judicial review. This trend may be seen as another attempt by the courts to bring the executive within the rule of law.

References

1) Blackstone, *Commentaries on the Laws of England.*
2) See *BBC v Johns* [1965] Ch 32; *Attorney-General v De Keyser's Royal Hotel* [1920] AC 508; *Burmah Oil Company v Lord Advocate* [1965] AC 75.
3) *Laker Airways Ltd v Department of Trade* [1977] 2 All ER 182.
4) *Council for Civil Service Unions v Minister for the Civil Service* [1984] 3 WLR 1174.

QUESTION 8

General Comment

A relatively simple and straightforward problem question concerning judicial review of administrative action. As with all problem questions Students should identify the relevant issues and then simply work through the problem logically discussing each point in the light of the relevant authorities.

Skeleton Solution

Introduction: public law remedy – application for judicial review under O.53; the requirement of locus standi.

The mini-bus service running from Redvale to Blacktown: possibility of substantive ultra vires; whether necessarily incidental to achieving the main purpose of the statute.

The daily coach service within Redvale provided by Henry: possibility of a breach of natural justice; the rule against bias; whether family relationship amounts to an interest; the right to be told the reasons for a decision.

The weekly mini-bus service to a shopping centre in Redvale: possibility of a breach of natural justice; whether procedural ultra vires; improper purpose or unreasonable exercise of discretion.

Suggested Solution

As this case concerns the public law functions of a public law body, John must, if he wishes to attack the legality of the decisions to grant the subsidies, apply for judicial review under O.53 of the Rules of the Supreme Court: *O'Reilly* v *Mackman* (1). Firstly however John will have to obtain leave of the court to apply for judicial review. Accordingly his application must, generally speaking, be made promptly, and in any event within three months from the date when grounds for the application first arose and he must establish the necessary locus standi. In this respect the order provides that the court shall not grant leave unless it considers that the applicant has a sufficient interest in the matter to which the application relates.

Regarding locus standi, the courts have been careful not to give restrictive interpretations to the meaning of sufficient interest. It remains in each case a question of fact and law to be determined in the light of all the circumstances of the case and should usually be considered together with the substantive legal merit of the applicant's case (2). Recent cases illustrate that the courts are becoming more liberal in the granting of locus standi (3). For example the fact that John is a ratepayer may give him a sufficient interest in the granting of subsidies from the rate fund. Also the fact that he is a mini-bus owner who applied unsuccessfully to provide a service within Redvale may also give him a suffient interest to challenge the award of subsidies to those operators who were successful in their applications.

With regard to the mini-bus service running from Redvale to Blacktown, John may be able to challenge this on the grounds that in providing the subsidy for this service the authority is acting ultra vires.

It is a fundamental principle of English law that no person or body should be permitted to exceed its lawful powers. Parliament, by statute, confers powers upon subordinate administrative authorities and these subordinate authorities can only do that which Parliament has authorised them to do in the parent statute. All acts of administrative authorities must therefore, in general, be justified by reference to some statutory power. Accordingly the courts must ensure that subordinate administrative authorities only do that which Parliament, in the relevant Act, has authorised them to do. If an authority exceeds its statutory powers, then the courts must declare its actions to be ultra vires and void. Where, for example, an administrative authority has acted in excess of its statutory powers or in excess of its jurisdiction this may amount to substantive ultra vires. In such cases it is the role of the court, by examining the parent Act, to determine the extent of the specific powers conferred upon the administrative authority by Parliament and ensure that those powers are not exceeded. If they are, then the actions of the authority will be ultra vires and void: *Attorney-General v Fulham Corporation* (4).

In the present case for consideration the Rural Mini-Buses Act 1986 provides that each District Council shall have the duty to subsidise such mini-bus services within its area as it shall consider necessary in the interests of the community. The parent statute therefore authorises the Council to subsidise mini-bus services within Redvale District. Prima facie therefore, in subsidising a minibus service to Blacktown, which is outside Redvale District, the Council is exceeding its statutory powers and acting ultra vires.

However in such cases the courts do have a discretion and may allow acts which although themselves are not directly authorised in the parent statute are nevertheless considered to be necessarily incidental to achieving that which is authorised in the Act (5). The subsidy of the service to Blacktown may fall into this class. Blacktown may for example be a major local shopping centre used by the people of Redvale and the provision of the subsidy for what may be an important local service may be considered an integral part of the Council's public transport policy for Redvale. However it can also be argued that as all District Councils are under a duty to provide such subsidies, the District Council for Blacktown should also contribute to the service if it is considered to be necessary in the interests of the community.

Regarding the daily coach service within Redvale provided by Henry, this may also be ultra vires. Although the service is provided within Redvale it involves a coach and the Act specifically refers to mini-buses. This particular subsidy may also be challenged on the ground that it was granted in breach of natural justice as Henry is the brother of Ivan, the Chairman of the Council. It is one of the most important principles of judicial review of administrative action that certain powers must be exercised in accordance with natural justice. Traditionally natural justice comprises two procedural rules; firstly the rule that no man is to be condemned without a hearing and, secondly, that no man should sit as a judge in his own cause. Since 1967 a third limb of natural justice has appeared, the so-called duty to act fairly.

The rule that no man should be a judge in his own cause requires that people affected by judicial and administrative decisions have a right that the decision maker should be impartial. No one should be a judge in a matter in which he is interested. The rule is not limited to pecuniary interest. As in the case of *Metropolitan Properties Ltd* v *Lannon* (6) other interests, such as professional or family interests, may also invalidate a determination.

We are not told what part, if any, Ivan played in the award of the subsidy to the coach service operated by his brother Henry. If he did not participate at all, then all well and good. But if, as Chairman of the Council, Ivan did participate in the decision to award the subsidy, his relationship with Henry undoubtedly amounts to an interest of a kind likely to raise a suspicion of bias in the mind of the reasonable man. The suspicion of irregularity in the award of this subsidy is further aroused by the fact that John's offer was cheaper than that of Henry. In such circumstances the decision to award the subsidy to Henry may be void.

As regards the failure to give a reason for this rejection, generally speaking the right to be heard does not require the giving of reasons to a mere applicant, but under the circumstances because John's livelihood may be affected by the decision he may have a legitimate expectation that reasons be given for the decision. In view of John's interest the failure to give reasons may also be a breach of the requirement of fairness. This also therefore may amount to a breach of natural justice.

Similarly, the decision to subsidise a weekly mini-bus service to a shopping centre in Redvale which is used almost exclusively by old age pensioners who are Ivan's constituents may also breach natural justice. If Ivan participated in the decision to award this subsidy, the fact that it benefits a section of the community on whom Ivan relies for his continuance in office may breach the rule against bias. It is doubtful however that this particular subsidy is ultra vires. The parent statute places the Council under a duty to subsidise certain mini-bus services within its district but it has a discretion in that it need only make a subsidy where it is considered necessary to do so in the interests of the community. Where such a discretion is conferred on an authority the courts require, inter alia, that the discretion will be exercised for its proper purpose, ie that purpose envisaged by Parliament when it passed the parent Act, and that the discretion will be exercised reasonably.

In the present case whatever Ivan's real motive may be it is almost certain that the provision of transport to take old people shopping is one envisaged by Parliament as being in the interests of the community and it is also reasonable in the sense that it is a decision which a reasonable body would have taken.

References

1) *O'Reilly* v *Mackman* [1982] 3 All ER 1124.
2) See *R* v *Inland Revenue Commissioners, ex parte National Federation of Self-Employed and Small Businesses Ltd* [1982] AC 617.
3) See *R* v *HM Treasury, ex parte Smedley* [1985] 1 All ER 589.
4) *Attorney-General* v *Fulham Corporation* [1921] 1 Ch 440.
5) See *Westminister Corporation* v *London and North Western Railway* [1905] AC 426.
6) *Metropolitan Properties Ltd* v *Lannon* [1969] 1 QB 577.

QUESTION 9

General Comment

This question involves discussion of the protection of human rights in the United Kingdom and the arguments for and against the adoption of the European Convention on Human Rights as a Bill of Rights. After introducing the present constitutional safeguards for maintaining individual liberty, the need for a Bill of Rights and the advantages of incorporating the European Convention should be argued. The problems of such a course of action may then be explored. A knowledge of Lord Wade's Bill to incorporate the Convention into United Kingdom domestic law would be useful.

Skeleton Solution

Introduction: the existing constitutional safeguards for protecting human rights in the United Kingdom.

The European Convention on Human Rights: the objects of the Convention and the machinery for enforcement.

The arguments in favour of adopting the Convention as a Bill of Rights for the United Kingdom.

The arguments against adopting the Convention: the problem of parliamentary sovereignty; politicising the judiciary.

Lord Wade's Bill to incorporate the Convention into domestic law.

Suggested Solution

The United Kingdom constitution is unwritten in the formal sense and accordingly lays great emphasis on the virtues of the common law and the legislative supremacy of Parliament. It relies heavily on the political process to ensure that Parliament does not override the basic rights and liberties of the subject, nor remove from the courts the adjudication of disputes between the citizen and the State arising out of the exercise of Executive power.

This traditional British approach to individual liberties is considered by many to be outdated and incapable of protecting individual rights from Executive encroachment. The critics advocate the creation of a new Bill of Rights for the United Kingdom. Accordingly, in 1978 a select committee of the House of

Lords was established to consider whether a Bill of Rights was desirable and, if so, what form it should take. The committee, while doubting that a Bill of Rights was desirable, nevertheless held unanimously that if there were to be a Bill of Rights, it should be a Bill to incorporate the European Convention of Human Rights into United Kingdom law.

The European Convention on Human Rights (1), prepared under the auspices of the Council of Europe, entered into force in September 1953. The Convention is a treaty under international law and its authority derives solely from the consent of those states who have become parties to it. The Convention declares certain human rights which should be protected by law in each state and provides political and judicial procedures by which alleged infringements of these rights may be examined at an international level. Every state party to the Convention has a duty to ensure that its domestic law conforms to the Convention, but a state is under no duty to incorporate the Convention itself within its domestic law. While about half the states who are parties to the Convention have incorporated it within their domestic law, others, including the United Knigdom, have not incorporated the Convention. Successive British governments have maintained that human rights are already adequately protected by law in the United Kingdom.

Those who argue in favour of adopting the European Convention as a Bill of Rights for the United Kingdom point out that human rights are not adequately protected under our present law and that further constitutional protection for human rights is therefore necessary. In support of their case they point to the ever increasing role of the state in economic and social affairs and the widespread public disillusionment with the parliamentary process and the 'undemocratic' electoral system which produces a legislature dominated and controlled by the Executive. There is also concern at the record of the United Kingdom under the European Convention on Human Rights and dissatisfaction with the performance of the courts in dealing with disputes between the citizen and the state. With the Executive every day assuming more statutory powers and in so doing eroding our common law liberties, so it becomes more vital to provide safeguards against the abuse of those powers.

Assuming that some form of Bill of Rights is needed in the United Kingdom, incorporation of the European Convention would probably be the easiest and most acceptable option available to the government. There is no dispute as to the rights protected. The Convention very wisely omits economic and social rights, over which considerable political controversy might arise, and is confined to certain basic rights and liberties which the framers of the Convention considered would be generally accepted in the liberal democracies of Western Europe. Incorporation of the Convention would also avoid the frequent humiliation suffered by the United Kingdom government before the European Court of Human Rights when, in the glare of international publicity, it is found in breach of its international obligations under the Convention. These foreign 'judges' would no longer be able to interfere with our law and instead breaches of the convention would be dealt with before our own municipal courts.

However, to be fully effective incorporation would have to enable the British courts to apply the Convention if necessary in preference to exisiting rules of statute or common law and this will entail grafting onto the present constitution an added power in the courts to give redress to the individual even against an Act of Parliament. Such an attempt would raise issues concerning the relationship of the courts to the political process, including the special difficulties inherent in the attempt by a supreme Parliament to bind itself.

There are therefore formidable legal and political problems in the incorporation of the European Convention as a new Bill of Rights for the United Kingdom (2). It is extremely difficult to bring about any enactment of fundamental rights that may not be violated by ordinary process of legislation and what is the value in having a Bill of Rights that cannot bind future parliaments? Also, is it desirable to have constitutional change likely to give greater power to the judiciary? Some argue that, in reviewing administrative decisions, the courts are already inclined to interfere in political disputes and should not be encouraged to extend this to the review of legislative decisions: political decisions should be made by democratically elected politicians, not by judges.

The House of Lords in 1979 did in fact approve a Bill proposed by the Liberal peer Lord Wade, that sought to incorporate the European Convention in United Kingdom law and provide a compromise which both enabled the United Kingdom to give better effect to its existing obligations under the Convention, and respond positively to the domestic movement for the greater protection of human rights. However the Bill failed to receive government support in the House of Commons. It remains to be seen therefore whether future decisions of the European Court of Human Rights will influence government thinking in favour of incorporating the Convention.

References
1) See Beddard, *Human Rights and Europe*, 2nd edn, 1980.
2) See Jaconelli, *Enacting a Bill of Rights, the Legal Problems*, 1980.

UNIVERSITY OF LONDON
INTERMEDIATE EXAMINATION IN LAWS 1987
for External Students

CONSTITUTIONAL LAW

Thursday, 11 June: 10.00 am to 1.00 pm

Answer FIVE of the following NINE questions

1 To what extent, if any, do you agree with the statement that 'conventions constitute probably the most discussed and least definable source of the constitution' (Norton).

2 What difference, if any, would reforming the electoral system make to the British constitution?

3 Parliament wishes to promote affirmative action and decides to allow women to be paid more than men for the same work. It passes the Turning the Tables Act 1987, s1 of which states:
   'This Act is to be given effect notwithstanding any decision of the European Court of Justice or any provisions of Community law or any provisions of the European Communities Act 1972.'
   Would a British judge still give primacy to Community law if this new Act came into conflict with it?

4 What contribution, if any, does the House of Lords make to the British constitution?

5 One of the most difficult constitutional problems today is striking a balance between central government control and local government autonomy. Discuss.

6 To what extent, if any, did the House of Lords in the *Council of Civil Service Unions* v *Minister for the Civil Service* (GCHQ case) change the role of the judges in reviewing the royal prerogative?

7 When, and in what circumstances, will judges quash administrative decisions?

8 What difference, if any, has the Public Order Act 1986 made to English law?

9 What differences, if any, would incorporation of the European Convention on Human Rights into British law, make to the British constitution?

QUESTION 1

General Comment

A relatively difficult question. Unless you can deal with the specific point raised concerning the definition of conventions you should not attempt this question. The danger with such a question is that your answer becomes too general and there is the temptation to fill it out by simply producing a list of conventions.

Skeleton Solution

Introduction – what are conventions of the constitution?

The difficulty of defining conventions. The lack of written form; their political nature; lack of legal form; effect of disagreement; absence of pre-existing usage; flexibility.

Why conventions are discussed. Distinction between law and convention; why conventions are obeyed; the advantage of conventions over legal rules.

Suggested Solution

A great many of the rules of the British constitution, which are observed by the sovereign, the Prime Minister, Ministers, Members of Parliament, the judiciary and civil servants, are not contained in Acts of Parliament or judicial decisions, but are to be found in those rules of conduct called constitutional conventions. These have been described as 'rules of constitutional behaviour which are considered to be binding by and upon those who operate the constitution but which are not enforced by the law courts... nor by the presiding officers in the Houses of Parliament.' (1) These conventions of the constitution are obeyed by those to whom they apply not because of the threat of any legal sanction in case of breach, but because of the political difficulties which may follow if they are not obeyed.

Some conventional rules are very well known and have great authority but many others have been developed on a very informal basis so as to avoid the sort of strictness one usually associates with changes in the law. This informality associated with conventions of the constitution often means that, while some may be publicly recorded, others are not formulated in writing, having simply evolved as practice over a period of time. It is for this reason that at a given moment in time it may be impossible to ascertain whether practice on a certain matter has crystallised into a conventional rule. This, together with the fact that they operate in a political context, often means that disputes may arise about the existence and content of conventional rules. Whereas disputes about the existence and content of legal rules are settled by judicial decisions, no formal judicial mechanism exists to settle disputes concerning conventional rules.

Problems may arise therefore when attempting to identify conventional rules. By their definition conventions of the constitution are forms of political behaviour based upon usage and regarded as obligatory, but at the same time lacking legal sanction. But when or how does such a non binding usage become binding? One answer is of course that usage becomes binding because those to whom the usage applies consider that there is an obligation on their part to continue to behave in that way. But the dominant motive is not always apparent. Is the usage obeyed out of a sense of obligation or for some other reason? Also, what if there is substantial disagreement as to the existence or content of a convention. Political expediency or personal prejudice may result in divided interpretations of the obligation, if any, to be assumed. Certainly the opinions of politicians may differ as to the scope of the conventions they should observe. The fact that conventions may be created without any evidence of pre-existing usage also results in problems of identification.

Their non-legal nature also means that conventions are very flexible in the sense that they may lose their binding force or undergo a change in content without the need for any formal mechanism being followed. Conventions established by express agreement may be superseded or changed by agreement. Decisions taken by the Prime Minister or the Cabinet about the way Cabinet is to operate, for example, may be superseded by new decisions. Changes in circumstance may result in a convention losing its force, or indeed, the fact that a convention has been disregarded with impunity. Other conventions disappear with general acquiescence.

It is therefore probably true to say that conventions constitute the least definable source of the constitution. They are also probably the most discussed source especially as regards their interrelationship with the legal rules of the constitution. The differences between law and convention, the reasons why conventions are obeyed, whether or not conventions should be codified as law and the attitudes of the courts towards conventions are all matters which have occupied constitutional writers for many years and no doubt will continue to do so into the future.

Reference
1) Marshall & Moodie, *Some Problems of the Constitution*, 5th edn, (1971) pp22–23.

QUESTION 2

General Comment

This is a very straightforward question involving discussion of the present electoral system and the effect reform would have on the British constitution.

Skeleton Solution

Introduction. The operation of the relative majority system.

The problems with the present system. Parliamentary seats not allocated on a proportional basis; discrimination against small parties; wastage of votes; problems with constituency size.

The advantages of the present system. Simplicity; results in strong government; constituency link with MP.

Effect of reform. Loss of the advantages of the present system; election of a Parliament but not a government.

Suggested Solution

Under the present parliamentary electoral system the United Kingdom is divided into 650 parliamentary constituencies, each of which returns a single member to the House of Commons. Each elector may vote for one candidate only and the successful candidate is the one who receives the highest number of valid votes in the constituency. This system of 'first past the post' is known as the simple majority system as wherever there are more than two candidates in a constituency, the successful candidate need not have received an absolute majority of votes, but simply a majority over the runner-up. This system has the advantage of being very simple, but as a means of providing representation of the electorate in Parliament it is very crude. It is a system which, according to its critics, is not truly democratic and one which has several inherent disadvantages, which, it is argued, can only be overcome by reform.

Certainly any reform of the present electoral system will seek to remedy the major problem that at present the system does not ensure that the distribution of seats in the House of Commons is in any way proportionate to the national distribution of votes.

There is no consistent relationship between the number of votes cast nationally for a political party and the seats which they obtain. This is well illustrated by the June 1983 election results. The Conservative Party polled 42.4 per cent of the votes cast and won 397 seats. The Labour Party polled 27.6 per cent of the votes cast and won 209 seats. But the Liberal/SDP Alliance polled 25.4 per cent of the votes cast and won only 23 seats. The Alliance therefore was under-represented in relation to their national vote, while the Conservative Government achieved the largest parliamentary majority since the war, but received one of the smallest percentages of votes cast. Under this system a Conservative vote thus carried more weight than an Alliance vote.

This tendency of the system to exaggerate the representation of the large parties and reduce that of the smaller parties leads to the allegation that the present electoral system makes no provision for the representation of minority interests. It discriminates against the smaller parties whose support is evenly spread throughout the country rather than being concentrated in particular constituencies. Votes for the smaller parties are, in effect, wasted votes. It doesn't matter whether the person elected has one more or twenty thousand more votes than his nearest rival. So where there are more than two candidates a person may be elected by less than 50 per cent of the total votes cast in that constituency. The votes for the losing candidate have no parliamentary importance, they are in a sense wasted. This system, it is argued, perpetuates the two party system and helps destroy any possibility of consensus politics in the United Kingdom.

A further problem arises from the constituency basis of the present system. If votes are to carry equal weight throughout the country each constituency must be of equal size. The size of each constituency is determined by the Boundary Commissioners who keep the situation under constant review and try to ensure that each constituency has the same number of voters in it. However disparity does exist between constituency populations and as a result the weight of your vote may vary according to where you live.

Reforming the electoral system would therefore help remove these problems and help achieve fairer representation for all political parties in the House of Commons. But it must always be remembered that the present electoral system has considerable advantages and that these advantages may be lost as a result of any reform. For example the voting procedure itself is very simple and easy to understand, ensuring quick results. The outcome of the election is known within a matter of hours of the close of poll. The system also ensures a close link between the Member of Parliament and his constituency. The constituents know who their parliamentary representative is and can approach him with their problems. He in turn will serve their interests, in the knowledge that their continued support is necessary if he is to be re-elected.

But the major advantage claimed for the present system is its tendency to produce an absolute majority of seats in the House of Commons for one party. The function of a general election is to elect a government as well as a parliament and the present system does precisely that, producing strong government. The United Kingdom system avoids the problems, often found in European countries, which use different electoral systems, of coalition or minority governments which can find it difficult to govern effectively because of their unstable electoral position.

Despite these advantages there is a case for reforming the electoral system so as to secure better representation of minority parties and a distribution of seats which bears some relation to the votes cast, the most favoured alternative systems being the alternative vote system, the party list system and the single transferable vote system. The adoption of any one of these systems would bring about changes to the British constitution which, while welcomed by some, would be abhorrent to others.

The major result of adopting these systems is that they will help achieve legislative representation which accords with the relative electoral strengths of the political parties. Minority parties and independent candidates will therefore stand a better chance of election and the number of wasted votes will be reduced. But while these systems may to an extent maintain a local basis for representation, they may weaken the link between members of Parliament and constituents. These systems of election are also complex. Most important, however, is the likely result that the traditional two party system may be destroyed. To some of course this may be no bad thing but, if the European experience is repeated and one party is less likely to secure an absolute majority of seats in the House of Commons, this will lead to minority or coalition governments giving smaller parties political importance out of all proportion to their popular support. Such a system of government is totally alien to the British tradition.

QUESTION 3

General Comment

A relatively simple question concerning the effect of membership of the European Communities on the sovereignty of the Westminster Parliament.

Skeleton Solution

Introduction. The European Communities Act 1972.

The principles of direct applicability and the supremacy of Community law over national rules. Section 2(1) and s2(4) of the European Communities Act 1972.

The sovereignty of Parliament. Express repeal and the doctrine of implied repeal. Effect of Community law.

Effect of parliamentary legislation expressly contrary to Community law. *Macarthys Ltd* v *Wendy Smith*.

The position with regard to the Turning the Tables Act 1987.

Suggested Solution

The United Kingdom became a member of the European Communities with effect from 1 January 1973, by virtue of the Treaty of Accession 1972. For the Treaty of Accession and the Community treaties and law to have legal effect in the United Kingdom it was necessary for Parliament to pass legislation incorporating them into domestic law. This was achieved by the European Communities Act 1972.

The legal regime of the European Community is founded upon the principles of direct applicability rules over conflicting national rules. Certain rules of Community law contained both in the treaties and in regulations made by the Council or the Commission are directly applicable in that, of their own force, they create legal rights and duties enforceable in municipal courts Community law also forms part of the national law of every member state. The European Court of Justice has held that Community law prevails over national law to the extent that they are inconsistent with one another. These two principles are given effect in the law of the

United Kingdom by virtue of s2(1) and s2(4) of the European Communities Act 1972.

By virtue of s2(4) of the European Communities Act 1972 therefore all United Kingdom legislation shall only take effect to the extent that it is consistent with Community law however clearly it may appear from the United Kingdom legislation that it is intended to have effect notwithstanding any Community law to the contrary. It is clear both from the treaty and from statements made by the European Court of Justice that Community law should prevail over national law in all circumstances. Any United Kingdom constitutional law doctrine of the legislative sovereignty of Parliament is irrelevant. This approach taken by the European Court of Justice runs completely contrary to the traditional doctrine of the sovereignty of Parliament as enunciated in *Vauxhall Estates Ltd v Liverpool Corporation* (1) and *Ellen Street Estates v Minister of Health* (2). Certainly the doctrine of implied repeal as set out in *Ellen Street Estates v Minister of Health*, that later United Kingdom legislation always, by implication, repeals earlier legislative provisions with which it is inconsistent, would not survive.

But what about the situation such as that under the Turning the Tables Act 1987, where Parliament legislates expressly contrary to Community law. In such a case it may be possible to treat s2(4) as amounting to a rule of interpretation that there shall be a presumption that the United Kingdom Parliament, in passing legislation, intends to legislate consistently with Community law. This approach allows that if the United Kingdom Parliament were to make it clear in a piece of legislation that it intended to legislate contrary to Community law or that it intended the legislation to take effect notwithstanding any provision of Community law to the contrary, then the United Kingdom legislation would prevail over the inconsistent Community law. This is the approach that was favoured by the Court of Appeal in *Macarthys Ltd v Wendy Smith* (3). A man had been employed as a stockroom keeper at £60 per week. Subsequently a woman was employed in this position at £50 per week. She took the matter to an industrial tribunal on the grounds that this was contrary to law. Two questions arose. Firstly was this contrary to article 119 of the Treaty of Rome which provides that each member state shall ensure and maintain the application of the principle that men and women should receive equal pay for equal work. Secondly, in the event of a conflict between the United Kingdom legislation and article 119 of the Treaty, which should prevail in English courts?

In the Court of Appeal Lord Denning MR felt that if there were a conflict between the United Kingdom legislation and article 119 of the Treaty, article 119 should prevail since this is required by s2(1) and s2(4) of the European Communities Act 1972. Lord Denning here assumed that Parliament, when it passes legislation, intends to fulfil its obligations under the treaty. But he felt that if the time should come when Parliament deliberately passes an Act with the intention of repudiating the treaty or any provision in it or intentionally of acting inconsistently with it and says so in express terms, then it would be the duty of the United Kingdom courts to follow the statute of Parliament. But unless there is such an intentional and express repudiation of the treaty, it is the duty of the United Kingdom courts to give priority to the treaty.

Thus Lord Denning put forward the view that if Parliament in an Act stated an express intention to legislate contrary to Community law or notwithstanding Community law, then in that one situation the United Kingdom court would give preference to the United Kingdom legislation over the Community law.

This amounts to a retention of the doctrine of express repeal of earlier law by later legislation, but involves the abandonment of the doctrine of implied repeal as far as Community law is concerned. In this approach it is neither consistent with the traditional United Kingdom doctrine of the sovereignty of Parliament, nor with the Community doctrine of the supremacy of Community law over national rules. However, it is yet to be seen how the United Kingdom courts would act if faced with a United Kingdom Act of Parliament expressing an intention of Parliament to legislate contrary to Community law. Regarding the Turning the Tables Act 1987 therefore the position is far from clear. The court may be inclined to uphold the express wish of Parliament and give effect to the Act notwithstanding article 119 of the Treaty of Rome. However the European Court of Justice would almost certainly declare this to be invalid and hold that s1 of the 1987 Act amounts to a blatant repudiation by the United Kingdom of its international obligations under the European Community Treaties.

References

1) *Vauxhall Estates Ltd* v *Liverpool Corporation* [1932] 1 KB 733.
2) *Ellen Street Estates Ltd* v *Minister of Health* [1934] 1 KB 590.
3) *Macarthys Ltd* v *Wendy Smith* [1981] 1 All ER 111.

QUESTION 4

General Comment

The annual House of Lords question. The question involves discussion of the role of the House of Lords as the second chamber in our bicameral parliamentary system and the effects to the constitution which would arise if the lords were not there.

Skeleton Solution

Introduction. General position of the House of Lords within the constitution.

The role of the House of Lords. The work of the Judicial Committee; role of the House as a revision chamber for public Bills; role of Lords as a check on the Executive.

Effects on the British constitution if the House of Lords abolished. Need for change in House of Commons procedure; need for written constitution.

Suggested Solution

The House of Lords is the second chamber in our bicameral parliamentary system. To its critics, the House of Lords as presently constituted is undemocratic, out-dated and unsuitable in a modern society. Many therefore favour reform, so that for example its composition becomes more democratic. Others, however, wish to go further still and see the total abolition of the House of Lords. But those in favour of abolition fail to realise that the House of Lords makes a valuable contribution to the British constitution. Despite the problems regarding its composition, the fact remains that the House of Lords does perform a valuable service within the present parliamentary system and if abolished many of its functions would still have to be performed by some other body, presumably the House of Commons. In 1965, the Government White Paper 'House of Lords Reform' referred to seven functions of the House of Lords. An examination of each of these functions serves to illustrate the contribution made by the House to the effective working of our constitution and highlight some of the problems that might result if the House of Lords ceased to exist.

Firstly, the House of Lords acts as the final court of appeal for the whole of the United Kingdom in civil cases and for England, Wales and Northern Ireland in criminal cases. The judicial work of the House is separate from its other functions and only involves the Judicial Committee, drawn from the Lord High Chancellor, the Lords of Appeal in Ordinary and Lords who hold or who have held high judicial office. Nevertheless it is extremely valuable to have the senior judiciary present in the legislature and able to contribute during the passing of Bills. Of course, if the House of Lords did not exist a new 'supreme court' would have to be established to take its place, unless of course the Court of Appeal were to become the final appeal court for England and Wales.

Secondly, the House of Lords provides a forum for free debate on matters of public interest, Wednesday in particular being traditionally set aside for special debate on a wide range of subjects. Apart from the fact that these debates are usually of a very high standard, a standard that would perhaps never be reached in the Commons, even if the time were available, their loss would not pose any great constitutional problem.

Thirdly, and perhaps most importantly, the House acts as a revising chamber for public Bills brought from the House of Commons. About one half of the time of the House of Lords is devoted to the consideration of public Bills. The majority of this time is spent on revising Bills which have already passed the Commons, where the great majority of government legislation is introduced. The House of Commons does not have the time to fully debate all the legislation it has to pass each session and the use of procedures for the curtailment of debate, such as the guillotine, often means that Bills are passed by the Commons without really being considered at all. A second chamber is therefore required to examine and revise such Bills. This is the greatest contribution made by the House of Lords to the British constitution and it is probably true to say that as far as this particular function is concerned, if the House of Lords did not exist then it would have to be invented. If the House ceased to exist then the procedures of the House of Commons for enacting legislation would have to be changed if the present standard and volume of legislation were to be maintained. This could be achieved by membership of the House of Commons becoming full-time and by making even more use of committees. However, even then the volume of legislation may still prove to be too great, necessitating either a shortening of the procedure by which a Bill is enacted or making more use of subordinate legislation, which some would argue is already over used as it is. Certainly some fundamental changes would have to be made to the procedures of the House of Commons.

Also it must be remembered that the House of Commons, because of the distortion produced by our electoral system, is largely controlled by a government which does not represent even 50 per cent of the electorate. A second chamber is thus required to at least delay substantially controversial legislation which may be unpopular with the majority of the people of the country. If the House of Lords were not there then the only way to control a government with an absolute majority in the House of Commons may be to have either a written constitution or a Bill of Rights containing entrenched clauses, perhaps requiring a referendum for amendment. Recent experience has shown that the House of Lords, with its independent membership, is the only check that exists on the present Conservative government and frequent defeats have been inflicted by their Lordships, thus helping to weaken executive control of the legislature.

The House of Lords also initiates public Bills. While the more controversial and important Bills almost invariably begin in the House of Commons, Bills which are relatively uncontroversial in party political terms are regularly introduced in the House of Lords. If the House did not exist these Bills would have to be dealt with by the Commons thus adding to its already overburdened workload. Similarly, the subordinate legislation and the private legislation at present dealt with by the House of Lords would also fall to be wholly dealt with by the Commons if the second chamber did not exist.

It can be seen therefore that the House of Lords makes a very great contribution to the effective and efficient working of the British constitution.

QUESTION 5

General Comment

A very topical question concerning the conflict between central and local democracy.

Skeleton Solution

Introduction. Unitary nature of the United Kingdom; the role of local government.

Central government control of local authorities. Finance; regulations; inspection; default powers; abolition.

The reasons for conflict. Maintenance of national standards; national economic policy.

Relationship between central and local government. Partnership or central dominance; problem of conflict of democracies.

Suggested Solution

Although the United Kingdom is a unitary state there is a highly developed system of local government. The organs of local government serve two broad purposes. Firstly, they enable many public services to be administered at a level nearer the people for the benefit of whom the service is provided. Secondly, they enable local political opinion to be organised and expressed. Local authorities, however, although representative bodies chosen by popular election, have not the autonomy of Parliament; indeed they are dependent upon Parliament for their powers.

The powers of local authorities derive either expressly or by implication from statute and they are exercised subject to the doctrine of ultra vires. The application of these rules in disputed cases is a matter for the courts and no local authority can determine the extent of its own powers. But within the limits of its powers, and subject to the performance of any statutory duties laid upon it, a local authority has a discretion in deciding how it is to administer the services for which it is responsible. In practice however this discretion is subject to many forms of direct and indirect pressure from central government and especially recently there has developed an increasing tendency for central government to restrict the freedom of local authorities to decide their own policies.

The array of local authority controls available to central government is formidable. Perhaps some of the most effective are those concerned with local authority finance. The services provided by local government will of course require expenditure and the two main sources of local authority finance to meet this expenditure are rates and grants from central government. But central government departments not only have the power to make grants but also to withhold them. They also have the power to control borrowing for capital projects. Most important today however is 'rate capping' whereby central government may set the maximum rate in the pound to be levied in any one year by any local authority designated by the Secretary of State.

As well as these powers over local authority finance, central government departments also have powers to prescribe rules for the conduct of local services. This may be achieved directly by regulations, or indirectly by the introduction of parliamentary legislation. Certain services, for example the police and education, are subject to central government inspection. Relevant central government departments also have the power to confirm or refuse to confirm by-laws, compulsory purchase orders, educational schemes, senior appointments etc, to conduct local inquiries under certain statutory powers and to entertain appeals in respect of certain local authority decisions, for example refusals of planning permission. Central government departments may also exercise default powers, by removing responsibility for the conduct of a service from one authority to another or by taking over responsibility for the service centrally or by issuing a mandatory order or obtaining from the courts an order of mandamus to compel the authority to carry out its statutory duties.

By its very nature therefore local government implies a measure of local self government. Local authorities do not operate as mere agents of central departments subject to the latter's full direction and control. But, because of central government's responsibility for national policies some of which, for example education and housing, depend completely upon local implementation, it is inevitable that claims have to be made by central government departments to supervise or control local authority activities, both for the overall maintenance of standards of service and reasons of national economic policy.

This relationship which results from these claims of central government and from the desire of local authorities for some autonomy is sometimes described as a partnership. However in reality it is central government that dominates the relationship. This is inevitable. Increasingly party politics is infiltrating local government and where the political composition of a local authority differs from that of the central government there is great scope for conflict. Local authorities are now responsible for the exercise of many powers and duties and spend vast sums of public money. They can therefore seriously frustrate the plans of the central government. But in any conflict it is usually the central government that wins. Central government controls Parliament and Parliament is supreme. Legislation may be enacted to control the functions of local authorities or even abolish authorities in some cases. Local authorities must not stand in the way of central government policy. But the problem is of course that local authorities are elected just as central government is elected and they too have their mandate. The great problem is striking a balance between these two conflicts of democracy.

QUESTION 6

General Comment

This question concerns the powers of the courts to review the prerogative acts of the Crown. Students should state the traditional powers of the courts in relation to the royal prerogative and then consider the implications of the GCHQ case. This is a very straightforward and relatively easy prerogative question, but knowledge of the GCHQ case is vital.

Skeleton Solution

Introduction. Definition and examples of the prerogative.

The traditional role of the courts in relation to the prerogative. The existence of the prerogative; its extent; who is entitled to its benefit; the effect of statute upon the prerogative; non-justiciability of a validly exercised prerogative.

The implications of the GCHQ case. Situations in which the House of Lords may be prepared to review a prerogative act.

Suggested Solution

According to Blackstone the prerogative is 'that special pre-eminence which the King has, over and above all other persons, and out of the ordinary course of the common law, in right of his royal dignity' (1). Today the prerogative consists mainly of a miscellaneous collection of residual executive governmental powers which are considered to be necessary to enable the government to function. These are powers enjoyed by the Crown but not by the subjects of the Crown and include, for example, the power to conduct foreign relations, to declare war and make peace, to regulate the disposition of the armed forces, to appoint and dismiss ministers, to dissolve Parliament, to assent to Bills, to grant honours etc. The prerogative also includes certain immunities and privileges, such as the Queen's personal immunity from suit or prosecution.

Generally, the executive derives its powers from two legal sources, statute and the prerogative. Where the Executive purports to act under powers conferred by statute, then, in the absence of any clause in the parent statute purporting to exclude the jurisdiction of the courts, the courts may review the action taken, and where necessary declare it void on the grounds of ultra vires or breach of natural justice. However, where the executive purports to act under the prerogative, and in so doing directly affects the rights of an individual, then traditionally the court's power is limited to the consideration of preliminary issues, namely the determination of the existence of the claimed prerogative and, if it is found to exist, its extent. This was for example the approach taken by the courts in such cases as *Attorney General* v *De Keyser's Royal Hotel* (2), and *Burmah Oil* v *Lord Advocate* (3). Once it is established that the conduct complained of is an exercise of the prerogative, the courts cannot challenge its use. The only 'remedy' the aggrieved individual has is a political remedy, for example by trying to have the matter raised in Parliament.

The role of the judiciary in relation to the prerogative has therefore been limited to the consideration of preliminary issues. With regard to the existence of a purported prerogative act the court's main task is to ensure that no new prerogatives are created. Only those prerogatives already recognised at common law will be upheld. As Diplock LJ said in *BBC* v *Johns* (4):

> 'It is 350 years and a civil war too late for the Queen's courts to broaden the prerogative. The limits within which the executive government may impose obligations or restraints on the citizens of the United Kingdom without any statutory authority are now well settled and incapable of extension'.

If the prerogative claimed is found to exist then the court will next consider its extent.

Once it is established that the act complained of is an exercise of the prerogative the traditional view was that the courts cannot challenge its use. They can, however, seek to contain its exercise in accordance with common law principles. For example the courts can consider whether the body or person purporting to act under the prerogative is entitled to the benefit of the prerogative. To be entitled to the benefit of the prerogative the person or body concerned must be entitled by statute or otherwise to benefit from the privileges, rights or immunities of the Crown. The court must also consider whether the existence or exercise of the prerogative power has been affected by statute. For example the Crown Proceedings Act 1947 abolishes the immunity of the Crown from being sued in contract and tort, while leaving the personal immunity of the Sovereign intact. The prerogative may not, however, be impliedly abolished by statute. In such cases the prerogative is merely placed in abeyance and if the statute is repealed the prerogative will be revived. If a statute does conflict with a prerogative without expressly abolishing the prerogative, the courts must give effect to the statute and treat the prerogative as being in abeyance – see *Attorney-General* v *De Keyser's Royal Hotel*. However, a statute which conflicts with a prerogative may expressly provide that the prerogative be left intact. For example, s33(5) of the Immigration Act 1971 provides that the powers conferred under the Act should be additional to any prerogative powers. Finally, the courts must consider whether the prerogative imposes a duty on the Crown to compensate the subject for damage caused by its exercise, as for example was the case in *Burmah Oil* v *Lord Advocate*.

So while the courts were prepared to consider the existence and the extent of a purported prerogative power they traditionally declined to go any further and review the merits of the actual exercise of the prerogative. However, recent cases indicate a shift in favour of granting judicial review in respect of the exercise of the prerogative in certain circumstances. This view, first expressed by Lord Denning MR in *Laker Airways* v *Department of Trade* (5), that the courts can intervene where a prerogative discretion is exercised improperly was recently considered by the House of Lords in *Council for Civil Service Unions* v *Minister for the Civil Service* (6), where their Lordships were called upon to consider whether the courts had the power to review, on the grounds of procedural irregularity, an instruction made in the exercise of a power conferred under the royal prerogative. Their Lordships were of the opinion that simply because a decision-making power was derived from a common law and not a statutory source it should not, for that reason only, be immune from judicial review.

According to Lord Diplock, judicial review had developed to a stage where one could classify under three heads the grounds on which administrative action was subject to control by judicial review: 'illegality, irrationality, and procedural impropriety'. As regards procedural impropriety, his Lordship saw no reason why it should not be a ground for judicial review of a decision made under powers of which the ultimate source was the prerogative.

However, Lord Roskill thought that the right of challenge could not be unqualified. It must depend upon the subject matter of the prerogative power that was exercised. Prerogative powers such as those relating to the making of treaties, the defence of the realm, the prerogative of mercy, the granting of honours, the dissolution of Parliament and the appointment of ministers, as well as others, were not, he thought, susceptible to judicial review because their nature and subject matter was such as not to be amenable to the judicial process. It was also pointed out that prerogative decisions would usually involve the application of government policy of which the courts were not the appropriate arbiters.

Their Lordships agreed therefore that executive action based on common law or the use of a prerogative power was not necessarily immune from review. This was especially so in the present case where the prerogative derived from an Order in Council, which was virtually indistinguishable from an order deriving from statute. In such cases the decision might be reviewed by the courts just as it would have been if it had rested on statutory powers.

Therefore the GCHQ Case, in theory at least, does seem to have changed the role of the judges in reviewing the Royal Prerogative in that the fact that the source of executive power is the prerogative and not statute will not necessarily deprive the citizen of the right of challenge as to the manner of its exercise, providing that the nature and subject matter of the particular prerogative in question are considered by the courts to be susceptible to judicial review.

References

1) Blackstone *Commentaries on the Laws of England.*
2) *Attorney-General* v *De Keyser's Royal Hotel* [1920] AC 508.
3) *Burmah Oil Company* v *Lord Advocate* [1965] AC 75.
4) *BBC* v *Johns* [1965] Ch 344.
5) *Laker Airways* v *Department of Trade* [1977] 2 All ER 182.
6) *Council for Civil Service Unions* v *Minister for the Civil Service* [1984] 3 WLR 1174.

QUESTION 7

General Comment

A rather general question concerning judicial review of administrative action.

Skeleton Solution

Introduction. Rules of the Supreme Court O.53.

Grounds for judicial review. Illegality; irrationality; procedural impropriety.

Suggested Solution

An application for an order of certiorari to quash an administrative decision is made by way of an application to the High Court for judicial review under O.53 of the Rules of the Supreme Court. The applicant must obtain leave of the court for his application to be heard and must establish the necessary locus standi, that is he must be shown to have a sufficient interest in the matter to which the application relates. If the court is satisfied as to the merits of the applicant's case and providing that the locus standi requirement is satisfied, it may then consider the substantive grounds on which judicial review may be exercised.

Generally speaking executive action will be the subject of judicial review on three separate grounds. The first is where the authority concerned has been guilty of an error of law in its action, as for example purporting to exercise a power which in law it does not possess. The second is where it exercises a power in so unreasonable a manner that the exercise becomes open to review under the principles set out by Lord Greene MR in the case of *Associated Provincial Picture Houses Ltd* v *Wednesbury Corporation* (1). The third is where it has acted contrary to what are often called the principles of natural justice. In the case of *Council of Civil Service Unions* v *Minister for the Civil Service* (2) Lord Diplock devised a new nomenclature for each of these three grounds, calling them respectively 'illegality', 'irrationality' and 'procedural impropriety'.

By illegality as a ground for judicial review is meant that the decision maker must understand correctly the law that regulates his decision-making powers and must give effect to it. According to Lord Diplock, whether he has or not is a justiciable question to be decided, in the event of dispute, by those persons, the judges, by whom the judicial power of the state is exercisable. It is a fundamental principle of English law that no person or body should be permitted to exceed its lawful powers. The starting point for judicial review of administrative action therefore is the doctrine of ultra vires founded upon the doctrine of parliamentary sovereignty. Administrative authorities must be restrained from exceeding their powers and inferior tribunals must be prevented from exceeding the limits of their jurisdiction.

Ultra vires may be classified as being either substantive or procedural. Substantive ultra vires occurs where an administrative authority acts in excess of its statutory powers or in excess of its jurisdiction. As regards excess of power, it is the role of the court, by examining the parent Act, to determine the extent of the specific powers conferred upon the administrative authority by Parliament and ensure that those powers are not exceeded, an example being the case of *Attorney-General* v *Fulham Corporation* (3). As for excess of jurisdiction, all administrative authorities have limited jurisdictions. Where an authority acts in excess of its jurisdiction as laid down in the parent Act, its acts will be ultra vires and void.

Procedural ultra vires occurs where a statute not only creates a body to perform some task on behalf of the executive but in so doing also lays down a procedure that the body should follow in performing its functions. Where a procedural requirement is laid down in the parent Act, for example consultation with interested parties or the giving of notice, failure on the part of the administrative authority to follow that prescribed procedure may, depending upon the nature of the requirement, result in its decision being ultra vires.

The second ground for judicial review envisaged by Lord Diplock, that of 'irrationality', applies in his Lordship's view to a decision which is so outrageous in its defiance of logic or of accepted moral standards that no sensible person who had applied his mind to the question to be decided could have arrived at it. It is of course implied by the courts as a matter of statutory construction that Parliament did not intend the powers it has conferred upon an administrative authority to be abused and in particular the courts will always imply that Parliament did not intend the administrative authority to act unreasonably and will therefore render administrative action ultra vires. However, unreasonableness is a subjective concept and opinions can vary as to whether a particular decision is reasonable or not. Judicial review is concerned with the legality of decisions not their merits.

The courts therefore have given the word 'unreasonable' a somewhat specialised meaning in the context of administrative law. According to Lord Greene MR in the case of *Associated Provincial Picture Houses Ltd* v *Wednesbury Corporation* a decision may be ultra vires if it can be proved to be unreasonable in the sense that the court considers it to be a decision which no reasonable body could take. He said that a decision would be unreasonable if it failed to observe certain principles. A person entrusted with a discretion must direct himself properly in law. He must call his attention to the matters which he is bound to consider. Finally he must exclude from his consideration matters which are irrelevant to what he has to consider.

A growing number of decisions seem to illustrate that the courts are now willing to invalidate administrative action on the grounds that there is an absence of evidence to justify it. Also if a power is granted to an administrative authority for one purpose, it cannot be used to fulfil another purpose, the case of *Congreve* v *Home Office* being an example. The failure to exercise a discretionary power will also be ground for review. If an administrative authority upon which a power has been conferred delegates the right to exercise that power to another body, or fetters itself in the free exercise of that power, then its actions will be construed by the court as ultra vires and void. Fraud or bad faith will also render a decision open to review.

Lord Diplock described his third head on which administrative action is subject to control by judicial review as 'procedural impropriety'. His Lordship includes in this not only the failure to observe basic rules of natural justice but also the failure by an administrative tribunal to observe procedural rules that are expressly laid down in the legislative instrument by which its jurisdiction is conferred.

The rule that certain powers must be exercised in accordance with natural justice is one of the most important principles of judicial review of administrative action. The traditional view of natural justice is that it comprises two procedural rules. Firstly the rule that no man is to be condemned without a hearing. A person is entitled to notice of the case he has to meet and must be afforded a fair opportunity to answer the case against him and to present his own cause. People affected by judicial and administrative decisions have a right that the decision-maker should be impartial. Natural justice will therefore be breached where the person taking a decision has an interest in the case or where the person taking the decision is biased. Recently a third limb of natural justice has appeared, the so-called duty to act fairly. In many respects this duty encompasses both of the traditional rules, but it may possibly apply to a wider range of decisions. The precise requirements of natural justice will vary with the circumstances of each case, such as the nature of the decision being taken, the status and interest of the applicant, etc.

References

1) *Associated Provincial Picture Houses Ltd v Wednesbury Corporation* [1948] 1 KB 223.
2) *Council of Civil Service Unions v Minister for the Civil Service* [1984] 3 All ER 935.
3) *Attorney-General v Fulham Corporation* [1921] 1 Ch 440.

QUESTION 8

General Comment

A relatively straightforward question concerning the new Public Order Act. students should know the changes introduced by this Act and compare the new provisions with those existing at common law and under the Public Order Act 1936.

Skeleton Solution

Introduction. General provisions of the Public Order Act 1986.

Abolition of common law riot, rout, unlawful assembly and affray. Introduction of statutory riot, violent disorder and affray.

Provisions relating to processions. Sections 12 and 13.

Provisions relating to assemblies. Section 14.

Provisions relating to racial hatred.

Causing fear or provocation of violence. Causing harassment, alarm or distress.

Miscellaneous provisions.

Suggested Solution

The Public Order Act 1986 was passed on 7 November 1986. Some provisions of the Act came into force on 1 January 1987. Most of the rest of the Act came into force on 1 April 1987. The Act firstly repeals certain provisions of the Public Order Act 1936. Secondly it abolishes the common law offences of riot, rout, unlawful assembly and affray. Third, it introduces new statutory offences to replace some of the common law offences abolished or statutory offences repealed. Fourth, it amends or repeals other statutory provisions including those concerning racial hatred. Fifth, it introduces new powers in relation to offences committed at or in connection with football matches. Sixth, it introduces miscellaneous provisions in relation to tampering with goods on sale and also mass trespass.

One of the main differences made to the law under the new Act is that the ancient common law offences of riot, rout, unlawful assembly and affray have been abolished and replaced by three statutory offences: riot, violent disorder and affray. The basis of these offences is no longer breach of the peace but fear for personal safety on the part of a person of reasonable firmness present at the scene.

As regards the Public Order Act 1936 this is largely repealed. Section 3 has been repealed and replaced by a new provision of greater scope and effect and has been extended to certain public assemblies. As was already the case under the old 1936 Act, s12 of the 1986 Act gives the police the power to impose conditions on certain processions and under s13 the chief officer of police may in certain circumstances prohibit processions in his district. The major difference under the new Act however is that now the organisers of public processions must give advance notice in writing to the police not less than six clear days before the date of any procession which is intended to demonstrate support for or opposition to the views or actions of any person or body of persons; or publicises a cause or campaign; or which marks or commemorates an event.

Another new development under the 1986 Act is contained in s14 which confers a new power allowing a senior police officer to impose conditions in relation to public assemblies. Under this section, if the senior police officer, having regard to the time or place at which and the circumstances in which any public assembly is being held or is intended to be held, reasonably believes that (a) it may result in serious public disorder, serious damage to property or serious disruption to the life of the community, or (b) the purpose of the persons organising it is the intimidation of others with a view to compelling them not to do an act they have a right to do, or to do an act they have a right not to do, he may give directions imposing on the persons organising or taking part in the assembly such conditions as to the place at which the assembly may be (or continue to be) held, its maximum duration, or the maximum number of persons who may constitute it, as appear to him necessary to prevent such disorder, damage, disruption or intimidation. However there is still no power to ban an assembly. Section 16 defines 'public assembly' as an assembly of 20 or more persons in a public place which is wholly or partly open to the air.

Section 5A of the 1936 Act dealing with racial hatred has been restructured and amended to produce six new offences. Section 17 of the 1986 Act defines racial hatred as hatred against a group of persons in Great Britain defined by reference to colour, race, nationality (including citizenship) or ethnic or national origins. The Act creates six offences all of which require the consent of the

Attorney-General to institute proceedings. All of these offences concern conduct which is threatening, abusive or insulting and which is intended or which is likely, having regard to all the circumstances, to stir up racial hatred. They are: (i) using such words or behaviour or displaying such materials; (ii) publishing or distributing such materials; (iii) presenting or directing a public play which involves such words or behaviour; (iv) distributing, showing or playing a recording of such visual images or sounds; (v) certain participation in a broadcast or cable programme service which includes such images or sounds and; (vi) possessing such material or recordings with a view to its being displayed, published, distributed, broadcast or included in a cable broadcast service.

Section 5 of the 1936 Act has also been repealed, and replaced by two new offences. Section 4 of the 1986 Act creates the offence of causing fear or provocation of violence. A person is guilty of an offence if he uses towards another person threatening, abusive or insulting words or behaviour, or distributes or displays to another person any writing, sign or other visible representation which is threatening, abusive or insulting, with intent to cause that person to believe that immediate unlawful violence will be used against him or another by any person, or to provoke the immediate use of unlawful violence by that person or another, or whereby that person is likely to believe that such violence will be used or it is likely that such violence will be provoked.

Section 5 of the 1986 Act creates the controversial offence of causing harassment, alarm or distress. A person is guilty of an offence if he uses threatening, abusive or insulting words or behaviour, or disorderly behaviour, or displays any writing, sign or other visible representation which is threatening, abusive or insulting, within the hearing or sight of a person likely to be caused harassment, alarm or distress thereby. Section 5 provides for three specific defences. First, that the defendant had no reason to believe that there was anyone within hearing or sight of his or her conduct who was likely to be harassed, alarmed or distressed; second, that he or she was inside a dwelling and had no reason to believe that the conduct would have been seen or heard by anyone outside; third, that his or her conduct was reasonable.

The 1986 Act also creates several miscellaneous offences. Under s30 a court by or before which a person is convicted of an offence connected with football may make an exclusion order prohibiting him from entering premises to attend a prescribed football match. Section 38 creates various offences connected with contamination of or interference with goods. Finally, s39 gives the most senior police officer present power to direct trespassers to leave land. The officer may arrest anyone who, knowing that such a direction has been given, fails to leave as soon as is reasonably practicable or, having left, re-enters within three months of the direction.

QUESTION 9

General Comment

The question of incorporating the European Convention on Human Rights into British law is very topical. Although this question is phrased rather generally students should concentrate on the effects of incorporation on the sovereignty of Parliament and the role of the judiciary in interpreting and enforcing a Bill of Rights in the United Kingdom.

Skeleton Solution

Introduction. The need for a Bill of Rights.

Mechanism for incorporation of the European Convention on Human Rights into United Kingdom law.

Effects of incorporation on the constitution. The sovereignty of Parliament; the role of the judiciary.

Suggested Solution

Recently there have been increasing demands for the enactment of a Bill of Rights in the United Kingdom to safeguard the fundamental rights and freedoms of the individual. As the Executive becomes more powerful, controlling the legislature and interfering more and more in the lives of the citizen, some protection it is argued becomes necessary. The state has become prosecutor and judge in its own cause. Because of this the common law negative freedoms we enjoy are under constant attack and the judges are powerless to check the legislative supremacy of that agent of the executive, Parliament. In most countries there is a written constitution which is not just a sacred piece of paper but a statement that the people are the ultimate source of power, that the state and its legislature and its civil servants and laws are the servants of the people. It is argued that the enactment of a Bill of Rights in the United Kingdom will help to reassert the supremacy of the individual over the state.

To achieve this the simplest and perhaps most obvious answer is to look to the European Convention on Human Rights. The United Kingdom is a party to the Convention and successive

British governments both socialist and conservative have allowed citizens to petition the European Commission of Human Rights and seek enforcement of the rights and freedoms set out in the Convention in international law. Why not go one step further and incorporate the European Convention into domestic law so that its provisions may be enforced and applied by British judges in British courts? But if such incorporation did take place would it make any difference to the operation of the British constitution as regards the protection of fundamental rights and freedoms? Probably not.

This is because the enactment of a Bill of Rights in the United Kingdom involves the consideration of a theoretically insurmountable problem, the sovereignty of Parliament. A Bill of Rights is a piece of paper. It has no practical value unless it can be enforced against those having the power to take away the rights and freedoms of the citizen. But the United Kingdom Parliament is sovereign. There are no legal restraints on its legislative powers. This absence of legal restraint has three aspects: Parliament is legally competent to legislate upon any subject matter; no Parliament can bind its successors or be bound by its predecessors; and once Parliament has legislated no court or other person can pass judgment upon the validity of the legislation.

Parliament may therefore make or unmake any law. There is no area or subject matter outside the scope of its legislative powers. Parliament is also unable to limit its own legislative powers for the future. Parliament cannot bind its successors and a later Parliament is always, in theory at least, able to expressly repeal the legislation made by an earlier Parliament. Also, under the doctrine of implied repeal as expressed in *Vauxhall Estates* v *Liverpool Corporation* (1) the provisions of an earlier Act can always be repealed by implication by provisions in a later Act which are inconsistent with those in the earlier Act. Further, in *Ellen Street Estates Ltd* v *Minister of Health* (2) it was also held that Parliament cannot, by a statement in an earlier Act, effectively provide that the provisions of that Act cannot be repealed by implication by inconsistent provisions in a later Act. The role of the courts is also limited with regard to Acts of Parliament. For example the case of *Pickin* v *British Railways Board* (3) illustrates the point that once it is established that an Act has received the consent of the House of Commons, the assent of the House of Lords (or that it has been passed under the provisions of the Parliament Acts 1911–1949), and the assent of the Sovereign all the courts can do is apply it subject to their limited powers of statutory interpretation.

It can be seen therefore that even if the present Parliament enacts a Bill of Rights for the United Kingdom a later Parliament intent on restricting or abolishing the rights and freedoms contained in it may do so either by express enactment or even impliedly by the enactment of a later statute which conflicts with its provisions. The courts will be powerless to intervene. So long as Parliament remains sovereign there can be no entrenchment of legislation against future amendment or repeal. Only Parliament can limit its own sovereignty and such limitations must have been enacted in the form of statute. However no Parliament can bind its successors. Therefore whatever limitations are imposed upon the sovereignty of Parliament by one statute may be repealed by a subsequent Act. Therefore in theory at least it may be true to say that even if enacted, a Bill of Rights could be repealed tomorrow and the existence of the Bill will make no difference to this aspect of our constitution.

However in theory there are means by which limitations can be placed upon the sovereignty of Parliament. For example some statutes such as the Statute of Westminster 1931 contain limitations as to the scope and subject matter of parliamentary legislation. Others such as the Colonial Laws Validity Act 1865 contain limitations as to the manner and form of future legislation. The real check upon the sovereignty of Parliament however in practice remains public opinion. The government knows that it will have to face a General Election within a few years and this stark reality may have a restraining effect upon their legislative proposals and deter any attempted government tampering with the Bill of Rights. Of course these informal restraints are present and operating already to curtail Executive power and in this respect the presence of a Bill of Rights will make little difference.

One difference that would be made to the British constitution by the incorporation of the European Convention on Human Rights into British law concerns the role of the judiciary. A Bill of Rights would involve a shift of power from elected and accountable members of Parliament to judges who are neither elected nor accountable. These judges will be involved not just in making interim policy choices about what the law should be, pending action by the legislature, but in making final policy choices which some would argue they cannot be trusted to do. It will turn judges into legislators. Judges whose job it is to know and apply the law will be asked to create and form the law. In this respect it may be doubted that British court procedure is the best environment in which to thoroughly analyse the kind of problematic political questions such a Bill of Rights will raise.

References
1) *Vauxhall Estates Ltd* v *Liverpool Corporation* [1932] 1 KB 733.
2) *Ellen Street Estates Ltd* v *Minister of Health* [1934] 1 KB 590.
3) *Pickin* v *British Railways Board* [1974] AC 765.

UNIVERSITY OF LONDON
INTERMEDIATE EXAMINATION IN LAWS 1988
for External Students

CONSTITUTIONAL LAW

Friday, 17 June: 10.00 am to 1.00 pm

Answer *FOUR* of the following SEVEN questions

1 'The House of Lords is becoming more and more important in the legislative process. It is the House of Commons which really needs reform.'
  Discuss.

2 Assess the impact of the *Council of Civil Service Unions* v *Minister for the Civil Service* (1984) upon the justiciability of prerogative decision making.

3 'The principle of collective responsibility requires from each Minister a full and whole-hearted acceptance of the measures decided on by the Cabinet and of the policies underlying them' (Lord Wilson).
  Discuss the purpose and nature of this rule.

4 'Phrases like "the separation of powers" and " the rule of law" have no application to the British Constitution which rests solely on the principle of parliamentary sovereignty.'
  Discuss.

5 'Since we have no written constitution which fixes the boundary between central and local government, it can be shifted by the actions of successive governments.'
  Discuss.

6 Critically assess the following statement that 'the case for a Bill of Rights rests on the the belief that it would make a distinct and valuable contribution to the better protection of human rights.'

7 A University Law Faculty has 100 places for its LLB course but receives 2,000 applications. The Sub-Dean for Admissions asks her secretary to choose the 100 candidates with the best 'O' Level results. The secretary does this by looking at the

application forms. The Sub-Dean then writes to the unsuccessful applicants saying that 'after the most careful consideration, we have reluctantly decided not to offer you a place. If you would like to discuss this with me, please arrange an appointment through my secretary.' All 1,900 disappointed applicants try to arrange appointments. The Sub-Dean writes again to withdraw her offer to meet applicants because of 'pressure of work'. She adds that 'applicants have no right to a hearing before or after a decision to refuse them admission.'

Have there been any breaches of the principles of administrative law?

QUESTION 1

General Comment

Despite a first impression to the contrary this is not a question requiring in-depth consideration of reform of the Lords, but does require some consideration of the changes in the nature of the work done by the House of Lords. Detail needs to be provided of the contribution made by the House of Lords, and also the current proposals for reform of the House of Commons.

Skeleton Solution

Brief history of House of Lords decline and rise – consider powers of the upper house – impact of Thatcher years – guillotine – amendment powers – reform of the House of Commons – accommodation – hours – proceedings – conclusion.

Suggested Solution

The importance of the House of Lords as a constitutional institution has declined since the latter half of the nineteenth century, as the importance and dominance of the House of Commons has increased. The House of Lords has for centuries recognised the privileges of the House of Commons in respect of financial matters, and with the enactment of the Parliament Act 1911, its power to delay legislation passed by the House of Commons was effectively reduced to 25 months. The Parliament Act 1949 reduced this period even further to one of 13 months.

In the post war era the House of Lords came to be seen by many as something of an anachronism. Particular criticism was made of its hereditary membership, the absence of women, and its inherent Conservative bias. Reform was clearly necessary, and it came in the form of the Life Peerages Act 1958, and the Peerages Act 1963. The combined effect of these measures was to introduce life peers into the house (in addition to those who were already life peers appointed under the Appellate Jurisdiction Act 1876), and to increase significantly the number of women entitled to sit.

Many would contend that these measures went a long way towards revitalising the House of Lords as an important element in the constitution, giving it greater credibility as part of the legislative process, and broadening the range of expertise amongst the members of the house. Experience since 1958 has shown that it is from the ranks of 500 or so life peers who have been appointed, that the house has drawn its most valuable participants.

The importance of the House of Lords as regards the legislative process has undoubtedly grown since 1979. Since that year the country has been governed by successive conservative governments, each of which has enjoyed a healthy majority in the House of Commons. The result has been that the opposition parties have been left somewhat impotent in their efforts to challenge, delay or amend government proposals for legislation. It has thus fallen to the House of Lords, since 1979, to provide the government with really effective challenges to its legislative proposals.

An impotent opposition in the House of Commons is one likely to resort to 'wrecking' or 'timewasting' tactics, with the result that the government is likely to impose a time allocation order, or guillotine, on a Bill in the House of Commons to ensure that it passes through all its stages in the lower house in good time. The problem with guillotine orders is that any part of a Bill not considered before the time allotted for its consideration expires, has to be voted upon as it is. Hence the Bill may not be properly scrutinised by the House of Commons, prior to its being sent up to the House of Lords. The guillotine motion was relied upon as many times between 1979–1985, as it had been in the preceding 20 years. There is no guillotine motion in the House of Lords, thus any matters not fully considered by the House of Commons can be scrutinised for as long as is necessary.

More generally, the House of Lords can use its powers to amend certain types of legislation sent up from the House of Commons, and to delay the passage of legislation to allow more time for debate outside Parliament. Again, given the current balance of power within the House of Commons, it would appear that the House of Lords has been more and more prepared to stand up to the government and reject legislative measures that are seen as going too far. As evidence of this it is worthy of note that between 1979 and October 1986, the House of Lords inflicted 100 defeats on successive Conservative governments.

As regards which house of Parliament is in the greater need of reform it is difficult to say. There have certainly been more attempts at reform of the House of Lords in recent years, but many of these might be seen as being politically motivated, rather that being based upon any pragmatic research. There are undoubtedly certain aspects of the work of the House of Commons that might be seen as ripe for reform.

The accommodation provided for backbench MPs and opposition members is frequently criticised as inadequate, many members having to share rooms, one or two, such as Ken Livingstone, having no room at all. The use of nearby buildings to take the 'overflow' is not an ideal solution. The hours of work within the House of Commons are frequently criticised, with all-night sittings playing havoc not only with the health of members, but also their domestic lives.

The reliance upon the whip system in debates in the Commons ensures that the outcome of debates is usually a forgone conclusion, forcing members to fire rhetoric and propaganda at each other, rather than using their oratorical skills to persuade others to agree with a particular viewpoint.

More generally the behaviour of members in the House of Commons does not always reach the levels of courtesy and politeness that one would wish to see in the nation's legislative chamber. In this respect the introduction of the televising of proceedings in the House of Commons can only be a positive change. Either the country will see MPs as they really are, and quite possibly be appalled at times, or the presence of the cameras will have a salutary effect on standards of behaviour.

In many of these matters listed above, the House of commons could usefully learn from the lead already shown by the House of Lords.

In conclusion, it can be said that whilst the House of Lords has undoubtedly become more important in the legislative process in recent years, whether it remains so will depend largely on the composition of the House of Commons in the future. As regards reform, whilst the House of Commons would doubtless benefit from some reforms, it should not be assumed that the same could not equally be said of the House of Lords.

QUESTION 2

General Comment

A question requiring a brief explanation of the nature of prerogative power, the traditional approach of the courts, and the impact of the 'GCHQ' case. It is important that subsequent decisions are cited to illustrate the real effect of the decision.

Skeleton Solution

Background to judicial review of the prerogative–nature of 'GCHQ' case – extracts from speeches – survey of subsequent decision indicating caution of the judiciary – *ex parte Everett*.

Suggested Solution

Prerogative powers can be described as those powers of government emanating from the Crown, which are exercised on behalf of the Crown by ministers, and which are not based upon statute.

The traditional approach of the courts to the question of reviewing the exercise of prerogative powers, was that whilst they would not recognise any new categories of prerogative power, and would thus adjudicate upon the scope of prerogative powers, the courts would not question the exercise of what was accepted as being a prerogative power, eg *Blackburn* v *Attorney-General* (1), once the court accepted that the power to enter into treaties with other sovereign states was within the prerogative, it was held that the decision to sign any particular treaty could not be questioned by the courts. In *Gouriet* v *UPOW* (2) Lord Denning MR, in the Court of Appeal, suggested that the Attorney-General's decision not to lend his name to proceedings against the union could be challenged in the courts notwithstanding that it involved the exercise of prerogative power, but this was denied by Lord Diplock when the case reached the House of Lords. Lord Diplock was of the view that if the Attorney-General had used prerogative power improperly he would be answerable to Parliament for his actions under the doctrine of ministerial responsibility.

In *Council of Civil Service Unions* v *Minister for the Civil Service* (3), the Prime Minister claimed that it was her prerogative power to alter the terms and conditions of civil servants employed at 'GCHQ.' that could not be questioned by the courts. The House of Lords rejected the submission that a power exercised in the sphere of public law should be immune from judicial review simply because of its source.

Lord Diplock in particular felt that such a doctrine was not in keeping with the reality of the way in which administrative law had developed in recent years. Their lordships felt that the key question was now that of 'justiciability'. Was the matter with which the litigation was concerned one that the courts were competent to deal with? Was it a matter that it was proper for the courts to deal with?

Lord Fraser felt that there was no good reason as to why the prerogative powers relating to the governance of the civil service should not be brought within the scope of judicial review, but was happy to regard matters such as control of the armed forces, and the conduct of foreign policy as areas where the courts would be well advised to defer to the wishes of the administration; ie they were 'non-justiciable' issues. Lord Diplock went further and described the maintenance of national security as being a matter which was 'par-excellence a non-justiciable question'. Lord Roskill provided a more detailed survey of matters with which the courts would not concern themselves when he stated:

> 'Prerogative powers such as those relating to the making of treaties, the defence of the realm, the prerogative of mercy, the granting of honours, the dissolution of Parliament and the appointment of ministers as well as others are not, I think, susceptible to judicial review because their nature and subject matter are such as not to be amenable to the judicial process.'

Subsequent decisions have essentially fallen into a predictable pattern given the above views. As suggested, the treaty making powers of the Crown will not be tested in the courts, as has been illustrated since the 'GCHQ' case in *Ex parte Molyneaux* (4), which involved an abortive attempt to challenge the Anglo-Irish treaty.

The prerogative of mercy has traditionally been seen as a non-justiciable matter, as in *Hanratty* v *Butler* (5); that this remains the case is perhaps illustrated by *R* v *Secretary of State for the Home Department ex parte Harrison* (6), where it was held that in the absence of any suggestion that that the Secretary of State had acted in a biased or fraudulent manner, his refusal to exercise his prerogative power to make an ex gratia payment to an individual who had been imprisoned but subsequently acquitted, would not be questioned by the courts; see also *R* v *Secretary of State for the Home office, ex parte Chubb* (7).

The above references indicate a cautious approach being adopted by the courts to the reviewability of prerogative powers in the wake of the 'GCHQ' decision, and this is reinforced by the Divisional Court's ruling in R v *Civil Service Appeal Board, ex parte Bruce* (8).

The applicant was a civil servant who had unsuccessfully challenged his dismissal as an Inland Revenue Enforcement Officer before the Civil Service Board. He now sought judicial review of the Board's decision to uphold the validity of his dismissal. In dismissing the application for judicial review, Lord Justice May indicated that the prerogative powers exercised by the Appeal Board were not automatically reviewable as a consequence of the 'GCHQ' case. Much depended on the circumstances of the individual case, but generally the courts would not intervene where there was no substantial public law issue involved, and alternative statutory remedies, such as recourse to an Industrial Tribunal, were available.

In one area, however, it can be said that the 'GCHQ' decision has clearly widened the scope of judicial review as regards decisions based upon the exercise of prerogative powers. In *Secretary of State for the Home Department* v *Lakdawalla* (9) it was held that the refusal of a passport application could not be challenged in the courts, but that should now be considered in the light of the Court of Appeal's decision in R v *Secretary of State for Foreign and Commonwealth Affairs, ex parte Everett* (10).

After referring to the 'GCHQ' case, Lord Justice O'Connor stated that the reviewability of prerogative power depended upon the subject matter of the decision. Whilst the making of treaties was clearly not a justiciable issue, his Lordship felt that a court should be able to intervene if a passport was refused and no good reasons were given for the decision. Lord Justice Taylor indicated that an exercise of prerogative power should be reviewable by the courts where it involved an administrative decision affecting the rights and freedoms of an individual, such as in this case, the freedom to travel.

In conclusion it can be said that the real breakthrough made by the House of Lords in the 'GCHQ' case was the ruling that prerogative powers were not per se unreviewable. The courts have however been somewhat conservative in applying the principles of administrative law to such decisions since this breakthrough was made.

References

1) [1971] 2 All ER 1310
2) [1978] AC 435
3) [1984] 3 All ER 935
4) [1986] 1 WLR 331
5) (1971) 115 Sol Jo 386
6) [1988] 3 All ER 86
7) [1986] Crim LR 809
8) (1988) The Times 22 June
9) [1972] Imm AR 26
10) (1988) The Times 1 November

QUESTION 3

General Comment

Essentially a straightforward question requiring an explanation of what the doctrine of collective responsibility involves, an explanation of its purpose, and citation of relevant examples of ministerial practice to support the points made.

Skeleton Solution

Collective responsibility – unanimity on policy–confidentiality – examples of its observance – examples of its breach –reference to *Jonathan Cape* decision – consideration of the need for the doctrine and its importance.

Suggested Solution

As generally understood, the doctrine of collective responsibility is a constitutional convention whereby government ministers undertake to present a united front in public in support of government policy as formulated in Cabinet. If a minister is unable or unwilling to publicly support government policy the convention is that he or she should resign. The result is that a politician cannot, or at least should not, disown or criticise a policy which was being promulgated by a Cabinet from which he or she did not resign.

It can be argued that collective responsibility also embraces two other conventions. First, that a government which loses the support of the House of Commons should resign. Secondly that minister must maintain the confidentiality of information received as a consequence of Cabinet membership.

If a government loses a vote of no confidence in the House of Commons, convention dictates that all its ministers should resign, thus indicating that they all accept responsibility for the government's record. Similarly a minister is expected to resign where he or she loses the confidence of fellow Cabinet members, as they cannot be expected to defend in public the position of a colleague which is plainly no longer tenable.

The need for confidentiality in respect of cabinet meetings is obvious. If differences of opinion which surface during Cabinet discussions are made public it will become extremely difficult for Cabinet members to put on a later show of public unanimity.

The difficulty with the general propositions considered above, is that they are not necessarily borne out by the evidence of ministerial practice in the post-war era. Certainly there is evidence that ministers have resigned as a result of irreconcilable differences with Cabinet colleagues. The resignation of Michael Heseltine over the handling of the 'Westland affair' within the Cabinet is one of many, but there are frequently other factors behind such decisions.

The clearest example in recent years of the doctrine of collective responsibility being placed under very considerable strain, arose in relation to the differences within the Labour Cabinet of 1975 on the issue of continued EEC membership. Following a vote within the Cabinet which revealed a majority of 16–7 in favour of continued membership, an 'agreement to differ' was arrived at whereby those Cabinet members who were opposed to EEC membership were allowed to campaign against it outside Parliament but not within the House of Commons. Perhaps this is evidence of a convention that collective responsibility can be suspended at the discretion of the Prime Minister of the day in relation to selected issues? If this is correct it would certainly suggest that the description of collective responsibility as something requiring from ministers '... a full and whole-hearted acceptance of the measures decided on by the Cabinet and of the policies underlying them ...' goes too far.

More generally, it is widely acknowledged that there are always shades of opinion within any group of government ministers and that individual ministers can make speeches which involve veiled criticisms of government policy, provided they do not go too far. Again it is a matter ultimately to be resolved with reference to political expediency rather than legal principles. The key questions are the amount of freedom a particular Prime Minister is willing to give Cabinet members, and the extent to which views expressed find common support within the Cabinet. The level of resignations by so called 'wets' from successive Cabinets presided over by Mrs. Thatcher indicates the way in which dissenting voices are steadily purged if the Prime Minister does not believe in a 'broad church' approach to Cabinet membership.

As to the confidentiality of Cabinet proceedings, whilst it is well known that Cabinet ministers, as Privy Councillors swear an oath of confidentiality, it is equally well known that there is a steady flow of information as to the nature of Cabinet decisions and discussions in the form of unofficial and unattributed 'leaks'. On occasion these leaks turn into floods when an ex-minister decides to publish his or her political memoirs complete with telling tales of Cabinet infighting. The matter was considered by Lord Widgery LCJ in *Attorney-General v Jonathan Cape Ltd* (1).

The Attorney-General applied for an injunction to prevent publication of the diaries of the late Richard Crossman who had been a Labour minister during the mid 1960's. The Attorney-General had contended that the injunction was necessary to preserve the confidentiality of Cabinet proceedings, and also collective responsibility. The Lord Chief Justice recognised the importance of collective responsibility as a constitutional convention, but doubted whether the publication of details of Cabinet meetings that had taken place some 11 years previously would actually cause that much harm or embarrassment to those who had been involved. His Lordship doubted whether collective responsibility in itself was a sufficient basis for the granting of an injunction, preferring to rely on breach of confidence if a remedy was to be provided. Ultimately it was decided that an injunction would not be granted in this case, but might be if in a subsequent case the evidence of the harm caused by disclosures of Cabinet discussions was more compelling.

Does the doctrine of collective responsibility as it is understood within the British constitution serve any useful purpose? Much depends upon the way in which a Cabinet is run. If ministers discuss policies and consider a variety of proposals until they come up with a scheme that is agreeable to all because it is the best solution to a problem, then there is much to commend the idea that they should then present a united front on the subject in public. If, however, it is a case of policies being imposed on ministers with the ultimatum of 'support the measure or resign' it is a doctrine that is likely to dissuade freedom of thought within the Cabinet, and ensure that its membership represents a narrow band of opinion, which cannot be a healthy state of affairs. The doctrine undoubtedly places difficulties upon junior ministers who are not Cabinet members and thus not privy to Cabinet discussions, yet have to support decisions taken by the Cabinet.

On a broader level it can be said that the doctrine does help to encourage some degree of integrity on the part of ministers in that if they wish to accept the credit for the successes of the administration of which they are a part, they must also be prepared to accept the blame for the failures.

Ultimately, it is submitted, the difficulty with collective responsibility is that it is observed on an everyday basis by scores of ministers without the matter even being seen as worthy of comment. It is only when there is an apparent breach of the doctrine that it attracts publicity, with the inevitable cries that it is fast becoming a constitutional irrelevance. What is perhaps needed is a sense of proportion.

Reference
1) [1976] 1 QB 752

QUESTION 4

General Comment

Not a difficult question, but an explanation of the doctrine of the separation of powers, and of the rule of law is required. The statement assumes that the British constitution is based upon the doctrine of parliamentary sovereignty, and whilst this may well be true it is an assumption that needs to be considered.

Skeleton Solution

Explain doctrine of separation of powers – provide examples of breach and observance – comment on importance. Similarly analyse the rule of law – consider Dicey's three propositions – example of each – conclusions on importance. Consider the theory of sovereignty and what it means in practical terms for the constitution – give examples. Conclusion.

Suggested Solution

Is the doctrine of the separation of powers irrelevant in the British constitution? The doctrine is based on the principle that the powers of the legislature, judiciary, and executive should be in different hands, so as to provide for a system of checks and balances between each branch of government. Under the constitution of the United States for example, the legislature, in the form of Congress, can veto the President's nominations for Supreme Court appointments. Similarly, the Supreme Court can invalidate legislation enacted by Congress, on the ground that it is 'unconstitutional'.

If one examines the British constitution it is undoubtedly the case that one will find many examples of the doctrine being violated. Ministers, members of the Executive, are allowed to sit as members of the legislative body, the House of Commons. Judges have a role in creating law, by virtue of their powers to 'discover' or develop the common law, a clear example of which is provided by *Shaw* v *D.P.P.* (1); arguably this involves the judiciary in usurping, or at least duplicating, the functions of the legislature. Further many executive bodies such as tribunals and commissioners exercise 'judicial' functions, by determining the rights of an applicant to some benefit or compensation.

To suggest, however, that the doctrine of the separation of powers is thus of 'no application' to the British constitution is, it is submitted, to go too far. One of the main purposes of the House of Commons Disqualification Act 1975 was to simplify the law relating to the involvement of members of the executive in the legislature. As a result, the number of government ministers permitted to sit in the House of Commons is strictly limited at 95. Civil servants must resign their posts in order to stand for election to the House; police officers and members of the armed forces are also disqualified from membership of the House. The doctrine of the separation of powers is also reflected in the fact that a member of parliament, although unable to resign from office, can disqualify himself by taking an 'office of profit under the Crown', such as Stewardship of the Chiltern Hundreds.

If the doctrine is really of little significance to the British constitution, it is difficult to explain the importance attached to judicial review. By means of an application for judicial review judges are able to call upon their common law jurisdiction to adjudicate upon the legality of action taken by administrative agencies, which includes members of the executive such as ministers; for a striking example of this see *Padfield v Minister of Agriculture* (2).

It is not easy to determine the importance of the rule of law to the British constitution until one has explained what is meant by the concept. If one adopts a Dicean approach the rule of law encompasses three notions, firstly the absolute predominance of regular law as opposed to the influence of arbitrary power, secondly equality of all subjects before the law, and thirdly that so-called constitutional law is simply the law of the land applied to the constitution.

As to the first of these notions, Dicey rejected 'arbitrary' power as being contrary to the rule of law, but in the modern state legislation is frequently enacted granting to ministers powers to act as they think fit in a given situation. The existence of such subjectively worded powers does not mean, however, that ministers can become a law unto themselves. Again one comes back to the significant role played within the constitution by judicial review. In *Padfield v Minister of Agriculture* (above), the House of Lords confirmed that the courts would not be inhibited from invalidating a minister's action simply because he purported to act within a broadly drafted power.

Equality of subjects before the law is perhaps less easy to establish in English law, if for no other reason than one party to litigation may be able to afford a more competent legal advisor than the other. Even if one takes the proposition to mean that no one is above the law and that the law applies equally to all, difficulties will still arise by virtue of the number of exceptions that can be cited.

Parliamentary privilege prevents MPs from being sued in respect of statements made in proceedings in Parliament, the immunities of foreign diplomats are well known, and judges enjoy various legal privileges as an incident of their holding office. Further, children under the age of ten are not subject to the criminal law. It is submitted, however, that these examples do not actually undermine the argument supporting the existence of the rule of law in the British constitution, but in fact add strength to it, since they are all examples of exemptions granted and recognised by law. It is certain that they could all be abolished or amended by law.

The third aspect of Dicey's theory of the rule of law is the most questionable, and arguably the least relevant to the modern British constitution. Dicey's view seems to reject the idea that there could be a body of law known as 'public law' as distinct from the private law governing individual rights and duties. That Dicey should reject such an idea is not surprising given his suspicion that it might involve public bodies being above the law, or at least enjoying legal privileges in comparison with the private individual. Today it has to be accepted that there is a branch of law, dealing with government and administration which lawyers for convenience term as 'public law' but it has not necessarily resulted in the type of abuse Dicey might have feared.

Turning to parliamentary sovereignty, it would be foolish indeed to undermine the importance of this doctrine to the British constitution, since it is in many ways what marks it out as being different from many other constitutions. It does mean that the judiciary will refuse to invalidate legislation which has been enacted by Parliament, see *Pickin* v *British Railways Board* (3). It also means that Parliament can enact legislation effectively nullifying a decision by the highest court, see *Burmah Oil Co* v *Lord Advocate* (4) as followed by the War Damages Act 1965. Whether it is still as strong a constitutional force as it once was is, however, questionable. The contention that parliamentary sovereignty meant that no parliament could bind its successors has always seemed dubious as regards legislation granting independence to former colonies and dominions. Parliament could vote to repeal the Canada Act 1982, but it is unlikely that the Canadians would give any effect to such a measure by recognising it. The debate over whether membership of the EEC has resulted in loss of sovereignty has been raging for nearly twenty years, but it is submitted that regardless of legal theory, there may well come a time when the United Kingdom is so firmly enmeshed in Europe that withdrawal ceases to be a practical option. What price parliamentary sovereignty then?

In conclusion it is submitted that if one had to cite the most significant aspect of the British constitution it would be parliamentary sovereignty, but this would not be on the basis that concepts such as the rule of law and the doctrine of the separation of powers were either redundant or irrelevant.

References
1) [1962] AC 220
2) [1968] AC 997
3) [1974] AC 765
4) [1965] AC 75

QUESTION 5

General Comment

A question that proceeds on the assumption that the United Kingdom does not have a written constitution, so perhaps some thought should be given to that at the outset. It then proceeds to suggest that this accounts for the nature of the relationship between central and local government, an assertion that certainly needs careful analysis. Some examples of the distribution of responsibilities between central and local government will obviously be needed, as well as an examination of the extent to which the introduction of a written constitution would alter the situation.

Skeleton Solution

Explain relationship between central and local government – give examples of allocation of functions – reservation of powers to central government. Consider the operation of a written constitution – cite problem of express repeal – implied repeal. Higher law argument – supreme court. Conclusion.

Suggested Solution

Any statement to the effect that the United Kingdom does not possess a written constitution has to be considered very carefully. Whilst all would accept that there is no one constitutional document embodying the framework of government, not even the Bill of Rights 1688 coming near to this, it should equally be accepted that many important aspects of constitutional law are ascertainable in a written form, either as common law, or legislation. The Crown Proceedings Act 1947, the Parliament Acts 1911–1949, the Representation of the People Act 1983, and the House of Commons Disqualification Act 1975, are all examples of legislation dealing with matters that can broadly referred to as 'constitutional'. As regards the relationship between central and local government there is no shortage of 'black letter' law. The main piece of legislation is still the Local Government Act 1972, but in recent years nearly every parliamentary session has seen the enactment of additional legislation on the topic.

It is submitted that the statement under consideration really prompts two questions. First, whether the boundary between central and local government really can be shifted by the actions of successive governments, and if so, secondly whether a written constitution could prevent this from happening.

Local government is generally seen as a 'good thing' on the ground that it enables locally elected persons to determine the provision of local services and amenities. Traditionally, the matters entrusted to local government have included education, planning, housing, and environmental protection. All of these are areas where political differences are likely to be sharp, resulting in an uneasy relationship between central and local government, especially where central government is of a markedly different political persuasion to that of a particular local authority.

On the one hand government ministers will not be unhappy that these functions are the responsibility of local authorities, since it means that ministers will not be answerable to parliament for the day to day activities of local authorities; on the other there is a need for ministers to retain a considerable degree of ultimate control in order for at least minimum standards to be observed nationally in respect of matters such as education. In extreme cases ministers may be vested with default powers whereby the functions of a local authority can be taken over completely by the relevant minister.

Examples of the boundary between central and local government being shifted as regards the allocation of powers and duties are not difficult to find. The Education Act 1944 places a broad duty upon local education authorities to provide adequate education for their inhabitants. The Education Reform Act 1988, however, proposes that all schools should follow a national curriculum to be determined by central government, thus restoring to central government a good deal of the discretion that formerly rested with local government. By virtue of the Housing Act 1957, local authorities are under a duty to provide for homeless persons within their areas, but since the enactment of the Housing Act 1980, council tenants have had the right to buy the council accommodation in which they are living. Where a local authority appears to be 'dragging its feet' in implementing the right to buy, the Secretary of State can intervene to take over the 'right to buy' scheme in any local authority's area; see *Norwich City Council* v *Secretary of State for the Environment* (1). Further, under the Town and Country Planning Act 1971, the Secretary of State for the Environment can 'call in' a planning application and institute a public inquiry, rather than leave the matter to be determined by the local planning authority.

In addition to legislation empowering central government to take over the functions of local authorities, there has, in recent years been a marked increase in the volume of legislation introducing extra controls over local government. Many of these measures have been aimed at constraining local government expenditure, but others have dealt with a wide range of matters, from prohibitions upon political advertising, the introduction of competitive tendering, and the publication of the minutes of council meetings, to the prohibition upon the promotion of homosexuality, and limitations upon 'creative accounting'. To what extent would a written constitution affect any of the above? Implicit in the statement under consideration is the suggestion that a written constitution would clearly delineate the boundary between local government and central government. This could certainly be achieved with some precision, but its long term effectiveness would depend upon other constitutional reforms being introduced. If a written constitution were introduced in the form of a general Act of parliament, it could be repealed by any subsequent parliament. Even if some attempt were made to entrench such an Act, perhaps by requiring a two thirds majority in both the Commons and the Lords before it could be altered or repealed, it is submitted that a future Parliament could still repeal it on the basis of a simple majority vote. The reason for this is the adherence to the doctrine of parliamentary sovereignty, and its continued recognition by the courts; see *Pickin v British Railways Board* (2).

Further, under the doctrine of implied repeal as it is currently understood, any later Act of parliament which appeared to conflict directly with the 'written constitution' legislation, would be applied in preference; see *Vauxhall Estates Ltd. v Liverpool Corporation* (3). Hence even if an Act were passed which appeared to enshrine the rights and independence of local government, there would be nothing to prevent a subsequent parliament enacting legislation to abolish a specific local authority, or even a whole tier of local government, as was the fate of the GLC and other Metropolitan County Councils.

For a written constitution to prevent local government being at the mercy of central government, therefore, a fundamental change would have to be made in the frame work of government, amounting to a new constitutional settlement. The written constitution, enshrining the rights of local authorities, would have to be regarded as a kind of 'higher' law to which all other legislation was subordinate and with which all subsequent legislation was required to comply; see *Harris v Minister of Interior*

(4). This would also involve the creation of a constitutional court empowered to invalidate legislation which purported to conflict with the provisions of the written constitution.

In conclusion, it is submitted that local government will continue to be treated as a political football for as long as central government has the power to do so. The constitutional reforms necessary to prevent this being the case are so fundamental and far reaching that it seems most unlikely that the situation is going to change in the foreseeable future.

References
1) [1982] 1 All ER 737
2) [1974] AC 765
3) [1932] 1 KB 733
4) (1952) (2) SA 428

QUESTION 6

General Comment

The question seems to be inviting discussion on the issue of whether human rights are adequately protected by the British constitution as it stands at present, or whether the enactment of specific legislation is called for. Thus some consideration of the protection offered under domestic legislation and the common law is called for. Thought should be given as to how an effective Bill of Rights might be introduced, and to the question of its contents.

Skeleton Solution

Explain the protection offered under English law – stautory provisions – common law decision. Shortcomings of both – examples of breaches of human rights under the ECHR by the United Kingdom government. Problems of the contents of a Bill of Rights – problems of implementation.

Suggested Solution

The question invites discussion of the merits and demerits of a Bill of Rights being enacted. One could commence by pointing out that there is already a Bill of Rights on the statute book, that of 1688, but of course that legislation was not concerned with the rights of individuals so much as the relationship between Parliament and the Crown. Whilst the Bill of 1688 may have been effective to prevent individuals being subject to arbitrary prerogative power as exercised by the monarch in person, it did little to protect the individual citizen from the excesses of governmental power exercised under the guise of parliamentary sovereignty; indeed one might well contend that one of the failings of the 'Glorious Revolution' was to place too much power in the hands of the legislature, and thereby the government.

There have been a number of attempts in recent years to introduce a Bill of Rights aimed at strengthening the protection of individual rights under English law. The most recent took the form of a Private Member's Bill introduced by Sir Edward Gardner, the Human Rights and Fundamental Freedoms Bill (1986), which sought to incorporate the European Convention on Human Rights into English law. The Bill very narrowly failed in the Commons (1), but there was clearly considerable parliamentary support for such a measure.

The statement under consideration suggests that a Bill of Rights could make a distinct contribution to the better protection of human rights, thus prompting the question, distinct from what?

Under English law, individual rights are protected by either statute or common law. Examples of statutory protection are provided by the Race Relations Act 1976, Sex Discrimination Act 1975, and the Police and Criminal Evidence Act 1984. At common law decisions such as *Christie* v *Leachinsky* (2), under which a police officer was required to inform a suspect of the grounds for an arrest, or *Entick* v *Carrington* (3) under which the courts invalidated the practice of issuing general search warrants, have undoubtedly contributed to the protection of individual rights and liberties. Can it be said that this combined protection is so inadequate that a formal Bill of Rights is needed?

The problem with 'equal rights' or 'civil liberties' legislation is that such measures are always at the mercy of successive parliaments. As a consequence of parliamentary sovereignty they can always be amended or repealed. Further, it can be argued that when parliament places individual liberties on a statutory basis it can draft them in terms that make them more limited in operation than they were at common law. More generally, successive parliaments have fought shy of granting United Kingdom citizens positive statutory rights, such as the right to free expression, the right to information, and the right to privacy.

The failings of the common law are that it is sporadic in nature. The judiciary can only develop individual rights at common law if cases are brought before them. Whether or not this occurs is a haphazard affair, not the best way in which to tackle such a serious matter. In any event, any decision of the courts can be nullified by subsequent parliamentary action in the form of new legislation, which can even be retrospective if necessary. The courts have not always responded when called upon by litigants to defend or develop human rights. Mr Malone's arguments for a right to privacy fell upon deaf ears in *Malone* v *Metropolitan Police Commissioner* (4), the Vice-Chancellor concluding that as there was no English law governing the matter of telephone tapping, he would be usurping the function of parliament by holding that such action did amount to an invasion of the plaintiff's right to privacy regarding his communications.

On the basis of the above, Lord Scarman, amongst others, has contended (5) that a Bill of Rights is needed in the British constitution because individual rights are not adequately protected at present by statute and common law. Those who contend that Human rights are not violated by the United Kingdom, can be referred to the succession of findings against the United Kingdom by the European Court of Human Rights under the European Convention.

Matters in relation to which the British government, and by implication the British constitution has been found wanting are, the law of contempt, the law relating to telephone tapping, the rights of prisoners to communicate with lawyers, the rights of prisoners to be legally represented in prison disciplinary proceedings, detention without trial under the Prevention of Terrorism legislation, corporal punishment, and restrictions upon adult homosexuals in Northern Ireland.

If it is accepted that a human rights measure is needed, the next question that needs consideration is its content. Most of those who support the introduction of a Bill of Rights point to the European Convention on Human Rights as a suitable model, but how valuable would this be?

Three matters in particular should be borne in mind. First the Convention is selective in the rights it seeks to protect, it contains no reference to a right to education, health care, or employment. It reflects a 'Western' view of individual rights, as opposed to a 'Socialistic' view. Secondly, the Convention includes many limitations upon the rights set forth, and does allow signatory states to derogate from some of its provisions in certain circumstances. For example the Convention does provide for freedom of association, but goes on to recognise that governments can limit this right if it is in the national interests to do so, thus the Civil Service Unions involved in the 'GCHQ' union ban dispute, were not able to pursue their case under the Convention. Thirdly, a Bill of Rights can only be effective if it is protected to some extent from repeal or amendment by subsequent governments, and if subsequent legislation is applied only to the extent that it does not conflict with the Bill of Rights. To prevent changes being introduced by a subsequent parliament would involve a major constitutional change in the nature of parliamentary sovereignty, with a marked increase in the powers of the judiciary. The controversy surrounding the status and effect of the European Communities Act 1972 provides an example of the difficulties that could be encountered. Many would feel that human rights are not in sufficient peril in the United Kingdom to justify such a constitutional upheaval.

References

1) Debated on 6th February 1987, although it attracted 94 votes in support and only 16 in opposition, it was lost on the technical requirement that there had to be 100 MP's supporting the measure.
2) [1947] AC 573
3) (1765) 19 St Tr 1030
4) [1979] Ch 344
5) See report in *The Guardian* 14 November 1988

QUESTION 7

General Comment
A question requiring consideration of four aspects of the ultra vires principle, the rule against delegation, irrational selection policy, estoppel, and natural justice. The rubric accompanying the question does not specifically invite discussion of whether the matters in question should be challenged by way of writ or an application for judicial review, so it is suggested that a discussion of the public/private dichotomy is not required here.

Skeleton Solution
The rule against delegation – no abdication of power – irrational basis for selection – extent to which the University is bound by the unilateral undertaking – whether any breaches of natural justice have occurred.

Suggested Solution
It is submitted that there are four grounds upon which the proceedings outlined in the above question might have involved a breach of the principles of English administrative law. Each will be considered in turn.

a) *The rule against delegation*
The rule against delegation, or the rule against sub-delegation as it should perhaps be described, operates to ensure that power is exercised by the body in whom it has been vested.
  If, for example, a tribunal has been empowered under statute to determine claims for a benefit of some sort, and in the absence of any express power to do so it delegates this function to some other organisation, a violation of the ultra vires principle will occur, since a body which has not been properly empowered to act will in fact be taking the decisions. Prima facie the delegation of the task of selecting students, by the Sub-Dean for Admissions, to a secretary, would appear to be a violation of the rule against delegation, since it involves a sub-delegation of powers vested in the Sub-Dean by the University, but a number of factors might suggest otherwise.

First, the power in question is (presumably) not statutory in origin, hence arguments that the delegation under consideration is contrary to the intentions of Parliament are not really applicable. One could argue that officers of a private organisation are free to delegate their functions as they see fit, subject perhaps to a requirement that any such delegation should be reasonable. Secondly, it could be contended that the facts under consideration do not involve delegation of a decision making function, but merely the use of an agent ie the secretary, by the Sub-Dean. Such an argument might meet with approval in the courts provided the ultimate decision making power still rests with the Sub-Dean, and also the responsibility for the decisions made; compare *Ellis v Dubowski* (1) with *Mills v LCC* (2)

Generally, it is submitted that the key question is not whether the Sub-Dean can delegate tasks to her secretary, but whether this particular type of task can be delegated. As suggested above, the act of delegation itself, might be more properly challenged on the ground of irrationality (considered below).

b) *Irrational basis of selection*

The decision of the Sub-Dean to select university entrants on the basis of their 'O' Level grades could be impugned upon the ground that it involves the over-rigid application of an irrational policy. Administrative agencies are permitted to exercise discretion according to policies, in order to achieve fairness and consistency, but this must not result in the exercise of discretion becoming 'straight-jacketed' by the policy, and the policy itself must be sound. The facts of the question suggest that the policy of referring to applicant's 'O' Level grades is being applied with considerable rigidity. This could be challenged on the basis that the university has 'shut its ears' to applicants who, despite poor 'O' Level grades, might have 'something new to say'; see *R v Port of London Authority ex parte Kynoch* (3). Against this, it has to be recognised that the Sub-Dean is dealing with a large number of applications, and in such circumstances the House of Lords has recognised that the adoption of a policy may be desirable, so that the administrative machinery can operate more efficiently; see *British Oxygen Ltd.v Minister of Technology* (4). Perhaps a stronger ground of challenge is that the policy itself is unreasonable or irrational. A complainant would have to show that the basis of selection was one that no reasonable university admissions tutor would have adopted; see *Associated Provincial Picture Houses v*

Wednesbury Corporation (5). Alternatively, the selection process could be described as 'irrational' in the sense outlined by Lord Diplock in *Council of Civil Service Unions v Minister for the Civil Service* (6), wherein his Lordship spoke of a decision being challengeable because of its defiance of logic and moral standards, being one that no sensible person who had applied his mind to the matter in issue could have arrived at.

Given that most of those applying to university will not yet have their 'A' level grades, reference to 'O' level grades may be perfectly sensible, but it is perhaps irrational to ignore such matters as references from head teachers, and the work experience of mature applicants.

c) *Estoppel*

Can the Sub-Dean lawfully withdraw her offer to deal with enquiries from all the unsuccessful applicants? It might be contended that she is estopped from going back on her unilateral undertaking, see for example *Lever Finance Ltd v Westminster City Council* (7). It should be borne in mind, however, that estoppel is 'a shield not a sword', and that any party wishing to raise the issue must show that they have acted in reliance upon the undertaking. It is submitted that a better approach would be to suggest that the undertaking of the Sub-Dean to deal with disappointed applicants gave rise to a legitimate expectation on their part that they would be given a hearing, and that the refusal of any such hearing amounts to a breach of natural justice; see *Attorney-General of Hong Kong v Ng Yuen Shiu* (8). In that decision the Privy Council held that where a public body makes a unilateral public statement as to the way in which it intends to act, those likely to be affected have a legitimate expectation that the undertaking will be observed, unless it would involve the public body in acting contrary to its public law powers and duties. In principle there is no reason why the sub-Dean should not be required to act according to her original undertaking, but it might be pointed out that a hearing would be unlikely to achieve any result for those applicants who have not been successful.

d) *Breach of natural justice.*

Should all 2000 applicants have been given a hearing? Natural justice does not require that an oral hearing should be given to every person whose interests are to be affected by a decision. Broad guidelines as to the treatment that should be given are provided by the decision in *McInnes v Onslow-Fane* (9), wherein Megarry VC identified three types of case. First there is the 'forfeiture' case where the individual in respect of whom the decision is being made, stands to lose some existing right or privilege. Secondly, the 'legitimate expectation' case, where the individual expects to receive some benefit because of passed conduct or treatment. Thirdly there are the cases concerning 'mere applicants' who, in the words of the Vice-Chancellor, do not have any right to heard as such, but who can expect their cases to be handled in good faith, without bias or caprice. It is submitted that the present question is concerned with this latter category.

The failure to interview all applicants does not, therefore, constitute a breach of natural justice, especially as the rejection of an application does not cast any particular slur on the reputation of the applicant, bearing in mind that there are other institutions of higher education to which the applicants can apply. This view is further supported by *Central Council for Training in Social Work* v *Edwards* (10), wherein it was held that an applicant for a place at a polytechnic does not have a right to an interview prior to any decision being made, but if an interview is granted it should be conducted in accordance with the rules of natural justice. The way in which the applications have been processed in the present case (the reliance on 'O' Level grades) may, however, be evidence of 'caprice', in the sense that it involves irrationality on the part of the Sub-Dean, as to which see above.

References

1) [1921] 3 KB 621
2) [1925] 1 KB 213
3) [1919] 1 KB 176
4) [1971] AC 610
5) [1948] 1 KB 223
6) [1984] 3 All ER 935
7) [1971] 1 QB 222
8) [1983] 2 All ER 346
9) [1978] 1 WLR 1520
10) (1978) The Times 5 May

UNIVERSITY OF LONDON
INTERMEDIATE EXAMINATION IN LAWS 1989
for External Students

CONSTITUTIONAL LAW

Thursday, 15 June: 10.00 am to 1.00 pm

Answer FOUR of the following SEVEN questions

1. 'When an Englishman speaks of the conduct of a public man being constitutional or unconstitutional, he means something wholly different from what he means by conduct being legal or illegal.'
   Discuss.

2. Evaluate the statement that the Parliament Acts 1911 and 1949 represent an appropriate balance between the House of Commons and the House of Lords.

3. 'The sole justification for the present privileges of the House of Commons is that they are essential for the conduct of its business and the maintenance of its authority.' (Sir Barnett Cocks)
   Discuss.

4. 'If a mistake is made in a Government Department the Minister is responsible even if he knew nothing about it.' 'A Minister cannot be blamed for a mistake made if he did not make it himself.'
   Consider these contrasting views.

5. 'Incorporation of the European Convention on Human Rights into domestic law is unnecessary and undesirable in view of the right of individual petition to the Commission in Strasbourg.'
   Discuss

6. 'The Courts will rarely be deterred by attempts to exclude their power to review decisions of administrative bodies, whether made directly by ouster clauses in one form or another, or indirectly by statutory provisions' conferring wide discretionary powers formulated in subjective terms.'
   Explain and discuss with reference to relevant authorities.

7 To what extent, if at all, have recent actual and proposed changes to the Laws relating to State security curtailed freedom of expression?

QUESTION 1

Skeleton Solution

Explain the meaning of the quotation setting it in context by showing what would be meant by the words in a system with a written constitution. Then look at role of convention and statute in British constitution.

Suggested Solution

Today most countries of the world possess a 'constitution' ie a document or series of documents laying down the fundamental rules relating to the organisation of the state. In such countries if a person decries a law or an action as being unconstitutional or illegal what he means is that it offends against the higher law laid down in the constitution, which is normally protected from later legislative changes by the need to follow a more difficult prescribed legislative process ie the constitution is entrenched. To a degree the two adjectives are in these countries interchangeable. Even in such countries convention plays a part but a role which cannot be compared to the position of conventions in the British constitution. To discover the fundamental rules governing the constitution in Britain one has to look to various sources – statute, judicial decisions and conventions of the constitution. Conventions of the constitution are rules of political practice regarded as biding by those to whom they apply but which are not enforced by the courts or by Parliament. The important point to grasp is that although statute is the most important source of our constitution and a statute can always override a convention, nevertheless one would not understand how the British constitution operated without an understanding of conventions. For instance the existence of the Prime Minister, Cabinet and other ministers is dependent on convention and their relationships to each other and to Parliament are regulated by conventions of ministerial responsibility. Furthermore if one looks strictly at the legal powers of the Monarch those are immense until one appreciates the convention that for the most part the Monarch follows the advice of her government. Conventions are also important in the functioning of the legislature and even to the judiciary.

The quotation in the question is therefore alluding to the difference between statute and convention as a source of the British constitution. If an Englishman spoke of something as 'illegal' he would normally be referring to a breach of a statute or common law rules. If he is talking of something being 'unconstitutional' he would be taken to be referring to a breach of a convention. This is however somewhat of an oversimplification for sometimes in speaking of a breach of a statute or case law rule of constitutional importance the Englishman might at once describe the behaviour as 'unconstitutional' and 'illegal', but what is unconstitutional is not necessarily illegal, although it may be.

Mallory said 'for the Americans anything unconstitutional is illegal, however right or necessary it may seem; for the British, anything unconstitutional is wrong, no matter how legal it may be'.

Some conventions are well known and possessing great authority whilst others have developed on an informal basis. This means that some conventions are not even recorded in writing in public documents having evolved informally over a period of time. Indeed this is one of the reasons why disputes arise as to the existence and content of conventional rules. There is no judicial procedure or mechanism to settle disputes concerning such rules. One of the results of these uncertainties is that the phrase 'unconstitutional' is often used by politicians in circumstances where it may not strictly be appropriate, thus devaluing the term.

For example in 1932 the national government's agreement to differ and the 1975 Labour government waiver of collective responsibility, over the EEC referendum were both described by some commentators as 'unconstitutional' but these occasions were both without precedent and should, some would argue, merely be seen as developments and glosses on a convention.

The question arises as to the consequences of a breach of non-legal rules. These may be in the political area, resignation, reprimand or a warning. There are many examples of such consequences, for example, in November 1974 the Labour PM reprimanded three top ministers who had criticised the government's policy on South Africa (the ministers had supported a motion passed by the National Executive of the Labour Party).

The courts will not enforce conventions but conventions are taken into account. The Crossman diaries are a good example illustrating the 'grey area' between legal and non-legal rules. In that case the AG tried to prevent the breach of a conventional rule and to establish the existence of a legal obligation. It was held that former cabinet ministers could be restrained by injunction from publishing confidential information – there is a legal obligation to respect confidentiality. The court, however, must not be thought to have enforced a convention in this case. Collective responsibility (the convention in question) was no more than one factor taken into account by the judge in establishing the limits of the legal doctrine of confidence.

Whilst some non legal rules are not enforceable by the courts, some legal rules are also difficult to enforce eg the duty of the Secretary of State for Education and Science to promote and develop educational institutions (1).

Some jurists take the view that all constitutional rules ought to be enacted as law. To a large degree this is what would happen if the United Kingdom were to entrench a written constitution. If that were done a Supreme Court (or Law Lords in the House of Lords) would interpret constitutional articles. It is true that some areas would be quite difficult. For example, to anticipate every possible eventuality in which the Sovereign might be required to invite a new Prime Minister to form a government. Also it could be argued that even if all present non-legal rules were susceptible to a written code, new conventions could be born at any time (2). This argument, however, is not entirely satisfactory – the main point about codification is that all non-legal rules (conventions) are brought under a legal footing, namely, a constitution. Were conventions fully codified then the use in Britain of the phrases 'unconstitutional' and 'illegal' would alter to resemble that in other countries.

References

1) However, an article in a constitution has to be *interpreted*, and this will depend on the *facts* of each case
2) Note Wade and Bradley say that 'provisions contained in a written constitution' are not *all* suitable for judicial enforcement. This, however, may not be valid as some constitutional lawyers will maintain that *all* provisions/articles of a written constitution have equal standing; it is either an article or not.

QUESTION 2

Skeleton Solution

History prior to Parliament Act 1911 and relationship of Commons and Lords

First state what the two Acts provide for.

Main result of the Acts in practice.

Reform/abolition of the upper house.

Conclusion.

Suggested Solution

Before the Parliament Act 1911 there was wide spread recognition that since the House of Commons was the elected chamber its will should override that of the House of Lords, which, in those days, was entirely hereditary in composition. In law the legislature, the Queen in Parliament, had three equally important constituent parts – the Commons, Lords and Monarch but there were already in existence conventions to regulate the conduct of the House of Lords. It was the breach by the House of Lords of the convention that it would not interfere with the government's financial proposals passed by the Commons which gave rise to the 1911 Act. The 1949 Parliament Act was passed further to curtail the delaying powers of the House of Lords by a Labour government which was attempting to prevent its post war nationalisation programme being delayed by the House of Lords. The preamble to the 1911 Act clearly reveals that its reforms were intended only as a stopgap measure until radical reform of the House of Lords was undertaken. However such reforms of the Lords as there have been during the twentieth century cannot be classified as radical and have not removed the substantial influence of the hereditary peers.

The Parliament Acts 1911–1949 provide that, in certain circumstances, Bills may receive the royal assent after approval by the Commons alone. This may happen (1) in the case of a Money Bill if it has not been passed by the Lords within one month and (2) in the case of a Public Bill if it has not been passed by the Lords within one year.

The Parliament Acts do not apply to Bills which seek to extend the maximum duration of Parliament beyond five years. Also these

Acts do not apply to local and private legislation nor to delegated legislation – in this case the power of the Lords depends on whether the parent Act expressly empowers the Lords to approve or disapprove of the delegated legislation in question.

The procedure provided by the Parliament Act 1911 with regard to a Money Bill (which is, of course, also a Public Bill) is as follows. A Money Bill is defined as a Bill which deals with the imposition, repeal, remission, alteration or regulation of taxation or with the Consolidated Fund or the National Loans Fund and other financial matters including raising or guarantee or repayment of loans but Bills dealing with taxation, money or loans raised by local authorities or bodies for local purposes are not certifiable as Money Bills. Under s2 of the 1911 Act any certificate of the Speaker (to certify that a Bill is a Money Bill), 'shall be conclusive for all purposes, and shall not be questioned in any court of law.'

Once a Bill has been certified as a Money Bill then if it is not passed by the Lords within one month of the Bill reaching that Chamber it may be passed direct to the Royal Assent and thus become law. In the case of all other public Bills (with the one exception noted above) if a Bill is not passed by the Lords after the Commons have sent it to them in two separate sessions (with a lapse of a year between the second reading by the Commons in the first session and the third reading in the second session) then it may be passed direct to the royal assent. Until the Parliament Act 1949 the delaying period was greater – three sessions spread over two years.

From an examination of the wording of these provisions of the Parliament alone it would be possible to draw the misleading impression that the Commons always has its legislative way. Although in the last resort the Commons can always, by operating the Parliament Acts, override the opposition of the Lords to its legislative proposals in fact the Parliament Act 1911 was operated only to pass the Welsh Church Act 1914, the Government of Ireland Act 1914 and the Parliament Act 1949. In the 1970's on several occasions the Lords utilised their delaying powers to hinder controversial legislation until policy was changed and in the 1975 – 76 session the Labour government commenced the 1949 Act procedure but this was later rendered unnecessary by compromises. The Acts therefore operate mainly as a deterrent, the psychological effect of which is normally to ensure that in case of conflict between Commons and Lords, the Lords give way. However it may sometimes be the case that rather than face a delay of one year before legislative proposals become law, thereby disrupting the legislative timetable for later sessions, a government would rather compromise, modifying its Bill in some way so as to satisfy the Lords in order to gain a swift passage to the statute book. Thus in the 1983/4 session the Government suffered an amendment to its Local Government (Interim Provisions) Bill imposed by the Lords to ensure that pending abolition of the Greater London Council in March 1986 councillors, whose term of office would normally have expired in May 1985, would retain their seats rather than being replaced by representatives nominated by the London Boroughs, a Government proposal condemned by the Lords as essentially anti-democratic.

This is not an isolated example.

No assessment of the House of Lords' legislative role would be complete without consideration of its importance in relieving the Commons of work by its work in private legislation and by its initiation of non-controversial Bills, such as the Courts Act 1971. In addition the Lords is extremely valuable in its role as a revising chamber. It provides an added opportunity for the government or private member promoting a public Bill to modify the Bill in response to criticism or unforeseen circumstances. An even more important point is that the House of Lords sits as a whole on the committee stage of Bills and there is therefore available a wider perspective on the Bill since the Lords is made up not only of hereditary peers but also life peers who may be Law Lords or those who have been successful in careers in industry or education etc. These Lords may be more clearly aware of the practical effect of proposed legislation on a particular industry than MPs in the Commons who view their career as politics rather than becoming legislators at the end of a career outside Parliament!

Reform of the House of Lords was envisaged in the preamble to the 1911 Act. A new second chamber based on a popular vote was to be set up and the old hereditary structure was to be abolished. The views of Viscount Bryce are interesting to note at this stage. Bryce saw the functions of a second chamber to be (a) examination and revision of Bills brought from the Commons (b) initiation and discussion of non-controversial Bills (c) delay of Bills for a reasonable time in order only to alert public opinion (d) discussion of current issues of policy which the Commons had no time to discuss. No action was taken on reform however. In 1948 the question surfaced again and disagreement broke out. This led to the passing of the 1949 Act by the Labour Party. This did not settle the question – in 1967 another attempt at reform was made. Disagreement once more broke out leading to the Parliament (No 2) Bill 1968–69 which sought to eliminate the hereditary basis of the Lords. This, however, was not acted on.

Plainly the constant efforts at reform/abolition of the Lords show that 'an appropriate balance' has not been achieved. Recently the Labour Party has dropped its proposal to abolish the Lords. The present position is summed up – reform, yes, abolish, no. However the relationship between Commons and Lords has an appropriate balance in the sense that the Commons holds basic power. Whether or not the Lords will remain as the second chamber, the 1911–1949 Acts were successful in confirming the Commons as the chief legislative chamber. Viewing the situation in this context one could say that a 'perfect' balance was not achieved and there is still room for reform of the second chamber.

QUESTION 3

Skeleton Solution

Introduction – original necessity for privilege and set out privileges.

Examine privileges in detail pointing out whether they remain essential – freedom of speech, freedom from civil arrest, right to regulate composition and proceedings and to punish those in contempt or breach of privilege.

Conclude.

Suggested Solution

Many of the privileges of Parliament have their origins in the sixteenth and seventeenth centuries at a time when the House of Commons was striving to prove its independence and to prevent interference with its members and proceedings by the Monarch and others outside Parliament. The privileges were originally developed to safeguard the position of MPs individually and that of the House as a whole. Today the privileges established during these centuries still exist but a select committee in 1967 commented that some were no longer required as they had become obsolete and suggested reforms, which have still not been implemented.

At the beginning of each new Parliament the Speaker claims 'ancient and undoubted privileges' which consist of freedom of speech in debate, freedom from civil arrest and freedom of access via the Speaker to the Sovereign. The Commons also enjoys privileges in its corporate capacity such as the right to regulate its own composition, the right to take exclusive cognisance of matters arising within the precincts of the House and the right to punish both Members and non-members for breach of privilege and contempt.

Perhaps the most important of the privileges of the Commons is that of freedom of speech. It was enshrined in the constitution by Article 9 of the Bill of Rights 1689 and provides:

'Freedom of speech and debates or proceedings in Parliament should not be questioned in any court or place outside of Parliament.' Practically this means that no criminal prosecution can be launched nor can any civil action for defamation be commenced in respect of words uttered or written during 'debates and proceedings in Parliament.'

There is debate over the meaning of the phrase 'proceedings in Parliament' (*Strauss* case 1957) but it seems that for anything said in the House in the course of Parliamentary business (such as debates or committee hearings etc) the MP has immunity. Potentially MPs could abuse this privilege by knowingly making false statements in the House but it was considered that this danger was outweighed by the public interest in ensuring that MPs could speak freely when carrying out Parliamentary business. It should be noted that if an MP does abuse his privilege it is open to the House itself to punish him for contempt of Parliament or to expel him from the House as unfit (*Allighan* (1947)).

The privilege of freedom of speech also prevents those outside Parliament attempting to dictate to MPs how they should speak in debate and/or vote. Although it is acknowledged that MPs may maintain business and other interests outside Parliament there is a register of Members' interests in which each MP is supposed to declare his other activities. Article 9 has been used to stop such outside commitments being used to force an MP into a particular course of action in the Chamber (*Yorkshire Union of Mineworkers* case (1974)).

In these ways the privilege of freedom of speech remains important to the Houses of Parliament.

By contrast the privilege of freedom from civil arrest is obsolete and is long overdue for repeal. It provides that for the forty days before, during a session and for the forty days after it an MP may not be subject to civil (not criminal) arrest. Although this was needed when the usual method of enforcing a debt was to incarcerate the debtor in a debtors' prison which, in the absence of the immunity, could have effectively disenfranchised large numbers of voters it is no longer required when arrest in civil proceedings is rare indeed.

Freedom of access via the speaker to the sovereign is today merely a formality but the Common's powers to regulate its own composition and internal proceedings remain relevant. Election petitions are no longer determined by the Commons itself, but by an election court made up of High Court judges, but the Commons still determines when to move a writ for a by election to fill any vacancies which arise. It may also declare that a member is unfit and expel him from the House. The House regulates its own proceedings and the courts will not take cognisance of these procedures even when these conflict with statute as in *Bradlaugh* v *Gossett*, where an MP was refused permission by the Commons to make his oath of allegiance in a form permitted by statute. The court's refusal to interfere in Parliament's internal procedure is exemplified in *Pickin* v *BRB* (1) where the fact that notices had apparently not been given by promoters of a private Bill so as to satisfy orders of the House of Lords did not lead to the invalidity of the Act of Parliament subsequently passed. This attitude is one aspect of the doctrine of Parliamentary sovereignty and there has been criticism of the fact that the courts do not intervene in such cases.

One aspect of Parliament's right to regulate its own conduct is its jurisdiction to punish breach of privilege and contempt of Parliament. Breach of privileges, consists of abuse of privilege by a member or of any conduct by anyone MP or non-member which interferes with one of the privileges of Parliament. Contempt is a wider concept and consists of conduct which tends to bring the House into disrepute or detract from its dignity. whether the offence is breach of privilege or contempt, the penal powers of the House are the same. Members may be reprimanded or admonished by the Speaker or members may be suspended or expelled. Officials of the House may be dismissed or a member or stranger may be committed to prison for the duration of the Parliamentary Session. The Select Committee on Parliamentary Privileges recommended that the punitive powers of the Commons and Lords be curtailed and although no such reform has been formally made, in practice the Commons seems reluctant to do more than give a reprimand to outsiders found to be in contempt (even where as in 1986 the Committee of Privileges had recommended that a lobby correspondent be expelled for six months with his paper, The Times, being allowed no substitute for that period). The most severe penalty it uses in respect of MPs is suspension.

The procedure by which complaints of breach of privilege or contempt of Parliament are made is open to criticism. At present a member may complain to the Speaker and the Speaker may refer the matter to a Committee of Privileges. This committee can compel attendance of witnesses and production of documents. Failure to comply is a contempt. The Select Committee on Parliamentary Privileges in 1967 recommended that persons directly concerned in the Committee's investigation should have the right to attend the hearings, make submissions, call and examine witnesses. Also legal aid, with leave of the Committee, should be granted. These recommendations were not implemented.

Furthermore even when the Committee of Privileges has reached its conclusion on the evidence that decision is not binding on the House which may reject it (eg *Strauss* (1957)). This state of affairs can hardly be justified in cases where the Commons might take a harsher point of view without hearing the evidence. However normally the Commons as a whole take a more lenient view than the Committee.

It does seem that this area is ripe for reform but such reform is unlikely to materialise in the near future as it is not seen by political parties as a priority.

Reference

1) *Pickin* v *BRB* [1974] AC 765

QUESTION 4

Skeleton Solution

Discuss individual responsibility giving examples which are relevant. A lot depends on the attitude of PM of the day.

Suggested Solution

In any democratic state it is a requirement that the people who govern should be responsible to those whom they govern. In the UK, for instance, responsibility is collective ie the government as a whole is responsible to Parliament and responsibility is individual ie individual ministers are responsible to Parliament for decisions taken by them or their civil servants in their departments. The principle of individual ministerial responsibility developed historically before the doctrine of collective responsibility. Collective and individual responsibility are rules of convention and as such are flexible concepts since conventions are rules of political practice regarded as binding by those to whom they apply but everyone recognises that they are subject to exceptions. Neither of the two quotations is an accurate statement of the requirements of individual ministerial responsibility, which it is wellnigh impossible to formulate in a way which indicates in every case what the outcome will be for a minister who has made a mistake or whose department has in some way failed.

A minister is responsible for his or her personal acts whether or not he or she is a member of the Cabinet. Responsibility will also include general conduct in the relevant department and any acts or omissions done in the name of the department. The responsibility may be legal or political or a combination of these. It seems that the meaning of responsibility and the persons or bodies to whom it is owed will vary according to the circumstances.

One of the practical expressions of individual ministerial responsibility is that a minister is required to answer questions in Parliament with regard to the conduct of officials in his department although – questions may be disallowed because of the sub judice rule or because of national security. It is true that a minister need not accept responsibility if an official has committed a dishonest act, exceeded his authority or disobeyed instructions. He cannot, however, totally absolve himself and he will be required to explain in public what has happened. In this sense the minister will –

whether he is to blame or not – have to 'carry the can.'. The minister must also, of course, when required, explain government policy in relation to his department. In the event that the minister's replies fail to satisfy MPs or the Lords a motion to reduce the minister's salary or to censure him may result, but because of party discipline these are rare. In order to consider the truth or otherwise of the quotations it is now necessary to consider some precedents in detail categorising them, if possible, under one of the quotations.

Perhaps one of the clearest examples of a minister resigning because of a mistake, even though he knew nothing of it at the time it occurred, is that of Sir Thomas Dugdale who resigned as Minister of Agriculture as a result of the Crichel Down Affair in 1954: In doing so he took responsibility for alleged maladministration by Senior Civil Servants without his knowledge. Some commentators have sought to explain this resignation on the basis that compulsory purchase was involved, (a matter about which the electorate were extremely sensitive at the time) but it certainly stands as a most stringent example of the 'rule' in force, particularly since the maladministration affected only one family and was a matter of embarrassment rather than one where severe loss either financial or in terms of physical wellbeing was concerned.

Lord Carrington's resignation in 1982 as Secretary of State for Foreign Affairs together with those of the other Foreign Office ministers who resigned with him can also be seen as an example of the first quotation in that it could be argued that Lord Carrington was poorly advised during the negotiations with Argentina over the Falkland Islands but personally made no mistake. On the other hand one could argue that he himself was culpable in that the department's failure to predict the invasion was an indication that it was inefficient or ill run and that in his position he should himself have been better informed and better able to foresee the invasion.

In recent times a rather different attitude has been taken in relation to mistakes by civil servants; whereas formerly the minister maintained the anonymity of the civil servant and would take responsibility in certain recent cases the blame has been laid squarely at the feet of civil servants (who have sometimes been disciplined) whilst ministers have felt no compunction to resign. Examples of this include the Maze Prison breakout which was followed by resignation of civil servants but no ministerial departures and the occasion when an intruder entered the Queen's bedroom and the Home Secretary, Lord Whitelaw, saw no need for resignation. These two instances are surely examples of the 'rule' set out in the second quotation.

If the first quotation is correct then a fortiori it would be expected that any minister himself making a mistake would have to take responsibility for it and very likely resign. If one examines some recent resignations and calls for resignation one can see that ministerial mistakes do not necessarily result in resignation.

The second quotation also tends to imply that a minister who personally makes a mistake will be 'blamed'; and the concomitant of this would very likely be resignation. If one examines recent cases one can see that there is no hard and fast rule. Some mistakes by Ministers lead to resignations others merely to calls by the opposition for resignation. Whether a minister survives a mistake seems to depend upon factors such as whether he nevertheless retains the confidence of the Prime Minister and the Cabinet, the view of the backbenchers of his own party and the level of public outcry. For instance Sir Leon Brittan survived calls for his resignation as Secretary of State for Trade and Industry over allegations that he had misled the Commons about a letter from British Aerospace to the government during the Westland Helicopter Affair in 1986. His survival was due to the continued support of Prime Minister and Cabinet. However when his behaviour (in authorising a leak to the press of a letter sent by the law officers to Michael Heseltine and then arguably covering up what had been done) came to light, several weeks later not even the Cabinet's support could protect his position when the Conservative backbenchers withdrew their support from him and he was forced to resign. In December 1988 Edwina Currie resigned as a Health Minister after over enthusiastic and somewhat misleading comments on the level of salmonella infection in poultry production. Her fault was to alienate poultry producers who had suffered severe financial loss and the government was forced to mount a costly compensation scheme. The remarks cost Mrs Currie her job but was she simply unlucky? Had there been some other important news story on the day of her remarks perhaps the media and the public would have overlooked them entirely – they would not then have been a 'mistake' and there would have been no resignation.

A lot depends, therefore, on the attitude of the Prime Minister of the day, the Cabinet and backbenchers and the attitude of the public to the particular mistake. The two contrasting views expressed in the question, are neither taken singly nor together a sufficient explanation of the difficult and subtle convention of individual ministerial responsibility.

QUESTION 5

Suggested Solution

Two basic features of the (unwritten) constitution of the United Kingdom are (i) the legal supremacy of Parliament and (ii) the common law which protects individual freedoms. In the United Kingdom, therefore, individual freedoms are not guaranteed in any formal document, they are residual. Provided the individual does no civil or criminal wrong, he may do as he wishes. A person also knows that for every wrongful encroachment upon his liberty there is a legal remedy available in an independent court of justice.

In the United Kingdom, therefore, individual liberty is protected by the ordinary courts of law using common law. This protection of the courts is limited by the doctrine of Parliamentary sovereignty. The Queen in Parliament may legislate upon any subject so that whatever liberties are given today may be taken away tomorrow.

Our present unwritten constitution founded as it is partly on Acts of Parliament and judicial decisions, partly upon political practice, and partly upon detailed procedures established by the various organs of government for carrying out their own tasks, provides a complex and comprehensive system of government which some would argue has served the United Kingdom well. In particular, as all law in the United Kingdom, including laws relating to the constitution, may be enacted, repealed or amended by the Queen in Parliament using the same legislative procedure, our constitution is highly flexible and can adapt to meet changes in social, moral and political circumstances. Indeed this facility for gradual evolution has been one of the major contributions to the political and social stability of the United Kingdom. Nevertheless in recent years there have been increasing calls for reform of the United Kingdom constitution by adoption of a written Bill of Rights and the model most often suggested is the European Convention on Human Rights, to which the UK has been a signatory since 1951 and which has been in force since 1953. In the UK, unlike other European countries such as West Germany, the Convention did not, merely by signature, become part of our domestic law. An Act of Parliament would be required to effect this. Under the present arrangement the United Kingdom is bound by the treaty in international law only, which means that the issue of breach of the Convention cannot be raised before a British Court. If a individual or group feel that they have discovered a breach of the convention then, since 1966, it has been possible for this to be raised with the European Commission on Human Rights. States too may refer another signatory to the Convention to the Commission if a breach of the Convention has occurred. However in a number of respects it may be argued that these rights to refer an alleged breach are insufficient protection for our human rights. First if an individual wishes to complain he must first exhaust all his rights under the national law before complaining within one year of the final decision in a British court. Since legal aid applies only in such a small number of cases it will in many cases be prohibitively expensive to take a case as far as the Lords before a reference to the Commission (in itself an expensive undertaking). It is also an extremely lengthy procedure, which again deters potential complainants. Once a matter is referred to the Commission an attempt is made to settle the dispute, but failing this it may be referred to the European Court of Human Rights. However if an individual has complained then the matter can only be referred to the Court if the European Commission decide this is the correct course of action. Once the European Court makes its judgement then, although an individual case may be settled, if English law does not coincide with the Convention there may be further delay before the necessary reforming enactment is introduced.

In *Attorney-General* v *Times Newspapers Ltd* (1) the House of Lords made a pronouncement that the European Court subsequently decided conflicted with article 10 of the European Convention on Freedom of Expression, but not until 1981 was the substantive law reformed by the Contempt of Court Act 1981.

The level of complaints to the European Commission against the British Government and English law has been consistently high and that together with anxieties over the situation in Northern Ireland and the defects of the system mentioned above has caused many to believe that incorporation of some Bill of Rights is now necessary and desirable.

The opponents to incorporation of the European Convention put forward a number of arguments. First that since the UK is already bound to its provisions in international law there is no need to go further, second that to have such a Bill of Rights would put too much power into the hands of the judiciary and third that to incorporate the Bill would be futile since the doctrine of Parliamentary sovereignty means that any later Parliament could simply choose to depart from its provisions.

The second objection, which is said to make incorporation of the convention undesirable, is that the courts would be asked to use the convention as a yardstick to pronounce on the validity of any pre-existing Act of Parliament (and possibly on subsequent Acts too). This places non-elected judges in a position to refuse to put into operation legislation duly passed through Parliament in which elected representatives sit. The judges, so the argument runs, are not trained to do this and since they do not answer to the electorate it would be inappropriate to allow them to have this effect.

Proponents of the European Convention argue that for it to be fully effective as a safeguard of human rights it should be entrenched in some way against later repeal. However this would, of course, be difficult from the constitutional point of view because of the doctrine of Parliamentary Sovereignty which includes as one concept the idea that no Parliament is bound by its predecessors. To achieve entrenchment it would probably be necessary to adopt a written constitution adjusting the relationship of Parliament and the Courts. Even so some more limited form of legislation could be attempted. Perhaps a Bill could be worded somewhat similarly to the European Communities Act 1972 so as to overrule pre-existing legislation and subsequent legislation except where Parliament made it clear that subsequent legislation should prevail.

Incorporation of the European Convention into domestic law has been kept a live issue during the 1980's by the efforts of backbench members of the Lords and Commons who have made various attempts at legislation. Unfortunately each attempt by Private Members' Bill has run out of time and/or support and it seems unlikely that a Bill of Rights will soon be incorporated despite the fact that many people, including eminent law lords, now regards this as both desirable and necessary.

Reference

1) *Attorney-General* v *Times Newspapers* [1974] AC 273

QUESTION 6

General Comment

Give an introduction as to the development and purpose of administrative law (use as much caselaw as possible). Comment on the areas where administrative law will not enter.

Skeleton Solution

Introduction – administrative law. Explanation of ouster clauses.

Subjectively worded powers – *Padfield* v *Minister of Agriculture*.

Time limit ouster clauses – *R* v *Secretary of State for the Environment, ex parte Ostler*.

Anisminic type clauses – *Anisminic* and *Re Racal Communications Ltd*.

Conclusion.

Suggested Solution

Administrative law is the law relating to the control of governmental power, and in particular with the legal controls upon the exercise of those powers by subordinate administrative authorities. Judicial review is the means whereby the courts achieve this control. In reviewing administrative action the court is not so much concerned with the merits of an actual decision but rather with the process by which that decision was reached.

At one stage the court's control could, it was thought, be avoided by the use either of subjectively worded powers in a statute or by the insertion of an ouster or privative clause removing the courts' jurisdiction. Nowadays the courts apply various principles where a subjectively worded power is at issue in order to assess whether the power has been used correctly and the various types of ouster clauses have generally been interpreted narrowly by the courts.

An example of a subjectively worded power would be one where 'if the Minister thinks fit…' he may carry out an action or 'in the Minister's discretion' he may …. Nowadays there is no doubt that in such cases the courts will review the exercise of such a power by a Minister or other public authority to ensure that he has acted reasonably. They will consider, inter alia, such factors as the following – whether the statute is being used for the correct or merely an ulterior purpose, whether the relevant matters have been taken into account in making a decision and the irrelevant ones discounted, whether there has been bad faith, whether the rules of natural justice (if applicable) have been applied, whether the authority has reached a decision that no reasonable authority could make. There is no exhaustive list of these rules and many cases could equally well be explained as falling foul of several of the rules enumerated above.

In *Padfield* v *Minister of Agriculture* (1) a subjectively worded power that a committee of investigation would investigate 'if the Minister in any case so directs' was at issue. The Minister's refusal to place a complaint by milk producers before such a committee was reviewed by the court because the Minister had failed to carry out the purposes of the Act.

This modern view of the law can be contrasted with older cases such as *Liversidge* v *Anderson* (2) where the court refused to intervene in the detention of a person under a power given to the Home Secretary during the Second World War to detain persons he believed to be of hostile origins or associations.

Ouster clauses may be found in several main forms. First clauses which impose a time limit (usually six weeks) outside which no appeal or application for review may be made and second clauses which provide that the decision of a body 'shall be final and shall not be called in question in any court of law'. These clauses are treated differently.

The time limit clauses are frequently used in statutes in areas such as compulsory purchase and town and country planning where many are affected by a decision. In these circumstances it is obviously important that a decision is rapidly reached and cannot after many months be set aside and therefore the courts have taken the view that the time limit clause should stand and no challenge be allowed at a later date, even where the complainant at the time time of the decision could not have known of the factor which, it is alleged, has tainted the decision. In *R* v *Secretary of State for the Environment ex p Ostler* (3), Ostler discovered that a decision taken many months before had been made by giving undisclosed assurances to certain objectors which affected his interests. He attempted to challenge the decision outside the six week limit. He failed, the court upholding the ouster clause.

The second type of ouster clause, commonly called an Anisminic clause, has caused much controversy in its treatment by the courts. In *Anisminic Ltd* v *Foreign Compensation Commission* (4) the Foreign Compensation Act 1950 provided by Section 4 that the decision of the Commission (a tribunal) should be final and should not be called into question in any court of law. When the Commission under a mistake of law withheld compensation from Anisminic, Anisminic applied for judicial review notwithstanding Section 4 of the Act. Anisminic was successful in the House of Lords. The Lords took the view that a clause of this type could prevent review by the court where the decision making body had remained within its jurisdiction but where it had exceeded its jurisdiction the clause would not prevent review. Since the tribunal was a lay body it would not have been intended by Parliament that they should decide the legal effect of words and actions, therefore a mistake of law took the Commission beyond its jurisdiction and the ouster clause did not operate to prevent review.

During the early part of the 1970s the Court of Appeal seemed to be taking the view that any mistake of law made by a decision making body of any type, which led it to reach a decision wrong in the eyes of the court, would take the body beyond its jurisdiction so that a clause attempting to oust review would fail to work. However this attitude was dealt a decisive blow by the House of Lords in *Re Racal Communications Ltd* (5). In that case a High Court judge was empowered under the Companies Act 1948 to order the production of management accounts etc upon certain conditions being shown. There was in the Act a provision to the effect that his decision was final etc. He refused to order the production owing to what was alleged was a mistake of law and the Court of Appeal therefore allowed an appeal but the House of Lords reversed the Court of Appeal.

The Lords took the view that a mistake of this sort by the judge (if indeed there was one) would leave him acting within his jurisdiction so that the ouster clause would prevent review.

To summarise the effect of these decisions one can state that an Anisminic ouster clause prevents review of a decision made within jurisdiction but not of one made outside jurisdiction. It may be very difficult to decide what mistake is jurisdictional in effect but where one is dealing with lay bodies, such as tribunals the courts seem to be prepared to treat any mistakes of law as taking them outside jurisdiction whereas, should the decision maker be a judge, his mistakes of law may, or may not, take him beyond his jurisdiction depending upon their gravity.

In conclusion in the case of time limit ouster clauses the courts are prepared in the public interest to see their jurisdiction to invalidate a decision set aside once the time limit is past (but this will not prevent claims for damages in appropriate cases). In the case of other ouster clauses and subjectively worded powers the courts are keen to protect their jurisdiction to review although they are interested in the process of decision making rather than the merits of a decision.

References

1) *Padfield* v *Minister of Agriculture* [1968] AC 997
2) *Liversidge* v *Anderson* [1942] AC 206
3) *R* v Secretary *of State for the Environment, ex parte Ostler* [1977] QB 122
4) *Anisminic Ltd* v *Foreign Compensation Commission* [1969] 2 AC 147
5) *Re Racal Communications Ltd* [1981] AC 374

QUESTION 7

Skeleton Solution

This answer could be very long. Important statutes to outline are The Official Secrets Act (and the new Act) and the Broadcasting Act. Contempt of Court is also important as is s159 Criminal Justice Act 1988.

Suggested Solution

The Official Secrets Acts 1911–1939 are the major Acts protecting state security. Section 1 provides that it is an offence punishable with 14 years imprisonment if a person goes into or passes any prohibited place or makes any major sketch or collects records prejudicial to the safety or interest of the state. *Chandler* v *DPP* (1) plainly shows that the 1911 Act is not restricted to spying, but includes acts of sabotage and acts of physical interference. Section 2 provides that it is an offence:

'if any person having in his possession or control ... any document ... communicates the document to any person other than a person to whom he should communicate it.'

This section is the 'catch all' section and covers a vast area. The Franks Committee estimated that there are over 2,000 possible charges that can be brought under s2. It is also unclear if s2 requires a guilty mind (mens rea).

Freedom of expression is restricted under this Act and the question arises as to whether or not the new Official Secrets Act due to come into face at the end of 1989 expands freedom of expression or hinders it?

It is right that certain secrets must be kept in any state and vital secrets are protected in the new Act. If we view, however, the function of the democratic state to be that of the efficient protection of information so that the country is run properly – not just refusal to disclose information – then the new Act can be severely criticised. The test to be applied is the balance struck between access to information to citizens and protection to servants of the state so that they can in fact run the country properly.

Under the new Official Secrets Act no new rights to information are provided for and ministers will continue to be able to withhold information embarrasing to their case. It is true that the vast bulk of information will no longer be protected by the criminal law but in the past civil servants were more likely to be disciplined or sacked for breaches of the Act rather than facing criminal prosecution (except in exceptional cases like Tisdall and Ponting). Many breaches of the old statute went unpunished.

The new Act makes it an offence for a member of the security and intelligence services or retired members to disclose any information relating to that work he has obtained while so employed. There is an offence relating to other Crown servants or government contractors who make damaging disclosures of information they have obtained about the security services. Damaging disclosures in relation to defence and international relations are also offences by Crown servants. A Crown servant also commits an offence if he discloses information he has received as such which results in the commission of an offence, facilitates an escape from custody or inhibits the detection of crime or arrest of offenders.

Where information is leaked from a foreign source and where information 'likely to be useful in the commission of a crime' is leaked it is outside the ambit of the Act. This is an improvement on the original Official Secrets Bill.

The concept of absolute offences is less strict than in the Official Secrets Act presently in force. The areas covered have been reduced in the Act but there is no prior publication defence. Therefore it is of no avail to show (i) no harm was done or (ii) that the matter was already widely published. This is particularly disturbing – an editor can be caught for repeating words forbidden today which had been widely published yesterday but not then forbidden.

(When Mr Douglas Hurd assured the public that this provision would be used sensibly there is still doubt about this especially in view of the Peter Wright affair.) No public interest defence will be allowed – so information revealing exceptional abuse of authority will not be a defence. Mr Hurd has said that a form of public interest defence will exist because in some areas the prosecution would have to show a disclosure caused 'harm to the public interest'. The Act itself does not use the words 'public interest' so if a specific form of harm can be shown, a jury will have to convict. For more than a century a public interest defence has existed. In the Spycatcher cases, Lord Griffiths continued to defend this principle – in exceptional circumstances a civil servant could be 'relieved of his duty of confidence' so that he could 'alert his fellow citizens to the impending danger'.

A case can be made, therefore, that the new Act should seek to uphold this principle because secrecy can be damaging in these 'exceptional circumstances'.

The government, recently moved to prevent unnecessary secrecy rulings in Crown Courts and s159 of the Criminal Justice Act 1988 provides for the first time the right to question judges' decisions to close their doors to the public or impose reporting restrictions in criminal trials. This means that, for example, journalists would have the right to contest reporting restrictions.

It was journalists led by Jim Brooks which led to the recognition by the European Commission on Human Rights that the lack of method to appeal against a judge's secrecy order is a potential breach of human rights. As reported in *The Independent* (24 June 1989) it seems there is concern that draft rules accompanying s159 may lead to more secrecy and reporting restrictions. Do these new draft rules reflect Parliament's intention when it provided for an appeal system? These rules are drawn up by the Lord Chancellor's department in consultation with a committee of advisers including the Lord Chief Justice of England.

The rules seem to provide for appeals by way of written representation only when a justice closes his doors to the press. This, it is submitted, may negate the 'open justice' principle. The rules also provide for a new category of secrecy in relation to witnesses or 'any other person.' There is no provision for an expedited appeal. The Court of Appeal's decision is final and the matter cannot be tested in the House of Lords. The Lord Chancellor's department have said that the draft rules were designed for practicality, expediency and in the interests of national security. The paper appeal provides a quick method of appeal and nothing confidential is likely to leak out inadvertently (2).

Contempt of court is another area where freedom of expression can be curtailed. The position is now governed by the Contempt of Court Act 1981. This act was partly in response to an appeal made by the *Sunday Times* to the European Court of Human Rights. The European Court had said that the test was too widely drawn in the United Kingdom and had the effect of unlawfully silencing a newspapers right to freedom of expression. Under the act there can be contempt regardless of 'intent to do so', this is the 'strict liability rule', however, there are defences under s3 eg 'innocent publication … etc' (see also *R v Griffiths* (3)). Contemporaneous reporting and reporting a discussion 'in good faith of public affairs' are two further defences.

The protection of journalistic sources is given a limited defence only. (See *Secretary of State for Defence v Guardian Newspapers Ltd* (4).) This limited defence is provided for in s10 of The Contempt of Court Act 1981. Disclosure will not be required 'unless it be established' (that disclosure) 'is in the interests of justice or national security or for the prevention of disorder or crime.'

The 'Death on the Rock' programme screened by Thames Television on 28 April 1988, against the government's wishes, illustrates a crisis with regard to freedom of expression.

This programme was 'a lightning conductor for the intense feelings that the Gibraltar shootings evoked in the minds of the British public ... The conflict was essentially one of divergent personal attitudes and value rather than of party political divisions (5). (All of the British public would understandably resent the IRA's brutal campaign of violence). Some people however, felt that the security forces were fully entitled to take such measures as were necessary to protect the people of Gibraltar and the Royal Anglian Regiment from planned assassination. Others, whilst abhorring the IRA's objectives and tactics, felt that the security force's actions (whether in Northern Ireland or elsewhere) fell outside the specific limitations of the rule of law by which they are bound. The question concerned the Broadcasting Act 1981 – did the programme 'Death on the Rock' offend against the due impartiality requirements? The Windlesham Rampton Report vindicates the objectivity of the television programme (6).

It is true, therefore, that the human rights jurists may now look to television more than newspapers when allegations of contempt (or 'trial by television') are made.

A new Broadcasting Act 1989 [1990] provides that where the minister is of opinion that an item to be broadcast would promote or incite crime or undermine the authority of the state, he may order a person/company not to broadcast such item. The Home Secretary can issue an order under this act requiring all television companies to refrain from broadcasting the forbidden item. This will include an interview or discussion of a person who appears or is heard on the particular programme and the person is representing or purports to represent a terrorist organisation or where the words support such an organisation.

To try to curtail terrorism is perfectly understandable in any civilised society. This new Broadcasting Act, however, has been subject to severe criticism. Since the government's ban on broadcasting interviews etc with IRA members and sympathisers except during election campaigns, television companies have shown programmes with a particular person in view but whose words/voice is not broadcast. A television reporter may then report about the events. This is less than satisfactory and raises the question as to the usefulness of the Act. It might be more practical to leave the discretion in the hands of the directors of the various television companies.

References

1) *Chandler* v *DPP* [1964] AC 763
2) See report *The Independent* 27 June 1989; see also leading article.
3) *R* v *Griffiths* [1957] 2 QB 192
4) *Secretary of State for Defence* v *Guardian Newspapers* [1984] 2 WLR 268
5) See The Windlesham/Rampton Report on *Death on the Rock*.
6) 'Whatever view is taken of the state of public opinion and the legitimacy of public opinion and the legitimacy of government intervention, the making and screening of "Death on the Rock" proved that freedom of expression can prevail in the most extensive and the most immediate of all the means of mass communication.' (Windlesham Rampton Report).

UNIVERSITY OF LONDON
INTERMEDIATE EXAMINATION IN LAWS 1990
for External Students

CONSTITUTIONAL LAW

Wednesday, 13 June: 10.00 am to 1.00 pm

Answer *FOUR* of the following SEVEN questions

1. 'Parliamentary experience of recent years has demonstrated that collectively Members (of the House of Commons) can exercise the political will necessary to provide the parameters within which the Government can govern, albeit of necessity in a limited and generally negative way.'(Norton)
   Discuss.

2. To what extent can the relationship between central and local government be described as a partnership?

3. 'Prerogative powers are essential to the smooth operation of government.'
   Do you agree?

4. 'In a country such as the United Kingdom which has an unwritten constitution based largely on parliamentary sovereignty, it is by no means clear that the enactment of a Bill of Rights is desirable, or that such a Bill could be protected from amendment or repeal'.
   Discuss.

5. 'With a perfect Lower House it is certain that an Upper House would be scarcely of any value. But ... beside the actual House (of Commons) a revising and leisured legislature is extremely useful.' (Bagehot)
   Discuss.

6. 'When the security of the State is under threat the rights and freedoms of the individual must give way to the greater interests of society as a whole.'
   Discuss in the light of recent changes in the law.

7 The Blankshire County Council has statutory responsibility for organising refuse collection. The County Council normally act on the recommendation of the Environmental Health Committee. Councillor Smith, the Chairman of the Environmental Health Committee is a director of Kleenit Ltd, a company based in Blankshire which wishes to bid for the Blankshire refuse collection contract. The Environmental Health committee decides:

i) that it wishes a Blankshire based company to have the contract;

ii) that it will not consider bids from former employees of the County Council;

iii) that it will leave the final decisions to its Chairman.

The Chairman awards the contract to Kleenit Ltd and his decision is forwarded to the County Council, which approves it. Advise Smurf, a former employee of the Blankshire County Council, who also runs a highly successful refuse collection business in an adjoining county, and who made a lower bid than Kleenit Ltd for the Blankshire contract.

QUESTION 1

Suggested Solution

The starting point of the constitution is the representation of the electorate in Parliament, which is the supreme and sovereign law maker. Developed from this is the notion that the electorate thereby makes its preferred choice of government. However, for obvious practical reasons, elections cannot be held every year, nor can referendums be held on all points of importance that arise during a government's term of office. Thus, the accountability of government directly to the electorate is only periodic and it is this situation that gives rise to the fear of the possibility of an 'elective dictatorship', with a carte blanche to govern in whichever way it pleases for the term of its office.

To a certain extent this is an ill founded fear since the final reckoning will ultimately come with the dissolution of Parliament. Of more concern, however, is the situation that arises where, for the most part, a government's policies and style of government finds general approval, but where particular measures are potentially constitutionally threatening.

In such circumstances, government becomes indirectly accountable to the representatives of the electorate in Parliament and as such Parliament is termed the 'watchdog' of Executive action. Since the Commons is the elected chamber and the focus of most political activity, without dismissing the important work of the Lords, it must clearly be the area where the ground rules of governmental activity are laid down.

Thus in purist theory, the political arm of the Executive are collectively responsible to Parliament in general and to the House of Commons in particular. The idiomatic traditions of Parliament provide the forum for the supervision of government. The experience of recent years has brought much attention to bear on how effective these complex constraints and restrictions are when the Commons is effectively dominated by the party that holds office.

Before considering in detail the general parliamentary restrictions on government activity, it must be made clear that the mere fact that a party commands a majority in the House does not guarantee a majority of votes. Even where the whip system that urges members to comply is in strict operation, a member cannot be forcibly compelled to vote with the government. Although the price of such rebellion might be suspension from the parliamentary party, as Nicholas Winterton MP seems bound to discover at the time of writing, such defiance often has a profound political consequence and may be the prompt for revision of legislation when the action is taken in concert.

As well as such purely political considerations, the application of conventions relating to the accountability individually and collectively of ministers establishes a further set of checks which are enforced through Parliament. The intense political embarrassment caused by ministerial or departmental misfeasance usually finds its focus in parliamentary questions or debates, where, on serious issues, the choice of either a convincing explanation or resignation is expected to be forthcoming.

Similarly, where decisions are made at Cabinet level, ministers are held collectively to account to Parliament. As De Smith observes, if a minister dissents he should resign first, and then publicly distance himself from the subject in contention. However, the purist theory lacks a little in substance, since a suspension of the convention is possible and the government attitude seems to be enshrined not a little in Mr Callaghan's remark that ' ... I certainly think the doctrine should apply, except in cases where I announce that it does not.' This indeed indicates the extent of the 'flexibility' of our unwritten constitution.

Parliament, if it feels so inclined, may censure the government with a motion of no confidence where the government is held to be collectively responsible. Of convention, such a motion, if it were successful, would prompt the resignation of the government. In recent years, however, Mrs Thatcher has been censured without subsequently leaving office. Once again it is the 'flexible' constitution at work. The significance of such a motion is to be viewed more in terms of a political tactic and a method of attracting media attention.

A more direct and effective control of government is the need for parliamentary approval for the financing of government initiatives. Since Parliament holds the country's purse strings, the government must inspire enough confidence in the Commons, at least to provide funding for new policies. The structure of government finance is necessarily complex, but the parliamentary system is structured so as to cope with these rigours. Central to this system is the Public Accounts Committee, which, although reflecting the parliamentary representation of the parties, has such a non-partisan reputation that it is, by convention, chaired by a member of the opposition. Although it primarily seeks out financial irregularities, it also monitors extravagant spending and imprudent contractual transactions.

Extensive powers of discovery and enquiry were conferred on the Treasury and Civil Service Committee, which was set up in 1979, to the extent that scrutinising Treasury policy is within the Committee's brief. In such ways Parliament tacitly defines the parameters within which the Executive can finance its policies.

Aside from these financial controls, the standing orders and procedures of the Commons provide adequate opportunities for confrontation of the government by the opposition and their own back benchers on contentious issues. Debating opportunities on the Queen's speech, budget and on Opposition Days, motions of censure and others and emergency debates take on more significance with the eye of the country fixed on television.

The committee system now mirrors the departmental organisation of central government with the setting up of twelve new Departmental Select Committees to examine the expenditure, administration and policy of various designated government departments. Their powers are the same as those of the Treasury and Civil Service Committee and are brought together under the auspices of the Liaison Committee. The force of the House's authority and powers to punish for contempt are behind these committees.

The teeth of the Defence Select Committee were tested during the 'Westland Affair' when it sought to discover the names of civil servants who were responsible for the leaking of a letter from the Solicitor General. Although the government achieved a compromise, the Committee never conceded that in law there were any governmental restraints on the exercise of its functions.

The Departmental Select Committee system is generally regarded as a forum for more in-depth and informed discussion than is available elsewhere in Parliament. Furthermore, their unanimous, but often powerfully critical reports, such as that of the Foreign Affairs Committee on government proposals to raise fees for overseas university students, have certainly had effects on Executive policy. However, the paucity of free debating time means that only a handful of the reports have had full discussion on the floor of the House of Commons.

Parliament's role as the arena for airing criticism of the government has been significantly augmented by the advent of television cameras, as we have observed before. Certainly the parliamentary proceeding that most captivates the imagination of the electorate is Question Time, when the government at least appears to be under the most stringent attack. The extent to which the request for oral or written answers to questions to any minister is actually laying down the parameters of government, rather than political point scoring, is somewhat questionable. However, it is clear that the electoral fortunes of a party or MP may be decided in the cut and thrust of these brief sessions, something of which the government is clearly aware. However, De Smith's view that 'a question to a minister is rather a method of ventilating a grievance than of securing a remedy' is perhaps the most realistic approach.

In addition to the practical limitations of parliamentary questions as a method of scrutinising the government, certain questions may be refused if they lie outside the sphere of competence of a minister. Answers may not be forthcoming if the matter is sub judice, or simply because an answer would cost more than £250, the current ceiling for expenditure on parliamentary answers.

A final method available to members to ensure the maintenance of the standards of government is by directing the Parliamentary Commissioner for Administration to investigate alleged maladministration. However, this function is one that is seldom exercised collectively, and therefore merits no detailed discussion.

Thus, having explored the way in which members might scrutinise the Executive, we must assess the truth of Norton's assertions. In our parliamentary system, strong reliance is placed upon adherence to conventions. The effect of disapproving motions relating to conventions of responsibility cannot be denied; recent resignations in the last parliamentary session underline this. However, the change in attitude towards, for example, the motion of censure, demonstrates that reliance on convention as a method of Executive control is unsatisfactory, particularly when a government commands a sizeable majority in the Commons.

Equally, there are limits on the extent to which control of the government can be exercised by intermittent rebellions of back bench members, who stand to lose their status within the parliamentary party and with the electorate.

Financial control holds out the most practical promise as delineating the parameters of government, but once again is subject to the control of the majority party in the House, which is almost always subject to strict party discipline.

It is therefore in the arena of the debating floor and during Question Time, which, due to its high media profile, is of great significance in terms of public opinion, that the democratic check on the executive finds its strongest weapon. Where MPs collectively know that public opinion supports them against government policy, even back benchers of the party in power may find a reserves of courage to criticise and rebel.

Conversely, the committee system is increasingly being regarded as the part of the Commons where much of the serious work goes on. With its smaller and more informed membership, and its greater opportunities for detailed and lengthy scrutiny, as well as the tendency of committees to be less partisan or concerned with political point scoring, this forum has become in many ways a powerhouse of the democratic process. Opportunities exist not only to criticise, but to make searching enquiries of the way in which the process of government is carried on.

It is difficult to envisage, however, what Norton's conception of a positive way of providing the parameters within which government can govern would amount to. Obviously, the doctrine of the separation of powers prevents excessive interference by the legislature in Executive functions. Thus, the positive function of members must be to maintain and enforce the constitutional safeguards against abuse of Executive power. Since these safeguards are largely in the nature of conventions, then following the general view that they are adhered to since their breach would result in political embarrassment, Parliament's only significant function is to heighten the electorate's awareness of government threats to the constitution. It is arguable that this role is better performed by the media, although it cannot compel ministers to account. More importantly parliamentary committees can extract information in a way that need not be as self-consciously populist as the methods employed on the floor of the House of Commons.

In the final analysis, any weaknesses or limitations in the methods available to members who wish to lay down the parameters for good government have to be put down to the inherent weaknesses of our constitution. Additionally, it must be remembered that excessive interference in Executive functions by the legislature is constitutionally undesirable.

QUESTION 2

Suggested Solution

The relationship between central and local government is often expressed in terms of a partnership, but as De Smith comments, if it is 'it is a partnership between a rider and a horse'. The measure of autonomy once enjoyed by local authorities has been somewhat eroded over recent years, particularly by the effects of government spending restrictions, the new form of finance for local authorities and by the legitimisation of 'opting out' by services whose control had been the cornerstone of their power.

However, it must be appreciated that since the rise of the Liberal Party under Joseph Chamberlain, central government has come to depend on a more 'grass roots' attitude towards politics, developing local issues and using pilot schemes organised and administered by local authorities as role models to illustrate not only the way in which a government appreciates the needs of the electorate, but, more recently, to prove ideological points.

The dependency of central government on local government is illustrated by the great weight afforded to Local government representations when, as often happens, a government department will consult on a local issue. Frequently, local authorities will be instrumental in the instigation of legislation.

However, a vast array of central controls are in place to promote effective and cost efficient services. The change in methods of funding away from the rates which were payable direct into local government coffers to the community charge which is distributed by the Treasury according to central government perception of need effectively robs regional authorities of control of expenditure. This is so even though poll tax rates are set locally since the controversial use of 'poll tax capping' denies true freedom in the determination of financial goals.

The true power of local authorities has traditionally stemmed from their powers to administer and control the essential services. However ultimate control must of necessity lie with central government to ensure the maintenance of minimum standards nationwide. In matters such as planning and environmental issues there is always a final veto or appeal direct to the Secretary of State for the Environment. As De Smith observed: 'No one reading through two years' output of Town and Country Planning Regulations will doubt the reality of central control over matters of procedure and substance'.

Briefly, we may wish to outline the various methods of governmental regulation of local authorities. As we have already noted executive control by ministers and their departments acting in a supervisory or judicial function is a primary technique applied to ensure compliance with statutory obligations. Generally, no power of a local authority exists or may be exercised without Parliament's implicit sanction. This will usually be found in the form of specific statutory enactments or the interpretation of Acts of Parliament by the courts with regard to the vires of a local authority's exercise of powers. In pursuance of the maintenance of standards in the provision of services within the control of a local authority, inspection either generally by the National Audit Office with regard to expenditure or consequent to a specific statute such as s77(2) of the Education Act 1944, may be carried out. Normally such functions of inspectors are accompanied by the power to make formal or informal compliance orders.

The appointment and dismissal of certain local authority officers also is subject to the sanction of central government. The 1988 Local Government and Housing Act put effective restrictions on those who can hold such offices when they seek regional political appointments. Even the qualified legislative power to create by-laws is subject to the confirmation and approval of the appropriate minister, as are any schemes, proposals or plans where statute places the requirement of ministerial assent.

Ultimately, the Local Government Act 1972 provides the machinery for a review of local government areas in the form of boundary commissions. In recent years governments have shown more than a willingness to 'reform' certain problematic or overpowerful councils. Perhaps most significant of all was the abolishment of the Greater London Council by the Local Government Act 1985. Currently, there are plans to review the status of an independent Local Authority for Kingston in London. This may be the ultimate central government sanction against habitually non-compliant authorities!

A more serious and insidious erosion of the independent power of regional government stems from the newly created concept of 'opting out'. Hospitals, formerly under the control of local health authorities, may now create self governing trusts, taking the administration and funding decisions away from regional authorities substituting direct accountability to the Department of

Health. In a similar vein, schools may establish their own individual control, again accountable direct to the Department. Although the uptake of this option has not been great, the potential for usurpation of these traditional powers is significant.

Thus, in conclusion we must relate our review of central government's relationship with local authorities to the concept of partnership suggested by the question. Partnership intimates an equality of status and a degree of mutuality. There can be no doubt that the administrative burden, practical requirements for good government and the appreciation of local needs dictate that there will always be a demand for some kind of local executive function. However, the term government must be viewed in the context of a degree of executive freedom that the encroaching controls and fetters stemming from Whitehall and Westminster would seek to prevent. In this light the partnership is certainly that between a senior partner and his junior, if not analogous to that between master and servant.

QUESTION 3

Suggested Solution

Prerogative powers stem from the historic rights and privileges of the monarch and as such represent a separate root of authority from that which devolves from the supremacy of Parliament. Although prerogatives can be traced even in the modern day to the sanction and approval of the monarch, vital prerogatives are largely exercised by central government. In addition they are now regarded as being subject to the scrutiny and approval of Parliament and of the courts. Moreover any possibility of prerogative powers usurping the legislative supremacy of Parliament has long been disregarded. In fact statute may suspend or eliminate existing prerogatives and the courts have expressed unwillingness to recognise the existence or unnecessary extension of such powers. Certain prerogatives were explicitly abolished with respect to the monarchy in the preamble to the Bill of Rights 1689.

As such it is hard to define precisely the nature of the modern prerogative; however certain elements may be clearly identified. Firstly the prerogative is residual to the will of Parliament as had been made clear by the Bill of Rights and more recently the Crown Proceedings Act 1947. Secondly, prerogative powers derive from the common law and are therefore interpreted by the courts who may delineate the parameters within which they may be lawfully exercised. As a matter of practice most significant powers of this kind, by convention, are normally exercised by the government of the day. There are certain personal prerogatives of the Queen however conventionally even these are subject to scrutiny or veto. Prerogatives such as the giving of the Royal Assent or the appointment of Prime Ministers are regulated by convention and it is inconceivable in the modern constitutional framework that these conventions will be departed from. This is not to say however that prerogatives could be dispensed with even where they seem to be purely a matter of form. Their exercise contrary to convention, for example where the monarch uses her powers against the wishes of the government of the day, may be justified in circumstances where that government seeks to act unconstitutionally and all conventional methods of controlling central government powers are ineffectual. It is because this situation seems such an unlikelihood that Royal prerogatives have the semblance of being ossified by the traditional mores of constitutional behaviour.

Thus, the application of these more formalised prerogatives are not essential for smooth government in routine circumstances, but relate to situations where there is serious constitutional conflict. However, there are a panoply of prerogative powers that, although they inhere in the Crown and are exercised in the name of the monarch, are principally at the disposal of the agencies of central government to facilitate the exercise of the executive function.

Certain of these relate to the fundamental administration of affairs of state. Matters such as disposition of armed forced which require swift and sometimes, for the purposes of national security, secret decisions are subject to prerogative powers. The defence of the realm, which is primarily the responsibility of the Crown, must be dealt with in a decisive manner and in consequence decisions relating to the armed forces, such as the extent to which protection of citizens must be provided, are subject to the exclusive privilege and cognizance of the Crown. This is illustrated by the decision in *China Navigation Company v AG* in which it was stated by Scrutton LJ: 'that the administration of the army is in the hands of the King who unless expressly controlled by an Act of Parliament cannot be controlled by the court'. To some extent this unquestioning view of privilege and the notion that the Crown may give conclusive certification of the needs of national security represents the old view of prerogative. It is clear from developments in legal thinking with regard to Crown privilege that the courts feel more able to scrutinise circumstances where national security is used to cloak arbitrary governmental action. Possibly the most significant developments in the sphere of judicial conceptions of prerogative are to be found in *CCSU v Minister for Civil Service* where the House of Lords decided that simply because a decision making power derives from the common law as opposed to statute this did not exclude the possibility of judicial review on the grounds of illegality, irrationality or procedural impropriety. In this case a decision implemented through the Privy Council pursuant to the exercise of prerogative preventing staff at the GCHQ from remaining members of a union was challenged on the basis of a failure to consult resulting in unfairness. The attitude in this case follows closely the rationale of Lord Denning in *Laker Airways Ltd v Department of Trade* which identified the prerogative as being a discretionary power exerciseable on the basis of necessity in such situations where the law has made no alternative provision for decision making frameworks.

This attitude, it is submitted, represents a realistic assessment of the circumstances when these powers may be exercised legitimately and their role in facilitating smooth and efficient government. The parliamentary attitude to central government effecting vital decisions without the explicit approval of its members is a somewhat sceptical one for although a minister may, by convention, be accountable after the event this does not prevent such actions being taken. Since in constitutional theory statute is the supreme source of law which the courts must follow it is clear that where a prerogative power exists Parliament may either abolish it or place it in abeyance. Indeed the courts, when faced with conflicts between statute law and purported exercises of this privileged Crown capacity, have given precedents to the former and shown scant regard for contentions that the Crown may pick and choose which source of law to follow. This was the case in *AG v De Keyser's Royal Hotel* where compensation for damages were payable in pursuance of the Defence of the Realm Consolidation Act 1914, regardless of a claim of immunity based on prerogative. Furthermore it was contended in *Malone v Metropolitan Police Commissioner* that even if such a claim succeeds the Crown may still be under a duty to compensate for lawful exercise of this decision making facility.

Less restrictions seem to attach to the exercise of Crown discretions in the sphere of foreign affairs, such as the making of treaties and matters relating to overseas interests generally. Where prerogatives are exercised for the purpose of foreign policy, judicial interference is less common, primarily because Parliament is regarded as the more appropriate and competent authority to scrutinise such matters, which seldom have full legal standing without parliamentary approval.

The exercise of the modern prerogative and its status in legal theory thus, to a great extent, reflect the practical need for executive power in circumstances and times where prompt execution of governmental decisions are required. The way in which these powers have devolved to the organs of central government mirror the general centralisation and development of the Executive function, necessitated by the complex and fast moving nature of modern society. Where possible, it is clear, the parliamentarians' dislike of extra parliamentary power has stripped the Crown and its servants of prerogatives and this is as it should be within our constitutional framework. The courts, also, have shown their disdain of the use of prerogative to execute policy decisions that lack the authority of statute, where the motive seems to be an arbitrary political one as in the *Laker Airways* case. In stressing the common law basis for prerogative powers, jurists such as Lord Denning clearly recognise that this 'pre-eminence of the Crown' is to be regarded as a complement to the supreme authority of Parliament, as a governmental weapon of last resort. Having said this, however, it would be hard to conceive of Parliament and the courts allowing the continued existence of certain elements of the prerogative if they did not genuinely believe them to be vital for the efficient administration of the country. One need only look at governmental action concerning the current 'Gulf crisis' to understand the proper place of prerogative powers. By virtue of statutory instrument, sanctions were imposed, and using prerogative powers and following the responsibilities placed by treaties, created in pursuance of the prerogative, the government has been able to implement emergency measures to deal with this situation. However, it is significant that Parliament was recalled to examine the steps taken, even in this emergency situation.

QUESTION 4

Suggested Solution

The notion of a bill of rights is that a document consisting of fundamental rights for citizens may be given the full force of law and invested with such constitutional significance that the creation and application of laws and the actions of administrative bodies must conform with its content and spirit. In countries that have experienced the turmoil of revolution or that have gained independence from imperial powers a bill of rights is frequently the highest source of constitutional law. It is a measure of the significance attached to such documents that the terms 'constitution' and 'bill of rights' are often used interchangeably in common parlance.

However, the United Kingdom has a bill of rights in name only. The 1689 Bill of Rights, although providing certain guarantees against arbitrary legal penalties, deals primarily with the respective powers of the monarchy and Parliament. There are certain other guarantees of personal rights embodied in municipal and Community legislation, but there is no single piece of legislation, let alone one that has the legal supremacy of, say, the American Constitution. This is not to say, however, that there is no demand for one. The Westminster model of democracy may be a reassurance against monarchic dictatorship, but the mechanism and nature of executive government, coupled with the 'first-past-the-post' electoral system is not an effective prophylactic against other forms of dictatorship and the piecemeal erosion of civil liberties. In recent years, both of the main opposition parties have called for constitutional reform. This may be, to a certain extent, based on the belief that such reform would improve electoral chances, but it must be accepted that with the extremely strong majority held by the present government and the seemingly inexorable periods of radical government, interspersed by brief and frenetic elections, there is a genuine apprehension that a similar situation would have less happy results for personal freedoms.

Since it is obvious that such political situations are not entirely unprecedented or beyond the conception of those who are concerned with such matters, why, we must ask, has no bill of rights been passed into law? There are three, or more, possible reasons; that it is undesirable, unnecessary or impracticable.

Before delving deeper into these assertions one might make some general observations as to the 'British conception' of the protection of rights. One assumes that somehow we have managed without a bill of rights and since we do not apparently live in a state that constantly restricts our freedom, someone must have thought out a system that guarantees our rights. Jurists have expressed the opinion that general statements of principle, that, in the words of the American Constitution are 'self-evident', have no greater guarantee than the earnest goodwill of the judiciary and Parliament. The experience of many former Commonwealth countries which were given Westminster style government and a bill of rights to boot, confirms the fallibility of a bill of rights without the right sentiment in the hearts of those who must govern by it. However, it does also emphasise the fragility of a reliance on benevolent paternalism.

It is not simply the experience of less established democracies that fuel these suspicions. Under the Republican administration in America, the appointment of averred opponents of the existing content of the Constitution has led to an increase in concern about civil liberties issues such as abortion and the freedom of expression. The issue of Supreme Court 'packing' lends credibility to the notion that a general declaration of the rights of the individual is open to illiberal as well as liberal interpretation. Such an argument may be even stronger in the United Kingdom where the impartiality of judges has been questioned on occasions when there is a serious assertion of civil liberties.

Conversely, it may be suggested that by investing the courts with more power as a consequence of their role in the interpretation of such a constitutional document, the pursuit of a coherent 'rule of law' may inspire them to follow more liberal lines. Such a view may be reinforced by the perceptible changes in the review of administrative actions and attitudes towards conflicts between British legislation and Community obligations.

It is this attitude that draws us to the primary argument for the undesirability. The most vehement critics of justiciable rules intended to protect civil liberties hold up the spectre of 'rule by judges'. A bill of rights for the United Kingdom would be undemocratic, they assert. The argument runs that although a bill of rights is designed to protect the rights of the general public, a bill of rights would also, however, fetter politicians, the democratic representatives of the people, from carrying out their mandated obligations, without constant concern as to whether their legislative actions will fall foul of the judiciary who are not democratically accountable.

This argument rather smacks of the assertion that we should not have a bill of rights because the electorate may not like the consequences, which may be true. Alternatively, it may reveal the possibility that politicians find the idea undesirable because it may lead to considerable inconvenience and an unwelcome limitation on their legislative power.

Whichever the reason it is certain that, at the present time, there is by no means a consensus as to the desirability of a bill of rights and in a parliamentary democracy such as ours it is mandatory that a majority of politicians are in agreement before there is any possibility of this sort of constitutional change.

Some jurists consider that, although legal safeguards of individual rights are necessary, adequate mechanisms already exist. If their contention is correct then a bill of rights is undesirable because it is superfluous. This belief is primarily fuelled by various international treaties to which the United Kingdom is party. The principal example must be the European Convention on Human Rights, which provides a forum for the review of particular human rights violations and a court which may adjudicate on alleged breaches of the Convention. The parameters of the Treaty are wide, although not all-embracing; however its application is slow, to say the least, resulting in only a small proportion of the petitioners satisfying the Commission, which processes applications for hearings in the European Court of Human Rights, that no adequate legal remedy exists in national law. Furthermore, as was discovered in *Malone v United Kingdom* [1984] Ch 344, national courts cannot apply the Convention directly, and need not even take it into account. This is as a result of the failure of the British Parliament to enact the Convention as municipal legislation.

Certain of the obligations created by our membership of the European Community, such as Article 119 of the Treaty of Rome, which prevents certain types of employment discrimination on the basis of gender, have, as Lord Denning observed in *Macarthys Ltd v Wendy Smith*, the full force of law. If the Community were to adopt the 'Social Charter' this would no doubt go even further to protect vital civil liberties and basic human rights. However, Community measures apply principally to the commercial aspects of life, and, as such, do not deal with other freedoms and rights in equal need of protection. Moreover, there is nothing, at least theoretically, to prevent Parliament, even at this late stage, from revoking or refusing to implement its European obligations.

If we can therefore accept that there is a vacuum in this area of constitutional law and that at some point in the future a majority of Parliament will be in favour of passing a bill of rights, we must examine its potential status in law. Obviously, as a simple Act of Parliament it would have the status of all Acts of Parliament; namely it would be good and binding law unless and until it was repealed, and as such all would have to abide by it. However, it would be up to the normal democratic processes to safeguard the Act itself and in circumstances where a new Parliament consisted of those who saw this bill of rights as unnecessary or undesirable, it could lose its status at the stroke of the legislative pen.

Thus, a simple Act of Parliament could not provide the monolithic certainty that one would expect of a cornerstone of the constitution, at least so far as the legal theory goes. Thus, one is faced with the problem of entrenching a bill of rights for the United Kingdom. The experience of earlier Parliaments who have sought, by drafting clauses against repeal, to challenge the concept that no Parliament can bind its successors, shows us, as in the case of *Vauxhall Estates/Ellen Street Estates* that a later Parliament, simply by stating something different, can implicitly repeal an earlier Act. Even if we could assume the judiciary would treat our Bill of Rights with the same reverence as the European Communities Act 1972, which seeks to have all legislation construed in accordance with its provisions, the situation would be doubtful. It seems that entrenchment would require something more than good draftsmanship, since even the requirement for a weighty majority of Parliament to modify or abolish this document could itself be set aside by Parliament.

It would therefore seem that nothing short of a complete restructuring of the constitutional tenets of the United Kingdom would give the desired effect, namely that Parliament was made less supreme than a constitutional document enshrining rights. But how may one Parliament surrender the sovereignty of all future Parliaments even in the name of a constitutional form of 'perestroika'. Perhaps the abolition of the Lords would provide an opportunity to move the legal goal posts, by adding the proviso that subsequent Parliaments were subject to the bill of rights. However, in theory, there would be nothing to prevent this itself from being overturned.

It soon becomes clear that when one pursues constitutional theory to its bitter end, ultimately one concludes that the constitution is as it is and its flexibility means that democratic change may be made, but constitutional guarantees cannot be written in stone. Such an attitude may be seen to be at the same time a truism and an absurdity. It is the nature of the British, and other constitutions that they have been created and added to by historical forces and certain documents have become, by dint of the democratic will and the writings of jurists, sacrosanct, such as the Bill of Rights 1689 or the Reform Bill of 1832. There is nothing but a continuing respect for the democratic forces that created them and for the certainty that they provide, through the passing ages, to keep them from repeal, and should the democratic will exist then these may be swept away. It is clear from the constitutional changes in the Soviet Union, for example, that rules of the constitution, however monolithic and theoretically entrenched, may in practice always be discarded.

Assuming that the legislature are willing and the general public support such a measure, a bill of rights could be passed and would remain in force as long as it was still desired. It is likely that a government that would not respect the will of the electorate would certainly not be too concerned about the constitutional niceties of entrenchment, even if it were possible.

QUESTION 5

Suggested Solution

An instinctive answer to the present question is 'nothing is perfect'. The truth of this statement is not diminished by the context of the question. The Houses of Parliament are invested with supreme constitutional power to legislate on all matters, but with responsibility to represent the interests, not only of the electorate, but all members of society. This is obviously a grave responsibility and in terms of work load an arduous one. In the light of this it is certainly not difficult to support the implicit assertion of the question that a legislature consisting of two chambers (a bicameral legislature) is not only convenient, but extremely desirable from a practical and constitutional point of view.

Much has been said in criticism of the present membership of Parliament and these observations have given rise to consideration of reform by some of the major political parties, particularly of the Upper House. This synopsis has largely been derived from democratic concerns.

The principal objections to the current constitution of the Commons relate to the election of members in accordance with the 'first past the post' system which does not proportionately represent the various minorities that, taken as a whole, make up the electorate. Nor can it truthfully be said that the combined number of seats of both Houses provide an adequate forum in terms of manpower to represent these views. One way of achieving constitutional perfection (which of course is in the eyes of the beholder, or jurist, or politician) may be to compensate for the inadequacies of both Houses by a radical overhaul of just one. A strong argument for this is that the long standing traditions and complex conventions that provide for the, by and large, smooth running of the legislature would be disrupted intolerably by attempted reform of both Houses.

In essence this is in keeping with the ethos behind bicameralism; that having two chambers, with different constitutions, is desirable since each can complement and regulate the other. As it stands, there is much justification for the present system. This centres around the practical difficulties of coping with the legislative burden, and around the peculiar skills of the House of Lords.

In essence, the simplest of the arguments in favour of the bicameral system is that two Houses can cope with twice the amount of legislation. This means that non-controversial Bills that are unlikely to be rejected outright in the Commons stage may be introduced in the Lords, leaving the Commons to grapple with more contentious legislation that might be radically altered in the Lower House. By having two forums, opportunities for debating or quizzing government ministers are doubled. These popular assertions may, however, be countered by the contention that these ends might more easily be achieved by shortening the legislative process, reducing the parliamentary 'holidays' and delegating more of the routine legislation to departments and more of the scrutiny of government to the committee system. The democratic desirability of diverting business off the floor of the House, especially into the hands of the government, or of distracting busy members from their constituency duties, is debatable. The justification for such measures, as opposed to retaining extra politicians and an alternate venue, are largely of a financial nature, however, and do not diminish the fact that for practical purposes the bicameral system is still preferable.

A more serious function of any second chamber is as a constitutional safeguard against incompetence or imbalance in the first chamber. The Lords, as they stand, comprise a reservoir of expertise and talent in all manner of matters and as such can contribute considerably to the more technical aspects of the content of legislation. Moreover, in the present electoral system, where the 'first past the post' system can occasionally lead to the predominance of one political party in the Commons, the House of Lords provides a balance of membership that represents the long-term views of the country.

Much has been said in criticism of the methods of appointment of the Lords, based on the misconception that Lords are created predominantly in consequence of the hereditary system. The constitution of this chamber on the basis of merit has been ensured by the Life Peerages Act 1958 and the Peerage Act 1963. Although this creates a situation that may be termed as 'undemocratic', the membership of the Upper House is more and more determined by the leaders of the main parties in the Commons. Thus, the appointees, although representing the views of the electorate over the years, albeit indirectly, are insulated from the less desirable side of democracy, the constant worry about the security of one's seat and the need to put forward 'popular' policies. This allows an objective view of legislative problems and a practical approach to their resolution. Given a situation where the second chamber is one with less constitutional power, then this provides the perfect situation where, providing the chamber contains a genuine cross-section of interests and experience, a pragmatic and informed base is given to the legislature which is not swayed by transitory movements in public opinion.

This reserve of informed and experienced ability may also initiate reform in areas that are perhaps not at the forefront of the minds of Commons members. This is well illustrated by the circumstances that led to the passing of the Sexual Offences Act 1967, which can honestly be said to have been originated as a backbench bill in the Lords.

Amendments to the Foreign Compensation Act 1969 and the Local Government Act 1972 illustrate how such expertise has proved, in hindsight, more than advantageous. This revising capacity coupled, in the present situation, with the power to remit bills for reconsideration, acts as an active filter of the Commons' output ensuring that both the practical substance and the political content is well considered. Although this has occasionally resulted in confrontation, which has been resolved in favour of the Lords (as with the Aircraft and Shipbuilding Bill in the mid 1970s) and in favour of the Commons (as with the Trade Union and Labour Relations Bill of the same era), usually a balance is struck. There is no doubt that this function, regardless of the politics of the government of the day, has enhanced the public's opinion of the Lords and is a strong recommendation for the retention of a second chamber. One must note that the Lords may be as wayward as they feel is necessary since the threat of deselection will not sway them from their resolve.

One cannot, however, disregard criticisms of the current second chamber even though, as De Smith observes, they tend to emanate from 'the eccentric and the naive'. There is a genuine concern that there is an inbuilt Conservative majority in the Lords, although this can be easily rectified by a government with the right mandate and political will. However, there is a more deep-seated mistrust of bodies that are not directly electorally accountable which has spawned the idea of an elected second chamber. To elect a second chamber on the same basis as the first would merely operate as an expansion of the Commons. To elect a second chamber in an alternative manner would necessarily lead to the question of which House truly represented the democratic will of the people and there would certainly be a power struggle of some description. The problems of such an upheaval, leaving aside the problems of electoral administration, more or less justify the general, if somewhat complacent, attitude of most jurists that we should let sleeping dogs lie. Irrespective of proposals, such as those of the Conservative Review Committee 1978, there have been no concerted efforts at reform since 1968.

Thus, whether reform of the system is imminent or unlikely, it seems manifest that a second revising and scrutinising chamber can perform a useful political and practical role. This function may be seen as desirable, if not necessary, regardless of the perfection of a Lower House. The situation may be summed up in terms of the assertion that two heads are better than one, and although this is no guarantee of constitutional perfection, two chambers must be seen as better than a single elected House.

QUESTION 6

Suggested Solution

In the modern world, threats to the security of some or all of the nation, may come in a large variety of forms, often considerably different from those experienced in the past. Principally, the development of systems that allow a complex society to function smoothly also make it vulnerable. From the terrorist's bomb on a plane to security considerations in defence establishments, law makers have been forced, by the circumstances of recent years, to curtail the freedoms that individuals have come to expect. Some prohibitions seldom have been placed 'across the board', but their effect has been felt in many areas of everyday life.

In extremis, it is conceivable that in circumstances of dire emergency, where civil authorities, due to internal or external disruption, abrogate their power in favour of military authorities, such a situation, although unlikely, would amount to the imposition of martial law. This term is something of a misnomer since it is a state where normal civil laws are in suspense in favour of the discretion of senior military commanders. Such a situation would certainly involve the individual's rights giving way to that of society. However, it is clear from such authorities as we have that the courts may still review whether the circumstances justify imposition of this extreme measure and may also exercise judicial review. Thus, in *Egan* v *Macready* [1921] IR 265, a court felt able to declare that the prerogative purported to be exercised by military authorities had been superseded by statute. Furthermore, if Dicey is to be believed, liability would be incurred by military authorities for any unnecessary harm once civil law was restored. It is, however, more likely that the military would be indemnified by subsequent statute against legal actions arising out of the period of martial law.

A more common occurrence, relatively speaking, is the nation being forced onto a war footing, either where there is no official state of war in existence, or where there is actual hostility. Powers relating to the declaration and conduct of war are primarily matters of prerogative.

Since the prerogative allows for the internment and deportation of enemies and the requisition of their property, as well as the tactical destruction or confiscation of property generally, individual rights and freedoms may be curbed. Such powers are currently being seen at work in the Persian Gulf, where sanctions prohibit the carrying on of all but humanitarian trade with Iraq and Britain has retained for the military forces in the Gulf the right of interception of property and vessels. This may directly interfere with the trading interests of individuals within this country. The current crisis has also seen the expulsion of diplomatic and other Iraqi nationals. Most of these prerogatives relate to the conduct of affairs outside the United Kingdom or are exercised against those who are not British subjects. However, in other war situations, citizens might find their commercial and proprietary interests affected by such prerogative powers. Although, as in the case of the *Burmah Oil Co v Lord Advocate* [1965] AC 75, the courts may review such actions and award compensation, indemnification of the Crown, in a similar manner to that effected by the War Damage Act 1965, would be likely to prevent redress from being made. Furthermore, it must be remembered that even where the exercise of prerogative is compensated for, the rights of the individual still take a back seat to the immediate requirements of national security and as such are held in suspense until the immediate crisis has passed.

The immediacy of the crisis is largely the yard stick that the courts have used to determine the extent to which the Crown may set aside considerations of individual rights. In interpreting the Defence of the Realm Acts 1914–1915 and the Emergency Powers (Defence) Acts 1939–1940, the judiciary have given considerable weight to the degree of emergency at any given time. Under these statutes, wide discretionary powers are conferred on the Crown, enabling it to make regulations that it deems necessary for the safety of the nation, including the suspension of normal peace time courts. Such an order was not itself made, but regulations relating to the internment of British subjects were viewed by the courts with varying degrees of approval in various stages of the First and Second World Wars.

It is not only in times of war or military threat that wide legislative powers can be adopted by the Crown. In states of emergency the Emergency Powers Acts 1920 and 1964 provide for legislation by Orders in Council when the provision of essential services is disrupted. The breadth of the powers is such that a court might find it difficult to declare such Orders ultra vires. The necessity of positive affirmation by Parliament is intended to provide a constitutional safeguard, but this does not of itself guarantee the rights of individuals, except insofar as the Act prohibits excessive criminal sentencing, forced labour or military conscription and the outlawing of normally legitimate strike actions. However, the increased powers of the police and the stricter regulation of trade union activities has meant that in the last decade other methods have been used to ensure the supply of essential services, in contrast to the frequent use in the 1970s of these provisions.

These modern methods of control reflect what some writers, such as De Smith perceive as a change in the nature of the threats to the security of the state. The 1980s have been marked by a sharp increase in public disorder, relating to industrial, political and leisure activities. Furthermore, there has been an increasing sensitivity to the dissemination of information both factually and subjectively generated. Whether such attitudes genuinely reflect a new form of threat to national security or the re-emergence of historical trends, accompanied by deepened insecurity amongst authorities, is open to debate. Nonetheless, in response to the changing situation, there has been a perceptible change in tactics. Instead of the sweeping invocation of emergency powers, the legislature has chosen to put into place more or less permanent structures that may be employed by subordinate authorities at their discretion. Although it is arguable whether violent disorders constitute serious threats to the security of the state, or at least the level of disorder that has prompted such measures, it is principally the police who now have wider powers in given circumstances to curtail the rights of the individual. Additionally, more and more activities are required to be performed only with authorisation and due compliance with regulatory stipulations. To enumerate the panoply of recent legislation that directly or indirectly tackle matters relating to the security of the state would be quite a considerable task. Therefore, our survey must confine itself to certain notable examples of the 'new tactics'.

The difficult area of the retention and security of official secrets and the consequence scrutiny, resulting in the introduction of a Bill reforming previous official secrets legislation, promises to tighten the reign on the free dissemination of information, which will lead to a 'knock-on' effect for free speech. Equally, the broadcasting reforms provide for a system of vetting material that is potentially harmful to the viewer, and as a result is certain to narrow the channels for more controversial forms of entertainment. The Public Order Act 1986, which regulates all manner of potential threats to the Queen's peace, prohibits, by virtue of s5, the use of communications and representations likely to cause harassment, alarm or distress to a person exposed to them. Similarly, material and communications that might induce racial conflict is liable to criminal sanction under ss17–23. To what extent these measures are intended to protect the state, rather than society, is debateable, but certainly the thinking behind such legislation is to prevent inflammatory situations from developing.

The Police and Criminal Evidence Act 1984 and the Public Order Act 1986 confer on the police significant powers with regard to freedom of movement and expression. The former allows for the use of road blocks and searches as a preventative measure, whilst the latter reforms and codifies public order laws imposing more coherent powers for the policing of demonstrations, processions and assemblies. Coupled with these measures are the requirements in most circumstances for due authorisation to organise these activities.

One must finally observe that other measures relating to the prevention of terrorism give rise to the prevention of the full exercise of certain public rights. Most recently, it has been announced that the free movement and free expression of persons in airport premises is to be restricted by the imposition of imprisonable sanctions for those who enter aircraft without authorisation or make misleading statements about the contents of baggage. Thus, it has been widely observed, a person exercising free speech by joking that he has a bomb in his suitcase might theoretically be convicted by virtue of these measures.

One is faced with a difficulty in these areas of relevance to the question. The security of the state is not seriously at risk by most of the activities that are envisaged by these statutes. The primary use of these laws is to protect society. However, since it is largely viewed by the courts that deciding what matters relate to state security is to be decided by central government, one must assume that the government's views on this matter must be conclusive. Since the head of the present government does not acknowledge the concept of society, one must assume that the state's security and society's safety are interchangeable concepts, and as such all criminal law must relate to the greater or lesser extent to state security.

The perceived change in tactics seems to confirm this view, since a shift in reliance on the concept of a transient national emergency to that of building safeguards into the everyday laws of the land must reflect a belief that the problem has changed. This might be an admission of the view that the Queen's peace is no longer prevalent throughout the land, which would indicate a siege mentality that requires individuals to relinquish their rights from day to day as new threats emerge. Alternatively, there might be a view that administrative convenience is better served by placing individual liberty in second place. This change must either signal the belief that the state has become more vulnerable or sensitive or that the democratic safeguards of using 'laws of last resort', which are brought out of the legislative armoury in times of dire emergency, are less important than they were. The fact that the Emergency Powers Act was used five times by the Heath government in the 1970s would appear to confirm the first synopsis. The complexities of the modern state make it more dependent and therefore more vulnerable and the facilities available to those who seek to threaten it have become equally sophisticated. As a result of such progress individual rights are placed between the rock of potential threats and the hard place that are the reinforced walls of the state.

QUESTION 7

Suggested Solution

Smurf's predicament may be resolved by reference to contractual law or by gaining satisfaction from seeing the criminal law take effect; however, his most likely course of action is to consider judicial review of the council's decision. However, we shall consider some general principles relating to the matter before directly addressing the possibility of judicial review.

In participating with his company in the tendering process, Smith has a pecuniary interest in the matter before the Environmental Health Committee. The interests of council members are governed by ss94–98 of the Local Government Act 1972, which requires them to declare their interests as soon as practicable and to renounce their speaking and voting rights unless the interest is exceedingly remote. Aside from the dispensation of the Secretary of State for the Environment when circumstances necessitate, non-compliance with these rules is a criminal offence and decisions taken with the participation of a disqualified officer may be overturned. In *R v Hendon RDC, ex parte Chorley*, the unanimous decision of a council regarding land use was quashed due to one member being the estate agent of an interested party. This finding was based on the rule against bias 'nemo judex in sua causa', which we will consider later. However, we can see that there is a certain analogy with the present situation.

Another point to consider is the existence and powers of the Local Commissioners, created by the Local Government Act 1974, Part III, who have powers to investigate maladministration in local government. In the absence of a statutory definition, one must be guided by the options of the courts, such as that in *R v Local Commissioner for Administration, ex parte Bradford City Council* [1979] 2 All ER 881, for guidance as to the ambit of their powers. However, should Smurf wish, he could have his complaint investigated and if maladministration is proved, the authority may be obliged to pay compensation for any injustice suffered.

It might also be to Smurf's advantage to remember that local government employees remain personally liable for torts they commit, whether or not these are committed in the course of their duties. There may also be an independent tort in which the council might be liable, relating to the wilful misuse of powers, causing economic loss as was suggested by *David v Abdul Cader* [1963] 1 WLR 834. As already suggested, there may also be remedies in the law of contract along the lines of *Harvela Investments Ltd v Royal Trust Company of Canada* [1984] 3 WLR 1280 CA.

However, it is the prospect of judicial review of the administrative action of the council that would possibly be the most appealing method of seeking redress, if not to Smurf, then to his legal adviser. The first consideration of the Council may be deemed to be an irrelevant consideration. The motivation behind ensuring that a Blankshire company receives the contract is almost certainly based on the desire to improve employment prospects in the area. If this is so, then the situation must be seen as analogous to the situation in *Roberts v Hopwood* [1925] AC 578 where the court held that 'principles of socialistic philanthropy ... in the world of labour' were irrelevant considerations. However, this is an issue of motivation, so that a genuine reason for ensuring provision by a local company might negate Smurf's claim, as might the fact that if such a policy was given as an election pledge, then the authority would seem to be bound to follow their mandate according to the suggestions of Lord Wilberforce in *Secretary of State for Education and Science v Tameside MBC* [1977] AC 1014. However, even this view may not protect the council from Smurf's legal action, since in *Bromley LBC v GLC* [1983] 1 AC 768 losing rate-payer's money even in pursuance of an election mandate was deemed to be outside the scope of the authority's powers and probably in breach of fiduciary duty. Since the purpose of the tender process would seem to be to obtain a service as cheaply as possible and to the highest standards, then unreasonable fetters on this objective would appear to achieve the same problem situation.

It would be unlikely, however, that Smurf would succeed purely on the grounds of unreasonableness, since the 'stringent test' following the Wednesbury principles demands that a decision must be such that no reasonable body could possibly make. It is clear that none of these fall into this category. However, Smurf might consider that there has been an unreasonable fetter on the discretion of the committee in laying down hard and fast rules. In *R v Port of London Authority, ex parte Kynoch Ltd* [1919] 1 KB 176 the court made it clear that an administrative body should not 'shut its ears' to alternatives to a desired policy. Thus, Blankshire CC should not predetermine to award the tender to a certain category of company regardless, although there is nothing wrong with having a general policy where exceptions are considered.

If Smurf were to attempt to establish ultra vires on the grounds that delegation of the decision was a breach of the principle (delegatus non potest delegare) he would be given short shrift by the courts, since it is not only acceptable, but common practice, for local authorities to legitimately delegate powers to committees and for those committees to sub-delegate. However, it is clear that his strongest argument would be on the basis that there was a failure to declare a pecuniary interest which resulted in a breach of the rule against bias, as mentioned above. Moreover if 'bad faith' could be established, in spite of the heavy burden of proof required, then the case would be arguable on the basis of ultra vires due to the abuse of administrative power.

Remedies would be available to Smurf if he could satisfy the requirement for locus standi laid down by Order 53; that is he must show that he had sufficient interest in the matter. This might be easily established on the face of the facts. Thereafter he would apply for leave to issue a writ either claiming damages or to compel compliance or to quash the decision of the body.

However, ultimately Smurf might find the second criteria impossible to counter, for although other circumstances would seem to be in his favour, the prohibition of awarding the tender to former members of the council might be totally supportable if the reason why the service was put out to tender was due to the ineptitude or misfeasance of employees. This view would be justified by the decision in *Cummings* v *Birkenhead Corp* [1972] Ch 12. However, the caveat remains that the administrative body must remain willing to consider alternatives. Although the committee has the power to make recommendations that are usually acted upon and it has sought to fetter itself with a concrete ruling, the final decision is up to to the County Council which is not specifically bound by the decision and therefore could consider other bids, irrespective of the committee's decision. As such, although the impropriety of the chairman might lead to his dismissal and to criminal charges, as well as the nullification of the decision, since there is no mandatory duty upon the Council to adopt the committee's findings it could be argued to be merely a body of enquiry and, as such, not subject to the rules of natural justice. As such the issue would be abuse of power, but even so there would be no way to compel the Council to accept Smurf's bid if the conduct of former employees was an issue and fair consideration was given by the Council to alternatives to the committee's representations. Even without such circumstances damages are available where harm can be shown. However the prerogative remedies are not available as of right and are largely to ensure compliance with legal duties. Unless there is a legal duty placed upon the Council to accept the lowest bid, irrespective of whether other considerations or irrelevant considerations have been taken into account and Smurf would have otherwise won the contract, then such remedies would not compel the authority to award him the contract.

Smurf would be well advised to find out more about the circumstances of the decision and the precise nature of the decision making process.